LOGIC

Informal, Symbolic and Inductive

SECOND EDITION

Chhanda Chakraborti

Department of Humanities and Social Sciences

Indian Institute of Technology Kharagpur

PHI Learning Private Limited

Delhi-110092

2026

In fond memory of ***Shri Asoke K. Ghosh*** *(October 1942 – February 2024), Founder Chairman and Managing Director of PHI Learning, whose vision endlessly inspires.*

The Legacy Continues....

Published by Pushpita Ghosh, PHI Learning Private Limited, Rimjhim House, 11, Patparganj Industrial Estate, Delhi-110092 and Printed by Gopsons Printers Pvt. Ltd., A-14, Sector-60, Noida, Gautambudh Nagar, Noida, Uttar Pradesh-201301.

₹1150.00

LOGIC: INFORMAL, SYMBOLIC AND INDUCTIVE, Second Edition
Chhanda Chakraborti

ISBN-978-81-203-3248-5 (Print Book)
ISBN-978-93-5443-123-4 (e-Book)

The export rights of the book are vested solely with the publisher.

To

My Students

at IIT Kharagpur and BITS Pilani

CONTENTS

PREFACE

The advice, suggestions, and encouragement from family, friends, colleagues, critics and students have been the key factors in bringing out the Second Edition of this book.

The most important addition to the previous edition has been the Appendix on *Basic Set Theory.* This addition is the result of taking into account the suggestions of several colleagues from different Indian universities (here, Department of Philosophy, Allahabad University deserves special mention) and their syllabi requirements. It covers all the fundamental concepts, principles and operations in Basic Set Theory.

Certain sections in Chapter 3 on Fallacies also have been rewritten. I believe that these modifications will make the text more accessible to the diverse readers.

Also, for the Second Edition, the entire manuscript has undergone editorial changes and revisions. In this work, my debt of gratitude has grown. I remain indebted to colleagues and students who have come forward with their suggestions and helpful comments. In particular, I must mention the invaluable support of my IIT Kharagpur students of Symbolic Logic course in Autumn 2006, who, while learning the subject, have volunteered to also carefully read the First Edition. In particular, I wish to thank Balachandra Suri, batch of 2004, student of Physics, and Ambuj Saxena, batch of 2002, student of Mechanical Engineering, for their excellent and systematic work. They have provided remarkable assistance. However, I know that there were many like the ones I mentioned in the class, equally alert and equally helpful. I take this opportunity to thank all of them, named and unnamed, and appreciate their support.

I also take this opportunity to thank all those who have used this book, and invite them once more to convey constructive suggestions to further improve the book.

Chhanda Chakraborti
IIT Kharagpur

PREFACE TO THE FIRST EDITION

Any logic text written in English today should give some account as to why it deserves to be added to the already existing list of books. My aim in writing this text is to promote more interest in the subject that I have been teaching for years. I have been fortunate to have had the opportunity to teach courses on logic in both India and the US to students from varied academic disciplines—engineering, science, and other subjects. In every class, I have observed the same sequence: the onset of interest in logic, the eagerness to master certain skills, and the inevitable healthy competition to hone the skills to reach higher levels of knowledge. Each time, the infectious enthusiasm of the students has reaffirmed my faith in logic as an interesting subject of study. This book is a result of that collective interest. It is an effort undertaken particularly for the students of this subject.

A textbook on logic has many challenges to face. One such challenge is how to strike a balance between the breadth and the depth of the subject. One has to cover certain topics as the prescribed 'syllabus', while also trying to give an overview of the field. For example, while teaching Western logic, it is not desirable to completely avoid Aristotelian logic, but one also has to devote enough space to modern Propositional and Predicate logic, and Induction. I hope that this book has found a balance.

This book covers Propositional logic, First Order Predicate logic, and Inductive logic. In addition, it includes chapters on Informal logic. For, it considers acquaintance with informal logic as an invaluable tool for improving reading, writing and thinking skills. In recent times, in several countries such as USA and Canada, informal logic or critical thinking has carved a niche of its own in the college and university curricula. It gives the benefit of having the requisite skill for identifying correct reasoning without invoking the abstract and complex mechanism of formal logic. Recognizing this trend, informal logic has been covered in the first few chapters of this text.

From a pedagogical point of view, the concern was to present the basic and relatively easier concepts first to the students, before proceeding on to the intricacies of more formal systems. Thus, the overall organization of the book is as follows. It has three main parts, addressing **Informal logic**, **Symbolic logic,** and **Induction,** individually. Each part is then divided into several chapters. Each chapter is broken down into several sections. For easy reference for both the instructors and the students, the list of contents provides the headings of the main sections as well as the major subsections in a chapter.

Since both teaching and learning logic require a certain amount of hands-on participation, a major requirement for a textbook in logic is copious and varied sets of exercises. I have tried to include exercises after each section, and also wherever possible. At the end of the book, Solutions to Selected Exercises (marked by '*') from each set have been provided as pointers.

Also, the presentation style needs to be pedagogically attractive while maintaining formal rigour. The language of the text needs to be easy flowing even when the material by nature is unavoidably dense. Moreover, the links among the chapters should be a justifiable one so that the entire material appears to the students as a well-structured, cohesive whole. I have sincerely tried to keep this balance in this book. It is a book mainly for the students —the aim is to make them read and learn by themselves.

A lively, interactive learning is needed for developing a certain level of skill in logic. Within Symbolic logic, Propositional logic of course is included as a staple. The presentation of Propositional logic takes the students through atomic sentences and the construction of complex sentences with connectives. I have shown step-by-step how to create a truth table and also how to implement the truth-table technique for determining various logical features.

In addition, this book covers the topic of truth trees. The aim is not only to equip the student with another technique that applies equally well and sometimes even better to the problems of Propositional logic, but also to teach how to make use of the truth-table definitions in a more effective way.

Predicate logic has been introduced through an initiation into Aristotelian Categorical logic. It has been my personal experience that, in general, learning Categorical logic eases the comprehension of the concepts of Predicate logic.

In the Appendices, several important topics have been discussed for those who want to learn more. Each Appendix item has a number of references meant for further reading in any of these topics. Indian logic and the nature of inference of Indian logic have been specially inserted to create a wider awareness about Indian logic as a separate field of study. Too often, I have seen students going away with the belief that Western logic is the only kind of logic possible. The addition of Appendices on Indian logic is to eradicate such false beliefs.

I would sincerely appreciate receiving any constructive suggestions for improving the contents and would be greateful to the readers who may venture to point out any errors that might have crept into the text.

Chhanda Chakraborti
Indian Institute of Technology Kharagpur

ACKNOWLEDGEMENTS

I would first like to thank the wonderful students I had at Birla Institute of Technology and Science (BITS) Pilani, Indian Institute of Technology (IIT) Kharagpur, and also in University of Washington, Seattle, and University of Utah, Salt Lake City. Wherever I have taught logic, the student feedback has been indeed gratifying. This, I believe, has more to do with logic than with me. Their interest in the subject, which I have seen so many times to rekindle my interest in the subject, has played a definite role in shaping the idea of writing this book. While teaching them, I have learnt from them. To them and to the others whom I may meet in the future, I dedicate this book.

With fondness, I also thank my logic teachers, Prof. Pranab Kumar Sen, Prof. Sutapa Saha, Prof. Marc Cohen, to mention a few, for igniting the initial spark of my interest in the subject. I also thank with deep gratitude Prof. P.K. Mukhopadhyay who has opened my eyes to the subtleties of Indian Logic, specially of the Nyaya System.

I am grateful to The Swedish Institute for its generous support and for making it possible to work on this book and to finish it on time. With great fondness I remember Karin Dif of the Swedish Institute and her dedication to work.

This book was started at IIT Kharagpur with the initial four chapters written there. I acknowledge the support received from the Continuing Education Programme, IIT Kharagpur for starting this project.

I am thankful to the Department of Philosophy, Lund University, Sweden for providing all kinds of support, academic and technical. The Department has been remarkably hospitable during my stay at Lund University from September 2004 to May 2005. I am grateful for the warmth and kindness I have received and also for the enjoyable work environment. In particular, I am grateful to Dr. Eric Olsson for his helpful suggestions and comments he made on some of the chapters of this book.

I am indebted to the Department of Humanities and Social Sciences, IIT Kharagpur for granting me leave from my official duties. I deeply appreciate the enabling support that the Department has extended to me.

I would fail in my duty if I do not mention the help and support received from the editorial team of Prentice-Hall of India, the publishers of the book, to attain a level of quality. I treasure their collaboration.

Finally, I am indebted to my family: my husband, Prof. Nirupam Chakraborti, and my daughter, Shankhamala Chakraborti. Their love and consideration have sustained me throughout the long, solitary period when I penned this book. With great fondness I acknowledge the special contribution of my daughter, Shankhamala, to this book. In spite of her busy schedule, she drew four pictures for this book, which can be seen on pages 13, 376, 388, and 409 of this book.

Chhanda Chakraborti

INTRODUCTION

The most formidable weapon against errors of every kind is Reason. I have never used any other, and I trust I never shall.

—Thomas Paine, *The Age of Reason*, 1794

The inclusion of the study of logic as a formal discipline in the university curricula has a long-standing tradition in academic institutions in India as well as in the West. The reason is perhaps a felt-need that without training in logic the ratiocinative abilities of a student remain impaired. However, most people consider themselves quite capable of reasoning and of applying logic even though they do not have a formal training in the subject. Charles Peirce, an American Philosopher, observed that:

> Few persons care to study logic, because everybody conceives himself to be proficient enough in the art of reasoning already. But I observe that this satisfaction is limited to one's own ratiocination, and does not extend to that of other men.
>
> —Charles Peirce, *The Fixation of Belief*

Peirce's observation reveals about a person's ego about himself and how he rates others through it. But it also brings to light an important fact that how one sees oneself as proficient in logic has very little to do with what one's actual proficiency in logic is. For, while it is true that most people consider themselves skilled in reasoning, it is also true that they make all kinds of errors in reasoning. Moreover, most people do not know how to identify and establish which is correct reasoning and which is not. So, though most of us can reason without a formal training in logic, study of logic is needed at least to learn how to discern correct reasoning from incorrect reasoning. Cynics may observe that in these days thinking clearly and being rational may be detrimental to one's mental and physical well-being. However, the fact remains that the study of logic helps one to learn the basic principles of clear and systematic way of correct reasoning.

Higher education is meant to enrich the intellectual prowess of the learners and to promote a respect for reason. It is not enough to know the answers to the questions asked; it is equally important to learn to question the answers. A critical, systematically inquiring mind is the end result of a proper intellectual training. Study of logic is an effective tool for achieving these goals. Furthermore, mere delivery of information to the students does not teach them how to organize or systematize their thoughts, or how to assess what they have received. While teaching some effective, time-tested methods for processing, analyzing and evaluating information, study of logic also teaches how to enrich one's intellectual life with a logical approach. This book is a humble contribution to the concerted effort for betterment of our thinking capacities through the study of logic.

The instrumental value of logic is well known in many disciplines such as Philosophy, Mathematics, and Computer Science. While including logic in their curricula, different disciplines also impact logic from their perspectives. Hence, there are several ways to teach logic. Mathematics teaches logic almost as an extension of algebra or calculus with lemmas and proofs, computer science teaches it with more emphasis on its applicability for enriching programming power or for building 'thinking machines'. Philosophy, of which logic has always been an integral part, approaches logic somewhat differently. For, its key concerns are of a different kind.

This textbook has been written keeping in mind logic as a subject of Philosophy. In Philosophy, a distinction between Western and Indian logic has always been maintained for a variety of important reasons, and the students of Philosophy are exposed to both kinds of logic, but separately. In conformity with that tradition, this book is on Western logic. However, in the Appendices (**Appendix E and Appendix F**), some sections on Indian logic have been introduced, particularly for those who, not being Philosophy students, may never get an opportunity to have an idea about what Indian logic is.

This book is devoted to the traditional Western logic. More specifically, it is on Symbolic logic, with Propositional and First Order Predicate logic forming its main body. The discussions on Aristotelian Categorical logic and Inductive logic come also as part of this traditional package. However, the aim of this book is also about other kinds of logic that exist at present within the field of Western Logic. Western logic has many subdivisions, and has also undergone many transformations. This book has an Appendix (**Appendix C**), specifically to acquaint the student with some of these alternative possibilities in Western logic.

The text uses ordinary language as the backdrop to articulate and demonstrate the concepts and problems of logic as has come to be the norm in teaching Western logic to Philosophy students. The principal goal is to teach how to apply logic in ordinary and systematic thinking in the context of language use. However, personally I have seen that year after year, students, who were not Philosophy students and were unexceptionally from engineering or science disciplines of premier educational Institutes of India, have enjoyed learning logic with this material. I have enjoyed their enjoyment of learning the subject. This personal experieence gives me the confidence to assert that the material in this book should not disappoint those who are not Philosophy students from using this book though it caters more to the needs of Philosophy students.

CHAPTER 1

PRELIMINARIES

1.1 What is Logic?

Logic, a branch of Philosophy, is dedicated to the study of reasoning. Its systematic and rigorous nature has prompted some to describe it as the *science of reasoning*.

Reasoning is a process of knowing that we use for inferring what is not directly given. It is a fundamental human mental activity that we regularly use for acquiring knowledge. For example, climbing stairs requires an intricate coordination between inputs from the eyes and different muscles in the body. This coordination involves habitual reasoning covering simple things such as how far the leg has to go up to get onto the next step, to complicated items, e.g., how much pause there must be between the steps so as not to stumble.

Sometimes, we use reasoning knowingly. For instance, when we go out during the monsoon season, we take a peek at the sky in order to decide whether or not to carry an umbrella, our decision involves reasoning.

We also use reasoning as part of our understanding of common social behaviour. For example, we do not actually see what other people want or what their intentions are. All we see is an expression on the face, or a gesture, sometimes certain eye movements and the body language. Using these, we then try to infer his or her intentions.

Reasoning occupies a major role in our decision-making process. The more complex the decision is, the more important the role of reasoning becomes. Consider, for example, a decision about where to invest in the stock market. Or, the decision about choosing the right future career for yourself. These are some examples of the more complex kind of the reasoning that we do.

Studies suggest that reasoning is what has evolved in our thinking as a tool for survival. If we could not reason from the given and from the obvious, as a race humans would not have survived this long. Seeing a charging tiger in your way is ineffectual if you cannot reason how to get out of its way.

Though the subject matter of logic is reasoning, *does it teach us to reason*? From what we have stated, one thing should be obvious, namely, that, as a matter of fact, we know how to reason *whether we know logic or not*. Logic, thus, does *not* teach us *to reason;* it teaches us how to *reason correctly.* Study of logic helps us learn how to *distinguish good reasoning from bad reasoning*. It provides us criteria for evaluating reasoning as good or bad, and also for justifying the legitimacy of that assessment.

How important is the role of logic? There are different opinions among philosophers regarding this. Aristotle saw logic primarily as an **instrument (*organon*)** for advancement of knowledge. He took it as the indispensable tool for any systematic study, be it Philosophy or Physics or Geometry. According to him, its role is to ensure cogency, soundness, and overall rationality in the deliberations.

The ancient Indian thinkers also saw in logic a similar instrumental value. Scholars (see, for example, Matilal[1]), maintain that Indian logic evolved from a felt-need to have a well-reasoned, systematic discussion on the extensive practice of debating prevalent at that time. The concern clearly was to promote the notion and the practice of a *good* debate, as opposed to the pointless, destructive debates (e.g., *vitanda*). Rules of correct public speaking had to incorporate the rules of logical thinking.

The Stoics, a group of philosophers in Ancient Greece, viewed logic as more important than *merely* as a tool. They considered logic as an integral part of our thinking, and also as integral to the language, we use.

Philosophers may disagree amongst themselves about the role of logic and about the level of priority they want to ascribe to logic, but the consensus is that logic as a branch of study *is connected to reasoning in a special way.* An etymological examination of the word 'logic' can provide us a clue

[1] Matilal, B.K., 1997, *Logic, Language, and Reality: Indian Philosophy and Contemporary Issues.* Motilal Banarasi Dass, New Delhi; Matilal, B.K., 1998, *The Character of Logic in India.* J. Ganeri and H. Tiwari (Eds.), Oxford University Press.

about the nature of that connection. The English word *Logic* is derived from the Greek word *Logos*, which roughly means 'reasoned discourse' or 'a systematic study'.

Logos in Greek ⟶ Logic in English

But then, one might point out that there is nothing unique about such characterization of logic since every other study, e.g., Anthropology, Biology, Geology, or Psychology, has to be a *reasoned discourse* also. For, each of their names ends with a 'logy', which is the remnant of the root '*Logos*'. Thus, Anthropology is supposed to be a reasoned discourse on humans, Biology on living creatures, Geology on the earth, and so on. The answer, however, lies there. Indeed, these other subjects are reasoned discourses, but they are reasoned discourses *about some specific domain or the other*, as the first part of their names suggest, e.g., 'Bio' (life), 'Geo' (earth). In contrast, the term 'logic' has no reference to any particular domain; it is *not* a reasoned discourse *about some other domain. It is supposed to be a discourse on reasoning itself.* It is a study of reasoning, its nature and various kinds, of the rules that should be observed to regulate reasoning to differentiate it from the spurious kinds, and also of proof procedures in order to demonstrate the validity of one's reasoning.

EXERCISE 1.1

1. Give five different examples of reasoning in everyday life from your own experience.

2. In each of the following cases, determine whether any 'reasoning' is taking place, and then describe what is being reasoned:

*a. The Rector told Sameer to wait.

b. If a is greater than 199, and b is greater than 1, $a + b$ has to be greater than 200.

c. We know that not everyone was inside the library when the theft took place. We also know that the theft was the job of an insider. We can eliminate those who were not present in the library at the time of the theft from being directly involved with the theft.

d. We know now that the earth is not stationary, and that it is not at the centre of the universe.

*e. There are some very good reasons for death penalty. For one thing, it is said to serve as a deterrent for those who would commit capital offences.

3. Explain why it is said that logic does not teach us how to reason, but it teaches us *how to reason well.*
4. *What is the etymological meaning of the term 'logic'? Does this meaning give us the clue about the subject matter of logic, as it may in the case of biology?

1.2 Laws of Thought

It is one of the pivotal assumptions of traditional western logic that there are certain fundamental principles which govern human thinking. They are considered as fundamental in the sense that without these laws reasoning cannot take place.

In the western tradition, the concept of **laws of thought** can be traced back to Aristotle (384–322 BCE), the eminent Greek thinker, who is considered to be the pioneer of western logic. Before him, the geometricians and the arithmeticians used *proofs* in their respective domains. Aristotle was the first to extend the study of formal proof in the domains beyond the realms of geometrical and mathematical thinking. He was also the first to investigate the patterns embedded in human reasoning and the way in which reasoning is processed.

As part of his project, Aristotle was trying to describe the basic laws by which human thought (and reasoning) can occur. As examples of foundational laws, he identified the following three laws:

- Law of Identity
- Law of Non-Contradiction
- Law of Excluded Middle

These are now explained below:

Law of Identity

This law says: Everything is identical (same) to itself.

Examples

1. If anything is *A*, then it is *A*.
2. A square is a square.

Alternatively, it asserts that if any proposition is true, then it is true. Violation of this law implies that it is possible for a thing to *not to be* itself with everything remaining the same within the same frame of reference.

Law of Non-contradiction

This law states that nothing can be both *A* and not *A*. The same attribute cannot at the same time both belong and not belong to the same subject in the same aspect within the same frame of reference.

> *Example*
>
> 3. A square cannot be at the same time both a square and not a square with everything remaining the same.

Alternatively, the law asserts that no proposition can be both true and false.

Law of Excluded Middle

This law states that for everything, it has to be either *A* or not *A*. There is no middle ground, i.e., it cannot be 'not either'.

> *Example*
>
> 4. A thing has to be either a square or not a square.

Alternatively, it asserts that any proposition must be either true or false.

Aristotle identified these laws as the *necessary conditions* for human thought: without them, thought cannot occur. He also held them as *laws of thought*, i.e., as fundamental principles for human rational thinking.

Along with him, western logicians consider them as 'laws' in the sense of being general principles that hold universally true about human thinking. They are also called 'laws' in the sense that they are seen as rules which govern the intellectual operations of human mind such that the operations 'obey' the 'laws of thought', just as the natural phenomena are supposed to obey the 'laws of nature'.

At least in **classical logic,** the Aristotelian laws of thought remain fundamental and indisputable till date. Their widespread influence can be seen in the works of logicians belonging to different ages from medieval to the modern.

George Boole, one of the greatest mathematicians of 19th century and one of the founders of mathematical logic, fully supported this Aristotelian notion. He considered these laws as inextricably linked to the constitution of human intellect[2]. Boole's aim was to show the mathematical character of logic and to come up with a calculus for logic just as there is an algebra

[2] Boole, George, *An Investigation of the Laws of Thought,* Dover, New York, 1958, Chapter 1.

for mathematics. In his effort, he used the three laws of thought as the bedrock for his system.

However, Boole added a few more laws to the list of three traditional laws of thought identified by Aristotle. For example, he mentioned the Law of Commutativity for Conjunction and the Index Law.

Law of Commutativity for Conjunction

Boole expressed this law as

$$(e \bullet a) \equiv (a \bullet e)$$

If two statements are joined by 'and', the order in which the statements are placed is immaterial. The truth or the falsity of the conjunction remains unaffected.

Example

5. Being a metallic object and a water carrier is equivalent to being a water carrier and a metallic object.

The Index Law

Boole expressed this law as

$$(c \bullet c) \equiv c$$

Asserting a statement is equivalent to its assertion in conjunction with itself.

Example

6. Being a metallic object and a metallic object is being a metallic object.

Boole believed that the truth of the laws of thought does not require the validation from extensive observation; their truth is immediately obvious as a matter of necessity. He claimed that on this point the laws of thought differ from the laws of nature, such as the Law of Gravitation, which are essentially based on empirical observations, being either causal hypotheses or the end-result of inductive generalization.

Gottlob Frege (1848–1925), another founder figure in the history of mathematical logic, also held that some of the rules of logic are laws of thought. According to him, violations of these laws only show the irrationality of the violators themselves.

The subject of 'laws of thought', however, is not entirely free of controversy. Questions have been raised from time to time about their nature and status. As, for instance, people have asked:

- Are there really such 'laws', or are they merely working assumptions from our side?
- Is it absolutely necessary for a logical system to accept *all of these 'laws'?*
- Is it absolutely necessary for a logical system to accept *any of these 'law'*?

There have been criticisms of the Law of Identity on the ground that it is possible for an utterance, such as "The Sun is shining", *to be true in a certain time and place* and *to be false in another time and place*. So, the Law of Identity does not seem to be universally true. In answer, it has been proposed that we need to make the time and place reference of an utterance a part of its truth-making circumstance. What the Law of Identity affirms is that with respect to that specific time and place the statement "The Sun is shining", if true, will be true; or, if false, will be false.

Similarly, the universality of Law of Contradiction has been questioned, because in some special circumstances apparent contradictions such as "the floor is wet" and "the floor is not wet", both may be true. For example, consider the situation where the floor is only partly wet. Again, to answer this charge, inclusion of the reference to the time and place of an utterance has been taken into consideration.

The Law of Excluded Middle has been criticised along similar lines. For example, it has been argued that it is not always possible to draw such a sharp line between truth and falsity to claim universally that a thing is either *A* or not-*A*. It is possible that about a certain individual we may not be able to decide whether "he is mature" is true or "he is not mature" is true. The vagueness in certain concepts, it has been argued, asks for some element of indetermination.

Debates over these criticisms and further questions that these have evoked have led many to view these principles more as *convenient logical rules* or *axioms* for a system instead of as the inviolable "*laws* of thought". However, just as there are the skeptics, there are also the believers who try to defend the centrality of these principles in human reasoning. For example, there have been some efforts recently which try to show that these 'laws' are rooted in human biology and in the way in which the human beings have evolved[3]. This implies that in a way they are inextricably linked the way the humans reason.

EXERCISE 1.2

1. Explain in what sense the laws of thought may be called 'laws'?

[3] See, for instance, William S. Cooper, *The Evolution of Reason: Logic as a Branch of Biology,* Cambridge University Press, Cambridge, 2001.

2. Explain how a violation of the Law of Identity can lead to a violation of the Law of Non-contradiction.

3. *Explain how a violation of the Law of Non-contradiction can lead to a violation of the Law of Excluded Middle.

4. What was George Boole's contribution to the 'laws of thought'?

1.3 Kinds of Logics

Over time, logic has flourished as a subject. Like any other active field of study, it too has grown in many directions. Today, logic is both a branch of philosophy and a branch of mathematics. Its applications are well known in the area of artificial intelligence.

This book aims primarily to acquaint the readers with the basics of what is known as **classical logic** *or* **classical first order logic**. It is also at times called **formal logic,** because proponents of this logic mostly believe that statements in natural language have underlying *logical forms*. In their view, the expressions in logic exhibit these latent *deep structures* or the logical forms. If the deep structure of the form is correct, only then a piece of reasoning in natural language is valid.

However, note that there are many other kinds of logic. Among these varieties, in this section only a short introduction to Informal Logic has been provided. For a discussion of many 'other' kinds of logics and their difference from the traditional formal logic, see **Appendix C** of this book.

Informal Logic

This recently developed logic mainly focuses on the kind of reasoning that occurs informally, as for example, in our everyday exchange of words, in media reports, in advertisements, in legal briefs, political debates, and so on. Its development comes from a felt-need to apply logic to ordinary situations and for sound decision making in everyday circumstances, without invoking the intricacies of formal logic. In situations such as these, we often also find that the training in formal logic does not help much. The study of informal logic has found a prominent place in the curriculum of educational institutions, particularly in UK, USA and Canada.

Informal logic aims at providing us with tools to assess and analyze the ordinary kind of reasoning as may be found in public documents or articles, and to improve the required skills of an ordinary reasoner. It also warns us of *fallacies* and shows us ways to avoid them. Fallacies are *patterns of bad reasoning,* which seem like acceptable pieces of reasoning, but which actually contain *logical defects*. This logic is supposed to make significant contribution in improving our communication skills by giving us tips for better argumentative skills and techniques for better persuasion powers. The book briefly discusses Informal logic in Chapters 2 and 3.

The main difference in the case of informal logic is the relative absence of formalism. It is not a formal system of logic. Thus, you will not find any axioms and theorems in it. Yet, it makes use of principles or rules for an organized approach to logical problem solving.

Keywords

Classical formal logic: Classical formal logic is the traditional system of logic. This book acquaints the reader with this system.

Law of excluded middle: For everything, it has to be either *A* or not-*A* where *A* is any predicate.

Law of identity: Everything is identical to itself.

Law of non-contradiction: Nothing is both *A* and not–*A* where *A* is any predicate.

Laws of thought: Rules or central axioms of classical formal logic which used to be considered as inviolable laws ruling all human thinking. They are supposed to be the fundamental principles; without following these, human reasoning cannot take place. Aristotle proposed the first three laws of thought, to which subsequently there have been some additions.

Logic: Study of reasoning.

Reasoning: A basic epistemic activity by which we draw or elicit more information from what is already known.

Part A

INFORMAL LOGIC

CHAPTER 2

INFORMAL LOGIC: ARGUMENTS

2.1 Claims

In Chapter 1, logic was described as a systematic study of reasoning. It was portrayed as a study that is supposed to help us differentiate between *good* and *bad* kinds of reasoning. In this sense, logic can be called a discourse to inculcate **critical thinking** in us.

Roughly speaking, **critical thinking** is reflective thinking as opposed to blind, uncritical acceptance. It is a way of thinking that encourages us to examine *why* one has to accept, or believe, or do something, *before* any decision is taken. Therefore, it involves:

- Demanding and examining the *reasons* or *grounds* behind a proposal.
- Evaluating whether these *reasons* or *grounds* can provide adequate support for the decision.

For example, suppose you need a two-wheeler, and a fellow that you have never met before comes up with the proposal that you can buy from him a brand new scooter at a much lower cost than the market rate. If you

are a critical thinker, before taking any decision regarding the purchase, you would start asking questions such as these: Why a brand new item is being sold at a rate lower than the market rate? How did he know that you need a scooter, when you do not remember ever meeting him before?

The central issue of critical thinking, thus, is to decide whether or not to accept or reject a **claim** on the basis of the reasons or justifications provided. *A claim is a statement that can be determined as either true or false*. Given below are some examples of **claims**. Each of these is a statement which is either true or false:

Examples

1. Watching TV from a close distance harms eyesight.
2. Thailand is not in Asia.
3. Whales live in water but they are mammals.

There are also statements which *cannot* qualify as claims simply because the consideration about truth or falsity does not apply to them at all. These are the **non-claims.** Grammatically, they are expressions, but they are not candidates to which truth or falsity can be assigned meaningfully. The following are some examples of **non-claims:**

Examples

4. Start writing now! (a command)
5. What time is it? (a question)
6. Hi Asha! (a greeting)

These non-claims are to be distinguished from other kinds of statements which cannot be determined as true or false *at present*. Best examples of this kind are the statements about future predictions, e.g., *it will rain tomorrow*. Since the future is uncertain to us, we cannot determine *at the moment* whether statements such as these are true or false. Nonetheless, statements of the latter kind, strictly speaking, are claims. For, considerations about truth or falsity do apply to them. With the passage of time, in principle, it is possible to determine their truth or falsity. The best way to determine whether the statement *it will rain tomorrow* is true or false is to wait until tomorrow, when it will have a definite truth value.

In this book, *our concern will be only with the claims*: statements to which truth or falsity can be meaningfully assigned and statements which can be determined as true or false. Non-claim statements do not come within the purview of our discussion.

EXERCISE 2.1

1. What is critical thinking? How is the study of logic connected to critical thinking?

2. Explain how the following case is an example of critical thinking:

Rita got an e-mail forwarded by her friend Shilpa that you can get a free Tokia cell phone from the leading cell phone company, provided Rita sends a copy of this mail to twenty other persons with a copy to the Senior Manager, Sales Division of Tokia. The mail looked authentic with a name of Marketing Manager of Tokia at the bottom of the mail. Shilpa said that she had already sent twenty copies of this mail, which included the mail sent to Rita, and a copy to the Sales Manager of Tokia. Rita thought about this and looked up the address of the Marketing Manager on the Tokia company webpage on the Internet. She then wrote directly to the Marketing Division Manager asking whether the claim the e-mail message is true. She promptly got a reply that the message is a hoax to promote chain letters and to harass Tokia company, and that Tokia has no intention to honour that claim in the e-mail message.

3. Check which of these are claims and which are not. Justify your reasons:

a. *Oh my God!

b. Lata Mangeshkar is one of the finest singers in the world.

c. The end-term examination will be held on January 19, if it cannot be held for some reason on the earlier date of December 2.

d. *I never thought Mr. Barman would win the election.

e. Can airlines ticket prices be affected by the oil price?

f. The sentence (b) above in this exercise set is a non-claim.

g. Medicines based on cannabis can cause harm to people who use the medicines.

h. Amnesty International says nearly 4000 people were executed in 2004.

i. Return the book at once and bring back the library card with you!

j. In 2001, Perry Wacker, a Dutch lorry driver was sentenced to 14 years in prison for his part in the deaths of 58 Chinese illegal immigrants who were found suffocated in the back of Perry Wacker's lorry when it was searched at the ferry port in Dover last June after arriving from Belgium.

2.2 Arguments: Basic Characteristics

Claims can be of different kinds. They can be *simple* or *complex* by nature. In Section 2.1, Examples 1 and 2 on claims provide some idea about simple claims. Advertisements that we encounter everyday in newspapers or on TV, on the other hand, are examples of long and complex claims made about some product or the other. Claims can be articulated, or can sometimes be expressed only as innuendo or as an insinuation. They can also be *supported* or *unsupported*; i.e., in some cases *reasons* for accepting them may be provided along with the claim, in which case the claim is called *supported*. In the absence of any reasons given, a claim remains *unsupported* or *unargued for*.

Since critical thinking is about accepting or rejecting a claim on the basis of reasons provided, we would be interested only in the supported claims. Claims that are supported can have a very special structure, namely, that of an argument.

An **argument** is a set of claims that has a *central* or *principal claim which is at issue and is to be argued for*, and other claims that are offered *as reasons* or *supporting evidence* for accepting or believing in that principal claim. Arguments are of great interest to logicians.

Conclusion: The principal claim that is argued for is called the *conclusion*.

Premises: The other claims that are offered as supporting reasons in the argument for the conclusion are called *premises*.

Arguments thus are structured pieces of articulated critical reasoning. Every argument must have a conclusion and a premise or some *premises*.

The simplest examples of arguments are those which have *one premise* and *one conclusion*. The following argument is an example of that kind. It has one principal claim or conclusion: *we are in for an unusually hot summer*, and one premise or supporting reason: the *data from Meteorological Office shows lower temperatures in the region in previous years*.

Example

7. We are in for an unusually hot summer because the data from Meteorological Office shows lower temperatures in the region in the previous years.

But, as we shall soon find out, arguments can also have many premises. In fact, it is more common to have several premises for a conclusion.

Arguments have certain special characteristics:

Arguments are not claims: Arguments are constructed out of a number of claims, but *they themselves are not claims*. For, they are not statements of any kind, and claims are statements. Hence, strictly speaking, the terms which apply to claims do not always apply to arguments, and vice versa. For instance, claims are *true* or *false* but, strictly speaking, the epithets *true* or *false* do not apply to arguments. For arguments, we have a separate set of evaluative terms such as *valid*, *invalid*, *sound* and *unsound*, which will be discussed later in a subsequent chapter. In a technical sense, these terms, e.g., *valid*, *invalid*, do not apply to claims. People loosely call claims or statements *valid* when they mean that they are *true*.

Claims	**Appropriate terms:** true, false.
Arguments	**Appropriate terms:** valid, invalid, sound, unsound.

Every set of claims is not an argument: An argument is a set of claims, but *every set of claims is not an argument*. Arguments are not just a list of statements. There has to be a *special relationship among the claims in the set* in order to qualify as an argument. There has to be a claim in the sense of conclusion as mentioned above, and other claims have to act as premises to support it. Thus, a descriptive passage or an explanation may be a set of claims, but it may not be an argument. Similarly, stories or reports may contain claims, but generally do not qualify as arguments.

No fixed number on how many premises: There is no fixed number of how many premises an argument can have: some may use a single premise, while others may have multiple premises. There is therefore no restriction on the number of premises. The following two examples are both arguments, but the first example has only one premise (*Cigarette smoking is a preventable cause of death*), whereas the second example has two premises (*All physical objects have mass, and this table is a physical object*).

Examples

8. Cigarette smoking is a preventable cause of death, so cigarette sales should be banned.
9. All physical objects have mass; this table is a physical object; therefore it has mass.

Incidentally, this may cause some of you to wonder whether there is any restriction on how many conclusions an argument can have. Remember, strictly speaking, one argument at a time can have one central claim or conclusion. But complex arguments may contain more than one connected conclusion in them. We shall see some examples of these in our discussion below.

Format of an argument may not always be simple: The format of arguments need not be always so simple as in Example 8 or Example 9.

Sometimes, a whole argument can be incorporated within one single statement. Consider the following:

Example

10. It is a mistake to argue that computers cannot think like humans because computers are products of humans, because humans are also products of humans.

The premise of Example 10 is "humans are also products of humans", and the conclusion is "It is a mistake to argue that computers cannot think like humans because computers are products of humans". However, the conclusion itself contains an argument complete with a *premise* (computers are products of humans) and a *conclusion* (computers cannot think like humans).

There may be unstated premises: Sometimes all the premises may not be stated explicitly, some may be assumed or some may be suppressed. When the situation is like this, a proper analysis of an argument will require bringing the relevant premises out or to state them all explicitly.

To take an example, in *The Adventure of the Blue Carbuncle*, Sherlock Holmes finds an old hat. He has no idea who the owner of the hat is, yet he tells a lot about the owner to Dr. Watson. One of his claims is that the owner is the highly intellectual type. Dr. Watson, as usual, does not see any connection. To explain, Holmes puts the hat on his head and shows that the hat is oversized as it touches the bridge of his nose. Then Holmes says: It is a question of cubic capacity. A man with such a large head must have something in it. To Holmes, this argument may seem very obvious. However, if we try to explicate the premises he has used, then we find that there are many unstated and questionable assumptions in it. Analysis of the argument may lead to the following structure:

Premise 1: This is a large hat.
Premise 2: Someone (male) is the owner of this hat.
Premise 3: The owners of large hats are owners of large heads.
Premise 4: People with large heads got to have something in it, namely, large brains.
Premise 5: People with large brains are highly intellectual.
Premise 6: The owner of this hat has a large head.
Premise 7: The owner of this hat has a large brain.
Conclusion: Therefore, the owner of this hat is highly intellectual.

There can be missing premises: Arguments with missing premises or presumed premises require sensitive and skilled handling. For, insertion of premises, where not overtly stated, needs deeper understanding about various factors, such as the context in which the argument is being offered, the assumptions being made, the target audience, and the speaker's intention. For the sake of simplicity, we shall be focusing only on those arguments which are well articulated, namely, where all the premises are stated.

Arguments have a standard format: For the purpose of logic, there is a standard format for arguments, i.e.,

Premises

∴ Conclusion

In the standard format, premises need to be stated first. They also have to be separated from the conclusion. It is desirable to use some *separating line* between the two kinds of components. In addition, it is better to use some conclusion marker symbol before the conclusion.

Unfortunately, however, arguments may not always be in a proper format. To put arguments in the standard format, one has to do the following:

- ✓ Separate the premises from the conclusion.
- ✓ State the premises first in a sequential order and, if necessary, number them.
- ✓ Then state the conclusion with a conclusion marker, such as the symbol '∴', or any of the conclusion-indicator words (see Section 2.3)

Standard format of an argument

Premise 1
Premise 2
⋮
(*Therefore*) *Conclusion*

Example 9 "All physical objects have mass and this table is a physical object, therefore this table has mass", in its standard format, should be written as follows:

Example

11. *Premise 1:* All physical objects have mass.
    Premise 2: This table is a physical object.
    Conclusion: Therefore This table has mass.

Arguments, their analysis and their evaluation are among the central topics in logic. Informally, it is the goal of logic to promote critical thinking through such analysis and evaluation.

EXERCISE 2.2

1. Which of the following statements are true? Justify your answer:

a. *Arguments are nothing but sets of claims.

b. An argument may have only one premise.

c. Premises form the support basis for advancing the conclusion.

d. There can be no argument without a conclusion.

e. In an argument in standard format, the conclusion may be missing.

f. Every argument is a claim but not every claim is an argument.

g. *All premises in an argument may not be explicitly stated.

h. The proper format places the conclusion first followed by the premises.

2. Arrange the arguments below in standard format:

a. The chase for a unified theory is a questionable pursuit. For, everything except the existence of universe is explainable to some extent; however, there is no one theory that explains it all.

b. People want a clean livable environment; they want safety and economic security for themselves and their family. Therefore, any government that can take good care of these basic demands will be popular.

c. * Since each person has a right to liberty and property, the government should leave individual citizens free to exchange their labour and property as they freely choose.

d. The kidnapped West German envoy was killed by the rebels since the Guatemalan Government refused to negotiate with the rebels. Also, the rebels asked for £2,70,000 as ransom which they did not get.

e. The Vietnamese Government has launched a nationwide clean-up of poultry farms to try to stop the spread of bird flu. For, Bird flu has killed almost 50 people since its resurgence in South East Asia in December 2003, and containment of this infectious disease is very important for many reasons.

f. Genetically transformed food crop could be dangerous; we are confronted with a very powerful technology the world has ever known, and it is being rapidly deployed with almost no thought whatsoever to its consequences.

g. "There is a difficulty with Darwinism. While Lamarckism appears to be not only refutable but actually refuted (because the kind of acquired adaptations which Lamarck envisaged do not appear to be hereditary), it is far from clear what we should consider a possible refutation of the theory of natural selection. If, more especially, we accept that statistical definition of fitness which defines fitness by actual survival, then the survival of the fittest becomes tautological, and irrefutable"†.

*h. "...History in the strict sense is dependent on human testimony. Since this is not available with respect to the development of the world of life we must be satisfied with something less satisfactory. The only evidence available is that provided by the fossils"††.

2.3 Recognizing an Argument

How does one recognize an argument? Given a passage, is there any way to tell whether it contains an argument or not? Unfortunately, the answer to this question cannot be a straightforward *yes*. For, the task is not an easy one. Sometimes, the presence of certain key words in a set of claims may provide us *the linguistic clue* that there is an argument there. It could be the presence of **words** that indicates the presence of a premise such as:

Premise-indicator words: Since For Because Given that

Or, it could be the presence of words that indicate the presence of a conclusion such as:

Conclusion-indicator words: Therefore Hence It follows that So Consequently Thus

We need to remember, however, that language use is a dynamic activity. A word, whether it is a premise-indicator or a conclusion-indicator, may *usually* indicate the presence of an argument, but in a different context, it may serve an entirely different function. Consider the following examples:

Examples

12. I have been living on this campus **since** 1994, and my children grew up here.
13. The project work has to be finished by summer, **since** funding for it will not be available from autumn semester.

Example 12 shows that the word 'since' does not necessarily indicate the presence of an argument. For, in Example 12 'since' is used to indicate a passage of time, not to indicate a reason. So, though the example contains two claims, is really not an argument. In Example 13 on the other hand,

† Karl R. Popper, *Federation Proceedings, American Societies for Experimental Biology*, Vol. 22, 1963, p. 964.

†† Thompson, W.R., *Introduction to The Origin of Species,* E.P. Dutton & Co., New York, 1956.

'since' signals the presence of a supporting reason or a premise "funding for it will not be available from autumn semester" for the principal claim or the conclusion "The project work has to be finished by summer". Therefore, it may be useful to remember that recognizing the presence of an argument in a passage takes more than a mere blind search for certain keywords.

One can recognize the presence of an argument by relying upon one's logical understanding of the contents in a passage. For example, the following is an argument. Recognizing this argument will require a close reading and comprehension of the passage, and an awareness of the logical relationship that exists among the statements in the passage. Though there is not a single special word to indicate the presence of a premise or a conclusion, the reader can still make out by following the flow of logic that the first statement in the following example is the conclusion, and the remaining are the premises. This shows that the presence of the premise-indicators or conclusion-indicators is not absolutely mandatory for recognizing the presence of an argument in a passage.

Example

14. For astronomy, desert mountaintops make good sites. Their height places them above a certain part of the atmosphere, enabling a star's light to reach the telescope without covering the entire depth of atmosphere. Also, the dry climate of the desert makes it relatively cloud-free.

EXERCISE 2.3

1. Do these passages contain arguments? Explain.

a. Obviously, there exists neither an absolute nor a generally accepted line of demarcation between pure and applied science. The distinction between analytical and empirical sciences is one of the most favoured categorizations of our time but it is not always accepted. Quine (1953), for instance, tried to use Gödels' incompletablity theorem to express doubt over this distinction.

b. *If an industry pollutes the environment and the citizens affected have to bear the cost (health hazards, medical cost, physical ailment, etc.), the market prices of its commodities will no longer reflect the true cost of producing the commodity. The result is the decline of the welfare of the society as a whole. Hence, if an industry pollutes, it is only fair to make it pay for the damages caused.

c. I have been sitting here for three hours, and I have not seen anyone coming out of the school gate.

d. In 2004, for the first time in more than four decades, US infant mortality has increased. For, older women are putting off motherhood. Also, couples are having multiple babies via fertility drugs.

e. Life insurance companies like their policy holders to be in good health. Some companies have three different premium classifications: standard, preferred, or preferred plus. You're rewarded with lower premiums if you're super-healthy and haven't smoked in five years because that reduces your chances of dying soon. Being just 'normally healthy' requires that you haven't used nicotine in the past three years and still gets you lower premiums. A standard rate requires that you have not used nicotine within the past year.

f. A housewife's work has no results: it simply has to be done again. Bringing up children is not a real occupation, because children come up just the same, brought up or not. (Germaine Greer, *The Female Eunuch*)

g. *...The paleontologist...deals with morphology and sees order in its change. He witnesses major trends...He sees what appear to be highly adaptive types of organisms side by side with what appear to be adaptive 'monstrosities.' He sees groups of organisms, apparently in their prime, fade and disappear through 'short' periods. And he may ask: "All this through shift in gene frequencies, in genetic shift through differential reproduction and slow change through successive populations?"†

h. It has taken biologists some 230 years to identify and describe three quarters of a million insects; if there are indeed at least thirty million, as Terry Erwin of the Smithsonian Institute estimates, then, working as they have in the past, insect taxonomists have 10,000 years of employment ahead of them.

2.4 Deduction and Induction

It is customary in the western tradition to classify logic into two broad types: **deductive** and **inductive**. This classification is based on the idea that the way we reason can be broadly categorized into two groups: **Deduction and Induction.** Though this categorization is very popular, it is not at all easy to pinpoint where exactly the line between the two types of reasoning should be drawn.

One of the ways in which the distinction can be attempted is to look at the general pattern of the argument types and to look into what we expect from them.

† Everett C. Olson, *Evolution After Darwin*, Vol. 1, Sol Tax, editor (University of Chicago Press, 1960), pp. 535–37.

Deductive Arguments

From a *good* **deductive argument,** our expectation is that, *if* all its premises are true, then its conclusion *must* be true. The joint truth of all the premises of a *good* deductive argument is supposed to *guarantee* the truth of the conclusion. Consider the following example:

Example

15. All human beings are mortal.
    All Indian voters are human beings.
    Hence, all Indian voters are mortal.

Example 15 is a deductive argument, and a *good* deductive argument. Given the truth of the two premises of the example, there is no way for the conclusion to be false. The truth of the conclusion here seems to be already *contained* in the truth of the premises. The deduction merely helps to elicit that *contained* information. This, as mentioned earlier, is the expectation from deductive arguments: that the premises will provide **conclusive support** for the conclusion.

Conclusive support means support which leaves no room for doubt for the truth of the conclusion. Failure to do so is held as a defect in a deductive argument. Those which fail to demonstrate support conclusively for their conclusion are considered as *bad* deductive arguments. Consider the example given below:

Example

16. All human beings are mortal.
    All whales are mortal.
    Hence, all whales are human beings.

Given that the premises of Example 16 are all true, the conclusion does not follow. Thus, the truth of the conclusion is still not guaranteed from the truth of all the premises.

Inductive Arguments

In contrast, there are other kinds of arguments, the **inductive arguments,** which differ from deductive arguments in having conclusions that do not rely upon merely explicating the information that might be implicitly contained in the premises. Typically, inductive arguments have conclusions which go beyond that which is covered, explicitly or implicitly, by the premises. This is known as the **inductive leap**: A jump from the known to the yet unknown, or from the cases observed so far to the yet unobserved cases.

The Usual Format of Induction

1.	Case 1:	ϕ
2.	Case 2:	ϕ
3.	Case 3:	ϕ
⋮	⋮	
n.	Case n:	ϕ

$n + 1$. Therefore, Case $n + 1$ also will be a ϕ case.

This inductive format can be seen in the following example:

Example

17. All students at IIT Kharagpur so far observed have black hair.

    Therefore, the student who will join IIT Kharagpur 10 years from now will also have black hair.

Or, consider generalizations such as the following example which too instantiates this characteristic feature of inductive reasoning:

Example

18. Mr. Rao had asked for a fruit after his lunch every day for the past 6 days. Therefore, today also he will ask for a fruit after his lunch.

One of the major differences between deductive and inductive reasoning is that by nature inductive arguments do not aim at providing conclusive evidence for their conclusions. Between their premises and their target conclusion, there always remains a gap. The joint truth of all the premises can *at best* provide **partial support** in terms of probability for the truth of the conclusion. The stronger the evidence is from the premises, the better will be the inductive argument. However, *at best* a good inductive argument can provide a very high degree of probability (close to 1), but can never yield conclusive support.

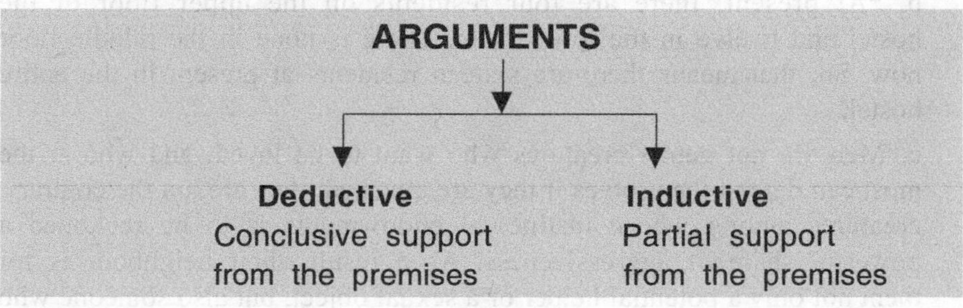

Since by nature the two types of arguments are different, the criteria for evaluation for each type also differ. For deductive arguments, the criteria of *validity* and *soundness* are used. These concepts will be discussed separately in Chapter 4. As for inductive arguments, we use the evaluative terms 'strong' or 'weak', depending upon the kind of support the premises provide.

Example

19. 99% of the residents of this town have ration cards. Hence, Ms. Puri, who is a resident of this town, is likely to have a ration card.

Example 19 is an instance of a 'strong' inductive reasoning, because its premises, which cover most of the relevant cases, provide a strong probabilistic support for its conclusion. On the other hand, premise of the following example offers little support for its conclusion and, therefore, is a 'weak' inductive argument.

Example

20. Two snakes that I have spotted were brown. So, snakes in this locality are all brown.

Most of the chapters in this book will discuss deduction and deductive arguments. Induction and issues related with it will be covered separately in Chapter 15.

EXERCISE 2.4

1. Construct your own examples of deductive and inductive arguments.

2. Deductive or inductive? Identify in each of following the type of argument and then rate it as 'good' or 'bad' with justification.

a. Common business practices differ markedly among nations. All forms of bribery of Government personnel are considered wrong in the United States. Whereas many forms of petty bribery of lower Government personnel are not only common in Mexico but also are universally accepted as the common practice.

b. *At present, there are four residents on the upper floor of the hostel and twelve in the lower floor. There is none in the middle floor now. So, that means there are sixteen residents at present in the entire hostel.

c. Men are not gentle creatures who want to be loved, and who at the most can defend themselves if they are attacked; they are, on the contrary, creatures among whose instinctual endowments is to be reckoned a powerful share of aggressiveness. As a result, their neighbour is for them not only a potential helper or a sexual object, but also someone who tempts them to satisfy their aggressiveness on him, to exploit his capacity for work without compensation, to use him sexually without his consent, to seize his possessions, to humiliate him, to torture him, and to kill him. *Homo homini lupus*[1]. Who, in the face of all his experience of life and of history, will have the courage to dispute this assertion? …Anyone who calls to mind the atrocities committed during the racial migrations or the invasions of the Huns, or by the people known as Mongols *under* Jenghiz Khan and Tamarlane, ...or even, indeed, the horrors of recent World War—anyone who calls these things to mind will have to bow humbly before the truth of this view. (Sigmund Freud, excerpt from *Civilization and Its Discontent*, Tranl. James Strachey, New York, W.W. Norton: 1962.)

d. Shashi had not locked the gates yesterday. Either the watchman or Shashi locks the gates. Therefore, the watchman must have locked the gates.

e. The members of the Bannerjee family are all related to the Chatterjee family. And every member of Chatterjee family is related to the Mukherjee family. So, the entire Bannerjee family is related to the Mukherjee family.

f. *A large number of studies show that obesity in children is linked to watching too much TV. Children who are mostly outdoors and are involved in physical activity do not show obesity. Studies show that those who watch four or more hours of TV everyday show a greater proportion of body fat than those who watch for two hours or less.

2.5 Analysis of Arguments

Arguments in everyday life rarely appear in isolation. They usually come within the context of a discussion which may include a lot of different information that may or may not be pertinent to the argument. Analysis of an argument, therefore, first requires the *isolation of the argument,* once identified, from its extraneous surrounding. This requires a careful pruning of all that is not relevant without affecting the argument. The extra material comes into the argument for a variety of reasons.

First, people often take a roundabout way to reach the point. Some get distracted. They start discussing something and in association bring in other points before continuing with the topic started. *Second*, some people tend to repeat their points. Their aim might be better communication with their audience or emphasis on the points covered. *Third*, in reasoning with everyday language people often use phrases or words to embellish their points. Sometimes

[1] Man is a wolf to man (translation).

the extra material comes in the form of expressions which are used to counter possible attacks on the premises of an argument. Ordinary arguments routinely use expressions with such strategic functions as:

(a) **To assure the audience of the value of the premises:** Expressions such as "Recent studies show that...", "A reliable source has claimed that...", "I can assure you that...", etc. are used to indicate that the premises in the argument have evidence which, though not provided with the argument, can be produced on demand.

***Example* (of Assuring term)**

21. It is already well established that arsenic is present in the aquafiers of this region. What we need, therefore, is a safe method to counter this pollution of water.

(b) **To guard the truth of the premises:** Usually, guarding is done by weakening the claims with expressions such as 'most' instead of 'all', 'Perhaps', instead of 'Surely', 'It seems that', instead of 'I know' 'almost always', instead of 'always', etc. This protects the claims in the argument against strong criticism.

***Example* (of Guarding term)**

22. Perhaps the data in the survey were collected from a small area. It seems that enough care has not been taken while preparing the questionnaire either. So, the findings of this survey and the claim of their universality remain questionable.

(c) **To discount obvious objections against the premises:** Generally, the pattern is to anticipate an objection by citing it in the claim and then by trying to discount it. Typically, the terms 'but', 'although', 'though', 'yet', 'nevertheless', etc. are used for this purpose.

***Example* (of Discounting term)**

23. Although the accommodation is not spacious, it is very reasonably priced. Even if it is located near a noisy factory, it is not dirty. So, overall it is a good place to be in.

Though an argument may be strewn with terms such as these for various argumentative reasons, they do not always have logical significance for the argument. Therefore, sometimes they can be dropped without affecting the meaning or the logical worth of the argument. As, for instance, in Example 21 above, the expression "It is well established that" can be dropped from the argument before putting the argument into standard form.

However, elimination of extra material from the argument requires skill, care and a deep understanding of the argument. For example, suppose someone argues: "Recent studies show that HIV does not always lead to full-blown cases of AIDS, so we know that HIV does not always lead to full-blown cases of AIDS". In this case, dropping the assuring term "Recent studies show that..." can only make the argument trivial: HIV does not always lead to full-blown cases of AIDS, so we know that HIV does not always lead to full-blown cases of AIDS. Therefore, in this case, dropping the assuring term is not advisable. It must be remembered that there is no mechanical method to decide when a material would be extra or unnecessary, and when it would not be. Paring an argument needs enough discretion to know how to keep its core intact and what not to omit to make it better.

Once the extra material from the argument is carefully isolated then, for further analysis of the argument, one needs to:

✓ Separate the premises and the conclusion

✓ Arrange the sub-arguments, if there are any

For this purpose, diagramming the argument may be of some definite advantage. The method of diagramming is explained below in the next section.

EXERCISE 2.5

1. If you can spot them, mark the Guarding terms as G, the assuring terms as A, and the discounting terms as D in the following arguments:

a. Given the economic strength of the Euro, it is very likely that the Euro will play an important role as an international currency. It seems that Euro may even eventually challenge the US dollar as the leading international currency.

b. *The close connectivity between countries may lead to undesirable economic consequences. Although close connection between countries promises greater economic growth, it may also cause undesirable economic fluctuation. Like a plague, any adverse economic condition or implementation of one economic policy by one country could be easily transmitted to another.

c. Many economists have described the economic aspects of intellectual property rights (IPRs) and have suggested solutions for individual countries. Perhaps, the best advice for developing countries is to find ways of cooperation among them to protect their intellectual property rights.

d. The generation gap is visible in many ways. The elders do listen to rock and pop, still they prefer the old bands and the music when they were young. They send their children to westernized schools, yet frown on the trendy western clothes that the youngsters wear today.

e. Architects and engineers, perhaps, inevitably regard the subject of town planning and of city improvements from opposite standpoints. The engineer probably considers a new roadway as essentially a fresh artery for traffic, whereas the average architect seems more concerned about providing the citizen with a picturesque perspective than with lessening the labour by which he earns his daily bread.

f. The Marburg virus, which has killed 140 people in a major outbreak in Angola in 2005, is a severe and highly contagious form of haemorrhagic fever caused by a virus from the same family—the filoviruses—as Ebola. Experts say it is possible that patients spread the virus by producing an aerosol of tiny infected droplets when they cough and splutter. About one in four people infected with the virus die, usually from shock or liver failure. However, in areas where medical support is poor, the death rate can be much higher.

2. What is the crucial difference between 'assuring' and 'guarding'? What is the consequence of not adopting the 'discounting' measure?

2.6 Diagramming Arguments

A **diagram** of an argument helps reveal the inner logical relationships within an argument. This is helpful both for gaining a better understanding of how an argument works and for assessing its worth. Diagramming brings out the role of a premise or a premise set quite clearly. From that, one can easily evaluate the worth of the support of that premise or premise set for the argument. It is possible to have more than one conclusion in an argument. For the sake of simplicity, our discussion will be confined to arguments with only one conclusion.

The steps in logical diagramming of an argument are as follows:

(i) *Identify the components.* In analyzing the structure of an argument, the first and the foremost task is to identify the components, i.e., the premise statements and the conclusion statement. You may try by identifying the conclusion first and looking for the supporting premises for it. For this purpose, the conclusion markers may be of help. Otherwise, the context and the content in the passage may make the conclusion evident. Consider, for example:

> She seems happy. There is a spark in her eyes. Her face looks calm and rosy.

Reading the statements together should tell you that the first statement "she seems happy" is the conclusion, while the rest are supporting evidence for that claim.

(ii) *Use a mark such as numbers 1, 2, etc., to identify each statement.* Before diagramming, one has to mark the components to uniquely show the position of each statement in the diagram. So, in order of their occurrence in the argument, a number is assigned to each of the components. You may leave out the premise-indicator words or the conclusion-indicator words. For example, we may use 1,2, and 3 to identify the argument given above:

> She seems happy [1]. There is a spark in her eyes [2]. Her face looks calm and rosy [3].

(iii) *Use certain symbols.* This is to capture the nature of the logical relationship existing among the components. For example, use a downward arrow '⇓' to indicate the logical flow from a premise to a conclusion. The following example shows you how to use the arrow to describe the logical relationship in a given argument.

Example

The following argument has one premise and one conclusion:

✓24. Because every object's temperature is above absolute zero, motion at the atomic level is always present.

'Because' is a premise-indicator word. We can set it aside for our diagramming task. So, after marking, the argument may look like this:

✓(Because) every object's temperature is above absolute zero [1], motion at the atomic level is always present [2].

This can be represented as follows:

(iv) *Properly represent the logical relationship.* There could be arguments in which a number of premises may *jointly* lead to the conclusion.

To indicate the nature of that collective support, *link all the jointly supporting premises* before indicating the logic flow to their conclusion. This shows that each of the statements thus linked is equal in status and has the same evidential worth in terms of support. This is particularly true about *conjunctions*. Consider Example 9 in this chapter.

Example

25. All physical objects have mass, and this table is a physical object, therefore it has mass.

After marking, the argument looks like this:

All physical objects have mass [1], and this table is a physical object [2], (therefore) it has mass [3].

Clearly, neither [1] nor [2] alone leads to [3]; but they do it jointly. The 'and' works as a conjunction. The diagram must capture this characteristic. Here is how it could be done:

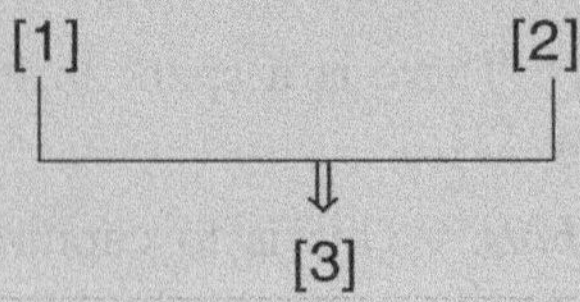

In contrast, it is possible that, though an argument may have several premises, some or all of them may lend support to the conclusion *independently*, i.e., not jointly. In such cases, the diagram should reflect that point of difference as may be seen in the following example. There is no need to link the premises in such cases and their independent support for the conclusion may be represented by separate arrows:

Example

26. Contrary to what many people may think, a positive test for HIV is not necessarily a death sentence. For one thing, the time from the development of the antibodies to the full-blown clinical symptoms may take 2–10 years, depending upon the person's health status. For another, various reports now indicate that a significant number of people who test HIV positive may never develop clinical AIDS.

Using a sequence of numbers, we may mark its components as follows:

Contrary to what many people may think, a positive test for HIV is not necessarily a death sentence [1]. (For one thing), the time from the development of the antibodies to the full-blown clinical symptoms may take 2–10 years, depending upon the person's health status [2]. (For another) various reports now indicate that a significant number of people who test HIV positive may never develop clinical AIDS [3].

The first statement or [1] is the conclusion in this case, and [2] and [3] are premises. However, the phrases such as 'For one thing' indicates that [2] independently provides the support to the conclusion; similarly, [3] also lends support independently. The diagram may be depicted as follows:

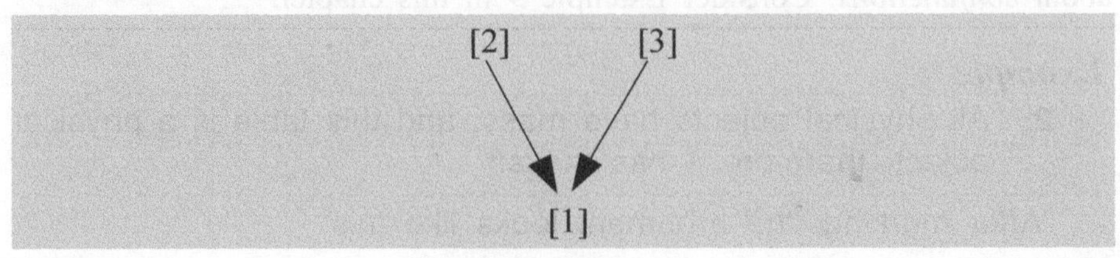

The difference in premise-conclusion relationship, as depicted in this diagram, should be noticeable when contrasted with the diagram of Example 25.

For exclusive disjunctions or 'either-or' in the sense of only one is possible, but not both, use the same branching procedure. For, 'either-or' in this sense indicates just one of the possibilities.

(v) *Treat sub-arguments with equal care:* It is possible that an argument may be complex enough to involve one or more sub-arguments. This happens when a conclusion of one argument becomes the premise for another argument. Thus the same statement may serve as a conclusion and as a premise in the same passage. Accordingly, the diagram should represent that situation in which arguments may be nested within another argument.

Given a complex passage, the first task should be to identify the conclusion or conclusions. It is often helpful to reconstruct the argument backwards from the conclusion.

Given below is an example of an argument in which we have already marked component statements with individual numbers.

Example

27. Multinationals (MNCs), which operate in more than one country, present ethical dilemmas for their managers [1]. One set of dilemmas is caused by the fact that environmental laws or labour policy of one country may not be effective constraints on a multinational [2]. For, the multinational has the ability to shift its operations to another country which offers it less stringent laws and policies [3]. Another set is caused by the quandary of deciding which of the different sets of norms and standards the multinational should follow in its various operations in different countries [4].

The main conclusion in this case is [1]. Its two premises are [2] and [4]. However, between [2] and [3], one can spot a premise and conclusion relationship also: [2] is the conclusion supported by [3]. Accordingly, the diagram will be:

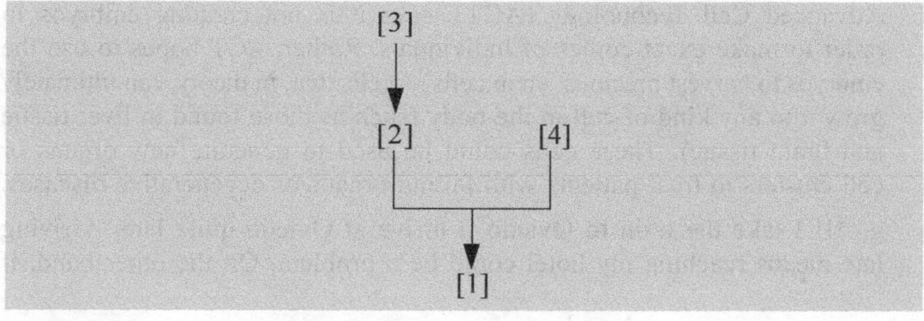

EXERCISE 2.6

1. Draw a diagram for each of the following argument, arranging the sub-arguments in order and by numbering the components:

   a. *Research findings are often questionable. Due to pressure of meeting deadlines, external and internal competitions, researchers sometimes cannot be as careful as they should be. Little errors slowly mount up and, as a result, the data becomes unreliable.

   b. Since no one had actually directly seen chemical bonding, scientists who use this concept must rely upon indirect evidence from experiments.

   c. Speculation over the existence of a 'southern land' was not confirmed until the early 1820s when British and American commercial operators and British and Russian national expeditions began exploring the Antarctic Peninsula region and other areas south of the Antarctic Circle. So, several exploration 'firsts' into Antarctica were achieved only in the early 20th century. Thus, the history of scientific research in Antarctica is fairly recent.

   d. Either the geographical location of the island has shifted or the satellite observational data is inaccurate. For, the island now shows 5 degree to the north of where it used to be. The Tsunami was caused by one of the most powerful earthquakes in the world history and it had the power to displace parts of geographical plate.

   e. If we are really protective about rights not being exploited, used, or abused without consent, then we would object against the use of animals in casual dissection for science education. The usual explanation for this disparity is that non-human animal life is considered less valuable than human life because other species lack certain traits that qualify humans for rights. But in suffering they are our equals. So, it goes to show that we are not really as consistent in our rationality as we would like to think.

   f. It is difficult to decide about whether human cloning is ethically right or wrong. George Bush, the US President, and conservative religious groups are pushing for a complete ban on human cloning because they think human cloning is morally wrong. However, the company responsible, Advanced Cell Technology (ACT), says it is not creating embryos in order to make exact copies of individuals. Rather, ACT hopes to use the embryos to harvest precious 'stem cells'—cells that, in theory, can ultimately grow into any kind of cell in the body (such as those found in liver tissue and brain tissue). These cells could be used to generate new organs or cell clusters to treat patients with failing organs or degenerative diseases.

   g. *If I take the train to Oviedo, I arrive at Oviedo quite late. Arriving late means reaching my hotel could be a problem. On the other hand, if

I fly to Oviedo, I have to buy the air-tickets now. Buying air-tickets now will mean I have to check their prices first. So, whichever transport I use, I shall reach Oviedo.

h. Hundreds of civilian deaths in the US–led invasion of Iraq could have been prevented by abandoning two misguided military tactics. The use of cluster munitions in populated areas caused more civilian casualties than any other factor in the military operations of the coalition. US and British forces used almost 13,000 cluster munitions, containing nearly 2 million sub-munitions, that killed or wounded more than 1,000 civilians. Also, 50 strikes on top Iraqi leaders failed to kill any of the intended targets, but instead killed dozens of civilians. The US 'decapitation' strategy relied on intercepts of senior Iraqi leaders´ satellite phone calls along with corroborating intelligence that proved inadequate. As a result, the US military could only locate targets within a 100-metre radius—clearly inadequate precision in civilian neighbourhoods.

i. Tapping into solar energy is a wise choice while the Sun is there. For, solar energy is created deep within the core of the Sun. Energy generated in the Sun's core takes a million years to reach its surface. Every second 700 million tons of hydrogen are converted into helium *ashes*. In the process, 5 million tons of pure energy is released; therefore, as time goes on the Sun is becoming lighter.

2.7 Validity, Soundness and Consistency

A crucial difference between a *good* and a *bad* deductive argument is that in the *good* deductive argument the conclusion *follows from* the given premises, whereas in a *bad* deductive argument the conclusion does not follow.

Validity and Invalidiy

This characteristic of *good* deductive arguments is known as **validity**. An argument is **valid** if and only if *it is not possible* for all its premises to be true and its conclusion to be false.

Example

28. Paris is in France.
    France is in Europe.
    Therefore, Paris is in Europe.

Example 28 is a valid argument; given the truth of all its premises, it is not possible for its conclusion to be false.

An argument is **invalid**, on the other hand, if and only if it is possible for its conclusion to be false even when all its premises are true.

Example

29. A is taller than C.
    B is taller than C.
    Therefore, A is taller than B.

Example 29 is an invalid argument. Even if we suppose that both its premises are true, there is no necessity why its conclusion must be true. Even though A and B are taller than C, there remains a possibility that A and B may be of the same height. The possibility of falsity of its conclusion, in spite of the truth of the premises, makes Example 29 invalid.

It is to be noted that just because an argument has false premises, it does not mean that it must be invalid. *A valid argument can have false premises.* In that case, since some or all its premises may be false, we cannot say that it is possible for the conclusion to be false *while the premises are all true*. Therefore, technically we cannot call it invalid.

Examples

30. A triangle has three angles.
    The sum of the three angles of a triangle is 190 degrees.
    Hence, If one of the angles of the triangle is 90 degrees, the sum of two other angles must be 100 degrees.
31. All cats have six legs.
    All six-legged creatures have wings.
    Therefore, all cats have wings.

In both Examples 30 and 31, the conclusions follow *given the truth of their premises*. So, they are valid. We know that the second premise of Example 30, "The sum of the three angles of a triangle is 190 degree", is false. However, if we suppose it to be true, then the conclusion follows. Similarly, both the premises of Example 31 are false. However, if we suppose them to be true, then the conclusion follows. Technically, therefore, both Examples 30 and 31 are valid.

Similarly, it has to be noted that an invalid argument can have a true conclusion. The premises can be true and the conclusion may also be true, yet the all important logical link between them may be missing.

Example

32. 12 is greater than 3.
    15 is greater than 3.
    Hence, 15 is greater than 12.

The premises and the conclusion of Example 32 are all true; yet the truth of the conclusion does not *follow* from the truth of the premises. This makes the argument invalid.

Now we can state the possibilities of validity and invalidity of an argument as follows:

Premises	Conclusion	Valid	Invalid
True	True	Possible	Possible
True	False	Not possible	Possible
False	True	Possible	Possible
False	False	Possible	Possible

Clearly, the possibilities of giving valid arguments with obviously false premises leading to absurdly false conclusions such as those in Example 31 indicate that requirement of validity from a *good* deductive argument may not be adequate. For, you might be thinking: Why should we bother about whether arguments are valid or not, when valid arguments can clearly have false premises and false conclusions! What is the point of having validity when the conclusion follows, but follows as a falsity or only *trivially*? Considerations such as these show that we need to have a stricter requirement in order to have more satisfactory kind of arguments.

Soundness and Unsoundness

This is why the concept of **soundness** is required. A **sound argument** requires *both* that:

✓ The argument must be valid.
✓ And the premises of the argument must be true.

An argument which violates any of these two conditions or both is **unsound**.

The conclusion of a sound argument must be true. By definition, a sound argument has to be valid. If an argument is valid, then it is not possible for the argument to have all true premises and a false conclusion. In addition, soundness requires that its premises must be all true. It follows from the definition of soundness that the conclusion of a sound argument must be true.

Soundness is a stricter requirement. For, this rules out the earlier possibility of cases of *vacuous validity* by virtue of having false premises.

Consistency

It is an extra requirement from a good argument, deductive or inductive, that its premise set should not be internally inconsistent. That is, it should *not* be the case that the truth of one of its premises cancels or is in conflict with the truth-claim of another. A set of statements is **consistent** if and only if there is at least a possible situation in which every member of that set is true. It is **inconsistent** if and only if no such possibility exists for the members of the set.

The requirement of consistency within the premises is there to ensure logical compatibility of the premises. The premises act as the support base for a conclusion. If that base within itself suffers from internal incompatibility or lack of cohesiveness, the result is disastrous for the conclusion. The argument then becomes trivial. Standard logic holds that from an inconsistent set of premises *anything follows* in a vacuous sense. For, an inconsistent premise set at best can lead to inconclusiveness, However, technically speaking, it is not a situation where the conclusion is false in spite of its premises being true. Therefore, any argument with an inconsistent set of premises will be valid, but that validity has no real logical worth.

We can sum up the discussion above as follows:

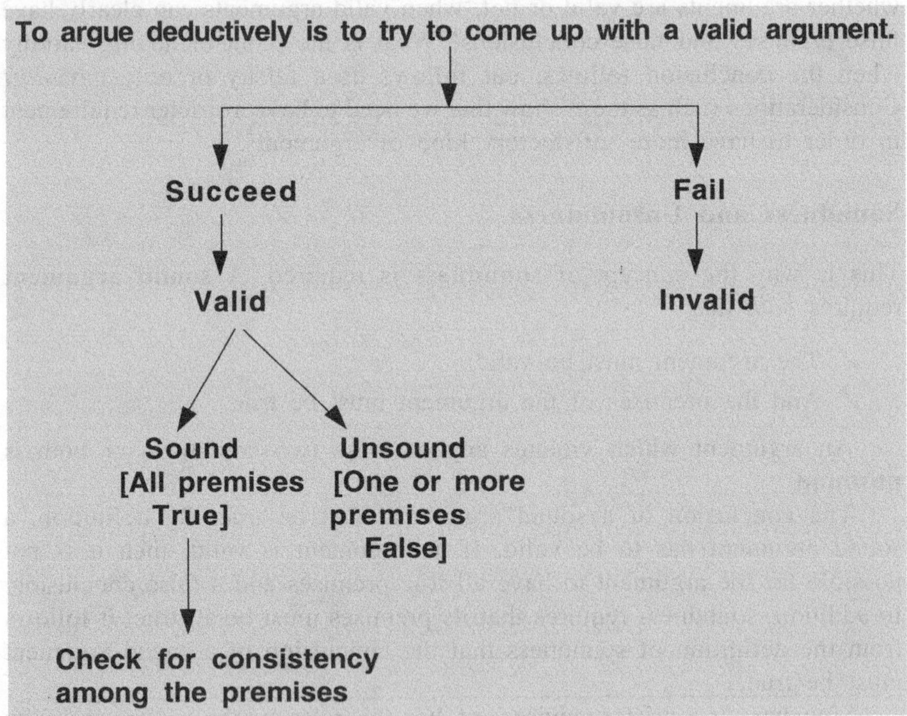

EXERCISE 2.7

1. True or False? Explain your answers. Where applicable, give examples of your own to justify your answer.

a. *All sound arguments are valid.

b. All valid arguments are sound.

c. No argument with false premises can be valid.

d. No argument with false premises can be sound.

e. *An argument which has all true premises and a true conclusion must be sound.

f. An argument with false premises but true conclusion must be invalid.

g. A valid argument with false premises but true conclusion may be sound.

h. An argument with false premises but true conclusion may be valid.

i. Any argument with a true conclusion must be valid.

j. *An argument with all true premises must be sound.

2. Suppose that an argument has a set of inconsistent premises. Can it be valid? Can it be sound? Explain.

2.8 Informal Evaluation: An Example

Suppose that we have been asked to rate the following argument which was sent as a letter to the editor of a newspaper.

> My thoughts on IIT–JEE (Joint Entrance Examination) Test are strong. This test does not tell us much more than whether the teachers are teaching the materials to us or not. If the teachers would and could teach us the things we need to know for the test, then may be we could actually score high in JEE. It is not like students are going to go home everyday and study huge books of the size of encyclopedias so that we can get a high score in the test. The things that we learn and remember come from school and our teachers. If they don't teach us what we need to know, then we will probably never know it. I say that we just get rid of JEE and any other test out there that are like JEE.

✓ The first task for an informal evaluation is to read the passage carefully. The aim should be to follow the thought pattern of the reasoner as closely as possible. The given passage contains a certain view about the Joint Entrance Examination (JEE) and few claims about the way the teachers teach for this examination. Based on that, it is finally claimed that JEE, and similar tests, should be abolished.

✓ Next, we need to identify the extra material in the argument, i.e., the material which, strictly speaking, is neither a premise nor a conclusion. Also, we need to identify the assuring, guarding and discounting terms, if present, to have a better grasp of the reasoner's argumentative technique. In the given argument, the first statement is more of an introductory remark which cautions the reader about the strong comments to come. It can be omitted without affecting the flow of the argument. There are also a few guarding terms, as can be seen below:

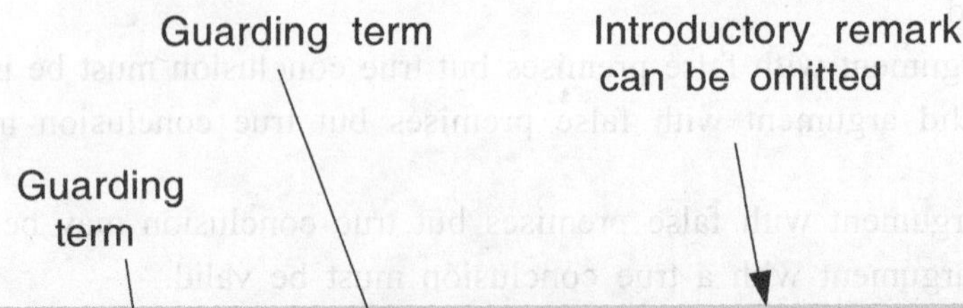

[My thoughts on IIT-JEE (Joint Entrance Examination) Test are strong]. This test does not tell us much more than whether the teachers are teaching the materials to us or not. If the teachers would and could teach us the things we need to know for the test, then may be we could actually score high in JEE. It is not like students are going to go home everyday and study huge books of the size of encyclopedias so that we can get a high score in the test. The things that we learn and remember come from school and our teachers. If they don't teach us what we need to know, then we will probably never know it. I say that we just get rid of JEE and any other test out there that are like JEE.

The presence of the guarding term shows that the reasoner is trying to soften the claims and thereby trying to avert direct refutation of some of his premises.

√ Once we have thus identified the extra material and the terms performing argumentative techniques, we next need to put the argument in the standard format to make it ready for evaluation.

In Standard Format

Premises:

1. This test (IIT-JEE) does not tell us much more than whether the teachers are teaching the materials to us or not.
2. If the teachers would and could teach us the things we need to know for the test, then may be we could actually score high in JEE.
3. It is not like students are going home everyday and study huge books of the size of encyclopedias so that we can get a high score on the test.

4. The things that we learn and remember come from school and our teachers.
5. If they don't teach us what we need to know, then we will probably never know it.

Conclusion:

6. ∴ I say that we just get rid of JEE and any other test out there that are like JEE.

√ For evaluation, we now consider (a) whether, given the truth of the premises, the conclusion follows, and (b) whether the premises are all true.

The conclusion states that JEE and similar tests should be terminated. We need to check whether the premises can support that claim. The premises in this case do not support the elimination of the examination. The premises talk about what the reasoner considers to be the fault of the teachers and the students' supposed dependence on the teachers for scoring high in JEE. If for argument's sake we suppose that all of that is true, even then the premises do not warrant the strong claim advanced in the conclusion. For, the situations mentioned, if true, can be rectified and thus JEE need not be discontinued.

Moreover, the premises are not all true. Premise 1 characterizes JEE in a certain way, which need not be the universal view on JEE. Many would contest its truth, as the JEE is also widely considered as a test to examine the student's own command over certain subjects. Since premise 1 is not obviously or incontrovertibly true, the beginning of the argument with premise 1 brings in a biased attitude in the argument which undermines its worth. Premises 2, 3 and 4 are presumptuous. They wrongly assume that the JEE candidates are not capable of self-learning and that they are also incapable of reading big-sized textbooks on their own. Moreover, they indicate that for scoring high in JEE, one has to depend completely on whether the subject has been taught by the teacher or not. Each of this is untrue; for, successful JEE candidates have to show presence of mind in unknown problems. JEE candidates are also independent learners; and successful candidates may bear evidence of negotiating huge and dense material, no less than an encyclopedia at times, on their own.

Premise 5 sums up the underlying assumption of this argument which, as discussed above, is highly questionable.

Thus, on an informal evaluation the argument is unsatisfactory on various counts. Its premises are doubtful; hence they cannot provide a firm or conclusive support for the conclusion advanced. Moreover, even if we grant the premises to be true, the conclusion, being too strong, remains unwarranted.

Keywords

Argument: A structured set of claims with a principal claim that is at issue, and other claims that are offered as supporting reasons for the principal claim.

Assuring terms: Terms used to assure the audience of the evidential support of the argument.

Claim: A claim is a statement that can be determined as either true or false.

Conclusion: The principal claim in an argument that is argued for.

Conclusion-indicator words: Words which usually suggest the presence of a conclusion, e.g., therefore, thus, so, etc.

Conclusive support: If the premises are true, the conclusion cannot but be true.

Critical thinking: Giving reasons for one's beliefs, and evaluating reasons given by others before accepting a suggestion.

Deductive arguments: Arguments from which our expectation is that if its premises are true its conclusion must be true.

Discounting terms: Terms used to ward off objections by anticipating them.

Guarding terms: Terms used for defensive strategies against possible objections.

Inductive arguments: Arguments from which our expectation is that its premises will provide probabilistic support as far as possible, for the conclusion.

Inductive leap: A jump from certainty to uncertainty. A characteristic trait of inductive arguments.

Non-claim: A statement which has no truth-claim. About it, it is not pertinent to ask whether it is true or false.

Partial support: Premises offering some evidential support for the conclusion but not absolute certainty.

Premise: A claim that is offered as the supporting evidence for the conclusion in an argument.

Premise-indicator words: Words which usually suggest the presence of a premise, e.g., since, for, etc.

CHAPTER

INFORMAL LOGIC: FALLACIES

3.1 Introduction

Defects in an argument may show up in more ways than one. There could be **genuine mistakes** or **accidental slip-ups** about some facts. For instance, suppose someone argues:

Example

1. Since India is below the equator line, its weather pattern will be like other countries in the southern hemisphere.

The error in its premise is a **factual error**. For, in reality India and, in fact even Sri Lanka, which is further south of India, lie above the equator line. The factual error in the premise could be a genuine mistake: the person may not have checked the map closely enough lately or is using the information from a less than credible source etc. Nonetheless, it creates a defect in the argument as it undermines the support for its conclusion. Because of this error in the premise, the conclusion does not follow from it.

However, factual errors of this kind are to be separated from **fallacies**. A **fallacy** is a **logical error**. Its presence in an argument makes the argument defective. For, with its presence in the argument, the purpose of the argument gets compromised.

The fallacies can show up as:

- ✓ Intentional mischiefs.
- ✓ Or, as cases of failure to distinguish between what is logically acceptable and what is not.

Sometimes people intentionally play tricks with their arguments to gain a quick point over not-so-careful opponents. Or, sometimes they try to divert the attention of the audience purposely by raising interesting but irrelevant points or by making personal attacks on the opponent. These are ploys to **create distraction** in the audience. The logical point gets lost while attention and time are given to points which have no logical significance for the argument. This is a defect because the argument, in the final analysis, fails to do what it is supposed to do, namely, persuade people on argument's own merit. Similarly, people try to suppress or omit information because full disclosure of information may not lead to the desired result. For instance, suppose someone argues:

Example

2. Infant mortality rate has certainly reached a satisfactory level. For, what used to be 70% has now declined to 66%.

The proponent clearly wants to argue that the rate is a satisfactory one. However, all that is said in the premise is that the rate has dropped somewhat. There is no mention about why we have to accept this 66% infant mortality rate as a cause for satisfaction. There is no mention, for instance, about whether this level is globally accepted as a satisfactory level, or about the competent body who has certified this as a satisfactory level. If these omissions are not unintentional, then we have reason to believe that such facts have been overlooked because their inclusion in the argument probably will not lend support to the conclusion.

There are other kinds of defects, which creep into an argument because of lack of logical discernment. Due to lack of training or due to ignorance, people commit mistakes that are logical in nature.

Fallacy of Composition

For example, if someone assumes that just because parts of a composite have a certain property, the composite as a whole also must necessarily have that same property, then the error is not factual by nature. It is a serious logical error known as the **fallacy of composition**. Fallacy of composition arises when a person reasons from the characteristics of individual members of a class or group to a conclusion regarding the characteristics of the entire class or group (taken as a whole). More formally, the 'reasoning' would look something like this:

- Individual F things have characteristics A, B, C, etc.
- Therefore, the (whole) class of F things has characteristics A, B, C, ...

This line of reasoning is fallacious because the mere fact that individuals have certain characteristics does not, in itself, guarantee that the class (taken as a whole) has those characteristics. For, what is true about the parts need not always be true about the whole, as can be seen from the example below:

Example

3. Sub-atomic particles are invisible to the naked eye, and material objects are made of sub-atomic particles. Therefore, material objects such as the human body, a building, etc. are invisible to the naked eye.

This is not to say that every case of part to whole inferences is mistaken. There could be cases where one can legitimately infer the features of the whole from the features of the components. For example, if a certain kind of wood is used for making an entire bed, then it is *not* illogical to claim that the whole bed and its legs have the same quality. The point is that such inferences must be based on sufficient evidence and examination. Example 3 points out what can happen if we blindly infer from the property of a part to the property of a whole. The inference from parts to the whole, unless executed with caution, may lead to a defect in the argument.

Fallacy of Division

Similarly, a **fallacy of division** may arise if we uncritically infer that what applies to the whole necessarily applies also to its parts. For example, it is fallacious to argue that if a team is awarded with a medal, it means every member of the team individually has been awarded with a medal. Or, it is fallacious to argue that since the book is interesting every page of the book also must be interesting.

All these defects, which are logical in nature, in general, are called **fallacies.**

EXERCISE 3.1

1. What is the key point of difference between a factual error and a fallacy?

2. *Consider the following claim and answer: Correct or Incorrect? Why? If the pen is black every molecule of the pen also must be black.

3. Why should one try to avoid fallacies in one's arguments?

3.2 Kinds of Fallacies

The taxonomy of fallacies is long. Medieval logicians have done a remarkable job of classifying them under certain headings. Recent informal logicians have augmented this list further. We shall mention only some of the kinds of fallacies below. The list is not intended to be exhaustive.

There are special fallacies connected to the two broad groupings of arguments: deductive and inductive. Deductive arguments, which leave open the possibility that their conclusion may be false while all its premises are true, instantiate **deductive fallacy**.

Deductive Fallacies

Two very well-known patterns of deductive fallacies are:

- ✓ **Denying the antecedent**
- ✓ **Affirming the consequent**

In a statement of the form 'If…then…', the part between the *if* and the *then* is called the **antecedent**, and the part after the *then* is called the **consequent**. The two above-mentioned fallacies are specially associated with the statements of 'if…then…' form. They arise from a misunderstanding of the nature of such statements. Examples of these are given below:

Examples

Affirming the consequent

4. If someone has diabetes, his eyes may be affected.
   Sheena's eyes are affected.
   Therefore, Sheena has diabetes.

Denying the antecedent

5. If someone has diabetes, his eyes may be affected.
   Ashish does not have diabetes.
   Hence, Ashish's eyes cannot be affected.

If refers to a *sufficient condition*, i.e., a factor which can lead to the effect. It, however, is not claimed as the *only* condition. Thus, the statement *If someone has diabetes, his eyes may be affected* merely states that diabetes is *one of the conditions* for which one's eyes may be affected. There could be other factors, such as eye infection, through which also the eyes can be affected. Therefore, from the facts that "If someone has diabetes, his eyes may be affected," and that someone's eyes are affected, it does *not* follow that he or she has diabetes. Thus, in Example 4, the conclusion may come out as false. Similarly, in Example 5 the conclusion does not follow in spite of the truth of the two premises. Just because Ashish does not have diabetes, it does *not* mean his eyes cannot be affected, as there could be other factors present.

Non sequitur is a Latin expression which means "it does not follow." To say that an argument is a *non sequitur* is simply to say that the conclusion does not follow from the premises. This term would apply to any argument that has a conclusion which does not follow from its premises. It is often used, however, to specially refer to the two deductive fallacies mentioned above.

Inductive Fallacies

Inductive fallacies usually occur when the premises of inductive arguments fail to provide the desirable amount of probabilistic support for their conclusions. Some inductive fallacies are listed below:

✓ **Illicit or hasty generalization:** The cases observed are too small to support an inductive generalization about a population, of which these cases are members.

Example

6. a. I have met two Americans and both were dishonest, so all Americans are dishonest.
   b. My grandmother at 82 can walk faster than me, can still remember everyone's name, and is healthy. All people who are of that age must be very strong and healthy.

✓ **Fallacy of generalization based on unrepresentative samples:** A subtype of illicit generalization, where the sample is unrepresentative of the whole population.

Example

7. The tiger that I saw was white, so all tigers must be white.

As we know, white tigers are rare among tigers. It is a mistake to rely upon two chance sightings of the unrepresentative white tigers to claim a universal statement about the skin colour of tigers as a whole.

✓ **False analogy:** Induction based upon the comparison of two samples when the samples being compared are almost dissimilar. The analogy falls apart as a weak analogy, and in the process it harms the argument.

Example

8. a. Tables have four legs, elephants have four legs too. Hence, tables, just like elephants, are animals.

b. Employees in an organization are like nails. Just as one has to use the hammer to hit a nail on the head to make it work, similarly an employee also needs to be hit on the head to make him work.

✓ **Fallacy of exclusion:** In an induction, the total relevant information needs to be examined. The fallacy occurs when relevant evidence which would undermine an inductive argument is excluded from consideration. The requirement that all relevant information be included is called the *principle of total evidence.*

Example

9. Sree is a 35-year old woman, and most women of her age are married, hence she too must be married.

The information left out is that at least some women of 35-year of age may remain unmarried, or, consider another example:

Example

10. Plumbers all overcharge, so Kali too, being a plumber, has overcharged.

The error comes from hiding the fact that there could be honest plumbers too who do not overcharge and Kali could be one of them.

There are many other kinds of fallacies. Given below is a list of some of them.

Fallacies of Ambiguity

This group of fallacies emerges from unclarity left in the premises, intentionally or unintentionally, by the use of terms or expressions that allow more than one interpretation. Specific examples of this kind are:

✓ **Equivocation:** Where the same term is used with two different meanings.

Example

11. He told me to *cane* (to use the cane material to weave the parts of chair) the chairs, so I *caned* (beaten them, with a cane) them, and the chairs came apart.

✓ **Amphiboly:** Where the sentence allows more than one interpretation.

Example

12. Only sons marry only daughters.

Fallacies of Relevance

In this kind of defective cases, the premises somehow fail to be relevant to the truth of the conclusion. Thus, they fail to perform their duty in an argument.

(i) Appeal to inappropriate authority: The reason of citing an authority in the premises is to lend some credibility to the argument. An appeal to authority is a fallacy with the following form:

1. Person A is (claimed to be) an authority on subject S.
2. Person A makes claim C about subject S.
3. Therefore, C is true.

This fallacy is committed when the person in question is not a legitimate authority on the subject. More formally, if person A is not qualified to make reliable claims in subject S, then the argument will be fallacious.

This sort of reasoning is fallacious when the person in question is not an expert. In such cases the reasoning is flawed because the fact that an unqualified person makes a claim does not provide any justification for the claim. The claim could be true, but the fact that an unqualified person made the claim does not provide any rational reason to accept the claim as true.

When a person falls prey to this fallacy, she is accepting a claim as true without there being adequate evidence to do so. More specifically, the person is accepting the claim because she erroneously believes that the person making the claim is a genuine expert and therefore the claim is reasonable. Since people have a tendency to believe authorities (and there are, in fact, good reasons to accept some claims made by authorities), this fallacy is a fairly common one.

Example

13. a. My friend says Einstein's relativity theory is bogus, hence the relativity theory is all nonsense.
    b. The lottery agent thinks that this ticket will win, so I must buy this lottery ticket.

If the friend happens to be someone who has no credible background in physics, then he or she is an inappropriate authority to appeal to for support. Citing the opinion of such a source can have no bearing on the truth of the conclusion. It is very important to decide who can be cited as an authority in a particular situation. Usually, it is the context which decides who can be cited as an authority. Kapil Dev could serve as an authority on Indian cricket, but he may not be an appropriate authority when settling claims about, say, interior decoration. In the professional world, however, the issue takes on a more serious form. Citations in an article or book, for instance, require full and detailed disclosure of sources, mainly to keep the fallacy of inappropriate authority at bay.

(ii) Ad hominem: Translated from Latin, *ad hominem* means *against the person.* This fallacy occurs when an argument is rejected, instead of by meeting it on a logical ground, by raising some irrelevant point about the person proposing the argument. The personal attacks may be abusive and directed at the character of the proponent, or at his circumstances (e.g., nationality, or ethnic background), or even at his actions to show he does not practice what he preaches.

Example

14. a. We need not give consideration to the issue of womens' reservation bill because the issue is raised by the bob-cutwallihs (women sporting bob-cut hairstyle).
    b. The testimony of Kamalesh is not acceptable because his father used to drink and gamble.

(iii) Appeal to common practice or to the popularity of the belief: When 'most people do it' or 'everyone believes' is used as the ground for advocating a point. It is a fallacy because the fact that most people do or believe something does *not* make an action or a belief right or acceptable.

Example

15. There is nothing wrong in dumping the industrial waste in the Ganges river because all the factories situated in the riverbank routinely do that.

(iv) Truth is relative: To claim x must be the case because x seems to be true to the proponent of the argument. The Relativist Fallacy is also committed when a person rejects a claim by asserting that the claim might be true for others but is not for him/her. It is fallacy because what seems true for me is not relevant for the truth of x.

In this context, relativism is the view that truth is relative to Z (a person, time, culture, place, etc.). This is not the view that claims will be true at different times or of different people, but the view that a claim could be true for one person and false for another at the same time.

Example

16. a. Prabal must be innocent, for he seems so innocent to me.
    b. Contradictions in arguments may be bad for others, but I do not think they are so bad, so my contradictory argument is just as good as an argument without contradiction.

Fallacies of Causing Distraction

These are generated by various ploys used for either diverting the attention of the audience from the issue at hand, or for unfairly influencing the audience.

(i) False dilemma: To give the impression that one has to choose among them when actually there are more options. Information about a legitimate option is suppressed to unfairly influence the audience to sympathize with the choices given. This is illegitimate and fallacious because the audience is misled to believe that if they do not agree with one of the options, the other option must be accepted.

Example

17. a. We have to cut down the state government expenses on public health, or else the state expenditure on primary school education must be slashed.
    b. If you are not agreeing with me, then you must be my enemy.

(ii) Argument from ignorance: To assume that if something cannot be proved as false, then it must be true. Or, conversely, if something cannot be proved as true, then it must be false. The choices need not be so restrictive. Also, lack of evidence does not constitute evidence to the contrary.

Example

18. a. We cannot demonstrate that Darwinian Evolution is the truth, hence we must regard it as a false theory.
    b. There is nothing on file to disprove that he is the thief; therefore, he must be the thief.

(iii) Slippery-slope argument: It is a type of negative reasoning that argues from consequences and urges not to take certain action. It presupposes the context of a graded series or a connected sequence of steps. Typically, it is argued that once the first action is taken at step *n*, there is no stopping. By virtue of the series being a gradation of steps, there will be a snowballing effect and something undesirable must hold true finally at the end of the series. Therefore, at step *n*, we must refrain from taking the action.

Example

19. We cannot allow for tuition increase of Rs. 20 per month. For, once we allow that, pretty soon the tuition hike will reach an exorbitant stage.

This is a fallacy because it overlooks the possibility that even among gradual and serial steps the situation may completely change from where we started.

The fallacy may also exhibit itself in other ways. It may be argued that in a connected series, once we accept something about a certain step 1, since there is not much difference between step 1 and step 2, the same applies for every two adjacent steps and therefore what we held at step 1 will hold true finally at the end of the series.

Example

20. There is no significant difference between those who marginally pass the JEE test and marginally fail it, hence there is no difference between those who pass the JEE test and those who do not.

This is a fallacy because it overlooks the possibility of a real difference emerging at the end of the series. Just because the line between the borderline cases are not very clear, it does not follow that in every case the line cannot be drawn.

A variety of this fallacy, sometimes called the **Heap argument,** is to overlook the existence of a series of steps between two opposite ends and to argue that if one end is the case, the other end cannot be reached.

Example

21. Giving one paisa to a beggar is not going to make him rich, so no matter how many one paisa you give to a beggar, you cannot make him rich from being poor.

(iv) Posing a complex question: Two unrelated claims, with one of them usually more desirable than the other, are placed together to create the impression that they must be accepted or rejected together, when actually one may be accepted without the other.

Example

22. a. Do you not want to improve the living standard and allow the businesses to run their activities completely freely?
    b. Do you accept that you are absent minded and also a liar?

(v) Red herring or **smoke screen:** To 'win' in an argument by presenting an irrelevant issue and thereby being able to divert the attention from the argument.

Example

23. Taxes must be raised, for we do not want the quality of life of an average person to come down.

Causal Fallacies

Causal fallacies arise from some mistake in reasoning based on cause, such as:

***Post hoc ergo propter hoc* or the fallacy of false cause:** The English translation of *Post hoc ergo propter hoc* is "after this, therefore because of this". This is a fallacy which assumes x to be the cause of y just because (i.e., when there is no other evidence) y occurs after x. Evidence only consists of x occurring before y. However, since all preceding phenomena are not causes of succeeding phenomena, it is a mistake to assume causal relationship here.

Example

24. On last three tests I used a blue pen to write the answers and I got low marks; hence using blue pen is the cause of getting low marks.

Quite often, this leads to a sub-variety:

Overlooking a common cause: Two events, occurring within a regular interval from each other, are held as cause and effects when there could be a common cause for both.

Example

25. Being four-legged and having a tail are two properties that are regularly associated (e.g., in cows, horses), so an animal has a tail because it has four legs.

This is a fallacy because both the features in an animal are caused by a third factor; namely, the genetic material.

Fallacies of Vacuity or Missing the Point

This group of fallacy occurs when the premises or the conclusion in an argument, instead of trying to establish what they are supposed to, offer empty reasoning.

(i) Circular reasoning: Where the conclusion is used as a premise.

Example

26. Iraqis are bad because that is what they are.

(ii) Begging the question: Where the argument relies upon (explicitly or implicitly) the point at issue, i.e., when the conclusion is assumed to be true in the argument. This is a fallacy because the arguments are supposed to establish the truth of the conclusion, and not assume that it is true already.

Example

27. God must exist, for who else can create the universe?

(iii) *Ignoratio elenchi* or proving the wrong conclusion: Where an argument, which is set out to prove one conclusion, proves a different conclusion instead.

Example

28. We must get rid of JEE Test, because it requires a very serious and painstaking effort for years and many who try cannot clear it.

The intended conclusion in the example is that we must get rid of JEE Test, but what the argument has managed to establish is that JEE is a rather hard test.

Fallacies of Definition

(i) Too wide definition: When a definition covers more than it should, that is, a definition should help identify the right samples and leave other cases out. A too wide definition includes even those examples that should have been left out.

Example

29. A human being is a mammal.

This is a fallacious definition which fails to uniquely identify the humans, as there are numerous non-human mammals, such as whales, tigers, elephants.

(ii) Too narrow definition: A too narrow definition covers less than what it should cover.

Example

30. Roses are red flowers.

This definition of a 'rose' fails to include pink, yellow and all the other colours that a rose can have.

(iii) Incomprehensible definition: Where a definition is harder to understand than that which is being defined.

Example

31. Having an idea is to generate the findings of an intense, abstract cognitive experiment.

(iv) Conflicting definition: Where the definition contains self-contradiction.

Example

32. All the software packages in this library are: (a) legally purchased, (b) certified as virus free, (c) available in the intranet, and (d) those copied from the private collections of various gracious library users.

If the software is freely copied from other users, then, it is not legally purchased.

EXERCISE 3.2

1. Identify the fallacies in the following cases:

a. Opium induces sleep in us because it has a sedative effect on our nervous system.

b.* Whenever I see Preetpal, something bad happens to me. He came to see me on last Wednesday and later in the day the bus I was riding on met with an accident. Sunday morning he came to my house and I got a call in the evening that my grandmother is not well. Yesterday we met and I injured my toe within an hour. He is the cause of my bad luck.

c. The number series is made of numbers such as 1, 2, ... Each number that makes up the number series is a finite quantity. Therefore, the number series 1, 2, 3, …. must also be finite.

d. When it comes to our stand about the neighbouring countries, we must choose between war and cowardice: we should either fight them or sit back in disgrace like a coward.

e. The minister said that if prices rise, then citizens will suffer. I see a lot of citizens are suffering, therefore the prices of commodities must have gone up.

f. A table is a four-legged wooden object.

g. *Everyone that I know cheats in the exam, then how can cheating in exam be wrong?

h. All Indians must be vegetarians because the Indians that I have met were all vegetarians.

i. Enough evidence has not been uncovered which helps us to conclude that Swaraj is innocent, therefore he must be guilty.

j. I find it hard to believe how a 1000 ton rocket can fly through the air and not fall. Therefore, no man has really landed on the moon.

k. The flu virus infects if we come close to the infected person. The measles virus also infects in a similar way. Therefore, a computer infected with virus also can infect another computer if it is put too close to the infected computer.

l. If you want to ban guns because guns kill people, then you should also ban cars because cars kill people too!

m. An elephant consumes more food than a human can. Therefore, all elephants put together consume more food than do all the humans on the earth put together.

2. Provide a suggestion in each case of 1 (a)–(j) to show how the fallacy can be avoided. You may rewrite the arguments/statements to indicate how the situation can be improved.

3.3 How to Avoid Fallacies

From the fallacies listed above, one can form some idea about what logical errors to avoid in one's argumentation. By knowing about fallacies, our aim is to avoid being misled by them. Most fallacies, when they are not intentional, are the result of hasty and uncritical thinking.

To argue effectively, therefore, one must exercise care and caution. We expect from a good argument that:

a. Its conclusion should *follow* from its premises.

b. Its premises should be true, effective and justified.

So, one needs to take care in the selection of the premises. Once the premises are selected, one needs to check the following:

- **Authenticity** of the premises: How credible are they? What is the level and the source of evidence supporting them?
- **Relevance** for the argument: Are they pertinent to what the conclusion proposes? Are they raising pertinent points?
- **Power of persuasion** of the premises: How effective are they to convince someone that the conclusion must be the case? Are they in any way presumptuous? Are they assuming, in some way, what they are set out to prove?

We expect that:

A logical argument should be a sincere effort to logically establish a point and not by rhetorical tricks or by deception. The rhetorical efforts may win the crowd, but they often are not worth much logically. An argument based on tricky manoeuvers or on pure verbal gymnastics is empty in the final analysis.

- ✓ In particular, if definitions are used, whether they are free of general defects.
- ✓ If causal reasoning is used, whether the causal relationship is properly understood.
- ✓ Choice of words are precise or not. Vagueness and ambiguity are to be avoided as far as possible. Also, it is better to stay within what is warranted. For example: Where the evidence points to only *some* cases, it is a logical error to claim support for *all* cases.

While reasoning, our goal should be to produce a well-reasoned, compelling argument. A number of factors, for instance, mistaken beliefs, peer pressure, desire to win at any cost, short-term goals, lack of judgement, and impulses, come in the way of reaching that goal and lead to fallacies. The aim of this chapter is to create awareness among critical thinkers about these common errors and tendencies.

Keywords

Authenticity: A concern for credibility for the premises. The more authentic the premises are, the better their support is for the conclusion.

Factual error: Error due to some mistake about the factual data, such as overlooking the most recent data or not knowing the data.

Fallacy: Logical errors which are to be avoided.

Logical error: Error in logical thinking or in logical analysis.

Part B

SYMBOLIC LOGIC

CHAPTER

SYMBOLIC LOGIC: INTRODUCTION

4.1 Historical Background

In the history of western logic, **Symbolic logic** is a relatively recent development. What sets symbolic logic apart from traditional logic is its leanings towards mathematics and symbolization. In this section, a brief summary of the factors which led to its development is recounted.

ZENO OF ELEA
(estimated to be born in 490 BCE)

Aristotle is regarded as the Father of Logic in the western tradition. It is to be noted, however, that he was not the first logician. Much before him there were reputed logicians such as Zeno of Elea; and even during and after Aristotle, there were a number of noteworthy logicians in Greece. The reason why Aristotle is still acknowledged specially is because of his special contribution to logic. Aristotle was the first to visualize in logic the possibility of a *science of sciences,* in the sense of being a study which can serve as the backbone of all other scientific queries. He was the first to propose that logic is the indispensable tool (*organon*) which can provide a set of correct ways or rules for correct reasoning that will be applicable in all scientific studies and discussions. His concern is understandable, as his own scientific interests were many: physics, botany, biology (Darwin wrote that he learnt his Biology from Aristotle), zoology.

In addition, he formulated treatises on poetics, politics, ethics, and metaphysics. In any case, validation of new thoughts, particularly argumentative issues, has to come from somewhere, and logic in his view had that potential. He organized logic to fit this role of the judge and came up with the idea of **logical structures** underlying the language content in any argument. If the content provides the **matter** or the material for the argument, then these logical structures are supposed to be the **form** or the mould to which the matter can be cast. He proposed a set of valid and invalid **forms of reasoning,** such that any individual argument exhibiting any of these forms could be readily identified as valid or invalid. He used these argument forms as the standard of validation for syllogistic reasoning. From Aristotle's idea of deep-seated forms, today's formal logic has imbibed its core belief: that there are certain correct forms for thinking, which provide the backbone for correct reasoning, regardless of the content.

Aristotle's conception of logic as a formal study of valid inferences reigned supreme as the only perception of logic for about 2000 years. Through the dark ages till 18th CE, it continued its hold on the logicians as the *only* kind of logic possible. In medieval Europe, through the Arab traders, writings of Aristotle came back to Europe along with those of Plato and other Greeks. Once Aristotelian logic was discovered by the medievals, it was wholeheartedly accepted by the scholars of that era. When repetition and analysis of dogmas, unquestioned beliefs and inherited religious precepts set the limits to human intellectual activity, medieval scholars, particularly the theologians, relied on Aristotelian logic to advance their claims. History shows that Aristotelian logic continued its reign even in the post-medieval times. Even after the Renaissance and the upheavals that it caused in the sciences, in 1787, we find Kant commenting that the fact that Aristotelian logic has not been able to make a step in advance, behooves us to consider it as *completed* and *perfect*, i.e., of which no further improvement is possible.

The journey into the logical realms beyond the Aristotelian scheme came gradually via a revaluation of our expectations from logic. The first murmurs of dissatisfaction with Aristotelian logic came from the Humanists scholars of renaissance in the 15th century. Their objection was that Greek logic, though it was not false in any respect, only helped the rhetoricians; it was unattractive as a subject when compared to Greek literature and philosophy.

The signs of changes to come became more visible in 17th CE with the rise of a new physics, i.e., the physics of Galileo, and a new faith in mathematics. The reawakened Europe shared the vision of Galileo who remarked: "Nature is written in a code, and the key to the code is mathematics".

GALILEO
(1564-1642)

There was a rising feeling that nature is waiting to be discovered and logic is not the right tool for that discovery but mathematics is. During the Greek period, Plato had insisted on the study of Geometry as a prerequisite for illumination. In a similar way, in 17th CE, the study of mathematics became the rage in the scientific world. Moreover, research in mathematics at that time was bustling with new creative energy. Mathematics was taking a new direction in Algebra. Many Algebraic discoveries were being made, new methods were being tried out, and the mathematicians of that time believed that their discoveries were completely novel in comparison to the traditional geometric ways of looking at things. As a result, Aristotelian logic was dislodged from its prestigious position as the *indispensable tool* for thinking.

GEORGE BOOLE
(1815-1864)

Against this background of ascendancy of the mathematical method, **George Boole** rediscovered logic and its potential. The early Megarians and the Stoics had developed some basic principles of propositional logic about the connectives such as conjunction, negation, disjunction and conditionals. Boole rediscovered this logic and formulated it like a **calculus**.

This was the turning point which ushered in the modern era in logic. Boole showed that the algebraic formulae can be used to express logical relations with the connectives, such as conjunction, negation, disjunction and conditionals. He also showed that one can do algebra, an abstract calculus, with entities other than numbers. From Boolean Algebra, modern logic has received the theory of truth functions, the disjunctive normal forms, and conjunctive normal forms.

GOTTFRIED WILLHELM LEIBNIZ
(1646-1716)

Though Boole was the first to demonstrate, he was not the first to think along the line of mathematization of logic. Before him, Leibniz had already noted certain resemblances between disjunction, conjunction of concepts, and addition and multiplication operations. Though he did not find it easy to formulate the resemblances, Leibniz clearly thought that logic has a tremendous potential for a **scientifically designed universal language that would be mathematical in character.**

Thus, logic and interest in logic were revived, and the mathematical development of logic was started by George Boole's project drew the attention of his contemporaries and interest in logic, particularly as the possibility of its expression in mathematical terms grew. Through the efforts of many, an **algebra for logic** took shape fast. J.Venn, an ardent admirer of Boole, in 1881, used diagrams of overlapping regions, some topological models to illustrate the relations between classes, to pictorially present the truth conditions of propositions.

Lewis Carroll, of the *Alice in Wonderland* fame, devised a scheme, somewhat similar to Venn's, for determining the validity of syllogisms. At the same time, Augustus De Morgan (1806–1871), an English mathematician, and Charles Sanders Peirce (1839–1914), an American philosopher, independently devised a very precise, almost mathematical notation system for relational arguments. This type of arguments, though neglected by Aristotelian logic, was very common in mathematics. The contributions of De Morgan, Peirce, William Stanley Jevons (1835–1882), et al., helped further liberate logic from its Greek fixation.

GOTTLOB FREGE
(1848-1925)

While Boole and others were interested in the mathematization of logic, Gottlob Frege (1848–1925), a German philosopher and mathematician, attempted something revolutionary. He tried a final reduction of mathematics into logic by a philosophical analysis of the concept of number. This is known as the **thesis of logicism:** That all mathematics can be reduced to logic. For this endeavour, he invented a language: a Begriffsschrift (language of thought) to free logical thinking from the dominion of ordinary language and its grammar. The invented language was meant only for logic. The Begriffsschrift makes use of a logical notation that makes it possible to express sentences of larger complexity than Aristotle's logic did. This achievement of Frege brought in the revolution in the way logic was perceived and ushered in the age of symbolic or mathematical logic. Frege is considered to be the Father of Modern Symbolic Logic.

However, there were other important contributors to the development of symbolic logic. Independently, based on the works of Boole and Peirce, Giuseppe Peano (1958–1932), an Italian mathematician, was also working on development of a more rigorous logic for mathematics and on a thorough study of foundations of mathematics. For this project, he too felt, as Frege did, that a separate symbolic notation system would make it noticeably easier to express thoughts that would be long and difficult to express in ordinary language.

GIUSEPPE PEANO
(1958-1932)

In 1900, Bertrand Russell, a British philosopher, mathematician, and social commentator, met Peano at a Congress[1] and was struck by the rigour in his thinking and also by the symbolic notation that Peano had developed. Bertrand Russell was fascinated by both Peano's and Frege's projects. At that time, Russell was working on his *Principles of Mathematics*. While going over Frege's work, Russell discovered (1901) a paradox (known as Russell's paradox or "Set of all sets: is that a set itself?" paradox) that some sets can be both said to be a member of themselves and yet must be greater than all the member elements.

BERTRAND RUSSELL
(1872–1970)

[1] In his autobiography Russell wrote about this meeting as follows: "The Congress was the turning point of my intellectual life, because there I met Peano."

The fame of the first discovery of this paradox, however, goes to Cesare Burali-Forti (1861–1931), an Italian mathematician, who, as early as in 1897, noted this set-theoretic paradox. Cantor devised a similar paradox two year later. Russell's discovery, however, became more famous. Russell, after his discovery, communicated to Frege about this paradox. The significance of this paradox was immense for Frege who realized that the discovered paradox showed a fatal flaw in his project also. When he and A.N. Whitehead (1861–1947) finally brought out the *Principia Mathematica* or *Principles of Mathematics (1911),* Russell added an appendix "The Doctrine of Types" as his first attempt to resolve this paradox. Symbolic Logic, as we know it today, came to be known and accepted mainly through the work of Russell and Whitehead.

Symbolic logic of today owes its origin primarily to Frege and Russell, and then to Peano and many others. If they had helped the genesis of symbolic logic, other 20th CE mathematicians and philosophers such as Brouwer, Gödel, Cantor, Hilbert, Wittgenstein, Tarski, Zermelo, Gentzen must be acknowledged for joining in their effort and for their worthy contributions towards its steady growth.

EXERCISE 4.1

1. True or false? Explain your reasons in each case.

a. Aristotle believed that actual arguments are valid by virtue of the underlying form or logical structure that they may have.

b. *Boole brought in the theory of truth functions.

c. The post-Renaissance interest in mathematics was one of the factors behind the fall of Aristotelian logic from its prestigious position.

d. Frege's Begriffsschrift was not an artificial language.

e. Long before Boole, Leibniz saw the similarities between certain logical operators and some mathematical operators.

f. *Western Logic began with Aristotle.

g. Russell's paradox, as the name suggests, was first discovered by Bertrand Russell himself.

2. What are the factors which led to the development of symbolic logic?

3. What is the thesis of logicism? How is it different from what Boole was trying?

4.2 Basic Components

Symbolic Logic, as we have seen, is a relatively recent logic which has strong connections with mathematics. This is the reason why symbolic logic also goes by the name **mathematical logic**. It is also called **formal logic** as it primarily deals with the **structures** or **forms** of reasoning. Its formal nature is shown in its insistence on demonstration or proof, and in its rigorous proof procedures based on the forms of reasoning.

As explained above, symbolic logic was developed with the aim of being a universal scientific language. Hence, a set of very precisely defined **symbols** forms the core of its vocabulary. The objective of its proponents was thus to avoid the vagueness, ambiguity and imprecision that they found bothersome in the ordinary everyday language. Symbolic expressions are also supposed to contribute towards economy in communication. Special symbols help express ideas in a compact manner, which would otherwise take a long sequence of words to express.

Symbolic logic, as a formal study of logic, requires acquaintance with the following three basic components:

1. A language: A collection of well-formed expressions to which meaning can be assigned. The part of language, which includes the symbols and the formal rules with which well-formed sequences of symbols are differentiated from arbitrary collections of symbols, is known as the **syntax** of the language.

Symbolic logic uses a special, artificial language that works as the intermediary between ordinary language and logical operations. That is, in order to do the logical operations on them, arguments and their components need to be first translated into a language consisting of only symbols. For the translation, symbolic logic uses a set of permitted symbols along with five basic connectives (see Chapter 5 for details), and their symbolic representations.

2. Semantics: A system which tells us how to interpret or assign meaning to the well-formed sequences of symbols. Symbolic logic is a two-valued system, i.e., every statement in it has to be either true or false. Its semantics consists of various well-defined rules and methods for assigning truth and falsity to the sequences of symbols.

3. A proof system: A formal procedure with a collection of rules (Forms of reasoning) that can be applied to derive other facts from the well-formed, meaningful expressions within the system.

In this book, from Chapters 5–12, we introduce the syntax, semantics and the proof procedure of both propositional and predicate logic, which together constitute the body of symbolic logic.

EXERCISE 4.2

1. Why does Symbolic logic use symbols?
2. What is the difference between syntax of a language from its semantics?

Keywords

Algebra for logic: A system of logic built with the model of mathematics in mind and which uses symbols like Algebra.

Form: The structure or the mould into which the matter or content is to be cast.

Formal logic: The logic which is primarily concerned with the structures or forms of reasoning and formal concepts.

Forms of reasoning: Formal structures of reasoning.

Logicism: The theory that mathematics can be reduced into logic by conceptual analysis.

Mathematical logic: Same as Symbolic Logic.

Matter: Content or the material.

Proof procedure: Formal derivation as a systematic procedure for demonstration.

Semantics: The part of language which tells us how to interpret or assign meaning to the well-formed sequences of symbols.

Symbolic logic: A relatively recent logic which has strong connections with mathematics.

Syntax: The part of language which includes the symbols, and the formal rules by which well-formed sequences of symbols are to be formed.

Universal language: The idea that a scientifically designed language which would be mathematical in character and would act as the bridge language for scientific purposes among the scientists of different languages.

CHAPTER 5

PROPOSITIONAL LOGIC: SYNTAX AND SYMBOLIZATION

5.1 Sentence, Proposition and Statement

With this chapter we shall begin our formal approach to symbolic logic. However, before we begin the formal exposition, we need to settle a very important question, namely,

> *What is the analogue in everyday language of what formal logic or symbolic logic primarily deals with?*

As you go through this chapter and others that follow, you will find that symbolic logic makes prolific use of '*p*' and '*q*' and other symbols to express its well-formed formulas. For example, in the following sections of this chapter you will be introduced to '$p \bullet q$', '$p \vee q$', '$\sim p$', etc. What do these '*p*', '*q*' refer to in our everyday language?

How are we supposed to interpret in terms of our everyday language, what these formulas try to tell us?

We can also formulate the question mentioned above semantically as follows:

> *What kind of items in everyday language can be properly said to be true or false in the logical sense? Or, what are the basic truth-bearers?*

'Being true' or 'being false' is seen as a property in logic. It is also considered to be an important property. For, when an argument is valid, its conclusion needs to be true when its premises are true. So, premises and conclusions should be something that can be true or false. Before we can approach the formal notions of validity in logic, it is important for us to be able to identify which items can be properly called the bearers of the property of 'being true' or 'being false'. And intuitively that identification has to make sense in terms of what we know about our everyday language.

Philosophical literature offers three possible candidates as the answer to these questions: Sentences, propositions and statements. I shall first explain these three terms and then give you the commonly held answer.

Sentences: A *sentence* is to be understood as *any* grammatically correct and complete strings of well-formed expressions in our everyday language. The following are examples of sentences:

Examples

1. Shops are closed on Sundays.
2. Fruits are nutritious.
3. Come here!
4. Are you alright?

On the other hand, the following are *not* sentences:

Examples

5. Fruits nutritious
6. Closed are

Note that 'sentence' represents a broad category which includes many different types of sentences. For example, it covers the interrogative kind (*Are you alright?*), i.e., the sentences, the main verb of which is in the interrogative mood. It also includes the command type (*Come here*!), the main verb of which is in the imperative mood. In addition, it covers the declarative sentence (*Fruits are nutritious*), the main verb of which is in the declarative mood.

Philosophers make a distinction between:

- Sentence tokens
- Sentence types

A **sentence token** is a physical item. In the case of a written sentence, the sentence token is the marks created by ink or some other material on a piece of paper. In the case of a spoken or uttered sentence, the sentence token is the string of produced sounds.

A **sentence type,** on the other hand, is abstract. It is the pattern exhibited by sentence tokens.

Example

7. a. Fruits are nutritious
   b. Fruits are nutritious
   c. Fruits are nutritious

Three tokens of the same sentence type

Alternatively, we can also understand a sentence type as the pattern for a set of similar sentence tokens. For example, the imperative sentence type is the common pattern for all sentence tokens, the main verb of which is in the imperative mood.

Examples

8. Come here!
9. Stand still!
10. Listen to me!
11. Shut the door!

Similarly, a declarative sentence type is the type for sentences, the main verb of which is in the declarative mood.

Examples

12. Today is Sunday.
13. Pines are evergreen trees,
14. Sand deserts are dry places.

Propositions: A proposition is to be understood as what is common to a set of synonymous declarative sentences.

Statements: A *statement* is to be understood as what is said when a declarative sentence is uttered or inscribed. Or, we can understand it as the *content* of what is uttered or inscribed. Note that every kind of sentence cannot be a proposition or a statement. For example, an interrogative sentence is a sentence but not a proposition or a statement, given the definitions above. For, only declarative sentences come under the purview of a proposition and a statement.

Note also that propositions and statements are close enough. Though it is difficult to give a very precise definition of synonymy (means the same), in a situation of a set of synonymous declarative sentence tokens, what is common among them (the proposition) and their content (the statement) may coincide. Consider the following tokens:

Examples

15. I am alright (said by A)
16. You are alright (said by B to A)
17. *Main thik hoon* (said by A in Hindi)

As ordinarily understood, the proposition expressed by these above given examples is the same as their content or the statement that they make.

It is time now to come up with the answer to the questions posed in the beginning of this section:

> *What is the analogue in everyday language of what formal logic or symbolic logic primarily deals with?*
>
> *Or, What kind of items in everyday language can be properly said to be true or false in the logical sense? Or, what are the basic truth-bearers?*

Though controversies exist, philosophers in recent times agree that sentences in general *cannot* be called properly true or false. For, there can be sentences which are neither true nor false. As for example, the interrogative sentences such as "Are you alright?"

Thus, they maintain that "propositions are the items which logic basically deals with. They are the items which can be properly said to be true or false". Since statements are close to the propositions, it will not be an error to consider them also as the basic topic of what logic deals with.

In Chapter 2, in the Informal Logic section I introduced the term 'claim' as statements which can be true or false. That informal notion can be now used in formal logic to understand what a proposition or a statement means.

Note that throughout in this book, I have preferred to use the term 'statement'. Like many other logicians, I have used it as equivalent to 'proposition'. If you find in other logic books discussions about propositions, note that what has been discussed in this book about statements is equivalent to them.

The kind of logic that we are about to learn now has been called *propositional logic*. Sometimes, it has been called propositional calculus by those who are keen to emphasize the analogy to mathematical calculus. I have opted for the expression 'propositional logic', as you may have noted from the heading of this chapter. However, while explaining the propositional logic, I have consistently used the term 'statement' for the reason cited above. This terminological preference should not create any difficulty for your approach to the subject.

5.2 Simple and Compound Statements

Propositional logic is **the logic of propositions.** It is that section of symbolic logic which considers **simple statements** as its atomic or the most basic units. That is, this logic assumes that simple statements are *not* further analyzable. So, propositional logic does not look into the sub-structures that could be present in simple statements themselves, to find logically relevant information. The discussion of further analysis of simple statements into its substructures has to wait until we take up predicate logic from Chapter 10 onwards. At present, in Chapters 5–9 only propositional logic will be discussed.

By **simple statements**, here we mean *structurally simple* statements, i.e., statements which do not contain any other statement as component.

Examples

18. Some Indians are Brahmins.
19. Mishra is a dentist.
20. New Delhi is the capital of India.

Each of Examples 18–20 is structurally simple in the above-explained sense: neither has another statement as a component. Examples 18–20 happen to be short statements. From this, we should **not** conclude that all simple statements are short. It is perfectly possible for a structurally simple statement to be rather long; and in spite of its structural simplicity, such a statement may convey many complex thoughts at the same time. Consider, for instance. "A recent film on two tribal queens has raised the hackles of Andhra tribals for alleged distortion and trivialization of the struggle of the tribal queen". Though it is a structurally simple statement, it is neither as short as the above examples, nor does it express a simple thought as Examples 18–20 do.

The simple statements form the foundation of the language of propositional logic. The language of propositional logic follows a model somewhat comparable to a *building block* or a *Lego*[1] model. The simple statements are supposed to be the starting points. The idea is to generate more and more complex structures by combining these simple statements with the help of **connectives**. Connectives are words or terms in the language which allow combination of statements, e.g., *and, but, either-or, if-then*. Complex structures obtained from such combination of simple statements and at least one connective are called **compound statements.** These are statements which have other statements as structural components.

Examples

21. [Some Indians are Brahmins], **and** [some Indians are vegetarians].
22. **If** [Mishra is a dentist] **then** [he will be able to solve my dental problems].

[1] 'Lego' is a toy set, which comes with small pieces, out of which toy buildings and other models can be constructed.

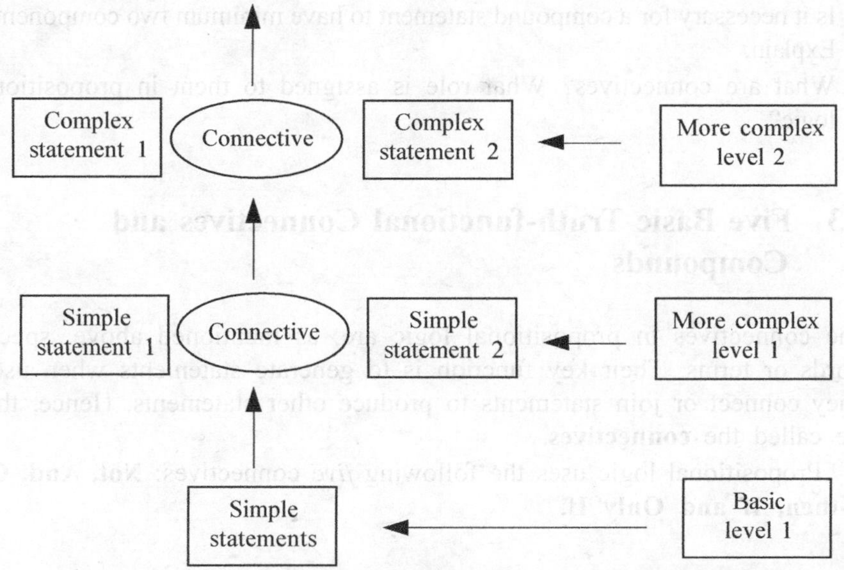

Fig. 5.1 The model of language of propositional logic.

Examples 21 and 22 show how simple statements can be connected to create longer, and structurally more complex statements. Example 21 uses the connective 'and' Example 22 uses 'if-then'. In each example a square bracket has been put around the component simple statements to identify the components.

EXERCISE 5.2

1. Which of the following are simple statements? Justify your answer.

a. Summer months in India are getting warmer.

b. *Four of us can go by car and the rest can take the train.

c. As one gets older, chances of changing jobs with equal pay and benefits become lesser, unless one is exceptionally talented.

d. Political affiliation of student groups often causes violence in the campus, leading to a general degradation of the quality of life in academia.

e. *Movies reach out to a lot of people.

f. Education is a very important public responsibility which is vital to a democracy and requires a strong and informed participation.

g. We shall go to Madurai or to Kanyakumari.

***2.** Explain in what sense the simple statements have been understood as 'simple' in propositional logic.

3. Is it necessary for a compound statement to have minimum two components? Explain.

4. What are connectives? What role is assigned to them in propositional logic?

5.3 Five Basic Truth-functional Connectives and Compounds

The connectives in propositional logic are, as mentioned above, special words or terms. Their key function is to generate statements when used. They connect or join statements to produce other statements. Hence, they are called the **connectives.**

Propositional logic uses the following *five* connectives: **Not, And, Or, If-then, If and Only If.**

Not [or **It is not the case] (Negation)**

This is a **monadic** or **unary** connective. For, at a time it can connect *only one* statement. It is represented by the symbol '~' **(called tilde).**

NOT | Statement |

Propositional logic reads sentences with 'not' somewhat differently, as can be seen from the table below:

Simple statement	**Colloquial 'not' statement**	**'Not' in propositional logic**	**In symbolized form**
Mishra is a dentist	Mishra is not a dentist	a. **Not** (Mishra is a dentist) b. **It is not the case** (Mishra is a dentist)	~ Mishra is a dentist

It is important to remember that in propositional logic, negations, i.e., statements with explicit 'not' or its equivalent in them, are compound statements. They have only one component, namely, the statement that is negated. Nonetheless, since it has another statement as a component, a negation is a compound statement.

It is possible that the negated component itself may be a compound statement. The statement in column above has a single simple component. However, in comparison, consider the following negation: ***It is not that***

Suresh will have to go and Paresh must stay back: The statement that is being negated itself is a compound statement with two simple components.

A negation is true if its component is false, and it is false if its component is true. So, its truth conditions can be listed as follows:

Component statement	**Its negation**	**Truth-value of component**	**Truth-value of its negation**
India is in Asia	India is not in Asia	T (True)	F (False)
Milton is the writer of *Othello*	Milton is not the writer of *Othello*	F (False)	T (True)

And (Conjunction)

A compound statement composed by the connective 'and' is called a **conjunction**. Its components are called **conjuncts**. The symbol chosen to express conjunction is **'•' (dot).**

The '•' and the other three connectives listed below in this section are **dyadic** or **binary** connectives. They are called so because at a time they can connect two statements.

Examples of conjunction are as follows:

Examples

23. Mishra is a dentist **and** he owns a car.
24. Some Hindus are Brahmins **and** some are not.

Both Examples 23 and 24 are compound statements. However, in Example 24, one of the conjuncts, 'some are not', is actually a compound statement, being a negation.

From the viewpoint of propositional logic, several English connectives are treated as equivalent to 'and' for example: *but*, *however*, *moreover*, *though*, *although*, *yet*, etc. Consider the following examples:

Examples

25. Some Hindus are Brahmins **but** many are not.
26. Some Hindus are Brahmins; **however,** many are not.
27. Some Hindus are Brahmins **though** many are not.
28. Some Hindus are Brahmins **although** many are not.

The nuance in each case may be different, but propositional logic will treat Examples 25–28 as conjunctions, i.e., as 'and' statements and will symbolize each as: (Some Hindus are Brahmins) • (many are not).

The conjunction is true only when both the conjuncts are true; it is false in every other case. If p and q are any two conjuncts, then the truth conditions for $(p \bullet q)$ will be:

p	q	$p \bullet q$	
True (T)	True (T)	True (T)	← The only condition in which a '•' is true
True (T)	False (F)	False (F)	
False (F)	False (F)	False (F)	
False (F)	False (F)	False (F)	

Sometimes, the sense of conjunction or the grouping of the conjuncts may not be explicit. However, in their symbolic representation the true character of the conjunction will have to be brought out. Consider these cases:

Examples

29. Kolkata, Mumbai, New Delhi, and Chennai are all big cities in India.
30. Jaya is rich and smart.
31. Anurag stays, Saurabh leaves.

Though it has only one 'and' in it, Example 29 is actually a conjunction with four conjuncts:

(Kolkata is a big city in India) • (Mumbai is a big city in India) • (New Delhi is a big city in India) • (Chennai is a big city in India).

Similarly, Example 30 is actually a conjunction of two statements: Jaya is rich and Jaya is smart. Example 31 has a comma that conveys the sense of conjunction and, when symbolized, its character as a conjunction should be preserved.

However, not all uses of 'and' are to be symbolized as •. Consider the following:

Examples

32. Bill and Hillary Clinton are married.
33. He took off his clothes and went into the swimming pool.

It would be a mistake to translate Example 32 as "(Bill Clinton is married) • (Hillary Clinton is married)". For, that would mean that each of them is separately married, but not that they are married to each other. Similarly, it would be a mistake to translate Example 33 with a •. For, the 'and' in Example 33 is actually an 'and then', as there is a distinct order or sequence that is intended, and it is not reversible. "He went into the pool and took off his clothes" is a very different statement meaning wise than what is given in Example 33.

Either-Or (Disjunction)

The compound statement formed by connecting two statements by 'or' is called a **disjunction**. Its components are called **disjuncts**. The symbol to represent *or* is ' ∨ ' (called 'vee' or 'wedge'), which is also a dyadic connective.

Statement 1	**OR**	Statement 2

Examples of disjunction are:

Examples

34. Either we go for camping or we go for swimming.
35. Either the conference will be held with support from the hosting organization or with the support of external agencies.

English 'either-or' statement	Disjunction in propositional logic	In symbolized form
Either we go for camping or we go for swimming	(we go for camping) or (we go for swimming	(we go for camping) ∨ (we go for swimming)

Usually, our understanding of 'either-or' is in an exclusive sense such that one of the disjuncts, if it is true, excludes or cancels the other. The examples of this **exclusive or** (sometimes called **XOR)** are:

Examples

36. Sumeet is either from Orissa or from Uttar Pradesh.
37. The number must be either odd or even.

The intended sense in both Examples 36 and 37 is that only one of the options holds, but *not both*. For two statements p and q, truth conditions of this 'exclusive or' are:

p	q	p **exclusive or** q
T	T	F
T	F	T
F	T	T
F	F	F

However, the disjunction in propositional logic represented by '∨' is **not** an exclusive or. It is an **inclusive or**, which is true *when either of the disjuncts is true and also when both the disjuncts are true*. Its truth conditions, for any two statements p and q, are as follows:

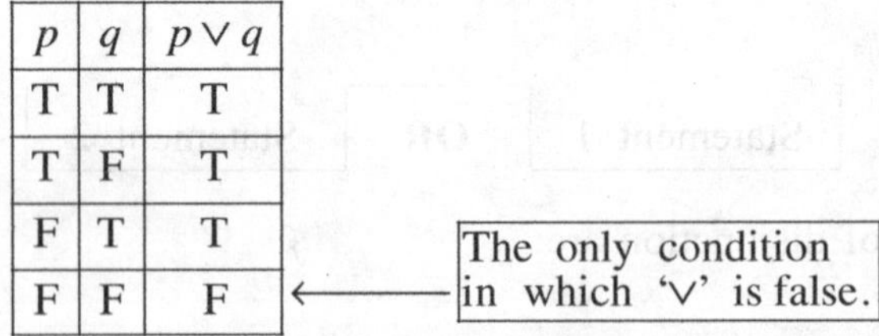

p	q	$p \vee q$
T	T	T
T	F	T
F	T	T
F	F	F

The three connectives 'not', 'and', 'or', as discussed above, are also known as the **Boolean operators** or **Boolean connectives**. For, these were first used by George Boole (see Chapter 4), the English logician, as part of his system of logic. You will find that these operators have gained widely diverse applications in various programming tasks, logic gates, for search in an electronic database, etc.

If-then (material conditionals)

A compound statement composed of two statements by the connective 'if-then' is called a **material conditional** in propositional logic. For example:

Examples

38. If switch A is pushed, then the machine will stop.
39. If Kamal boards the superfast train, (then) he will arrive here by tomorrow morning.

The component between the 'if' and the 'then' is called the **antecedent**. In Example 38, "switch A is pushed" is the antecedent. The component statement that follows the 'then' is called the **consequent**. Sometimes, the 'then' is not mentioned, as may be the case in Example 39. Even then, the comma in Example 39 indicates the division of the components. The statement "he will arrive here by tomorrow morning", which follows the comma, is the consequent.

If	Antecedent	**Then**	Consequent

The symbol for 'if-then' in propositional logic is '$\supset$' (called the **horseshoe** or the **hook**). As mentioned earlier, it is a dyadic connective, at a time connecting only two statements. The format for translation is: antecedent $\supset$ consequent.

Colloquial English 'if-then' statements	**In symbolized form**
If switch A is pushed, then the machine will stop.	(Switch A is pushed) $\supset$ (the machine will stop)

There are many kinds of 'if—then' statements in English, exhibiting different kinds of relationships between the antecedent and the consequent. Examples of various kinds of conditionals are as follows:

Examples

40. If successors of even numbers are odd numbers, then 5 is an odd number.
41. If ABC is a triangle, then the summation of its angles comes to 180 degrees.
42. If a piece of wax is left in the hot sun, then it will melt.
43. If you clean up your room, then I'll buy you the toy you want.

Example 40 expresses a logical relationship between the antecedent and the consequent, whereas Example 41 conveys a definitional relationship. By definition of a triangle, the consequent follows. Example 42 exhibits a causal connection based on experience, and Example 43 is a promise, the fulfillment of which depends upon a certain behaviour.

Philosophically, it is a highly controversial issue whether the '$\supset$' or the material conditional can truly represent the English 'if-then' statements and their diverse uses. **Appendix B** at the end of this book presents a summary of the great philosophical controversy that exists on this issue. Those of you who are interested in the philosophy of logic or the philosophy of language, or simply on the issue of how much of this logic applies to ordinary everyday language, may find the entire debate interesting and informative. In this section, however, we do not intend to go into that debate. In Section 5.2, we shall simply say that propositional logic, through the beliefs of its founders and practitioners, has adopted a rather simplified approach towards its material conditionals.

Propositional logic maintains that the common core meaning of all conditionals is that they are considered to be false *when the antecedent holds true, but the consequent fails to occur*. For instance, Example 42 will be considered as false when a piece of wax is left out in the hot sun but it does not melt. That is, if we take *p* and *q* as any two antecedent and consequent, respectively, then $p \supset q$ is false when *p* happens, but *q* does not; or when $(p \bullet \sim q)$ is true. Thus, $p \supset q$ is true whenever $(p \bullet \sim q)$ is false, or whenever $\sim (p \bullet \sim q)$ is true. Its truth conditions, therefore, are as follows:

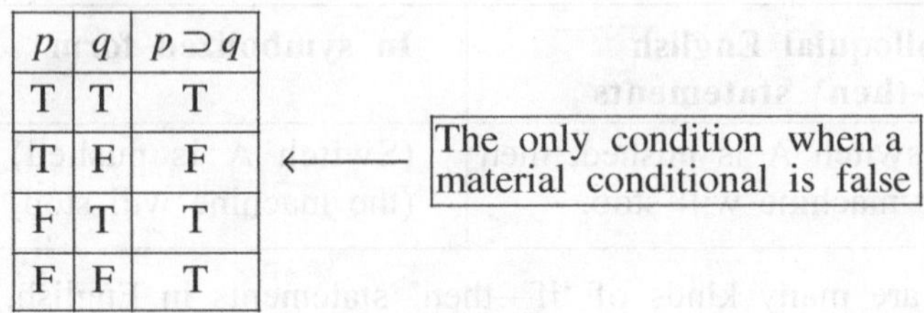

p	*q*	$p \supset q$
T	T	T
T	F	F
F	T	T
F	F	T

The first and the third row of this table show that a material *conditional* will be true *whenever its consequent is true*, irrespective of what value its antecedent has—true or false. Similarly, the third and fourth rows show that a material *conditional* is true *whenever its antecedent is false*, irrespective of what value the consequent has—true or false.

In English, there are many other ways to express a conditional. Some examples are given below:

Examples

44. *Given that* Tina will go, Rina will follow.
45. Rina will follow *provided that* Tina will go.
46. Rina will follow *if* Tina will go.
47. Tina will go *only if* Rina will follow.

In propositional logic, Statements 44–47 will be translated as "If Tina will go, then Rina will follow", or as "(Tina will go) ⊃ (Rina will follow)".

The antecedent in $p \supset q$ is also known as the **sufficient condition**. Its occurrence is supposed to be sufficient to bring about the consequent. However, that does *not* mean without it the consequent cannot occur; for, there could be other sufficient conditions too for the consequent to happen. If *p* then *q* does *not* mean only if *p*, then *q*.

The consequent, on the other hand, is sometimes called the **necessary condition,** i.e., if it is not true, then the antecedent too cannot be the case. For, if the consequent has not happened, one can assume that none of the sufficient conditions, along with the antecedent, have happened.

If and only if (equivalence or **material biconditional)**

A compound statement composed by the connective "if and only if" ("*iff*" for short) is called an equivalence or a biconditional statement. The symbol '≡'(triple bar) is used for *if and only if*.

Statement 1	**If and only If**	Statement 2

Examples of equivalence are:

Examples

48. A student can register for the courses if and only if she has completed the admission procedures.
49. We book the hotel if and only if the vacation plan is confirmed.

English 'if and only if' statements	**Equivalence in propositional logic**	**In symbolic form**
We book the hotel *if and only if* the vacation plan is confirmed.	(We book the hotel) *if and only if* (the vacation plan is confirmed.)	(We book the hotel) ≡ (the vacation plan is confirmed).

The truth conditions for '≡' are as follows:

p	q	$p \equiv q$
T	T	T
T	F	F
F	T	F
F	F	T

The point to note is that '≡' is true *whenever both the components have the same value*. It is true either when both components are true or when both are false, as can be seen from the first and fourth rows of the table. Thus, $p \equiv q$ is true *iff* $[(p \bullet q) \vee (\sim p \bullet \sim q)]$ is true. It is false *whenever the components have different values,* as can be seen from the second and third rows of the table.

The $p \equiv q$ or p *iff* q can be also seen as a conjunction of two conditionals: p *if* q, and p *only if* q. Symbolically, according to propositional logic, p *if* q is $q \supset p$, and p *only if* q is $p \supset q$. So,

$$(p \equiv q) \equiv (p \supset q) \bullet (q \supset p).$$

The same can be alternatively expressed as: p is both the *sufficient and necessary condition* of q.

This ends the introduction to the five basic connectives in propositional logic. The syntax of propositional logic is as follows:

1. If p is a statement in propositional logic, then so is $\sim p$.
2. If p and q are statements in propositional logic, then so is $p \bullet q$.
3. If p and q are statements in propositional logic, then so is $p \vee q$.
4. If p and q are statements in propositional logic, then so is $p \supset q$.
5. If p and q are statements in propositional logic, then so is $p \equiv q$.

Nothing else is a well-formed statement in propositional logic unless it is formed by repeated application of rules 1–5 mentioned above.

EXERCISE 5.3

1. *What is the difference between a monadic and a dyadic connective?

2. In total how many connectives are used in propositional logic? How many of these are monadic?

3. What is the difference between an inclusive and an exclusive or? Explain using your own examples.

4. What are the alternative ways to express an 'if-then' in English? Can you think of examples other than the ones given in the book?

5. True or false? Justify your answer:

a. *A material conditional may be false if it has a true antecedent.

b. A conjunction is true if at least one of the conjuncts is true.

c. A disjunction is true if at least one of the disjuncts is true.

d. If a material bi-conditional is false, at least one of its atomic components, namely, one of the simple statements as its components, must be false.

e. If a material bi-conditional is true, at least one of its atomic components, namely, one of the simple statements as its components, must be false.

f. *The '$\vee$' is true if both disjuncts are true.

5.4 Alternative Notations

In this book we have used a set of five symbols to represent the five basic truth functional connectives. However, you will often find that different symbols are being used for the same connectives as there are wide uses of these connectives in different disciplines such as mathematics, computer science, and programming languages. Accordingly, there are many variants available as symbols for the same connectives. Sometimes these alternative symbols are chosen purely for the sake of finding them on the keyboard. For example, for negation you may find the symbol '—' (a dash or the mathematical subtraction symbol) or sometimes '¬' (a dash with a tiny tail) is being used. You may even find some using a simple bar above a statement to indicate a negated statement as in $\overline{A}$. Similarly, for other connectives, sometimes different symbols are used.

If you encounter these different symbols, you simply need to remember that, as long as the truth tables for the connectives remain the same, the difference in the symbols does not matter. What you have learnt above in this book about the five basic connectives will hold true.

Still, for the beginners, a list of some alternative symbols used for the five connectives is given below. This is given so that you are aware of the different usages and can treat them as superficial differences. If you see some other symbol other than the one that you are used to, you will know how to interpret it in terms of your known symbols and not feel obstructed by them.

Name of connective	**Symbol used in this book**	**Some alternative notations**
Not or It is not the case	~ (tilde or curl)	-, ¬, !
And	• (dot)	&, *, ∧, &&
Inclusive Or	∨ (vee or vel)	+, |, ||
If then or material conditional	⊃ (horseshoe or the hook)	→
Equivalence or Biconditional	≡ (triple bar)	↔

5.5 Truth-functionality

Instead of numerical values, symbolic logic deals with **truth values**. It is based upon only **two** truth values, truth (T) and falsity (F). Hence, it is called a **bi-valued system**. All its statements will be either true or false and, similarly, its compounds will also be either true or false.

Broadly speaking, compound statements can be of two types depending on how the truth value of the compound is determined. A compound is **truth functional** *iff* its truth value is entirely determined by the truth values of its simple or atomic components, or, in other words, it is a function of the truth values of its simple or atomic components.

In the case of a truth-functional compound, the input values will be truth values, T or F, of the simple components, and the output will be the truth value of the compound. For instance, the truth value of Example 51 which is a negation or is a '~' statement, is entirely a function of what the truth value of "New York is the capital of USA" is. It is true *iff* "New York is the capital of USA" is false, and it is false *iff* "New York is the capital of USA" is true. This makes Example 51 a truth-functional compound.

Similarly, for Example 50 we need not look anywhere else but into the truth values of the components to know what its truth value is.

Examples

50. (Mars is uninhabited) • (it is the fourth planet in the solar system).
51. ~ (New York is the capital of USA).

Propositional logic is a logic based on the notion of truth functionality. The concept of truth functionality is crucial for propositional logic; otherwise, it does not know how to deal with the truth values of its compound statements. All its five basic connectives, '~', '•', '∨', '⊃', '≡', are all **truth-functional operators**. They are supposed to yield only **truth-functional compounds**. A look at the tables of truth conditions of each of the connectives shows that, in order to know the truth value of the compound, all we ever need to know is what the truth values of its components are.

A sentential connective is used truth functionally *iff* it is used to generate a compound statement from atomic components in such a way that if its component atomic statements are replaced by other atomic statements of **equivalent truth value**, its own truth value will remain the same.

EXERCISE 5.5

1. What is a bi-valued system? Can any statement of propositional logic be neither true nor false?
2. What is the mark of a truth functional compound statement? Explain with your own examples.
3. *How many truth values are being used in the following table for an unknown connective '*'?

p	q	$p * q$
T	T	T
T	F	Undecided
F	T	Undecided
F	F	F

4. Given that A is true, B is false, C is true, and D is unknown, what can you tell about the truth value of each of the following?

a. $*(A \bullet C) \supset (D \vee C)$
b. $D \supset \{(A \vee C) \equiv A\}$
c. $(\sim B \supset D) \supset \sim (\sim C \bullet A)$
d. $(B \bullet D) \supset [(A \bullet C) \supset (B \vee C)]$
e. $*D \equiv (A \bullet B)$
f. $\sim [(B \bullet C) \bullet \sim (C \bullet B)]$
g. $\sim [(A \bullet B) \vee \sim (B \bullet A)]$
h. $[A \vee (B \vee C)] \bullet \sim [(A \vee B) \vee C]$
i. $[B \vee (A \bullet C)] \vee [(B \vee A) \bullet (B \vee C)]$
j. $[B \bullet (A \vee C)] \bullet [(B \bullet A) \vee (B \bullet C)]$
k. $[A \bullet (B \vee C)] \bullet \sim [(A \bullet B) \vee (A \bullet C)]$
l. $*[[(\sim B \bullet A) \bullet (C \bullet \sim D)] \bullet \sim [(A \bullet \sim B) \bullet \sim (\sim C \bullet D)]$
m. $\sim D \bullet D$
n. $\sim (D \vee A) \vee A$
o. $(\sim A \vee D) \bullet (\sim D \vee C)$
p. $\sim [\sim D \vee (\sim B \vee A)] \vee [\sim (\sim D \vee A) \vee (\sim D \vee B)]$

5. What property of the statements in questions 4 (a)–(p) allows you to compute the truth value of the whole statement in each case? Explain.

5.6 Non-truth-functional Connectives

A compound statement is a **non-truth-functional compound** *iff* its truth value depends on something other than the information about the truth values of its components.

Examples

52. (Harappa had a civilization) *before* (the Aryans came into India).
53. Mihir believes that (Elvis Presley is still alive).

Both Examples 52 and 53 are non-truth-functional compounds, and the connectives used in each, namely, *before* and *Mihir believes that* are **non-truth-functional connectives**. For, in Example 52, the truth values of the two components, "Harappa had a civilization" and "the Aryans came into India", alone do not determine what the truth value of Example 52 will be. In order to know whether it is true or false, one has to depend on further information about the historical course of events in the Indian subcontinent. This is why Example 52 is not a truth-functional compound.

Similarly, whether truly "Elvis Presley is still alive" or is dead does not completely determine the truth value of Example 53. Its truth value further depends on a psychological fact about Mihir: on whether he truly believes that Elvis Presley is alive or not. Therefore, it too is a non-truth-functional compound.

It is to be noted that all truth-functional statements are compound statements, as can be seen from the examples above. However, all compound statements are not truth functional, as can be seen from Examples 52 and 53. Propositional logic is concerned *exclusively with truth-functional compounds*, and non-truth-functional connectives or compounds do not fall within its purview.

EXERCISE 5.6

1. What is a non-truth-functional connective? Explain using at least one of your own example.
2. Why are non-truth functional connectives not part of the propositional logic?

5.7 Variables and Constants

Propositional logic is about statements. In order to symbolize statements, a proper system of representation is required.

In case we want to refer to actual or specific simple statements such as "**M**ars is a planet", "Mars is the fourth **p**lanet in the solar system", the convention in propositional logic is to use an *appropriate capital letter* from the alphabet for each simple or atomic statement. Within the same context, a capital letter should not represent more than one statement. For example, we may use the capital letter M to represent "Mars is a planet". If used in the same context, M should *not* also represent "Mars is the fourth planet in the solar system". Some other capital letters, such as P, may be used to represent "Mars is the fourth planet in the solar system". Because of their unique reference to a specific simple statement in a given context, capital letters such as A, B, C ... will be referred to as **statement constants**. Within a given context, their value will remain constant.

Specific statement	Represented by statement constant
Mars is a planet	M
Mars is the fourth planet in the solar system	P

In comparison, sometimes we do not wish to refer to any one particular statement but would like to make some comments about statements in general. For instance, when we want to say that the truth conditions of '•' are of a certain kind, obviously we want to keep our reference non-specific. Instead of referring to particular statements, we mean for *any two* statements, when conjoined by the '•', the special truth conditions will hold. In cases of such non-specific reference, the convention is to use lowercase alphabets p, q, r. These will be referred to as **statement variables**. For, they are **placeholders** which can be replaced by various statement constants in different contexts. In Section 5.2, the syntax rules for propositional logic exhibit the use of statement variables p, q to refer to statements in general. For, the combination procedures that these syntax rules talk about apply to statements in general in propositional logic.

EXERCISE 5.7

1. Given that p is true and q and r are false, what can you tell about the truth value of each of the following?

a.* $[(p \bullet r) \supset (q \bullet p)] \equiv [q \vee r]$

b. $[\{(p \supset q) \supset r\} \supset (q \supset r)] \supset [q \supset (p \supset r)]$

c. $\sim [\sim p \vee [\{(q \supset p) \supset (q \bullet r)\}]]$

d. $\sim [(p \vee q) \vee \sim (r \vee \sim p)]$

e.* $[p \vee (q \bullet r)] \bullet \sim [(p \vee q) \bullet (p \vee r)]$

f. $[p \equiv (q \supset r)] \supset [r \supset (p \equiv q)]$

g. $[\sim p \vee (q \equiv r)] \equiv [\sim q \supset (r \bullet (p \supset q))]$

h. $\sim [[(\sim p \bullet q) \vee (\sim r \vee q)] \supset [\sim (\sim p \bullet \sim (q \equiv r))]$

2. Did you know which statements the p, q, r in Question 1 above stand for? Explain then how you could still know which of them are true and which of them are not. What results do questions 1(a)–(h) actually show?

3. Replace the variables in 1(b) by constants and provide a suitable statement for each constant.

5.8 Scope of a Connective

Whenever more than one connective are used in a statement, there rises a chance of ambiguity. Consider the statement: "$M \bullet L \vee C$". It is ambiguous because it allows two different interpretations:

$M \bullet (L \vee C)$ $(M \bullet L) \vee C$

If *M* is "The market survey will be done", *L* is "The product will be launched", and *C* is "The product will be considered for improvement", then the meaning of the statement changes depending upon which interpretation is selected. $M \bullet (L \vee C)$ asserts that "The market survey will be done, and the product will be either launched or considered for improvement", whereas, $(M \bullet L) \vee C$ asserts quite a different statement, namely, "Either the market survey will be done and the product will be launched, or the product will be considered for improvement". What makes one interpretation true does not make the other true. $(M \bullet L) \vee C$ is true if *C* alone is true, it does not really matter what truth values *M* and *L* may have. However, the truth of *M* is crucial for the truth of $M \bullet (L \vee C)$, and moreover, it is required that at least one of *L* or *C* must be true in order to make $(L \vee C)$ true. So, depending upon which interpretation is taken up, the truth conditions and the truth value of the statement $M \bullet L \vee C$ differs significantly, and may create a serious problem for the proper evaluation of the statement in propositional logic.

Removal of ambiguity such as in the above case is desirable. More so, because in sentential logic, no logical connective gets precedence over any other, unless specifically mentioned. For this purpose, devices such as parentheses '( )', curly brackets, '{ }', square brackets, '[ ]', are used to remove ambiguity.

Devices such as parentheses and square brackets help demarcate clearly the **scope of each connective.** The **scope** of a connective is the range of its operation or the extent of its operation within the statement. For instance: in the case of negation or '~', its scope is always over that which it negates. In '~*Q*', the component *Q* is under the scope of '~'. The scope of dyadic connectives, such as '∨', '•', etc. always ranges over the two components that they connect.

When there are several connectives in use, the **main connective** is that truth-functional connective in the statement which has the *maximum scope*. The scope of the main connective covers the entire statement, and all the component statements.

Examples

54. $\sim [(D \supset E) \vee (F \vee G)]$
55. $\sim D \supset (E \vee (F \vee G))$

In Example 54, the square brackets indicate that '~' ranges over the whole statement and all the components; the scope of '⊃' is only over $(D \vee E)$, whereas the scope of the second '∨' is only over $(F \vee G)$, and the first '∨' ranges over $(D \supset E)$ and $(F \vee G)$, both as its two disjuncts.

Therefore, in Example 54, '~' is the main connective as it has the maximum scope.

In Example 55, on the other hand, '⊃' is the main connective which ranges over $\sim D$ as the antecedent and also over $(E \vee (F \vee G))$ as the consequent. The scope of the '~' in Example 55 is only over D, the only statement that it negates.

Examples 54 and 55 also bring out the importance of using parentheses and brackets for marking the scope of a connective. Without them, the statements would have been ambiguous. In general, whenever more than one connective is to be used, devices such as parentheses should be used as a practical necessity.

EXERCISE 5.8

1. Explain, with two examples of your own, the scope of a connective. Why is understanding the scope of a connective important?

2. Identify the main connective in each case:

a. $[(A \vee B) \vee D] \supset \sim E$

b. $(T \bullet M) \bullet (C \supset Q)$

c. $(R \vee S) \equiv \{\sim L \bullet (G \bullet A)\}$

*d. $\sim [(G \vee (A \supset B)]$

e. $\sim K \supset [(J \supset K) \vee (\sim J \supset \sim K)]$

5.9 Symbolization

The key to the symbolization in propositional logic is to follow the given statement closely. One should:

- Pick out the atomic or simple statements in the given statement.
- If a list of capital letters to be used as the translation key is not provided, then select an appropriate and unique capital letter for each distinct simple statement.
- Read the statement carefully to understand the grouping of the statements.
- Look out for punctuation marks such as comma to identify the main and the subordinate connectives.
- Replace each simple statement by the chosen capital letter.
- Replace each English connective by the appropriate connective from propositional logic.

Examples of Negation

56. She does not dance. $\sim D$
57. Vivek will not run in the marathon. $\sim V$
58. This tree is not evergreen. $\sim E$

Examples of Conjunction

59. Aveek will join, but Sheela too must join. $A \bullet S$
60. Mother and father-both will come. $M \bullet F$
61. Rabindranath and Bankim Chandra were both visionaries. $R \bullet B$

Examples of Disjunction

62. Either Milan or Shiva will perform. $M \vee S$
63. You call him at seven or eight in the morning. $S \vee E$

Examples of Material Implication

64. If I see him, then I shall tell him. $S \supset T$
65. Given that the economy is good, the job market will expand. $E \supset J$
66. You can score high provided you work hard. $W \supset S$

Examples of Material bi-conditional

67. The Job market will expand if and only if the economy is good. $J \equiv E$
68. The plan is good just in case it is safe. $G \equiv S$

Some slightly more complex examples are given in the following table.

Examples of English statements	**Symbolization key**	**In symbolized form**
69. Mona read the book and she didn't like it	M: Mona read the book L: Mona liked the book	$M \bullet \sim L$
70. Harsh will play *iff* Mehta and Sridhar are not in the team	H: Harsh will play M: Mehta is in the team S: Sridhar is in the team	$H \equiv (\sim M \bullet \sim S)$
71. If it either rains or snows, we shall have the party inside only if we have the consent from the club.	R: It rains S: It snows P: We shall have the party inside C: We have the consent from the club	$(R \vee S) \supset (P \supset C)$

72. We do not need to raise taxes or show deficit if wasteful Government spending is curbed.	T: We need to raise taxes D: We show deficit G: Wasteful Government spending is curbed	$G \supset (\sim T \vee D)$

It is to be noted that in the symbolization key, certain expansions are necessary and also that only simple statements are to be represented by capital letters. In Example 69, '*L*' stands for the simple statement "Mona liked the book" which is an expansion based on the given statement. Also, it represents the basic simple statement that "she didn't like it" negates. This helps the symbolization to bring out the logical structure in a clearer fashion.

EXERCISE 5.9

1. Symbolize the following statements using the symbolization key provided. [M: We are going to the mountains, G: The weather is good]

a. We are not going to the mountains.

*b. We are going to the mountains only if the weather is good.

c. We are going to the mountains though the weather is not good.

d. Either we are going to the mountains or the weather is not good.

e. We are going to the mountains just in case the weather is good.

f. It is not that we are not going to the mountains.

2. Translate into English the following symbolized statements. Your translation should be as idiomatic and free-flowing as possible.
[A: Aveek will win, B: Balaram will win, C: Champa will win]

*a. $A \vee (B \vee C)$

b. $\sim A \bullet (\sim B \bullet \sim C)$

c. $C \supset \sim (B \bullet A)$

d. $A \equiv (\sim B \vee \sim C)$

*e. $(\sim A \bullet \sim B) \vee [(\sim B \bullet \sim C) \vee (\sim A \bullet \sim C)]$

3. Translate the following using the symbolization key provided:

*a. Iraq is in turmoil now, either it will lead to a prolonged internal war in that country or to an international conflict. [I: Iraq is in turmoil now, P: It will lead to a prolonged internal war in that country, C: It will lead to an international conflict.]

b. If Ranen passes with good marks grade, then he may easily get a good job and make a lot of money or he may go abroad for higher studies and earn a lot of money and respect. [A: Ranen passes with a good academic result, J: Ranen may easily get a good job, M: Ranen may make a lot of money, B: Ranen may go abroad, R: Ranen may earn a lot of respect.]

c. The meaning of life is love; the goal of life is to connect with others; but we tend to forget these truths. [M: The meaning of life is love, G: The goal of life is to connect with others, T: We tend to remember these truths.]

d. If Mona wears green but Jay wears blue, then Bobby wears Red if I wear white. [G: Mona wears green, B: Jay wears blue, R: Bobby wears Red, W: I wear white.]

e. It is not that if a problem exists, a solution has to exist; also it is not that there will be a unique solution given that a problem exists. [P: A problem exists, S: A solution has to exist, U: There will be unique solution.]

f. Jaya's being rich is both necessary and sufficient condition for her being famous. [R: Jaya is rich, F: Jaya is famous.]

*g. Given that Israel buys more weapons, either Jordan will ask for international aid or both Iraq and Palestine will protest against external intervention in the Middle-East crisis. [I: Israel buys more weapons, J: Jordan will ask for international aid, Q: Iraq will protest against external intervention in middle-east crisis, P: Palestine will protest against external intervention in middle-east crisis.

5.10 Complex Symbolizations

Not Both

Suppose that you are operating with a shoestring budget and have to plan a menu, you have to take the following decision in the given example:

Example

73. Ice-cream and Kulfi will **not both** be served.

The statement, when paraphrased, becomes: It is not the case that both Ice-cream and Kulfi will be served. Suppose 'I' stands for "Ice-cream will be served" and 'K' for "Kulfi will be served". Accordingly, the translation will be: $\sim (I \bullet K)$. It is a negation of a conjunction. This means that *at most* one of them may be served.

On the other hand, suppose you have taken the following decision as in the given example:

Example

74. Ice-cream and Kulfi **both** will **not** be served.

In that case, what you mean is that "Ice-cream will not be served and Kulfi will not be served". Your budget does not support any of them, so neither will be served. Accordingly, the translation will be: $\sim I \bullet \sim K$. The different scope of the '~' in each case creates a very important difference between Examples 73 and 74.

Neither-Nor

Consider the statement:

Example

75. **Neither** Ice-cream **nor** Kulfi will be served.

It means, as in Example 73 given above, "Ice-cream will not be served and Kulfi will not be served". Its translation also will be the same: $\sim I \bullet \sim K$. One may also read 'neither-nor' as 'not (either-or)', Accordingly Example 75 can also be translated as $\sim (I \vee K)$.

However, it will be a mistake to treat 'neither-nor' statements as disjunctions. Example 75 should **not** be translated as: $\sim I \vee \sim K$, i.e., "Either Ice-cream will not be served or Kulfi will not be served". $\sim I \vee \sim K$ is true when at least one of the disjuncts is true; it is true when, for instance, only ice-cream is not served but Kulfi is served. However, that is not what Example 75 means: it disallows the serving of both Ice-cream and Kulfi. Therefore, one has to be careful while translating 'neither-nor' statements.

Unless

Consider the following example:

Example

76. Bharati will go, unless she has other commitment.

Example 76 means: "If Bharati does not have other commitment, then she will go". Translated, it incase: $\sim C \supset G$. 'Unless' can be also interpreted as 'if not'.

EXERCISE 5.10

1. Translate the following using the given symbolization key:

*a. Chocolates are neither nutritious nor good for teeth. [N: Chocolates are nutritious, T: Chocolates are good for teeth.]

b. The factory will shut down unless the debts in the market are quickly paid back and the raw material supply is back to normal. [F: The factory will shut down, D: The debts in the market are quickly paid back, R: The raw material supply is back to normal.]

c. If this is the only possible world, then not both its improvement and its transformation are possible. [O: This is the only possible world, I: Its improvement is possible, A: Its transformation is possible.]

d. Education is not useful if it neither prepares the youth to shoulder the social responsibilities nor enables them to stand on their feet. [U: Education is useful, P: It prepares the youth to shoulder the social responsibilities, E: Education enables the youth to stand on their feet.]

e. Both India and Pakistan will play Cricket only if it is a friendship match series, unless there are reasons for security concern for the players. [I: India will play Cricket, P: Pakistan will play Cricket, F: It is a friendship match series, S: There are reasons for security concern for the players.]

f. If Rony gets the highest marks, then not both Deepa and Elena will be happy. [R: Rony gets the highest marks, D: Deepa will be happy, E: Elena will be happy.]

h. If politicians are responsible only if the citizens are responsible; then politicians are neither honest nor self-respecting. [P: Politicians are responsible; C: Citizens are responsible, H: Politicians are honest; S: Politicians are self-respecting.]

*i. The fact, that if this substance is an acid then it contains hydrogen ions is both a sufficient and necessary condition for this substance to be corrosive and sour to the taste. [A: This substance is an acid; H: This substance contains hydrogen ions; C: This substance is corrosive; S: This substance is sour to the taste.]

j. Neither it is the case that if an artist is rich then he is not talented, nor is it true that if the artist is talented then he is rich. [R: An artist is rich, T: An artist is talented.]

k. If Sri Lanka agrees, but neither India nor Pakistan agrees, then it is not the case that only if Bangladesh agrees, the series will be played. [C: Sri Lanka agrees; I: India agrees; P: Pakistan agrees; B: Bangladesh agrees; S: The series will be played.]

5.11 Tips for Translation

Translation is one of the areas in propositional logic which requires some caution. The first job while translating is to read the statement to be translated and find out what the main connective is. For this purpose, often the **first word** of the statement is a key. For example, if the statement starts with an 'if', the main connective is likely to be the '⊃'. If the first word is 'Either', the main connective will be a '∨'. The '•', as the main connective, does not require any special first word. One has to look out for the key position of 'however' or 'but' In between statements to find out the scope of a '•'. So, even if there are no easy to detect first word, the presence of a 'however' or 'but' as an important divider in the statement may indicate the '•' as the main connective. Similarly, the usual place for 'if and only if' is at the middle of a statement, and not at the beginning.

Punctuation marks often give us the clue, for example, a comma (,) or a semicolon (;), indicates a certain way of grouping the components. Parentheses and brackets should reflect the grouping indicated by the punctuation marks.

Once the main connective is identified, the components require equally careful attention. The process is the same: one has to first identify the main connective in each component and, if there are subcomponents, then the same process has to be repeated for them also until all the components are translated. A connective within the scope of another connective may create some confusion, particularly if both the connectives are the same. For example, in "If either it snows or rains, we have the party inside provided we have the consent of the club" (Example 71), the first word 'if' indicates that the main connective will be '⊃'. Its antecedent is "either it snows or rains", the main connective of which will be a '∨' as indicated by 'either'. The consequent is indicated by a comma and the consequent is another '⊃' statement, as 'provided' indicates. The scope of this '⊃' is within the scope of the main '⊃', and that has to be reflected by the use of parentheses.

Keywords

Antecedent: The statement between the 'if' and the 'then' in a conditional statement. Symbolically, it is the component on the left of the '⊃' symbol.

Binary or **Dyadic connective:** Connective which at a time can connect two statements. '•', '∨', etc. are all examples of this kind.

Bi-valued system: A logical system which believes in two truth values, truth and falsity. Every statement in such a system is either true or false.

Compound statements: A statement containing at least one statement as its component.

Conjunct: Each statement conjoined by 'and' or '•' is a conjunct.

Conjunction: A compound statement whose main connective is the 'and' or in symbol '•'.

Connectives: Words or symbols used as connectors between statements.

Consequent: The statement after the 'then' in a conditional statement. Symbolically, it is the component on the right side of the '⊃' symbol.

Disjunction: A compound statement whose main connective is the 'or', or symbollically '∨'. Also known as the 'either-or' statement.

Disjuncts: Each component statement of a disjunction is a disjunct.

Equivalence: A compound statement whose main connective is the 'if and only if' or the symbol '≡'. Also known as the bi-conditional.

Exclusive 'or': The English 'or' used in an exclusive sense in which only one and exactly one of the options is true, not both.

If-then or **Material conditional**: A compound statement whose main connective is '⊃'. It is true either when the antecedent is true, or when the consequent is false, or both.

Inclusive 'or': The English 'or' used in a sense which leaves open the possibility that both the disjuncts may be true, or at least one of them will be true. The '∨' of sentential logic is used in this sense.

Negation: A compound statement, the main connective of which is 'not' or '~'.

Proposition: Is true or false. What is common to a set of synonymous declarative sentences.

Propositional logic: A section of symbolic logic which takes simple statements as its most basic units. Also, known as **propositional calculus.**

Sentence: A grammatically correct and complete string of expression in everyday language. Could be neither true nor false.

Sentence token: Physical in nature.

Sentence type: Abstract in nature.

Simple statements: Statements which contain no other statement as components. Also known as atomic statements.

Statement: What is said when a declarative sentence is uttered or written.

Truth-functional compound: Compound statements, the truth value of which is the function of or is completely determined by the truth values of their components. These are compounds formed by truth-functional connectives, such as conjunction, negation and disjunction.

Truth-functional connectives: A connective is truth functional if the truth value of the statements formed by it is completely determined by the truth value of the component statements.

Truth values: The logical value of a statement, such as 'true' or 'false'.

Unary or **Monadic connective:** A connective which at a time can connect only one statement. '~' is the only monadic connective.

CHAPTER

PROPOSITIONAL LOGIC: SEMANTICS AND TRUTH TABLES

6.1 The Basics

A **truth table** is a two-dimensional array, i.e., it is formed by rows and columns. Basically, it is a method by which one can mechanically find out the truth values of compound statements or sets of compound statements, and for that it is not necessary to know the actual truth value of their components. We shall now find out how to construct a truth table.

Rows

As mentioned above, a truth table will have rows and columns. The rows of a truth table are supposed to provide *all possible* truth value situations for a given set of statements. The first step in constructing a truth table is to know *how many rows* will be needed.

We have to understand that each row in a truth table presents a possible combination of the truth values of the atomic components in a compound statement. Each row also lists what the corresponding output or the final truth value of a compound will be for a particular combination of truth values for the components. Each row in Table 6.1, for instance, lists

Table 6.1 Example of Rows in a Truth Table

p	q	$p \equiv q$
T	T	T
T	F	F
F	T	F
F	F	T

a possible combination of truth values for the component atomic statements, p and q, of the compound $p \equiv q$. The first two columns exhaust the possible combinations. The last or final column of the table gives an exhaustive list of all truth values of $p \equiv q$, with respect to the combination of truth values of p and q as mentioned in each row. The second row, for example, presents a possible scenario when p will be true and q will be false. The second row in the final column tells us that for that specific combination of truth values, $p \equiv q$ will be false.

How many rows should there be in a truth table? That number is determined by the following formula:

$$\textbf{Number of rows} = 2^n$$

The 2 in the formula stands for the "number of truth-values". Since propositional logic deals with only two truth values, namely truth and falsity, in this context 2 remains a constant. The superscript n in the formula stands for the "number of discrete atomic components" in a given compound statement. The compound statement in Table 6.1, for instance, has only two simple components, p and q. Therefore, the number of rows in Table 6.1 are: $2^2 = 4$. A statement with only one atomic component will require $2^1 = 2$ rows, whereas a statement with four different atomic components will require $2^4 = 16$ rows in total.

Columns

The columns in a truth table help us to gradually compute and display *all possible* truth values of the truth-functional compound statements, given all possible truth-value assignments for the components.

How many columns should there be in a truth table? There is no formula for that. The number will depend upon the number of atomic components in a compound statement and also on the level of structural complexity present in the statement. For, in a truth table, a column for each of the atomic component has to be constructed separately. These first few columns will be used as the **reference columns,** i.e., columns representing all possible truth-value combinations for the simple or atomic components. These will be referred to whenever we need to consult the truth value of the components. Then, step-by-step, other columns are added for each truth-functional compound present in the statement.

How to Construct a Truth Table

For constructing a truth table, first we need to know *how many rows are needed.* We can easily compute that using the 2^n formula explained above. Once we know the number of rows required, the next step is to learn *how to systematically build the columns.*

The first step for constructing columns is to set up the reference columns. Reference columns, as explained above, will list possible ways of assigning truth values to the atomic components. The number of atomic components will be fixed in a statement. Consider the statement:

$$(A \bullet C) \supset \sim D$$

It has three atomic components: *A*, *C* and *D*. If we are trying to construct a truth table for this statement, we need to set up three separate columns for each of the components, and then fill the columns with all possible truth values for the components.

There are various ways to distribute the truth values to the atomic components. However, we shall follow the following procedure:

Alphabetic arrangement of atomic components: We shall arrange the atomic components *alphabetically* and accordingly assign a column each for them. Consider again the statement:

Example

1. $(A \bullet C) \supset \sim D$

First, the table for this statement will need $2^3 = 8$ rows. Second, the need to assign separate columns to each atomic component, *A*, *C*, *D*. Alphabetically arranged, the order of the columns will be as shown in Table 6.2.

Table 6.2 Example of Alphabetic Arrangement

A	*C*	*D*

Note that each column has eight rows.

Next we have to learn to systematically list arrangements of truth values to the atomic components. For that, the following procedure may be adopted:

In the first column, the first component symbol will get *R*/2 (read *R* divided by 2) **rows of consecutive T-s**, and *R*/2 **rows of consecutive**

F-s; where R **is the number of rows** in the table. The second symbol in the second column will get $R/4$ T-s and $R/4$ F-s consecutively, the third symbol in the third column will get $R/8$ T-s and F-s, etc.

Let us try to understand this using an example. Consider Table 6.3 as an instance.

Table 6.3 Example of Distribution of T-values

A	*C*	*D*		
T	T	T		
T	T	F		
T	F	T		
T	F	F		
F	T	T		
F	T	F		
F	F	T		
F	F	F		

Remember our statement $(A \bullet C) \supset \sim D$ requires eight rows. So, in this case:

$$R = 8$$

In Table 6.3, the first component A in the first column gets

$$R/2 \text{ T-s i.e., } 8/2 = 4 \text{ T-s}$$

consecutively for the first four rows, and then,

$$8/2 = 4 \text{ F-s}$$

consecutively in the last four rows.

The second component C gets $R/4$, i.e., $8/4 = 2$ T-s and then 2 F-s consecutively until all eight rows are filled. The third component D gets $R/8$, i.e., $8/8 = 1$ T and 1 F alternately until the eight rows are filled.

Our reference columns are now set. We can add other columns to the table following the truth values of the connectives as per their definitions given in Chapter 5.

The process of building the columns will follow the *order of increasing scope*. Connectives with the relatively lesser scope are first computed, then the ones with the larger scope. Thus, further columns are assigned to compound components in ascending order of complexity. The final column will belong to the main connective, which obviously will have the largest scope.

Table 6.4 Example of Columns of Increasing Slope

A	C	D	$\sim D$	$A \bullet C$	
T	T	T	F	T	
T	T	F	T	T	
T	F	T	F	F	
T	F	F	T	F	
F	T	T	F	F	
F	T	F	T	F	
F	F	T	F	F	
F	F	F	T	F	

In Table 6.4, for example, after the reference columns, the fourth column is assigned to ~D which has the least scope in the statement. The truth conditions of the '~' has been followed to compute the truth values of ~*D*. The value of ~*D* for each row has been computed with reference to the column of *D*.

The fifth column in Table 6.4 computes the truth values of $A \bullet C$. For, the next large connective is '•' which ranges over both *A* and *C*. In order to find out the values of $A \bullet C$, we refer to the values of *A* and *C* as found in the reference columns under the respective atomic letter.

Finally, we try to construct the last column which will record the truth values of the entire statement $(A \bullet C) \supset \sim D$ the main connective of which is '$\supset$'. In order to compute the value of '$\supset$', we check the truth-values listed in the column for $A \bullet C$ (antecedent) and the values listed in the column for ~*D* (consequent) in the fifth and fourth column, respectively. This is how the truth values in the final column are determined for the given compound $(A \bullet C) \supset \sim D$, as shown in Table 6.5. The completed table shows that the given statement is false only when all its atomic components are true. It is true in every other possible truth value assignment.

The truth table method is *exhaustive* as it is meant to present *all* possible truth-value situations. It is an *effective method* also, in the sense that, following a certain algorithm, it can yield definite result within a finite number of steps.

Table 6.5 Example of a Complete Truth Table

A	C	D	$\sim D$	$A \bullet C$	$(A \bullet C) \supset \sim D$
T	T	T	F	T	F
T	T	F	T	T	T
T	F	T	F	F	T
T	F	F	T	F	T
F	T	T	F	F	T
F	T	F	T	F	T
F	F	T	F	F	T
F	F	F	T	F	T

The truth table method, as explained above, can be put to various uses which serve in consonance with the interest of propositional logic. The sections below will show some of these uses. For instance, Section 6.2 introduces the concept of classification of statements on the basis of certain forms, namely, tautology, contradiction and contingency, so that in Section 6.3 we can see how the truth table method can help us determine which class a given statement belongs to. Similarly, from Section 6.4 onwards, several applications, which are particularly useful for propositional logic of the truth table method, are explained.

EXERCISE 6.1

1. How many rows will there be in the truth table of the following statements? Why? Justify your answer.

a. $*\{(B \vee D) \equiv E\} \supset \{\sim G \supset (H \bullet D)\}$

b. $A \equiv (A \equiv \sim A)$

c. $(B \bullet C) \supset \{B \vee (C \vee \sim C)\}$

2. How many consecutive T-s and F-s will the reference column of E have in the truth table of $\{(B \vee D) \equiv E\} \supset \{\sim G \supset (H \bullet D)\}$? Why? Justify your answer.

3. Construct a truth table for each of the following:

a. $*(H \bullet K) \bullet (H \supset (K \supset H))$

b. $A \equiv (B \equiv A)$

c. $(\sim M \bullet K) \supset (\sim L \vee M)$

d. $\sim (N \equiv P) \vee (R \supset (Q \supset P))$

e. $\sim (D \vee \sim E) \vee (G \bullet \sim (I \supset J))$

f. $(M \vee \sim T) \supset [T \vee (M \supset T)]$

g. $[A \bullet (B \vee \sim C)] \vee \sim [\sim B \supset (A \equiv C)]$

h. $(A \supset B) \supset [A \supset (B \supset A)]$

4. Symbolize each of the following and construct a truth table for each:

I: I am invited. *B*: I buy the black suit.

T: Ela books the Town Hall. *R*. It rains.

*a. I do not buy the black suit unless I am invited.

b. I buy the black suit if and only if I am invited and Ela books the Town Hall.

c. If it rains then neither I buy the black suit nor Ela books the Town Hall.

d. It is not the case that Ela books the Town Hall but I am not invited.

e. Either I am invited and I buy the black suit or it rains and I do not buy the black suit.

6.2 Statement Forms

In propositional logic, actual statements are symbolically represented by appropriate capital or uppercase letters, e.g., A, B, C. Because these sentence letters have a fixed reference in a given context, they are called **statement constants.** The statement "$(A \bullet C) \supset D$", for example, is an actual statement. The sentence letters in it are A, C, D. These constants in this context will each represent exactly one statement and no more. The constants characteristically have a unique reference.

Statement variables, on the other hand, are place-holder symbols. They do not have any fixed reference; rather, because of their general nature, their reference can vary. These are called variables as they can be replaced by various actual statements. Lower case letters such as p, q, r etc. are used to represent the statement variables. Consider, for example, the statement "$(p \bullet q) \supset r$". It is a sequence made exclusively of statement variables. Its meaning is not supposed to be fixed. For, p, q, r may be replaced by A, C, D, and we shall get "$(A \bullet C) \supset D$", or, they may be replaced by M, N, P, and we shall get "$(M \bullet N) \supset P$".

A **statement form** is a sequence of statement variables. Consider the following examples:

Examples

2. $p \bullet q$
3. $p \equiv (q \vee r)$
4. $(p \bullet q) \supset r$

A statement form is supposed to represent the bare logical structure of a statement, when all its content is set aside. Several actual statements may share the same statement form. For example, the statement form $p \bullet q$ represents the basic structure of all the following statements: $A \bullet B$, $D \bullet M$, etc. As mentioned above, the form $(p \bullet q) \supset r$ can be shared by $(A \bullet C) \supset D$ as well as $(M \bullet N) \supset P$.

A statement form is a sequence of statement variables such that, when the statement variables are substituted by actual statements, the result is an actual statement. The substitution should be consistent, i.e., within the context of the same situation the same actual statement should replace a certain statement variable throughout. Actual statements, thus obtained by properly substituting the variables by constants, are called the **substitution instances** of the statement form.

However, since there are more than one way to interpret what 'form' or structure a statement may have, there can possibly be some confusion about how to decide what exactly would be the statement form of a given statement. Consider the following:

Examples

5. $A \bullet B$
6. $D \bullet (E \equiv F)$
7. $(H \vee J) \bullet (K \equiv L)$

In a sense, the statement form $p \bullet q$ can be said to represent the underlying bare structure present in all of them. For, in all of them the main connective is '$\bullet$'. Thus, all three can claim to be the substitution instances of $p \bullet q$. Yet, internally Examples 6 and 7 exhibit a different kind of structural complexity which is not present in Example 5. This is where we need to look into the concept of **specific statement form** for help.

A specific statement form: That statement form in which actual statements result by consistently substituting **a** *different* or unique simple statement *for each distinctly different statement variables*. If we wish to find out the specific statement form for Examples 5–7 above, then we find that the statement form $p \bullet q$ cannnot be the *specific statement form* for all of them. It is the specific statement form of *only* Example 5 $A \bullet B$, and not of Examples 6 and 7. There are two discrete statement variables in $p \bullet q$, and when each is replaced properly by a different simple statement, we get examples such as $A \bullet B$. On the other hand, for Example 6, the specific statement form should be "$p \bullet (q \equiv r)$" and for Example 7, the specific statement form should be "$(p \vee q) \bullet (r \equiv s)$".

Since a specific statement form better represents the inner logical structure of a given statement; henceforth we shall refer to it whenever we speak of statement forms.

Depending on the kind of specific statement form that they reveal and the properties of these forms, we can classify statements into three major groups:

- Tautology or truth-functionally true
- Contradiction or truth-functionally false
- Contingency or truth-functionally indeterminate

Tautology or **truth-functionally true:** A specific statement form, which has only true substitution instances, is called a tautology or a truth-functionally true form. Its falsity is logically impossible. Statements with these kinds of specific forms are also known as tautologies. This class of statements are *always* true, i.e., they are true in every possible truth value assignment.

Examples

8. $\sim p \vee p$
9. $q \supset q$
10. $p \equiv p$

Alternatively, we can define a statement *p* as a tautology or as truth-functionally true *iff p* is always true.

Contradiction or **truth-functionally false:** A specific statement form, which has only false substitution instances, is called a contradiction or truth-functionally false. Its truth is a logical impossibility.

Examples

11. $p \bullet \sim p$
12. $q \equiv \sim q$

Statements, which have this type of specific forms, are known as contradictions. Alternatively, a statement *p* is a contradiction or truth-functionally false *iff* it is always false.

Contingent or truth-functionally indeterminate: This brings us to the third category of statements and specific statement forms, which are neither tautology nor contradiction. This group is called the contingents or truth-functionally indeterminate. They are neither always true nor always false. Unlike the tautologies or contradictions, their truth or falsity is not a matter of logical possibility or impossibility, but is contingent upon the facts of the world. The following examples show that, depending upon which actual statements we choose for *p* and for *q* and what their truth value are with respect to the facts of the world, each of examples given below may be true or false. Even if we do the full truth table for each of them, we shall find that the final columns in these tables will contain neither all T-s nor all F-s.

Examples

13. $p \bullet q$
14. $p \vee q$
15. $p \equiv q$
16. $p \supset q$

With this knowledge about the three types of statements, we can now proceed to see how, given a statement, the truth table method can help us determine which type it is.

EXERCISE 6.2

1. Determine which of the following are actual statements:

a. $A \vee (P \bullet B)$

b. $*(q \vee p) \vee r$

c. $\sim (p \bullet r) \supset (q \supset p)$

d. $[S \equiv (R \supset V)] \bullet D$

2. What is the difference between a statement variable and a statement constant?

3. What are specific statement forms? Explain with three examples of your own.

4. True or false? Justify your answer in each case.

a. A material conditional ($\supset$) with a contradiction as its antecedent will always be false.

b. *A conjunction ($\bullet$) with a tautology as one of the conjuncts will be true.

c. A contingent statement can be a component of a truth-functional compound statement, which is a tautology.

d. The final column of a truth table for a contingent statement must contain at least one F.

e. *A statement is a tautology *iff* its negation is a contradiction.

f. A material conditional with a tautology as its consequent will be a contingent statement.

6.3 Using Truth Tables to Determine Tautology, Contradiction and Contingent Statements

We can use the truth table method for determining the type of the statement form or statement by simply constructing a truth table for the given statement or statement form and by checking its truth value in the final column.

Testing for Tautology

A tautology, by definition, will be always true since a tautology is true in every truth value assignment. In other words, there will be no truth value assignment in which it will come out as false. Our test by truth table method will be simple: A statement or a statement form will be a tautology *iff* its truth table has only T-s in the final column. It will not be considered a tautology if there is even one F in the final column.

We shall use the following two examples to instantiate this method:

Examples

17. $p \supset p$
18. $K \supset (J \vee K)$

Of these, as can be seen from the use of variables and constants, $p \supset p$ is a statement form constituted of only variables, whereas $K \supset (J \vee K)$ is an actual statement. Our first task will be to construct a truth table for each of them following the instructions given in Section 6.1.

Table 6.6 Truth Table for $p \supset p$

p	$p \supset p$
T	T
F	T

Table 6.7 Truth Table for $K \supset (J \vee K)$

J	K	$J \supset K$	$K \supset (J \vee K)$
T	T	T	T
T	F	F	T
F	T	T	T
F	F	T	T

After constructing the table, we look for the values in the final column, each of which has been shaded for attention. Since there are only T-s in the final column, and since the rows in each table exhaust the possible truth value assignments for the given statement, in each case we have shown that the given statement or statement form is a tautology. It should be noted that since the statement form $p \supset p$ is a tautology, statements which have this form also will be tautologies, For example:

$$A \supset A, (B \vee T) \supset (B \vee T)$$

Testing for Contradiction

Similarly, a **contradiction** is false on every possible truth-value assignment. Accordingly, our test by truth table method for a contradiction will be: A statement or a statement form will be a contradiction *iff* its truth table has only F-s in the final column. It will not be considered a contradiction if there is even one T in the final column.

Examples

19. $q \bullet \sim q$
20. $(D \bullet S) \bullet (D \bullet \sim S)$

Table 6.8 Truth Table for $q \bullet \sim q$

q	$\sim q$	$q \bullet \sim q$
T	F	F
F	T	F

Table 6.9 Truth Table for $(D \supset S) \bullet (D \bullet \sim S)$

D	S	$\sim S$	$D \supset S$	$D \bullet \sim S$	$(D \supset S) \bullet (D \bullet \sim S)$
T	T	F	T	F	F
T	F	T	F	T	F
F	T	F	T	F	F
F	F	T	T	F	F

Testing for Contingent

For **contingent** statements, we follow the same method. A statement or statement form is contingent *iff* its truth table contains at least one T and at least one F in the final column.

Examples

21. $p \vee r$
22. $(A \bullet C) \supset \sim D$

Table 6.10 Truth Table for $p \vee r$

p	r	$p \vee r$
T	T	T
T	F	T
F	T	T
F	F	F

Table 6.11 Truth Table for $(A \bullet C) \sim D$

A	C	D	$\sim D$	$A \bullet C$	$(A \bullet C) \supset \sim D$
T	T	T	F	T	F
T	T	F	T	T	T
T	F	T	F	F	T
T	F	F	T	F	T
F	T	T	F	F	T
F	T	F	T	F	T
F	F	T	F	F	T
F	F	F	T	F	T

EXERCISE 6.3

1. True or false? Justify your answer in each case by the truth table method.

a. *$p \supset (p \bullet p)$ and $p \supset (q \vee \sim q)$ are both tautologies.

b. $q \supset \sim q$ is a contradiction.

c. A disjunction made of a contingent statement and a contradiction will always be a contradiction.

d. A conjunction made of a contingent statement and a contradiction will always be a contradiction.

e. A bi-conditional ($\equiv$) statement with two contingent statements must always be a contingent statement.

2. Use truth tables to determine whether the following statement forms are tautologous, contradictory or contingent:

a. $\sim p \equiv p$

b. $\sim p \supset p$

c. $q \supset (q \supset q)$

d. $*(q \supset q) \supset q$

e. $(p \bullet q) \equiv \sim(\sim p \vee \sim q)$

f. $(p \bullet q) \supset p$

g. $(p \bullet q) \bullet (q \bullet p)$

h. $(p \supset q) \supset \{\sim(q \supset r) \supset \sim(r \supset p)\}$

6.4 Using Truth Tables to Check Validity and Invalidity

In our earlier discussion (Section 2.7) on validity, an argument has been defined as **valid** *iff it is not possible* for all its premises to be true and its conclusion to be false, and **invalid** *iff* it is possible for all its premises to be true and its conclusion to be false. After the introduction of formal concepts such as truth functionality and truth value assignment, we are now going to redefine validity in terms of these concepts as follows:

> An argument is truth functionally valid *iff* there is **no** truth value assignment, on which all the premises are true but the conclusion is false. In other words, it is valid *iff* on every truth value assignment, in which the premises are true, the conclusion too is true.
>
> An argument is truth-functionally invalid *iff* it is not valid in the above-mentioned sense. In other words, an argument is invalid *iff* there is **at least one** truth value assignment on which all the premises are true but the conclusion is false.

As the truth table method depicts truth value assignments of given truth-functional compounds clearly and exhaustively, we can easily employ the truth table method to determine validity and invalidity of arguments in the following way. An argument, in its simplest form, consists of premises and a conclusion. We may read the argument as a claim that the conclusion follows if the premises hold true. For example, consider the following argument:

Example

23. The electoral process is fair.
    The electoral body is vigilant and is not under coercion of any sort.
    Therefore, the elected candidate represents the choice of the majority of the people.

We may try to understand this argument as a claim that the elected candidate represents the choice of the majority of the people *given* or if the electoral process is fair and the electoral body is vigilant and is not under coercion of any sort. Thus, given an argument, we may reformulate it by forming out of its premises and conclusion a **corresponding material conditional**. The premises may be used to form an iterated conjunction. That is, if an argument has n premises, we may form a conjunction of the form $(p_1 \bullet p_2 \bullet p_3 \bullet ... \bullet p_n)$. This conjunction may be treated as the **antecedent of the material conditional**. The conclusion will form its **consequent**. Thus, given an argument of the form p, q, and therefore r, we may read it as a corresponding material conditional of the form $(p \bullet q) \supset r$.

Given this interpretation of an argument in terms of its corresponding material conditional, we may now define the test of validity or invalidity as follows:

> We construct a truth table for the corresponding material conditional and check the final column of this truth table. If it has all T-s, then the corresponding argument is **valid**. Even if there is just one F in the final column, the corresponding argument is **invalid**.

All T-s in the final column of the material conditional indicate that there is **no** truth value assignment in which the conjunction of all the premises of the given argument (the antecedent of the material conditional) is true, while the conclusion (consequent) is false. As per our definition of validity given above, this situation satisfactorily shows that the corresponding argument must be valid. The presence of at least one F in the final column indicates that there is at least one such truth value assignment. According to the definition of invalidity given above, this situation indicates that the corresponding argument must be invalid.

Using Truth Tables to Determine Validity/Invalidity of an Argument

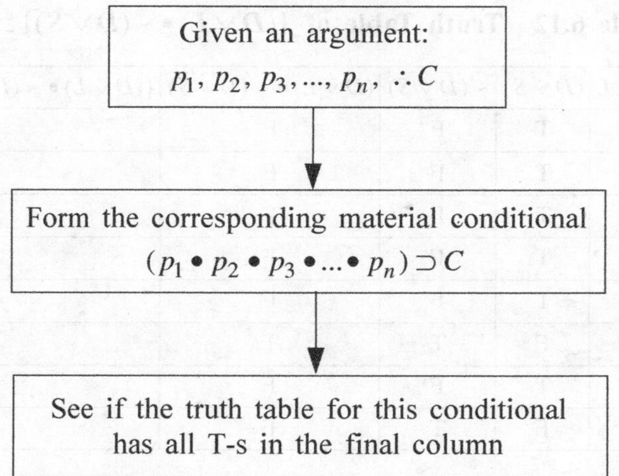

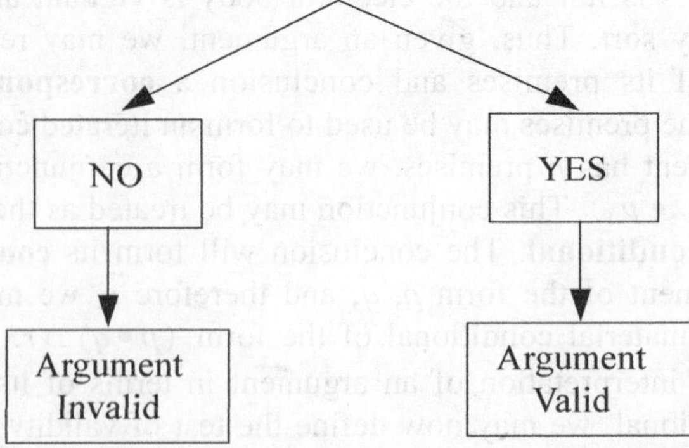

We now show, with the help of examples, the truth table test for validity and invalidity.

Example

24. Either the doorman or the librarian forgot to close the elevator door. Subsequent investigation shows that it is not the case that either the doorman or the secretary forgot to close the elevator door. It follows that it was the librarian who forgot to close the elevator door. (D, L, S).

In symbolized form, the argument can be translated as:

$$(D \vee L),\ \sim(D \vee S),\ \therefore L$$

The corresponding material conditional is

$$\{(D \vee L) \bullet \sim(D \vee S)\} \supset L$$

The full truth table of this conditional is as given in Table 6.12.

Table 6.12 Truth Table of $\{(D \vee L) \bullet \sim(D \vee S)\} \supset L$

D	L	S	$D \vee L$	$(D \vee S)$	$\sim(D \vee S)$	$(D \vee L) \bullet \sim(D \vee S)$	$\{(D \vee L) \bullet \sim(D \vee S)\} \supset L$
T	T	T	T	T	F	F	T
T	T	F	T	T	F	F	T
T	F	T	T	T	F	F	T
T	F	F	T	T	F	F	T
F	T	T	T	T	F	F	T
F	T	F	T	F	T	T	T
F	F	T	F	T	F	F	T
F	F	F	F	F	T	F	T

The final column of Table 6.12 with all T-s shows that the corresponding argument given in Example 24 must be **valid.** The shaded sixth row shows that the only situation in which the conjunction of the premises is true, the conclusion is true as well.

Example

25. Either the **d**oorman or the **l**ibrarian forgot to close the elevator door. However, it is not the case that both the librarian and the **s**ecretary forgot to close the elevator door. Therefore, it is the doorman who forgot to close the door. (D, L, S)

In symbolized form, the argument can be translated as

$$(D \vee L),\ \sim(L \bullet S),\ \therefore D$$

The corresponding material conditional is

$$\{(D \vee L) \bullet \sim(L \bullet S)\} \supset D\,.$$

We test the validity of Example 25 by constructing the full truth table of this conditional as in Table 6.13.

Table 6.13 Truth Table to Test Validity Example 25

D	L	S	$D \vee L$	$L \bullet S$	$\sim(L \bullet S)$	$(D \vee L) \bullet \sim(L \bullet S)$	$\{(D \vee L) \bullet \sim(L \bullet S)\} \supset D$
T	T	T	T	T	F	F	T
T	T	F	T	F	T	T	T
T	F	T	T	F	T	T	T
T	F	F	T	F	T	T	T
F	T	T	T	T	F	F	T
F	T	F	T	F	T	T	F
F	F	T	F	F	T	F	T
F	F	F	F	F	T	F	T

The full truth table for the conditional above establishes the corresponding argument in Example 25 as **invalid**. Coincidentally, the shaded sixth row shows that there is at least one truth-value assignment in which both the premises are true but the conclusion is false. It is to be noted that this one row is enough to establish the invalidity of the given argument.

There may be other ways to use the truth table to establish validity or invalidity. For instance, one may construct the truth table only up to the last but one column and, instead of having a separate column for $(p_1 \bullet p_2 \bullet p_3 \bullet ... \bullet p_n) \supset C$, one may just compare the columns for $(p_1 \bullet p_2 \bullet p_3 \bullet ... \bullet p_n)$ and for C, to see whether C is ever false when the conjunction of premises is true. In the case of Example 25, for instance, one may just compare the column for $(D \vee L) \bullet \sim (L \bullet S)$ and the column for D, which happens to be the first column. The result will be the same. However, in this book we have followed the convention of constructing a separate final column for $\supset$. For us, this will be the method for constructing a truth table for determining the validity or invalidity of an argument.

Fortunately, Examples 24 and 25 do not contain long and complex premises which require an increased number of columns. However, there can be arguments with premises and conclusion which have structural complexity. Consider the following example:

Example

26. $(p \vee q) \bullet (p \supset q), (\sim p \bullet q) \vee p, \therefore (p \supset q) \bullet (q \supset p)$.

The table for this argument will require separate columns for $\sim p$, $p \vee q$, $p \supset q$, $\sim p \bullet q$, $(\sim p \bullet q) \vee p$, $(q \supset p)$, $(p \vee q) \bullet (p \supset q)$ and for $(p \supset q) \bullet (q \supset p)$. For the sake of convenience, we suggest that the important columns be numbered. So, instead of reiterating the entire long and complex formula at the head of a column, we may refer simply to the numbers. For example, we can rewrite the truth table for Example 25 as in Table 6.14.

Table 6.14 Rewritten Truth Table of Example 25

(3)			(1)		(2)		
D	L	S	$D \vee L$	$L \bullet S$	$\sim (L \bullet S)$	$1 \bullet 2$	$(1 \bullet 2) \supset 3$
T	T	T	T	T	F	F	T
T	T	F	T	F	T	T	T
T	F	T	T	F	T	T	T
T	F	F	T	F	T	T	T
F	T	T	T	T	F	F	T
F	T	F	T	F	T	T	F
F	F	T	F	F	T	F	T
F	F	F	F	F	T	F	T

EXERCISE 6.4

1. Use truth tables to determine whether the following arguments are valid or invalid:

a.*(i) $K \bullet (H \supset J)$

(ii) $J \equiv H$

(iii) $\sim J$

$\therefore \sim K$

b. (i) $E \vee (F \bullet \sim G)$

(ii) $(G \supset F) \equiv E$

(iii) $\sim E \vee F$

$\therefore \sim (F \vee G)$

c. (i) $(L \equiv \sim M) \bullet M$

(ii) $[M \vee \{(N \supset O) \bullet N\}] \supset \sim L$

$\therefore M \supset \sim L$

d. (i) $B \supset T$

$\therefore (B \supset T) \supset (B \supset T)$

e. (i) $R \supset (S \supset T)$

(ii) $R \supset S$

$\therefore R \supset T$

*f. (i) $(A \equiv C) \vee (\sim A \equiv C)$

$\therefore (\sim A \equiv \sim C) \vee \sim (A \equiv C)$

2. Symbolize the following arguments and use truth tables to determine their validity or invalidity:

a. Sohail and Tina will go to Bangalore. So, Sohail will go to Bangalore. (S, T)

b. If it is not the case that you do not like me, then it is not the case that I do not like you. You do not like me, if I do not like you. Therefore, if I like you then you like me. (Y: You like me, I: I like you)

c. Dharitri and Srishti will go to the picnic. However, not both Dharitri and Garima will go to the picnic. Therefore, Garima will go to the picnic. (D, S, G)

d. If development has to be sustainable, then our natural non-renewable resources must be conserved. So, either our natural non-renewable resources must be conserved if development has to be sustainable, or our natural resources will be depleted and war will be inevitable. (S, C, D, W)

e. Although the number of undergraduates studying engineering has grown steadily over the years, there will be a shortage of engineering teachers if the number of people receiving Ph.D. degree in Engineering does not increase and also the number of people willing to teach engineering does not increase. The number of undergraduates studying engineering has grown steadily over the years. Therefore, there will be a shortage of engineering teachers. (U: The number of undergraduates studying engineering has grown steadily over the years, S: There will be a shortage of engineering teachers, R: The number of people receiving Ph.D. degrees in Engineering is increasing, W: The number of people willing to teach engineering is increasing)

f. If you are sober, you may drive yourself home even late at night, but if you are inebriated, you should have someone else drive you home. You are either sober or inebriated. So, either you may drive yourself home even late at night or you should have someone else drive you home. (S, D, I, E).

6.5 Shorter Truth Table Method and Invalidity

A **shorter truth table** is, as its name suggests, a truth table in its short form: with just one single row. To establish the invalidity of an argument in propositional logic, one needs to demonstrate at least one set of possible truth conditions in which the premises are all true but the conclusion is false. So, demonstration of invalidity by constructing just one row, instead of a full truth table, is very effective.

What is required for a shorter truth table is the construction of a crucial row. Our task will be to try to assign truth values to the component simple statements in such a way that it will make each of the premises true and the conclusion false. The assignment of truth-values must be **consistent**, i.e., it should not be the case that the same simple component is assigned T in one place and an F in another.

If it is possible to construct such a row with consistent truth assignments to the simple components, then **it is sufficient to establish the invalidity** of the argument being tested. This row stands for a particular row in the relevant full truth table. Barring human errors, if no such assignment of truth values is possible, we shall take this as an indication that the argument may be valid. However, the full demonstration of validity requires the construction of an exhaustive, full truth table.

Let us take an example to instantiate the process of constructing a shorter truth table:

Example

27. a. $A \supset B$
    b. $C \supset D$
    c. $B \vee C$
    ∴ $A \vee D$

First, the argument has to be laid out in the format of a row. Just as in the full truth table, in this row for a shorter truth table we have to assign individual reference columns for each of the simple components and then separate columns for each of the premises and the conclusion if they are truth-functional compound statements. For constructing a shorter truth table, the argument in Example 27, therefore, needs to be arranged with separate columns with appropriate headings in the following way:

A	B	C	D	$A \supset B$	$C \supset D$	$B \vee C$	$A \vee D$

The first four columns are reference columns for the four simple components in the argument. Then a column each for the three premises and the conclusion has been allocated. However, it is to be noted that, unlike the full truth table, in shorter truth table technique we do *not* start our truth value assignment from the simple components. Instead, we start our truth value assignment from the **compound statements.** We are trying to see if we can make the conclusion false while making all the premises true. So, to make $A \vee D$ false, both A and D must be false. We note down these values of A and D in the reference columns and also wherever in the premises A and D have occurred. Thus, we generate the following table:

A	B	C	D	$A \supset B$	$C \supset D$	$B \vee C$	$A \vee D$
F			**F**	**F**	**F**		**FFF**

From the above, the truth values of other simple components also become clear. For example, since $C \supset D$ must be true as a premise and since its consequent D is false, C as the antecedent has to be false. If C is false (F), then in premise $B \vee C$, B must be true (T); else $B \vee C$ will become false. Following these observations, we can now construct the entire row as follows:

A	B	C	D	$A \supset B$	$C \supset D$	$B \vee C$	$A \vee D$
F	**T**	**F**	**F**	**F T T**	**F T F**	**T T F**	**F F F**

The constructed single row is the shorter truth table which shows that the argument given in Example 27 is invalid as there exists at least one possible truth-value assignment on which the premises are all true while the conclusion is false.

While constructing the shorter truth table for Example 27, the truth conditions of the premises and the conclusion helped us significantly. We started out from the conclusion $A \vee D$, and since a '$\vee$' statement is false under only one circumstance, we could immediately know what the values of *A* and *D* must be; and from there we went on to deduce the values of the other components. However, things may not always so simple or so decisive. Consider the following example:

Example

28. a. $(O \vee P) \supset Q$
    b. $Q \supset (P \vee R)$
    c. $O \supset (\sim S \supset P)$
    d. $(S \supset O) \supset \sim R$
    $\therefore P \equiv Q$

The conclusion of Example 28 can be false in two conditions (a) when *P* is true and *Q* is false, or (b) when *P* is false but *Q* is true. Accordingly, we may try constructing the shorter truth table as follows:

O	P	Q	R	S	$(O \vee P) \supset Q$	$Q \supset (P \vee R)$	$O \supset (\sim S \supset P)$	$(S \supset O) \supset \sim R$	$P \equiv Q$
									T F
									F T

Given these possibilities, we have a choice. We may pick the first choice (a) which has *P* as true and *Q* as false. However, as we start repeating this truth-value assignment, it becomes clear from the first premise "$(O \vee P) \supset Q$" that this assignment is *not* feasible as it makes the first premise false. If *P* is T and *Q* is F, no matter what value *O* has, the truth value of $O \vee P$ will be true, then the truth value of $(O \vee P) \supset Q$ will be false. Thus we are left with the second choice: *P* is false and *Q* is true. We may begin our row as follows:

O	P	Q	R	S	$(O \vee P) \supset Q$	$Q \supset (P \vee R)$	$O \supset (\sim S \supset P)$	$(S \supset O) \supset \sim R$	$P \equiv Q$
	F	T			F T	T F	F		F F T

From the above, we can see that the value of *R* has to be true to make the premise $Q \supset (P \vee R)$ true. If *R* is true, ~*R* has to be false.

O	P	Q	R	S	$(O \vee P) \supset Q$	$Q \supset (P \vee R)$	$O \supset (\sim S \supset P)$	$(S \supset O) \supset \sim R$	$P \equiv Q$
	F	T	T		F T	T F T	F	F	F F T

Since ~*R* is the consequent of the fourth premise $(S \supset O) \supset \sim R$, $(S \supset O)$ as the antecedent has to be false in order to make the premise true. This settles that, of the remaining simple components, S has to be true and O must be false. Now we have the following complete shorter truth table:

O	P	Q	R	S	$(O \vee P) \supset Q$	$Q \supset (P \vee R)$	$O \supset (\sim S \supset P)$	$(S \supset O) \supset \sim R$	$P \equiv Q$
F	F	T	T	T	F F F **T** T	T **T** F T T	F **T** F T F	T F **T F**	F **F** T

As it clearly shows, one truth value assignment for which the premises are true but the conclusion is false, the shorter truth table establishes that the given argument in Example 28 must be invalid.

It is possible that an argument may be shown as invalid for *more than one* truth-value assignments. For example, consider the following argument:

Example

29. a. $(Q \bullet P) \equiv (D \vee B)$
    b. $C \supset (D \bullet P)$
    c. $Q \equiv A$
    $\therefore\ A \bullet B$

Since '$\bullet$' is false under three different conditions, the conclusion of this argument given in Example 29 is false under three truth-value assignments for $A \bullet B$. Accordingly, we may start out as follows:

A	B	C	D	P	Q	$(Q \bullet P) \equiv (D \vee B)$	$C \supset (D \bullet P)$	$Q \equiv A$	$A \bullet B$
									T F
									F T
									F F

In the process of testing whether each of these three assignments makes the premises true and the conclusion false, we find out that the second possibility; namely, A is false and B is true, is not feasible. For, it makes at least one of the premises false. If A is false, then in order to make the premise $Q \equiv A$ true, Q has to be false. If Q is false and B is true, then the first premise $(Q \bullet P) \equiv (D \vee B)$ becomes false. For, if Q is false, the value of $Q \bullet P$ is false no matter what value P has; and if B is true then the value of $D \vee B$ is true no matter what the value of D is. However, if $Q \bullet P$ is false and $D \vee B$ is true, then the first premise $(Q \bullet P) \equiv (D \vee B)$ becomes false. Since this is not the desired outcome, we have to rule out that possibility.

As for the remaining two possible truth value assignments, we find that both can fit into our general plan of coming up with consistent truth-value assignment for making the premises true and the conclusion false:

A	B	C	D	P	Q	$(Q \bullet P) \equiv (D \vee B)$	$C \supset (D \bullet P)$	$Q \equiv A$	$A \bullet B$
T	F	F	F/T	F/T	T	T F/T F/T F	F F/T F/T	T T	T F
F	F	F	F	F/T	F	F F/T F F	F F F/T	F F	F F

The above shorter truth table shows two possible truth-value assignments which make the argument in Example 25 invalid. The '/' as in 'F/T' indicates that the component can be either T or F. For multiple possible truth-value assignments such as this, it is enough to present **any one** of the assignments. It will perfectly serve the purpose of proving invalidity.

EXERCISE 6.5

1. Use the shorter truth-table method to show that the following arguments are invalid:

a. (i) $C \vee D$
   (ii) $C / \therefore \sim D$

b. (i) $M \supset N$
   (ii) $N / \therefore M$

*c. (i) $(X \supset Y) \bullet (U \supset V)$
   (ii) $Y \supset V / \therefore X \supset U$

d. (i) $L \supset M$
   (ii) $(K \bullet M) \vee \sim N / \therefore N$

e. (i) $[G \equiv (\sim G \supset G)] \supset \sim G / \therefore G$

f. (i) $A \vee \sim B$
   (ii) $C \supset B$
   (iii) $A / \therefore B$

g. (i) $D \equiv E$
   (ii) $E \equiv (F \vee D)$
   (iii) $(F \vee E) \equiv G$
   (iv) $\sim F / \therefore (D \vee E) \vee G$

h. (i) $S \supset (N \supset M)$
   (ii) $M \supset (P \supset Q)$
   (iii) $S \supset N$
   (iv) $Q \supset S / \therefore P \supset Q$

i. (i) $J \bullet \sim L$
   (ii) $\sim L \vee (R \bullet W)$
   (iii) $(R \vee \sim J) \bullet (R \vee \sim W)$
   (iv) $J \vee (S \bullet T) / \therefore T$

j. (i) $\sim(P \equiv L)$
(ii) $(T \bullet P) \supset Q$
(iii) $\sim(P \vee Q) \bullet (Q \vee L)$
(iv) $P \supset (S \supset Q) \,/\, \therefore S \supset P$

k. (i) $((L \supset M) \supset N) \supset P$
(ii) $(P \supset (M \bullet N)) \supset L$
(iii) $M \vee N \,/\, \therefore L \equiv P$

l. (i) $B \supset (B \vee H)$
(ii) $Q \supset (Q \vee H)$
(iii) $(B \vee H) \bullet (Q \vee H) \,/\, \therefore B \bullet Q$

m. (i) $(U \vee \sim A) \bullet (B \supset X)$
(ii) $C \supset (V \supset W)$
(iii) $A \supset (N \supset D)$
(iv) $A \vee B$
(v) $(U \vee X) \supset (C \bullet V) \,/\, \therefore B \bullet \sim(C \bullet A)$

n. (i) $D \supset (E \equiv G)$
(ii) $E \vee (S \vee M)$
(iii) $G \supset (T \supset S)$
(iv) $\sim(\sim T \bullet D)$
(v) $H \supset (A \vee E) \,/\, \therefore G \supset (E \supset A)$

o.* (i) $K \supset (A \bullet B)$
(ii) $\sim L \vee \sim M$
(iii) $L \supset (K \vee C)$
(iv) $C \supset (B \supset M)$
(v) $G \supset (A \supset K) \,/\, \therefore \sim(K \equiv G)$

6.6 Using Truth Tables to Check Logical Consistency

In Chapter 2, a set of statements has been defined (see Section 2.7) as **consistent** *iff* there is at least one possible situation in which every member of that set is true. The set is supposed to be **inconsistent** *iff* no such possibility exists for the members of the set. We shall now modify these definitions of consistency and inconsistency in terms of truth-value assignment as follows:

> A finite set of statements is truth-functionally **consistent** *iff* **there is at least one** truth-value assignment on which all the members of the set are true.

A finite set of statements is truth-functionally **inconsistent** *iff* it is not consistent in the above sense; i.e., *iff* **there is no** truth value assignment on which all the members of the set are true.

Thus understood, we can utilize the truth table method to help us determine whether a given set of statements is consistent or inconsistent. We need to construct a truth table in which all the members of a given set of statements appear. In that table, we look out for a **line** or a **row** on which **all the statements are true**. Since the truth table displays all possible truth value interpretations of the set being tested, the set is **consistent** *iff* there is such a row. It is **inconsistent** *iff* there is no such row.

Consider the following set:

Example

30. $\{(A \supset B), (A \vee \sim B), \sim A\}$

Is this set consistent? We shall find out the answer using the truth table method in the following way. First we shall construct the truth table:

A	B	$\sim A$	$\sim B$	$A \supset B$	$A \vee \sim B$	
T	T	F	F	T	T	
T	F	F	T	F	T	
F	T	T	F	T	F	
F	F	T	T	T	T	←

The set in Example 30 is shown as consistent since the last row (indicated by an arrow) presents the possible truth value assignments on which each member of the set is true.

Example

31. $\{C, (\sim C \vee D), \sim D\}$

Is this set consistent? Using the truth table method, we find the answer as follows:

C	D	$\sim C$	$\sim D$	$\sim C \vee D$
T	T	F	F	T
T	F	F	T	F
F	T	T	F	T
F	F	T	T	T

The truth table shows that there is no truth value assignment possible on which every member of the set can be true at the same time. The set therefore is inconsistent.

EXERCISE 6.6

1. Use truth tables to determine which of the sets are consistent:

a. $\{M, N, O\}$

b. $\{[(A \supset B) \bullet (C \supset D)],\ (A \vee C),\ (B \vee D)\}$

c. $\{(P \equiv Q),\ [(P \bullet Q) \vee (\sim P \bullet \sim Q)]\}$

d. $*\{(T \equiv R), T, (\sim T \vee \sim R)\}$

e. $\{(C \supset D),\ (\sim D \supset \sim C)\}$

f. $\{(G \equiv (J \bullet K)), \sim J, (\sim B \supset B)\}$

g. $\{\sim [L \vee (H \supset M)],\ [M \equiv (\sim L \vee \sim H)],\ [H \equiv (L \vee M)]\}$

h. $\{[(A \bullet B) \bullet C],\ [C \vee (B \vee A)],\ [A \equiv (B \supset C)]\}$

2. For each of the following sets of statements, either show that the set is consistent by constructing an appropriate shorter truth table or show that the set is inconsistent by constructing a full truth table:

a. $\{[P \supset P) \supset Q],\ \sim P,\ \sim Q\}$

b. $\{[R \vee (W \bullet U)],\ [W \equiv (R \vee U)],\ (U \vee \sim U)\}$

c. $\{\sim (D \bullet H),\ \sim (H \bullet N),\ \sim (D \bullet N),\ (D \vee (H \bullet N))\}$

d. $\{B \equiv (\sim B \supset B)\}$

e. $*\{(A \equiv \sim D),\ (\sim D \supset (E \bullet A)),\ \sim (\sim A \vee \sim E)\}$

3. Symbolize each of the following passages and determine whether the set is consistent by constructing a truth table:

a. If the entry to the garden is visible from the Sentry Box, then the sentry will see anyone entering the garden. The sentry has neither seen anyone entering the garden nor has seen anything unusual. The entry to the garden is visible from the Sentry Box. (E, S, U)

b. Turku is in Sweden if it is not in Finland. Turku is in Finland *iff* the map of Finland found on the Internet is correct. The map of Finland found on the Internet is correct, or Turku is in Sweden. (S, F, M)

c. Neither sugar nor butter is desirable *iff* consumption leads to health problems. Consumption leads to health problems *iff* butter is desirable. Sugar is not desirable *iff* consumption does not lead to health problems. (S, B, C)

6.7 Using a Consistency Test for Checking Validity

An argument, after all, is a set of statements. We may use a test of consistency as an alternative test for validity for an argument. For a valid argument, it is not possible for the premises to be true when the conclusion is false, whereas for an invalid argument, exactly that possibility holds. We shall now interpret this understanding of validity in terms of consistency or inconsistency of a set:

> An argument is valid *iff* the set consisting of all the premises and the negation of the conclusion is **inconsistent**.
>
> An argument is invalid *iff* the set consisting of all the premises and the negation of the conclusion is **consistent**.

Suppose we want to know if the following argument is valid or not:

Example

32. $\sim A \supset \sim B$
    $B \vee C$
    $\therefore \sim A \supset C$

In order to test its validity, we construct a truth table for the premises and the negated conclusion $\sim (\sim A \supset C)$ as follows:

A	B	C	$\sim A$	$\sim B$	$\sim A \supset \sim B$	$B \vee C$	$\sim A \supset C$	$\sim (\sim A \supset C)$
T	T	T	F	F	T	T	T	F
T	T	F	F	F	T	T	T	F
T	F	T	F	T	T	T	T	F
T	F	F	F	T	T	F	T	F
F	T	T	T	F	F	T	T	F
F	T	F	T	F	F	T	F	T
F	F	T	T	T	T	T	T	F
F	F	F	T	T	T	F	F	T

The truth table makes it clear that there is not even one possible truth value assignment on which the premises and the negated conclusion are simultaneously true. Hence the set consisting of premises and the negated conclusion is inconsistent. Thus, the given argument must be valid. In contrast, had there been even a single row on which the premises and the negated conclusion had come to be true, that would be an indication of the invalidity of the argument.

The relation between validity and consistency brings to us a curious and startling consequence:

> An argument with an inconsistent set of statements as its premises is always valid.

The reason for this lies in the fact that being inconsistent, the premises cannot all be made true in any truth value assignment. Since they are mutually inconsistent, the truth of one will cancel the truth of another among them. Given this, we cannot ever show that the conclusion is false *while the premises are all true* simply because the premises are never true at the same time. Thus, the argument, technically speaking, will be valid, irrespective of what the conclusion may be or how irrelevant the conclusion may be.

Are these kind of trivially 'valid' arguments desirable? The answer has to be: No. It is worth noting that the requirement of soundness (see Section 2.7) helps us to eliminate these kinds of empty or vacuous cases of validity. Possibility such as this should also bring to focus why consistency is prized in reasoning. Inconsistent sets of statements are not entirely meaningless, especially if the inconsistency is not an explicit kind such as $A \bullet \sim A$. The main problem with a set of inconsistent statements is that it means too much as it leads to anything and everything.

6.8 Using Truth Tables to Check Logical Equivalence

We can redefine logical equivalence between two statements as follows:

> Statements p and q are truth-functionally equivalent *iff* there is no truth value assignment on which p and q have different truth values. Two statements are not truth-functionally equivalent *iff* there exists *at least one row* in the truth table in which the two statements *do not have the same truth value* under the same truth-value assignment to the components.

This makes determining by the truth table method—whether two statements are equivalent or not an easy task. We simply need to construct a single truth table where both the statements appear. Then we compare the columns meant for each and check if the two statements have the **same truth value** on every truth-value assignment.

Consider the two statements in the following example:

Example

33. $(W \bullet Y) \supset H, W \supset (Y \supset H)$

Are these two statements equivalent? In order to know that, we construct a truth table for both as follows:

H	W	Y	$W \bullet Y$	$(W \bullet Y) \supset H$	$Y \supset H$	$W \supset (Y \supset H)$
T	T	T	T	T	T	T
T	T	F	F	T	T	T
T	F	T	F	T	T	T
T	F	F	F	T	T	T
F	T	T	T	F	F	F
F	T	F	F	T	T	T
F	F	T	F	T	F	T
F	F	F	F	T	T	T

Then we compare the columns for $(W \bullet Y) \supset H$ and $W \supset (Y \supset H)$, both of which have been shaded. We find that for every possible truth condition in each row, the two statements have identical set of truth values. This helps us decide that the given two statements are logically equivalent to each other.

Consider another pair:

Example

34. $(E \equiv H) \equiv E$, $(H \bullet {\sim} E) \supset H$

Are these two equivalent? We try to determine this by the same method. The full truth table for both is as follows:

E	H	${\sim} E$	$E \equiv H$	$(E \equiv H) \equiv E$	$H \bullet {\sim} E$	$(H \bullet {\sim} E) \supset H$
T	T	F	T	T	F	T
T	F	F	F	F	F	T
F	T	T	F	T	T	T
F	F	T	T	F	F	T

From this table we find that the second and fourth row show that the statements do not have the identical truth value for every possible truth-value assignment. Clearly, the given statements in Example 34 are not equivalent.

A curious consequence is that all truth-functionally true statements or tautologies turn out to be logically equivalent. For, they will all have only T-s in the final columns. Thus, technically speaking, for every possible truth assignment, there will be identical truth values. Consider the following example:

Example

35. $S \vee \sim S$, $\sim (J \bullet \sim J)$

The truth table for both will be like this:

J	S	$\sim J$	$\sim S$	$S \vee \sim S$	$J \bullet \sim J$	$\sim (J \bullet \sim J)$
T	T	F	F	T	F	T
T	F	F	T	T	F	T
F	T	T	F	T	F	T
F	F	T	T	T	F	T

As per our definition of truth table test for logical equivalence, both these tautologies are equivalent to each other. It should be easy to see from this why all tautologies must be logically equivalent to each other.

Similarly, all truth-functionally false statements or contradictions also can be claimed to be logically equivalent to each other. For every possible truth-value assignment, they will all have identical columns with all F-s.

EXERCISE 6.8

1. Using truth tables, decide which of the following pairs of statements are logically equivalent to each other.

a. $(A \vee B)$, $\qquad \sim (\sim A \vee \sim B)$

b. $\sim (A \bullet B)$, $\qquad (\sim A \vee \sim B)$

c. $A \supset (B \supset A)$, $\qquad (B \bullet \sim B) \vee (A \supset A)$

d. $\sim (C \supset D)$, $\qquad \sim (\sim C \vee D)$

e. $C \vee (D \bullet E)$, $\qquad \sim C \supset (D \vee E)$

f. $*H \supset (I \supset J)$, $\qquad (H \supset I) \supset J$

g. $\sim (K \bullet L) \equiv (L \equiv \sim M)$, $\qquad (K \bullet L) \supset \sim M$

h. $[D \vee \sim (A \bullet B)] \supset \sim A$, $\qquad [A \vee \sim (D \bullet B)] \supset \sim D$

i. $(P \bullet \sim Q) \vee (P \vee Q)$, $\qquad P$

2. For each of the following pairs of statements, either show that the statements are logically equivalent by constructing a full truth table or show that they are not logically equivalent by constructing a shorter truth table.

a. M, $\qquad M \vee P$

b. M, $\qquad M \bullet P$

c. D, $D \supset D$

d. $A \vee \sim A$, $(T \equiv W) \supset (T \equiv W)$

e. $S \equiv J$, $\sim S \equiv \sim J$

*f. $V \bullet (P \vee L)$, $(V \bullet P) \vee L$

g. $(C \supset E) \supset (E \supset C)$, $(C \equiv E) \vee (\sim C \vee E)$

h. $G \supset [H \supset (G \supset H)]$, $H \supset [G \supset (H \supset G)]$

i. $(N \equiv O) \bullet Q$, $Q \bullet O$

3. Symbolize each of the following pair of statements and determine for each pair whether they are logically equivalent by constructing truth tables:

a. (i) The shareholders can be apprised *iff* the acquisition deal is made final and the top management approves. (S, A, M)

(ii) Unless the top management approves, the acquisition deal will not be made final and the shareholders cannot be apprised.

b. (i) The oilseed crop was not good in the first, third and the seventh year, but it was good in the eighth year. (F, T, S, E)

(ii) Neither the first nor the third was a good year for oilseed crop, and not both seventh and eighth years were good for oilseed crop.

*c. (i) The inflation rate will not increase provided the economy is flourishing. (I, E)

(ii) If the economy is not flourishing then the inflation rate will increase.

d. (i) Although the car has been recently serviced, the air-conditioning is not going to function well unless the battery has been recharged. (A, B, C)

(ii) The car has been recently serviced, and if the battery has been recharged, the air-conditioning is going to function well.

Keywords

Contingent: A statement form, or alternatively, a statement which is neither always true nor always false.

Contradiction: A specific statement form which has only false substitution instances. Alternatively, it is a statement which is always false.

Reference columns: The first few columns in a truth table representing all possible truth-value combinations for the simple or atomic components.

Shorter truth table: A single row truth table generally used for establishing the invalidity of arguments in propositional logic.

Specific statement form: A statement form from which actual statements result by consistently substituting a different or unique simple statement for each distinctly different statement variable.

Statement form: A sequence of statement variables.

Statement variables: Statement place-holders which do not have any fixed reference and can be replaced by various actual statements, denoted by symbols such as *p*, *q*, *r*.

Substitution instances: Actual statements obtained as a result of properly substituting the variables in a statement form by constants.

Tautology: A specific statement form, which has only true substitution instances. Sometimes the term is loosely used also for the always true substitution instances.

Truth-functionally false: Same as contradiction.

Truth-functionally indeterminate: Same as contingent.

Truth-functionally true: Same as tautology.

Truth table: A two-dimensional array formed by rows and columns by which one can mechanically find out the truth values of compound statements or sets of compound statements.

CHAPTER 7

PROPOSITIONAL LOGIC: TRUTH TREES

7.1 Introduction

The truth tree is a technique or a method used in logic. The name 'truth tree' is based on an analogy with a tree. As we shall find out in this chapter, the procedure results in an arrangement that looks like an *upside down tree*: the root comes first, and from it the branches gradually come down.

The truth tree method, like the truth table, is a mechanical procedure. Simply by following a set of rules, and without getting into the semantics, one can obtain an answer by using this technique. If the correct procedure is followed, it is very effective, and can provide an exhaustive answer correctly.

Truth trees have a distinct advantage over truth tables. Though they can do everything that the truth tables can, the truth trees often require **less work** than the truth tables. From an operational point of view, they are relatively easier to handle. Truth tables start to get unwieldy when the number of atomic components gets increasingly higher. For example, a statement, which has eight different atomic components, will have $2^8 = 256$ rows in a truth table and, depending upon the structural complexity involved, it may have a similarly large number of columns. In cases such as these, the prohibitively high numbers become a source of problem for constructing a truth table and managing it. With truth trees, however, the situation need not necessarily be so. Trees, as we shall see, remain economical even with a large number of atomic components in the truth-functional compounds.

Also, the truth trees apply to both propositional and predicate logic, whereas the truth tables apply only to propositional logic. In predicate logic, truth trees lose their effectiveness somewhat, because some of them in special circumstances involving quantified statements do not terminate in a finite number of steps. Then again, in the domain of predicate logic, no method remains effective in the technical sense. However, in the domain of propositional logic, the effectiveness of truth trees is unquestionable. They provide a graphically detailed visual display, thus making their point clear not only to the intellect but also to the eye. In this, they are similar to truth tables.

Truth trees are also known as the **Semantic tableaux systems**. Tableaux systems were first suggested by the Dutch logician, Evert W. Beth[1] (1908–64). Since then, the tableaux have undergone several versions in the hand of many logicians. Owing to the ease of learning and also to their potential for easy implementation, truth trees have gained wide acceptance not only among the logicians, but more recently among the computer scientists, especially in the field of automated theorem proving. In particular, in the areas of modal and temporal logic and in applications such as in verification, truth trees are often hailed as *the* most effective tool.

7.2 How to Generate a Truth Tree

The first step in constructing a truth tree is to get acquainted with the **rules of decomposition** for the truth trees. In this context, **decomposition** means breaking a statement or a string of symbols down to its literals following certain rules. These rules are listed now.

A **literal** in this context is an atomic component statement such as '*A*' or its negation, e.g. '~*A*'. Decomposition stops when a compound has been broken down to its literals.

Rules of decomposition are basically lists or records of the truth condition or conditions of different types of statements. The first rule, called the *Double Negation Decomposition rule*, for example, lists the truth condition of its only atomic component, *P*. It tells us that ~~*P* will be true when *P* is true. Similarly, the rule *Biconditional Decomposition* or '$\equiv D$' (Rule No. 8 in the list below) lists the condition or the conditions in which $P \equiv Q$ is true. From its truth table, we know that $P \equiv Q$ is true whenever its components have the *same* truth value—either when both *P* and *Q* are true or when both of them are false, i.e. when ~*P* and ~*Q* are true. The truth tree rule $\equiv D$ lists exactly those two separate set of conditions for $P \equiv Q$. In each of the rules given below, the string to be decomposed is listed on top. The decomposed components are listed below in bold letters.

For each rule, the full name is first mentioned and then for easy reference its shorter abbreviation is also mentioned within brackets. For instance, the first rule may be referred to by the abbreviated form '~~D' (*tilde tilde D* or *double negation D*).

---

[1] Beth, E.W. 1955. Semantic Entailment and Formal Derivability. Reprinted in K.J.J. Hintikka (Ed.), *The Philosophy of Mathematics*, Oxford University Press, Oxford, 1969.

Truth Tree Rules

1. *Double Negation Decomposition* ($\sim\sim D$)

$$\sim\sim P\ \checkmark$$

$$\mathbf{P}$$

2. *Conjunction Decomposition* ($\bullet D$)

$$P \bullet Q\ \checkmark$$

$$\mathbf{P}$$

$$\mathbf{Q}$$

3. *Negated Conjunction Decomposition* ($\sim\bullet D$)

$$\sim(P \bullet Q)\ \checkmark$$

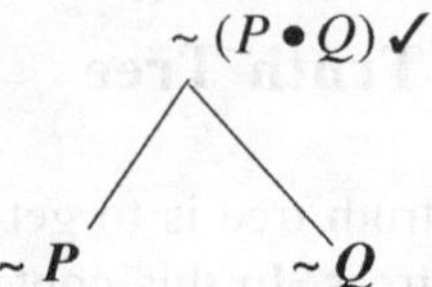

$$\sim\mathbf{P} \qquad \sim\mathbf{Q}$$

4. *Disjunction Decomposition* ($\vee D$)

$$P \vee Q\ \checkmark$$

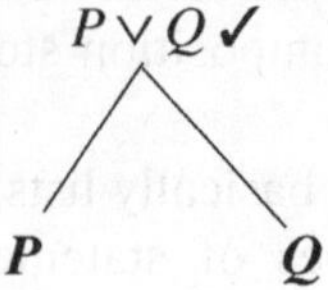

$$\mathbf{P} \qquad \mathbf{Q}$$

5. *Negated Disjunction Decomposition* ($\sim\vee D$)

$$\sim(P \vee Q)\ \checkmark$$

$$\sim\mathbf{P}$$

$$\sim\mathbf{Q}$$

6. *Conditional Decomposition* ($\supset D$)

$$P \supset Q\ \checkmark$$

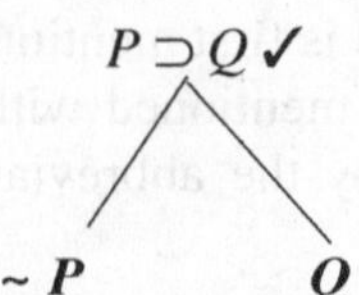

$$\sim\mathbf{P} \qquad \mathbf{Q}$$

7. *Negated Conditional Decomposition* $(\sim\supset D)$

$$\sim(P \supset Q)\checkmark$$
$$P$$
$$\sim Q$$

8. *Biconditional Decomposition* $(\equiv D)$

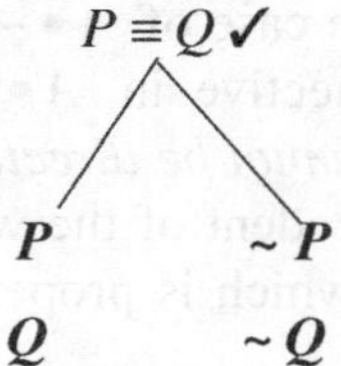

9. *Negated Biconditional Decomposition* $(\sim\equiv D)$

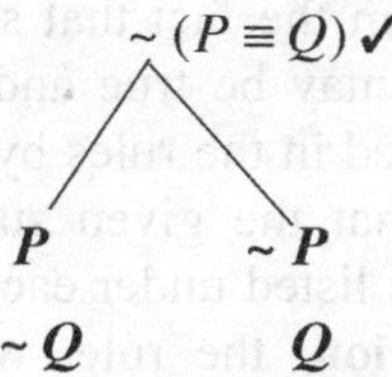

The **second step** in constructing a truth tree is to form the **trunk** or the **root** of the tree. This involves listing a given finite set of truth functional statements as a **vertical column** or as the trunk or the root of the tree.

It is important to remember that to list a statement either in the root or in the 'branch' of a truth tree is to assign it the truth value T. Therefore, further decomposition will enter statements or atomic components which will be assigned the truth value T.

For easy reference and also to avoid ambiguity, we shall maintain a convention of assigning a number to each of the statements on the left-hand side of the tree, as shown in Example 1 below. We shall also include a column on its right as the justification column, where the rules used will be cited along with the number of the line on which the rule has been applied. No line of justification should contain more than one rule citation, or reference to more than one previous line.

Now, consider the set $\{A \bullet \sim B, C\}$. In order to build the tree, the root will have to be first arranged as shown in the following example:

Example 1:

1. $A \bullet \sim B$
2. C

This vertical column or root will serve as the source set for the rest of the tree. Next, we need to know which rule to apply to which statement. For that, one needs to look only at the *main connective* of the statement. Then, following the appropriate rule of decomposition, each member of the set can be decomposed one after the other. Only one rule is to be applied at a time in a step.

We need to remember that decomposition rules apply only to **whole statements**, not to compounds which are parts of the larger compound statements. For example, in the case of $A \bullet \sim B$, one needs to apply the $\bullet D$ rule as '$\bullet$' is the main connective in $A \bullet \sim B$. However, in the case of $(A \bullet \sim B) \supset C$, the $\bullet D$ rule *cannot be directly applied* just on the $(A \bullet \sim B)$ part, which serves as the antecedent of the whole compound $(A \bullet \sim B) \supset C$. The only decomposition rule which is properly applicable to $(A \bullet \sim B) \supset C$ is the $\supset D$ rule.

It is also important to understand when and why a rule branches out (e.g. $\vee D$ rule), and why some of them do not result in branches (e.g. $\bullet D$ rule). This difference comes from the fact that some statements allow more than one condition in which it may be true and some have only one such condition. **Branching,** represented in the rules by the bifurcated lines, stands for **inclusive 'or',** indicating that the given statement may be true when either or both of the possibilities listed under each branch are true. The **non-branching** represents **conjunction**: the rule, which lists the decomposed component or components directly below the string, as in the case of $\sim\sim D$ or $\bullet D$ rule, indicates that the given string is true *only* under the condition or conditions listed below it.

A statement, once it has been decomposed, must be **checked** (use the symbol ✓). This becomes crucially important when the 'trunk' contains several compound statements. Otherwise, one may overlook one or two compound statements which should have been decomposed.

A branch on which an atomic or simple statement and its negation both occur is called a **closed branch**. Since this situation indicates that the truth conditions listed in that branch contains a contradiction, the branch is closed down as an eliminated possibility. The mechanism to indicate a closed branch is to put an '×' under that closed branch. No further entries are made on a closed branch.

A tree which has each of its branches closed is a **closed tree.**

In contrast, a branch which is not closed is an **open branch**. Open branches allow for further entries to be made. For larger trees, it is important to remember that the decomposed components of a compound statement must be listed at the bottom of *every open branch directly coming out of the compound.*

A **completed open branch** is a finite open branch that contains only literals and checked compound statements. This shows that the decomposition has been thoroughly carried out.

A tree with at least one completed open branch is an **open tree.**

A tree, each of whose branches is either closed or is a completed open branch, is called a **completed tree.**

Examples are in order. Consider the set of statements mentioned in Example 1 above in this section. The tree for this set $\{A \bullet \sim B, C\}$ will be as follows. First, one has to arrange the statements given as a vertical column as the 'root'. Then, each new line that is generated from this root must be entered following the format of the decomposition rule used. Each new line must be numbered serially on the left-hand side. On its right-hand side, the abbreviated name of the rule by which this new entry has been obtained must be entered. Following these guidelines, the tree for this set $\{A \bullet \sim B, C\}$ will be as follows.

Example 2

1. $A \bullet \sim B$ ✓		Given set
2. C		
3. A	1, $\bullet D$	Open tree, completed open branch
4. $\sim B$	1, $\bullet D$	

In Example 2, the 'root' has two statements listed. These have been assigned numbers 1 and 2. Among them, statement 2 'C' is already a literal since it is an atomic or simple statement. The only statement to be decomposed therefore is the statement 1 or the compound '$A \bullet \sim B$'. The decomposition of statement 1 starts at line 3 and ends at line 4. Since its main connective is a '$\bullet$', a '$\bullet D$' rule is applied to it. On the right-hand side of both lines 3 and 4, this $\bullet D$ rule is referred to as the justification for the new lines entered in the tree. Since it is the same statement 1 which has been decomposed in lines 3 and 4, on both the lines line 1 has been referred to. Once decomposed, statement 1 must be checked off, i.e., the sign ✓ is to be put against it to indicate that the compound has been decomposed.

Since there are no further decomposition to be done, the tree for Example 2 stops here. Only one branch has come out of the 'root', and it is a **completed open branch** containing only literals and checked compound statements. The tree is also an **open tree** as it has a completed open branch. Compare this 4-line tree, in terms of the amount of work needed, with the truth table that has to be drawn for this set, and you will find the advantage of learning about the truth trees. This set will require a truth table which will have eight rows and minimum four columns.

Consider another set $\{A \bullet \sim B,\ C,\ \sim A \vee \sim C\}$, We start the tree as in the following example:

Example 3

1. A • ~ B
2. C
3. ~ A ∨ ~ C

Example 3 has three statements as its members, two of which are compounds. Each of these has been entered on the vertical column or the 'root'. We then start the decomposition. On the right-hand column, we mention the line number and the rule used as the justification, and check the compound that has been decomposed:

Example 3 (continued)

1.	A • ~ B ✓	
2.	C	
3.	~ A ∨ ~ C	
4.	A	1, • D
5.	~ B	1, • D

If we stop at line 5 after decomposing "*A* • ~ *B*", then our tree will not be complete. For, the 'root' contains another statement "~ *A* ∨ ~ *C*" which is not a literal and till line 5 it has not been decomposed. So, we must decompose it in order to complete our tree.

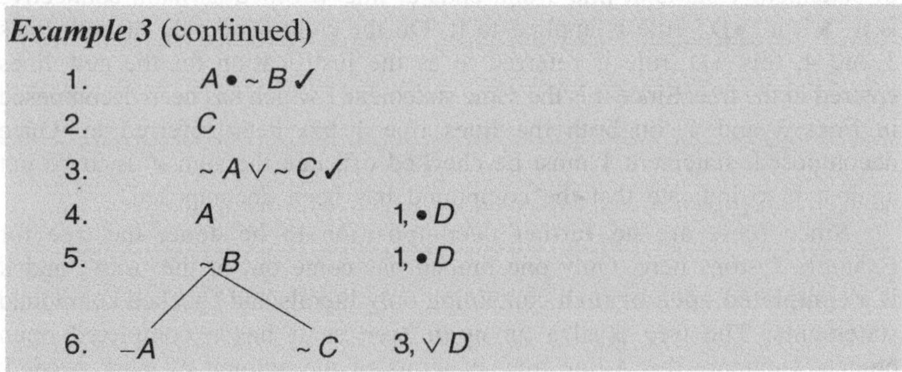

As we decompose it on line 6, we find that since "~ *A* ∨ ~ *C*" is a disjunction, two branches have come out of our tree. By displaying '~ *A*' and '~ *C*' on the same line, rather than one below the other, and on two different branches, we show that making either of them true is enough to make "~ *A* ∨ ~ *C*" true. The tree is now **completed.** We now trace each of its branches finishing at the 'root' to look out for the literals. For, a literal occurring on a branch is true.

As we trace the branches of the completed tree in Example 3, we find that each branch contains **a literal** and **its negation.** The left-hand branch contains '*A*' on line 4 and '~ *A*' on line 6, whereas the right-hand branch contains *C* on line 2 and ~ *C* on line 6. If we have to assign truth values to the literals, then on the left branch both 'A' and '~A' will have to be true, and on right branch both '*C*' and '~ *C*' will have to be true. So, since the branches offer two possibilities, either '*A*' and '~ *A*' will have to be true, or '*C*' and '~ *C*' will have to be true. However, neither of these alternatives is possible. Therefore, we declare each of these branches as a 'closed branch', as explained above, by placing an '*x*' below each of them. The completed tree has been fully worked out below. To draw attention to the contradiction occurred, in each branch the literal and its negation have been encircled. Since each of its branches is closed, the tree is, as mentioned above, a closed tree. We mention this next to the tree as our comment on the tree.

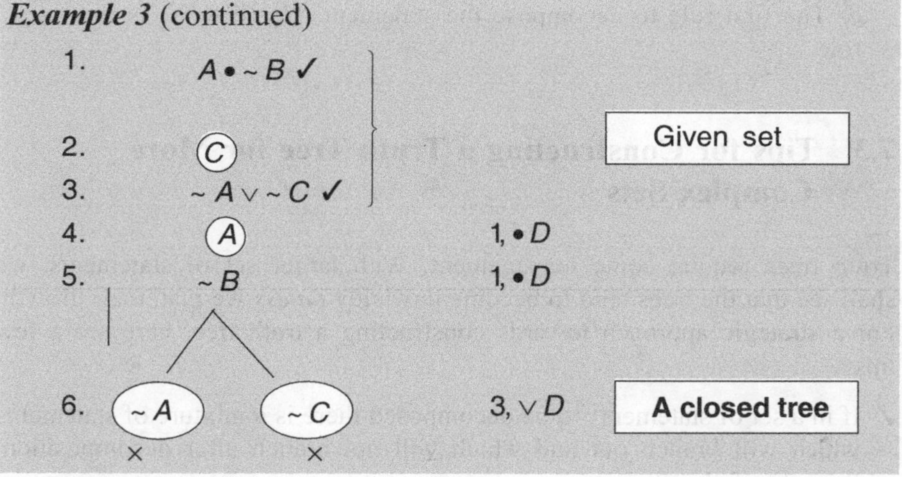

Generating a tree, therefore, requires:

✓ Listing a finite set of truth-functional statements as a vertical column as the root.

✓ Decomposing the statements, where possible, as per the decomposition rules to the literals.

✓ Checking off the decomposed statements.

✓ Terminating a branch as soon as a literal and its negation both appear on a branch.

✓ Checking for closed branches.

✓ Terminating the tree when there are no statements left for further decomposition.

EXERCISES 7.1–7.2

1. What do we gain by learning about the truth trees when we already know how to do truth tables? Explain with your own example.
2. *In the context of truth trees, what is decomposition? What does a rule of decomposition tell us?
3. Cite two rules of decomposition which branch out. Why do some of the rules of decomposition branch out?
4. Which of the following claims are true? Justify your answer.
   a. If a truth tree is closed, then every statement in the tree either has been decomposed or is a literal.
   b. *An open tree cannot have a closed branch.
   c. A closed tree cannot have an open branch.
   d. *The number of branches in a truth tree must be greater than one.
   e. The first rule to decompose the statement "$J \vee (W \equiv K)$" is the '$\equiv D$' rule.

7.3 Tips for Constructing a Truth Tree for More Complex Sets

Truth trees require some management. With larger set of statements, we shall see that the trees tend to become unwieldy *unless* we plan their growth. For a strategic approach towards constructing a truth tree, here are a few tips:

✓ If in a set of statements to be decomposed there is a mixture of statements which will branch out and which will not branch after decomposition, the rule of thumb is:
Always decompose the **non-branching statements** *first.*

✓ Decompose those statements first that will rapidly generate closed branches. Since closed branches do not require any further attention, this operation helps one to 'trim' the tree and keep the growth in check. The attention then can be focused only on the remaining open branches.

✓ If none of the above tips is applicable to the set to be decomposed, try decomposing the most complex statement first.

✓ Results of decomposing a statement must always be entered on every open branch *that runs through the statement being decomposed.*

Recommendations 1–3 are meant to prevent a lot of unnecessary branching, entries and complexities in the tree. Consider the set of statements in the following example:

$$\{\sim A \bullet \sim B,\ D \equiv \sim B,\ \sim(\sim B \vee A),\ L \supset (B \bullet \sim D)\}$$

Some of these statements branch out after decomposition and some do not. Also, decomposing some of them will generate closed branches faster. If we follow guidelines, 1 and 2, then the tree for this set looks like the one in the following example:

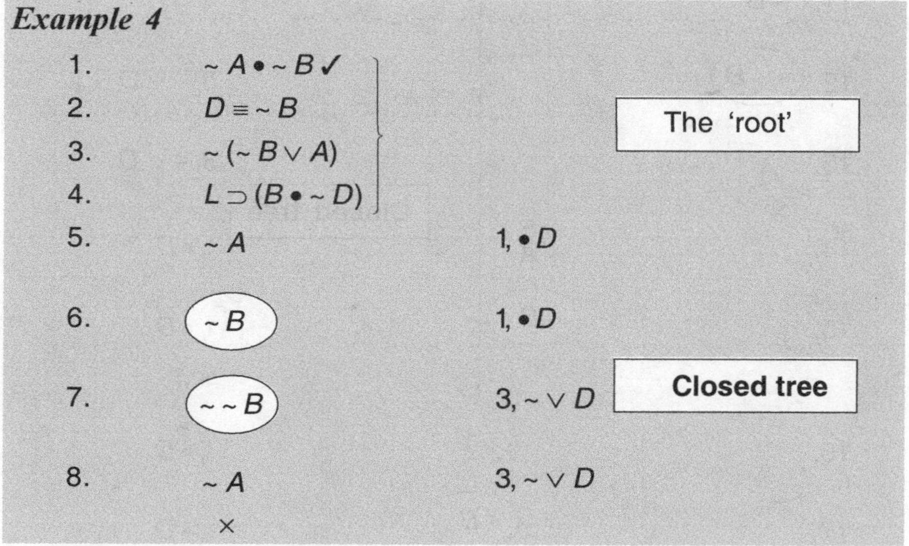

However, if we want to see what happens if we do not follow this, then the tree may look like the one in the following example:

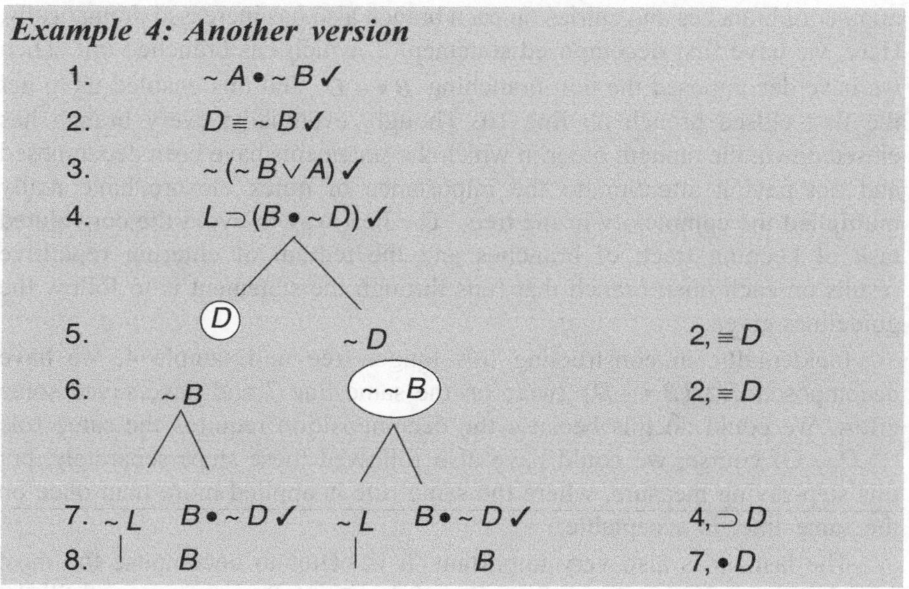

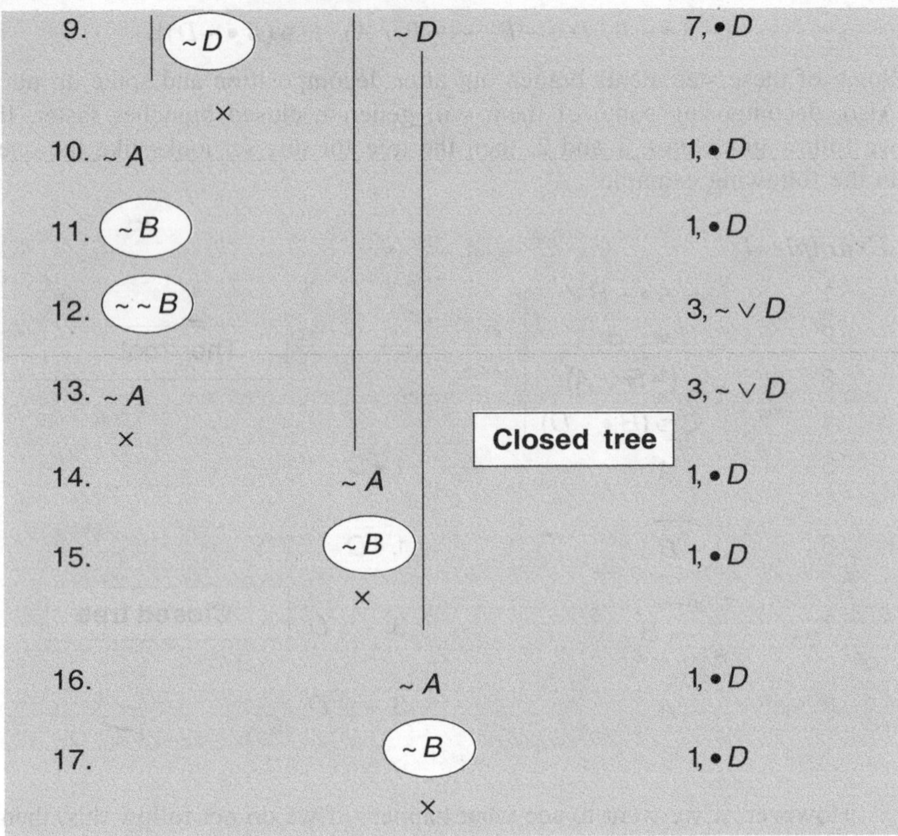

The latter version of tree for Example 4 above has 17 steps. The number of branches and entries on each branch also has increased dramatically. Here, we have first decomposed statement 2, which has branched out. Then we have decomposed the non-branching $B \bullet \sim D$, and this enabled us to get the first closed branch on line 10. Though, eventually, every branch has closed down, the random order in which the statements have been decomposed and not paying attention to the importance of quick closure have really multiplied the complexity in the tree. The best way to avoid the convoluted task of keeping track of branches and the tedium of entering repetitive results on each open branch that runs through the statement is to follow the guidelines given.

Incidentally, in constructing this longer tree in Example 4, we have decomposed $L \supset (B \bullet \sim D)$ twice on the same line 7 and have saved some effort. We could do this because the decomposition requires the same rule '$\supset D$.' Of course, we could have also followed these steps separately, but this step-saving measure, where the same rule is applied more than once on the same line, is acceptable.

The last tip is also very important. It is better to decompose the most complex statements at the earliest. For, if they are left undecomposed till the end, chances are that the results of decomposing them will have to be entered on many open branches, and particularly on every branch that runs through the statement being decomposed. In the longer version of Example 4 above, the results of decomposing $\sim A \bullet \sim B$ had to be entered on each of the three remaining branches on lines 10–11, 14–15, and 16–17 respectively. This is because each of these branches runs through $\sim A \bullet \sim B$ as their common root.

This point can be appreciated from the following example: $\{(J \equiv B) \vee (A \bullet B)\}$. The tree for this is worked out in the following example:

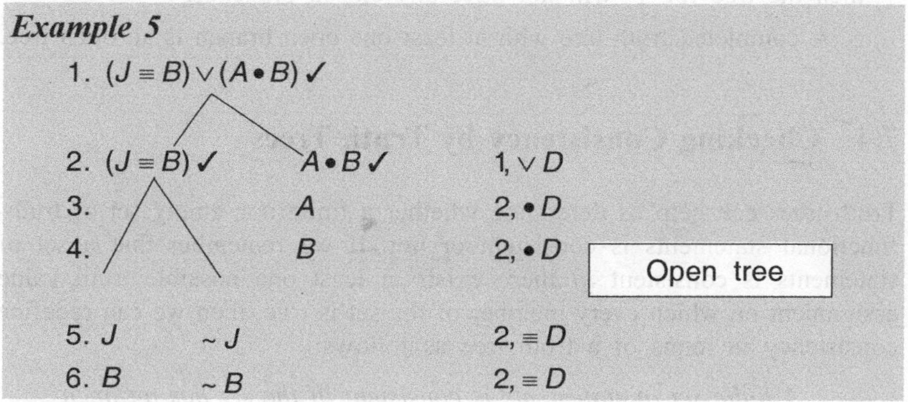

Example 5 has only one statement, a disjunction, to decompose. So, on line 2 by the '$\vee D$' rule, we have two branches. The non-branching $A \bullet B$ is decomposed first and the results are entered on lines 3 and 4. It is to be noted that the results of this decomposition are not entered on the other branch which has $J \equiv B$. Only a continuing line has been drawn under $J \equiv B$ through lines 3 and 4 until it is decomposed on line 5. Similarly, the results of decomposing $J \equiv B$ is entered only on the left-hand branch, and *not* on the right-hand branch under $A \bullet B$. That is so because the left-hand branch happens to be the only open branch *that runs through the statement being decomposed*. So, the results of decomposition need not be entered on every open branch, but only on those open branches that stem out of the statement being decomposed.

EXERCISE 7.3

1. Which of these will result in a closed tree? Justify your answer with a worked-out tree for each of the following:

a. $*\{(C \vee D),\ (\sim C \vee \sim D)\}$

b. $\{(C \vee D),\ (\sim C \bullet \sim D)\}$

c. $\{(C \vee D), (C \supset \sim D), (C \equiv D)\}$
d. $\{(L \vee (A \bullet \sim A)), (\sim\sim A \supset B), \sim C\}$
e. $\{(B \supset E), (B \vee (N \bullet C)), \sim (N \vee (B \bullet E))\}$
f. $\{(H \equiv K), \sim (H \supset J), (H \vee (J \vee K)), \sim\sim (H \bullet \sim\sim K), J\}$

2. Which of the following claims is false? Elucidate your answer.

a. *If there are six atomic statements in the members of a statement set Γ, then a completed truth tree for Γ will have six branches.

b. If none of the statements in the set Γ has a negation sign or a '~', then the tree for Γ will not have any closed branches.

c. A completed truth tree with at least one open branch is an open tree.

7.4 Checking Consistency by Truth Trees

Truth trees can help us determine whether a finite non-empty set of truth-functional statements is consistent or not. If we remember that a set of statements is consistent *iff* there exists at least one possible truth value assignment on which every member of the set is true, then we can redefine consistency in terms of a truth tree as follows:

> *A finite set of statements is consistent iff the set has an open tree.*

Recall that an open tree is a tree that has at least one completed open branch, i.e., an open branch which contains only literals and checked compound statements. An open tree need not be a completed tree.

The open tree with at least one completed open branch shows that there is **at least one** possibility in which the literals listed on that branch can all be true at the same time. For, listing a statement or a literal in any segment of a truth tree is to assign it the truth value 'true'. Once we have such a completed open branch, it is easy to determine whether there are any truth value assignments on which all the members of the set that we are testing are true. For this, we need to carefully trace the open branch, starting from the *bottom* and finishing at the *root*. We pay attention only to the **literals** (an atomic statement or its negation) and record them. If the literal is an atomic statement, such as '*A*', on that branch, we assign it the truth value T; if the literal is a negation of an atomic statement such as '~*A*', then we assign the atomic statement A the truth value F. This process is known as the **recovery of the partial assignment of truth values**. The truth values, thus recovered, of the literals tell us of at least one possibility when every member of the 'root' is true on these truth value assignments. Thus we come to know whether a set is consistent by the truth-tree method.

This is demonstrated below in the following example with the set $\{(A \supset B), (C \bullet D), (E \bullet (B \vee D)\}$. We are testing whether it is consistent by the truth-tree method as follows:

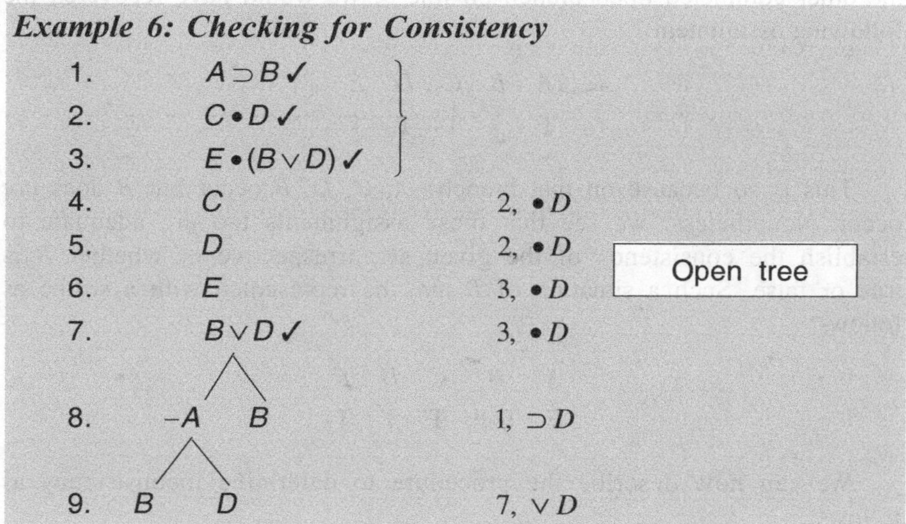

Example 6: Checking for Consistency

1.	$A \supset B$ ✓		
2.	$C \bullet D$ ✓		
3.	$E \bullet (B \vee D)$ ✓		
4.	C	2, $\bullet D$	
5.	D	2, $\bullet D$	Open tree
6.	E	3, $\bullet D$	
7.	$B \vee D$ ✓	3, $\bullet D$	
8.	$-A$ B	1, $\supset D$	
9.	B D	7, $\vee D$	

In the above example, we have followed the tips for strategic decomposition for a tree. First, the non-branching statements have been decomposed, for example, statements 2 and 3. After that the branching statements 1 and 7 have been decomposed. On line 9, the compound statements in the tree have all been decomposed, as indicated by the check marks.

The tree at line 9 is an open tree though it is *not* a completed tree. The same entries on line 9 should be entered on the right-hand branch on line 8 under *B* so as to make it a completed tree. However, for checking consistency, we do not need to go any further. On line 9 we have two completed open branches which contain only the literals and checked compounds. That is sufficient to mark it an open tree.

For recovery of partial truth-value assignment from the **leftmost branch** of these two completed open branches, we shall start from the bottom. Tracing the leftmost branch gives us the following literals: *B*, *~A*, *E*, *D*, *C*. Following the above mentioned procedure of assigning truth value to the atomic components, we generate the following partial assignment in alphabetical order:

A	*B*	*C*	*D*	*E*
F	T	T	T	T

This shows that there is at least one truth-value arrangement for the atomic components on which every member of the set that we are testing $\{(A \supset B), (C \bullet D), (E \bullet (B \vee D)\}$ is true. Since we have found at least one truth-value assignment on which every member of the set is true, the set therefore is **consistent**.

Note that, if we had tried to recover the truth-value assignment from the other completed open branch on line 9, we would have recovered the following assignment:

A	*B*	*C*	*D*	*E*
F		T	T	T

This is so because on that branch ~*A*, *C*, *D*, *E* occur but *B* does *not* occur. Nonetheless, we see that these assignments too are adequate to establish the consistency of the given set, irrespective of whether *B* is true or false. Such a situation of *B* may be represented with a stroke as follows:

A	*B*	*C*	*D*	*E*
F	T/F	T	T	T

We can now describe the procedure to determine inconsistency as follows:

> *A finite set of truth-functional statements is inconsistent iff the set has a closed tree.*

A closed tree has its every branch closed, which means every branch of it contains a contradiction. This means that there is not even a single possibility of recovering truth-value assignments on which every member of the set will be true together.

Given this understanding, we may now recall that the set $\{A \bullet \sim B, C, \sim A \vee \sim C\}$ in Section 7.2, Example 3 is an inconsistent set. Another example of inconsistent set may be the following:

$$\{(\sim B \bullet C) \bullet (\sim A \vee B), (A \bullet C)\}$$

The corresponding tree is given in the following example:

Example 7

1.	$(\sim B \bullet C) \bullet (\sim A \vee B)$ ✓		
2.	$A \bullet C$ ✓		
3.	$\sim B \bullet C$ ✓	1, •*D*	
4.	$\sim A \vee B$ ✓	1, •*D*	
5.	Ⓐ	2, •*D*	Closed tree
6.	*C*	2, •*D*	

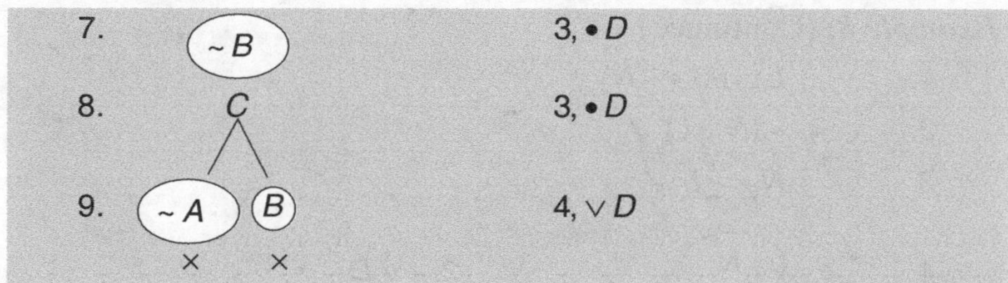

This is a completed tree, each branch of which is closed and contains a literal and its negation. The set therefore is inconsistent.

Here is another example:

$$\{L \supset (M \bullet \sim N),\ \sim (N \vee L),\ N \equiv \sim L\}$$

The tree for this set can be started as follows:

Example 8

1.	$L \supset (M \bullet \sim N)$	
2.	$\sim (N \vee L)$ ✓	
3.	$N \equiv \sim L$	
4.	N	2, $\sim \vee D$
5.	L	2, $\sim \vee D$

After line 5 of Example 8, we find that we are confronted with a choice: which statement to decompose first? Both statements 1 and 3 are the branching types. At this point, which one should we start decomposing first? In a sense, the order does not matter. For, if decomposition finally will yield an open tree, then any order of decomposition will. And the same stands also for a closed tree. If the tree closes down, then any order of decomposition will lead towards that result. However, as we have seen in Section 7.3, sometimes the order of decomposition becomes extremely important to make a difference to the complexity of the tree. While constructing a tree, the aim always should be to keep the tree as simple as possible by making the number of branches to the minimum so that we get to work with the least number of open branches.

With the given example, therefore, our choice also should be guided by this strategy. Both statements 1 and 3 will branch out when decomposed. However, there is a difference. Decomposing statement 1 will immediately yield two branches with $\sim L$ and $(M \bullet \sim N)$, but neither will close shortly. On the other hand, decomposing $N \equiv \sim L$ will immediately give us two branches containing $\sim N$ and $\sim L$, thus leading to two closed branches. Hence, in this case, the right choice is to proceed with statement 3 first.

Example 8: (Continued)

1.	$L \supset (M \bullet \sim N)$		
2.	$\sim (N \vee L)$ ✓		
3.	$N \equiv \sim L$ ✓		
4.	$\sim N$		2, $\sim \vee D$
	$\sim L$		
5.			2, $\sim \vee D$
6.	N	$\sim N$	3, $\equiv D$
7.	$\sim L$	$\sim\sim L$ ✓	3, $\equiv D$
	×		
8.		L	7, $\sim\sim D$
		×	

Closed tree

This tree in Example 8 shows that the given set is **inconsistent**. Note that the tree has proved the set as inconsistent *without* decomposing every compound statement in the 'root'. Statement 1 has not been decomposed since, from the other statements, a closed tree has been generated. What this shows is that we have accomplished a goal in an economical and concise manner. If we had chosen to decompose statement 1 first, then we would still have a closed tree eventually, but it would have been a more complex tree.

EXERCISE 7.4

1. Construct truth trees to determine which of the sets of statements is consistent. If a set is consistent, recover a partial truth-value assignment from your tree, which establishes the following:

a. *$\{(M \bullet N), (M \bullet \sim N)\}$

b. $\{(A \vee B), \sim (B \bullet \sim A)\}$

c. $\{D \vee (J \bullet \sim J), (L \bullet \sim P)\}$

d. *$\{(M \bullet N), (M \vee (\sim N \bullet O))\}$

e. $\{\sim (\sim (E \vee \sim H) \bullet G), \sim ((E \vee \sim H) \bullet G)\}$

f. $\{\sim (J \vee B), (B \supset (K \bullet \sim J)), (B \equiv \sim J)\}$

g. $\{(B \equiv J), (H \equiv J), (\sim H \vee B)\}$

h. $\{(D \vee (E \vee F)), (D \supset F), \sim(\sim E \vee E)\}$

2. Symbolize, with appropriate sentence letters of your choice, and use the truth-tree test on the following passages to test the consistency of the statements:

a. At least one of the staff, Chandan, Divyendu, Esha, came to the office last night. If Esha came, then Divyendu also came. Not both Chandan and Divyendu came. Esha came *iff* Chandan did not come.

b. Either Thailand will agree to the trade offer or both Myanmar and Indonesia will have to be approached. Sri Lanka is interested in the trade offer. Malaysia and Indonesia have been approached and Vietnam will be interested in the trade offer if Thailand does not agree to the trade offer. If Sri Lanka is interested in the trade offer, then Myanmar will be approached.

c. The employees with fixed scale salary will get the health insurance coverage, and the employees on contract will not get it. If the board of directors do not approve, then the employee with fixed scale salary will not get the health insurance coverage.

7.5 Truth Trees and Tautology, Contradiction and Contingent Statements

We know that the statements in standard bi-valued truth-functional logic can be either of the three types: tautology or truth-functionally true, contradiction or truth-functionally false, and contingent or truth-functionally indeterminate. We can use the technique to determine tautology, contradiction and contingent statements based on the following reasoning: Since a truth-tree records only truth conditions, if a tree for a given statement is a closed tree, then it shows that there is no truth value assignment on which the statement can be true. On the other hand, if the negation of the statement results in a closed tree, then the negated statement must be always false and, therefore, the statement itself must be always true.

Testing for Contradiction

As a test for contradiction, we shall state:

A statement S is a contradiction or a truth-functionally false statement iff the set of the statement i.e. {S} has a closed tree.

Consider the set below which a single statement exists as its member:

$$\{[P \supset (Q \vee R)] \bullet \sim ((P \supset Q) \vee (P \supset R)]\}$$

In order to find out whether its member is a contradiction or not, we work out its tree as in the following example:

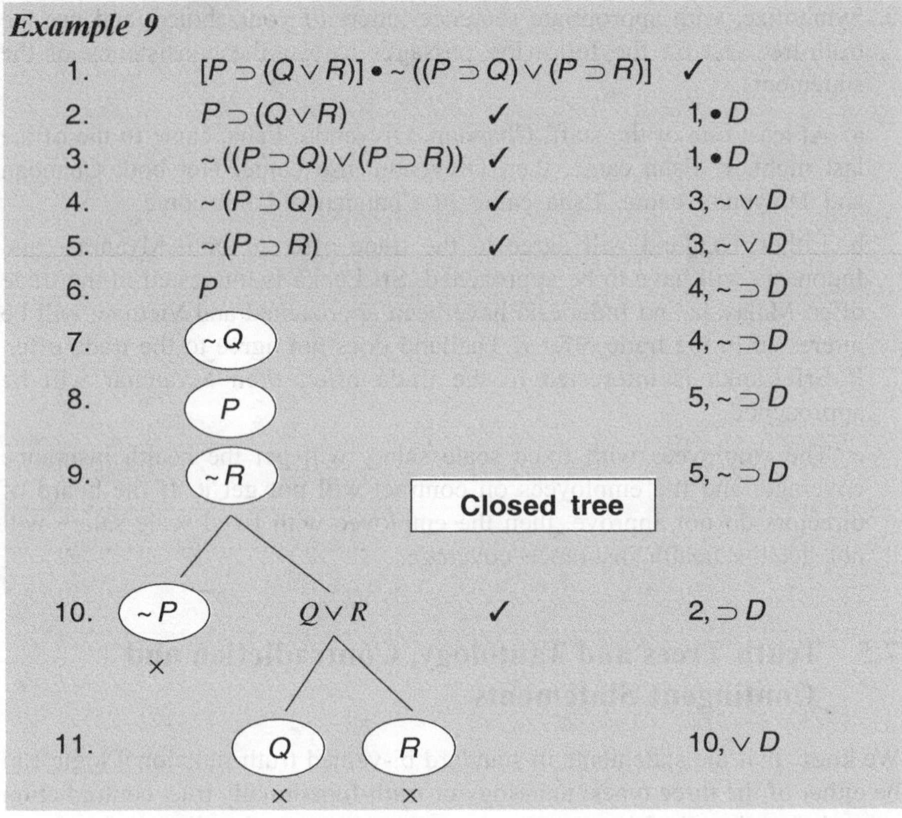

All the branches of the tree in Example 9 are closed, so there is no truth value assignment on which the statement in question is true. In its corresponding truth table, there will not be any row on which the statement will have the truth value T. Hence, the set

$$\{[P \supset (Q \vee R)] \bullet \sim ((P \supset Q) \vee (P \supset R)]\}$$

is inconsistent, and its only member is a **contradiction** or **truth-functionally false statement**.

Testing for Tautology

We shall also further assert:

> A statement *S* is a *tautology* or *a truth-functionally true* statement *iff* the set of the *negated statement* i.e. {~*S*} has a closed tree.

As explained above, if the tree for the negated statement ~*S* is a closed tree, then there is no truth-value assignment on which ~*S* is true. Therefore, ~*S* is always false, and hence *S* must be always true or a tautology.

Consider the example:

$$(C \supset R) \supset [\sim R \supset \sim (C \bullet J)]$$

We do not know which kind of statement it is. Suppose we do a tree for the statement itself as in Example 10:

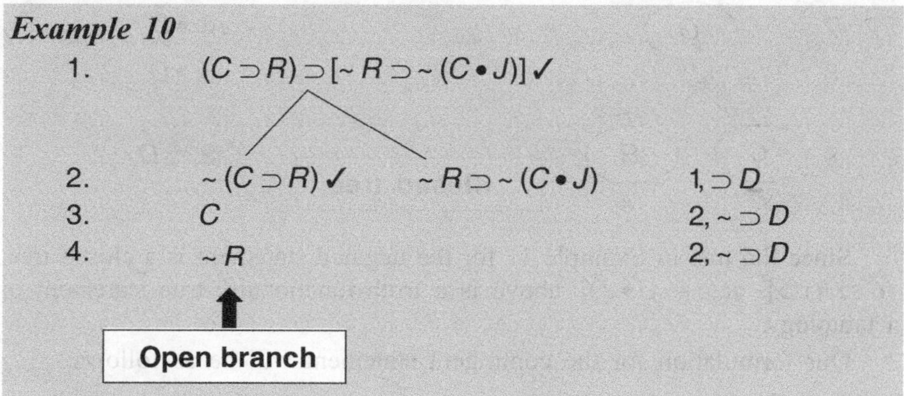

Line 4 of this tree shows that the tree is going to be an **open tree**. Though the right-hand side branch is still not decomposed, the left branch is an open completed branch, which contains only literals and the checked compound statements. Although more work can be done on the right-hand branch, none of that is going to close the left-hand branch. At this juncture, we can safely conclude that the statement we are testing is **not a contradiction**.

Testing for Contingent

We shall also further assert:

> A statement *S* is a *tautology* or *a truth-functionally true* statement *iff* the set of the *negated statement* i.e. {~*S*} has a closed tree.

However, we cannot conclude from this that the statement must be a tautology. For, it could still be either a tautology or a contingent. Many statements which are not tautologies have trees with open branches and many tautologies have trees with only open branches. We can definitely find out its nature by doing another tree for its negation. The following example gives the tree for the negated statement:

Example 11

1.	$\sim\{(C \supset R) \supset [\sim R \supset \sim(C \bullet J)]\}$		✓
2.	$C \supset R$	✓	1, $\sim\supset D$
3.	$\sim[\sim R \supset \sim(C \bullet J)]$	✓	1, $\sim\supset D$
4.	$\sim R$ (circled)		3, $\sim\supset D$
5.	$\sim\sim(C \bullet J)]$	✓	3, $\sim\supset D$
6.	$C \bullet J$	✓	5, $\sim\sim D$
7.	C (circled)		6, $\bullet D$
8.	J		6, $\bullet D$
9.	$\sim C$ (circled) × R (circled) ×		2, $\supset D$

Closed tree

Since the tree in Example 11 for the negated statement is a closed tree, $(C \supset R) \supset [\sim R \supset \sim(C \bullet J)]$ above is a truth-functionally true statement or a tautology.

Our formulation for the contingent statement will be as follows:

> A statement S is a *contingent* or a *truth-functionally indeterminate statement iff* neither the set $\{S\}$ nor the set of the *negated statement* $\{\sim S\}$ has a closed tree.

We shall take a simple example to establish the point: $A \vee B$. First we do the tree for $A \vee B$ and then a tree for its negation $\sim(A \vee B)$.

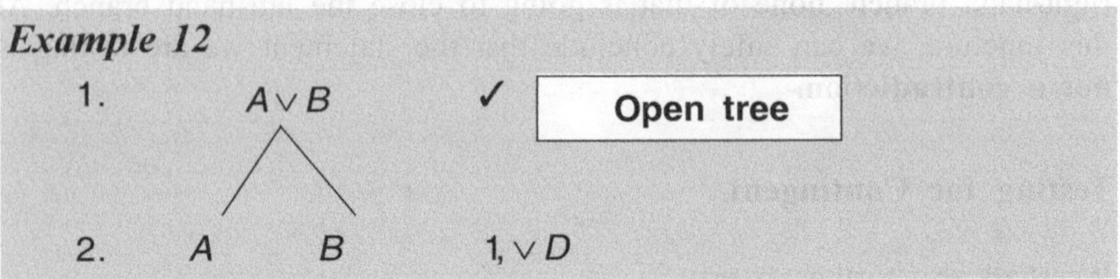

The tree for $A \vee B$ is open. This shows that it is not a contradiction. Here is the next tree for $\sim(A \vee B)$.

Example 13

1. $\sim(A \vee B)$	✓	
2. $\sim A$	1, $\sim\vee D$	**Open tree**
3. $\sim B$	1, $\sim\vee D$	

The tree for '$\sim(A \vee B)$' is also open. This rules out the possibility that it is a tautology. Since there are only three admissible kinds of statements, it must therefore be a contingent statement.

EXERCISE 7.5

1. Use the truth-tree method to determine for each of the statements below whether it is a tautology, contradiction or contingent.

a. $(G \bullet \sim G) \vee (G \supset H)$

b. $\sim J \vee \sim J$

c. $*D \supset (D \equiv D)$

d. $(B \supset L) \vee (L \supset B)$

e. $\sim (C \vee A) \bullet \sim (\sim C \bullet \sim A)$

f. $(N \bullet (R \vee O)) \supset \sim (N \vee O)$

g. $(S \supset K) \equiv (\sim S \vee K)$

h. $((V \supset X) \bullet V) \supset \sim X$

2. Which of the following claims is true? Justify your answer.

a. If a completed tree for a statement has at least one open branch and at least one close branch, then the statement must be contingent or truth-functionally indeterminate.

b. If a statement is a tautology, then the completed tree for it will have each one of its branches open.

c. *If a statement is a tautology, then the completed tree for its negation will have each one of its branches closed.

d. If a set of statements α has an open tree and a set of statements β has an open tree, then the combined or the union set of α and β also will have an open tree.

7.6 Checking Validity and Invalidity by Truth Trees

We can apply the truth tree method to test whether an argument is valid or invalid. From our discussion on truth-tables in Section 7.5, we understand the validity of an argument as a situation where there is *no* truth-value assignment on which every member of the premise set Γ is true and the conclusion C is false. In other words, if the argument is valid, then the set of $\{\Gamma, \sim C\}$ will be inconsistent. This can be expressed in terms of truth tree as:

> An argument is *valid iff* the *set consisting of the premises and the negation of the conclusion has a closed tree.*

On the other hand,

An argument is *invalid iff* the *set consisting of the premises and the negation of the conclusion* has an *open tree.*

This is so because the open tree shows that the set is consistent. In other words, it shows that there is at least some possible truth-value assignment on which the negation of the conclusion is true, therefore, the conclusion is false while all the premises are true. Needless to say, this is the basic condition for invalidity.

In order to test arguments for validity or invalidity, therefore, we need to do the following:

- ✓ List the premises one by one and the negated conclusion in the 'root' of the tree. This assumes that the argument is invalid.
- ✓ Start decomposition as per rule.
- ✓ If the completed tree is closed, then the assumed set is inconsistent, hence the actual argument with unnegated conclusion is valid.
- ✓ If the completed tree is open with at least one open completed branch, then the argument is invalid.

We shall instantiate the test procedure with the following argument as an example:

$(\sim C \vee \sim D) \supset G$

$H \bullet \sim G$

$\therefore C$

Is this argument valid or invalid? Here is the tree with the premises and the **negated conclusion**:

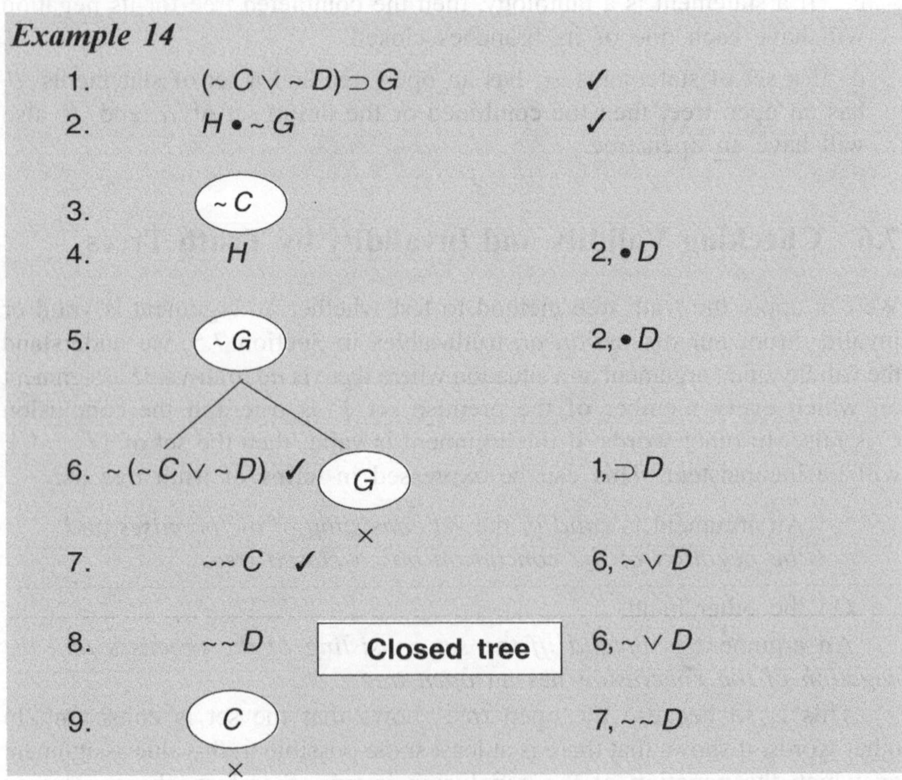

The tree is closed. This shows that the given argument must be valid. Here is another example:

$\sim J \bullet \sim K$

$(L \supset \sim J) \equiv \sim K$

M

$\therefore L \bullet M$

Is this argument valid or invalid? For a decisive answer, we shall construct a tree as explained above:

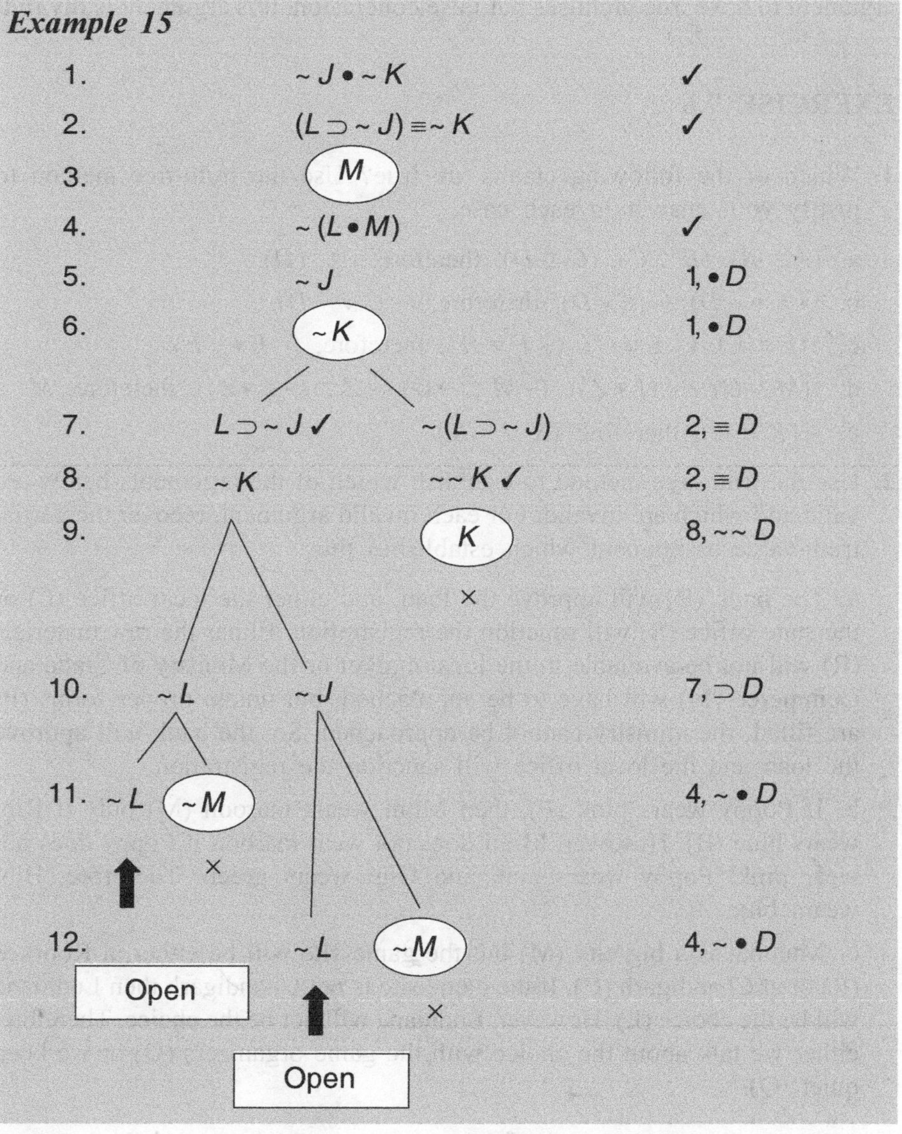

The tree in Example 15 is an open tree as it has two completed open branches as indicated above. Because these branches are open, we can recover a partial truth-value assignment from either of them on which the premises of the argument will be true but the conclusion will be false. Tracing any of them from the tip of the branch to the root, the following truth values of the atomic statements can be recovered:

M	J	K	L
T	F	F	F

The recovered truth values establish that, since it is possible for this argument to have true premises but false conclusion, this argument is **invalid**.

EXERCISE 7.6

1. Which of the following claims are true? Use the truth-tree method to justify your answer in each case.

a. $(A \supset B)$, $(B \supset C)$, $(C \supset D)$, therefore, $(A \supset D)$.

b. $(\sim C \bullet \sim D)$, $\sim (C \bullet D)$, therefore, $(\sim C \vee \sim D)$.

c. *$(E \equiv F)$, $(\sim E \equiv G)$, $(\sim F \equiv H)$, therefore, $(\sim E \bullet \sim F)$.

d. $((M \equiv O) \vee \sim (L \bullet Z))$, $(\sim M \supset \sim O)$,$(\sim Z \supset (\sim L \bullet Z))$, therefore, M.

e. $\sim (K \equiv K)$, therefore $(K \vee \sim K)$.

2. Use the truth-tree method to establish which of the arguments below are valid and which are invalid. For each invalid argument, recover the partial truth-value assignment which establishes this.

a. The bank (B) will approve the loan, and either the local office (L) or the state office (S) will sanction the registration. Either the raw materials (R) will not be available in the local market or the Ministry of Trade and Commerce (M) will have to be approached, but unless proper forms (P) are filled, the ministry cannot be approached. So, the bank will approve the loan and the local office will sanction the registration.

b. If Poppy wears pink (P), then Mimi wears maroon (M) only if Bibi wears blue (B). However, Mimi does not wear maroon if Poppy does not wear pink. Poppy wears pink and Gigi wears green. Therefore, Bibi wears blue.

c. Mumbai is a big city (M) but the game site will be either at Roorkee (R) or at Chandigarh (C). If the game site is not Chandigarh then Ludhiana will be the choice (L). However, Ludhiana will not be the choice. Therefore, either we talk about the choice with the game organizers (O) or we keep quiet (Q).

d. The members will not vote for the Bill (M) if their party high command orders them (O), and their party high command will order them if and only if the Bill allows more privatization (P) and also invites direct foreign investment (I). But the Bill invites direct foreign investment only if the country's law permits it (L), and indeed the country's law permits it. Therefore, the members will not vote for the Bill.

3. Suppose we are told that a completed tree for premises and the conclusion of an argument is open. Does this show that the argument is valid? Does this show that the argument is invalid? Justify your answer with example of arguments.

7.7 Checking Logical Equivalence by Truth Trees

Two statements p and q are logically equivalent *iff* there is no truth value assignment on which p and q have different truth values. So, p and q can be said to be logically equivalent *iff* $p \equiv q$ is a tautology. We can express the same idea in terms of the truth trees as

> p and q are *logically equivalent iff* the *set* $\{\sim (p \equiv q)\}$ *has a closed tree.*

It follows that p and q cannot be logically equivalent if the set $\{\sim (p \equiv q)\}$ has an open tree. For, that will establish the presence of recovering at least one possible set of truth value assignments on which p and q will not have the same truth values.

The procedure, as in the case of testing for validity, requires us to start with the **negated equivalence** claim. We begin with the assumption that the given two statements are *not* equivalent. We illustrate the procedure with the following two simple examples:

Is $M \supset N$ logically equivalent to $\sim (M \bullet \sim N)$? The truth-tree method can settle this question in the following way. As shown in the following example, the negation of the equivalence claim between the two statements $M \supset N$ and $\sim (M \bullet \sim N)$ is listed in the tree as the 'root'. We look for the result to our proposed question in the worked-out tree:

Example 16

1.	$\sim \{(M \supset N) \equiv \sim (M \bullet \sim N)\}$ ✓		
2.	$M \supset N$ ✓	$\sim (M \supset N)$ ✓	1, $\sim \equiv D$
3.	$\sim\sim (M \bullet \sim N)$ ✓	$\sim (M \bullet \sim N)$ ✓	1, $\sim \equiv D$

4.	$M \bullet \sim N$ ✓		3, ~~ *D*
5.		M	2, ~ ⊃ *D*
6.		$\sim N$	2, ~ ⊃ *D*
7.		$\sim M$ $\sim\sim N$	3, ~ • *D*
8.		× N	7, ~~ *D*
		×	
9.	M		4, • *D*
10.	$\sim N$	**Closed tree**	4, • *D*
11.	$\sim M$ N		2, ⊃ *D*
	× ×		

A closed truth tree for the negated equivalence claim in Example 16 shows that the claim is inconsistent. Therefore, we can safely conclude that the statement $M \supset N$ is logically equivalent to $\sim(M \bullet \sim N)$.

Let us take another example: Is $M \supset N$ logically equivalent to $\sim(M \vee \sim N)$? We find the result by the truth-tree method in the same way. The negation of the equivalence claim between $M \supset N$ and $\sim(M \vee \sim N)$ is first taken as the 'root' or the beginning assumption. The detailed tree is given in the following example:

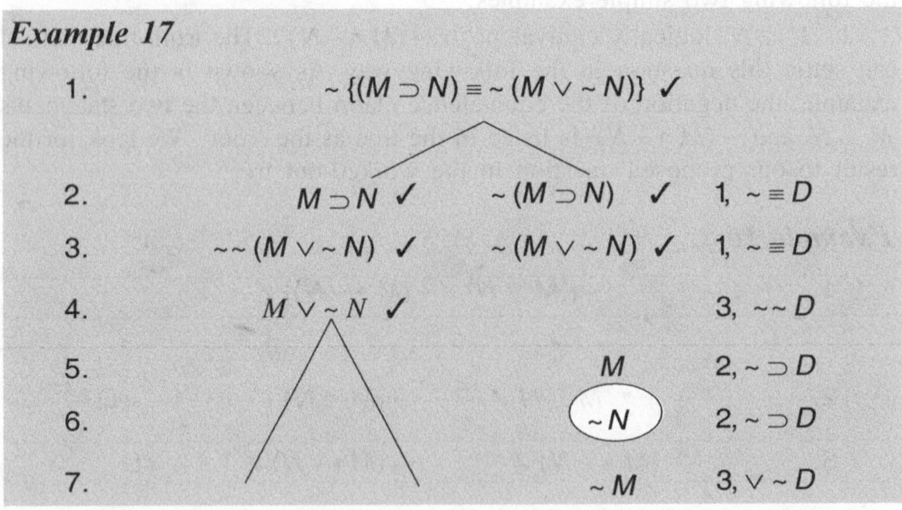

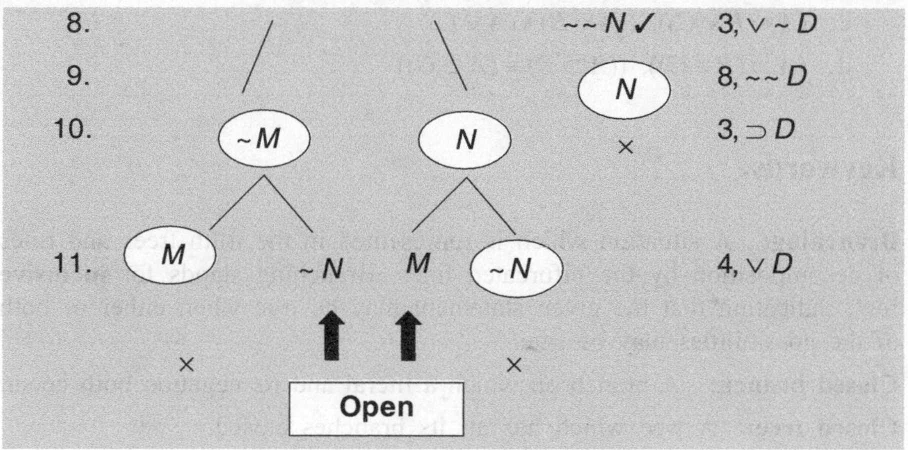

The open branches on the tree shown in Example 17 establishes that there is at least one possible set of truth values for which the two statements in question will *not* be equivalent. We recover these truth values from the open branches. Since there are two open branches, from these we can recover two sets of values, as given below. The left-hand open branch shows that when ~*N* and ~*M* are true, the statements will not be equivalent. The right-hand open branch shows that, when *M* and *N* will be true, the statements will not be equivalent. Accordingly, we have listed both sets of truth values. However, any one of them is sufficient to establish our claim that the two statements are **not** equivalent.

M	*N*
F	F
T	T

EXERCISE 7.7

***1.** If any two statements, p and q, are logically equivalent, will the truth tree for $\{p \equiv q\}$ be open?

2. If any two statements, p and q, are logically equivalent, will the truth tree for $\{p \equiv \sim q\}$ be open?

***3.** If any two statements, p and q, are logically equivalent, will the truth tree for $\{p, q\}$ be open?

4. Use the truth-tree method to determine which of the following pairs are logically equivalent. For those that are not equivalent, recover a partial assignment to establish this.

a. $\sim (A \vee B)$, $(\sim A \vee \sim B)$

b. $\sim (A \vee B)$, $(\sim A \bullet \sim B)$

c. $(A \bullet (B \vee C))$, $((A \vee B) \bullet (A \vee C))$

d. $(A \supset (B \equiv C))$, $((A \supset B) \equiv (A \supset C))$

Keywords

Branching: A situation which is represented in the truth trees and rules of decomposition by the bifurcated lines. Branching stands for **inclusive 'or'**, indicating that the given statement may be true when either or both of the possibilities may be true.

Closed branch: A branch on which a literal and its negation both occur.

Closed tree: A tree which has all its branches closed.

Completed open branch: A finite open branch that contains only literals and checked compound statements.

Completed tree: A tree, each of the branches of which is either closed or is a completed open branch.

Decomposition: Breaking a string of symbols or a compound statement down to literals, following certain rules.

Literal: An atomic or simple statement or its negation, such as *A* or *~A*.

Open branch: A branch that is not closed.

Open tree: A tree with at least one completed open branch.

Semantic tableaux systems: Same as truth trees.

CHAPTER

DERIVATIONS

8.1 Argument Form

From our discussion in Chapter 2, we know already that an argument is composed of statements, one of which is the conclusion and the rest are supporting premises. An **argument form** is a form or structure composed only of statement forms such that all its substitution instances will be arguments. Basically, it is an array of symbols with only statement variables and not actual statements.

Consider the following three arguments:

Example 1

A. 1. If this figure is a triangle, then the sum of its three angles is equal to 180°.
   2. This figure is a triangle.
   3. Therefore, the sum of its three angles is equal to 180°.

B. 1. If Honshu is in Japan, then it is in Asia.
   2. Honshu is in Japan.
   3. Therefore, Honshu is in Asia.

C. 1. If she passes the physical fitness test, then she will play tomorrow.
   2. She has passed the physical fitness test.
   3. So, she will play tomorrow.

The contents of arguments A–C are different as each of them is about a different thing. However, there is a distinct *pattern* or *form* here; namely,

1. If p then q.		1. $p \supset q$
2. p	In Symbols ⟹	2. p
3. Therefore, q.		3. $\therefore q$

This array of symbols and statement variables is not an argument itself, but an argument form. If we replace each occurrence of each distinct statement variable in the form consistently by the same statement wherever that variable occurs in the argument form, we get an actual argument such as any of the three arguments above. The argument resulting from this substitution is said to *have that form.* Alternatively, we can say that each of the arguments A–C is a substitution instance of this argument form.

Each of the following symbolized arguments is also a substitution instance of the same argument form:

1. $p \supset q$
2. p
3. $\therefore q$

D. 1. $G \supset \sim A$
2. G
3. $\therefore \sim A$

E. 1. $\sim (C \vee D) \supset (A \supset B)$
2. $\sim (C \vee D)$
3. $\therefore A \supset B$

F. 1. $(E \vee (F \supset G)) \supset (I \supset K)$
2. $E \vee (F \supset G)$
3. $\therefore I \supset K$

Types of Argument Forms

A **valid argument form** has no substitution instance which is invalid. In other words, if an argument form is a substitution instance of a valid argument form, then it *cannot* have all its premises true and its conclusion false. A valid argument form will have only valid arguments as its substitution instances.

An argument form is an **invalid argument form** if it has even one invalid argument as a substitution instance.

How can we tell if an argument form is valid or not? Moreover, how do we prove that an argument form is valid or is not valid? The truth-table method can help us to answer both of these questions satisfactorily. We can take the help of the truth-table method to demonstrate the validity or invalidity of an argument form. Let us test the argument form mentioned above:

1. $p \supset q$
2. p
3. $\therefore q$

We first set up a complete truth table of the argument form as follows:

p	q	p	$p \supset q$	q
T	T	T	T	T
T	F	T	F	F
F	T	F	T	T
F	F	F	T	F

The truth table shows us that only in the first row (shaded) the premises p and $p \supset q$ are all true; in the rest of the rows at least one of them is false. It also shows us that, when the argument form has all its premises true, i.e., in the first row, it also has its conclusion q true. Therefore, this is a valid argument form. It is commonly known as the **Modus Ponens (M.P.)**. If an argument is a substitution instance of it, the argument cannot be invalid.

This implies that we can now call an argument valid by virtue of its being the substitution instance of a valid argument form. The advantage of this is that it lessens the burden of proof. For example, by demonstrating the *Modus Ponens* as a valid argument form, we have shown in one stroke that each of abovementioned arguments, *A–C* and *D–F* in our examples, is valid without constructing a separate truth table for each of them. All we need to do to justify the claim of their validity is to refer to Modus Ponens as the valid argument form that they have.

Let us now test another argument form that is closely similar to the Modus Ponens:

1. $p \supset q$
2. q
3. $\therefore p$

We construct its truth table in the same way:

p	q	$p \supset q$	q	p
T	T	T	T	T
T	F	F	F	T
F	T	T	T	F
F	F	T	F	F

We find that it contains at least one row, namely, the third (shaded), in which both the premises are true but the conclusion is false. This shows that it is an *invalid* argument form, and that it is possible for one of its substitution instances to have true premises but false conclusion. This particular invalid argument form is commonly known as the **fallacy of affirming the consequent**. Given below is an English substitution instance of this fallacy:

Example 2

1. If he has diabetes, then he has problem in his eyes.
2. He has problem in his eyes.
3. Therefore, he has diabetes.

This argument is invalid. For, if he has eye problems due to eye diseases like conjunctivitis, cataract, glaucoma or trachoma, then though the premises will be both true, it is possible for the conclusion to be false.

8.2 The Proof Procedure: Formal Derivation

Truth tables and truth trees both, as we have seen in Chapters 6 and 7, are helpful for demonstrating validity of arguments. Both procedures, however, tend to become unwieldy and tiresome as the complexity present in the arguments increases. Truth tables steadily become cumbersome and error-prone as the number of atomic statements becomes larger than three. As we know from our discussion in Chapter 6, the number of rows in a truth table is decided by the formula 2^n, where n is the number of atomic components. So, a 7-variable argument, for example, will demand a truth table with 128 rows. As validity is an exhaustive notion with no room for chances of invalidity, this makes the truth table a particularly difficult choice for the demonstration of validity, which requires us to ensure a T in each and every row in the final column. The same demand on completed truth trees also requires keen attention to all the branches and sub-branches. This too can prove to be a challenge when arguments have a large number of premises which decompose into numerous components.

For these and other historical reasons, most practicing logicians, mathematicians and computer scientists prefer to demonstrate validity through a proof procedure called **formal derivation**. Its aim is to establish the validity of arguments. However, this is not the way to establish invalidity. The shorter truth-table method that we have learnt in Section 6.5 is still the most efficient way to establish invalidity of arguments.

The main vehicle for a formal system is its module for 'derivation' or 'proof'. The derivation procedure that we shall look into in this chapter is called *formal* derivation because it relies on the *valid argument forms*, and not on the truth or falsity of the individual statements involved, to show how the conclusion can be *derived* or deduced from the given set of premises. The overall function of formal derivation is to deduce the logical consequences from the premises. It uses the valid argument forms as the *logical rules* to determine which consequences can be correctly or validly drawn from the premises.

The logical rules, being valid argument forms themselves, have a special quality. They are all **truth-preserving**, i.e., they will never lead us to falsity if we start out with truth. This preservation of truth is an essential concept for validity. As we shall see, the formal derivation procedure relies heavily on this truth-preserving quality of the valid argument forms.

Format of a Derivation

The format for this procedure will be as follows:

1. ✓ The proof will start by first listing the given premises or assumptions for an argument. Each line should have a unique line number for easy reference.

Suppose that we need to demonstrate the validity of the following argument by formal derivation procedure:

Example 3

1. $B \supset A$
2. B

$\therefore A$

The proof will start first by listing the premises as lines in the proof, as follows:

1. $B \supset A$
2. B

It is customary to mention the conclusion in this list as the target. Usually, the conclusion is mentioned with a separator line or a '/' followed by a '$\therefore$' symbol. For example, the proof above may be written with its conclusion in the following way:

1. $B \supset A$
2. B $\qquad\qquad$ / $\therefore A$

This completes the set-up for derivation.

2. ✓ Now the derivation will proceed by adding new lines to these already given lines. Each subsequent new line, which is *not* a given premise but has been obtained by deducing from the previous lines, must have a *justification* (about why it should be allowed). The justification should be in terms of the valid argument form or the logical rule used for deduction. The justification with the name of the rule and the number of the lines used should be entered on the *right-hand side* of the new line.

In the example above, we need to demonstrate how *A* can be derived from the given two premises. *A* happens to be the consequent of the first premise which is a conditional. If we recall our discussion of valid argument forms from Section 8.1, then we know that *Modus Ponens* (M.P.) is a valid argument form which allows us to detach a consequent from a conditional *provided* the conditional and its antecedent are both separately true. In other words, M.P. guarantees that given $p \supset q$ and *p*, we can safely derive *q*.

In the following example, we use this valid argument form as the logical rule or the justification of this example:

Example 4

1. $B \supset A$
2. B
3. A 1, 2, M.P. ⟸ Justification

And our proof is complete. Note that it is much shorter than a proof by truth tree or a truth table. Its efficiency comes from relying as a rule of inference on an argument form that is *already known to be valid*.

Note that we can use the abbreviated name of the valid argument form in the justification. In line 3 of Example 4, instead of *Modus Ponens*, we simply write M.P. However, it is more important to note that every previous line that has been used to deduce line 3 must be mentioned in the justification. The application of M.P. requires the use of both lines 1 and 2. So, both of them should be mentioned, separated by a comma, in the justification.

Consider another similar example where we show how *A* can be validly derived from the given three premises:

Examples 5

1. $L \supset B$
2. $B \supset A$
3. L

$\therefore A$

The formal derivation of this argument will be as follows:

Example 5 (Continued)

1. $L \supset B$
2. $B \supset A$

3. *L*	
4. *B*	1, 3, M.P.
5. *A*	2, 4, M.P.

In Example 5, the same valid argument form M.P. has been used as justification twice on two different occasions. What would have required a 16-row truth table for 4-statement letters and a tree with several lines of decomposition has been accomplished in 5 lines in total.

3. ✓ The proof, as should be clear from the above two examples, terminates when the conclusion of the given argument is reached by deduction. Obviously, the conclusion will be the last line of the derivation of the argument whose validity is to be established.

8.3 Derivation Rules: Rules of Inference

We shall use 18 valid argument forms in total as rules for applying in formal derivations. Out of these, nine are **rules of inference**. They are rules which tell us what can be validly inferred from a certain kind of premises. In our formal derivations, we shall follow them exactly to decide what can be legitimately inferred in a situation and what cannot be.

Given below is a list of these nine rules of inference. With each rule, you will find its complete name and the abbreviated name for your easy reference. As before, the symbol '∴' will indicate which is the conclusion. The statements preceding it will be the premise or the premises.

It is crucial to remember the requirements of each rule. Some rules require two premises before the conclusion can be validly deduced and some require only one. Also, they allow certain inferences only from statements of a certain form. Unless this point is recognized, application of these rules in derivations may go wrong.

It is also very important to remember that the rules of inference *work in one direction*: only from the premises to the conclusion shown and not from the conclusion back to the premises. Details about each rule are given in the explanation which follows the list.

Rules of Inference

1. Modus Ponens (M.P.)

1 $p \supset q$

2. p

$\therefore q$

2. Modus Tollens (M.T.)

1. $p \supset q$

2. $\sim q$

$\therefore \sim q$

3. Hypothetical Syllogism (H.S.)

1. $p \supset q$
2. $q \supset r$

$\therefore p \supset r$

4. Disjunctive Syllogism (D.S.)

1. $p \vee q$
2. $\sim p$

$\therefore q$

5. Constructive Dilemma (C.D.)

1. $(p \supset q) \bullet (r \supset s)$
2. $p \vee r$

$\therefore q \vee s$

6. Destructive Dilemma (D.D.)

1. $(p \supset q) \bullet (r \supset s)$
2. $\sim q \vee \sim s$

$\therefore \sim p \vee \sim r$

7. Simplification (Simp.)

1. $p \bullet q$

$\therefore p$

8. Conjunction (Conj.)

1. p
2. q

$\therefore p \bullet q$

9. Addition (Add.)

1. p

$\therefore p \vee q$

Modus Ponens and Modus Tollens

These two valid argument forms are closely related. These are also frequently used in proofs. We discuss each of them now. **Modus Ponens (M.P.)**, as we have seen above, tells us that anytime we have a conditional or a statement of the form $p \supset q$ *and* its antecedent 'p', we can validly infer 'q'. The important point is that we have to have *both* the premises, that is, q cannot be inferred by *Modus Ponens* from $p \supset q$ alone, nor from p alone. In Section 8.2, we have seen two examples of how M.P. can be applied and one of them used M.P. twice.

M.P. requires that one of its premises must be a conditional or a statement of the form $p \supset q$. It cannot be applied unless this requirement is met exactly. Consider the following attempt at a proof:

Example 6

1. $B \vee (C \supset D)$			
2. $G \bullet E$			
3. C			
4. D	1, 3, M.P.	×	**Wrong!**

The argument in Example 6 has three premises which are listed in lines 1–3. However, the derivation in line 4 has gone completely wrong because it involves an *incorrect application* of the valid argument form M.P. Line 1 has a statement which has the form of a disjunction or of a statement of the form $p \vee q$. The application of M.P. on line 1 therefore is unauthorized. Moreover, in this case, M.P. has been applied to $C \supset D$ which appears as a part within the statement $B \vee (C \supset D)$ This move is also not authorized by M.P. Note that the rule requires $p \supset q$ and p, both as stand-alone statements, and not as components of other statements.

Modus Tollens (M.T.) tells us that anytime we have a statement of the form $p \supset q$ *and* the negation of its consequent or $\sim q$ as stand-alone statements, we can validly infer $\sim p$ from both the statements. A simple instance of its application is given below:

Example 7

1. $L \supset (J \equiv K)$
2. $M \vee L$
3. $\sim (J \equiv K)$
4. $\sim L$ **1, 3, M.T.**

Example 7 has three premises listed on lines 1–3. On line 4, a new line is inferred using M.T. and lines 1 and 3. We could do this because lines 1 and 3 match the exact statement forms which M.T. requires for its application. $L \supset (J \equiv K)$ is a statement of the form $p \supset q$, and $\sim (J \equiv K)$ is the negation of its consequent. Thus, we were able to derive '$\sim L$' from them.

In a proof, you may have to apply more than one rule of inference to reach the target conclusion. However, *only one rule* has to be applied at a time. The following example shows a case where both M.P. and M.T. have been used.

Example 8

Suppose we are asked to prove the validity of the following:

1. $\sim A \supset (B \supset C)$
2. $\sim C$
3. $\sim A$
4. $\sim B \supset (D \vee E)$

$\therefore D \vee E$

Formal derivation:

1. $\sim A \supset (B \supset C)$
2. $\sim C$

3. $\sim A$
4. $\sim B \supset (D \vee E)$
5. $B \supset C$ **1, 3, M.P.**
6. $\sim B$ **5, 2, M.T.**
7. $D \vee E$ **4, 6, M.P.**

While learning about M.P. and M.T., you have to be careful not to confuse them with two invalid argument forms which are very similar to these. These argument forms are:

Fallacy of Affirming the Consequent	**Fallacy of Denying the Antecedent**
1. $p \supset q$	1. $p \supset q$
2. q	2. $\sim p$
3. $\therefore p$	3. $\therefore \sim q$

In Section 8.1 (see pages 163-164), we did a truth table demonstration of the invalidity of the argument form of Affirming the Consequent. We can do the same now for the argument form Denying the Antecedent:

p	q	$p \supset q$	$\sim p$	$\sim q$
T	T	T	F	F
T	F	F	F	T
F	T	T	T	F
F	F	T	T	T

The truth table analysis shows that, whenever p is false and q is true, we will have a situation in which the premises will be true but the conclusion will be false. This shows that the argument form is invalid. Therefore, arguments of the same form cannot be trusted.

The main point to remember is that, from a statement of the form $p \supset q$ and the assertion of the consequent, we cannot validly infer that the antecedent must be the case. Similarly, from a statement of the form $p \supset q$ and the negation of the antecedent, we cannot validly infer the negation of the consequent.

Hypothetical Syllogism (H.S.) and Disjunctive Syllogism (D.S.)

The Hypothetical Syllogism (H.S.) rule shows how from two conditionals a third conditional statement can be derived, *provided* the consequent of one of the conditionals is the antecedent of the other conditional. In other words, the rule says that, whenever we have two conditionals of the form $p \supset q$ and $q \supset r$, we can combine the information from these two premises to legitimately deduce a conditional which has the antecedent of the first conditional as its antecedent and the consequent of the second conditional as its consequent. This shows that '$\supset$' is transitive. For this reason, the rule is also known as the *chain rule*. Here is a simple example:

Example 9

Suppose we have the following to prove:	*Its formal derivation:*	
1. $B \supset D$	1. $B \supset D$	
2. B	2. B	
3. $D \supset E$	3. $D \supset E$	
4. $E \supset A$	4. $E \supset A$	
$\therefore A$	5. $B \supset E$	**1, 3, H.S.**
	6. $B \supset A$	**5, 4, H.S.**
	7. A	**6, 2, M.P.**

Disjunctive Syllogism (D.S.), on the other hand, tells us that, given a statement of the form $p \vee q$, where we know that *at least one* of the statements is true, and then given a further information that one of them is definitely not true, we can very safely infer that the other statement must be true.

Given below is an example of a proof where all the four rules that we have learnt so far are applied:

Example 10

Argument	**Formal Derivation**	
1. $S \vee (T \supset V)$	1. $S \vee (T \supset V)$	
2. $\sim U \supset (V \supset W)$	2. $\sim U \supset (V \supset W)$	
3. $S \supset U$	3. $S \supset U$	
4. $\sim U$	4. $\sim U$	
$\therefore T \supset W$	5. $\sim S$	**3, 4, M.T.**
	6. $T \supset V$	**1, 5, D.S.**
	7. $V \supset W$	**2, 4, M.P.**
	8. $T \supset W$	**6, 7, H.S.**

Constructive Dilemma (C.D.) and Destructive Dilemma (D.D.)

The dilemma rules require us to have a conjunction of two separate conditionals as one of the premises, i.e., a statement of the form $(p \supset q) \bullet (r \supset s)$. In addition, **Constructive Dilemma (C.D.)** needs a premise which says that either of the antecedents of these two conditionals is true, i.e., a statement of the form $p \vee r$ is true. Given that both of these premises are true, the C.D. rule then allows us to validly infer either of the consequents of the two conditionals to be true, i.e., a statement of the form $q \vee s$ is true.

The **Destructive Dilemma (D.D.)** also needs $(p \supset q) \bullet (r \supset s)$ as a premise but, in addition, it needs a statement which says that either the consequent of this conditional is not true or the consequent of the other is not true, i.e., a statement of the form $\sim q \vee \sim s$ is true. From these two premises, we can validly infer that either of the antecedents is not true, i.e., a statement of the form $\sim p \vee \sim r$ follows. In a way, the statement utilizes what we learnt from M.T.

Given below is an example of a formal derivation which shows the application of C.D. and D.D. along with a few other rules that we have learnt. In the example, the argument is not given separately from the derivation. The conclusion which is to be derived is indicated by the symbols '/' and '∴'.

Example 11

1. $(M \supset N) \bullet (O \supset P)$		
2. $M \vee O$		
3. $(N \vee P) \supset (\sim B \vee \sim D)$		
4. $(G \supset B) \bullet (H \supset D)$		
5. $\sim\sim G$		
6. $(K \bullet L) \supset H$	$/ \therefore \sim (K \bullet L)$	
7. $N \vee P$		**1, 2, C.D.**
8. $\sim B \vee \sim D$		**3, 7, M.P.**
9. $\sim G \vee \sim H$		**4, 8, D.D.**
10. $\sim H$		**9, 5, D.S.**
11. $\sim (K \bullet L)$		**6, 10, M.T.**

Simplification (Simp.) and Conjunction (Conj.)

Both of these rules are quite intuitive. Simplification says that, if we know that both p and q are true, i.e., a statement of the form $p \bullet q$ is true, then it follows that one of them is true.

Conjunction rule employs the same observation in a different way. It says that any time we know that any two statements p and q are true, we can validly infer that their conjunction $p \bullet q$ must be true.

Addition (Add.)

The Addition rule employs the truth condition of a disjunction. We know that a disjunction is true anytime at least one of its disjuncts is true. The Addition rule uses that to say that anytime we know that any statement p is true, we can infer *any* disjunction as long as the disjunction has p as one of its disjuncts. Thus, for example, if we know that A is true, by the Add. rule we can infer from it $A \vee B$, or even a complex statement, like $A \vee (B \equiv (D \vee T))$. This makes Add. a very useful rule in derivations, particularly when the components you are looking for are not found in the premises. You can bring them into the proof by the Add. Rule. Here is an example which employs Simp., Conj. and Add.:

Example 12

1. M	
2. $(I \bullet B) \bullet J$	
3. $(I \bullet M) \supset (I \supset (K \bullet L))$ $/\therefore (K \bullet L) \vee (Z \supset W)$	
4. $I \bullet B$	**2, Simp.**
5. I	**4, Simp.**
6. $I \bullet M$	**5, 1, Conj.**
7. $I \supset (K \bullet L)$	**3, 6, M.P.**
8. $K \bullet L$	**7, 5, M.P.**
9. $(K \bullet L) \vee (Z \supset W)$	**8, Add.**

It should be noted that in Example 12 in the justification on line 6 it is desirable that we mention the two lines used for conjunction in the exact order in which they have been used. Because '*I*' occurs on line 5 and '*M*' occurs on line 1, and we want to have '$I \bullet M$' on line 6, the justification should say "5, 1, Conj". The justification "1, 5, Conj.", for instance, refers to a string of symbols $M \bullet I$, which have the same elements but in a different order.

Also, line 9 of Example 12 shows the power the rule of addition has. $Z \supset W$ is part of the conclusion we want to derive. However, neither it nor its component statement letters occur anywhere in the premises. The rule of Addition nevertheless makes its derivation as a disjunct easy on line 9 once on line 8 we have validly inferred $K \bullet L$. The point to note is that the rule of Addition is flexible about what you wish to add as the 'q' when it says:

1. p
2. $\therefore p \vee q$

Just as on line 8 'p' is a compound statement $K \bullet L$, similarly on line 9 'q' too is a compound $Z \supset W$.

EXERCISE 8.3

A. For each of the following and for every line in the proof that is *not* marked as a premise with a letter 'P', provide the justification by mentioning *which lines* were used to derive it and *which rule* of inference was used.

A1.
1. H — P
2. $H \supset R$ — P
3. R
4. $R \vee S$

*A2.
1. L — P
2. $K \supset N$ — P
3. $\sim N$ — P
4. $\sim K$
5. $L \bullet \sim K$

A3.
1. $A \supset B$ — P
2. $A \vee C$ — P
3. $C \supset D$ — P
4. $(A \supset B) \bullet (C \supset D)$
5. $B \vee D$

A4.
1. $\sim H \vee \sim I$ — P
2. $[(G \supset H) \bullet (J \supset I)] \bullet (A \supset B)$ — P
3. $(G \supset H) \bullet (J \supset I)$
4. $\sim G \vee \sim I$

*A5.
1. $C \supset D$ — P
2. $\sim F$ — P
3. $D \supset E$ — P
4. $F \vee C$ — P
5. $E \supset G$ — P
6. $C \supset E$
7. $C \supset G$

8. C

9. G

B. Prove the validity of the following arguments by constructing a formal derivation:

B1. *1. $(S \supset (T \bullet V)) \bullet (U \supset W)$

2. $\sim (T \bullet V)$

3. Q $/ \therefore \sim S \bullet Q$

B2. 1. F

2. $G \supset H$

3. $J \supset M$

4. $W \supset G$

5. $F \supset B$

6. $H \supset J$

7. $B \supset W$ $/ \therefore M$

B3. 1. $(M \bullet N) \vee O$

2. $\sim (M \bullet N)$

3. $(O \supset P) \bullet (D \supset E)$ $/ \therefore P \vee E$

B4. 1. $\sim A \supset (B \supset C)$

2. $\sim C$

3. $\sim A$

4. $\sim B \supset (D \vee E)$ $/ \therefore D \vee E$

*B5. 1. $[(K \bullet P) \supset [K \supset (M \bullet N)]$

2. $(K \bullet P) \bullet L$ $/ \therefore M \vee N$

B6. 1. $G \vee (H \vee I)$

2. $(H \supset J) \bullet (I \supset K)$

3. $(J \vee K) \supset (G \vee I)$

4. $\sim G$ $/ \therefore I$

B7. 1. $(\sim A \bullet B) \supset (\sim C \vee \sim D)$

2. $F \supset (\sim G \supset H)$

3. $(\sim C \vee \sim D) \supset E$

4. $(\sim G \supset H) \supset (J \equiv \sim K)$

5. $\sim E \vee \sim (J \equiv \sim K)$ $/ \therefore \sim(\sim A \bullet B) \vee \sim F$

B8. 1. $(P \bullet Q) \supset R$

2. $(S \vee T) \supset U$

3. $(P \bullet Q)$
4. $\sim R \vee \sim U$
5. $(W \bullet X) \supset (S \vee T)$ $\quad / \therefore \sim (W \bullet X)$

B9.
1. $[(X \vee (\sim T \bullet V)) \vee Y] \supset [Z \supset (A \equiv B)]$
2. $[(X \vee (\sim T \bullet V)] \supset [(U \supset V) \supset K)]$
3. $X \supset [(A \equiv B) \supset (U \supset V)]$
4. X $\quad / \therefore Z \supset K$

*B10.
1. $K \vee \sim (B \vee R)$
2. $K \supset (L \equiv W)$
3. $\sim (B \vee R) \supset (K \vee \sim T)$
4. $\sim (L \equiv W) \bullet \sim M$ $\quad / \therefore \sim T$

8.4 Derivation Rules: Rules of Replacement

In Section 8.3, we learnt about the rules of inference that we can use in formal derivation. However, they allow strictly *one-directional inferences*. In contrast, we are now going to learn about 10 equivalence rules which we can use in the formal derivation. Strictly speaking, they are not inference rules. However, these will be referred to as **Rules of Replacement** because these equivalences are to be used in formal derivations to derive new lines. It will be important to remember that they have some major differences from the previous nine rules. In contrast to the rules of inference, these new rules allow:

✓ Replacement of a statement by its logically equivalent statement

✓ Replacement in both directions as will be indicated by the '≡' symbol

✓ Application to parts of a statement as well as to statements as a whole

As before, given below is a list of replacement rules with their names and abbreviated forms.

Rules of Replacement

10. De Morgan's Theorems (De. M.)

$\sim (p \bullet q) \equiv (\sim p \vee \sim q)$

$\sim (p \vee q) \equiv (\sim p \bullet \sim q)$

11. Commutation (Com.)

$(p \vee q) \equiv (q \vee p)$

$(p \bullet q) \equiv (q \bullet p)$

12. Association (Assoc.)

$[p \vee (q \vee r)] \equiv [(p \vee q) \vee r]$

$[p \bullet (q \bullet r)] \equiv [(p \bullet q) \bullet r]$

13. Distribution (Dist.)

$[p \bullet (q \vee r)] \equiv [(p \bullet q) \vee (p \bullet r)]$

$[p \vee (q \bullet r)] \equiv [(p \vee q) \bullet (p \vee r)]$

14. Double Negation (D.N.)

$p \equiv \sim\sim p$

15. Transposition (Trans.)

$(p \supset q) \equiv (\sim q \supset \sim p)$

16. Material Implication (Impl.)

$(p \supset q) \equiv (\sim p \vee q)$

17. Material Equivalence (Equiv.)

$(p \equiv q) \equiv [(p \supset q) \bullet (q \supset p)]$

$(p \equiv q) \equiv [(p \bullet q) \vee (\sim q \bullet \sim p)]$

18. Exportation (Exp.)

$[(p \bullet q) \supset r] \equiv [p \supset (q \supset r)]$

19. Tautology (Taut.)

$p \equiv (p \vee p)$

$p \equiv (p \bullet p)$

Note that each of these rules is stated as equivalences with '≡' as the main connective. As stated earlier, this indicates that we can infer the left-hand side of the '≡' from the right-hand side and vice versa. So, if Rule 16 or Material Implication is to be taken as an example, then not only $p \supset q$ can be replaced legitimately by $\sim p \vee q$, but also $\sim p \vee q$ can be replaced by $p \supset q$. And this replacement can take place anywhere within a statement to a part of the statement and also to the whole statement. Consider the statements in the following example. They show different ways of replacement by Rule 16, Material Implication or *Impl.*

Example 13

1. Suppose we have a premise # n. $\sim A \vee B$
   we can derive # n+1. $A \supset B$ n, Impl.
2. Or, if we have a premise # n. $A \supset (G \bullet (H \vee K))$
   we can derive # n+1. $\sim A \vee (G \bullet (H \vee K))$ n, Impl.
3. Or, if we have a premise # n. $(C \bullet D) \vee (\sim A \vee B)$
   we can derive # n+1. $(C \bullet D) \vee (A \supset B)$ n, Impl.

De Morgan's Theorems (De.M.) and Commutation (Com.)

De Morgan's theorems, named after the 19th century English logician and mathematician Augustus De Morgan, born in 1806 in India, are two powerful rules of equivalence:

$$\sim (p \bullet q) \equiv (\sim p \vee \sim q) \qquad \sim (p \vee q) \equiv (\sim p \bullet \sim q)$$

Together, they show the conditions of interchangeability of negation of '•' and '∨', and the negation of '∨' and '•'. The first one shows how negation of '•' can be converted into a disjunction with negated components and vice versa. The second one shows the logical equivalence between negation of a '∨' and a conjunction with negated components. These rules are used in Boolean Algebra and Set Theory and have found wide applications in Electrical Engineering and discrete mathematics.

We can do a truth-table test of their claim of validity as follows:

p	q	$\sim p$	$\sim q$	$p \bullet q$	$\sim(p \bullet q)$	$\sim p \vee \sim q$	$p \vee q$	$\sim(p \vee q)$	$\sim p \bullet \sim q$
T	T	F	F	T	F	F	T	F	F
T	F	F	T	F	T	T	T	F	F
F	T	T	F	F	T	T	T	F	F
F	F	T	T	F	T	T	F	T	T

The shaded parts of this truth table prove their equivalence by showing that (*a*) $\sim(p \bullet q)$ and $(\sim p \vee \sim q)$ have identical truth values under the same truth conditions, and (*b*) $\sim(p \vee q)$ and $\sim p \bullet \sim q$ too have the identical truth-values under the same truth conditions. Even intuitively, if we ponder over what we learnt in Section 5.8 about translation of 'not both', i.e., $\sim(p \bullet q)$, we find that it is equivalent to saying 'either *not this* or *nor that*' i.e., $\sim p \vee \sim q$. Similarly, when we think about 'neither nor' i.e., $\sim(p \vee q)$, we find that it is equivalent to saying '*not this* and *not that*', i.e., $\sim p \bullet \sim q$. De Morgan's theorems certify these intuitions as correct.

The **Commutation Rule** also gives two equivalences:

1. $(p \vee q) \equiv (q \vee p)$
2. $(p \bullet q) \equiv (q \bullet p)$

The rule tells us that when the main connective in a statement is either a '∨' or a '•', the order of the components is *reversible* without any change in the truth value of the statement. A truth table can easily show their equivalences. However, even without a truth table, we can intuitively understand their legitimacy. If it is true that "either Joy or Tulip will come", then so is "either Tulip or Joy will come", and vice versa. Similarly, if it is true that "Tulip and Joy will come", then so is "Joy and Tulip will come", and vice versa.

It is important to remember that the commutation of order holds only for the '∨' and '•' statements. Intuitively, it also holds for the '≡', though the Commutation Rules do not cover it. However, commutation does *not* hold for '⊃'. For example, the statement "If you pay me the price, then I give you the merchandise" for obvious reasons is not equivalent to the statement "If I give you the merchandise, then you pay me the price".

Here is a simple example which shows the application of both of De. M. and Com. Rules:

Example 14

1. $\sim(B \vee D)$ $/\therefore \sim D$
2. $\sim B \bullet \sim D$ 1, **De. M.**
3. $\sim D \bullet \sim B$ 2, **Com.**
4. $\sim D$ 3, Simp.

Association (Assoc.) and Distribution (Dist.)

The **Association Rule** tells us that when we have compound statements formed only by repeated occurrences of '$\vee$', twice or thrice, the parentheses can be moved to make alternative groups of components without altering the truth value of the statement. Similarly, when we have compound statements formed only by repeated occurrences of '$\bullet$', the parentheses can be moved. So, the Association Rule certifies that a statement $[p \vee (q \vee r)]$ can become $[(p \vee q) \vee r]$ and vice versa; and $[p \bullet (q \bullet r)]$ can become $[(p \bullet q) \bullet r]$ without any loss in the truth-value. Since this is intuitively obvious, we do not need a truth-table test to prove its legitimacy.

As before, the Association Rule does not hold for compound statements formed by repeated occurrences of '$\supset$'. It does *not* attest the move from $C \supset (D \supset E)$ to $(C \supset D) \supset E$, for these two statements are not equivalent.

The **Distribution Rule** is another powerful rule that shows that a conjunction statement, which has a disjunction as a component is equivalent to a disjunction which has one conjunct distributed over each of the two disjuncts. In other words, $[p \bullet (q \vee r)] \equiv [(p \bullet q) \vee (p \bullet r)]$. Similarly, in $[p \vee (q \bullet r)] \equiv [(p \vee q) \bullet (p \vee r)]$, it is seen that, how a disjunction statement, which has a conjunction as a component, is equivalent to a conjunction which has one disjunct distributed over each of the two conjuncts. The two equivalent argument forms show that when a conjunction is distributed it becomes a conjunction; and when a disjunction is distributed the result is a conjunction. The application of this rule has a similarity to how a multiplication operates. The main connective, '$\bullet$' or '$\vee$', becomes the sub-connective within the components, and the sub-connective becomes the main connective.

The following is an example of how these two rules can be put to use along with a few others that we have already learnt:

Example 15

1. $\sim[L \vee (\sim M \vee N)]$ $/\therefore (N \vee L) \vee \sim(N \vee \sim M)$
2. $\sim[(L \vee \sim M) \vee N]$ **1, Assoc.**

3. $\sim(L \vee \sim M) \bullet \sim N$	2, De. M.
4. $(\sim L \bullet \sim\sim M) \bullet \sim N$	3, De. M.
5. $(\sim L \bullet M) \bullet \sim N$	4, D.N.
6. $\sim L \bullet M$	5, Simp.
7. $(\sim L \bullet M) \vee N$	6, Add
8. $N \vee (\sim L \bullet M)$	7, Com
9. $(N \vee \sim L) \bullet (N \vee M)$	8, **Dist**

Note that, in Example 15, though on lines 6 and 7 we have used the same rule De. M. on different parts of the statement, we have used two separate lines for each application of the rule. In general, the rule of thumb is to use one rule at a time and one application at a time.

Double Negation (D.N.)

The double negation rule tells us that *any* statement is equivalent to the negation of its negation, and vice versa. In a bi-valued system, this means that a true statement is equivalent to the claim of falsity of its falsity. Since this is one of the most intuitive rules, we shall not test it by truth table and shall move on to the discussion of the other rules.

Transposition (Trans.) and Material Implication (Impl.)

The **Transposition** and the **Material Implication Rules** are particularly useful for situations involving conditional statements. The Transposition rule (or Trans.) says that a conditional statement is equivalent to a conditional which has its antecedent and consequent in reverse positions with a negation sign attached to each. So, also, obviously, $(\sim q \supset \sim p) \equiv (p \supset q)$; for, $(\sim q \supset \sim p)$ is equivalent to $(\sim\sim p \supset \sim\sim q)$ which, by the Double Negation Rule, is equivalent to $(p \supset q)$.

The Material Implication Rule (Impl.) holds good only for the truth-functional '$\supset$' statements. It shows how a '$\supset$' statement is convertible into a disjunction and a disjunction is convertible into a material implication. The confirmation of this rule $(p \supset q) \equiv (\sim p \vee q)$ comes from the truth table of '$\supset$' itself. Thus, $(p \supset q)$ is true if and only if either p is false or q is true, or both.

The following derivation shows how these rules can be used on conditional statements and utilized for the benefit of the derivation:

Example 16

1. $C \supset (A \bullet \sim B)$
2. $\sim C \supset A$ $\quad /\therefore (A \bullet \sim B) \vee A$
3. $\sim A \supset \sim\sim C$ **2, Trans.**
4. $\sim A \supset C$ 3, D.N.
5. $\sim A \supset (A \bullet \sim B)$ 4, 1, H.S.
6. $\sim\sim A \vee (A \bullet \sim B)$ **5, Impl.**
7. $A \vee (A \bullet \sim B)$ 6, D.N.
8. $(A \bullet \sim B) \vee A$ 7, Com.

Material Equivalence (Equiv.), Exportation (Exp.), and Tautology (Taut.)

The **Material Equivalence (Equiv.) Rule** simply states the truth conditions of a materially equivalent statement. $p \equiv q$ is true *iff* both p implies q and q implies p; and that is captured by the statement $(p \equiv q) \equiv [(p \supset q) \bullet (q \supset p)]$. Another way to put it is, $p \equiv q$ is true when both of p and q are true together or false together, and that is captured by the statement $(p \equiv q) \equiv [(p \bullet q) \vee (\sim p \bullet \sim q)]$.

The **Exportation Rule (Exp.)** gives expression to the intuitive idea that, if both p and q together imply r, then p implies that if q then r. The reverse is also true. If it is true that you have to have a visa and a ticket to fly to Amsterdam, then it follows that if you have a visa, then if you have a ticket then you can fly to Amsterdam, and vice versa.

The two equivalences that come under the **Tautology Rule** help reduce the size of a statement by eliminating redundant statements. For example, $A \supset \sim A$ can be reduced to $\sim A$ as is shown by the proof below:

Example 17

1. $A \supset \sim A \ /\therefore \sim A$
2. $\sim A \vee \sim A$ 1, Impl
3. $\sim A$ **2, Taut.**

Given below is another proof which shows how all three of these rules, along with others, can be used in a derivation:

Example 18

1. $(\sim K \bullet P) \equiv (\sim P \vee R)$ $\quad /\therefore (\sim K \bullet P) \supset R$
2. $[(\sim K \bullet P) \supset (\sim P \vee R)] \bullet [(\sim P \vee R) \supset (\sim K \bullet P)]$ **1, Equiv.**
3. $(\sim K \bullet P) \supset (\sim P \vee R)$ 2, Simp.
4. $\sim K \supset [P \supset (P \vee R)]$ **3, Exp.**

5. $\sim K \supset [P \supset (P \supset R)]$	**4, Impl.**
6. $\sim K \supset [(P \bullet P) \supset R)]$	**5, Exp.**
7. $\sim K \supset (P \supset R)$	**6, Taut.**
8. $(\sim K \bullet \supset P) \supset R$	**7, Exp.**

EXERCISE 8.4

A. For each of the following, for every line in the proof that is *not* marked as a premise with a letter P, provide the justification by mentioning *which lines* were used to derive it and *which* Rule of Replacement or Rule of Inference was used.

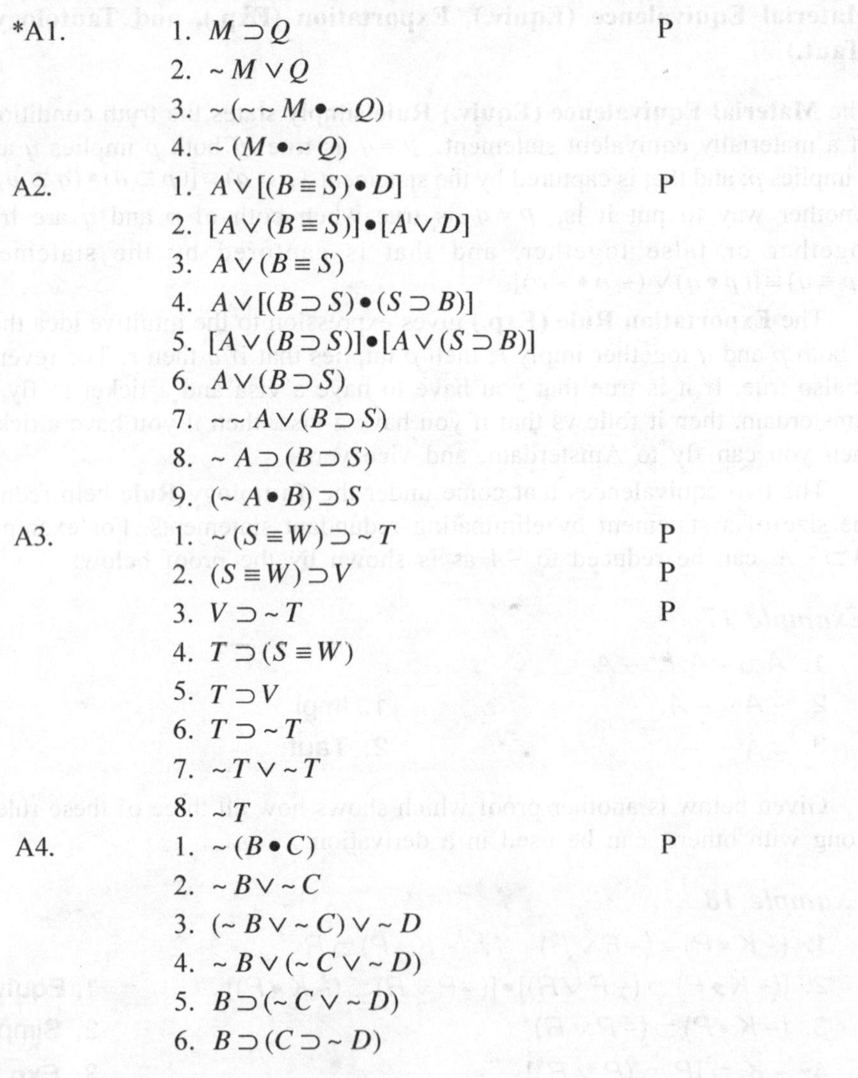

*A1.	1. $M \supset Q$	P
	2. $\sim M \vee Q$	
	3. $\sim(\sim\sim M \bullet \sim Q)$	
	4. $\sim (M \bullet \sim Q)$	
A2.	1. $A \vee [(B \equiv S) \bullet D]$	P
	2. $[A \vee (B \equiv S)] \bullet [A \vee D]$	
	3. $A \vee (B \equiv S)$	
	4. $A \vee [(B \supset S) \bullet (S \supset B)]$	
	5. $[A \vee (B \supset S)] \bullet [A \vee (S \supset B)]$	
	6. $A \vee (B \supset S)$	
	7. $\sim\sim A \vee (B \supset S)$	
	8. $\sim A \supset (B \supset S)$	
	9. $(\sim A \bullet B) \supset S$	
A3.	1. $\sim (S \equiv W) \supset \sim T$	P
	2. $(S \equiv W) \supset V$	P
	3. $V \supset \sim T$	P
	4. $T \supset (S \equiv W)$	
	5. $T \supset V$	
	6. $T \supset \sim T$	
	7. $\sim T \vee \sim T$	
	8. $\sim T$	
A4.	1. $\sim (B \bullet C)$	P
	2. $\sim B \vee \sim C$	
	3. $(\sim B \vee \sim C) \vee \sim D$	
	4. $\sim B \vee (\sim C \vee \sim D)$	
	5. $B \supset (\sim C \vee \sim D)$	
	6. $B \supset (C \supset \sim D)$	

*A5. 1. $W \equiv X$ P
2. $W \vee X$ P
3. $(W \bullet X) \vee (\sim W \bullet \sim X)$
4. $[(W \bullet X) \vee \sim W] \bullet [(W \bullet X) \vee \sim X]$
5. $[\sim W \vee (W \bullet X)] \bullet [(W \bullet X) \vee \sim X]$
6. $[W \supset (W \bullet X)] \bullet [(W \bullet X)] \vee \sim X]$
7. $W \supset (W \bullet X)$

B. Prove the validity of the following arguments by constructing a formal derivation. You may use both the Rules of Inference and the Rules of Replacement:

*B1. 1. $\sim L \vee M$
2. $\sim N \supset \sim M$ $/ \therefore L \supset N$

B2. 1. $(A \supset B) \bullet (C \supset B)$
2. $D \supset (A \vee C)$
3. D $/ \therefore B$

B3. 1. $(G \bullet H) \vee (I \bullet J)$
2. $G \supset \sim G$ $/ \therefore I$

B4. $S \supset L$ $/ \therefore S \supset (L \vee W)$

*B5. $J \supset (K \supset L)$ $/ \therefore K \supset (J \supset L)$

B6. 1. $P \vee (\sim Q \vee P)$
2. $Q \vee (\sim P \vee Q)$ $/ \therefore (P \bullet Q) \vee (\sim P \bullet \sim Q)$

B7. $O \supset (R \bullet S)$ $/ \therefore O \supset R$

B8. $(U \vee V) \supset W$ $/ \therefore U \supset W$

B9. 1. $X \supset Y$
2. $X \supset Z$ $/ \therefore X \supset (Y \bullet Z)$

*B10. 1. $\sim K \vee (J \equiv B)$
2. $\sim K \supset K$ $/ \therefore (B \supset J) \bullet K$

8.5 Strategic Tips for Doing Derivations

By now you are probably aware of the fact that formal derivations are somewhat like puzzles. As in the case of puzzles, there is no one way to solve them or there is no algorithm to solve them. So, often the problem could be a 'starting problem', i.e., where to start from. Also, like puzzles, solving formal derivations requires some strategic planning. Though the conclusion is provided, its derivation may not be obvious from the premises. However, like puzzles, the premises may supply some clues. And the rules of inference and replacement indicate the permissible moves. Together, they permit many possibilities. Thus, there are many available steps to take at any given point in a proof, but *not all of them may be helpful for reaching the conclusion ultimately*. So, there is need for pruning. You have to learn to foresee which steps are redundant, which lead to nowhere after a while and which would be productive in the long run. Overall, you need to formulate some kind of a strategy right from the beginning of the proof. As your strategies become better, you become better at formal derivations.

Some general suggestions are given here so that you can use them for your next set of exercises. Of course, as you work on the derivation problems, you will find out what works for you, and you are going to develop some of your own strategy. Nonetheless, these are given here to get you started.

1. ✓ Know your rules well: Perhaps, the most important point is to *know your rules well enough*. With 9 Rules of Inference and 10 Rules of Replacement, altogether you have 19 rules. Merely memorizing them will *not* do. Mastery over the rules requires you to *understand* what they actually empower you to do.

2. ✓ Goal analysis: In a derivation, the given conclusion only tells you where you need to be. In the derivation, however, you will have to ask yourself *what you need in order to get there*. This is known as *goal analysis*. The conclusion that you are supposed to derive is the target or the goal, and we have to look for intermediate steps which will lead us closer to this goal. The intermediate steps thus will be our sub-goals, derivation each of which will bring us to the conclusion.

This is where the rules help. You have to learn how to put them to use to get what you want. Knowing the rules well will give you a clearer picture of what you can possibly do at any stage in the derivation. It will also save time and number of moves you need to make. For example, in the following simple example, you can derive $\sim C \vee \sim E$ quickly if you realize what **M.T.** can do for you. Consider:

1. $(C \bullet E) \supset \sim (B \vee A)$		
2. $B \vee A$	$/ \therefore \sim C \vee \sim E$	
3. $\sim\sim (B \vee A)$		2, D.N.
4. $\sim (C \bullet E)$		1, 3, M.T.
5. $\sim C \vee \sim E$		4, De. M.

If, on the other hand, your acquaintance with the rule base is not so close, you might do something like the following which reaches the same conclusion but takes a few more steps and more time:

1. $(C \bullet E) \supset \sim (B \vee A)$		
2. $B \vee A$	$/ \therefore \sim C \vee \sim E$	
3. $\sim\sim (B \vee A) \supset \sim (C \bullet E)$		1, Trans.
4. $(B \vee A) \supset \sim (C \bullet E)$		3, D.N.

5. $\sim(C \bullet E)$ 4, 2, M.P.
6. $\sim C \vee \sim E$ 5, De. M.

Since this was a simple derivation, the number of steps did not really matter. However, in longer and more complicated proofs, it may create a significant difference.

3. ✓ Which rule to apply? The next tip is to look out for argument forms and find out which rules they correspond to. Look into *every premise* for fresh information. Find out the main connective in the statement and also pay close attention to the sub-connectives within the components. This is a sound strategy if you want to know your options. If, for example, you find that the main connective is '⊃', you immediately know that **M.P., M.T., H.S., Trans**. are among the possibilities. Since '⊃' is easily convertible into '∨', there are also possibilities of applying **D.S.** and **Impl.**

4. ✓ Elimination of the extra: Next, try to reduce the 'excess baggage'. In a derivation, you will often find many premises offering lot of information. If you consider the conclusion as the target, then anything that is not related to the conclusion or does not help to get at it is superfluous. Also, the links which help us to get closer to the conclusion, *after* they have been utilized, become redundant in the proof. So, use rules to clean up the unnecessary details so that the conclusion comes into sharper focus. For example, when some statement occurs at two different places, look for the possibilities to use **H.S.** to eliminate some common term. **Simp.** works very well on conjunctions for eliminating unnecessary items. Sometimes, application of **Equiv.** opens up the possibility of using **Simp.** to remove the clutter as may be seen in the following example:

1. $[E \vee (\sim D \supset H)] \equiv [\sim G \vee (H \vee K)]$
2. $\sim G \bullet \sim E$ $\quad /\therefore \sim D \supset H$
3. $\{[E \vee (\sim D \supset H)] \supset [\sim G \vee (H \vee K)]\} \bullet \{[G \vee (\sim H \vee K)] \supset [E \vee (\sim D \supset H)]\}$ 1, Equiv.
4. $\{[\sim G \vee (H \vee K)] \supset [E \vee (\sim D \supset H)]\} \bullet \{[E \vee (\sim D \supset H)] \supset [\sim G \vee (H \vee K)]\}$ 3, Com.
5. $[\sim G \vee (H \vee K)] \supset [E \vee (\sim D \supset H)]$ **4, Simp.**

The **Simp.** move in line 5, which removes a large chunk of statement letters, would not have been possible without the **Equiv.** step on line 3. The derivation, of course, does not stop at line 5. However, it comes closer to the conclusion with the removal of the excess 'baggage' as can be seen from the remaining steps below:

6. $\sim G$ **2, Simp.**
7. $\sim G \vee (H \vee K)$ 6, Add.
8. $E \vee (\sim D \supset H)$ 5, 7, M.P.
9. $\sim E \bullet \sim G$ 2, Com.

10. $\sim E$ 9, Simp.
11. $\sim D \supset H$ 8, 10, D.S.

5. ✓ Attention to the details: It is always advisable to pay close attention to the single atomic statement letters or negations of single statement letter. These often become handy to make the crucial moves. On line 6 above, the occurrence of $\sim G$ by **Simp.** made it possible to detach $E \vee (\sim D \supset H)$ on line 8 by M.P. Similarly, the occurrence of $\sim E$ helped us to finally reach our destination.

6. ✓ Back calculation: As a strategy, the importance of *working back from the conclusion* perhaps cannot be emphasized enough. The conclusion in a given derivation is the fixed target. When you are in a dilemma about how to start or where to start from, use the conclusion to ask yourself what you need to get at the conclusion and what you already have in the premises. This kind of thinking eventually has to be done *before* you actually start writing the proof.

We can take the previous proof as a case in point. At the starting point, we had:

1. $[E \vee (\sim D \supset H)] \equiv [\sim G \vee (H \vee K)]$
2. $\sim G \bullet \sim E$ $/\therefore \sim D \supset H$

Your question should be: How to get to $\sim D \supset H$? You can see that it is there in $E \vee (\sim D \supset H)$ on the left-hand side of premise 1. If you can get $E \vee (\sim D \supset H)$ isolated somehow, then you can get at $\sim D \supset H$. However, you will need to cancel E. Since $E \vee (\sim D \supset H)$ is a disjunction, the best rule to apply in that case to cancel E will be **D.S.** However, for application of D.S., you will need $\sim E$. If you look at premise 2, you will find that $\sim E$ is already there. All it needs is **Com.** and **Simp.** steps. Therefore, since you have found a way to get $\sim E$, at this point, your immediate goal is how to get $E \vee (\sim D \supset H)$.

If we write this backward calculation, then it may look somewhat like the following:

1. $[E \vee (\sim D \supset H)] \equiv [\sim G \vee (H \vee K)]$
2. $\sim G \bullet \sim E$ $/\therefore \sim D \supset H$
3. How do I get $\sim D \supset H$? **From $[E \vee (\sim D \supset H)]$**
4. How do I cancel the E in $[E \vee (\sim D \supset H)]$? **D.S. is a possibility**
5. How do I get a '$\sim E$' for D.S.? **From premise 2, by Com. and Simp.**
6. So, how to get $[E \vee (\sim D \supset H)]$? **...**

Similarly, working from backward would show you that you can get $[E \vee (\sim D \supset H)]$ from premise 1 if the equivalence can be broken down to parts. Equivalence Rule allows for two ways of breaking an equivalent statement down. However, you should realize that the conjunction form makes your job easier. For, you can then apply **Simp.** to chop off the extra parts that you do not need.

However, even after breaking down the equivalence, you have the statement:

$$\{[E \vee (\sim D \supset H)] \supset [\sim G \vee (H \vee K)]\}$$
$$\bullet\{[\sim G \vee (H \vee K)] \supset [E \vee (\sim D \supset H)]\} \qquad \text{1, Equiv.}$$

Which part do you eliminate and, more importantly, why? This is where you need to ask yourself: with what I have, which of the options lead me to the conclusion? You will find that if you retain $\{[E \vee (\sim D \supset H)] \supset [\sim G \vee (H \vee K)]\}$, you do not have any legitimate way to take $[E \vee (\sim D \supset H)]$. On the other hand, you have some possibility of **M.P.** application if you retain $\{[\sim G \vee (H \vee K)] \supset [E \vee (\sim D \supset H)]\}$. For, premise 2 shows that you already have '$\sim G$', and it should occur to you that from there it is a simple **Add.** step to get $\sim G \vee (\sim H \vee K)$.

As a beginner, you may not realize the power of the **Addition Rule**. As a result, you do not notice the chance of using it, or when you see the chance, you do not feel confident to use it. So, some of you may get stuck at $\sim G$ and may not see how from there you can get to $\sim G \vee (H \vee K)$. May be you would not even think about **Add**. These stumbling blocks, however, will go away as you practice more. Initially, you should get to know the rules well and have your focus on where you have to reach to use these rules.

If you are completely stuck with a derivation, as it may happen often, just keep trying. Try with different premises. Try breaking them down. As long as you are following the rules, and deriving consequences validly, your efforts are worth a lot.

Here is a slightly difficult proof:

1. $(J \supset \sim K) \bullet \sim L$
2. $K \supset (\sim J \supset L)$ $\quad /\therefore \sim K$

Since there is no other move possible, we shall try the simplest move namely, we shall use Simp. on the first line and isolate the components for further use:

3. $.(J \supset \sim K)$ — 1, Simp.
4. $\sim L \bullet .(J \supset \sim K)$ — 1, Com.
5. $\sim L$ — 4, Simp.

The '$\sim L$' on line 5 seems promising provided we can use it for M.T. on line 2. However, before that, line 2 needs some rearrangement by the Exportation Rule in the following way:

6. $(K \bullet \sim J) \supset L$ — 2, Exp.

Then we use the M.T. on it:

7. $\sim(K \bullet \sim J)$	6, 5, M.T.

This gives us a lead about how to get rid of '~J' by De. M. and D.N, and H.S.:

8. $\sim K \vee \sim\sim J$	7, De. M.
9. $\sim K \vee J$	8, D.N.
10. $K \supset J$	9, Impl.
11. $K \supset \sim K$	10, 3, H.S.

The rest should be a further contraction by the rules of Impl. and Taut.:

12. $\sim K \vee \sim K$	11, Impl.
13. $\sim K$	12, Taut.

EXERCISE 8.5

Construct a formal proof of validity or a formal derivation to establish the validity of the following arguments, in each case using the given symbols:

***1.** If it does not rain and the sky is clear, then we can go for either swimming or biking. If it does not rain then if we go for swimming, then we have to take the van. There is no rain and the sky is clear. We shall not go for biking. Hence, we shall take the van. (R, C, S, B, V)

2. If the Chennai supplier agrees, then the merchandise can be offloaded at Mumbai. Either we order for an additional supply if Chennai supplier does not agree, or we can call up Ernakulam. Faizabad has been already asked and we cannot call up Ernakulam. Provided the merchandise can be offloaded at Mumbai, the demurrage cost will be saved. So, either the demurrage cost will be saved or we order for an additional supply. (C, M, A, E, F, D)

3. If the monsoon is normal, then if the seeds are sown at the right time, then there will be a good harvest. If the seeds are sown at the right time, then people will be happy if there is a good harvest. Therefore, if the monsoon is normal, then if the seeds are sown at the right time, then people will be happy. (N, S, H, P)

4. If exams are held on time then the grades will be out on time, and if a fixed calendar has to be followed then the calendar has to be prepared before the academic year starts. If grades will be out on time, then transcripts can be sent out on time, and if the calendar has to be prepared before the academic year starts, then the work needed for the current year will get delayed. If transcripts can be sent out on time, then the work needed for the current year will not get delayed. If exams are held on time, then a fixed calendar has to be followed. Hence, the exams will not be held on time. (E, G, F, P, T, W)

***5.** If the allotments are irregular, then if the petrol pump ownership decisions were made during the Petroleum Minister's tenure, then an expert panel has to be formed. If both an expert panel is formed and a report is submitted, then the Supreme Court will look into the case. If the distribution does not link the Petroleum Minister, then a report is submitted but the Supreme Court will not look into the case. Therefore, if the allotments are irregular, then the distribution links the Petroleum Minister if the petrol pump ownership decisions were made during the Petroleum Minister's tenure. (I, O, E, R, S, D)

6. If either the law is toned down or foreign direct investments are allowed on new ventures, then both European and Japanese firms will become interested. If either the Japanese firms become interested or the domestic industry gets extra protection, then the transnationals will be able to start ventures in the domestic soil. But the transnationals will not be able to start ventures in the domestic soil and the European firms will not become interested. So, neither the law will be toned down nor foreign direct investments will be allowed to start new ventures. (L, F, E, J, D, T)

7. If a faster growth is desired, then production has to increase and the cities will grow richer. However, if economic growth for all sections of society is desired, then the rate of economic growth will be much slower. Either a faster growth is desired or an economic growth for all sections of society is desired. Given that the cities will grow richer if the rate of economic growth will not be much slower, then one has to pay attention to Agriculture. Therefore, either one has to pay attention to Agriculture or economic growth for all sections of society is not desired. (F, P, C, G, R, A)

8. If I leave for Copenhagen today, then if I have to travel to the city centre, then I need a map. If I need a map and an address, then I have to call the office. If I have to travel only upto the hospital, then I need an address but I do not have to call the office. So, if I leave for Copenhagen today, then if I have to travel to the city centre, I do not have to travel only upto the hospital. (L, C, M, A, O, H)

9. If he attends the conference, then he must book his flight now. If he books his flight now, then either he will not be able to change the date of his travel or he will not be able to change the time of his travel. If he will not be able to change the time of his travel, then he has to pay the hotel now. But he cannot pay the hotel now, and he has to change the date of his travel. So, he will not attend the conference. (C, B, D, T, H)

***10.** If you remember bringing the key back, then the key is in the house and is safe. If the key is in the house, then it will be found. Given that if the reports of everyone are reliable, then no key has been sighted, and it will not be found. If the key is in the house, then you remember bringing the key back and the reports of everyone are not reliable. So, if the key is in the house, then the reports of everyone are not reliable. (R, H, S, F, E, K)

11. If either the book or the review is found, then we can cite the source. Therefore, if the book is found, we can cite the source. (B, R, C)

12. If I go to office then I stay till late, and if I go to market then I shall be able to pick up some vegetables. Either I go to office or I go to market. If I go to office, I shall not be able to pick up some vegetables, and if I go to market then I do not stay till late. If either I am not able to pick up some vegetables or I do not stay till late, then I shall order food from outside. If either I stay till late or I am able to pick up some vegetables, then I shall make the dinner myself. Therefore, either I shall order food from outside or I shall make the dinner myself. (O, L, M, V, F, D)

13. Either the river has overflowed, or the rain is continuous and the fields are flooded. If the river has overflowed, then the floodgates must be open and if the flood gates are open, then the fields are flooded. So, the fields are flooded. (R, C, F, O)

14. If the cafeteria is empty then we sit at the cafeteria, and if we go outside, then we go for bowling. Either the cafeteria is empty or we go outside. If the cafeteria is empty, then we don't go for bowling, and if we go outside, then we do not sit at the cafeteria. So, we sit at the cafeteria *iff* we don't go for bowling. (E, S, O, B)

***15.** If taxes are raised, then revenue will be generated. However, if unemployment increases, then people will be unhappy. So, if taxes are raised and unemployment increases, then revenue will be generated but people will be unhappy. (T, R, U, P)

16. If Patel wins the nomination, then campaign will be well financed, and if Desai gets the nomination, then victory will be assured. Therefore, if either Patel or Desai gets the nomination, either the campaign will be well financed or victory will be assured. (P, C, D, V)

17. If the course content is interesting and either the teaching is good or the exams are good, then both the teaching and the exams are good. So, if the course content is interesting, then if the teaching is good, the exams are good. (C, T, E)

18. You do not go to the wedding; if you go to the wedding *iff* your relatives are not there. It is not the case that either you do not go to the wedding or your relatives are there. So, you do not go to the wedding. (W, R)

19. If people want, then a re-election will be called. If a re-election is called and people vote freely, then order will be restored. Therefore, if people vote freely, then if people want, order will be restored. (W, R, V, O)

20. If I plant roses, then my garden will need a lot of care. If I plant marigolds, then my garden will bloom early. So, if I plant either roses or marigolds, then my garden will either need a lot of care or will bloom early. (R, C, M, E)

8.6 Indirect Proof

A more advanced derivation requires more powerful proof procedures. Also, certain valid arguments cannot be proved valid only with the 19 rules we have mentioned. Consider, for example:

$A \qquad / \therefore B \vee (B \supset C)$

In this section and in Section 8.7, we shall discuss two additional proof procedures which make our formal derivation procedure more powerful and complete, namely, the Indirect Proof and the Conditional Proof.

The **Indirect Proof (I.P.)**, as its name suggests, is a proof procedure that establishes the validity of an argument indirectly. It does not show how a given conclusion can be directly derived. Rather, it allows us to assume the *negation* of the given conclusion as an extra premise in the argument. Consider for example the following:

Example 19

1. $D \vee (M \bullet N)$
2. $D \supset N \qquad / \therefore N$

If you want to apply the I.P. procedure, then on line 3, you can add the negation of the conclusion, namely, $\sim N$, as an extra premise.

3. $\sim N$

On line 3, you can indicate this addition of an extra premise and also the kind of proof procedure you have opted for in two ways: Either by announcing the proof procedure as part of the justification on the right, in the following manner:

3. $\sim N$	I.P.

or by a bent arrow on the left and by asserting in the justification that it is an additional or assumed premise (A.P.), for example:

↦ 3. $\sim N$	**A.P.**

We shall follow here the *bent arrow format.* Then, from the original premises *and* the negated conclusion, we need to derive an explicit or obvious contradiction of the form $p \bullet \sim p$ by the use of the rules of inference and replacement that we have learnt. Consider the following:

4. $\sim D$	**2, 3, M.T.**
5. $M \bullet N$	**1, 4, D.S.**
6. $N \bullet M$	**5, Com.**
7. N	**6, Simp.**
8. $N \bullet \sim N$	**7, 3, Conj.**

Line 8 is an **explicit contradiction.** Thus, it establishes that the conjunction of the original premises *and* the negated conclusion cannot be right and, in fact, the negated conclusion must be false. Hence, it claims that the original, unnegated conclusion, namely *N*, must follow from the premises.

Note that the contradiction could be drawn because we assumed a new premise. So, all the lines from lines 3 to 8 are under that assumption. This is what we indicate by a bent arrow on the line where the assumption starts, namely, on line 3 in this case, and we continue the straight line ensuing from the bent arrow on the left side of the lines as a reminder of the assumption. Note the straight line on the left side of the proof.

Now, the additional premise that we assumed on line 3 using I.P. can be discharged, or withdrawn, having shown that the assumption leads to a contradiction. We indicate the withdrawal or the discharge of the assumption by drawing a horizontal line and by placing the original conclusion on a new line.

9. N	3-8, I.P.

Note that the justification refers to the technique I.P., and includes all the lines as a hyphenated block that are within the **scope of the assumption**. Instead of the usual way of referring to lines separated with a comma, e.g.,

'7, 3, conj', the end line of I.P. refers to the whole block which was derived with the additional premise as an assumption.

The scope of an assumption means the extent covered by it. *An assumption falls within its own scope.* For, it is the beginning point. It ends with the **discharge of the assumption** as indicated by the horizontal line. This is to say that the lines of proof under the horizontal line do *not* fall within the scope of the assumption.

The I.P. is also known as the **Reductio Ad Absurdum (R.A.A.)** method. For, it 'reduces' an assumption to an absurdity by showing that it implies a contradiction.

The general format for I.P. proofs, therefore, will be as follows where the conclusion let us suppose is q:

→ $\sim q$	A.P.
.	
.	
.	
$p \bullet \sim p$	
q	I.P.

Now, we can return to the argument that we started this section with:

1. A $\quad / \therefore\ B \vee (B \supset C)$

This strange argument is valid, because the conclusion is a tautology. However, since the premise is completely irrelevant to the conclusion, the straight derivation by the 19 rules does not help much. Now, it can be proved by the I.P. as follows:

1. A $\quad / \therefore\ B \vee (B \supset C)$	
→ 2. $(B \vee (B \supset C))$	A.P.
3. $. \sim (B \vee (\sim B \vee C))$	2, Impl.
4. $. \sim ((B \vee \sim B) \vee C)$	3, Assoc.
5. $. \sim (B \vee \sim B) \bullet \sim C$	4, De. M.
6. $. \sim (B \vee \sim B)$	5, Simp.
7. $B \bullet \sim B$	6, De. M.
8. $B \vee (B \supset C)$	2-7, I.P.

Note that the last line of proof does not fall within the scope of the assumption and thus does not depend on it.

EXERCISE 8.6

I. Prove the validity of each of the following, using the Indirect Proof technique. For the sake of comparison, you can construct a formal derivation for each and compare the length:

*1. 1. $R \supset (S \bullet T)$
2. $\sim S$ $\quad / \therefore \sim R$

2. 1. $J \vee B$
2. $J \vee \sim B$ $\quad / \therefore J$

3. 1. $D \supset (E \bullet F)$
2. $(E \vee G) \supset H$
3. $G \vee D$ $\quad / \therefore H$

4. 1. $(L \bullet M) \supset (N \bullet O)$
2. $M \supset \sim O$ $\quad / \therefore \sim L \vee \sim M$

*5. 1. $P \supset Q$
2. $R \supset P$
3. $R \vee (Q \bullet S)$ $\quad / \therefore Q$

6. 1. $(A \supset B) \bullet (C \supset D)$
2. $(B \supset F) \bullet (D \supset G)$
3. $A \vee C$ $\quad / \therefore (F \vee G)$

7. 1. $\sim H$
2. $(H \vee \sim L) \equiv L$
3. M $\quad / \therefore \sim (L \bullet M)$

8. 1. $S \supset (\sim U \supset \sim T)$
2. $S \supset T$
3. $\sim U \supset (S \vee V)$ $\quad / \therefore U \vee V$

9. 1. $(Z \vee \sim Z) \supset \sim (\sim X \bullet \sim Y)$
2. $(X \vee Y) \supset \sim V$ $\quad / \therefore \sim V$

*10. 1. $(R \vee N) \supset (P \bullet R)$
2. $N \supset P$
3. $\sim Q \supset (R \vee N)$ $\quad / \therefore Q \vee R$

8.7 Conditional Proof: Preliminary and Strengthened Version

A **Conditional Proof (C.P.)** is a proof that allows us to *assume* something that is not given as a premise or as true. In other words, using it we can add a premise as *assumed to be true*, and then we may try to derive the given conclusion. The derivation, however, will depend on this assumption; hence the proof will be *conditional* upon its truth. This is why the technique is called the conditional proof.

The procedure of conditional proof operates on the possibility: *what if '... ' were true?* We do not know that '...' is true, and the premises do not include it. However, we are entitled to explore: *suppose* that it is true, then what happens? The conditional proof allows us to work with that possibility for *a limited time* within the proof.

In order to separate the 'assumed to be true' premises from the given premises, we shall again follow *the bent arrow format*, as we did for the I.P. Just as we did for the I.P., the beginning of the assumption will be indicated by the bent arrow and the tail of the arrow will continue as a vertical line until we are ready to discharge the assumption by drawing a horizontal line.

However, you must remember that when you are withdrawing the assumption or discharging it, *you will always get a conditional statement back*. If you are starting out by assuming for example, 'what if *p*?', and then you have derived a conclusion, say *q*, once we withdraw or discharge the assumption in C.P. Then we shall get back a conditional of the form $p \supset q$, which has the assumption as its antecedent and the derived statement as its consequent. This makes sense intuitively. You asked 'what if *p*?', and whatever you inferred by assuming *p*, is conditional upon the fact that '*p*' is the case. Our format therefore will be as follows:

```
→ p            A.P.
  .
  .
  .
  q
─────────
p ⊃ q          C.P.
```

After discharge, the justification will include all the lines within the scope of the assumption as a block and refer to C.P. as the technique used.

Preliminary Version of C.P.

Now, you may ask, what do we assume in C.P.? The I.P. gave us a fixed starting point, namely, the negation of the given conclusion. But in C.P., what are we supposed to do? In the **preliminary version of C.P.**, the technique is supposed to be applied to only those arguments that have conditional statements as their conclusion. We are allowed to assume the *antecedent of the conclusion* to derive *the rest of the conclusion*. Consider the following example as an illustration:

Example 20

1.	$(A \vee B) \supset (C \bullet D)$	
2.	$(D \vee E) \supset F$ $/\therefore A \supset F$	
3.	→ A	A.P.
4.	$A \vee B$	3, Add.
5.	$C \bullet D$	1, 4, M.P.
6.	$D \bullet C$	5, Com.
7.	D	6, Simp.
8.	$D \vee E$	7, Add.
9.	F	2, 8, M.P.
10.	$A \supset F$	3-9, C.P.

The working principle in Example 20 is that, given a set of premises such as $\{p_1, p_2, \ldots, p_n\}$ and a conditional $q \supset r$ as a conclusion, using C.P. preliminary version, we can use 'q', the antecedent of the conclusion, as an assumed premise and then derive r from joint set of $\{p_1, p_2, \ldots, p_n\}$ and 'q'. The justification of this move can be found in the Exportation Rule which says: "$p \supset (q \supset r) \equiv (p \bullet q) \supset r$". If $\{p_1, p_2, \ldots, p_n\}$, then $q \supset r$, and by Exportation, $(p \bullet q) \supset r$.

Note that in Example 20 after line 3, our target is no longer to derive $A \supset F$. After assuming A, the goal is now to derive 'F', the remaining part of the conclusion. We have worked towards that end from lines 4–8 using the usual 19 rules. On line 9, when we have reached that target, we let go of the assumption by drawing a line. Because we started out with A as our assumption and have derived F on the basis of that assumption, by discharging the assumption we get back a conditional $A \supset F$ on line 10, which happens to be our original conclusion and is not dependent on the assumed condition.

It is not necessary that in a single proof you can do only one C.P. procedure. If you wish, you can *nest* one C.P. within another. For instance, given below is a proof which has a conclusion in which one can easily find the opportunity to use C.P. twice. So, in it one C.P. can be *nested* inside another as follows:

Example 21

1. $A \supset (B \supset C)$
2. $B \supset (C \supset D)$ $/\therefore A \supset (B \supset D)$

3.	→ A	A.P.
4.	→B	A.P.
5.	$B \supset C$	1, 3, M.P.
6.	$C \supset D$	2, 4, M.P.
7.	$B \supset D$	5, 6, H.S.
8.	D	7, 4, M.P
9.	$B \supset D$	4–8, C.P.
10.	$A \supset (B \supset D)$	3-9, C.P.

In Example 21, first we assumed *A*, and within it we also assumed *B*. After the second C.P. assumption, our target was to derive *D*. Note that when we are making more than one assumption, their *order of discharge* should be: Last in, First out (LIFO). The most recent assumption must be discharged first and the initial assumption must be discharged last. We should see that the vertical lines on the left-hand side of the derivation, indicating the scope of each assumption, do not cross or intersect.

Note also that *each assumption has its own limited scope*. For the innermost assumption, the scope ends at line 8. Line 9 is not within its scope. However, the scope of the original assumption made on line 3 extends up to line 9, so it includes the innermost assumption and all the lines it has helped to produce. This fact is reflected in the justification of line 10. Ultimately, however, all assumptions are limited in scope. They must all be terminated before the end of the proof.

It is important for you to remember that once an assumed premise is discharged, *we can no longer use it or use any line that depends on it to derive other new lines*. On line 9 of Example 21, for instance, we do not have any access to lines 4–8 any longer, as the assumption of line 4 has been discharged. All you will get to use is the conditional that comes to you as the result of the discharge.

You can make *any* number of assumptions, as long as each assumption is eventually discharged properly. *Proper discharging will always give you back a conditional.* And all assumptions that you make must be discharged before the proof ends, i.e., before the last line of the proof.

Strengthened Version of C.P.

The **strengthened version of C.P.** applies to all kinds of arguments, even to those which do not have conditionals as their conclusions. It comes with a lot of freedom: you can assume *anything* you want for the sake of the proof. The assumed premise does not have to be a part of the conclusion. However, this freedom comes with certain responsibilities: as already mentioned, every assumption made must be discharged properly and before the end of the proof.

In deciding what you need to assume, you have to think strategically in terms of your conclusion. For, no matter what you assume, you will have to discharge it properly, and as you do that you will get a conditional back. So, you need to know how you can use that conditional before you allow yourself to start an assumption. Here is a simple example:

Example 22

1.	$A \supset B$	
2.	$[A \supset (A \bullet B)] \supset C \quad / \therefore C$	
3.	→ A	A.P.
4.	B	1, 3, M.P.
5.	$A \bullet B$	3, 4, Conj.
6.	$A \supset (A \bullet B)$	3–5, C.P.
7.	C	2, 6, M.P.

Note that the conclusion of Example 22 is not a conditional statement at all. Note also that what is assumed in this Example 22 has no direct link to the conclusion, but is crucial to derive it. The strategy was to use M.P. to detach C from the second premise. So, the target was to derive $A \supset (A \bullet B)$ first. However, the following simple valid argument cannot be proved valid by the 19 rules in our system:

1. $A \supset B \quad / \therefore A \supset (A \bullet B)$

This is where the C.P. makes a difference. In fact, we should take this example as the sign of the power of C.P. Without this additional proof procedure, we cannot reach "$A \supset (A \bullet B)$" in Example 22 from "$A \supset B$".

Examples such as this show why we are introducing C.P. or I.P. The fundamental reason is to make our deduction system complete, or bring more proofs within our reach: especially we want to bring those proofs which cannot be directly proved by the 19 rules of formal derivation within our power. With C.P., our deduction system is *complete* in the sense that we can prove every valid argument in propositional logic in this system.

Here is another example of using C.P. The premise is a conditional and so is the conclusion. However, we need to proceed with a strategy:

Example 23(a)

1. $(A \vee B) \supset [(C \vee D) \supset E]$ $/ \therefore A \supset [(C \bullet D) \supset E]$
2. A — A.P.
3. $C \bullet D$ — A.P.
4. $A \vee B$ — 2, Add.
5. $(C \vee D) \supset E$ — 1, 4, M.P.
6. C — 3, Simp.
7. $C \vee D$ — 6, Add.
8. E — 5, 7, M.P.
9. $(C \bullet D) \supset E$ — 3-8, C.P.
10. $A \supset [(C \bullet D) \supset E]$ — 2-9, C.P.

Note that ultimately you need the conditional $A \supset [(C \bullet D) \supset E]$. So, if you start out by assuming $A \vee B$, then after discharging you will get back a conditional like this: "$((A \vee B) \supset ...$", which will not serve your purpose. So, your choice in this case is to start with the assumption A. Then you can proceed to detach $[(C \vee D) \supset E]$ by M.P. from premise 1. However, you need $[(C \bullet D) \supset E]$ for your conclusion. This is where a second C.P. becomes useful as you can see on line 3. As a beginner, you may make the second assumption later in the proof as in the following example, and continue as shown in Example 23 (a):

Example 23(b)

1. $(A \vee B) \supset [(C \vee D) \supset E]$ $/ A \supset [(C \bullet D) \supset E]$
2. $\rightarrow$ A — A.P.
3. $(C \vee D) \supset E$ — 1, 2, M.P.
4. $\rightarrow$ $C \bullet D$ — A.P.

.

.

Either way, you are fine. When you are at an advanced level with derivations, you will know how many assumptions you need to make and in what order. So you can save a lot of steps by assuming them at the right point in the proof.

EXERCISE 8.7

Construct formal derivation for each of the following using strengthened version of Conditional Proof.

***1.** $C \supset D$ $/ \therefore [(D \supset E) \supset (C \supset E)]$

2. $(N \supset P) \bullet (B \supset S)$ $/ \therefore (N \bullet B) \supset (P \bullet S)$

3. $(A \supset B) \bullet (C \supset D)$ $/ \therefore (A \vee C) \supset (B \vee D)$

4. 1. $E \supset F$
2. $E \supset (F \supset G)$
3. $E \supset (G \supset H)$ $/ \therefore E \supset H$

***5.** 1. $P \supset (T \bullet S)$
2. $Q \supset (S \bullet W)$ $/ \therefore (\sim T \bullet \sim W) \supset (\sim P \bullet \sim Q)$

6. 1. $(L \vee M) \supset [(N \vee O) \supset (\sim P \bullet Q)]$
2. $(\sim P \vee \sim R) \supset S$ $/ \therefore L \supset (N \supset S)$

7. 1. $A \supset B$
2. $(\sim A \supset C) \vee E$
3. $D \bullet \sim E$
4. $B \supset F$ $/ \therefore F \vee C$

8. 1. $I \vee (J \supset K)$
2. $[J \supset (J \equiv K)] \supset (T \vee U)$
3. $(T \supset I) \bullet (U \supset L)$ $/ \therefore I \vee L$

9. 1. $[A \supset C)] \bullet [D \supset C)]$
2. $(E \supset A) \bullet (F \supset D)$
3. $B \supset (E \vee F)$ $/ \therefore B \supset C$

***10.** 1. $P \vee [(K \supset P) \bullet (Q \supset P)]$
2. $M \bullet (K \vee Q)$ $/ \therefore P$

8.8 Proof of Tautology

We said that our deduction system is now *complete*. This means that every valid argument in propositional logic now can be demonstrated in our system as having a proof. This includes the proofs of **theorems** or **tautologies** also. A theorem is a logical truth, and its truth is provable *without* any contingent premises as added information. Its truth is supposed to be provable from the rules of logic alone. This is why the proofs of theorems or tautologies are called **zero-premise proofs.**

In this section, we show how the zero-premise proofs can be worked out in our system for proving tautologies or theorems. So far, every proof that you have worked on had some premises that were given for you to start with. However, for reasons explained above, a tautology is not going to have any premises. Yet, we have to use the derivation procedure for them. This is where C.P. or I.P. becomes very helpful. For, both allow one to assume a premise that is not given. Consider, for example, the proof of the following tautology $A \supset (A \vee B)$:

Example 24

→	1. A	A.P.
	2. $A \vee B$	1, Add.
	3. $A \supset (A \vee B)$	1-2, C.P.

We can also use the I.P. technique for the proof of the same theorem as shown in the following example:

Example 25

→	1. $\sim [A \supset (A \vee B)]$	A.P.
	2. $\sim [\sim A \vee (A \vee B)]$	1, Impl.
	3. $\sim\sim A \bullet \sim (A \vee B)$	2, De. M.
	4. $\sim\sim A \bullet (\sim A \bullet \sim B)$	3, De. M.
	5. .$(\sim\sim A \bullet \sim A) \bullet \sim B$	4, Assoc.
	6. $\sim\sim A \bullet \sim A$	5, Simp.
	7. $A \supset (A \vee B)]$	1-6, I.P.

When the theorem or tautology is in the conditional form, as is the case in Example 24 and 25, the C.P. could be easier to apply. When the theorem is not in the conditional form, as in the case of $\sim (A \bullet \sim A)$, for example, the wisdom of I.P. can be used to make the best of the situation.

EXERCISE 8.8

1. Prove that the following are theorems or tautologies by C.P. or I.P.:

1. $X \supset (X \vee Y)$
2. $X \vee (X \supset Y)$
3. $(X \bullet Y) \supset X$
4. $(X \supset Y) \supset [(Y \supset Z) \supset (X \supset Z)]$

*5. $(X \supset Y) \supset [(X \bullet Z) \supset (Y \bullet Z)]$

6. $[(X \supset Y) \supset Y] \supset (X \vee Y)$
7. $(X \supset Y) \vee (Y \supset Z)$

8. $[(X \supset Y) \supset X] \supset X$
9. $(X \vee Y) \supset [Z \supset (X \vee Y)]$
10. $(X \vee Y) \supset [[(X \supset Z) \bullet (Y \supset Z)] \supset Z]$
11. $(X \vee Y) \supset [(X \supset Y) \vee (Y \supset X)]]$
12. $(X \equiv Y) \equiv (\sim X \equiv \sim Y)$
13. $\sim (X \vee Y) \supset \sim X$
14. $(X \supset Y) \vee (X \supset \sim Y)$
15. $X \equiv (X \vee (X \bullet Y))$

8.9 How to Avoid Common Errors

While doing proofs, it is common for beginners to make certain mistakes. I list some of them here so that you know what to avoid.

1. Overlooking negation signs or dropping negation signs. Though this could be a result of oversight as happens when one is in a hurry or is stressed, this is a serious error. This can change the proof entirely, particularly when you are dealing with rules such as De. M. The remedy for this is to pay more attention. Also, you need to be careful to understand that the '~' in the beginning of the statement makes the statement a negation.

2. Applying Rules of Inference to parts of statements. Remember that Rules of Inference such as D.S. or M.P. cannot be applied to fragments within the whole statement. No matter how tempting it may seem, you cannot use Simp. on the conjunction which is an inner component of a statement which is not a conjunction itself, as for example, $(A \bullet B) \vee C$.

3. Reliance on too few rules. The rule-base for this system has 19 rules. Get acquainted with all of them. Otherwise, a tendency develops to use those and only those rules with which you were earlier acquainted, such as De. M., Dist. This restricts your imagination and creativity as for as formal derivations are concerned. For example, learn about the powers of Add. or Taut.

4. Exporting rules that are not given. The deduction system that we are learning is a formal system. Like all other formal systems, it has its own set of rules which we have to comply to. Just because you are used to using a rule like "$1 \vee 0 = 1$" in a different context, you cannot assume that it will be applicable in this system. In fact, it is not part of our system. So, if your proof relies upon a step of that nature, then on that line you cannot refer to any rule from our rule-base. Thus, your proof becomes questionable in our system.

Keywords

Argument form: A form or structure composed only of statement variables and symbols such that all its substitution instances will be arguments.

Discharging the assumption: Ending or withdrawing an assumption when its truth is no longer being assumed as a maneuver within the proof. Indicated by a horizontal line.

Explicit contradiction: An obvious contradiction that is a substitution instance of the statement form $p \bullet \sim p$.

Formal derivation: A deductive proof procedure that establishes the validity of an argument by deducing the logical consequences from given premises by valid argument forms.

Invalid argument form: An argument form which has at least one invalid substitution instance.

Natural deduction: Same as formal derivation.

Reductio Ad Absurdum (R.A.A.): Proof technique of reducing an assumption to absurdity by deriving explicit contradiction from it. Same as the Indirect Proof or I.P.

Scope of an assumption: The extent or the limit of an assumption, or lines in the proof which depend upon the truth of the assumption. The scope of an assumption includes the assumption.

Theorem: A logical truth.

Truth-preserving: The characteristic of preservation of truth, such that if we start from truth, we shall never end at falsity.

Valid argument form: An argument form which has no invalid substitution instance.

CHAPTER

ARISTOTELIAN SYLLOGISTIC LOGIC

9.1 Reasons for Going beyond Propositional Logic

In earlier chapters we have learnt about propositional logic. It is time to we talked about the limitations that propositional logic has. So far, we have been talking about only one particular type of statements, namely, the truth-functional, and about how to do logic with them. The proof techniques that we have so far learnt for assessing validity, for example, apply *only* to those arguments whose validity depends on the way in which simple statements are combined into truth-functional compound statements. For this reason, we cannot make use of these to assess other kinds of arguments, which do not contain truth-functional statements.

The following example presents an argument, the assessment of which lies beyond the reach of the proof techniques that we have learnt.

Example 1

Salil believes that logic classes are boring, and he told me so. So, I believe logic classes are boring.

Both "Salil believes that logic classes are boring" and "I believe logic classes are boring" are non-truth-functional statements (see Section 5.5 of this book). Since Example 1 contains non-truth-functional statements as its components, it remains inaccessible. Similarly, there can be other kinds of arguments to which the application of propositional logic may fail for other kinds of reasons. This appears to be a significant loss, because among these there can be arguments whose validity may be obvious. Yet, the demonstration of their validity would not be possible within the boundaries of propositional logic. The following examples present two such arguments:

Example 2

1. All cats are mammals.
2. Garfield is a cat.
3. Therefore, Garfield is a mammal.

Example 3

1. No friend of mine lives in an army base.
2. Aniruddha lives in an army base.
3. Therefore, Aniruddha is not a friend of mine.

In both the cases, the truth of the conclusion follows from their respective premises, but we cannot prove their validity using propositional logic. The reason is that propositional logic takes the simple statement as the 'atom' or the further irreducible unit, whereas in the arguments in Examples 2 and 3, information has been given at the sub-sentential level or at a level which requires further decomposition of the simple statements. In Example 2, premise 1 is a structurally simple statement, but on analyzing it we find that it states a relationship between the 'cats' class and the 'mammals' class.

We need to access this class relationship for understanding what premise 1 claims. Premise 2 is also a structurally simple statement, but it asserts that Garfield is a member of the same 'cat' class which we know, by premise 1, as a part of the 'mammals' class. Only through the understanding of relationships mentioned in the premises, can we appreciate the validity of the argument in Example 2. However, propositional logic has no way to do that. Instead, if we wish to follow the propositional logic translation technique on Example 2, we may end up showing it as *invalid*! For, since its premises and the conclusion are different simple statements, propositional logic can at best represent the case by using a different sentence letter each time as follows:

1. A
2. C

$\therefore M$

It should be obvious that this translation does *not* do justice at all in capturing the validity of Example 2. For, given that translation, it is easy to show it as invalid by simply assigning 'T' to A and C, and 'F' to M. The point is, however, that propositional logic has no other option than this.

Similarly, in Example 3, logically important information is given *within* the premises, which are structurally simple statements. Processing the information requires some sort of decomposition or analysis of the simple statements, which is not possible in propositional logic.

The failure in cases like Examples 2 and 3 only shows that the logical reach of propositional logic has limitations. Propositional logic will fail to capture information, which may be logically significant if that information is given in the *sub-sentential structure* of the statement. This is the reason why the translation technique of propositional logic cannot capture the significance of any of the following statements:

Example 4

1. You cannot fool all the people all the time.
2. For Desdemona, there was no one but Othello.
3. Some historians are gifted writers whose writings read like novels.

In each of these cases, the statement does not contain any other statement as its component. Yet, there is enough information given within the statement which is available only if we allow ourselves to go deeper into the inner logical structure of a simple statement.

For reasons like these, we need to go beyond propositional logic. In what follows, we shall step out of propositional logic and look into logics that allow us to further analyze statements, both simple and compound, to access information given in their interior structure. Our first destination is **Aristotelian logic** of categories and syllogisms.

Note that though there are enough conceptually stimulating points to learn from it, in this book we shall not go into the details of Aristotelian logic. This chapter will only try to present a brief overview of it. Its purpose is to get you acquainted with Aristotelian logic so that you are somewhat prepared for the First Order Predicate Logic, which we shall start from Chapter 10. There are other sources from which you can learn more about Aristotelian logic. Some of the recent publications on Aristotelian logic are listed below.

Socratic Logic: A Logic Text Using Socratic Method, Platonic Questions, and Aristotelian Principles, Peter Kreeft and Trent Dougherty, St Augustine's Press, 2003, ISBN: 1890318892.

Aristotelian Formal and Material Logic, Pierre Conway, (Paperback), University Press of America, 1995, ISBN: 0819199060.

9.2 Class and Categories

Aristotelian logic was developed by Aristotle and later on by medieval logicians. It deals with the logic of **classes.** A **category** or, in Greek, *kategoria,* is a predicate; it is one of the fundamental classes of things that we make use of in our conceptual framework. Following Aristotle, we can roughly define a **class** as "a collection of objects" or "entities", but it is not a haphazard or random collection of members. The members of a class are supposed to have a *common characteristic* or *property* that can be predicated about all of them. For instance, 'physical objects' is a class, of which all physical objects are members. A class of 'paperclips' will have only paperclips as its members. Similarly, we can talk of:

Class of Tennis players
Class of whales
Class of *Fortune* 500 companies

In each case, we make use of a different common characteristic or a class property to identify the class.

Classes and their relationships form the content of the **categorical propositions** or **categorical statements**[1]**.** Categorical statements are statements which assert something about the classes. Aristotelian logic is exclusively concerned with this kind of statements and with arguments that are formed out of these.

Typically, a categorical statement is viewed as a linguistic structure where the subject and the predicate are connected by a verb, preferably a 'to-be verb' such as 'is', 'are'. It is important to remember that each of

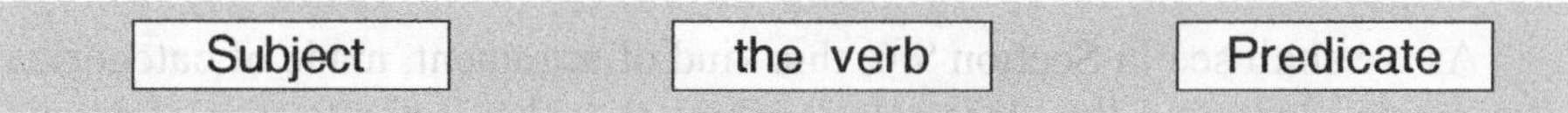

the subjects and the predicate terms in a categorical statement refers actually to a class. So, the actual picture of a categorical statement may be something like the following:

The following are some examples of categorical statements, in which the verbs have been highlighted so that the subject and predicate terms and the classes that they refer to can be easily identified:

Example 5

1. Bear cubs **are** cute animals.
2. Paperclips **are** handy objects.

Statement 1 of Example 5 asserts that the class of 'bear cubs' is related to the class of 'cute animals'. Similarly, statement 2 asserts the relation between the class of paperclips and the class of handy objects.

Now consider the statements in the following example:

---

[1] I shall refer to them as categorical statements instead of categorical propositions.

Example 6

3. Physical objects **are not** fictional entities.
4. Polar bears **are not** blue.

Example 6 brings to us statements which deny a relation between two classes. Statement 3 *denies* any relation between the class of 'physical objects' and the class of 'fictional entities'. Similarly, statement 4 *denies* that the class of 'polar bears' has any relation to the class of 'blue things'. Note that these too are **categorical statements**, or statements which assert something about class relationships even though it is an assertion of no relationship.

There can be arguments composed entirely of categorical statements. Consider the following example:

Example 7

College students are reckless people.
Reckless people are poor drivers.
∴ College students are poor drivers.

As we shall see in Section 9.6, this kind of argument, made of categorical statements alone and the class relationships that they refer to, are of special interest to Aristotelian logic.

You may have already noticed that relationships between two classes can be of different kinds. For example, the relationship between two classes, *A* and *B* can be expressed as follows:

(a) *Every* member of *A* may be also a member of *B*. In this case, *A* is said to be included or contained *wholly* in *B*. If you want the statement "paperclips are handy objects" to mean in this sense, then the statement actually asserts that every paperclip is also a member of the 'handy objects' class. The class of 'paperclips' is, in this sense, wholly contained or included in the class of 'handy objects'.

Or, (b) *Only some* members of *A* may also be a member of *B*. In this case, *A* is said to be only *partly* included in *B*. If you want "Bear cubs are cute animals" to have meaning then the statement asserts that only some bear cubs are also members of the class 'cute animals'.

Or, (c) There could be no relation at all, such that there will no common member that is common between the two classes. In Example 6, statements 3 and 4 are exemplars of this kind.

Considering these different kinds, Aristotelian logic lays down its requirements for a properly formed or **standard form** categorical statement in the following way:

Quality

Every categorical statement, in its standard form, is supposed to have a quality. That is, it is supposed to: (a) either *affirm* the class inclusion or containment in which it will have the quality of being **affirmative** (b) or *deny* the class inclusion or containment in which it will have the quality of being **negative**. Consider the following examples:

Example 8

5. College students are reckless.
6. Physical objects are not fictional.

Statement 5 is an affirmative categorical statement, whereas statement 6 is a negative categorical statement.

Quantity

Every categorical statement, in its standard form, is also supposed to have quantity. It is supposed to use quantity terms such as 'all' or 'some' to indicate its quantity.

(a) If the statement refers to *all the members* of the class mentioned by its subject term, then its quantity is **universal**, or (b) if it refers to only some members of the class mentioned by the subject term, then its quantity is **particular**. Consider the following example:

Example 9

7. All bear cubs are cute animals.
8. Some paperclips are objects made of plastic.

The quantity of statement 7 is universal, as every member of the 'bear cubs' class is asserted to be also a member of the class of 'cute animals'. On the other hand, the quantity of statement 8 is particular, as only some members of the class 'paperclip' are supposed to be also the members of the class 'objects made of plastic'.

You can now see that unless their quantity is specifically mentioned, categorical statements cannot be in standard form. Some of the earlier examples in this chapter, such as "Polar bears are not blue" for this reason, are not in standard form; for, their quantity is not clearly mentioned. In order to make them standard form categorical statements, we need to add appropriate quantity terms such as 'all' or 'some' to each of them.

EXERCISE 9.2

1. What is a class? Give three new examples and identify in each case the common characteristic.

2. Which of the following is a categorical statement and why?

*a. Either he did not notice the change or he approves of it.

b. Diamonds are stones used in tools for cutting glass.

*c. Weather predictions are claims that are often wrong.

d. If the car is kept in good condition, then we can take it for long-distance drive.

e. Doctors and lawyers are professionals.

f. No one younger than 18 years is eligible to vote.

3. What are the three major requirements for a standard form categorical statement? Explain.

4. Use the class names or terms 'Authors' and 'Famous people', to formulate the following:

*a. A categorical statement which denies the class relation for all members of the subject term.

b. A categorical statement which affirms the only some members of the subject term are also the members of the predicate term.

9.3 Categorical Propositions: A, E, I, O, and Venn Diagrams

Combining the quality and quantity requirements, there are four kinds of standard form categorical statements in Aristotelian logic, which are now described.

1. Universal affirmative: This kind of statement asserts that the subject class is *wholly* contained in the predicate class, or, that *every member of the subject class is also a member of the predicate class*. Because it refers to 'every member', its quantity is **universal**. Since it asserts a relationship, its quality is **affirmative**. Given that *S* and *P* are any two classes, its schematic form is

All S is P.

It may be illustrated by an actual example: ***All* students *are* athletes.**

We shall use the Venn diagrams to visually represent these class relationships. The relation expressed in the statement "All students are athletes" may be represented with diagrams either as Fig. 9.1(a) or as Fig. 9.1(b):

Though either way of depiction is correct, we shall follow the mode of representation by *two overlapping regions* as shown in Fig. 9.1(b). Moreover, we shall also follow the technique of *shading* to indicate that "a region is empty", i.e., it has no members.

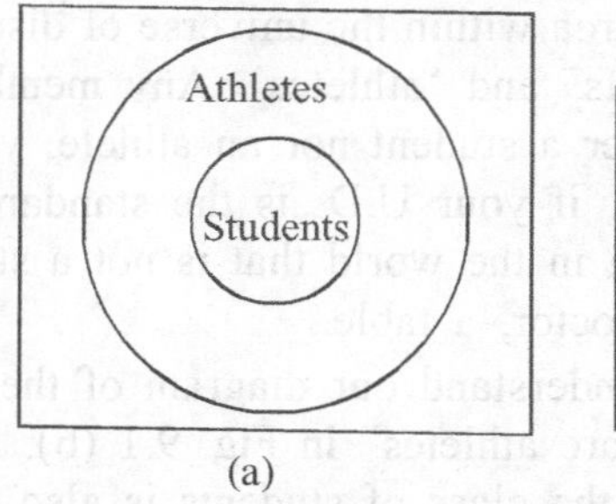

(a)

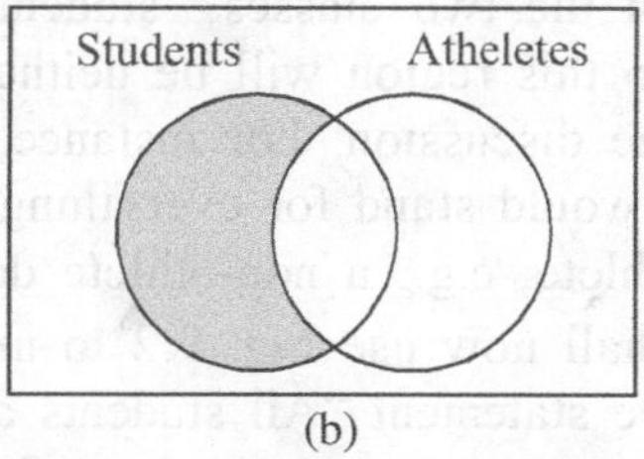

(b)

Fig. 9.1 Categorical Statement '*A*'.

In Fig. 9.1(b), the two circular regions represent two classes, 'students' (*S*) and 'athletes' (*A*). In Fig. 9.2 below, we have tried to explain how we read this diagram. $\bar{S}$ or $\bar{A}$ are symbols that have been used to indicate the regions which are *not S* or *not A*. They are called '*S*-bar' or '*A*-bar' to indicate the overbar on top of the letter symbols. By these symbols with overbars we refer to *complementary classes*, a concept that will be explained in Section 9.5. For the time being, we shall understand $\bar{S}$ and $\bar{A}$ respectively to designate the regions which are *not S,* and $\bar{A}$ to designate the regions which are *not A*.

Thus, Fig. 9.2 has four clearly marked regions: $S\bar{A}$, SA, $\bar{S}A$, and $\bar{S}\bar{A}$.

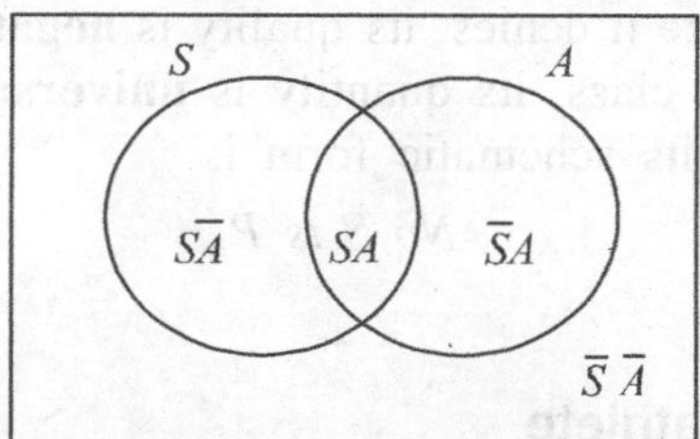

Fig. 9.2 Regions in Venn Diagram.

The $S\bar{A}$ region in Fig. 9.2 shows the area which belongs to 'students' class, but not to the 'athletes' class, whereas the $\bar{S}A$ shows the region which belongs to 'athletes' class but not to the 'students' class. The *SA* region shows where the two classes overlap—it is the area which can be said to belong to both classes. So if this region has a member, then the member belongs to both *S* and *A*. The region $\bar{S}\bar{A}$, on the other hand, marks the area which belongs to none of the two classes.

The rectangle outlining the diagram represents the **universe of discourse** (U.D.), which means the context or everything that is assumed or believed for the discussion. There are many kinds of things in the world, such as people, plants, animals, mountains, numbers, physical objects, events, places, etc. The collection of things that we are talking about on a given occasion constitutes the universe of discourse for that occasion. Usually, we assume the universe of discourse to include everything that is there. However, it can be restricted on certain occasions. For example, if you wish to restrict your discussion only to the human beings or to people, then that is possible too.

The $\bar{S}\,\bar{A}$ in Fig. 9.2 marks the area within the universe of discourse but not within the two classes, 'students' and 'athletes'. Any member which belongs to this region will be neither a student nor an athlete, yet will be part of the discussion. For instance, if your U.D. is the standard context, then $\overline{SA}$ would stand for everything in the world that is not a student and not an athlete, e.g., a non-athlete doctor, a table.

We shall now use Fig. 9.2 to understand our diagram of the universal affirmative statement "All students are athletes" in Fig. 9.1 (b). According to this statement, every member of the class of students is also a member of the class of athletes. This implies that the $S\bar{A}$ region (representing students who are not athletes) is empty, i.e., it has no members. There is no student who is not an athlete. In the language of Set Theory, we can represent this as

$S\bar{A} = \phi$, where the 'ϕ' stands for the null set or the empty set.

In Fig. 9.1 (b), this is what we have diagrammed by shading the $S\bar{A}$ area to indicate that it is empty.

2. Universal negative: This kind of statement asserts that there is no relation between the two classes, i.e., no member of one class is a member of the other class. Since it denies, its quality is **negative** and, since it refers to every member of a class, its quantity is **universal**. Given that S and P are any two classes, its schematic form is

No S is P.

Example

***No* student *is* athlete.**

According to this statement, the overlapping region between students and athletes, or SA, is empty. In the language of Set Theory, we can represent this as

$$SA = \phi$$

Diagrammatically, we may represent the situation as follows:

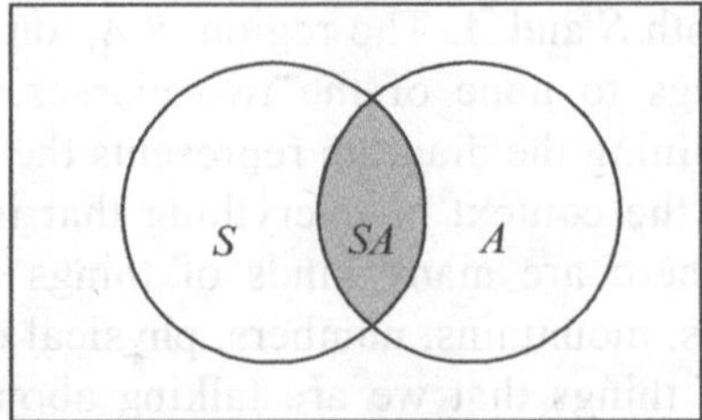

Fig. 9.3 Categorical Statement '*E*'.

3. Particular affirmative. This type of statement affirms that only some, not all, members of one class is also members of another class. Since it affirms that its quality is **affirmative**, but since it refers to some members, its quantity is **particular.** Given any two classes *S* and *P*, its schematic form is

Some S is P.

Example

Some students _are_ athletes.

Note that 'some' has an indefinite reference. For, it does not tell us exactly *how many*. We shall take the customary way to interpret some as 'at least one'. So, when "Some students are athletes" is asserted, we shall take it to mean that *at least one member* of the 'students' class is also a member of the class of 'athletes'. In other words, the region where both 'students' and 'athletes' overlap or the SA, is non-empty or has at least one member. In the language of Set Theory, we can represent this as:

$$SA \neq \phi.$$

Accordingly, we shall diagrammatically represent the situation described, not by shading, but *by placing an* '×' to indicate that the *SA* region has at least one member. Figure 9.4 shows this diagram of particular affirmative:

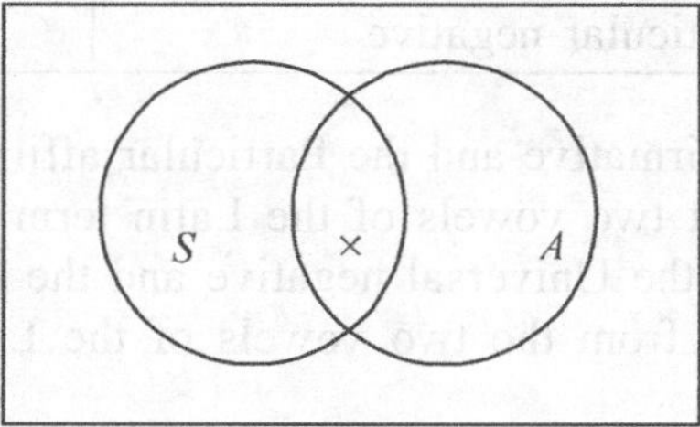

Fig. 9.4 Categorical Statement '*I*'.

4. Particular negative. A statement of this kind asserts that some members of a class are *not* members of another class. Its denial makes its quality **negative**, and its reference to 'some' members makes its quantity **particular**. Given any two classes *S* and *P*, its schematic form is:

Some S is not P.

Example

Some students are _not_ athletes.

Following our explanation of 'some', we may take it to mean that there is *at least one* student who is *not* an athlete. This implies that the region which is 'students' but not 'athletes', or $S\overline{A}$, is not empty. In the language of Set Theory, we can represent this as:

$$S\overline{A} \neq \phi$$

Diagrammatically we represent this as in Fig. 9.5.

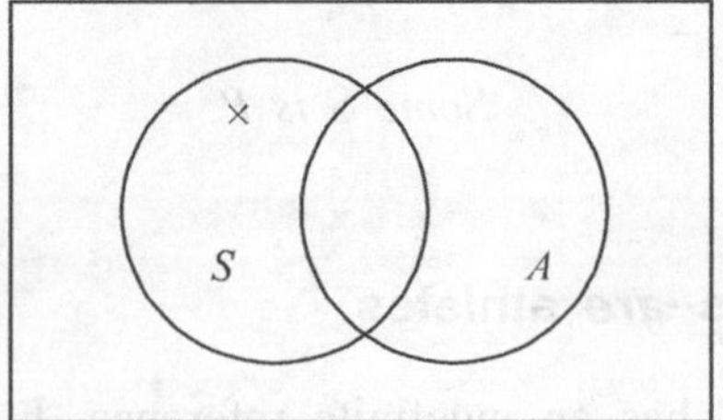

Fig. 9.5 Categorical Statement '*O*'.

This completes our discussion of the four standard forms of categorical statement. Each of the four standard form categorical statements has a code name, as you shall find in the following tabular representation.

Name of categorical statement	Code name
Universal affirmative	A
Universal negative	E
Particular affirmative	I
Particular negative	O

The Universal affirmative and the Particular affirmative get their names *A* and *I* from the first two vowels of the Latin term *affirmo*, which means "I affirm". Similarly, the Universal negative and the Particular negative get their names *E* and *O* from the two vowels of the Latin term *nego*, which means "I deny".

From now on, we shall refer to these four standard form categorical statements by their code names: *A*, *E*, *I*, *O*.

EXERCISE 9.3

1. Give two examples of your own for each of '*E*' and '*I*'.
2. State in terms of standard form categorical statements what each of the following Venn diagrams assert:

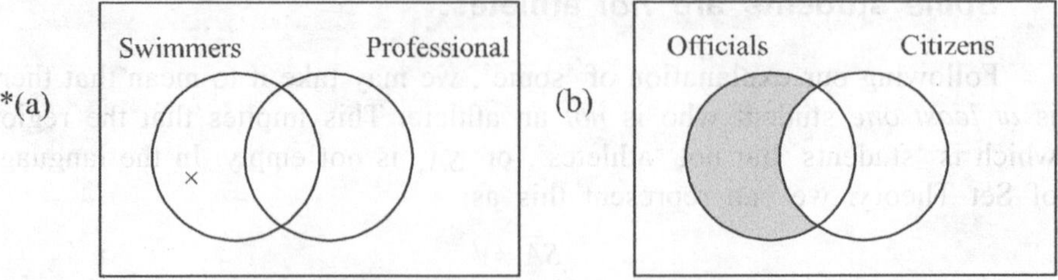

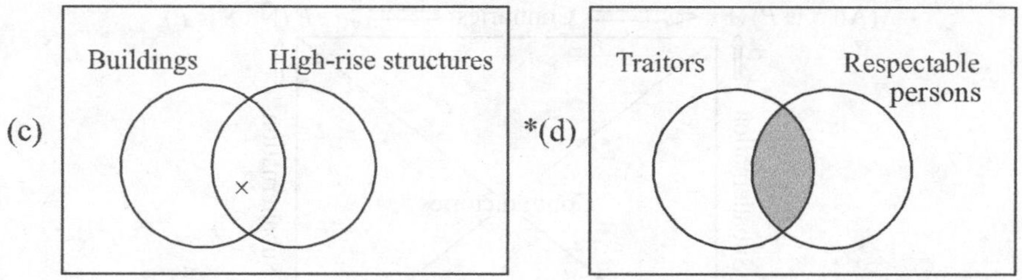

3. For each of the following categorical statements, draw a Venn Diagram that properly represents it:

   a. Some arguments are arguments made with categorical statements.
   *b. Some people are neither a doctor nor an engineer (assume 'People' as the Universe of Discourse for the diagram)
   c. None of the students were eligible.
   d. Every weapon is a thing that may be misused.
   *e. No competition with a lot of money at stake is an easy thing.
   f. Some ministers are not environmentally aware.

4. What is a universe of discourse? If the Universe of Discourse is 'the integers', what standard form categorical statement does this Venn Diagram represent?

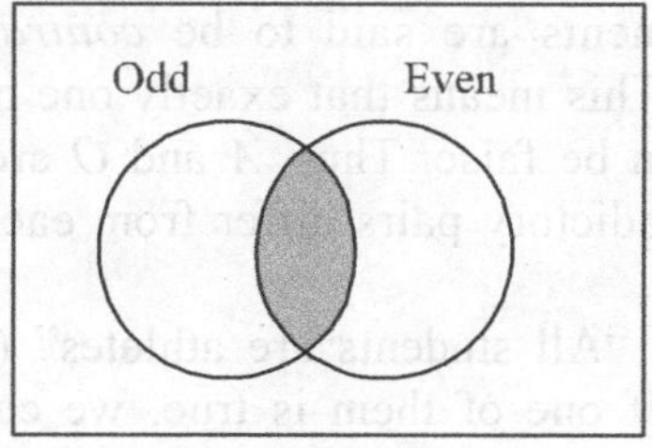

9.4 Traditional Square of Opposition

Earlier logicians of the Aristotelian tradition observed that the standard form categorical statements, *if they have the same subject and predicate terms*, may differ from each other in quantity or quality or both. They used the technical term **opposition** to refer to this kind of differences between categorical statements with same subject and predicate terms.

Various kinds of *opposition* show various kinds of truth relations that may hold between a pair of categorical statements with the same subject and predicate terms. These kinds of *oppositions* and the truth relations that they stand for are represented by a diagram called **the Square of Opposition** (see Fig. 9.6).

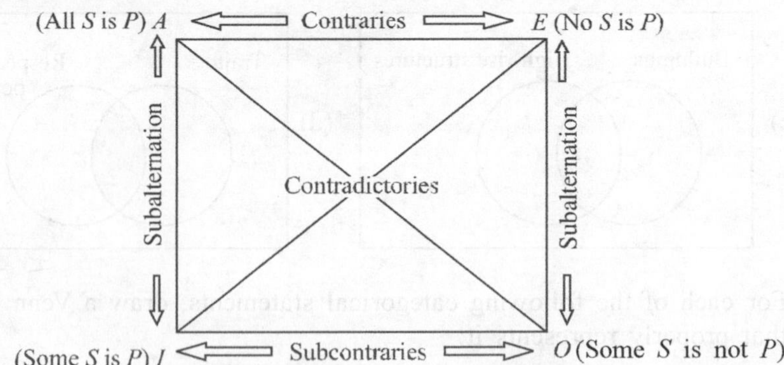

Fig. 9.6 The square of opposition.

As you can see, the square of opposition shows different relationships on each of its four sides and also diagonally from its two corners to the opposite corners. These relationships provide us the logical basis for some elementary inferences about the truth condition of one kind of categorical statement from another. If we know the truth condition of one, we should be able to infer *immediately*, that is, without the mediation of any other premise, what the truth condition of another categorical statement is, on the basis of the kind of *opposition* they have between themselves.

1. Contradictories. The contradiction relation runs diagonally in the square. Two categorical statements are said to be *contradictories* if one is the negation of the other. This means that exactly one of them can be true, and exactly one of them can be false. Thus, *A* and *O* are contradictories; so are and *E* and *I*. The contradictory pairs differ from each other in both quantity and quality.

Consider the pairs: "All students are athletes" (*A*) and "Some students are not athletes" (*O*). If one of them is true, we can validly infer that the other must be false. If one of them is false, we can safely infer that the other must be true.

2. Contraries. This relation is diagrammed on the top of the square of opposition between *A* and *E*. Two categorical statements are said to be *contraries* if both cannot be true at the same time, although both may be false at the same time. *A* and *E* are contraries in this sense. If one of them is true, we may safely infer the falsity of the other.

Consider the pairs: "All students are athletes" and "No students are athletes". Both cannot be true at the same time. If one is true, the other must be false. However, note that *both may be false at the same time*. If it is true that only some students are athletes, then it is false that "All students are athletes" and it is also false that "No students are athletes".

3. Subcontraries. This relation is shown at the bottom of the square of opposition between *I* and *O*. Two categorical statements are said to be

subcontraries if both of them cannot be false at the same time though both may be true together.

As in the case of *A* and *E*, *I* and *O* also differ from each other only in quality, However, there is an important difference between this pair and the *A*-*E* pair. "Some students are athletes" and "Some students are not athletes" cannot both be false, yet both may be true together about a student batch which includes both athletes and non-athletes.

4. Subalternation. Subalternation refers to a special kind of opposition which is not based upon contrasts as was the case in the other oppositions as stated above. Rather, the opposition holds between a universal statement and its corresponding particular statement. Note that this relation is diagrammed on the two sides of the square of opposition between *A* and *I* on the one hand, and between *E* and *O*, on the other. Two categorical statements are supposed to be in subalternation relation if the truth of the universal statement implies the truth of the particular, but the falsity of the particular implies the falsity of the universal. If "No student is an athlete" is true, it follows that "Some students are not athletes" is also true. If we know that it is false that "some students are not athletes" (i.e., all students are athletes), then it follows that "No student is an athlete" is false too.

The information given about the relationships shown on the Square of Opposition provides a basis for drawing several **immediate inferences**. By immediate inference, we mean an inference which can be drawn from a single premise. Given the relations in the Square of Opposition and given the truth value of any of the four standard form categorical statements, it is easy to make immediate inferences about the truth value of the others. In some cases, the immediate inference will yield a definite conclusion, and in some cases it may lead to inconclusive answers. Consider the following:

1. If we know that *A* is true: *O* must be false (by contradiction)
   I must be true (by subalternation)
   E must be false (by contrary).
2. If we know that *E* is true: *I* must be false (by contradiction)
   O must be true (by subalternation)
   A must be false (by contrary).
3. If we know that *I* is true: *E* must be false (by contradiction), *A* and *O* are undetermined. We cannot say anything definite about *A*, because from the truth of the particular, by subalternation, nothing follows about the truth value of the universal. It may be true, and it may not be true. Similarly,

since subcontrary relation allows both *I* and *O* to be true together and the truth of *I* does not stop *O* from being false, nothing conclusive can be said about the truth value of *O*.

4. If we know that *O* is true: *A* must be false (by contradiction), *E* and *I* are undetermined, but for reasons similar to what is explained above in 3.

5. If we know that *A* is false: *O* must be true (by contradiction) for *E* and *I* are undetermined. Nothing conclusive can be inferred about the truth value of *E* and *I*. *A* and *E* are contraries, and between such a pair both may be false. So, from the falsity of *A*, it neither clearly follows that *E* must be true nor follows that E must be false. Similarly, from the falsity of *A*, it follows neither that *I* must be false nor that it must be true. Thus, *E* and *I* are undetermined.

6. If we know that *E* is false: *I* must be true (by contradiction), *A* and *O* are undetermined. For reasons similar to those explained in point 5, nothing conclusive can be inferred about the truth value of *A* and *O*.

7. If we know that *I* is false: *E* must be true (by contradiction) *A* must be false (by subalternation) *O* must be true (by subcontrary).

8. If we know that *O* is false: *A* must be true (by contradiction) *E* must be false (by subalternation) *I* must be true (by subcontrary).

Aristotelian logic also discusses three other forms of immediate inferences, namely, Conversion, Obversion, and Contraposition. However, we shall discuss these in the next section.

EXERCISE 9.4

1. Can the immediate inferences based on oppositions hold if the categorical statements under consideration do not have the same subject and predicate terms? Explain.

2. *A. What can you infer about the truth or falsity of the following, if you assume "All politicians are corrupt" is true?

(i) No politicians are corrupt.
(ii) Some politicians are corrupt.
(iii) Some politicians are not corrupt.

B. What can you infer about the truth or falsity of the following, if you assume "All politicians are corrupt" is false?

(i) No politicians are corrupt.
(ii) Some politicians are corrupt.
(iii) Some politicians are not corrupt.

*C. What can you infer about the truth or falsity of the following if you assume "Some reptiles are not poisonous" is false?

(i) All reptiles are poisonous.
(ii) No reptiles are poisonous.
(iii) Some reptiles are poisonous.

D. What can you infer about the truth or falsity of the following if you assume "Some reptiles are not poisonous" is true?

(i) All reptiles are poisonous.
(ii) No reptiles are poisonous.
(iii) Some reptiles are poisonous.

3. What is the main difference between a pair of Contraries and a pair of Subcontraries?
4. What is the name of the opposition relation in which the categorical statements differ:

a. In quantity only?
b. In both quality and quantity?

9.5 Immediate Inferences

In Section 9.4, we have already been introduced to the idea of immediate inference, i.e., *inference from a single premise*. We saw how the square of opposition can serve as the basis for immediate inferences about the truth values of categorical statements which have the *same subject and predicate terms*.

In our everyday life, without realizing we do make use of immediate inferences. For example, suppose you hear the statement:

She currently works at Pune.

From this statement alone, based on your language skill you can infer a few things. Among other things, you can infer that:

She used to work earlier somewhere else.
She has relocated herself recently.
Pune may be a new city for her.

Each of the above conclusions can be independently drawn, but each would be a case of immediate inference.

Paul Grice, a philosopher, proposed a theory of "conversational Implicatures" as an example of everyday inferences that we draw as part of our ordinary life. But Aristotle's classical patterns of immediate inferences that we are going to learn about now are a specialty class.

There are three other kinds of immediate inferences in Aristotelian logic:

- Conversion
- Obversion
- Contraposition

These immediate inferences are not part of the square of opposition. They involve certain changes in their subject and predicate terms. Being immediate, each of these makes use of *only one premise*.

In these immediate inferences the main concern is to conserve logical equivalence. From a given truth, the conclusion should be only what analytically follows from that premise without altering the truth value.

In the remaining part of the section, we shall learn about these three kinds of immediate inferences, and their differences from each other.

Conversion

Conversion is the immediate inference process that results from simply **reversing** the subject and the predicate terms in the premise.

Schematically, the format is as follows:

Format of Conversion

Premise:	*S* is *P*.
Conclusion by conversion:	*P* is *S*.

Note that other than the change of the **position** of the terms, no further change in them is allowed by conversion. For example, a change in the quantity or quality of the premise is *not allowed* by conversion.

We may try to understand the process from some examples of actual statements as follows. For easy understanding, the subject and the predicate terms have been italicized in the examples of conversion:

Example 10

(a) Premise:	Some *ornaments* are *things made of gold*.

Conclusion by Conversion: Some *things made of gold* are *ornaments*.

(b) Premise: Some *whales* are *mammals*.

Conclusion by Conversion: Some *mammals* are *whales*.

Your next question might be: Does this operation yield valid immediate inferences? For, you might consider it odd that given a premise, we can legitimately infer something from it simply by reversing the positions of the subject and the predicate. So, our next concern is to find out where we can safely use conversion as a valid inference process. Our investigation, however, will be limited to categorical statements alone.

***I* statements:** Note that in the example above, we have already established that conversion can be safely applied to *I* statements. "Some *ornaments* are *things made of gold*" and "Some *whales* are *mammals*" are both *I* statements. We also saw that their truth values remain preserved by conversion. If it is true that "Some *whales* are *mammals*", then it follows as true that "Some *mammals* are *whales*". This means that when applied to *I* statements conversion preserves the truth value, and it is therefore a reliable valid inference process for *I* statements. We can also try to see whether the truth value is preserved by the Venn Diagram technique that we learnt in Section 9.3 of this book for plotting the categorical statements.

For this Venn diagram test, our *modus operandi* or the operational principle will be:

If the truth value of the premise is preserved in the conclusion, then the same diagram which plots the premise should also automatically plot the conclusion.

We shall only plot the premise. Remember that *we shall not try to plot the conclusion also*. If the inference is valid, then the same Venn diagram which plots the premise will also plot the conclusion.

Let us take our familiar *I* statement example:

Premise: Some *students* are *athletes*.

From this by conversion it follows:

Conclusion by conversion: Some *athletes* are *students*.

The Venn diagram is as shown in Fig. 9.7.

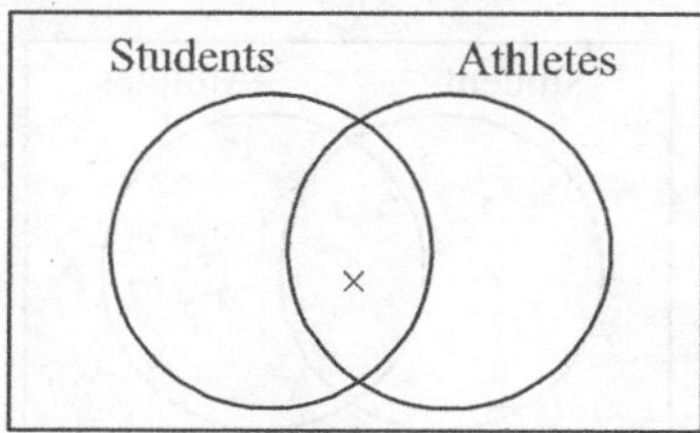

Fig. 9.7 Venn diagram of an '*I*' statement.

Figure 9.7 is a diagram for "Some students are athletes". The cross or '×' in the intersection of the two classes shows that. Note that the same diagram also shows that "Some athletes are students". Since this was a random example of *I* statement, by this Venn diagram technique we have shown that conversion is a safe inference process for *I* statements in general.

***E* statements:** We can similarly establish that conversion is safe for *E* statements in general. Consider as a random example the following:

Premise: No *students* are *athletes*.

Conclusion by Conversion: No *athletes* are *students*.

Intuitively, we should be able to see that the truth value of the premise is preserved in the conclusion. If "No *students* are *athletes"* is true, then it follows as true that "No *athletes* are *students*" We can strengthen this observation by drawing a Venn diagram for the premise (Fig. 9.8).

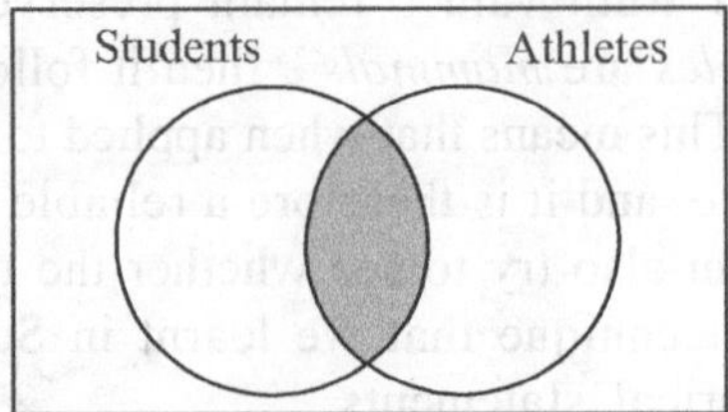

Fig. 9.8 Venn diagram of an '*E*' statement.

The same diagram which depicts the premise also depicts the conclusion by conversion. Since this was a random *E* statement, we can conclude that conversion is safe for *E* statements in general.

***O* statements:** For *O* statements, conversion is *not* safe. Consider the conversion of the following *O* statement:

Premise: Some *students* are not *athletes*.

Conclusion by conversion: Some *athletes* are not *students*.

Clearly, the conclusion is not logically equivalent to the premise. The premise is true if there is at least one student who is not an athlete. Clearly, that condition will not make the conclusion by conversion true. To support this claim, we can take the help of the Venn Diagram. Figure 9.9 illustrates the premise "Some *students* are not *athletes*".

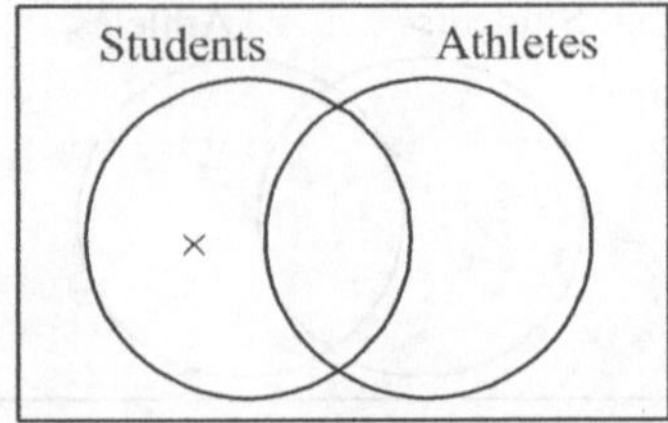

Fig. 9.9 Diagram of "Some students are not athletes".

The cross sign '×' in the students class shows that there is at least one member who is a student but is not an athlete. This depicts the premise. Unfortunately, however, it *does not thereby depict* the conclusion "Some *athletes* are not *students".*

"Some *athletes* are not *students"* or, the conclusion by conversion, is true if there is at least one athlete who is not a student. In order to have a confirmation of the truth of the conclusion, we need a different diagram as shown in Fig. 9.10.

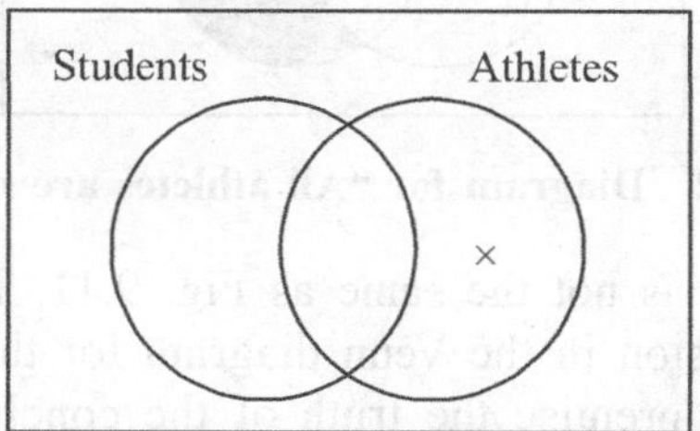

Fig. 9.10 Diagram for "Some athletes are not students".

It is obvious that Fig. 9.10 is not the same as Fig. 9.9. According to our operational principle, we are not supposed to have two different diagrams for a single inference. A single diagram made for the premise should also show the conclusion by conversion. This failure to plot the conclusion in the Venn diagram for the premises shows that from truth of the premise the truth of the conclusion does not follow. Since this was a random example of *O* statement, it shows that for *O* statements in general conversion is not safe.

***A* statements:** Strictly speaking, conversion for *A* statements does not hold good. It is very much possible for "All *students* are *athletes*" to be true, while its converse "All *athletes* are *students*" is false. "All *humans* are *mammals*" is true, but it does not follow that therefore it will also be true that "all *mammals* are *humans*"! We can depict the premise "All *students* are *athletes*" as in the following Venn diagram (Fig. 9.11):

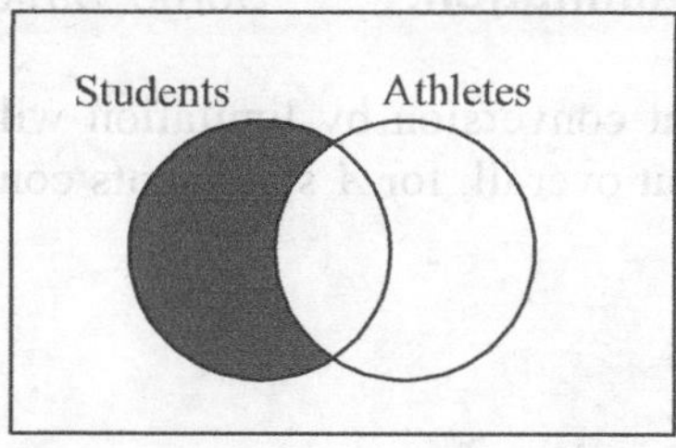

Fig. 9.11 Venn diagram for "All *students* are *athletes*".

Note that Fig. 9.11 does *not* depict the converse statement: "All *athletes* are *students*". The Venn diagram for "All atheletes are students" is given in Fig. 9.12.

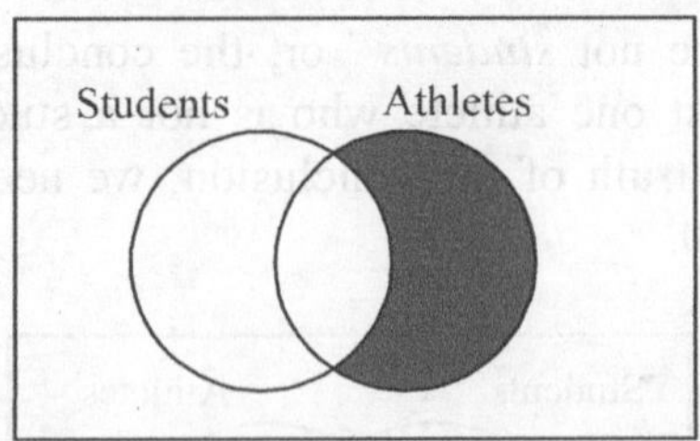

Fig. 9.12 Diagram for "All athletes are students".

Clearly, Fig. 9.12 is not the same as Fig. 9.11. This failure to plot the conclusion by conversion in the Venn diagram for the premises shows that from the truth of the premise the truth of the conclusion does not follow. Since this was a random example of *A* statement, it shows that conversion is not a reliable process for *A* statements in general.

Traditional Categorical logic suggests that in case of *A* statements, we may try a **conversion by limitation** which is a conversion after a limitation of the quantity of the statement in question. That is, it is suggested that we first limit the quantity of *A* statement, or perform a subalternation on it, and thus obtain its corresponding *I* statement. After that, we can safely use conversion on it since on *I* statements conversion is known as a safe process.

For example: Given "All *students* are *athletes*", we may obtain its subaltern "Some *students* are *athletes*". Then on that, we can use conversion by limitation as: "Some *athletes* are *students*". This is illustrated in the following example:

Example 11

Given:	All *students* are *athletes.*
Corresponding Subaltern:	Some *students* are *athletes.*
Conversion by limitation:	Some *athletes* are *students.*

Note, however, that conversion by limitation will work only if there is at least one student. But overall, for *A* statements conversion is not regarded as a safe process.

Obversion

For explaining what obversion is, we need to first explain what a **complementary class** is. Given any class *C*, its complementary class is just all those things that are not in *C*. A standard way of referring to the complementary of a class term is to use the prefix 'non'. Consider the following examples: Voters and *non-voters*, athletes and *non-athletes*.

Note that, unless restricted, a complementary class is a very large class. For example, if you want to know what counts as a non-athlete, you will find that it includes all that is not an athlete, such as the terminally ill, the dead, prime numbers, trees, shoes, etc. To restrict this, the context of an inference may be used as a specifier for deciding what the extent of a complementary class will be. For example, if you so wish, you can restrict the extent of the class of non-voters to human residents of a nation. Otherwise, it may include even the sticks and stones and every object in the world that cannot be considered as a voter.

Example 12

Class	Complementary class
• Voters	Non-voters
• Athletes	Non-athletes

If a class is C, it is customary to symbolically refer to its complementary class as $\overline{C}$, called C-bar or C with an overbar. You may have already noted the use of this symbol in Section 9.3 in our discussion of the use of Venn diagram for the categorical statements. If the class of voters is V, then its complementary class of non-voters is $\overline{V}$.

For obversion, the steps required are as follows:

Obversion

✓**Step 1:** Reverse the quality of the given statement. That is, if affirmative, change it into negative, and if negative, change it into affirmative.

✓**Step 2:** Replace the predicate term by its complementary term.

When you have practiced enough, you may combine the two steps and do obversion in one single step. But for the beginning, it is better to practice in two steps.

You need to remember that in obversion the quantity is *not* changed. Given a universal statement, you cannot obvert and change it into a particular; or the vice versa. Also, note that unlike conversion, we do *not* switch the class terms, that is, the subject and the predicate terms are not interchanged in obversion.

An example of obversion is as follows:

Example 13

Given:	All *students* are *athletes*
Step 1: *Change of quality.*	No students are athletes.
Step 2: *Replacing predicate by complementary:*	No students are non-athletes.

When is this process safe? The answer is: *always*. Obversion is the only immediate inference process that is valid for *any* categorical form of statement: *A*, *E*, *I*, *O*.

Categorical statement	Its obverse
All students are athletes. (*A*)	No students are non-athletes.
No students are athletes. (*E*)	All students are non-athletes.
Some students are athletes. (*I*)	Some students are not non-athletes.
Some students are not athletes. (*O*)	Some students are non-athletes.

Note that in all the instances given above, a categorical statement and its obverse must have exactly the same truth value. This ensures obversion as a valid inference process for any categorical statement.

Contraposition

Contraposition involves some elements from both conversion and obversion. The process to get a contrapositive of a given statement is:

Contraposition:

✓**Step 1:** Convert the statement: reverse the subject and the predicate terms.

✓**Step 2:** Replace both terms by their complementary terms.

A statements: For *A* statements, contraposition is a reliable process. Consider the simple example:

Example 14

Given: All students are athletes

Applying the process:

Step 1: All athletes are students.

Step 2: All non-athletes are non-students. (← the contrapositive)

If the given *A* statement is true, its contrapositive also will be true. We can also use the Venn diagram to verify this.

The Venn diagram for "All students are athletes" is given in Fig. 9.13.

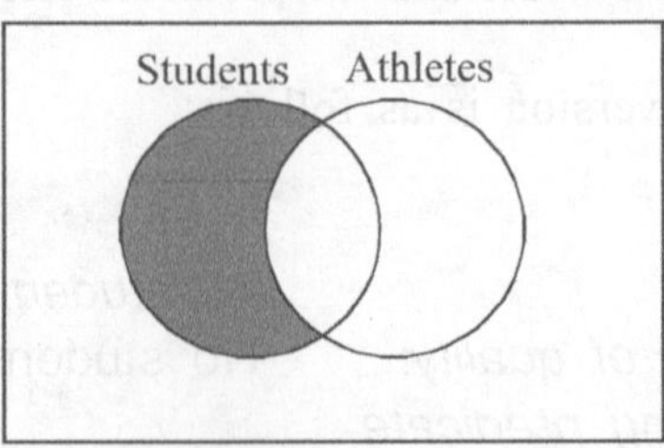

Fig. 9.13 Venn diagram for "All students are athletes".

Notice that the same diagram also depicts the contrapositive: All *non-athletes* are *non-students*. The non-athlete class is the region within the box but outside the two overlapping circles; namely the region $\overline{SA}$. Where there are no athletes, there are no students also. Within the circles, the region $S\overline{A}$, or the region which belongs to students but not to athletes, is also non-atheletes, but it is empty. Thus, the diagram also depicts the contrapositive. Since this was a random sample, it follows that for *A* statements, contraposition is a reliable and safe process.

O **statements.** For *O* statements, contraposition is a reliable inference process. Given that "Some students are not athletes" is true, the truth of "Some non-athletes are not non-students" will follow. The two 'not' and 'non' in the end of the contrapositive cancel each other out and the contrapositive simply means "Some non-athletes are students". Figure 9.14 depicts both the statements:

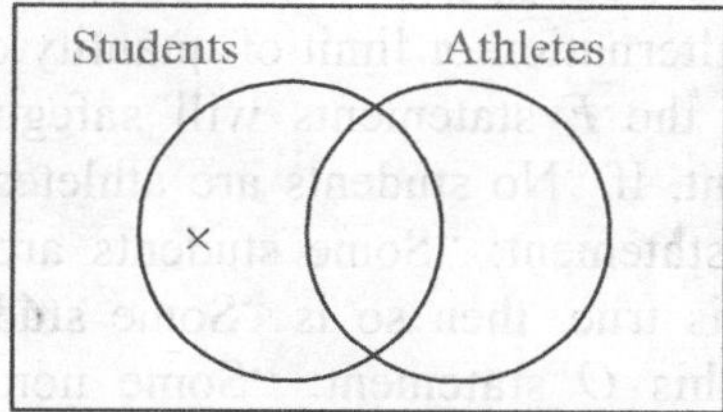

Fig. 9.14 Venn Diagram for "Some students are not athletes" and its contrapositive.

E **statements.** In general for *E* statements contraposition is *not* a safe process. Given "No student is athlete", its contrapositive will be: "No non-athlete is non-student". Intuitively, it should be clear that the two statements do not mean the same and they are not logically equivalent either. We can demonstrate this point by Venn diagram in the following way. The Venn diagram for "No student is athlete" is depicted in Fig. 9.15.

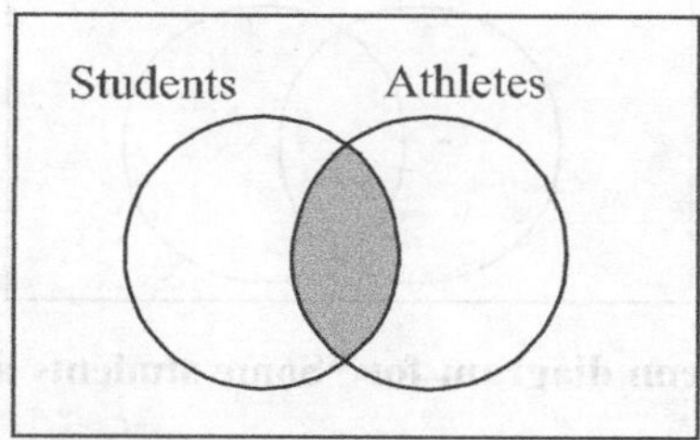

Fig. 9.15 Venn diagram for "No student is athlete".

The Venn diagram for "No non-athlete is non-student" is as in Fig. 9.16.

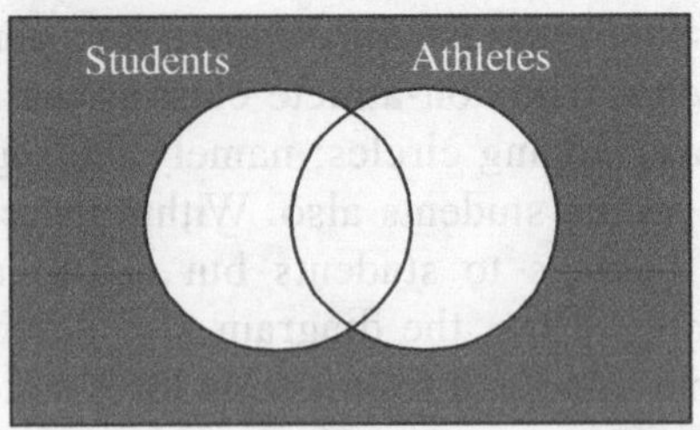

Fig. 9.16 Venn diagram for "No non-athlete is non-student".

There can be no question that the two diagrams, Figs. 9.15 and 9.16, are not the same. In Fig. 9.16 the area in which non-students and non-athletes overlap, namely, the region within the box but outside the two overlapping circles, is supposed to be empty, as has been shown in Fig. 9.16.

Traditional logicians have suggested a *contraposition by limitation* on *E* statements: we form the contrapositive on the corresponding *O* statement, after performing a subalternation or limit of quantity on a given *E* statement. This way the truth of the *E* statements will safeguard the corresponding contraposed *O* statement. If "No students are athletes" is true, then first we make its subaltern *O* statement: "Some students are not athletes". If "No students are athletes" is true, then so is "Some students are not athletes". Then we contrapose this *O* statement: "Some non-athletes are not non-students" which will be true. But again, we need to remember that the by limitation process applies only if there is at least one student.

I **statements.** Contraposition for *I* statements is simply not valid. The statement "Some students are athletes" does not have the same truth value as "Some non-athletes are non-students". The Venn diagrams also confirm this. For "Some students are athletes" the Venn diagram is as given in Fig. 9.17.

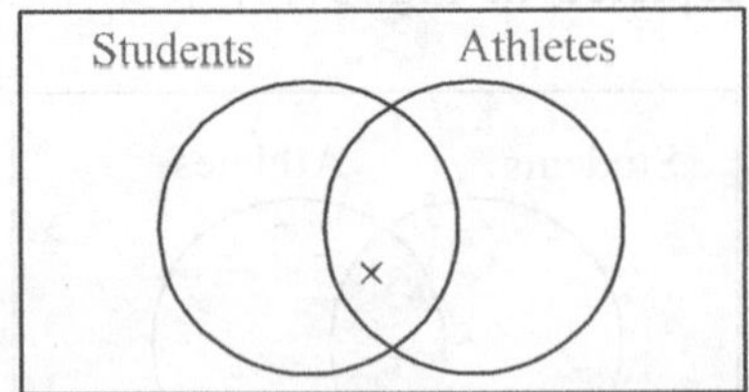

Fig. 9.17 Venn diagram for "Some students are athletes".

However, the Venn diagram for "Some *non-athletes* are *non-students*" is depicted in Fig. 9.18.

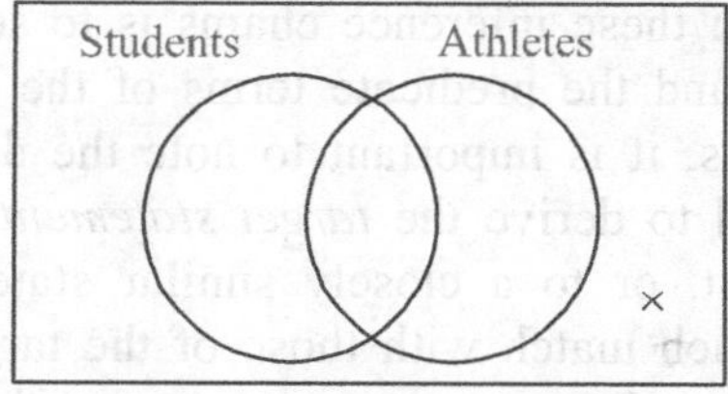

Fig. 9.18 Venn diagram for "Some non-athletes are non-students".

"Some non-athletes are non-students" is true if there is at least one member in the region which has non-athletes and non-students. The cross in Fig. 9.18 depicts that. But this figure is not the same as Fig. 9.17. Therefore, we can conclude that, from the truth of a given *I* statement as a premise, the truth of its contraposed does not follow.

The summary of the above is:

Conversion: Valid for *E* and *I*, not valid for *O*, and applicable by limitation to *A*.
Obversion: Valid for all types of categorical statements.
Contraposition: Valid for *A* and *O*, not valid for *I*, and applicable by limitation to *E*.

Successive Immediate Inference Chain

After learning about these immediate inferences, it is time to learn how to use them for furthering our knowledge. In Aristotelian logic, one of the ways is to use these inferences in a successive immediate inference chain. A successive immediate inference chain would mean an inference chain that is formed by repeated application of these three immediate inference patterns along with the immediate inferences we have learnt from the traditional square of opposition. The square of opposition has taught you about: (a) Contradiction, (b) Contrariety, (c) Subcontrariety, and (d) Subalternation. In addition, you have learnt about (e) Conversion, (f) Obversion, and (g) Contraposition. The aim in successive immediate inference chain is to learn to use these seven logical relations one after the other, as needed, to establish if, given two categorical statements, any logical relation exists between them.

The object is to find out and justify the truth value of a statement, given the information about the truth value of another statement. For example, given that you know that "All voters are citizens" is true, what can you infer about the truth value of "No non-citizens are voters"? Your answer could be based on a successive immediate inference chain as shown below:

Example 15

Given:	All voters are citizens	True
Obversion:	No voters are non-citizens	True, by obversion
Conversion:	No non-citizens are voters	True, by conversion on *E* statement

A good strategy in these inference chains is to see *if there is an exact match* in the subject and the predicate terms of the two given statements. If there are differences, it is important to note the differences. Let us call the statement we need to derive the *target statement.* The aim is to arrive at the target statement, or to a closely similar statement the subject and predicate terms of which match with those of the target statement. If there is difference in two complementary terms between the given and the target statement, then contraposition seems to be a step to consider. If the difference is of only one the complementary class, then obversion may be used. If the difference is simply a matter of reversal of positions of subject and predicate terms, then conversion is the step to be taken. Thus, once the exact match is arrived at in the subject and predicate terms of target statement, then you can use the square of opposition to infer the truth value of the target statement in comparison to the truth value of the given statement.

Note that in our Example 15 above, the difference between the given and the target statement is two-fold: there is one complementary term difference in the subject of the target statement, but also the position of the subject and predicate terms are reversed. This gives us the indication that there is scope to use obversion and conversion, both on the given statement to derive the target statement.

The given statement "All voters are citizens" is an *A* statement. Conversion cannot be used properly on it, and contraposition will not yield the result. So, we can try obversion to achieve the complementary class difference in the predicate term. In addition, we also get the change in the quality: from 'all' to 'none'. If the given statement is true, so will be its obverse: "No non-citizens are voters". Since obversion is safe on all categorical statements, its application preserves the truth value of the given statement. Then, the next step is to convert the *E* statement thus obtained. And we have our target statement. Since we know that conversion is valid for *E*, we can safely use it and preserve the truth value we started with. If the given statement is true, we can now claim that the target statement is also true.

Note that the target statement cannot be directly derived from the given statement. The given statement is an *A* statement, and from it by one step we cannot arrive at the target statement. Hence, a series of immediate inferences are linked up to derive the same. The trick here is to remember which inference process is safe for which categorical statements. Because, your goal will be to preserve logical equivalence, as far as possible.

There could be cases where you will not be able to determine the truth value of the target statement by this process. For all such cases, your answer will be "cannot be determined". The undetermined truth value may be because the two statements, the given and the target, are not logically related. But you should try by each step to maintain a truth value at each step before you come to the closest possible match in the subject and predicate terms before you make your judgment. For example, consider this problem:

Given "Some non-students are athletes" is true, what can you infer about the truth value of "All students are athletes"?

We start as follows:

Given: Some non-students are athletes True

There is more than one way of proceeding from the given statement. There is no obvious benefit of doing obversion on it. Since contraposition is not allowed on *I* statements, the only choice is conversion. By conversion, we get the converse:

Some athletes are non-students True, by conversion

Now, there is only one complementary class difference between the subject and predicate terms of the given and the target statement: non-students and students. Obversion on it may help us to get rid of the complementary term, and thus we get

Some athletes are not students True, by obversion

This gives us a match in the terms, but notice that we still do not have an exact match between the subject and predicate terms of the two statements. The subject term of the target statement is 'students', whereas the *O* statement we have derived has 'students' as its predicate. This does not allow us to make any comparison using the traditional square of opposition. You may be tempted to do a conversion on "Some *athletes* are not *student*" to arrive at an exact match. But note that conversion is not valid for *O* statements. Thus, in this case, we have to conclude that from the truth of the given statement, the truth value of the target statement cannot be determined.

As overall strategy for the successive immediate inference chains, it is wise to use the inference patterns one after the other to get as close as possible to the target statement. It is important also to get the subject and predicate terms also in the right order. For, as you know, unless two categorical statements have the same subject and predicate terms, no comparison among their truth values can be done using the traditional square of opposition. It is also advisable to use the immediate inference patterns, where applicable, to eliminate the complementary terms.

EXERCISE 9.5

1. Perform **conversion** on the following statements, where possible, and indicate which of these are logically equivalent to the given statement:

*a. Some parrots are pet birds.
b. No mammals are cold blooded creatures.
c. Some shoes are not made of leather.
d. No decent students are people who would get involved in illegal activities.
*e. All scholarly works are works of dedication.
f. Some TV channels are not channels worth watching.
g. All undergraduate students are applicants for projects.
h. Some drunken people are reckless drivers causing accidents.

2. Perform **obversion** on the following statements and indicate which of these are equivalent to the given statement:
a. All goats are herbivores.
*b. Some philosophers are non-conformists.
c. Some vases are fragile.
d. Some productions are not abundant processes.
e. No soldiers are non-citizens.
f. Some actors are professionals.
*g. All businessmen are profit-oriented.
h. No mothers who have minimum two young children are idle.

3. Perform **contraposition** on the following statements, where possible, and indicate which of these are equivalent to the given statement:
*a. Some light-bulbs are not blue things.
b. Some flying objects are identified objects.
c. All devout Christians are faithful people.
d. No non-philosophers are scientists.
e. All pensioners are frugal people.
f. Some cars which have air-conditioners are not energy efficient.
g. No environmentalists are warmongers.
*h. Some insects are carriers of diseases.

4. Given that "All traders are investors" is true, use **successive immediate inference chain** to answer what you can infer about the truth or falsity about the following. Indicate which of these cases cannot be determined and why.
*a. No non-investors are non-traders.
b. No traders are non-investors.
c. Some non-investors are not non-traders.
d. All non-traders are non-investors.

e. No non-investors are traders.
f. All non-investors are non-traders.
*g. No investors are non-traders.
h. No investors are traders.
i. Some non-investors are traders.
j. Some traders are not non-investors.

5. Given that "No politicians are honest" is true, use **successive immediate inference chain** to answer what you can infer about the truth or falsity about the following. Indicate which of these cases cannot be determined and why.

*a. Some non-politicians are not non-honest.
b. All non-politicians are non-honest.
c. No non-honest persons are politicians.
d. Some non-honest persons are politicians.
e. No non-politicians are non-honest persons.
f. All non-honest persons are non-politicians.
*g. All honest persons are politicians.
h. No honest persons are non-politicians.
i. All politicians are honest persons.
j. Some non-honest persons are not politicians.

6. Given that "Some animals are herbivores" is true, use **successive immediate inference chain** to answer what you can infer about the truth or falsity about the following. Indicate which of these cases cannot be determined and why.

*a. All animals are non-herbivores.
b. All animals are herbivores.
c. No animals are herbivores.
d. Some herbivores are animals.
e. All herbivores are non-animals.
f. Some animals are not non-herbivores.
g. No herbivores are animals.
h. Some non-animals are herbivores.
i. No non-animals are herbivores.
*j. Some herbivores are not non-animals.

7. Given that "Some economists are not forecasters" is true, use **successive immediate inference chain** to answer what you can infer about the truth or falsity about the following. Indicate which of these cases cannot be determined and why.

a. All non-economists are forecasters.
*b. No economists are non-forecasters.
c. No forecasters are economists.
d. Some economists are non-forecasters.
e. All economists are non-forecasters.
f. All economists are forecasters.
g. No non-economists are forecasters.
h. All non-forecasters are non-economists.
h. No forecasters are non-economists.
i. Some forecasters are economists.
*j. Some non-forecasters are economists.

9.6 Bringing Non-Standard Categorical Statements into Standard Form

Categorical statements may not always be stated in exactly one of the four standard forms. Just as we saw in propositional logic, categorical statements too can be expressed in various ways. However, before we can consider them using Aristotelian logic, we need to translate these non-standard categorical statements into standard forms. In this section, you will learn how to do such translations.

You will find that in some statements the predicate term may not be a class term but an **adjective** or an **adjective phrase**. Consider, for example, the statement: "All babies are cute". In addition, there may not be any quantity term as for example in "Human babies are born with a brain that weighs on the average 14 ounces". In each case, the predicate place is occupied by an adjective term or an adjectival description. In order to bring them into standard form, *the adjectives and adjectival descriptions must be replaced by terms designating a class of objects or entities,* of which the adjective or the adjectival description can be properly predicated. Also, a quantity term has to be added where there is none. Some of the ways in which the statements may be rephrased are as follows: "*All* babies are cute *beings*", and "All human babies are *creatures* born with a brain that weighs on an average 14 ounces".

Example 16

Statements in non-standard form	Statements in standard form
All babies are cute	All babies are cute beings
Human babies are born with a brain that weighs on the average 14 ounces	All human babies are creatures born with a brain that weighs on an average 14 ounces

You may also find categorical statements **the main verbs of which are not 'to be' verbs.** Consider for example: "Some bad doctors disgrace others" or "All teenagers seek guidance". In cases such as these, the predicate has to be *rephrased* so that a suitable *'to be'* verb can be brought in and the original expression can be attached to it as a defining property for a class. For example, the two statements cited may be translated into standard form as: "Some bad doctors *are* doctors who disgrace others" and "All teenagers *are* persons who seek guidance".

In some cases, the standard form elements **may not be arranged in the proper order**. Consider, for example, the statement "Bats are all blind" or "Gone are all days of youth". In cases such as these, we must first decide what the subject and the predicate terms are and then rearrange them in the subject-verb-predicate format, and then attach a suitable quantity word in front of them. Thus arranged, we shall have two standard form statements: "All bats are creatures that are blind" and "All days of youth are days that are gone".

Example 17

Statement in non-standard form	**Statements in standard form**
Bats are all blind	All bats are creatures that are blind
Gone are all days of youth	All days of youth are days that are gone

Often, the **quantity terms** used are either **not the standard form** 'all', 'some' or 'no', or they **are not specified**. In such cases, you need to *rephrase* or *explicate the quantity terms in terms of standard form quantity terms, after* examining the statement in its proper context. As an illustration, consider the following example:

Example 18

1. **Whoever** votes, is a good citizen.
2. **A** bat is a mammal.
3. **A** tiger has escaped.
4. **Any** day of the week is convenient.

Statement 1 in Example 18 has 'whoever' in it, which is comparable to the expressions 'every', 'he who…,' etc. In standard form it will be an 'A' statement: "All who vote are good citizens". Statement 2 also is an 'A' statement. Although the indefinite article 'a' does not clearly state that, when we examine the statement in its context we find that this 'a' means 'all'. In standard form, it will be: *All bats are mammals.* Statement 3 also contains 'a'. However, judging from the context, we can make out that the article 'a' in this case does not refer to all members of the class of tigers, but only to some particular member that has escaped. Accordingly, its standard form should be an 'I': "Some tiger is an animal which has escaped". Statement 4, which has 'any' in its standard form will again be an 'A' statement: "All days of the week are convenient days". The lesson to learn here is that in cases such as these it is better to be alert and to be sensitive to the context for translating correctly.

Note that there are categorical statements which may not even resemble categorical statements at all, particularly because they use **non-standard quantity terms**. As for example: "There are good human beings", or "Not everyone subscribes to Cable TV", or "Two students protested". Each of these, however, can be translated into standard form categorical statements as may be seen in the following example:

Example 19

Statements in non-standard form	Statements in standard form
There are good human beings	Some human beings are good human beings
Not everyone subscribes to Cable TV	Some people are not subscribers of Cable TV
Two students protested	Some students are persons who protested

The statement "Not everyone subscribes to Cable TV" is actually "(Not) everyone subscribes to Cable TV". It does not say no one subscribes to cable TV, but denies that everyone does, i.e., it is a denial of an 'A' statement. If you recall traditional Square of Opposition, then you will realize that a denial of an 'A' statement is an 'O' statement: "Some people are not subscribers of Cable TV". On the other hand, the statement "Two students protested" uses a numerical term for quantity. While translating into standard form, these numerical terms viz. One, Two, Three are all to be regarded as *Some*, in the sense of being *at least one*. Thus, the translation in standard form will be: "Some students are persons who protested". Similarly, quasi-numerical terms such as *many*, *most*, *few*, etc. too are to be regarded as *Some*, in the sense of not being *All*.

Some categorical statements **may not contain any quantity words** to indicate any quantity at all, e.g., "Cars are parked in front of the house" or "Whales are mammals". These can be rather problematic. Because they have no quantity terms, what the statements intend to express may be doubtful. Hence, they may be interpreted in different ways. So, we need to determine what they mean only by a careful examination of their context. The cited examples, however, fortunately are pretty straightforward. They can be safely rephrased in the standard form as: "Some cars are vehicles that are parked in front of the house" and "All whales are mammals". However, understandably, there can be statements where the intended meaning may not be so clear as in "Textbooks are useful" or "Logic problems are difficult". As already stated, translation of these into standard format requires careful attention to their contexts and what the user intends to assert.

There are **quasi-numerical terms** which require careful attention, such as *almost all*, *all but*, *except*, etc. Statements which use these expressions are called **exceptive statements** as they make exceptions in a general class. For example: "All but the first year students are eligible" or "All except the athletes are tired". These are actually compound statements which express *two assertions* rather than one. When translating these into standard form, choosing a single standard form categorical statement will not fairly represent them. Rather, they should be translated as a *conjunction* of two standard form categorical statements. For example: "All but the first year students are eligible" is to be translated in standard form as "All non-first year students are eligible" *and* "No first year students are eligible". Similarly, "All except the athletes are tired" in standard form is "All non-athletes are persons who are tired" *and* "No athletes are persons who are tired".

Example 20

Statements in non-standard form	Statements in standard form
All but the first year students are eligible.	All non-first year students are eligible, **and** no first year students are eligible.
All except the athletes are tired.	All non-athletes are persons who are tired, **and** no athletes are persons who are tired.

There are also statements which use the expression 'only' as in "Only citizens can vote". Statements which use this expression are known as **exclusive statements**. Rendering them as standard form categorical statements is very much possible, but it requires sensitivity towards their intended meaning. "Only citizens can vote", for example, does not only mean "All citizens can vote", but means something more than that. It means that *All those persons who can vote are citizens*. Its equivalent will be *No non-citizens are persons who can vote*. Though they are similar to the exceptive statements, the exclusive statements do not require an explicit conjunction to clarify their meaning in the standard form.

Finally, there may be reference to **quantity of places or times** as in the use of terms *wherever* or *whenever*. These too are translatable into standard form categorical statements. Consider the example: "The alarms ring wherever the safe is touched". The 'wherever' may be read as 'all places'. Thus, the statement can be rewritten as: "All places where the safe is touched are places where the alarms ring". Similarly, a statement such as "Dogs bark whenever a car passes by" may be translated into standard form categorical statement as follows: "All times when a car passes by are times when the dogs bark".

Example 21

Statements in non-standard form	**Statements in standard form**
The alarms ring wherever the light beam is intercepted.	All places where the safe is touched are places where the alarms ring.
Dogs bark whenever a car passes by.	All times when a car passes by are times when the dogs bark.

EXERCISE 9.6

1. Translate the following into standard form categorical statements:

a. Any mammal is a warm-blooded animal.
*b. Sheep are not hostile animals.
c. He who follows me will be rewarded.
d. Diplomats are overpaid and underworked.
e. Ten people have applied for the position.
f. Whenever trains come, the railway crossing gates are closed.
g. Only students are allowed free.
h. A day in peace is a day spent in heaven.
i. All that glitters in not gold.
j. A man-eater tiger has been spotted in the Sunderbans.
*k. Autumn days are short.
l. None but the brave deserves the praise.
m. Except the Asians, all other communities must report.
n. Most Europeans prefer bread.
o. A crocodile is a reptile.
p. Whoever comes, will be warmly received.
q. Rooms have air-conditioners.
r. Doors to the building are all sealed.
s. No decent human being will accept this offer.
*t. Few people have seen the Northern Lights.

9.7 Standard Form Syllogisms

A **syllogism** is a deductive argument which has exactly two premises and one conclusion and is composed exclusively of standard form categorical statements. So, the points to remember about a standard form syllogism are:

- It is composed of only **three standard form categorical statements.**
- A syllogism contains exactly **three terms** or **class names.**
- In the syllogism, each of these terms or class names occurs **exactly twice in the constituent statements.**

Major, Minor, and Middle Terms

The conclusion of the syllogism will have two terms as its subject and predicate. The predicate term of the conclusion is known as the **major term**, and the subject term of the conclusion is known as the **minor term**.

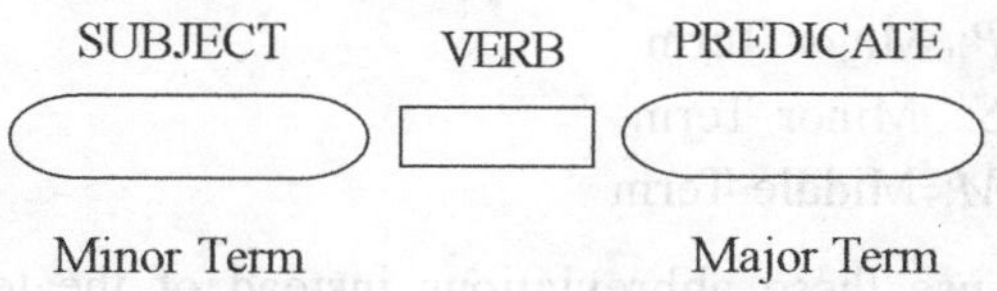

Fig. 9.19 The terms in a conclusion of a syllogism.

The only term left, or the third term, is called the **middle term**. The middle term occurs once in each of the two premises. Each major term and minor term also can occur only once more (apart from their occurrence in the conclusion) in the syllogism and, obviously each occurs in a different premise. The premise in which the middle term and the major term occur is known as the **major premise**. The premise in which the middle term and the minor term occur is known as the **minor premise**. Consider the following example:

Example 22

No objects made of gold are inexpensive objects.

Some ornaments are inexpensive objects.

Therefore, some ornaments are not objects made of gold.

According to the definition given above, 'ornaments' is the **minor term** in this example, and 'objects made of gold' is the **major term**. Each of these two terms appears once in the conclusion and once in one of the premises, but each in a different premise. *Inexpensive objects* is the only other term in this syllogism, and it is the **middle term**, occurring once in each of the premises. The middle term is called so since it acts as the mediating link between the minor and the major term. As per the definition given above, "No objects made of gold are inexpensive objects" is the **major premise**, and "Some ornaments are inexpensive objects" is the **minor premise**.

Standard form order: The standard form order for a syllogism is the following format:

- Major premise first
- Minor premise next
- Finally, the conclusion.

The syllogism given in Example 22 exhibits this standard format correctly. Any other sequence of the statements in a syllogism is *not* considered as in the standard format.

While referring to the schema or the formal structure of a syllogism, usually the following notation is used:

P: Major Term
S: Minor Term
M: Middle Term

Thus, if we use these abbreviations instead of the terms or the class names, the bare logical structure of the syllogism cited in Example 22 may be represented as follows:

Original syllogism	**Structure of the syllogism**
No objects made of gold are inexpensive objects.	No *P* is *M*
Some ornaments are inexpensive objects.	Some *S* is M
Therefore, some ornaments are not made of gold.	Therefore, some *S* is not *P*

This brings out the logical structure of the syllogism and the respective positions of the terms in it quite clearly.

Here are two more examples of syllogism and their respective structures in terms of *S*, *P*, *M*:

Example 23

1. All subscribers are persons who are listed.	All *P* are *M*
No persons who are listed are tax-evaders.	No *M* is *S*
Therefore, no tax-evaders are subscribers.	Therefore, no *S* is *P*

2. Some humans are creatures who have a long life span.	Some *M* are *P*.
All humans are mammals.	All *M* are *S*
Therefore, some mammals are creatures who have a long life span.	Therefore, some *S* are *P*

Mood of the Syllogism

According to traditional categorical logic, every syllogism is also supposed to have a **mood**. The mood is determined by the type of the standard form categorical statements the syllogism contains. Since a syllogism contains two premises and a conclusion, the mood of a syllogism is always represented by three statement letters given in the standard form order: major premise, minor premise, and conclusion.

Consider the first syllogism in Example 23 above: Its mood is **AEE**. The first letter represents the major premise: All subscribers are persons who are listed. The second letter represents the minor premise: No persons who are listed are tax-evaders. The third and the last letter represent the conclusion: No tax-evaders are subscribers.

For the second syllogism in Example 23, the mood is: **IAI.**

Figure of the Syllogism

Every syllogism is also supposed to have a diagram or a **figure.** The figure of a syllogism refers to the position of the major and minor term with respect to the position of the middle term in the premises.

Syllogisms can be diagrammatically represented in four precise ways:

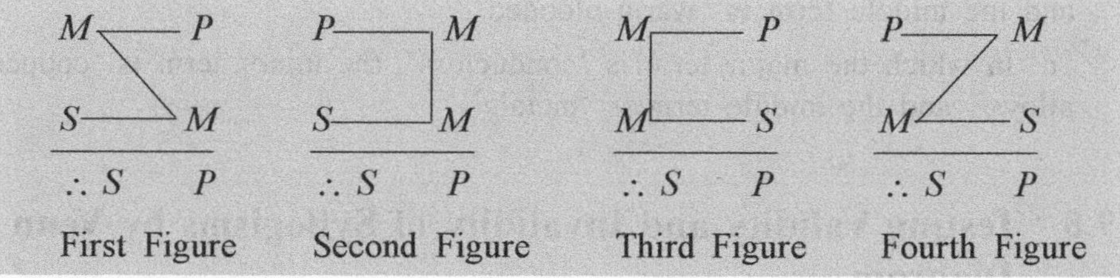

First Figure Second Figure Third Figure Fourth Figure

In first figure the position of the middle term (M) has to be the subject term of the major premise, and the predicate term of the minor premise. If we draw an imaginary line from the major term through the two occurrences of the middle term to the minor term, the first figure looks like an inverted 'Z'. The fourth figure on the other hand, looks like a 'Z'. Similarly, second figure looks like an inverted 'C', and third figure as a 'C'. But the positions of the terms are fixed. As shown in the figures above, the terms have to be exactly in the same positions. For example, if a syllogism has third figure it must have its middle term as the subject term in both major and minor premises. Every syllogism must have one of these four figures.

The traditional way to describe a standard form syllogism is to describe its mood and figure. For example, **EAE-1** would describe every syllogism which has the mood **EAE** and is in **first figure**. The schematic form of **EAE-1** is as follows:

No *M* is *P*
All *S* is *M*
∴ No *S* is *P*.

There can be in total 64 possible moods, and four figures. Thus, there can be exactly $64 \times 4 = 256$ possible standard forms for a syllogism. Out of these, the traditional logicians identified only a few as valid syllogistic forms. They also gave a name to each of the valid syllogistic form, such as "Barbara", "Cesares", etc.

EXERCISE 9.7

1. In the statements constituting a standard form syllogism, where should the middle term occur and how many times?

2. What is the right sequence of premises in a standard form syllogism?

3. How is it determined what the minor premise and major premise are in a syllogism?

4. Construct a standard form syllogism for each of the following cases:

*a. In which the major term is 'good actors', the minor term is 'comic role artists', and the middle term is 'astute observers of human life'.

b. In which the major term is 'mammals', the minor term is 'lizards', and the middle term is 'warm-blooded'.

*c. In which the major term is 'conductors', the minor term is 'copper alloys', and the middle term is 'metals'.

9.8 Testing Validity and Invalidity of Syllogisms by Venn Diagram

The form or the bare logical structure of the syllogism is very important in Aristotelian logic. For, traditionally this logic determines the validity or the invalidity of a syllogism exclusively by what form it has and independently of its content, or what the categorical statements of the syllogism are all about. As explained above (in Section 9.7), there are 256 possible forms for categorical syllogism. Out of these, following the traditional criteria, the medieval logicians accepted only 15 forms which were considered as valid *irrespective of the subject matter*. Each was assigned a unique name, such as 'Barbara', 'Camestres', etc. So, only syllogisms with these forms were considered as valid, no matter what their contents are.

Knowing what these forms imply requires a far more in-depth understanding of the various possible arrangements of terms in a syllogism than we have in this book. For us the task of determining the validity or invalidity of a syllogism will involve a more explicitly demonstrable technique, namely, the Venn Diagrams. In the rest of this section, this technique is explained in detail.

Since a syllogism necessarily involves three terms or class names, a Venn diagram of a syllogism will have three intersecting circles, as shown in Fig. 9.20.

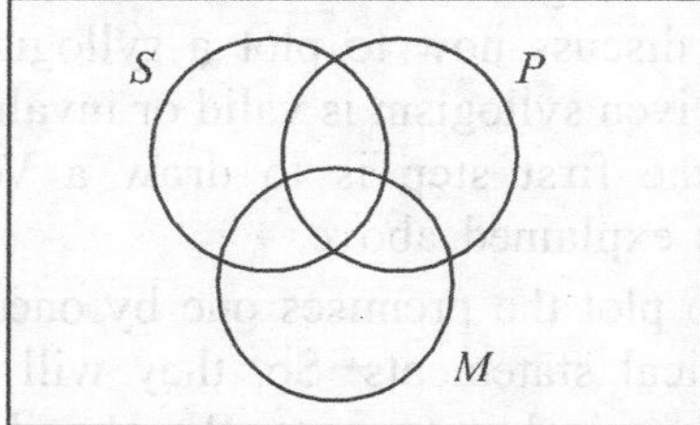

Fig. 9.20 Representation of a syllogism by Venn diagram.

With respect to *S*, *P*, *M*, the areas within this diagram may be marked, as can be seen in Fig. 9.21:

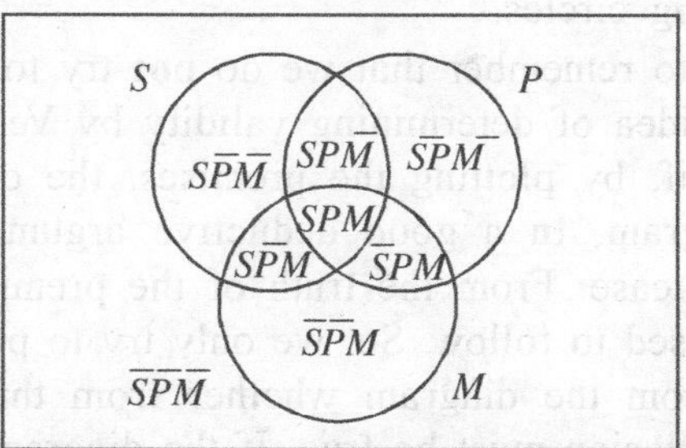

Fig. 9.21 The areas in the diagram.

Note that in Fig. 9.21, the rectangular outline, as before, represents the universe of discourse or UD. The areas within the three overlapping circles and the area outside of these circles have been identified by the letter signs to indicate which class each area represents. Thus we have eight areas within the diagram. $S\overline{P}\overline{M}$ stands for the class of *S*, where there is no presence of *M* or *P*. Similarly, $\overline{S}P\overline{M}$ represents the class of *P*, where there is no presence of *S* or *M*, and $\overline{S}\overline{P}M$ stands for the class of *M* where there is no *S* or *P*. However, there are areas where two or more classes overlap.

$SP\bar{M}$, for example, stands for the region where *S* and *P* intersect, but there is no presence of *M*. If in the diagram any member is shown to belong to this $SP\bar{M}$ region, it is supposed to be a member of both *S* and *P* without being a member of M. Similarly, $S\bar{P}M$ refers to the region where *S* and *M* intersect, but there is no presence of *P*, and $\bar{S}PM$ stands for the overlapping region between *P* and *M*, where there is no presence of *S*. There is only one area, *SPM*, where all three classes overlap. So, if, for instance, *S* refers to the class of women, *P* refers to the class of famous persons, and *M* refers to the class of entrepreneurs, then SPM stands for the class of famous women entrepreneurs. Of course, $\bar{S}\bar{P}\bar{M}$ represents the class of all things that are neither *S* nor *P* nor *M*, and yet falls within the universe of discourse. This is why this area is shown within the diagram but not within any of the overlapping circles.

Given this understanding of the areas within the Venn diagram for a syllogism, let us now discuss how to plot a syllogism on a diagram. Our task is to find out if a given syllogism is valid or invalid by the Venn diagram technique. For that, the first step is to draw a Venn diagram of three overlapping circles, as explained above.

The next step is to plot the premises one by one. The premises will be standard form categorical statements. So, they will be in one of the four standard forms for categorical statements. We already know how to plot *A*, *E*, *I*, and *O* in diagrams with two overlapping circles. We shall extend this knowledge to the diagram of three overlapping circles. In this, Fig. 9.21 with its marked areas will give us the pointers. Though the diagram will have three overlapping circles, at a time, however, you will need to deal only with two overlapping circles.

It is important to remember that we do **not** try to plot the conclusion. In fact, the whole idea of determining validity by Venn diagram is that a syllogism is valid if, by plotting the premises, the conclusion is already plotted in the diagram. In a good deductive argument, that is what is supposed to be the case. From the truth of the premises, the truth of the conclusion is supposed to follow. So, we only try to plot the premises, and then try to read from the diagram whether from this, the diagram also shows that the conclusion must be true. If the diagram does not show that the conclusion must be true, then the syllogism is invalid.

Consider the syllogism in the following example:

Example 24

All helpers for the charity event are volunteers.	All *P* are *M*.
No volunteer is a person recruited from outside the college.	No *M* is *S*.
Therefore, No person recruited from outside is a helper for the charity event.	No *S* is *P*.

In Example 24, the bare logical structure of the syllogism is given on its right. We test its validity first by plotting the major premise and then the minor premise. To understand the process better, each step shall be shown separately (see Figs. 9.22 and 9.23).

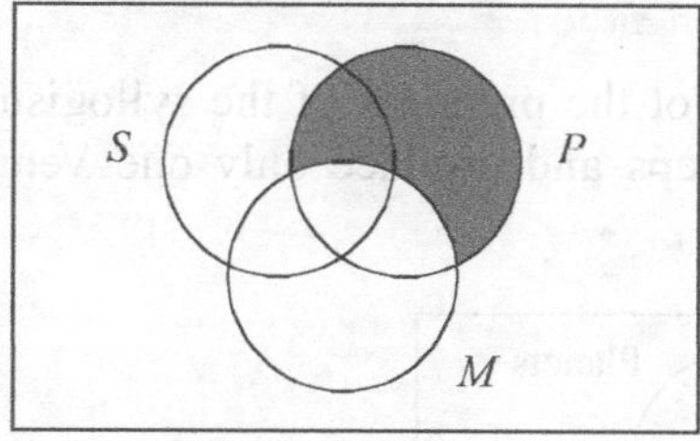

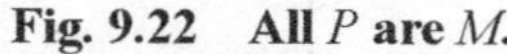

Fig. 9.22 All *P* are *M*.

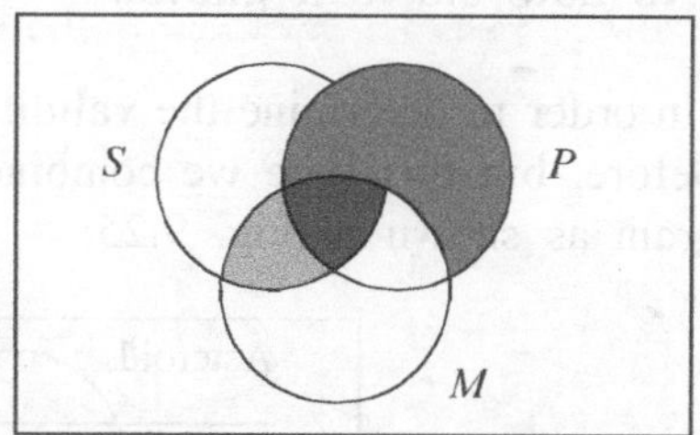

Fig. 9.23 All *P* are *M* and No *S* is *M*.

Figure 9.22 shows the situation after plotting the major premise, All *P* are *M*. As we know from our discussion of A statements (see Section 9.3), the way to plot it is to shade the entire region, that is, *P*, but not *M*. This in this context includes the areas $SP\overline{M}$ and $\overline{S}P\overline{M}$. We shade both of these areas, as shown in Fig. 9.22. It may help you to see *P* and *M* as the only two relevant circles at this point.

Then in Fig. 9.23, we add to this the information given in the minor premise that "No *M* is *S*". This requires that the area where *S* and *M* overlap must be shaded. In this context, this covers the areas *SPM* and $S\overline{P}M$. Again, while doing this, it may help as to focus only on *S* and *M* as the relevant circles.

Note, however, that Fig. 9.23, which has both the premises plotted on it, also show that the conclusion must be true, namely, that No *S* is *P*. While plotting the premises, the overlapping region between *S* and *P* has become completely shaded, which indicates that No *S* is *P*. This proves that the syllogism is **valid.** Given the premises, its conclusion follows.

Though for labelling the circles in the Venn diagram, we have followed the abbreviated class names *S*, *P* and *M*, it is also common to use the actual class names used in the syllogism, as in Fig. 9.24.

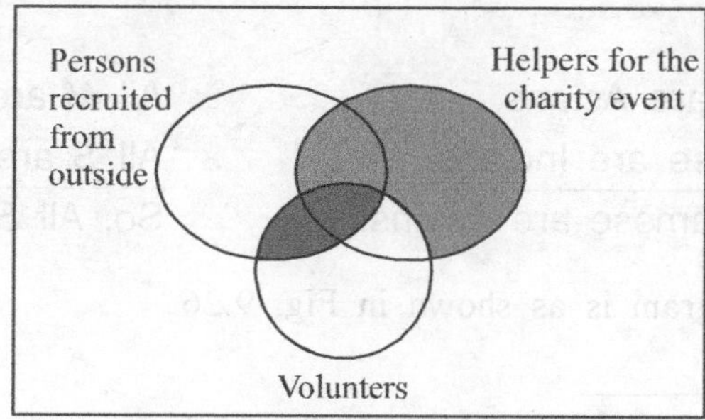

Fig. 9.24 Use of actual class names.

Here is another syllogism:

Example 25

No star is a planet.	No *M* is *P*.
No asteroid is a star.	No *S* is *M*.
No asteroid is a planet.	No *S* is *P*.

In order to determine the validity, we plot the premises of the syllogism as before, but this time we combine the steps and produce only one Venn diagram as shown in Fig. 9.25:

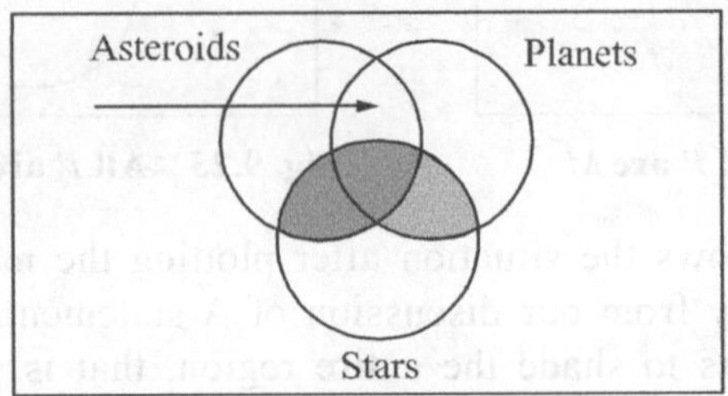

Fig. 9.25 Venn diagram for Example 25.

Plotting the major premise requires shading the area where stars and planets overlap, namely, the areas SPM and $\bar{S}PM$, and plotting the minor premise requires the shading of the intersection area between stars and asteroids, namely, the already shaded area SPM and $S\bar{P}M$. Note that by doing so, the diagram does *not* show that the conclusion too must be the case. We have not really established that no asteroid is a planet. As the arrow in Fig. 9.25 indicates, even after all the shading, there is still an unshaded area left in the diagram, where the classes of asteroids and planets intersect, which should have been shaded if the conclusion has to be the case. Because the entire overlapping area between asteroids and planets is not shaded, we have to admit that given the premises, it does not follow conclusively that no asteroids are planets[2]. The syllogism is thus shown by Venn diagram as **invalid**.

Here is another example:

Example 26

All Indians are Asians.	All *M* are *P*.
All Assamese are Indians.	All *S* are *M*.
So, All Assamese are Asians.	So, All *S* are *P*.

Its Venn diagram is as shown in Fig. 9.26.

---

[2]Incidentally, asteroids which are rocky or metallic objects are also known as minor planets or planetoids.

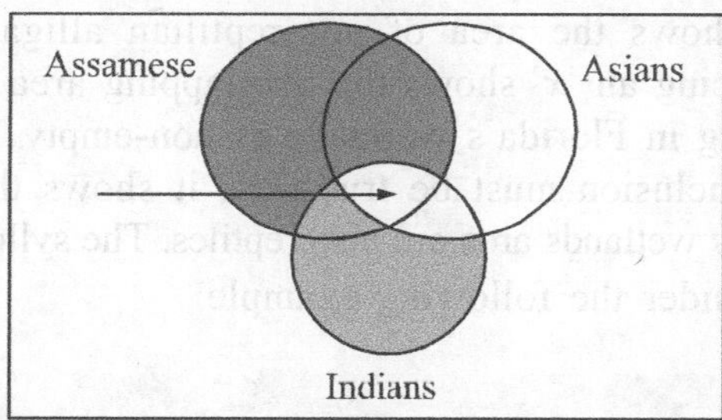

Fig. 9.26 Venn diagram for Example 26.

Plotting the major premise shades the area of non-Asian Indians, and plotting the minor premise shades the area of non-Indian Assamese. Have we thereby shown that all Assamese (who are Indians) must be Asians? Yes. In Fig. 9.26, the unshaded area marked by an arrow shows that the entire non-empty or unshaded region of Assamese class is also a part of the Asians class. This shows that the syllogism is **valid.** In order to be valid, the diagram for the premises must also include the plotting for the conclusion.

So far we have been dealing with syllogisms that are composed of universal statements. What happens when a syllogism is made of both universal and particular categorical statements, as is the case in the following example:

Example 27

All alligators are reptiles.	All *M* are *P*.
Some alligators are creatures that live in Florida's wetlands.	Some *M* are *S*.
So, some creatures that live in Florida's wetlands are reptiles.	So, some *S* are *P*.

When you have a combination of universal and particular statements among the premises, as a rule, *always plot the universal statement first.* Then, plot the particular statement. This is a safety rule so that the 'x' plotting the particular statement does not land in a shaded area, i.e., an area marked as empty. If we try to plot the particular statement first, we may place the 'x' in an area, which may become shaded after plotting the universal statement. Proper plotting of the syllogism in Example 27 leads to Fig. 9.27.

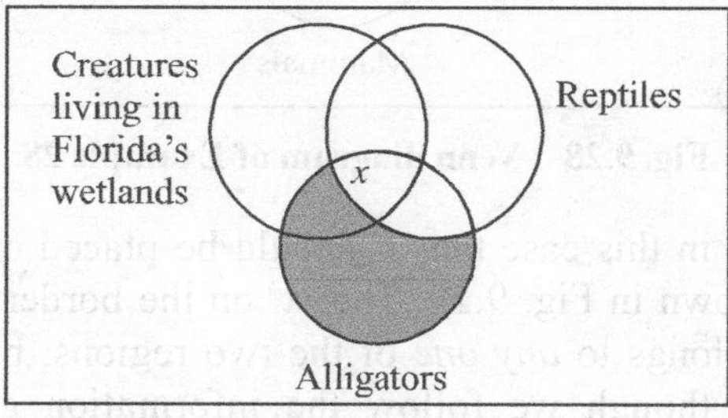

Fig. 9.27 Venn diagram of Example 27.

Figure 9.27 shows the area of non-reptilian alligators as shaded or empty, and by placing an '*x*' shows the overlapping area between alligators and creatures living in Florida's wetlands as non-empty. This automatically shows that the conclusion must be true, i.e., it shows that some creatures that live in Florida's wetlands area are also reptiles. The syllogism is thus **valid**.

However, consider the following example:

Example 28

All human beings are mammals.	All *P* are *M*.
Some underwater creatures are mammals.	Some *S* are *M*.
Therefore, some underwater creatures are human being.	Some *S* are *P*.

When you try to test it using the Venn diagram, a proper diagram may lead you to face a dilemma about the correct placing of the '*x*' as is required by the minor premise.

The major premise is easy to plot. As shown in Fig. 9.28, it requires that the area of non-mammal human beings should be shown as empty. The minor premise requires that the overlapping area between mammals and underwater creatures should be non-empty. This, however, poses a problem. For, the intersection area has two subareas in it: (a) the *SPM* area, i.e., the area of the underwater human mammals, and (b) the $S\bar{P}M$ area, i.e., the area of underwater creatures that are mammals but not human beings. But where to place the '*x*'? The interesting point is that placing it in area (a) makes the syllogism valid, whereas placing it in area (b) makes it invalid. The premises do not help us to reach a certain decision about this and, if we try to arbitrarily place the '*x*' is one area, then we are projecting a decision that is not warranted by the syllogism.

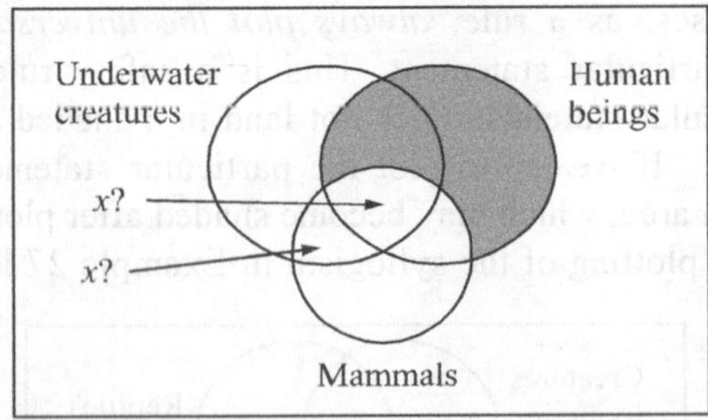

Fig. 9.28 Venn diagram of Example 28.

In all fairness, in this case the '*x*' should be placed on the *border of the two regions*, as shown in Fig. 9.29. The '*x*' on the border of the two regions indicates that it belongs to *any one* of the two regions, but does not specify the region. Thus, though we follow the information given in the minor premise, we do not go beyond it to place '*x*'.

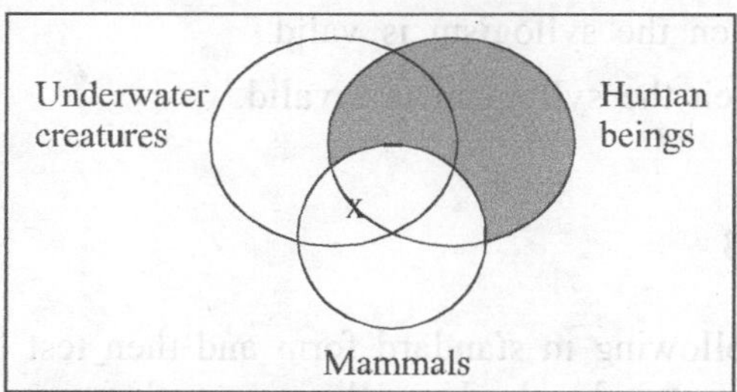

Fig. 9.29 The '*x*' on the border.

Now, if we examine the Venn diagram to see whether by proper plotting of the premises we have also plotted the conclusion or not, we find that we have not. In order for the conclusion "Some underwater creatures are humans" to be true, an '*x*' is needed in the overlapping area between the classes "Underwater creatures" and "Humans". We find that part of this area is shaded, and part, namely, the *SPM* area, is unshaded. However, there is no certainty that the '*x*' should land here. Moreover, if we examine the premises, we do not find anything that says that the conclusion follows from them. Rather, the conclusion seems to be patently false. This element of doubt in the truth of the conclusion, in spite of the truth of the premises, is enough to establish that the syllogism is **invalid**.

While this settles the matter with Example 28, perhaps further clarification is needed. What you need to learn from this example is that sometimes when clearer information from the premises is not forthcoming about its exact position, in all fairness, you may have to put an '*x*' on the border of two possible regions. In the case of Example 28, that led to the invalidity of the syllogism. From this, *you need not conclude* that a syllogism will be invalid whenever an '*x*' has to be placed on the border of two regions. Remember that the crucial test of validity or invalidity of a syllogism by the Venn diagram method is to ask whether the conclusion is clearly shown to be the case in the diagram merely by plotting the premises. In Example 28, this was not clearly shown and that is why the syllogism was invalid. No further conclusion from this is warranted.

Now, let us sum up what we have learnt. The steps involved in testing the validity or invalidity of a syllogism by Venn diagram are:

- ✓ Draw a Venn diagram consisting of three overlapping circles.
- ✓ Label the circles.
- ✓ Plot only the premises one by one.
- ✓ If there is a mixture of universal and particular statements among the premises, plot the universal premise before the particular statement.
- ✓ Check if by doing so the diagram shows that the conclusion must be the case.

✓ If yes, then the syllogism is valid.

✓ If not, then the syllogism is invalid.

EXERCISE 9.8

A. Arrange the following in standard form and then test the validity of the following syllogisms by the Venn diagram technique:

*1. No foreigners are residents, for, no foreigners are citizens and all citizens are residents.

2. No power-hungry person is a philosopher, and all active politicians are power-hungry persons; therefore, no philosophers are active politicians.

3. Some prime numbers are even, because some prime numbers are not odd numbers, and no even numbers are odd numbers.

4. All masterpieces are rare collectibles and all rare collectibles are commercially valuable items. Therefore, all masterpieces are commercially valuable items.

*5. Some residents of Kerala are Christians, because all residents of Kerala are Indians, and some Indians are Christians.

6. Some women are musicians, and some political dignitaries are women. Therefore, some political dignitaries are musicians.

7. No humans are cats, and all humans are mammals. Therefore, no cats are mammals.

8. No local cottage industries are Fortune 500 companies. For, no Fortune 500 companies are small scale enterprises and all local cottage industries are small scale industries.

9. All students are human beings. Therefore, no human beings are professors since no professors are students.

10. All employees of the company are insured by the company, but some board members are not employees of the company. Therefore, some board members are not people insured by the company.

B. Arrange the categorical statements, where necessary, into standard form syllogisms and translate the statements, where necessary, into standard form categorical statements *before* testing them with the Venn diagram technique:

*1. Elephants are not tigers and no elephants are carnivorous, so no tigers are carnivorous.

2. Each financially secure item requires government approval; for, every business project must be financially secure, and any business project requires government approval.

3. Not all food items are milk-products and every cheese is a milk product. Therefore, not every cheese is a food item.
4. No dairy product is a perishable item, for all seafood are perishable items, and no seafood are dairy products.
5. All the members are city dwellers, but one of the eligible persons does not live in the city. Therefore, a few eligible persons are not members.

9.9 The Problem of Existential Import

A categorical statement is said to have **existential import** if the class designated by its subject term is *assumed* to have at least one existing member, or, in other words, if the class designated by its subject term is *assumed* to be non-empty. This is easy to understand in cases of particular statements, for example:

Example 29

1. Some leaves are green.
2. Some leaves are not green.

If it is assumed that in these statements in Example 29 we are talking about some actually existing leaves, which in fact are green or not green, then these statements have existential import.

What about the universal statements, such as *A* and *E*? Do they also have existential import? Should we also assume that their subject terms too refer to classes with existing members? The classical logicians of Aristotelian tradition thought that *we should*. They assumed that we are referring to non-empty classes when we are using *A* or *E* statements. This seems to be their position, if we once more examine the traditional Square of Opposition. The Subalternation relation between *A* and *I*, or between *E* and *O* seems to presuppose existential import for all statements. One might say that the reason, why knowing that an *O* statement "Some Indians are not Asians" is false we can infer that its corresponding *E* statement "No Indians are Asians" must also be false is because the subject term *Indians* in both cases are assumed to refer to classes with at least one existing member.

The modern logicians, however, disagree on this point. It is safer, in their opinion, to not allow the *A* and *E* to have existential import. The main question is: When can we reasonably conclude that something exists? The opinion of the modern logicians is that *it is not logically safe or justified to assume existential import unless we have evidence*. Otherwise, the theory of logical validity may be compromised. Consider the statements in the following example.

Example 30

3. All winged horses are creatures faster than the Concorde.
4. No Hogwarts[3] students are people older than the Hogwarts Headmaster.

Statements 3 and 4 in Example 30 are *A* and *E* statements. If we have to follow the intuition of the classical logicians, then we have to say that these statements too have existential import, i.e. the subject terms *winged horses* or *Hogwarts students* refer to non-empty classes. But we know that there are no winged horses, and we also know that the Hogwarts students, no matter how real they seem when we read about them, are actually characters in a fiction!

Granting existential import to all categorical statements, including examples such as "All winged horses are creatures faster than the Concorde", has some serious adverse effects for the traditional Aristotelian logic. Since there are actually no winged horses, both the *A* statement "All winged horses are creatures faster than the Concorde" and its contradictory *O* statement "Some winged horses are not creatures faster than the Concorde" will both be false! This puts the traditional opposition of contradiction in jeopardy. For, in contradiction relation, exactly one of the pairs can be false at a time. So, it seems that we need to choose between the traditional relation of contradiction or the traditional assumption of existential import. Either existential import stays or the relation of contradiction stays!

It is possible that someone may try to salvage the situation by the following way: One might argue that we can keep out all the problematic categorical statements such as "All winged horses are creatures faster than the Concorde" or "No Hogwarts students are people older than the Hogwarts Headmaster" by adopting an overall assumption: that categorical statements will *always* have an existential assumption and their subject terms will never refer to empty classes.

Tempting as it may seem, this option, however, is not really very helpful. It has been criticised that this option will seriously and unnecessarily curb our power of expression through the use of categorical statements. We can not formulate any categorical statement which legitimately denies any member to a class. Consider, the statements in the following example:

Example 31

5. Some classes are classes that have no members.
6. All empty classes are classes without members.

---

[3]Hogwarts is the school of magic, created by the excellent creative imagination of J.K. Rowling in her Harry Potter series of books.

If this overall existential assumption becomes the norm, then we cannot even use statements such as statements 5 and 6 without contradicting ourselves.

Moreover, we should be able to use terms without making any existential commitment. For, sometimes we want to use terms specifically with the intention of keeping the class designated by the subject term empty. As, for example, the statement "All those who cheat in the exam will be expelled" does not presuppose the class of *cheaters in the exam*" to have existing members. Rather, its intended use is to keep that class empty. Also, sometimes we want to talk about theoretical entities without making any commitment about their existence. This is particularly true in the case of scientific principles. For instance, in science and mathematics we may refer to points, lines, frictionless planes, ideal gases, bodies in rest, or bodies not acted upon by any external forces but, while doing so, we may not want to commit ourselves to the claim that these entities actually physically exist.

For reasons such as these, **George Boole** and other modern logicians suggested that, instead of restricting on the kind of categorical statements we can use, it is better to restrict existential import only to *I* and *O* statements. This is known as the **Boolean interpretation**. Based on this view, we say that:

- *A* and *E* do *not* have existential import.
- Only *I* and *O* statements have existential import.

That is, all kinds of categorical statements are allowed, but we cannot assume the existence of individuals or entities mentioned in the subject term of the universal categorical statements, unless so specified. In fact, on Boolean interpretation it is an **existential fallacy** to assume existence where there is no evidence for such a claim.

According to Boolean interpretation, the universal statement *A* which claims *All S are P* is actually a conditional of the following kind: For any *x*, *if x* is *S*, then *x* is *P*. This does not commit us to say that there is at least one *x* and that *x* is *S*. It hypothetically or conditionally asserts that *if x* is *S*, then *x* is *P*. "All men are mortal" on Boolean interpretation would mean "if *x* is a man then *x* is mortal". Similarly, "No *S* are *P*" is actually a conditional assertion that *for any x, if x is S, then x is not P*. Thus, the statement "No leaves are green" would be taken to mean that "given any *x*, if *x* is a leaf, then *x* is not green". This does not commit us in any way to assume that the class of leaves is a non-empty class.

Obviously, this changes the traditional relations of oppositions drastically. Since *A* and *E* do not have existential import and *I* and *O* do, logically they become significantly apart. Thus, on Boolean interpretation the relation of subalternation is not acceptable. It is an existential fallacy to infer a statement which has existential import from premises which have none. From the truth of the universal, the truth of the particular cannot follow anymore. This is easy to understand from examples such as these:

Example 32

7. All winged horses are creatures faster than the Concorde. (*A*)

Note that on Boolean interpretation, statement 7 in Example 32 which is an *A* statement, conditionally asserts:

7′. For any *x*, if *x* is a winged horse then it is a creature faster than the Concorde.

Note also that because there is no winged horse, this makes the antecedent of the above conditional "*x* is a winged horse" false. Since a conditional with a false antecedent is always true, it too is true. Similarly, and *for the same reason*, this *E* statement too is true:

Example 33

8. No winged horses are creatures faster than the Concorde. (*E*)

Since there are no winged horses, the conditional "for any *x*, if *x* is a winged horse then *x* is a creature faster than the Concorde" too is true. Note that though the above mentioned *A* and *E* are true, from that we cannot infer that "Some winged horses are creatures faster than the Concorde" (*I*) is true. Nor can we infer that "Some winged horses are not creatures faster than the Concorde" (*O*) is true.

Because it has existential import, on Boolean interpretation, a particular statement such as "Some winged horses are creatures faster than the Concorde" is to be understood as a *conjunction* with an existential claim. It is necessary to assert: "There is some *x* which is a winged horse and *x* is a creature faster than the Concorde".

Example 34

9. Some winged horses are creatures faster than the Concorde.
9′. There is some *x* which is a winged horse **and** *x* is a creature faster than the Concorde.

In Example 34, statement 9′ is a much stronger claim than the conditional assertion made by the universal statements, and it is simply false. For, there is no *x* which is a winged horse; and a false conjunct makes the whole conjunction false. However, from its falsity, the falsity of "All winged horses are creatures that are faster than the Concorde" does not follow. We have already seen that "All winged horses are creatures that are faster than the Concorde" can be true particularly when there are no winged horses. This clearly makes subalternation unacceptable.

We have also shown above that because they have no existential import *A* and *E* both can be true together, as in the case of "All winged horses are creatures that are faster than the Concorde" and "No winged horses are creatures that are faster than the Concorde". Since *A* and *E* can be both true together, we have to give up the traditional relation of contrary too. For, according to the traditional definition, the contrary pairs both may be false together, but both cannot be true together.

Moreover, we have shown that because they have existential import, in Boolean interpretation *I* and *O* can be false together as in the case of "Some winged horses are creatures faster than the Concorde" and "Some winged horses are not creatures faster than the Concorde". This shows the relation of subcontrary between *I* and *O* as unacceptable. For, in the traditional definition, the subcontrary pairs may be true together but cannot be false together.

Thus, the fallout from the problem of existential import is that on Boolean interpretation in the Square of Opposition, only the relation of contradiction can remain. All other relations among categorical statements must be rejected.

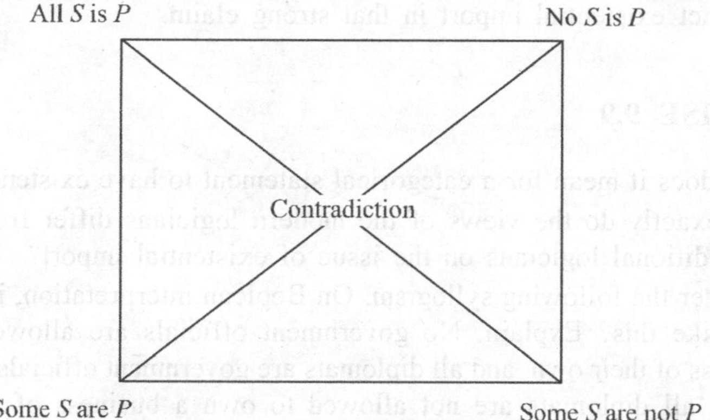

Fig. 9.30 Square of Opposition after Boolean interpretation.

Note that on this interpretation all immediate inferences by limitation, such as conversion by limitation or contraposition by limitation, are also rejected. For, by limitation processes assume that the subject class is not empty, or that there is at least one member in the subject class. Boolean interpretation disallows exactly that assumption. Therefore, after Boolean interpretation conversion by limitation on *A*, or contraposition by limitation on *E*, are to be discontinued.

The upshot from the Boolean interpretation is that the existence of members in the class, referred to by its subject term, is to be assumed only in the case of *I* and *O* statements. The existence of members in the class referred to by its subject term is *not* to be assumed in case of universal statements, *A* and *E*. If the existence of members of the subject term of a universal statement is intended, then one must assert this by adding an existential statement separately. Thus, if we wish to assert "All human beings are mortal" and wish to refer to existing human beings, it will have to be asserted *as a conjunction* as follows:

For any x, if x is a human being then x is mortal, and there is at least x and x is a human being.

To summarize, the effect of Boolean interpretation is:

✓ Only Contradiction relation survives in square of opposition

✓ Conversion: Valid only for *I* and *E*.

✓ Obversion: Valid for all.

✓ Contraposition: Valid only for *O* and *A*.

You may now realize that, in our Venn diagram of the four standard categorical statements, *A*, *E*, *I*, and *O*, we have followed this stricture. Our Venn diagrams of *A* and *E* merely state that a certain area is empty, thereby we do not wish to commit ourselves to assert that the rest of the regions must have existent members. Similarly, our Venn diagrams of *I* and *O* clearly assert the existence of at least one member in a certain region. There is a distinct existential import in that strong claim.

EXERCISE 9.9

1. What does it mean for a categorical statement to have existential import?
2. How exactly do the views of the modern logicians differ from those of the traditional logicians on the issue of existential import?

*3. Consider the following syllogism. On Boolean interpretation, is it valid to infer like this? Explain: No government officials are allowed to run a business of their own, and all diplomats are government officials. Therefore, almost all diplomats are not allowed to own a business of their own.

4. On Boolean interpretation, why is the contrary relation between *A* and *E* is no longer acceptable? Explain with your own examples.
5. On Boolean interpretation, can we still talk of existent human beings if we want to assert "all humans are mortals"? Explain.

Keywords

Categorical statements: Statements which assert something about the relationships between the classes referred to by their subject and predicate terms.

Category: A predicate or a fundamental class of things.

Class: A collection of objects or entities with a common characteristic.

Complementary class: For any class *C*, its complementary class will contain all the objects that are not in *C*. The usual way to refer is by the use of the overbar sign. For class *C*, the complementary class is $\bar{C}$.

Contraposition by limitation: Contraposition after a limitation of the quantity of the statement in question. Restricted application.

Conversion by limitation: Conversion after a limitation of the quantity of the statement in question. Restricted application.

Existential fallacy: To assume existence where there is no evidence to assume so. Or, to infer a particular statement with existential import from universal statements which in Boolean interpretation have no existential import.

Figure: Arrangement of major and minor terms with respect to the position of the middle term in the standard form syllogism.

Immediate inference: Inference from a single premise.

Major premise: Premise which contains the major term in a syllogism.

Major term: Predicate term of the conclusion of a syllogism.

Minor premise: Premise which contains the minor term in a syllogism.

Minor term: Subject term of the conclusion of a syllogism.

Mood: The three letters signifying the type of categorical statements a syllogism contains. The sequence in the letters must follow the standard form order of a syllogism.

Opposition: The differences in quantity and quality between categorical statements with same subject and predicate terms.

Particular affirmative: '*I*' statement. A categorical statement with particular quantity and affirmative quality.

Particular negative: '*O*' statement. A categorical statement with particular quantity and negative quality.

Quality: The affirmation or denial of class relationships in a categorical statement.

Quantity: 'How many' members of the class designated by subject term are intended. Standard quantity terms are 'all' or 'some'.

Standard form: Proper format.

Successive immediate inference chain: Inference chain formed by repeated application of immediate inference patterns.

Syllogism: A deductive argument which is composed exactly three standard form categorical statements, and three terms, each occurring exactly twice in the argument.

Traditional square of opposition: A diagram to depict the traditional oppositions among categorical statements with the same subject and predicate terms.

Universal affirmative: '*A*' statement. A categorical statement with universal quantity and affirmative quality.

Universal negative: '*E*' statement. A categorical statement with universal quantity and negative quality.

Universe of discourse (U.D.): The context or everything that is assumed or believed for a discussion.

CHAPTER

FIRST ORDER PREDICATE LOGIC: SYNTAX AND SYMBOLIZATION

10.1 Basics

Predicate logic, as its name indicates, is a logic concerned with predicates, or with predication of properties, and also with things or objects to which the predicates may be ascribed. In more formal terms, it is also known as **Quantification Theory** or the **Predicate Calculus**.

Predicate logic contains the entire Propositional logic that we have learnt in the previous chapters. In addition, as we shall see in this chapter, it also has a set of new vocabulary and a language of its own. It has its own grammar or *syntax* which helps us to formulate statements which are considered well-formed in this logic. In Chapter 11, we shall learn about its *semantics*, i.e. about how to capture or codify the meaning and truth-conditions of statements expressed in this language. Chapter 12 will introduce us to its deductive system, which with a set of new quantification rules, records, demonstrates and captures the inferences that are correct or valid in this logic.

Individual Constants

Like any other language, predicate logic has its own alphabets and rules to bind the alphabets into acceptable bunches. In Chapter 9, we have already seen that Aristotelian logic refers to entities as members of a certain class, (e.g. horses are members of the class of *horses*), and identifies classes by a common property that the class members share (e.g. the property of *being a horse*). We have also seen how in terms of their having or not having certain properties, we can identify them as members of this class or that class. Yet, for Aristotelian logic, reference to very specific items in the class is a bit problematic. Consider the statements in the following example:

Example 1

a. This diskette is damaged.

b. Kalidasa is a poet.

c. Freud is not a mathematician.

Each of these statements affirms or denies that a *specific individual or object* belongs to a certain class. By having the property of 'being a poet' Kalidasa, a very specific person, belongs to the class of the poets. Similarly, by not having the property of 'being a mathematician', Freud, the specific individual, does not belong to the class of mathematicians. In Aristotelian logic, these are known as **singular propositions**, which we shall refer to as singular statements.

Since there are only four standard forms for statements in categorical logic, singular statements had to be fitted into that scheme. It is customary in Aristotelian tradition to take *affirmative singular statements as 'A' or universal affirmative*, and *negative singular statements as 'E' or universal negative*. Thus, "Kalidasa is a poet" is interpreted as the '*A*' statement : *All members of the class which contains only Kalidasa are poets*. "Freud is not a mathematician" is interpreted as an '*E*' statement: No member of the class of which contains only Freud is a mathematician.

Predicate logic, however, has a very different way of capturing the *uniqueness* of the reference of the singular statements. Its vocabulary has **singular terms**, whose function is to denote a specific person or an object. Singular terms can be of two kinds: proper names and definite descriptions. It uses these singular terms uniquiely 'Kalidasa', 'Freud', 'Dr. Manmohan Singh' are examples of proper names. 'The even prime number', or 'the tallest mountain in the world' or 'the author of *The Hobbits*' are examples of definite descriptions.

Not every singular term designates something. In its normal use 'Sherlock Holmes' or 'Phantom' does not designate any specific person because there is no such person as Sherlock Holmes or Phantom. Similarly, the definite description 'the largest natural number' does not designate any specific member because there is no such number. What a proper name or definite description designates, if any, depends upon the context in which it is used. In its most familiar usage, 'Kalidasa' may designate the great Indian poet and dramatist who thrived during the reigns of Chandragupta II Vikramaditya and wrote unparallel Sanskrit plays such as *Abhinjnana Shakuntalam* and works in verses such as the *Meghdootam*. But in another context 'Kalidasa' may designate a different person. For example, you may know of a 'Kalidasa' who is your local grocer. Thus, a context is required in which the singular terms can be said to designate a particular individual. When we are dealing with a group of statements, as in an argument, the context that is assumed must remain the same for all the statements so that the same singular term designates the same thing in each of its occurrences in that set of statements. Its reference has to remain constant.

The singular terms are represented in predicate logic by the **individual constants**. These are small or lowercase letters from '*a*' to '*w*', with or without numerical subscripts. Their function is to denote *only one, unique individual* or *object* from the domain of discourse. Since their reference remains *fixed* or *constant* within a given context, they are called *individual constants.* Usually, an individual or entity is referred to by the first letter of its name. The singular term, *Kalidasa,* **which is a proper name,** may be referred to as '*k*', and *Freud* as '*f*'. For *this diskette,* which is a definite description, we may use the individual constant 'd_2'.

Singular term	Individual constant
Kalidasa	k
Freud	f
This diskette	d_2

Predicates

Predicates are linguistic expressions of properties. In other words, predicates are words or expressions that we use to refer to properties or attributes that things have. For example, we may use the predicate term 'red' to refer to the property of 'being red' that a flower has. We have already talked about individuals and how to refer to them in Predicate logic. Now, we have to learn how to refer to properties of these individuals in Predicate logic.

For predicates, Predicate logic uses the capital letters such as '*A*', '*C*' etc, with or without subscripts. These are known as the **predicate letters.**

Let us consider the statement:

This diskette is damaged

Predicate logic would interpret this statement as saying: "This diskette has the property of 'being damaged'". Or, 'being damaged' is predicated to this diskette. The property of being damaged may be symbolized by the predicate letter '*D*'.

Similarly, "is a poet" may be symbolized in Predicate logic by the predicate letter *P*, and "is a mathematician", by *M*.

Predicates	Predicate letters
Is damaged	D
Is a poet	P
Is a mathematician	M

N-Place predicates. Since different kinds of properties can belong to different number of individuals, predicates too are supposed to be ***n*-place**, where '*n*' stands for the number of individuals required for predication. Accordingly, for symbolizing such ***n*-place predicates**, we use ***n*-place predicate letters**. For example, **one-place predicate** letters refer to monadic properties or properties which require one individual for predication. For example, consider the predicate 'being a mathematician' which may belong to this individual or that individual, but needs only one individual for its expression "____ is a mathematician". Compare this to, for instance, **two-place predicates**, such as 'being the husband of', or 'being greater than'. Each of these two-place predicates requires two individuals or objects. Someone has to be husband of someone else, or something has to be greater than something else. Similarly, a **three-place predicate** may be 'being in between of' as in the linguistic expression "Kharagpur is in between Kolkata and Puri". A **four-place predicate** may be: "buying something for a monetary value". This requires four items or individuals as in 'someone *x* has to buy *y* from *w* for *u* amount'.

Prefix type notation: It is time now to learn how to express in Predicate logic predicates along with the individuals to whom these are predicated. In order to express predicates or properties and their relation to entities or objects, we shall use a **prefix type notation**, in which the predicate letters are *prefixed* or written to the left of the individuals or objects. Thus, our examples will be symbolized as shown below:

Singular statements	**Their symbolization in Predicate Logic**
This diskette is damaged	$\boldsymbol{Dd_2}$
Kalidasa is a poet	***Pk***
Freud is not a mathematician	**~*Mf***

In each of the symbolizations, the predicate letter has been highlighted to draw your attention to the prefixed notation. Note that in order to symbolize *Freud is not a mathematician* we have combined the '~' from propositional logic with the predicate logic vocabulary. Since predicate logic contains the propositional logic, this combination is perfectly alright. Predicates followed by the appropriate number of individual constants of predicate logic are the atomic statements of predicate logic. 'Being damaged' is a monadic property, and it is predicated to one object, hence 'Dd_2' is an atomic statement of predicate logic. Similarly, 'being a poet' and 'being a mathematician' are also monadic properties, and '*Pk*' and '*~Mf*' too are atomic statements of Predicate logic.

It is customary in Predicate logic to use the same prefix notation for symbolizing the *n*-**place predicates, where** *n*-**place predicates** are followed by *n*-constants or *n*-**variables** (Variables are discussed below in this section).

For example, the statement "12 is greater than 9" contains the two-place predicate 'greater than', where '*Gxy*' stands for *x* being greater than *y*. This statement can be rewritten as:

Gtn

where '*t*' stands for number twelve and '*n*' for the number nine.

The statement "Kharagpur is in between Kolkata and Puri" contains the three-place predicate 'being in between', where '*Bxyz*' stands for "*x* is between *y* and *z*", and '*g*' stands for Kharagpur, '*k*' for Kolkata and *p* for Puri, the statement may be translated as:

Bgkp

Both the two-place and three-place predicates are examples of *n*-place predicates. They express a certain specific relationship between the terms that they relate. They are also known as relational predicates. We shall take up the topic of **relational predicates** in Section 10.6.

For the time being, however, let us keep our discussion for the remainder of this section at a basic level with the one-place predicates.

***n*-place predicates**	**Their symbolization in Predicate logic**
12 > 9	*Gtn*
Kharagpur is in between Kolkata and Puri	*Bgkp*

Remember that in developing Predicate logic, we do not abandon the propositional logic. So, Predicate logic also contains truthfunctionally compound statements, such as: "Rushdie is arrogant but he writes well". Using the following symbolization key, the statement may be translated as follows:

Example 2

Rushdie is arrogant but he writes well.

Ax: *x* is arrogant. Translation in predicate logic: ***Ar* • *Wr***

Wx: *x* writes well.

r: Rushdie

Note that '*Ar* • *Wr*' is a **truth-functional compound statement** which has, as its conjuncts, atomic statements of predicate logic. As you know from previous chapters, this statement will be true *iff* both its conjuncts are true; it will be false otherwise. In the symbolization key, expressions such as '*Ax*' are to be understood *any x* that has a certain property. '*Ax*' stands for the key to translating *any x* who is arrogant. In the translation, we have replaced the '*x*' by the individual constant '*r*' which stands for Rushdie.

Individual Variables

This brings us to the discussion about **individual variables,** which Predicate logic also uses. Individual variables, like individual constants, are terms which stand for objects or individuals in the domain.

However, variables are by nature quite different from the constants. A variable is just a *place marker*, it is not like a name. Its reference does not remain as uniquely fixed as that of a constant. Variables serve the function of referring to unspecified individuals. For example, the mathematician may want to start a proof by stating "Let x be a number greater than 100", or a philosopher may want to state "Let us take any individual in the society". In these cases, the reference is to arbitrary entities within a specified class and the use of variables serves the purpose very well.

Variables also serve when you do not have enough information to refer to very specific individuals. Suppose that you know that someone in a batch got an '*A*' in logic, but you do not know who got it. You would perhaps want to assert a statement with unspecified reference as "Someone got '*A*' in logic".

Variables also help us to maintain generality in our discussion. For example, when we want to assert "take any natural number x, there is always a number y such that $x > y$", we do not want to mean any specific number. In the symbolization key for Example 2, when we used expressions such as '*Ax*' and '*Wx*' as keys to predicates, we used variables to keep the reference sufficiently general for the sake of translation.

In Predicate logic, to symbolize the individual variables, it is customary to use **lower case letters towards the end of the alphabets,** such as '*w*', '*x*', '*y*', etc., with or without numerical subscripts. In order to symbolize their relations to the predicates, we use the same prefix notations. For example, consider the expression:

y is a poet.

It may be symbolized as

$$Py$$

Note that as you do not know what or who that y is, '*Py*' is *neither true nor false*. Compare this with '*Pk*' (which stands for "Kalidasa is a poet") which you know from history is true. Expressions like '*Py*' are known as **propositional functions**, which are supposed to symbolize only a common pattern of all singular statements that may result by substituting the variable by an individual constant. If we, for instance, replace or substitute the '*y*' in '*Py*' by the '*k*', we shall get '*Pk*'. If we choose to replace the '*y*' by '*f*', then we get '*Pf*', and so on. '*Pk*' and '*Pf*' are exemplars of the common pattern represented by '*Py*'. In this sense, any singular statement is a substitution instance or a result of replacement of a propositional function.

This ends our introduction to the basic vocabulary of predicate logic. Before we can leave this section, one more explanation is needed. You may have noted in the title of this chapter that the Predicate logic that we are discussing is called the **First Order Predicate Logic**. The reason why it is called so is because, in the order of Predicate logics, it is the first or the most elementary kind of Predicate logic. In it, only simpler predications such as properties of individuals or objects are considered. There can be complicated predications where we need to consider *properties of properties* and *quantity of properties*, and that would be the Second Order Predicate Logic. In higher order logics, we can have variables standing for properties such as '*F*' or '*G*', etc., and property constants. In this book, we shall be concerned only with First Order Predicate Logic where our considerations will remain at a more basic level of predications about objects in terms of their properties.

EXERCISE 10.1

1. Symbolize the following statements using the symbolization key:

Sx: *x* is sincere.	*Hx*: *x* is hardworking.
Ix: *x* is intelligent.	*Bx*: *x* is handsome.
Rx: *x* is rich.	a: Anil.
s: Sunil.	n: Neel.

*a. Sunil is both rich and handsome, but he is not intelligent.

b. Neel is intelligent and handsome but not rich.

c. Anil is sincere and intelligent but not handsome.

d. If Anil and Neel are both intelligent, then they are also hardworking.

e. Sunil is neither intelligent nor sincere nor hardworking,

f. Either Neel is intelligent and handsome or he is intelligent and sincere.

g. It is not the case that Anil, Sunil and Neel are all rich.

h. At least one of Anil, Sunil and Neel is handsome.

i. At most two of Anil, Sunil and Neel are intelligent.

*j. Anil is sincere if and only if he is hardworking.

2. What is the difference between an individual constant and an individual variable? Explain with an example of your own.

***3.** Does the statement "some properties are coextensive" belong to First Order Predicate Logic? Justify your answer.

10.2 Quantifiers

Quantifiers are expressions in Predicate logic that state *how many* of the individuals or objects have the property in question. They do *not* state *which* one of the individuals have the property. A quantifier consists of:

- A left parenthesis or '('
- A quantifier symbol
- One of the individual variable symbols
- A right parenthesis or ')'

In predicate logic, we have two *quantifier symbols*:

- the inverted 'A' or $\forall$
- and the inverted 'E' or $\exists$

Thus, a quantifier symbol in Predicate logic will be any of the following kind:

$$(\forall x), (\forall y), (\forall w), (\exists x), (\exists y), (\exists z) \text{ etc.}$$

These quantifiers give us a way to symbolize quantity terms such as 'all', 'some', 'every', 'none', which may occur in statements about predications, as we have seen in Categorical logic. Predicate Logic uses only two kinds of quantifier symbols: **Universal Quantifier** and **Existential Quantifier**.

Universal Quantifier

The '$\forall$' corresponds to universal quantity terms such as 'all' or 'every' and their equivalent expressions in English. So, if you want to symbolize the statement, e.g. "Everything is a temporary thing" then we can translate the 'every' in terms of a quantifier as '$(\forall x)$'. Note that '$(\forall x)$' has all the components of a quantifier as mentioned above. It has the appropriate quantifier symbol along with an individual variable 'x', and it is enclosed within a pair of parentheses. '$(\forall x)$' stands for 'for all x' or 'for any x', or 'for every x'. It is known as the **universal quantifier**.

Suppose we want to state "Everything is a temporary thing" in predicate logic. Note that the statement has reference to things, a quantity term telling us how many of those things, and a property that belongs to those things. Your symbolization has to pay attention to all these aspects. We have a property 'being a temporary thing' in that statement, for which we shall need a predicate letter. Let us use 'Tx' to stand for 'x is a temporary thing'. For 'everything', we can use the universal quantifier. Your universe of discourse, unless it is restricted, will take care of the reference to things.

Tx: x is temporary.

In the beginning, in moving from English to language of predicate logic and back to English, you may find it useful to pass through a quasi-English paraphrase. Let us symbolize the statement "Everything is a temporary thing" in predicate logic step by step through such a paraphrase:

Example 3

Everything is a temporary thing.

Which can be paraphrased as:

Step 1. For all *x*, *x* has the property of being temporary
or, for all *x*, *x* is temporary.

Replacing the underlined segment where the property is predicated we come to step 2:

Step 2. For all *x Tx*

Now replacing the underlined quantity segment in For all *x Tx*, we arrive at step 3:

Step 3. $(\forall x)\ Tx$

If you want to say "Nothing is temporary", even then you need the universal quantifier. As is shown below, it will be useful to go through a paraphrase:

Example 4

Nothing is temporary.

Step 1. Rephrased: For all *x*, *x* is not temporary.

Step 2. Translated: $(\forall x)\ {\sim}Tx$

Existential Quantifier

The '$\exists$', on the other hand, stands for particular quantity terms such as 'some', 'a few', etc. and their equivalent terms in English. As a quantifier, it is used as '$(\exists x)$'. '$(\exists x)$' stands for the expression "There is at least one *x*". If we recall Boolean interpretation of the particular statements, then we know that particular statements carry an existential import. This existential import is acknowledged in the expression "There is at least one *x*". Not only the expression refers to the quantity (at least one) of things but also commits that at least one of the things referred to exists. '$(\exists x)$' is known as the **existential quantifier**.

Statements such as "Some things are temporary" may be paraphrased as

There is at least one *x* such that *x* is temporary.

Using the same way of translation as shown above, we may translate the English statement in predicate logic as

$$(\exists x)\ Tx$$

Similarly, "Some things are not temporary" will be rephrased as

There is at least one x such that x is not temporary.

Note that the 'not' or the negation appears only in the predication part, not in the quantity part. Translated, it will look like:

$$(\exists x) \sim Tx$$

It should be mentioned that it is not compulsory for translation with universal or existential quantifiers to use the variable 'x'. It does not matter which variable we use, as long as we use it from the letters set aside as variable letters and we use it consistently within the context. Thus, '$(\forall x)$ Tx' and '$(\exists x)$ Tx' may very well be symbolically represented as '$(\forall z)$ Tz' and '$(\exists u)$ Tu'.

Whenever statements are formed by placing a quantifier, whether universal or existential, *in front* of it, we have **general statements**. These are to be distinguished from other statements of predicate logic, such as the singular statements or the truth-functional compounds.

Symbolization of Categorical Statements with Quantifiers

Let us now revisit the four standard form categorical statements: *A*, *E*, *I* and *O*, and see how they can be translated into predicate logic. Suppose we start out with the simple '*A*' statement:

Every dog is a mammal.

There are two properties mentioned in this statement, 'being a dog' and 'being a mammal'. Accordingly, the symbolization key must have two predicate letters with a variable each for non-specific reference:

Dy: y is a dog.

My: y is a mammal.

Note also that the property of 'being a mammal' predicated to every member who has the property of being a dog. Clearly, we need universal quantifier in this case.

On Boolean interpretation, as we have seen in Chapter 9, universal statements are actually conditional statements with no existential commitment. Accordingly, we may paraphrase it as:

For every y, if y is a dog then y is a mammal.

The expression "if y is a dog then y is a mammal" may be translated with a truth-functional symbol '$\supset$'. Thus translated, it becomes

$$(\forall y)\,(Dy \supset My)$$

Using the same symbolization key, we may now translate the '*E*' statement 'No dog is a mammal" as:

$$(\forall y)\,(Dy \supset \sim My)$$

Note that "No dog is a mammal" can be paraphrased as:

For every *y*, if *y* is a dog, then *y* is a not mammal.

The statement does not deny the predication of the property of 'being a dog', but it denies the property of 'being a mammal' to every dog. This is the reason the translation "$(\forall y)\,(Dy \supset \sim My)$" has the negation sign '~' before '*My*'.

I and *O* statements, for obvious reasons, will require the existential quantifier. Let us take the *I* statement first:

Some dogs are mammals.

When paraphrased, we have to admit the existential import and also the property predication. It has to be stronger assertion than the conditional we state for the universal statements. Considering these aspects, the following may be the paraphrase for the *I* statement above:

There is at least one *y* such that *y* is a dog and *y* is a mammal

Translated, this becomes

$$(\exists y)\,(Dy \bullet My)$$

Note that a truth-functional symbol '•' from propositional logic has been used to denote that both properties belong to the '*y*' in question.

Similarly, we can paraphrase the *O* statement:

Some dogs are not mammals

as:

There is at least one *y* such that *y* is a dog and *y* is not a mammal. And it is translated as

$$(\exists y)\,(Dy \bullet \sim My)$$

As a rule, if we may use 'ϕ' (Greek letter 'phi') and 'ψ' (Greek letter 'psi') as two arbitrary predicate letters, the format for translating *A*, *E*, *I*, *O* is as follows:

$$(\forall y)(\phi y \supset \psi y) \qquad A$$

$$(\forall y)(\phi y \supset \sim \psi y) \qquad E$$

$$(\exists y)\,(\phi y \bullet \psi y) \qquad I$$

$$(\exists y)(\phi y \bullet \sim \psi y) \qquad O$$

This gives us the following four important equivalent forms of statements: *A* and its corresponding *O* are still contradictories, and so are *E* and its corresponding *I*. Hence:

A is true *iff* negation of *O* is true.

O is true *iff* negation of *A* is true.

E is true *iff* negation of *I* is true.

I is true *iff* negation of *E* is true.

These four equivalences are symbolically represented as follows:

$$(\forall y)(\phi y \supset \psi y) \equiv \sim (\exists y)(\phi y \bullet \sim \psi y)$$

$$(\exists y)(\phi y \bullet \sim \psi y) \equiv \sim (\forall y)(\phi y \supset \psi y)$$

$$(\forall y)(\phi y \supset \sim \psi y) \equiv \sim (\exists y)(\phi y \bullet \psi y)$$

$$(\exists y)(\phi y \bullet \psi y) \equiv \sim (\forall y)(\phi y \supset \sim \psi y)$$

These four equivalences are also known as **quantifier negation rules**. They allow us to replace a quantified expression by its equivalent expression, whether it is in the case of translation or in an argument involving quantified statements.

EXERCISE 10.2

1. Symbolize the following statements in Predicate logic using the given symbolization key:

Bx: *x* is a book. *Ix*: *x* is interesting.
Ex: *x* is expensive. *Gx*: *x* is good.
Rx: *x* is boring. *Wx*: *x* is well written.

*a. Some books are expensive but not interesting.
b. All books are interesting.
c. No good books are boring.
d. Not every book is expensive.
e. A book is good *iff* it is well written.
*f. It is not the case that some books are expensive.
g. There are books which are well written but not interesting.
h. Some good books are also expensive.
i. Some interesting and good things are books.
*j. No expensive things are good.

2. Symbolize the following statements in Predicate logic using the given symbolization key:

Ax: *x* is an ambitious person *Rx*: *x* is a ruthless person
Dx: *x* is a determined person *Cx*: *x* is a consistent person
Lx: *x* is a level-headed person *Sx*: *x* is shallow
n: Neera s: Sohini

*a. An ambitious person is also a determined person.

b. Neera is level-headed and consistent, but not all level-headed and consistent persons are ambitious.

c. Sohini is shallow *iff* all ambitious persons are shallow.

d. No level-headed person is both determined and shallow.

e. Ruthless persons are determined, but shallow persons are not.

f. Neera and Sohini are ambitious and ruthless.

g. It is not the case that some determined persons are shallow.

*h. All ambitious persons are determined, but a few determined persons are consistent.

3. Use your own examples of quantified general statements or English statements to explain why the quantifier negation rule

$$(\forall y)\,(\phi y \supset {\sim}\,\psi y) \equiv {\sim}\,(\exists y)\,(\phi y \bullet \psi y)$$

must be true.

10.3 Universe of Discourse

We have already encountered the concept of **universe of discourse** earlier in our discussion of categorical logic in Chapter 9. Still, we need to talk about it once more while trying to understand predicate logic and the quantifiers. As before, the collection of all the things that we are talking about on a given occasion constitutes our universe of discourse or, as it is sometimes called, the **domain of discourse**.

When we are using quantifiers, however, the universe of discourse stands for "all the individuals represented by the variable in the quantifier". For example, our standard reading of the universal quantifier '$(\forall x)$' is: 'For any x', or 'For every x', or 'For all x'. In this case, the universe of discourse is constituted by all that is assumed by the 'every x' or 'all x' in the universal quantifier. The existential quantifier '$(\exists x)$' too assumes a collection of things, out of which it singles out 'Some x' or 'At least one x' to refer to.

Unrestricted Universe of Discourse

Our usual practice is to have an **unrestricted universe of discourse**, which includes each and every diversely different thing that exists. It includes people, stones, stars, animals, numbers, atoms and, molecules, etc. In an unrestricted domain, the general statement '$(\forall x)\ Ix$' would mean that the property of 'being I' belongs to each and everything that exists in the universe: to the Sun, to the Hydrogen molecule, to number 4, etc.

Restricted Universe of Discourse

However, we may not be always interested in talking about such unrestricted universe of discourse. Sometimes we may want to restrict our discussion to some collection of things, which is less inclusive. For example, we might want to talk about the papers in the drawer of the office table. If we do so, then our universe of discourse will have to be restricted to only those things.

And note, every restriction of the universe of discourse will be reflected in the symbolization key, for it affects the reading of the statements in Predicate logic. So, now our symbolization key will be:

Universe of Discourse or U.D.: the papers in the drawer of the office table.

Suppose that we would like to predicate the property of 'being important' to this universe. In that case, our symbolization key will be:

Universe of Discourse or U.D.: the papers in the drawer of the office table

Ix: *x* is important.

Note that in this restricted universe of discourse, the general statement "$(\forall x)\, Ix$" would mean that "all the papers in the drawer of the office table are important". In this restricted universe of discourse, "$\sim (\forall x)\, Ix$" or "$(\exists x) \sim Ix$" means that "Not all papers in that drawer are important," or "there is at least one paper in that drawer which is not important."

Compare this situation with the same statements made in an unrestricted universe of discourse. As mentioned above, in an unrestricted universe of discourse, $(\forall x)\, Ix$ would mean that each and everything that exists, the Sun, the Hydrogen molecules, etc., is important; and $(\exists x) \sim Ix$ would mean that among the extremely diverse things that exist, at least one thing is not important.

The issue of restricted vs. unrestricted universe of discourse becomes clearer in our symbolization of universal statements such as:

All humans are mortals.

In an unrestricted universe, where we have statements like: "*Hx* : *x* is human" and "*Mx*: *x* is mortal", it would be wrong to translate these statements as any of the following:

$$(\forall x)\, Mx$$

$$(\forall x)\, (Hx \bullet Mx)$$

For, in an unrestricted universe, $(\forall x)\, Mx$ would mean that everything is mortal and $(\forall x)\, (Hx \bullet Mx)$ would mean that everything, including the

Sun, the Hydrogen molecule, is a human being and is mortal. In an unrestricted domain, the safe translation of the statement is

$$(\forall x)\,(Hx \supset Mx)$$

The rule of thumb is that *when no restriction is specified in the symbolization key, the universe of discourse is presumed to be unrestricted, the entire universe.*

There is an advantage in symbolizing in unrestricted universe of discourse. Sometimes, it allows us to display more logical structure. Consider the following example of an obviously valid argument:

Example 5

All humans are mortal.

Not everything is mortal.

Therefore, not everything is human.

The argument in Example 5 requires an unrestricted domain to demonstrate its validity. A less inclusive domain, for example, if we consider a universe of discourse consisting only of humans, may make its premises seem inconsistent and, consequently, may make it look like a bad argument. For, in that restricted universe, two of its premises would read as $(\forall x)\,Mx$ and $(\exists x) \sim Mx$.

EXERCISE 10.3

1. Symbolize the following statements of Predicate logic into flowing, idiomatic English using the given symbolization key:

   Px: *x* is a person. *Sx*: *x* is subject to the Law of Gravitation.

   Tx: *x* is tall. *Bx*: *x* is black.

   Mx: *x* has mass.

   a. $(\forall x)\,Sx$

   b. $(\exists y)\,(Py \bullet Ty)$

   *c. $\sim (\forall z)\,[(Pz \bullet Bz) \supset Tz)]$

   d. $\sim (\exists y) \sim Sy$

   e. $(\forall x)\,(Mx \equiv Sx)$

   *f. $\sim (\exists x)\,(Px \bullet \sim Mx)$

2. Translate the following statements in an unrestricted universe of discourse, and determine their truth value:

Ix: *x* is an integer.
Ox: *x* is odd.
Ex: *x* is even.

a. Every integer is either odd or even.
b. Either every integer is odd or every integer is even.

3. Try symbolizing the same two statements given in 2a and 2b using the following symbolization key and a restricted universe of discourse:

Universe of discourse: Integers.

Ox: *x* is odd.
Ex: *x* is even.

10.4 Scope of a Quantifier

A quantifier is used to interpret the question of 'how many' of a variable and, in order to do that, the variable must be within its **scope**. The **scope of a quantifier** indicates the extent of its interpretive power. A quantifier cannot be used to understand or interpret any variable that falls outside of its scope.

Every quantifier will have a scope or a range of its cover. By convention, *a quantifier falls within its own scope*. For instance, the '*x*' of '$(\forall x)$' or '$(\exists x)$' falls within the scope of the quantifier itself. This is why we can interpret the '*x*' as 'all *x*' in the former case and as 'at least one *x*' in the latter case. Then, if a quantifier is followed by a left parenthesis '(' or a left square bracket '[', its scope continues to the next matching parenthesis or bracket. Consider the following example:

Example 6

$(\exists y)(Dy \bullet My)$

$(\forall y)(Dy \supset My)$

The scope of the quantifiers in each of the two statements in Example 6 includes the variable in the quantifier itself and then extends from the next left-hand parenthesis bracket to the end of the matching parenthesis. This is shown in Example 6 by the use of bracket under each statement.

On the other hand, if a quantifier is *not* followed by a left parenthesis or bracket, then its scope extends only up to the first binary connective or to the end of the statement, whichever comes first. Consider the following example as a clarification:

Example 7

(a) $\underline{|(\forall y)\, Dy|} \supset Da$

(b) $\underline{|(\exists x) \sim Ax|}$

(c) $\underline{|(\exists x)\, Dx|} \bullet Aa$

In Example 7, none of statements has a left parenthesis or bracket after the quantifier. In the first example, as shown by the bracket under the statement '$(\forall y)\, Dy \supset Da$'. the scope of the universal quantifier starts with itself and ends before the first binary connective '$\supset$'. That is, it extends upto 'Dy', the antecedent of the '$\supset$'. The '*a*' of '*Da*' is not within its scope; moreover, it is a constant. In the second example, '$(\exists x) \sim Ax$', the scope of the existential quantifier starts with itself and ends with '$\sim Ax$', which also happens to be the end of the statement. The third example, $(\exists x)\, Dx \bullet Aa$, is similar to the first one. In it, the scope of the quantifier starts with itself and ends with '*Dx*' before the first binary connective '•'.

Difference between Quantified Statements and Truth-Functional Compounds

The important point to note is that in Example 7, the second statement "$(\exists x) \sim Ax$" alone is a **quantified statement** *because* the scope of the quantifier *includes the whole statement*. Quantified statements do not have any main connective though binary connectives such as '$\supset$' and '•' may occur in them. In quantified statements, the first quantifier is the main logical operator. The other two statements in Example 7 are *not* quantified statements, but **truth-functional compounds**. A truth-functional compound statement is a statement in Predicate logic but it contains a truth-functional connective that does not fall within the scope of any quantifier. In Example 7, the '$\supset$' of the first statement or the '•' of the third statement does not fall within their respective quantifiers. If we use the following symbolization key to translate them into English:

Universe of Discourse: All humans

Dx: *x* is dull

Ax: *x* is articulate

a: Armando

then, their differences become clearer:

1. '$(\forall y)$ *Dy* ⊃ *Da*' translates in English as "If everyone is dull, then Armando is dull".
2. '$(\exists x)$ ~*Ax*' translates in English as: "Someone is not articulate".
3. '$(\exists x)$ *Dx* • *Aa*' translates in English as: "Someone is dull and Armando is articulate".

Other examples of quantified statements are:

Example 8

a. $(\forall x)(Hx \supset \sim Mx)$

b. $(\forall z)(Az \supset \sim Bz)$

c. $(\forall y)\,Ky$

d. $(\exists y)(Cy \bullet Fy)$

Altering the scope or having a different scope can drastically affect what a statement asserts, and even change it from being a statement in predicate logic to being a non-statement in predicate logic. Consider the two statements in the following example:

Example 9

a. $(\forall x)(Hx \supset \sim Mx)$

b. $(\forall x)\,Hx \supset \sim Mx$

In Example 9, statement *a* is a quantified statement, all three occurrences of '*x*' in it fall within the scope of the universal quantifier '$(\forall x)$'. However, in statement *b*, "$(\forall x)$ *Hx* ⊃~ *Mx*", only the first two occurrences of '*x*' are within the scope of the universal quantifier and the '*x*' in '~*Mx*' is not within its scope. Thus, the '~*Mx*' is not interpretable, and hence it is not a well-formed statement of predicate logic.

Bound Variables

To understand the above-mentioned difference, we need to look at the difference between *bound* and *free* variables. An occurrence of a variable is **bound** if it is either part of the quantifier or lies within the scope of a quantifier. The variable is referred to as a **bound variable**.

Free Variables

The occurrence of a variable is **free** *iff* it is not bound in the above-mentioned sense. It is referred as a **free variable**. In Example 9, in the statement "$(\forall x)$ (*Hx*⊃~ *Mx*)", all three occurrences of the variable '*x*' is bound. The first occurrence is within the quantifier '$(\forall x)$', and the other two also fall within the scope of the quantifier. In the statement "$(\forall x)$ $Hx \supset \sim Mx$", on the other hand, the first two occurrences of 'x' are within the scope of the quantifier but the third occurrence in '$\sim Mx$' is free. Whenever one or more variables occur free in a statement, it is an **open statement** and open statements are *not* statements of predicate logic.

Let us remember that there are three kinds of statements of predicate logic, and we have already seen examples of these. These three types are:

(i) **Atomic statements:** Atomic statements of propositional logic and statements made on *n*-place predicates of predicate logic followed by *n* individual constants.

(ii) **Truth-functional compounds**

(iii) **Quantified statements** which begin with a quantifier, universal or existential, and every occurrence of every variable in it is bound.

EXERCISE 10.4

1. Which of the following are the statements of Predicate logic? For those that are not, explain why they are not.

a. $(\forall z)\ Bz \vee Py$

*b. $(\exists x)\ Dxx \bullet Cb$

c. $(\exists x)\ (\forall y)\ Axy$

d. $(\forall y)\ (\exists z)\ (Cyy \supset Dyz)$

e. $(\forall z)\ ((\exists x)\ Fxz \bullet Gzx)$

f. $(\exists y)\ (Hy \bullet Kya) \equiv (\exists x)\ Lxb$

g. $(\exists y)\ (Hy \bullet Kya) \equiv (\exists x)\ Lxy$

h. $(\forall y)\ (A \supset (\exists z)\ Mzy)$

*i. $(\sim \exists z)\ (Bz \vee Cz)$

j. $Dab \bullet Fbb$

k. $Nax \supset (\forall y)\ Pxy$

2. Indicate for each of the following whether it is an atomic statement, a truth-functional compound, or a quantified statement.

*a. $(\forall x)\ (Mx \supset Na)$

b. $\sim (\forall x)\ (Mx \supset Na)$

c. Da

d. $(\exists y)\ (Ray \vee Rya)$

e. $(\exists y)\ Ray \vee Raa$

f. $(\forall y)\ (Cy \supset (\exists z)\ Dz)$

*g. $(\forall y)\ Cy \supset (\exists z)\ Dz$

h. $(\exists z)\ (\ Fz \supset (\forall w)\ (Hw\ \equiv \sim Lwz))$

i. $\sim (\exists y)\ (Jy \vee Ky) \vee (\exists z)\ (Lz \vee Mz)$

j. $\sim [(\exists y)\ (Jy \vee Ky) \vee (\exists z)\ (Lz \vee Mz)]$

10.5 Basic Predicate Logic Symbolization

Symbolizing with Universal Quantifier

Universal quantifier will be used for all universal statements. From our discussion in Chapter 9 of categorical statements and some of the non-standard forms in which they may appear, you already know that the universal statements may come in many different guises. But usually, the terms 'All', 'No', 'None', 'Every', 'Each', etc. precede them. For example:

Every student is eligible to enter the competition.

But there can be notable exceptions. For instance, each of the statements in the following example is an '*A*' statement, but none of them use the terms mentioned above:

Example 10

Dogs are mammals.

A dog is a mammal.

Any dog is a mammal.

For translating these, let us use the following symbolization key:

Universe of domain: all physical objects.
Dx: *x* is a dog.
Mx: *x* is a mammal.

Each of the statements in Example 10 is to be symbolized as:

$$(\forall x)\ (Dx \supset Mx).$$

In the given context, each statement of Example 10 states that every dog is a mammal.

Similarly, consider the following example:

Example 11

No dogs are mammals.

Dogs are not mammals.

Both of the statements in the above example are to be translated, using the same translation key, as:

$$(\forall x)\,(Dx \supset {\sim} Mx).$$

Symbolizing with Existential Quantifier

The quantity terms 'someone', 'something', 'some' usually are to be symbolized by the existential quantifier '$(\exists x)$'. However, as we know, there can be variations. Consider the following example:

Example 12

Not all dogs are mammals.

There are dogs that are not mammals.

Both these statements in Example 12 may be translated as an '*O*' statement as follows: $(\exists y)\,(Dy \bullet {\sim} My)$.

Similarly, in the same universe of discourse, each of the following statements in the Example 13, though they do not use the quantity term 'some' explicitly is to be translated with an existential quantifier '$(\exists y)$' as : $(\exists y)\,Dy$.

Example 13

Dogs exist.

There is at least one dog.

There are dogs.

Each of the statements in Example 13 indicates that there is or there exists at least one thing which is a dog. For the same reason, '$(\exists y)\,Dy$' should also be the translation for: *"Something is a dog"*.

Symbolizing Rare Cases of 'Someone'

There can be exceptions, however. Not all 'someone' or 'something' require an existential quantifier. Consider, the following example:

Example 14

If something is dog, then it is a mammal.

What is meant by Example 14 is *not*:

There is at least one y such that it is a dog and it is a mammal.

For, the claim in Example 14 may be true even if there is no dog. It also does *not* mean: *There is at least one y such that if y is a dog then it is a mammal.*

For, this translates as

$$(\exists y)\ (Dy \supset My)$$

which is equivalent to

$$(\exists y)\ (\sim Dy \lor My).$$

This statement will be true if there is at least one thing in the universe of discourse that either is not a dog or is a mammal. This is very easy to satisfy, and is thus is a much weaker claim than what we want to assert in Example 14.

The proper paraphrase of Example 14 is an 'A' statement:

Every x is such that if x is a dog then x is a mammal.

Translated, this becomes

$$(\forall x)\ (Dx \supset Mx)$$

The best way to detect such exceptions is to attempt alternative paraphrases and then to ask oneself which version someone asserting the English statement would be the most likely to be endorsed.

Symbolizing 'Only'

You need to be careful about the 'only' statements also, and again the best way to approach their translation may be through a paraphrase. Consider the following example:

Example 15

Only dogs are mammals.

Its proper paraphrase is *not*: "All dogs are mammals". Rather, the statement of Example 15 says something more. Its proper paraphrase is:

For any z, if z is a mammal, then z is a dog.

Its proper translation, therefore, is

$$(\forall z)\ (Mz \supset Dz)$$

Similarly,

Example 16

Only mammals are dogs.

It should be paraphrased as

For any z, if z is a dog, then z is a mammal.

And translated as

$$(\forall z)\ (Dz \supset Mz)$$

Statements containing the phrase 'none but' are to be dealt with in a similar way. "Only dogs are mammals" and "None but the dogs are mammals" are equivalent, and both are to be translated as

$$(\forall z)\ (Mz \supset Dz)$$

Scope of a Quantifier in Symbolization

We have already mentioned about the difference between a quantified statement and a truth-functional compound. Sometimes, the grammatical structure of the English statement may be a good guide to decide whether the statement should be symbolized as a quantified statement and a truth-functional compound. Compare the statements in the following example:

Example 17

a. Something is a dog and a mammal.

b. Something is a dog and something is a mammal.

In statement (a), the entire statement is under the scope of one quantity term 'something', including the connective 'and'. Thus it is to be symbolized as a quantified statement as:

$$(\exists x)\ (Dx \bullet Mx)$$

In statement (b), on the other hand, there are two quantity terms. The whole statement is clearly a conjunction, the conjuncts of which are separated by the term 'and'. Its nature as a conjunction should be preserved by treating it as a truth-functional compound and its translation therefore will be:

$$(\exists x)\ Dx \bullet (\exists x)\ Mx$$

The two translations are absolutely different, and this difference is to be noted. In Table 10.1 we give some more examples of translations of both quantified and truth-functional statements:

Table 10.1 Examples of Translations of Quantified and Truth-functional Statements

English statement	Translation in predicate logic
All and only dogs are mammals.	$[(\forall z)\ (Dz \supset Mz) \bullet (\forall z)\ (Mz \supset Dz)]$ Or, $(\forall z)\ (Dz \equiv Mz)$
Something is a dog if and only if it is a mammal.	$(\forall z)\ (Dz \equiv Mz)$
Dogs are mammals or nothing is a mammal.	$[(\forall z)\ (Dz \supset Mz) \vee \sim (\exists z)\ Mz$

In Chapter 9, the following example of a valid English argument was presented which cannot be properly translated or shown as valid using the techniques of propositional logic:

All cats are mammals.
Garfield is a cat.
Therefore, Garfield is a mammal.

We can now symbolize the argument in predicate logic. We shall use the following key:

C*x*: *x* is a cat.
M*x*: *x* is mammal.
g: Garfield.

Translated, this becomes

$(\forall x)\,(Cx \supset Mx)$
Cg
$\therefore$ Mg

We shall show in the following chapters how arguments such as these can be easily shown to be valid.

'Anything' and 'Anyone'

Now, let us consider some more complicated claims as given in the following example:

Example 18

a. If everything is a dog, then Snowy is a dog.
b. If anything is a dog, then Snowy is a dog.
c. If anything is a dog, then that dog is a mammal.
d. Anything that is a dog is a mammal.

For translating these, let us mention Snowy specifically in our universe of discourse by an individual constant:

s: Snowy

The statement (a) of Example 18 is a clear truth-functional compound which translates as a conditional:

$$(\forall x)\; Dx \supset Ds$$

Statement (b) too is a conditional with a crucial difference in its antecedent as may be seen in the following translation:

$$(\exists x)\ Dx \supset Ds$$

Statement (a) asserts that Snowy is a dog if *everything* in the domain is a dog. Hence, we need a universal in its antecedent. However, the 'any' in the statement (b) does not function as 'every'. It asserts that Snowy is a dog even if there is at least one thing in the domain that is a dog. Clearly, it requires an existential quantifier in its antecedent.

Pronominal Cross Reference

Statements (c) and (d) of Example 18 establish that 'any' does not always mean 'at least one'. In statement (c), the reference of the quantity term 'anything' is carried back to the term 'that dog'. That is, the term 'that dog' refers back to the 'anything', and is within the scope of this quantity expression. This is known as **pronominal cross-reference.** In Predicate logic, pronominal cross-reference is indicated *by allowing one quantifier bind several variables*. Hence, the translation for statement (c) will be a quantified statement whose scope includes the whole statement:

$$(\forall x)\ (Dx \supset Mx)$$

This will also be the translation for statement (d).

You may find the following useful to remember: Where there is a pronominal cross-reference to a quantity term 'any', 'anyone', 'anybody', 'anything', etc., that quantity term should generally be symbolized as a universal quantifier with broad enough scope to cover the entire pronominal cross-reference within the statement. On the other hand, when the quantity term such as 'any' does not carry pronominal cross-reference, it can be generally symbolized by an existential quantifier.

EXERCISE 10.5

1. Symbolize the following statements in Predicate logic: U.D: persons

Px: x is a professor.	Sx: x is a student.
Ix: x is intelligent.	Ox: x is overworked.
Ux: x is underpaid.	Bx: x is busy.
Lx: x is lethargic.	

a. There are students who are intelligent and busy.

*b. Professors are overworked and underpaid.

c. A professor is busy *iff* she is overworked.

d. Busy students are not lethargic.

e. Professors and students are busy and overworked.

f. Only intelligent students are busy.

g. Anyone who is lazy is not a professor or a student.

h. Not all lethargic students are unintelligent.

i. Students are neither lethargic nor overworked.

*j. All and only students are overworked.

k. If somebody is a professor, then she is underpaid.

l. If someone is overworked, then all students are overworked.

m. Any student who is underpaid is also overworked.

n. A few underpaid professors are also busy.

2. Symbolize the following statements in Predicate logic:

Fx: *x* is found. *Px*: *x* is a person.

Ox: *x* is the owner. *Ix*: *x* will be informed.

Rx: *x* will be returned.

*a. If anything is found, some owner will be informed.

b. If anything is found, it will be returned.

c. If nothing is found, nothing will be returned.

d. A person is informed *iff* she is the owner.

e. Many found objects are not returned if there are no owners.

f. If anything is returned, then all owners are informed.

10.6 Multiple Quantifiers and Relational Predicates

In this section, we take up more complex types of statements in Predicate logic. For this, we need to first acquaint ourselves to multiply quantified statements and relational predicates.

Multiply Quantified Statements

Statements containing more than one quantifier are referred to as **multiply quantified statements**. Alternatively, they are known as **multiply general statements**. Usually, when in a statement more than one group of individuals are referred to, in order to keep the quantity reference to each group separate, we need a quantifier for each group.

We have already seen statements of predicate logic that contain more than one quantifier. But these have been the truth-functional compounds, and, in these, none of these statements have one quantifier falling within the scope of another quantifier. That is, we have seen instances such as the following:

$$(\exists x)\ (Dx) \bullet (\exists x)\ (Mx)$$

$$[(\forall z)\ (Dz \supset Mz) \vee \sim (\exists z)\ Mz$$

To see how quantified statements can have more than one quantifier and how to interpret statements in which *one quantifier is embedded within the scope of another quantifier*, we need to look at multiply quantified statements. Let us instantiate this point. Suppose we use the following symbolization key in an unrestricted universe of discourse:

Rx: *x* is a rule.

Bx: *x* will be broken.

Hx: *x* is a human.

Px: *x* will be punished.

In this universe, suppose we want to symbolize the following two examples:

Example 19

a. If any rule will be broken, then someone will be punished.
b. If anything is a rule, then if there are humans, then it will be broken.

Remember that we have an unrestricted domain, and two groups of items: rules and human. The same variable which will refer to rules *cannot be* used for referring to human beings. Assuming a standard context, a rule cannot be punished; humans can be. These subtleties should show up in the translation.

The paraphrase of Statement (a) of Example 19 is

If at least one rule is broken, someone will be punished.

We can safely interpret the 'someone' as 'some human' who will be punished. The paraphrase shows that it is a conditional statement. Thus, for its translation the paraphrase may be:

If there is at least one *x* such that *x* is a rule and *x* is broken, then there is at least one *x* such that *x* is a human and *x* will be punished.

Accordingly, its translation will be:

$$(\exists x)\ (Rx \bullet Bx) \supset (\exists x)\ (Hx \bullet Px)$$

Again, we have a truth-functional compound statement which uses two quantifiers but in which the scope of each quantifier is distinct from the other. We can use a different variable '*y*' when we select a new quantifier in the translation as

$$(\exists x)\ (Rx \bullet Bx) \supset (\exists y)\ (Hy \bullet Py)$$

However, since there is no scope-conflict between the quantifiers in this case, picking a different variable is not absolutely essential.

Compare the situation with statement (b) of Example 19 which, on the other hand, has a *pronominal cross-reference* (see Section 10.5) that connects the 'anything' in the antecedent to the 'it' in the consequent:

If anything is a rule, then if there are humans, it will be broken.

Hence it requires a universal quantifier that will range till the end of the statement. Thus, it should be translated as a quantified statement. Yet, note that in between there is another quantified statement 'there are humans' which should be translated as: $(\exists y)\ Hy$. This existentially quantified statement must be *embedded within the scope of the universal quantifier* that will range over the whole statement. Thus, we shall need for this translation two different quantifiers. Moreover, since we need to refer to two distinctly different groups of entities, rule and humans, one within the scope of the other, *it is best to use two separate variables.*

Given all these, statement b of Example 19 can be paraphrased as:

For any *x*, if *x* is a rule, then if *there is at least one y such that y is a human*, then *x* will be broken.

Accordingly, the translation of statement b of Example 19 will be:

$$(\forall x)\ [Rx \supset ((\exists y)Hy \supset Bx)]$$

Note that the scope of the existential quantifier '$(\exists y)$' ranges only over itself and '*Hy*', but the entire statement is under the scope of the universal quantifier '$(\forall x)$'. Statement b of Example 19 is an example of multiply quantified or multiply general statements with more than one quantifier in it with embedded scopes.

Relational Predicates

Multiply quantified statements and their overlapping scopes become important in some cases with ***n*-place predicates.** *n*-place predicates are also known as **relational predicates** as they express a certain relation among a group of individuals.

Note that the use of relational predicates does not necessitate the use of multiple quantifiers. Consider, for example, some of the statements we have seen in Section 10.1:

1. 12 is greater than 9.
2. Kharagpur is between Kolkata and Puri.

Note that each of the statements above contains *n*-place predicates ('is greater than', 'is between'), but neither requires quantifiers. These are simple statements with relational predicates that involve symbolization by the individual constants. They are fairly easy to translate.

There can also be *n*-place predicates or relational predicates with a single quantifier. Consider, for example, the statement: "Everyone knows Mahatma Gandhi" or "Sachin knows everyone". Their translation will be as shown in the following example:

Example 20

Px: *x* is a person.

Kxy: *x* knows *y*.

m: Mahatma Gandhi

s: Sachin

Everyone knows Mahatma Gandhi	Sachin knows everyone.
Translation: $(\forall x)\ (Px \supset Kxm)$	$(\forall x)\ (Px \supset Ksx)$

These too are relatively easy to translate, provided we remember the order mentioned in the relational predicate. For example, in "Sachin knows everyone" presents a different order of who knows whom in comparison to "Everyone knows Mahatma Gandhi". This order of *who knows whom* has been preserved in '*Ksx*' and '*Kxm*', respectively.

Examples of more complicated relational predicate symbolization with a single quantifier are now given.

Example 21

Bx: *x* is a book.

Axy: *x* is authored by *y*.

Rxy: *x* reads *y*.

m: Mahatma Gandhi

s: Sachin

a. Sachin reads some of Mahatma Gandhi's books.

Translation: $(\exists x)\ (Bx \bullet Axm) \bullet Rsx))$

b. If Sachin reads some books, then he (Sachin) reads only Mahatma Gandhi's books.

Translation: $(\exists x)\,(Bx \bullet Rsx) \supset (\forall y)\,[(By \bullet Rsy) \supset Ayn]$

The Statement (b) of Example 21 has two quantifiers in it but it actually is a truth-functional compound. Each quantifier ranges over only one relational predicate. Thus, it too is an extended example of relational predicate symbolization with single quantifiers.

Now, compare the following example with a relational predicate: 'is greater than':

Example 22

Given any natural number, there is a natural number greater than it.

Let us use the following symbolization key for translating this statement:

Universe of Discourse: Set of Natural Numbers

Gxy: *x* is greater than *y*

Note that for its proper translation, you need two variables and two quantifiers. For any natural number, there has to be *something else* or *other than* it. The paraphrase of the statement in Example 22 will be:

For any *y*, there is at least one *z* such that *z* is greater than *y*.

In the symbolization key, the property variable *Gxy* refers to any two *x* and *y*, which you may have to recast in terms of your chosen variables in your translation. Translated, Example 22 becomes

$$(\forall y)\ (\exists z)\ Gzy$$

Overlapping Quantifiers and Relational Predicates

Note that the symbolization of Example 22 shows relational predicate with multiple quantifiers of **overlapping scopes**. The scope of '$(\exists z)$' is embedded within the scope of the main quantifier '$(\forall y)$' which ranges over the entire statement. Yet, we can identify which will be greater than which. Note also that this multiply quantified statement has two quantifiers placed next to each other in a row, but the main operator is still identifiable. In general, the rule is that in a multiply quantified statement, the main logical operator is always *the quantifier with the maximum scope,* and usually it is *placed first*. When a quantifier is followed *immediately* by another quantifier, the scope of the first quantifier includes the scope of the second quantifier, *but not vice versa*.

Position of Multiple Quantifiers in a Sequence

While translating, this **positioning of quantifiers** is extremely important, as it can drastically affect the interpretation of the multiply quantified statement. For example, if we had translated as

$$(\exists z)\ (\forall y)\ Gzy$$

It would be wrong! For, by placing the existential quantifier in the first position then we have made it the prime logical operator. As a result, our statement claims that *there is at least one number such that it is greater than any other natural number*! And that would be a false claim, for the simple reason that there is no such natural number. In addition, it will not represent what the statement in Example 22 asserts. Thus, when two or more quantifiers are placed in a row, one has to be rather cautious about their ordering. Otherwise, the apparently innocuous switch of the quantifiers can lead to logically undesirable outcomes. Of course, there are instances when the ordering will not matter. Consider the following example:

Example 23

Some natural number is greater than some other natural number.

Using the same symbolization key, its translation is obtained as:

$$(\exists y)\ (\exists z)\ Gyz$$

Understandably, for Example 23, it will not matter which quantifier comes first.

There are four possible combinations in which quantifiers placed immediately one after the other can occur. They are as given below, and with each a paraphrase has been given to make it convenient to read them:

(i) $(\exists x)\ (\exists y)$ ... There is an *x* and a *y* such that...
(ii) $(\forall x)\ (\exists y)$ ... For every *x* there is a *y* or other such that...
(iii) $(\exists x)\ (\forall x)$ ... There is an *x* such that for every *y*...
(iv) $(\forall x)\ (\forall y)$ ... For every *x* and every *y*...

We have already seen the instances of (i)–(iii). As for (iv), we can use a different symbolization key:

Universe of Discourse: Persons
Lxy: *x* loves *y*

Using this key, the quantified statement:

$$(\forall y)\ (\forall z)\ Lyz$$

may be paraphrased as:

Every person *y* and every person *z* is such that *y* loves *z*.

We can further improve this paraphrase as:

Everyone loves everyone

Note that in this quantified statement also the ordering of the quantifier will not matter.

Using the same symbolization key,

(i) $(\exists x)$ $(\exists y)$ Lxy is to be interpreted as: Some person loves another person.

(ii) $(\forall x)$ $(\exists y)$ Lxy is to be interpreted as: Every person loves someone or other.

(iii) $(\exists x)$ $(\forall y)$ Lxy is to be interpreted as: There is a person who loves everyone.

This shows how positioning of quantifiers is extremely important for understanding multiply quantified or multiply general statements.

EXERCISE 10.6

1. Symbolize the following statements in Predicate logic:

Fx: x is found. Px: x is a person.

Ox: x is the owner. Ix: x will be informed.

Rx: x will be returned.

*a. If something is found, but there is no owner, then it will not be returned.

b. If any object is found, then some persons will be informed.

c. If any object is found, then if all found objects are returned, then it will be returned.

d. Some persons are not owners and some persons are not informed, but all returned objects are objects that are found.

e. If all persons are informed, then some persons are owners.

f. If all objects are returned, and only found objects are returned, then if there are any objects found, then some persons are the owners.

g. If every person is an owner, then if no objects are returned, then he will not be informed.

*h. If any person is an owner, then if some objects are not found, then some persons will not be informed.

2. Symbolize the following statements using the given symbolization key:

Dx: x is a dog. Px: x is a person.

Wx: x is whisky. Hxy: x hears y.

Lxy: x likes y. Sxy: x says y.

c: Professor Calculus h: Captain Haddock

t: Tintin s: Snowy

a. Tintin does not like all dogs, but he likes Snowy.

*b. Anything that one says, Professor Calculus cannot hear it.

c. Captain Haddock does not like anyone but he likes whisky.

d. Captain Haddock hears everything but he does not like what he hears.

e. Some persons like Professor Calculus, and some like Captain Haddock, but everyone likes Tintin.

*f. What Tintin says, Snowy likes.

g. If someone did not hear what Tintin said, it was either Professor Calculus or Captain Haddock.

3. Symbolize the following statements using the given symbolization key:

*a. There is no largest number. [*Nx*: *x* is a number, *Lxy*: *x* is larger than *y*]

b. None but the soldiers are braver than the fighter pilots. [*Sx*: *x* is a soldier, *Fx*: *x* is a fighter pilot, *Bxy*: *x* is braver than *y*]

c. Not all sons of teachers are teachers. [*Tx*: *x* is a teacher, *Sxy*: *x* is the son of *y*]

d. No tent is waterproof unless it is specially coated, or everything that is a tent is waterproof. [*Tx*: *x* is a tent, *Wx*: *x* is waterproof, *s*: *x* is specially coated]

e. Any professor who cannot make any of her students learn, ought to be fired. [*Px*: *x* is a professor, *Sx*: *x* is a student, *Fx*: *x* ought to be fired, *Mxy*: *x* can make *y* learn]

f. If everything that a person eats is food, then some foods are not healthy. [*Px*: *x* is a person, *Fx*: *x* is a food, *Hx*: *x* is healthy, *Exy*: *x* eats *y*]

g. Anyone who takes politicians seriously ought to be seen by a psychiatrist. [*Px*: *x* is a person, *Yx*: *x* is a psychiatrist, *Ox*: *x* is a politician, *Txy*: *x* takes *y* seriously, *Oxy*: *x* ought to be seen by *y*].

h. Students of an unpopular professor are either bored by that professor or receive bad grades from that professor. [*Sxy* *x* is a student of *y*, *Ux*: *x* is unpopular *Px*: *x* is a professor, *Bxy*: *x* bores *y*, *Gxy*: *x* gives bad grades to *y*]

*i. Not all co-authors of a book are happy with each other. [*Px*: *x* is a person, *Cxy*: *c* coauthors a book with *y*, *Hxy*: *x* is happy with *y*].

4. Use the symbolization key to construct fluent English readings for the following statements:

Cx: *x* is a cake.
Tx: *x* is a time.
Hxyz: *x* has *y* at *z*.
Oxy: *x* is on the other side of *y*.
Wx: *x* is a woman.
Dxy: *x* is done at *z*.
Px: *x* is a person.
Exyz: *x* eats *y* at *z*.
Gx: *x* is grass.
Gxy: *x* looks greener than *y*.
Wxy: *x* is the work of *y*.

*a. $(\forall u)\ (\forall w)\ [((Gu \bullet Gw) \bullet Ouw) \supset Guw)]$
b. $(\forall x)\ (\forall y)\ [(Cx \bullet Py) \supset \sim (\exists z)\ (Tz \bullet (Eyxz \bullet Hyxz)]$
c. $\sim (\exists x)\ [Tx \bullet (\forall y)\ (\forall z)\ ((Wy \bullet Wzy) \supset Dzx)]$

10.7 Complex Symbolizations in Predicate Logic

In Chapter 9, we saw the following example of a valid English argument, which cannot be translated properly using the methods of propositional logic:

> No friend of mine lives in an army base.
> Aniruddha lives in an army base.
> So, Aniruddha is not a friend of mine.

Now we can start our discussion on translations involving more and more complexity and multiple quantifiers with the symbolization of this example in Predicate logic. First, we need an appropriate symbolization key such as the following:

Fxy: *x* is a friend of *y*.
Lxy: *x* lives in *y*.
a: Aniruddha.
Ax: *x* is an army base.
m: me

Let the universe of discourse be unrestricted. The first premise is a general statement which essentially claims:

No things of …. type are things of …. type

This makes it an '*E*' statement, and it can be translated either as an '*E*' statement or by the Quantifier Negation rule as a negated '*I*' statement. If we want to keep it simple and opt for an '*E*' format, then we can start the paraphrase as:

For any x, if x is a friend of mine, then x does not live in an army base.

or, as

For any x, if x is a friend of mine, then it is not the case that x lives in an army base.

The part "For any x, if x is a friend of mine" is easy to translate as

$$(\forall x)\ (Fxm \supset ....$$

However, "it is not the case that x lives in an army base" can be paraphrased as

It is not the case that there is a y such that it is army base and x lives in y.

Note that 'army bases' is a different group of items and, in order to refer to its quantity, you need a second quantifier in addition to the quantifier that ranges over x, which has been identified as a 'friend of mine'. Note also that a universal quantifier will not be suitable for ranging over army bases, as clearly you do not want to say x lives in every army base that exists. Thus, the translation of the other part of the statement is

$$\sim (\exists y)\ (Ay \bullet Lxy)$$

Put together, the translation of the first premise is

$$(\forall x)\ (Fxm\ \supset \sim\ (\exists y)\ (Ay \bullet Lxy))$$

The second premise requires the use of an existential quantifier, for you need to say that *there is an x such that it is an army base and Aniruddha lives in it*. Translated, it becomes

$$(\exists y)\ (Ay \bullet Lay)$$

You need to be careful about the ordering in '*Lax*' to make sure that it is Aniruddha who lives in the army base and not vice versa!

The conclusion, "Anirudha is not a friend of mine", which will use two constants, is translated as:

$$\sim Fam$$

Again, you need to be careful about ordering of the constants to make it clear who is not a friend of whom.

In general, as said earlier, paraphrases help to translate in predicate logic. For, then phrases and words are unpacked and you realize whether you need more quantifiers and of what kind. Consider, for instance, the seemingly simple statement given with following example:

Example 24

Everyone loves a lover.

Let us use the following key:

Universe of Discourse: All persons.
Lxy: *x* loves *y*.

Note that the statement in Example 24 is different for "everyone loves everyone". Rather, its paraphrase is

Every person *x* is such that *x* loves a lover.

Note that the 'a' in 'a lover' does not designate some particular lover, but refer to *all* lovers. When paraphrased, then becomes

Every person *x* is such that for every person *y* if *y* is a lover then *x* loves *y*.

We can replace the 'every person *x*' and 'every person *y*' with two lined-up universal quantifiers and start the translation as follows:

$$(\forall x)\ (\forall y)\ (\text{if } y \text{ is a lover then } x \text{ loves } y)$$

'*x* loves *y*' will simply be '*Lxy*'. However, we need to unpack "*y* is a lover". In order to do that, we take it that a lover is a person who loves someone or the other, that is, if there is at least one person that this person loves. So, we can replace "*y* is a lover" by

There is a *z* such that *y* loves *z*
This is symbolized as

$$(\exists z)\ Lyz$$

Put together, "everyone loves a lover" is symbolized as

$$(\forall x)\,(\forall y)\ [(\exists z)\ (Lyz \supset Lxy)]$$

Again, 'Anyone', 'Anything', 'Someone', 'Something'

Let us take another statement along with a new symbolization key in an unrestricted universe:

Example 25

Anyone who buys anything is envied by someone.
Px: *x* is a person.
Bxy: *x* buys *y*.
Exy: *x* envies *y*.

There are three quantity terms in Example 25: 'anyone', 'anything', and 'someone'; so we need three quantifiers. The first, 'any' in 'anyone', has pronominal cross-reference from "envied by someone"; the person who buys is obviously the one who is envied. Hence it requires a universal quantifier. The second, 'any' of 'anything', does not have pronominal cross-reference, and is equivalent to 'at least one thing'. This means it will require an existential quantifier. Finally, the 'someone' has to be a person and certainly needs an existential quantifier. Paraphrased, Example 25 becomes.

For every x such that [if (x is a person, and there is at least one y such that x buys y) then there is some z such that z is a person and z envies x]

When translated all together, we have the statement

$$(\forall x)\ [(Px \cdot (\exists y)\ Bxy)) \supset (\exists z)\ (Pz \cdot Ezx)]$$

Compare this statement with another:

Example 26

Everyone envies whatever anyone buys.

The quantity term 'whatever' is equivalent to 'all' or everything', and will be replaced with a universal quantifier. The first 'everyone' is clearly universal. The last 'anyone' however, is a person and is a 'someone'. Thus, Example 26 can be paraphrased as.

For every x such that (if x is a person then (for every y (if there is some z such that z is a person and z buys y then x envies y.)))

Translated this becomes

$$(\forall x)\ [Px \supset (\forall y)\ [(\exists z)\ (Pz \bullet Bzy) \supset Exy)]]$$

Finally, let us translate:

Example 27

Anyone who envies himself/herself does not buy anything.

This statement requires two quantifiers. The first 'anyone' is a universal quantifier, as it has the pronominal cross-reference from being the one who does not buy anything. The last 'anything' refers to something, and requires an existential quantifier.

When paraphrased, it becomes

For every w such that if (w is a person and w envies w) then (it is not the case that there is a y such that w buys y).

When translated, this will be:

$$(\forall w)\ [(Pw \bullet Eww) \supset \sim (\exists y)\ Bwy]$$

Symbolizing Quantity of Places and Times

In Section 9.5, we have learnt how there may be reference to **quantity of places** or **times** in the use of terms such as *wherever*, *whenever*, *somewhere*, *sometimes*, *never*. These too are translatable into Predicate logic. Consider the example: "The alarms ring whenever the safe is touched". The *whenever* has a quantity reference to time and it may be read as "at all times". Thus, the statement can be paraphrased as: "All times when the safe is touched are times when the alarms ring". Given the following symbolization key:

Example 28

Ax: *x* is an alarm.

Tx: *x* is a time.

Uxy: *x* is touched at *y*.

Rxy: *x* rings at *y*.

s: The safe

"The alarms ring whenever the safe is touched".

Translation: $(\forall x) [(Tx \bullet Usx) \supset (\forall y) (Ay \supset Ryx)]$

Similarly, a statement such as "Dogs bark whenever a car passes" by may be translated into Predicate logic by a paraphrase such as: "All times when a car passes by are times when the dogs bark".

Consider also the statement:

The sages never tell a lie.

The "never" in the statement contains quantity reference to time and should be read as: "no times". The paraphrase should be:

"It is not the case that there is a time when someone who is a sage tells at least one lie".

It can be symbolized in the following way with the given symbolization key:

Example 29

Lx: *x* is a lie.

Sx: *x* is a sage.

Tx: *x* is a time.

Txyz: *x* tells *y* at *z*.

"The sages never tell a lie".

Translation: $\sim [(\exists y) (Ty \bullet (\forall z) (Sz \supset (\exists x) (Lx \bullet Tzxy))]$

Similarly, the line from the famous song from *The Wizard of Oz*:

"Somewhere over the rainbow the skies are blue".

It should be paraphrased as

"There is at least one place, such that is over the rainbow, where all things that are skies are blue".

Accordingly, its translation will be as follows:

Example 30

Px: *x* is a place.

Sx: *x* is a sky.

Bx: *x* is blue.

Oxy: *x* is over *y*.

Ixy: *x* is in *y*.

r: The rainbow.

Translation: $(\exists x)\,[(Px \bullet Oxr) \bullet (\forall y)\,((Sy \bullet Iyx) \supset By)]$

EXERCISE 10.7

Symbolize the following using the given symbolize key:

***1.** Doctors treat well all and only those patients that they are treated well by. [*Dx*: *x* is a doctor, *Px*: *x* is a patient, *Txy*: *x* is treated well by *y*]

2. Any doctor who does not treat some of his patients well are not liked by anyone. [*Dx*: *x* is a doctor, *Px*: *x* is a patient, *Hx*: *x* is a human, *Lxy*: *x* likes *y*, *Txy*: *x* is treated well by *y*]

3. No time is a bad time when Romeo is with Juliet. [*Tx*: *x* is a time, *Bx*: *x* is bad, *Ixyz*: *x* is with *y* at *z*, *r*: Romeo, j: Juliet]

4. Some times are bad, and some times are good, but all times are good when someone you love is with you. [*Tx*: *x* is a time, *Bx*: *x* is bad, *Gx*: *x* is good, *Px*: *x* is a person, *Lxy*: *x* loves *y*, *Wxyz*: *x* is with *y* at *z*]

***5.** Some sailors have a friend in every port. [*Sx*: *x* is a sailor, *Px*: *x* is a port, *Fx*: *x* is a friend, *Hxy*: *x* has *y*, *Ixy*: *x* is in *y*]

6. An apple a day keeps the doctor away. [*Px*: *X* is a person, *Dx*: *x* is a doctor, *Ax*: *x* is an apple, *Yx*: *x* is a day, *Hxyz*: *x* has *y* in *z*, *Kxy*: *x* keeps *y* away]

7. No one trusts anyone with anything. [*Px*: *x* is a person, *Txyz*: *x* trusts *y* with *z*]

8. Do not put all your eggs in the same basket. [*Ex*: *x* is an egg, *Bx*: *x* is a basket, *Bxy*: *x* belongs to *y*, *Pxy*: *x* is put in *y*]

9. Anish has a son who is a musician and a daughter who is a lawyer. [*Sxy*: *x* is a son of *y*, *Dxy*: *x* is a daughter of *y*, *Hxy*: *x* has *y*, *Mx*: *x* is a musician, *Lx*: *x* is a lawyer, a: Anish]

***10.** In some groups there are men and women scientists. [*Mx*: *x* is a man, *Wx*: *x* is a woman, *Sx*: *x* is a scientist, *Gx*: *x* is a group, *Ixy*: *x* is in *y*].

11. If a student is bored by all his or her professors, then all those professors are wasting their time. [*Px*: *x* is a professor, *Wx*: *x* is wasting *x*'s time, *Sxy*: *x* is a student of *y*, *Bxy*: *x* bores *y*].

12. Mrs. Lahiri has a flowering plant on each of her window sills, and a butterfly on each of her plants. [*Fx*: *x* is a flowering plant, *Wx*: *x* is a window sill, *Bx*: *x* is a butterfly, *Oxy*: *x* is on *y*, l: Mrs Lahiri]

13. Men in great place are servants of the sovereign or state; servants of fame; and servants of business. [*Mx*: *x* is a man, *Gx*: *x* is a great place, *Sx*: *x* is a sovereign, *Tx*: *x* is a state, *Fx*: *x* is fame, *Bx*: *x* is business, *Ixy*: *x* is in *y*, *Sxy*: *x* is the servant of *y*].

14. Some authors do not understand English Grammar as well as some of their readers do. [*Ax*: *x* is an author, *Rxy*: *x* is the reader of *y*, *Uxyz*: *x* understands *y* as well as *z*, e: English Grammar].

***15.** Romi loves Somi, and Somi loves Naomi; but for some reason no one loves everyone. [*Rx*: *x* is a reason, *Px*: *x* is a person, *Lxy*: *x* loves *y*, *r*: Romi, *s*: Somi, *n*: Naomi].

16. Electricians and carpenters are members of the labour unions, but some of the things in the rules of the labour unions are not clear. [*Ex*: *x* is an electrician, *Cx*: *x* is a carpenter, *Lx*: *x* is a labour union, *Rx*: *x* is rule, *Lx*: *x* is clear, *Ixy*: *x* is in *y*, *Oxy*: *x* is of *y*].

17. There is no place safer than Antarctica, but weird people are everywhere. [*Px*: *x* is a place, *Hx*: *x* is human, *Wx*: *x* is weird, *Sxy*: *x* is safer than *y*, *Axy*: *x* is at *y*, *a*: Antarctica].

10.8 Common Errors to be Avoided

While doing translation, you need to be careful about several points, some of which are, as have been already mentioned:

- ✓ Required number of quantifiers
- ✓ Pronominal cross reference
- ✓ Proper order of quantifiers
- ✓ Proper order of constants or variables while dealing with n-place predicates
- ✓ Right interpretation of 'a' or 'any'.

Above all, use your common sense and knowledge of the language. For instance, the following example may read like a conjunction when it should be translated as a disjunction:

Example 31

Cats and dogs are mammals.

We may paraphrase it as

For all x, if x is a cat then x is a mammal, and for all x if x is a dog then x is a mammal.

Translated, it becomes

$$(\forall x)\ (Cx \supset Mx) \bullet (\forall x)\ (Dx \supset Mx)$$

Or, we may paraphrase it as

For all x, if x is either a cat or a dog, then x is a mammal.

In that case, its translation will be:

$$(\forall x)\ ((Cx \vee Dx) \supset Mx)$$

Either translation is acceptable. However, what is *not* acceptable is:

$$(\forall x)\ ((Cx \bullet Dx) \supset Mx).$$

Changing Scope of a Quantifier

It is time to talk also about **changing the scope of the quantifiers.** While doing translations, there may be times when you may not be very sure whether a certain quantifier should be an embedded quantifier or it should be out and placed with the other quantifiers in a row to range over the entire statement. Your main worry might be whether you can do either of these *without distorting the meaning of the statement*, as this means usually a change in the scope of a quantifier.

If you have concerns such as these, it may be reassuring to know that there are situations when change of a scope of a quantifier does not affect the logical equivalence of the translation, but there are other cases where it does affect. It is these latter cases that you need to be careful about. For, these require that while you change *the scope of a quantifier, you also change the quantifier*. For example, you have already seen that we have symbolized:

Everyone loves a lover.

as

$$(\forall x)\ (\forall y)\ [(\exists z)\ (Lyz \supset Lxy)]$$

Note that you can also symbolize it in its equivalent form using only universal quantifiers:

$$(\forall x)\ (\forall y)\ (\forall z)\ (Lyz \supset Lxy)]$$

The major difference is that in the second version, the quantifier for z has become universal and is out with the other quantifiers ranging over the entire conditional, whereas in the first version it is an embedded existential quantifier ranging only over the antecedent of the conditional. How do we know that these are equivalent?

Remember that the general rule is that:

> When an existential quantifier has only the antecedent of a conditional within its scope, and its scope is then broadened to include the consequent of that conditional, the quantifier becomes universal quantifier.
>
> Similarly,
>
> when a universal quantifier has only the antecedent of a conditional within its scope, and its scope is then broadened to include the consequent of that conditional, the quantifier becomes existential quantifier.

Thus, where 'C' is any statement, the following quantified statement forms are equivalent:

$$(\exists x)\, Lx \supset C \quad \text{and} \quad (\forall x)\, (Lx \supset C)$$

$$(\forall x)\, Lx \supset C \quad \text{and} \quad (\exists x)\, (Lx \supset C)$$

These statements are logically equivalent, even though the first one is a truth-functional compound and the second is a quantified statement.

However, there are many cases in which the quantifiers do *not* change when their scopes are broadened or narrowed. For example, when the scope of quantifiers is changed from ranging over only the consequent of a conditional to the whole conditional, it does *not* require a change in the quantifier. Thus the following pairs are equivalent *without the change* in the quantifier, only the scope of quantifier changes:

$$C \supset (\exists x)\, Lx \quad \text{and} \quad (\exists x)\, (C \supset Lx)$$

$$C \supset (\forall x)\, Lx \quad \text{and} \quad (\forall x)\, (C \supset Lx)$$

Similarly, with change of scope over disjunctions and conjunctions, the quantifier does *not* require a change. The following are all pairs of equivalent statement forms:

$$(\exists x)\, Lx \vee C \quad \text{and} \quad (\exists x)\, (Lx \vee C)$$

$$(\forall x)\, Lx \vee C \quad \text{and} \quad (\forall x)\, (Lx \vee C)$$

$$C \vee (\exists x)\, Lx \quad \text{and} \quad (\exists x)\, (C \vee Lx)$$

$$C \vee (\forall x)\, Lx \quad \text{and} \quad (\forall x)\, (C \vee Lx)$$

$$(\exists x)\, Lx \bullet C \quad \text{and} \quad (\exists x)\, (Lx \bullet C)$$

$$(\forall x)\, Lx \bullet C \quad \text{and} \quad (\forall x)\,(Lx \bullet C)$$

$$C \bullet (\exists x)\, Lx \quad \text{and} \quad (\exists x)\,(C \bullet Lx)$$

$$C \bullet (\forall x)\, Lx \quad \text{and} \quad (\forall x)\,(C \bullet Lx)$$

Biconditionals or equivalences, however, are a completely different kind of case. The scope of a quantifier which does not extend over both sides of an equivalence *cannot* be broadened to cover both sides, nor the scope of a quantifier which ranges over the entire equivalence can be narrowed to cover only one side. Thus, "$(\forall x)\, Lx \equiv C$" is *not equivalent* to:

$$(\forall x)\,(Lx \equiv C)$$

It is also *not equivalent* to:

$$(\exists x)\,(Lx \equiv C)$$

Translations with equivalences therefore will require your skill with paraphrase and proper understanding of the given statement.

10.9 Identity as a Relational Predicate

Identity, or 'is' in the sense of being identical, is a relational predicate. Consider, for example:

Radha is cautious.

In the statement above, the word 'is' indicates that the property of 'being cautious' is a property of Radha.

Consider now a bit more complex example:

The morning star is the evening star.

In this statement, no property is predicated to 'Morning Star'. The role of the word 'is' here is to express identity between the two descriptions, the *morning star* and the *evening star*. Both expressions refer to the same star: Venus. Those of you who are familiar with this philosophical example perhaps know that expressions such as these require special treatment in Russell's theory of Definite Descriptions.

Similarly, consider the statement:

Rabindranath Tagore is Bhanu Singha.

Here too, the word 'is' indicates identity. It indicates that the person known as Rabindranath Tagore is the same as the person who is Bhanu Singha (Tagore used this penname while writing a special collection of songs).

In Predicate logic, we have to learn to deal with this notion of identity. We use the property *Ixy* to symbolize *x is identical with y*. Using this new symbol, we can now translate the two statements above as shown below:

Example 32

m: morning star.

e: evening star.

r: Rabindranath Tagore.

b: Bhanu Singha.

Ixy: *x* is identical with *y*.

a. *The morning star is the evening star* **Translation**: Ime

b. *Rabindranath Tagore is Bhanu Singha* **Translation**: Irb

The addition of identity as a relational predicate in our Predicate logic vocabulary has other added benefits too, particularly for bringing accuracy in our translations. We now give examples of situations where this new symbol '*Ixy*' can be effectively used.

At Least

Suppose you want to assert: "There are at least two doctors". Ordinarily, we might simply translate it as: $(\exists x)\ Dx$, where Dx stands for "x is a doctor". Note that this does not assure that *at least two* are doctors, and might be taken as misleading when there is only one doctor. With *Ixy* as a predicate, we now have a better way to represent the difference that we see between *at least one* and *at least two*. We use the following symbolization key:

Dx: x is a doctor.

Ixy: x is identical with y.

Given this, the translation of "There are at least two doctors" is:

$$(\exists x)\ (\exists y)\ ((Dx \bullet Dy) \bullet {\sim}\ Ixy)$$

The translation ensures that there is at least one x who is a doctor and at least one y who is y and they are not identical. This preserves what is indicated by "at least two".

We can use the same format to translate "There are at least three doctors" as:

$$(\exists x)\ (\exists y)\ (\exists z)\ [((Dx \bullet Dy) \bullet Dz) \bullet ((\sim Ixy \bullet \sim Iyz) \bullet \sim Ixz)]$$

This format can be further extended to also assert similar expressions such as: "at least four", or "at least five."

At Most

Identity as a predicate can be effectively used for translating statements such as: "There is at most one umbrella". This means that there is no more than one umbrella. It may be paraphrased as: "For any thing *x*, if it is an umbrella then for anything else *y* that is an umbrella, *x* is identical with *y*." For *Ux* as *x is an umbrella*, the translation of this statement therefore will be:

$$(\forall x)\ (Ux \supset (\forall y)\ (Uy \supset Ixy)$$

For the same reason, the translation of "There are at most two umbrellas" is:

$$(\forall x)\ (\forall y)\ [((Ux \bullet Uy) \bullet \sim Ixy) \supset (\forall z)\ (Uz \supset (Izx \vee Izy)]$$

Understandably, the same format can be further extended to symbolize "at most three", "at most four", etc.

Except

Symbolizing statements containing 'except' may sometimes be helped by the two-place Identity predicate. Consider for example: "Everyone except Toni has passed". Clearly, it is not enough just to state that Toni has not passed, for that is only half of what is asserted by the original statement. If we take *Px* as "*x* has passed" and *t* for Toni, then it may be translated as

$$(\forall y)\ [(\sim Py \supset Iyt) \bullet (Py \ \supset \sim Iyt)]$$

or, as

$$\sim Pt \bullet (\forall x)\ (\sim Ixt \supset Px)$$

Exactly

Consider the statement: "There are exactly two apples". The word exactly indicates that there are at least two, and any additional one is identical to either of these two, where *Ax* stands for *x* "is an apple", we may translate this statement as

$$(\exists x)\ (\exists y)\ ((Ax \bullet Ay) \bullet \sim Ixy) \bullet (\forall z)\ (Az \supset (Izx \vee Izy)]$$

In this reading 'exactly' is a combination of 'at least' and 'at most'.

Properties of Identity

Identity is a relation with three characteristics:

It is a **transitive** relation: if *x* is identical with *y* and *y* is identical with *z* then *x* is identical with *z*. That is,

$$(\forall x)\ (\forall y)\ (\forall z)\ ((Ixy \bullet Iyz) \supset Ixz)$$

Examples of other transitive relations will be: 'taller than', 'older than', etc.

Examples of relations which are *not* transitive are: 'being the mother of', '*x* knows *y*', etc.

It is a **symmetric** relation: if *x* is identical with *y*, then *y* is identical with *x*. That is:

$$(\forall x)\ (\forall y)\ (Ixy \supset Iyx).$$

Examples of symmetric relations are: "having the same age", "is the sibling of", "is the roommate of".

Examples of relations which are *not* symmetric are: "is the brother of", "is the wife of", "is in love with"; etc.

It is a **reflexive** relation: A relation is reflexive *iff* every object stands in this relation to itself.

Examples of other reflexive relations: 'being the same colour as', 'being the same height as', 'being in the same place as', etc.

Examples of relations which are *not* reflexive are: 'is the father of', 'is the square root of' etc.

EXERCISE 10.9

Translate the following statements using the identity as a relational predicate:

***1.** Mr Patnaik has only one son who is a musician and at least two daughters who are doctors. [*Mx*: *x* is a musician, *Dx*: *x* is a doctor, *Sxy*: *x* is the son of y, *Dxy*: *x* is the daughter of *y*, *UIxy*: *x* is identical with *y*, p: Mr Patnaik].

2. There is exactly one person whom everyone loves. [*Px*: *x* is a person, *Lxy*: *x* loves *y*, *Ixy*: *x* is identical with *y*].

3. At most three names are there. [*nx*: *x* is a name, *Ixy*: *x* is identical with *y*].

***4.** Only Rohit knows Samuel. [*Kxy*: *x* knows *y*, *r*: Rohit, s: Samuel, *Ixy*: *x* is identical with *y*].

5. At least three women have climbed the Nanga Parvat. [*Wx*: *x* is a woman, *Cxy*: *x* climbs *y*, *Ixy*: *x* is identical with *y*, *n*: The Nanga Parvat].

Keywords

Bound variable: If the variable is either part of the quantifier or lies within the scope of a quantifier.

Domain of discourse: Same as universe of discourse.

Existential quantifier: The '$(\exists x)$', which stands for "there is at least one x" and has existential commitment.

First order predicate logic: The most elementary kind of predicate logic, in which only simpler predications such as properties of individuals or objects are considered.

Free variable: If and only if the variable is not bound.

General statements: Statements formed by placing a quantifier, whether universal or existential, *in front* of them and allowing the quantifiers to range over the statements.

Individual constants: Small or lowercase letters from 'a' to 'w', with or without numerical subscripts.

Individual variables: Lowercase letters towards the end of the alphabets, such as 'w', 'x', 'y', etc., with or without numerical subscripts.

Multiply general statements: Same as multiply quantified statements.

Multiply quantified statements: Statements containing more than one quantifier.

Open statement: One or more variables occur free in a statement. These are not statements of Predicate logic.

Predicate calculus: Same as Predicate logic.

Predicate logic: A logic of predicates or properties, and things or objects to which the predicates may be ascribed.

Predicate letters: The capital letters such as 'A', 'C', etc., with or without subscripts.

Prefix type notation: The style of notation in which the predicate letters are prefixed or written to the left of the individuals or objects.

Pronominal cross-reference: Reference in a quantified statement carried from a pronoun to a term in the beginning of the statement.

Propositional functions: Symbolizing only common patterns of a group of singular statements that may result by substituting the variable by an individual constant.

Quantification theory: Same as Predicate logic.

Quantified statement: Statements in which the scope of the quantifier includes the *whole statement*.

Quantifier negation rules: Rules or equivalences between *A*, *E*, *I*, *O*, which follow from the Square of Opposition, but phrased as quantified expressions and their negations in Predicate logic.

Quantifiers: Expressions that state *how many* of the individuals have the property in question.

Restricted universe of discourse: Restriction of discussion to some collection of things, which is less inclusive.

Scope of a quantifier: The extent of the interpretive power of a quantifier.

Singular propositions: Statements which refer to specific individual as the subject term are known in Categorical logic as singular propositions.

Singular terms: Denote a specific person or an object. Can be of two kinds: proper names and definite descriptions. Represented in Perdicate logic by individual constants.

Universal quantifier: The '$(\forall x)$' which stands for "for all x" or "for any x", or "for every x".

Universe of discourse: The collection of all the things that we are talking about on a given occasion.

Unrestricted universe of discourse: Includes each and every diversely different thing that exists.

CHAPTER

FIRST ORDER PREDICATE LOGIC: SEMANTICS

11.1 Interpretations in Predicate Logic

The basic idea in semantics is that of assignment of truth value to the statements. So, in this chapter we shall discuss different ways to assign meaning to the statements of Predicate logic so that truth values can be assigned to them or their truth values can be determined.

Since determination of truth values is related to concepts such as consistency of a group of statements, or of validity and invalidity of arguments, we shall also discuss related topics such as evaluation and proof of the validity and invalidity of arguments composed of statements of Predicate Logic.

Truth Values and Interpretation in Predicate Logic

The semantics of Predicate logic is more complicated than that of Propositional logic. In Propositional logic we assign T or F to the atomic or simple statements, as these are the most basic units in that logic, and then we work our way up to the compounds to determine their truth values. That is *not* how Predicate logic semantics can begin. In Predicate logic, simple statements are not the most basic units and they are still analyzable in terms of predicates and individuals. Therefore, truth value assignment in Predicate logic has to start from a more basic level than in Propositional logic. Therefore, for example, the following is a statement in Predicate logic:

$$Eb$$

Note that '*Eb*' in itself is a simple statement in Predicate logic, but it is composed of predicate '*E*' and of an individual constant '*b*'.

Note also that unless we know what '*E*' stands for and '*b*' is, we cannot determine whether '*Eb*' is true or not. The truth value of '*Eb*' depends on *what meaning* the predicate and the individual constant has. That is, the truth value of '*Eb*' depends on the *interpretation* of the predicate and constant. The basic semantic concept in Predicate logic is that of an **interpretation**, because without it is not possible to carry out even the most elementary task in semantics in Predicate logic.

What is an Interpretation and How to Create One?

Interpretations in Predicate logic require interpretations of predicates and constants *with respect to* a universe of discourse (U.D.). The symbolization keys that we have been using so far can now be viewed as embodied examples of interpretations. We now give two examples of interpretations.

Example 1

A. U.D.: Set of natural numbers
 (i) *Ex*: *x* is even
 (ii) *b*: the number two

B. U.D.: Set of all mammals
 (i) *Ex*: *x* is a marsupial
 (ii) *b*: the largest elephant in Calcutta Zoo

While working on an interpretation, the first task is to specify a universe of discourse (U.D.). A U.D., as mentioned earlier, is a non-empty set consisting of certain things or individuals. In Example 1A, the U.D. is the set of natural numbers, whereas in Example 1B it is the set of all mammals.

Once the U.D. is specified, then the predicates need to be interpreted in relation to it. Thus, the predicate '*E*' is interpreted with respect to the U.D. chosen. We call the set of those things in the U.D. that a predicate picks out the **extension** of that predicate.

Thus, the extension of predicate '*E*' in the first interpretation A in Example 1 is the set of all even numbers. Whereas in interpretation B of Example 1, the extension of '*E*' is the set of all marsupials, i.e., the set of all mammals with a pouch, such as the Kangaroos, the Tasmanian devils, the possums.

An individual constant is interpreted similarly by assigning to the constant some member of the selected U.D. An individual constant, because it is like a name, must have an interpretation. That is, we must know which individual in the domain it stands for. Individual variables, on the other hand, do not require any interpretation.

In Example 1 in the two interpretations above, the assigned individual to '*b*' varies because what counts as members of U.D. in one case does not qualify in the other case. In the first interpretation, '*b*' is the number two, as is suitable to the U.D. selected for that interpretation. In the second interpretation, '*b*' is the definite description "The largest elephant in Calcutta Zoo", as is suitable to the U.D. selected for that interpretation.

We have a **full interpretation** when we know (a) which U.D. is specified, and (b) how to read the predicate and the constant letters in it. Once we have the full interpretation, we may determine the truth value of the statement. '*Eb*', for example, is true in the first interpretation, if we take the universe of discourse as a set of natural numbers, and '*Ex*' as *x* is even, and '*b*' refers to number 2. However, it is false in the second interpretation; for, no elephant, though it is a mammal, is a marsupial because elephants, no matter how large or small, are not pouched animals.

Interpretation of *n*-Place Predicates

Interpretation of *n*-place predicates needs careful attention. Consider, for instance, the following interpretation:

Example 2

U.D.: set of natural numbers

Gxy: *x* is greater than *y*

Note that in Example 2 the predicate '*Gxy*' does not pick out individual numbers from the U.D. in the same way '*Ex*' does in interpretation A of Example 1. '*Gxy*' stands for '*x* is greater than *y*', and its extension is a set of *pairs of numbers*, rather than a set of individual numbers. Moreover, these are *ordered pairs*, in the sense that in each pair there is a definite order as to which comes first and which comes second so that the relation of 'being greater than' can be expressed. If '*a*' is number 4 and '*b*' is the number 2, then '*Gab*' is true on the interpretation given in Example 2. On the other hand, if '*a*' is 2 and '*b*' is 4, then '*Gab*' says that number 2 is greater than number 4 and is, therefore, false.

Just as the extension of 2-place predicates will be a set of ordered pairs, the extension of other *n*-place predicates too will be a set of *ordered n-tuples*. For example, the extension of 3-place predicates will be a set of ordered triplicates in the U.D. For example, if '*Bxyz*' is interpreted as "*x* is between *y* and *z*", then '*Babc*' is true where '*a*' stands for your nose, '*b*' for your left ear and '*c*' for your right ear. '*Babc*' will be false on an interpretation, where '*a*' stand for your left ear, '*b*' for your right ear and '*c*' for your nose!

While we are on the subject of ordered *n*-tuples, let us remember that a relation can hold between an object and itself. Consider, for example, the case of the statement '*Wab*' on the following interpretation:

Example 3

U.D.: Sanskrit Literary works

Wxy: *x* and *y* are written by the same author.

a: *Abhijnana Shakuntala*

b: *Abhijnana Shakuntala*

In this example, both the names '*a*' and '*b*' have been interpreted as designating *Abhijnana Shakuntala*. The statement '*Wab*' is true since *Abhijnana Shakuntala* is written by the same author, Kalidasa.

As for constants, it is better to use different constants to designate different individuals. Sometimes different constants or names may refer to the same individual, for example, 'morning star' and 'evening star' may refer to the same Venus. An object may have more than one name. However, *we do not allow in Predicate logic that one name may designate more than one object.* It is always right to pick a different constant if the object is not the same.

Interpretation of Truth-Functional Compound

For interpretation of truth-functional compounds in Predicate logic, we use the information from the truth tables for the truth-functional connectives to determine the truth values of such statements. Consider, for example, the statement:

$$(M \supset N) \vee (\exists x)\, Bx$$

This statement contains two statement letters '*M*' and '*N*', that so an interpretation for the statement must interpret the statement letters also along with the predicate that occurs in that statement. Here is an interpretation for the statement:

Example 4

U.D.: unrestricted

M: T

N: F

Bx: *x* is breakable.

Hx: *x* is heavy.

Given that there is at least one breakable object in the U.D., the statement will be true because disjunctions with one true disjunct are true. The other disjunct '$M \supset N$' is false in this interpretation. But its falsity does not affect the truth of the entire statement if the other disjunct is true.

Now, consider a different statement which is a conjunction composed of two separate quantified statements:

$$(\exists x)Bx \bullet (\exists x)Hx$$

It is true on the same interpretation as in Example 4. For, '$(\exists x)\ Bx$' and '$(\exists x)Hx$' are both true as there are breakable objects and there are heavy objects, and conjunctions with both conjuncts true are always true.

In determining truth conditions for quantified statements, we need to be careful about the following things:

✓ Individual variables are not to be interpreted.

✓ The universal quantifier ensures that its reference is to *each* member of the U.D.

✓ The existential quantifier indicates that its reference is to at least one member of U.D.

To sum up, assignment of truth values to statements of Predicate logic are determined by *interpretations*. The interpretation consists of:

✓ Specification of U.D.

✓ Interpretation of statement letters

✓ Interpretation of predicates

✓ Interpretation of constants

EXERCISE 11.1

1. Find out the truth values of each of the following statements on the given interpretation:

U.D.: set of integers

A: T

B: F

Px: x is a positive number.

Rx: x is a prime number.

Sxy: x is the square root of y

a: 1

b: 164

c: – 2.

*a. $(Pb \supset Sca) \vee Rb$

b. $(A \vee B) \supset (Ra \bullet Pc)$

c. $B \equiv (Sab \bullet Pb)$

d. $A \equiv (\sim Pb \equiv \sim Pc)$

e. $[(B \vee Pb) \supset (Rc \vee Sbb)] \supset B$

*f. $\sim [\sim Sab \equiv (Pb \bullet Pa)] \equiv B$

2. For each of the following statements, construct a full interpretation on which the statement is true:

*a. $Bba \supset \sim Bab$

b. $S \supset (Cmp \bullet Dpm)$

c. $\sim (N \equiv \sim La)$

d. $(Mab \vee Obc) \vee Nbc$

3. For each of the following statements, construct a full interpretation on which the statement is false:

a. $(Dq \bullet \sim Dq) \vee Cpq$

*b. $(Baa \bullet Cba) \supset (Bab \bullet Bba)$

c. $(H \equiv \sim Gf) \equiv Jh$

d. $(Rcb \vee Rbc) \vee (Raa \vee Rbb)$

4. For each pair, construct a full interpretation on which one of the statements is true and the other is false:

*a. $Lc \supset Ld,\ Ld \supset Lc$

b. $(Maa \bullet Mab) \vee P,\ \sim P \equiv \sim (Maa \bullet Mab)$

c. $\sim Kc \vee Ndfe,\ Ncdf \vee \sim Ke$

d. $Baa \vee Cbb,\ Bab \supset Cba$

5. Find out the truth values of each of the following statements on the given interpretation:

U.D.: set of human beings

Ex: *x* is European

Nx: *x* is a North American

Fxy: *x* is the father of *y*

Pxy: *x* is the parent of *y*

*a. $(\exists y)\ (\exists z)\ (Fyz \supset Pyz)$

b. $\sim (\forall x)\ (Ex \vee Nx)$

c. $(\forall x)\ (Nx \supset Pxx)$

d. $(\exists w)\ (\forall u)\ ((Nw \bullet Eu) \bullet Fwu)$

*e. $(\exists y)\ Ey \supset (\forall x)\ (\forall z)\ (Pxz \supset Fxz)$

11.2 Truth-functional Expansions

When we want to ask whether quantified statements have certain semantic properties, we may often find the answers by considering their interpretations in a relatively small finite U.D. *Constructing truth-functional expansions* is a method to have these interpretations in a relatively smaller U.D.

A **truth-functional expansion** of a quantified statement is the expansion of the statement in terms of truth-functional formulations. The principles behind the truth-functional expansions are quite simple:

Expansion for Universally Quantified Statements

A **universally quantified statement** says something about *each and every member* in the U.D. So, it is true *iff* all of its substitution instances with each member in the U.D. are true. If we have a rather small finite U.D., and assign a name to each member of the U.D., then we can rephrase or *expand* the **universally quantified statement as a truth-functional conjunction**. For example, imagine a rather small universe which has only three entities: *a*, *b*, *c*. What would a universally quantified statement such as (∀ *x*) *Hx* mean in such a universe? Roughly, it would mean:

U.D.: {*a*, *b*, *c*}

(∀ *x*) *Hx* would mean a conjunction: *Ha* • (*Hb* • *Hc*)

In this limited universe, '(∀ *x*) *Hx*' will be an abbreviation for the conjunction mentioned above. It will be *true* only when *each of the conjuncts is true*, and *false if even one of the conjuncts is false.*

In that same U.D., a negative universally quantified statement (∀ *x*) ~*Hx* would mean:

~ *Ha* • (~ *Hb* • ~ *Hc*)

It too will be true *iff* each and every conjunct in its truth-functional expansion is true.

Expansion for Existentially Quantified Statements

An **existentially quantified statement**, on the other hand, says something about at least one member of the U.D. In a restricted U.D., we can rephrase or *expand* the **existentially quantified statement as a truth-functional disjunction**. In the same three element U.D. as mentioned above, the statement (∃ *x*) *Hx* would be an abbreviation for the following disjunction:

U.D.: {*a*, *b*, *c*}

$(\exists x)$ *Hx* would mean a disjunction : $Ha \vee (Hb \vee Hc)$

Similarly, $(\exists x){\sim}Hx$ in that same three elements U.D. would mean: ${\sim} Ha \vee ({\sim} Hb \vee {\sim} Hc)$.

These disjunctions will be true *iff* any one of the disjuncts is true and will be false only when all the disjuncts are false. Accordingly, in that universe, an existentially quantified statement will be true *iff* at least one of its substitution instances is true, and false *iff* no substitution instance of it is true.

In the case of truth-functional expansions, the U.D. has to be finite, as infinitely long conjunctions or disjunctions are *not* statements of Predicate logic.

Remember that in truth-functional expansions of a quantified statement, we *remove the quantifiers* so that the expanded statement is always a truth-functional compound, and not a quantified statement. However, the expansion *should match the truth conditions of the original statement* in a restricted U.D.

For applying these principles to construct a truth-functional expansion, we need to remember the following:

- ✓ Decide the size of the U.D. Usually a two-element or a three-element U.D. should be sufficient.
- ✓ Select as many distinct individual constants as there are members in the U.D.
- ✓ In the case of universally quantified statement, remove the quantifier and replace the statement by a reiterated conjunction, by replacing the variable by a constant from the U.D. If there are *n* constants, there will be *n* conjuncts. Each conjunct will be a substitution instance of the original statement.
- ✓ For existentially quantified statement, remove the quantifier and replace the statement by a reiterated disjunction by replacing the variable by a constant from the U.D. If there are *n* constants, there will be *n* disjuncts. Each disjunct will be a substitution instance of the original statement.

One may also expand a statement for a one-member U.D. for example, U.D.: {*a*}. However, note that in a single-element universe the semantic differences between the universally quantified and the existentially quantified statements are not distinguishable. For, in that U.D., the universally quantified statement $(\forall x)\, Gx$ is expanded as '*Ga*', and the existentially quantified statement $(\exists x)\, Gx$ is also expanded as '*Ga*'. Thus, it is advisable to choose a U.D. the size of which is greater than one.

Expansion for Relational Predicates

Now consider the following example:

Example 5

U.D.: {*a*, *b*}

Statement to be expanded: $(\forall z)\ (Dz \supset Fzz)$

For a two-element universe, containing just '*a*' and '*b*', we can expand the statement given in Example 5, by *first dropping the quantifier* and *then by replacing the resulting free variable 'z' in "Dz ⊃ fzz" once by 'a' and then by 'b'* in an iterated conjunction such as the following:

$$(Da \supset Faa) \bullet (Db \supset Fbb)$$

This new statement is the truth-functional expansion of the original statement and will be true only when each of the conjuncts is true.

Here is another example:

Example 6

Statement to be expanded: $(\forall z)\,(Dz \supset Fbc)$

Note that the given statement already contains two constants '*b*' and '*c*'. No matter what size U.D. you choose to expand this statement, you must include '*b*' and '*c*' in your expansion. So, your U.D. must include these constants. Suppose you decide on a three-element U.D., then your U.D. needs just another element because '*b*' and '*c*' are already in it. Let us suppose that the third element is '*a*'. Then, in that three-element U.D., the truth-functional expansion of the original statement in Example 6 will be:

U.D.: {*a*, *b*, *c*}

Statement to be expanded: $(\forall z)\ (Dz \supset Fbc)$

Expanded form: $(Da \supset Fbc) \bullet [(Db \supset Fbc) \bullet (Dc \supset Fbc)]$

Note that the '*Fbc*' does not get replaced, but only the variable freed by dropping the quantifier '*z*' gets replaced by each of the constants in the U.D. Since the given statement was a universally quantified statement, the expanded statement is a conjunction. The general point to learn from this example, however, is that *if a statement to be expanded contains any individual constants, we must use them in any expansion of the statement.*

Expansion for Multiply Quantified Statements

Now, consider an example which has **more than one quantifier**:

Example 7

$(\forall y)(Ky \supset (\forall x)\, Lxy)$

Note that Example 7 has one universal quantifier '$(\forall x)$' nested within the scope of another universal quantifier '$(\forall y)$'. Suppose we have a two-element universe to expand the statement in $\{a, b\}$. When we have more than one quantifier, we start with the outermost and remove the quantifier and replace the resulting free variable by the constants in the U.D., and then we move to the quantifiers in the inside, and do the same. The process usually is to start with the quantifier with the *largest scope* and then slowly move down to the *quantifiers with lesser and lesser scope.*

Thus, the first step in the expansion of the statement given in Example 7 is

Step 1: $[Ka \supset (\forall x)\, Lxa\,] \bullet [Kb \supset (\forall x)\, Lxb]$

We take off the main universal quantifier '$(\forall y)$', and replace all the occurrences of the freed variable '*y*' in the antecedent and the consequent of the statement, first by '*a*' and then by '*b*'.

In the next step, we replace each of the universally quantified statement that are components by eliminating the universal quantifier in each case and by expanding the resulting free variable by each of the elements in the U.D.:

Step 2: $[Ka \supset (Laa \bullet Lba)] \bullet [Kb \supset (\,Lab \bullet Lbb)]$

Note that in step 1, the term '$(\forall x)\, Lxa$' in the first conjunct and the term '$(\forall x)\, Lxb$' in the second conjunct themselves are universally quantified statements. Thus, each of these must be expanded as iterated conjunctions as shown in step 2.

Step 2 gives us the full truth-functional expansion of the statement given in Example 7. Note that while expanding, we have replaced the free variable exactly where it occurs in the statement, *leaving the rest of the statement intact.*

Let us consider an example with existential quantifiers in a two-element U.D: $\{a, b\}$:

Example 8

$(\exists x)(\exists y)\, Fxy$

The process will be the same, except that we shall expand it into an iterated disjunction. We first eliminate the outer existential quantifier and replace the resulting free variable:

Step 1: $((\exists y)\, Fay \vee ((\exists y)\, Fby)$

Then, we remove the '$(\exists y)$' in each of its occurrences and replace only the '*y*' that it frees. However, since each of the disjuncts is an existentially quantified statement itself, it must be expanded as an iterated disjunction itself. Thus, we obtain the following truth-functional expansion:

Step 2: $(Faa \vee Fab) \vee (Fba \vee Fbb)$

Finally, let us consider expansion of the statement which combines both universal and existential quantifiers in a two-element U.D:

Example 9

$Gm \vee (\forall x)(\exists y)\ Hxy$

For the reasons explained above, the two-elements U.D. in this case will contain '*m*' and with the addition of '*n*', the U.D. will be: $\{m, n\}$. The expansion will start by first removing '$(\forall x)$':

$$Gm \vee ((\exists y)\ Hmy \bullet (\exists y)\ Hny)$$

Then, we remove each occurrence of '$(\exists y)$' in the inside, and replace only the free variable, leaving the rest intact. Thus we obtain the full truth-functional expansion as follows:

$$Gm \vee [(Hmm \vee Hmn) \bullet (Hnm \vee Hnn)]$$

When we have thus expanded a statement of Predicate logic for a finite U.D., we may determine its possible truth values by constructing a truth table. For, in a full truth-functional expansion, there will be only atomic or truth-functional compounds. We treat each of the distinct atomic components of an expanded statement as independent. The truth value of one atomic component does not depend upon the truth value of another.

Thus, the possible truth values of the truth-functional expansion $(Da \supset Faa) \bullet (Db \supset Fbb)$ of the statement $(\forall z)(Dz \supset Fzz)$ will be a '2^4' or **16-row truth table**, as there are four distinct atomic components: *Da*, *Db*, *Faa*, and *Fbb*. Table 11.1 gives the truth table.

Table 11.1 16-row Truth Table

Da	*Db*	*Faa*	*Fbb*	$Da \supset Faa$	$Db \supset Fbb$	$(Da \supset Faa) \bullet (Db \supset Fbb)$
T	T	T	T	T	T	T
T	T	T	F	T	F	F
T	T	F	T	F	T	F
T	T	F	F	F	F	F

Table 11.1 (cont.)

T	F	T	T	T	T	T
T	F	T	F	T	T	T
T	F	F	T	F	T	F
T	F	F	F	F	T	F
F	T	T	T	T	T	T
F	T	T	F	T	F	F
F	T	F	T	T	T	T
F	T	F	F	T	F	F
F	F	T	T	T	T	T
F	F	T	F	T	T	T
F	F	F	T	T	T	T
F	F	F	F	T	T	T

From this truth table we come to know that the statement $(\forall z)\,(Dz \supset Fzz)$ is a contingent statement, for its truth-functional expansion is true on some interpretations and false on others.

EXERCISE 11.2

1. Provide a truth-functional expansion for each of the following statements for a one-element U.D.:

a. $(\forall z)\,(\forall y)\,(Mzy \equiv Myz)$

*b. $(\exists x)\,(\exists y)\,(Jxy \bullet Pb)$

c. $(\forall x)\,(Kx \supset (\exists y)\,Lyy)$

d. $(\forall z)\,Dz \supset (\forall z)\,Gz$

2. Provide a truth-functional expansion for each of the following statements for a two-elements U.D.:

a. $(\forall x)\,Cxk$

*b. $(\forall y)\,Hy \supset (\forall x)\,Ix$

c. $(\exists x)\,(\exists y)\,(Nxy \bullet Oy)$

d. $(\exists x)\,(Rx \bullet (\exists y)\,Syx)$

*e. $(\forall y)(Fy \supset (\exists x)\,(Ixy \vee Iyy))$

f. $(\forall z)\,(Gz \equiv {\sim}\,Hz)$

3. Provide a truth-functional expansion for each of the following statements for a three-elements U.D.:

*a. $(\exists x)\ Kx \bullet (\forall y)\ By$

b. $(\exists z)\ (Gz \equiv Hz)$

c. $(\forall u)\ Lu \lor \sim (\exists w)\ Mw$

4. Construct a truth-functional expansion of the statement: "$(((\exists x)\ Sx \bullet (\exists z) \sim Vz) \supset (\forall u) \sim Hu)$" for a one-element U.D. and then for a two-element U.D. Then construct a truth-table for each of the expansions. What does the truth-table in each case tell you about the statement?

11.3 Using Expansions to Prove Invalidity

As we know, to show that an argument is invalid, we need only show that *it is possible* for the premises to be all true while the conclusion is false. It is enough, therefore, to produce a counter-example. In Predicate logic, this counter-example could be an *interpretation* that makes the premises all true but shows the conclusion as false. Consider the following example:

Example 10

$(\forall x)\ (Ex \supset Fx)$

$(\exists x)\ (Tx \bullet Fx)$

$\therefore\ (\forall x)\ (Ex \supset Tx)$

In order to demonstrate that the argument in Example 10 is invalid, we need to come up with an interpretation that shows that the premises are all true but the conclusion is false. Here is a possible interpretation that serves the purpose:

U.D.: unrestricted

Ex: *x* is an elephant.

Fx: *x* is four-legged.

Tx: *x* is a table.

On this interpretation, both the premises turn out to be true. The first premise says that all elephants are four legged and the second premise says that there are some tables which are four legged. However, the conclusion, which says that all elephants are tables, turns out of be false.

In comparison to this method of finding an interpretation to show an argument is invalid, it is *easier*, however, to **prove invalidity** if we use the method of **truth-functional expansions.** All we need in the case of method of **truth-functional expansions** is to have a non-empty U.D. and the basic assumption will be that there is at least one individual in the U.D. That conforms to the claims made in each of the premises and the conclusion.

To each of the distinct atomic components of the expansion, we mechanically assign the truth values. We do not need to know what the properties mentioned in each of the statements stand for, and we can stipulate that a certain individual has or does not have a said property. The aim, as in the case of a shorter truth table, is *to find one possible set of truth values to the components which make the premises all true but the conclusion false*. That one possibility proves that the given original argument is invalid.

To exemplify this technique, we use the same argument given in Example 10. We take a two-element U.D.: $\{a, b\}$ to expand the quantified argument into truth-functional statements. The result is as follows:

Original argument

Premise 1: $(\forall x)\ (Ex \supset Fx)$

Premise 2: $(\exists x)\ (Tx \bullet Fx)$

$\therefore\ (\forall x)\ (Ex \supset Tx)$

Expanded form

Premise 1: $(Ea \supset Fa) \bullet (Eb \supset Fb)$

Premise 2: $(Ta \bullet Fa) \vee (Tb \bullet Fb)$

$\therefore\ (Ea \supset Ta) \bullet (Eb \supset Tb)$

Now, our job will be to construct a line of consistent truth value assignment to the atomic components which make the premises *true* and the conclusion *false*. We lay out the atomic components and the statements *in a row* as in Table 11.2. We also show here that the possible truth value assignments which would prove the argument as invalid:

Table 11.2 Proving Invalidity of Argument in Example 10

Ea	*Fa*	*Ta*	*Eb*	*Fb*	*Tb*	$(Ea \supset Fa) \bullet (Eb \supset Fb)$	$(Ta \bullet Fa) \vee (Tb \bullet Fb)$	$(Ea \supset Ta) \bullet (Eb \supset Tb)$
T	T	F	T	T	T	T	T	F

Note that this proves that the *original quantified argument* is invalid. Note also that the shorter truth table above shows *just one possible* set of truth value arrangements. There could very well be other alternative truth value assignments to prove the argument as invalid. For example, it is possible to achieve the same result by assigning '*Tb*' as false, and making the rest of the atomic components all true. However, as before, for proving invalidity, we need to show *only one* possibility. So, one truth value assignment among many alternatives will serve the purpose.

The general principle behind this technique is simple. The demonstration of invalid argument is understood as follows:

An argument in Predicate logic whose statements contain quantifiers is quantificationally invalid *iff* there exists **at least one** possible non-empty universe of discourse (or model) in which its truth-functional expanded form is invalid.

Thus, proving invalidity by constructing truth-functional expansion requires:

- ✓ Specifying a non-empty U.D.
- ✓ Expanding each of the quantified premises and conclusions into truth-functional statements
- ✓ Consistent assignment of truth values to each distinct atomic component so that in the expanded argument the premises are all true and the conclusion is false.

Here is another example of an argument, but more than one quantifier appear in it, and the quantifiers are nested within the scope of another quantifier:

Example 11

$(\exists y)(\forall z)(Fy \supset Gz)$

$(\forall z)(\exists x)(Gz \supset Hx)$

$\therefore \quad (\forall x)(\exists y)(Fx \supset Hy)$

In a simple two-element U.D. $\{a, b\}$, the expansions in small steps will look like what follows:

Premise 1

Step 1: $[(\forall z)(Fa \supset Gz) \vee (\forall z)(Fb \supset Gz)]$

Step 2: $[(Fa \supset Ga) \bullet (Fa \supset Gb)] \vee [(Fb \supset Ga) \bullet (Fb \supset Gb)]$

Premise 2

Step 1: $(\exists x)(Ga \supset Hx) \bullet (\exists x)(Gb \supset Hx)$

Step 2: $[(Ga \supset Ha) \vee (Ga \supset Hb)] \bullet [(Gb \supset Ha) \vee (Gb \supset Hb)]$

Conclusion

Step 1: $(\exists y)(Fa \supset Hy) \cdot (\exists y)(Fb \supset Hy)$

Step 2: $[(Fa \supset Ha) \vee (Fa \vee Hb)] \cdot [(Fb \supset Ha) \vee (Fb \supset Hb)]$

One of the possible truth value assignments for constructing the conclusive row for proving the invalidity of the argument may be as given in Table 11.3.

Table 11.3 Proving Invalidity of Argument in Example 11

Fa	*Fb*	*Ga*	*Gb*	*Ha*	*Hb*	$[(Fa \supset Ga) \bullet (Fa \supset Gb)] \vee [(Fb \supset Ga) \bullet (Fb \supset Gb)]$	$[(Ga \supset Ha) \vee (Ga \supset Hb)] \bullet [(Gb \supset Ha) \vee (Gb \supset Hb)]$	$[(Fa \supset Ha) \vee (Fa \vee Hb)] \bullet [(Fb \vee Ha) \vee (Fb \vee Hb)]$
T	F	F	F	F	F	T	T	F

One last comment before we leave the topic. For demonstrating invalidity, the size of U.D. may matter. Consider the argument given in Example 10.

$(\forall x)(Ex \supset Fx)$
$(\exists x)(Tx \bullet Fx)$
$\therefore\ (\forall x)(Ex \supset Tx)$

Though we know now that it is invalid and have demonstrated it to be so in a two-element universe, note that we cannot prove its invalidity in a single-element universe {a}. Where the U.D. contains a single element $\{a\}$, its truth-functional expansion is

$$Ea \supset Fa$$

$$Ta \bullet Fa$$

$$\therefore\ Ea \supset Ta$$

Note that, in this expansion, if we assign T to '*Ea*' and F to '*Ta*' to make the conclusion false, then we make the second premise '$Ta \bullet Fa$' also false! There is no consistent truth value assignment in a single-element U.D. on which the *all* premises can be shown as true while the conclusion is false. It is crucial therefore that for demonstration of invalidity of this argument, the size of U.D. be > 1.

This brings us to an important question. We just saw an example which cannot be shown as invalid in a U.D. which is < 2 in size. So, clearly, we cannot conclude that a given argument is not invalid if we cannot show its invalidity in a U.D. of certain size. A sufficiently large U.D. is needed for demonstration of invalidity. This brings us to the next important question: *How large a U.D. or model must we consider before we can confidently claim the invalidity for a given argument*?

A theoretically satisfying answer to this question is: for *n* discrete predicate symbols in an argument, we need a U.D. containing 2^n individuals. If an argument is not invalid for a U.D. containing 2^n individuals, then we take it that it is valid universally. The above-given argument has three distinct predicate symbols '*E*', '*F*', and '*T*'. A theoretically satisfying demonstration of its invalidity should thus have 2^3 or 8 elements in its specified U.D.

This, however, is the theoretical answer. For practical purposes, we usually do not need U.D. larger than three elements. In the above-given example, the invalidity became evident with a two-element U.D.

Problem of Proving Validity by Expansion or Interpretation

This also brings us to the question of **proving validity** in Predicate logic. If we are following the method of interpretation or that of constructing a truth-functional expansion, then the criterion of validity is:

> An argument in Predicate Logic is quantificationally valid *iff* there is **no** interpretation or there is **no** non-empty universe of discourse (or model) in which every premise is true and the conclusion is false.

Note that this makes the task impossible, as proving this involves proving something about the truth value of statements on *each and every one* of their interpretations and on *every possible interpretation*, not just on a selected few. In general, therefore, *neither the method of interpretation nor that of constructing a truth-functional expansion can be used to prove that a quantified argument is valid.* Proving validity in Predicate Logic is a different issue altogether. We shall save the discussion of the formal method of proving validity by Quantification Rules for Chapter 12.

EXERCISE 11.3

1. Prove that each of the following arguments is quantificationally invalid by the method of truth-functional expansions. Use a minimum two element universe:

*a. $(\forall y)\ (Dy \supset Ey) \supset (\exists y)Fy$
$(\forall y)\ (Fy \supset Ey)$
$\therefore (\forall y)\ ({\sim}\, Dy \vee Ey)$

b. $(\forall y)\ (Dy \supset Ey)$
Dd
$\therefore\ Ed$

c. $({\sim}(\exists x)\ Mx \supset (\exists x)\ Mx) \vee {\sim}\, Mk$
$\therefore\ (\exists x)\ Mx$

d. $(\exists x)\ (Mx \bullet Nx)$
$(\exists x)\ (Mx \bullet Ox)$

$\therefore$ $(\exists x)\ (Nx \bullet Ox)$

e. $(\forall x)\ (\forall y)\ (Pxy \supset Qxy)$

$\therefore$ $(\forall x)\ (\forall y)\ (Pxy \supset (Qxy \bullet Qyx))$

*f. $(\exists x)\ Sx$

$(\forall x)\ (Sx \supset Rxx)$

$\therefore$ $(\exists x)\ (\forall y)\ (Sx \bullet Rxy)$

2. Use the given symbolization key to translate the following argument pairs into Predicate logic. Then find out by the truth-functional expansion method which argument in each pair is quantificationally invalid.

a. U.D.: unrestricted, *Mx*: *x* is mortal, *Px*: *x* is a person.

(i) Everything is mortal, therefore, something is mortal.

(ii) Every person is mortal, therefore some person is mortal.

b. U.D.: set of people, *Sx*: *x* is a singer, *Dx*: *x* is a dancer.

(i) Not everyone is a dancer, therefore, someone is not a dancer.

(ii) No singer is a dancer, therefore, some singers are not dancers.

11.4 Quantificational Truth, Falsity, and Indeterminacy

A statement *p* is quantificationally true *iff p* is true on every interpretation.

A statement *p* is quantificationally false *iff p* is false on every interpretation.

A statement *p* is quantificationally indeterminate *iff p* is neither quantificationally true nor quantificationally false.

Quantificational truth, falsity and indeterminacy are analogues of tautologies (logical truths), contradictions (logical falsehoods), and contingent statements (truth-functionally indeterminate) of Propositional Logic. Note, however, that the above given definitions are given in terms of interpretations, and not in terms of their truth values.

The demonstration of quantificational truth or quantificational falsity is not an easy matter in Predicate logic. For, each requires that we go through *every possible* interpretation of the statement to ensure and in certain cases there may be *infinitely possible* interpretations.

Consider the following example:

Example 12

$(\exists y)\ (By \vee {\sim} By)$

Note that though we intuitively understand that the given statement has to be true, we cannot hope to show that Example 12 is quantificationally true by the method of interpretations. For, there can possibly be infinitely many interpretations of the property '*B*'. Similarly, the demonstration of its quantificational truth cannot also be accomplished by considering truth-functional expansions only for some finite U.D., but must be done for each and every possible U.D. And there can be infinitely many U.D.s possible for this statement. For example, if we take just the set of positive integers as one of the U.D.s, even then there are infinitely many elements in that U.D. We shall need to prove that our statement $(\exists y)\ (By \vee \sim By)$ is true for each and every element in that U.D. That alone gives us an infinitely long task. Then there can be other interpretations and other U.D.s too. Also, note that we cannot construct a truth table to prove the point because the given statement $(\exists y)\ (By \vee \sim By)$ is not a truth-functional compound.

We may reason instead, that no matter what '*B*' stands for in a given interpretation, and no matter what the interpretation is, in every interpretation at least one member in the selected non-empty U.D. will be either *B* or will not be *B*. Therefore $(\exists y)\ (By \vee \sim By)$ is true on *every* interpretation and is **quantificationally true**.

Similarly, consider the following example:

Example 13

$(\forall y)\ By \bullet (\exists z) \sim Bz$

Instead of trying to prove by the method of interpretations or of truth-functional expansions which require that we go through the infinitely possible interpretations that this statement in Example 13 may have, we can simply reason, without knowing what '*B*' stands for, or which interpretation we are talking about, that there is *no* interpretation, on which every member in the U.D. will be *B* and yet there will be some member in the U.D. which will not be *B*. Both quantified statements cannot be true at the same time. The statement given in Example 13, therefore, will be false in every possible interpretation and is **quantificationally false**.

In general, however, direct proof of quantificational truth or falsity is not so easy. It is *easier* to show that a statement is *not* quantificationally true or *not* quantificationally false. For, that requires *only one interpretation* where you show either that the statement is *false* in at least one interpretation (in case of showing it is *not* quantificationally true) or that the statement is *true* in at least one interpretation (in case of showing it is *not* quantificationally false).

However, we can use the method of interpretations or of expansions to prove that some statements in Predicate logic are **quantificationally indeterminate** or contingent. Consider the following:

Example 14

$(\exists y)\ By \bullet Ca$

We can successfully show that the given statement is quantificationally indeterminate by constructing its truth-functional expansion in the following way. Since the given statement already contains '*a*', let us choose a two-element U.D. $\{a, b\}$ for converting it into a truth-functional compound. In this U.D., the truth-functional expansion of the given statement is:

$$(Ba \vee Bb) \bullet Ca$$

Then, as is shown in the following tabular representation, we show by assigning truth values to each of the distinct atomic components that there is *at least one* possible truth value assignment on which the statement will be true and there is *at least one* possible truth-value assignment on which the statement will be false.

Ba	*Bb*	*Ca*	$(Ba \vee Bb) \bullet Ca$
T	T	T	T
F	F	T	F

The statement given in Example 14 is, therefore, quantificationally indeterminate.

We may obtain the same result by the method of interpretations. Here are two interpretations. In one, the given statement $(\exists y)\ By \bullet Ca$ in Example 14 turns out to be false and in the other turns out to be true:

Interpretation 1: U.D.: Set of all mammals

Bx: *x* is a bear.

Cx: *x* is a cat.

a: Rene Descartes

Interpretation 2: U.D.: Set of all natural numbers

Bx: *x* is even.

Cx: *x* is prime.

a: the number two

On interpretation 1, the statement asserts: "There is at least one bear and that Rene Descartes is a cat". It is false, as the conjunct '*Ca*' is false. Rene Descartes was not a cat but a man and an extraordinary philosopher and mathematician. Having one of the conjuncts as false makes the entire statement as a conjunction false.

On interpretation 2, the statement is true. For, it asserts: "There is at least one even number and number 2 is a prime number". With both the conjuncts true, the entire statement as a conjunction is true.

Alonzo Church Result

Before we end this section, there is an important theoretical point to share. Generally speaking, there is no *effective method* of deciding for every statement in Predicate logic whether a statement is quantificationally true, or quantificationally false, or quantificationally indeterminate. By *effective method* we mean always finding the correct answer by a finite number of mechanical steps. This is known as the **Alonzo Church result** (1936). Alonzo Church[1] showed that there is no such effective method for Predicate logic now and no such effective method will ever be found. The lack of an effective method in this respect is a major point of difference between Predicate logic and Propositional Logic. In Propositional Logic, the construction of truth tables gives us the effective method of deciding whether a statement is a tautology or a contradiction or contingent. There is no comparable way in Predicate Logic to determine the status of statements. Logicians Bernays and Schönfinkel[2], however, claim that for quantified statements which contain only one-place predicates, there is an effective method. And it is, as we mentioned in Section 11.3: for n discrete predicate symbols, we need a U.D. containing 2^n individuals to construct a truth-functional expansion and a full truth table of the expansion to determine the status of the given statement.

EXERCISE 11.4

1. Prove that each of the following statements is *not quantificationally true* by using both the method of constructing an interpretation and the method of truth-functional expansions:

*a. $(\forall x)\ Hx \supset (\forall x)\ Gx$

b. $(\forall x)\ (Hx \supset Gx) \supset (\forall x)\ Gx$

c. $(\exists x)\ Hx \supset (\exists x) \sim Gx$

d. $(\exists x)\ (Hx \vee Gx) \supset ((\exists x)\ Hx \supset (\exists x) \sim Gx)$

e. $(\forall x)\ (\exists y)\ Dxy \supset (\exists y)\ (\forall x)\ Dxy$

*f. $(\forall y)\ (Dya \vee Ey) \supset [(\forall y)\ Dya \bullet (\forall y)\ Ey]$

---

[1]Alonzo Church,"A note on the Entschedungproblem", *Journal of Symbolic Logic,* 1, 40-41, 101-102, 1936.

[2]P. Bernays and M. Schönfinkel, "Zum Entschiedungsproblem der mathematischen Logik", Mathematische Annalen, 99, 342–372, 1928.

2. Prove that each of the following statements is *not quantificationally false* by using both the method of constructing an interpretation and the method of truth-functional expansions:

a. $(\exists x)\ Hx \bullet (\exists x) \sim Hx$

*b. $[(\exists x)\ Hx \bullet (\exists x)\ Gx] \bullet \sim [(\exists x)\ (Hx \bullet Gx)]$

c. $\sim (\forall y)\ (\forall z)\ Fyz \equiv (\forall x)\ Fxx$

d. $(\exists w)\ ((\exists z)\ Bz \supset \sim Bw)$

e. $(\forall y)\ (By \supset Cy) \bullet (\forall y)\ (Cy \supset \sim By)$

f. $(\exists w)\ (\forall y)\ (Dyw \supset \sim Dwy)$

3. Prove that each of the following statements is *quantificationally indeterminate* by using both the method of constructing an interpretation and the method of truth-functional expansions:

a. $(\forall x)\ Bax \supset (\forall x) \sim Bax$

*b. $(\exists x)\ (Lx \bullet Mx) \supset (\exists x) \sim (Lx \vee Mx)$

c. $(\exists x)\ Lx \supset (\forall y)\ (My \supset Ly)$

d. $(\exists x)\ (Lx \supset Mx) \supset (\exists y)\ (Ly \bullet My)$

e. $(\forall x)\ (\forall y)\ [(Kxy \vee Kyx) \supset Kyy]$

f. $(Nd \bullet Ne) \bullet (\exists x) \sim Nx$

4. A truth-functional expansion of the statement "$(\exists x)\ Hx \bullet (\exists x) \sim Hx$" for a one member U.D. is $Hb \bullet \sim Hb$. Explain why this expanded statement "$Hb \bullet \sim Hb$" is quantificationally false. Then explain why this does *not* show that the original statement "$(\exists x)\ Hx \bullet (\exists x) \sim Hx$" is quantificationally false.

11.5 Quantificational Equivalence and Consistency

The constraints that exist for demonstrating quantificational truth and falsity exist also for demonstrating **quantificational equivalence**. For, in terms of interpretations, the criterion for determining quantificational equivalence is

> Two statements *p* and *q* of Predicate logic are *quantificationally equivalent iff* there is *no* interpretation on which *p* and *q* have different truth values.

Thus, for reasons explained above, the methods of interpretations or of constructing truth-functional expansions cannot be used effectively to show that two statements of Predicate Logic are quantificationally equivalent. For, that would require demonstrating their equivalence for *every possible interpretation* for the two statements. And that task, as we have seen in our earlier discussion on quantificational-truth and falsity, can be next to impossible as infinitely many interpretations may be possible. This cannot also be accomplished by considering truth-functional expansions only for some finite U.D.

Rather, the method of interpretations or the method of constructing truth-functional expansions is effective to show two statements are *not* quantificationally equivalent. For, that requires a much simpler task of showing *just one interpretation* in which the two statements have different truth values. Consider, for example the following two statements:

Example 15

a. $(\exists z)(Sz \bullet Tz)$

b. $(\exists z) Sz \bullet (\exists z) Tz$

We shall demonstrate that the two statements are *not* quantificationally equivalent: first, by the method of interpretation, and then by constructing truth functional expansions:

By the method of interpretation

U.D.: all human beings

Ix: *x* is short.

Mx: *x* is tall.

On this interpretation the statement (a) of Example 15 reads: Some human beings are both short and tall. Since this cannot be true in ordinary contexts, (a) is false. The statement (b) reads: there are some tall human beings and there are some short human beings. This is true in our everyday world. Since *on the same interpretation* the two statements show two different truth values, we conclude that the two given statements in Example 15 are *not* quantificationally equivalent.

By the method of truth-functional expansions We can show the same result by constructing the following two truth-functional expansions for the given two statements in a two-element U.D. $\{a, b\}$:

a. $(Sa \cdot Ta) \vee (Sb \cdot Tb)$ b. $(Sa \vee Sb) \cdot (Ta \vee Tb)$

The following shorter truth table shows that (a) and (b) can have different truth values on the same assignment of truth values to their atomic components:

Sa	*Ta*	*Sb*	*Tb*	$(Sa \bullet Ta) \vee (Sb \bullet Tb)$	$(Sa \bullet Sb) \bullet (Ta \vee Tb)$
F	T	T	F	F	T

The concept of **quantificational consistency** is understood as follows:

> A finite set of statements in Predicate Logic is quantificationally consistent *iff* there is *at least one* interpretation on which every member of the set is true.
>
> A finite set of statements in Predicate Logic is quantificationally inconsistent *iff* there is *no* interpretation on which every member of the set is true.

Consider the following example:

Example 16

{(∀y) *Dya*, (~ *Dba* ∨ (∃x) ~ *Dax*)}

To prove that the set given in Example 16 is consistent, we need just one interpretation on which all the members of the set are true:

U.D.: Set of positive numbers
Dxy: *x* is divisible by *y*
a: the number 1
b: the number 2

On this interpretation, the term '(∀ *y*) *Dya*' reads: all positive numbers are divisible by the number one. Since this is the case, '(∀ *y*) *Dya*' is true. The term '(~ *Dba* ∨ (∃x) ~ *Dax*)' is also true. On this interpretation, it reads as: Either 2 is not divisible by 1 or there is at least one number that 1 is not divisible by. The disjunct '(∃x) ~ *Dax*' is true because there is at least one positive number 1 is not divisible by, e.g., 3. This makes the disjunction '(~ *Dba* ∨ (∃x) ~ *Dax*)' true. So, on this interpretation every member of the given set is true. Thus we have established that the given set is consistent.

We can obtain the same result by truth-functional expansions. Since '*b*' and '*a*' already occur in one of the statements as constants, we expand the statements in a two-element U.D. {*a*, *b*} as follows:

Given the set:

{(∀y) *Dya*, (~ *Dba* ∨ (∃x) ~ *Dax*)}

We have the truth-functional expansions:

(*Daa* • *Dba*) and (~ *Dba* ∨ (~ *Daa* ∨ ~ *Dab*))

The following shorter truth table, establishes that the expanded statements are quantificationally consistent, as both of them are true on the same consistent truth value assignment:

Daa	Dba	Dab	(Daa • Dba)	(~ Dba ∨ (Daa ∨ ~ Dab)
T	T	F	T	T

Thus, we have shown that the set of statements given in Example 16 is quantificationally consistent.

Note that we *cannot* use the same methods of interpretations or truth-functional expansions to show that a set of statements is **quantificationally inconsistent**. For, we would have to show that *on every possible interpretation* at least one member of the set is false. Since interpretations may be infinitely many, this is not possible. This cannot also be accomplished by considering truth-functional expansions only for some finite U.D.

EXERCISE 11.5

1. Show that the statements in each of the pairs are *not quantificationally equivalent* by using both the method of constructing an interpretation and the method of truth-functional expansions:

a. (∃w) Bw ⊃ Ca, (∃w) (Bw ⊃ Ca)

*b. (∃w) (Bw • Cw), (∃w) Bw • (∃w) Cw

c. (∀y) Dy ∨ (∀y) Fy, (∀y) (Dy ∨ Fy)

d. (∃x) (Px ∨ Qb), (∃x) (Px ∨ Qc)

e. (∀y) (Py ≡ Qy), (∃y) Py ≡ (∃y)Qy

2. Show that the statements in each of the set are *quantificationally consistent* by using both the method of constructing an interpretation and the method of truth-functional expansions:

*a. {(∃y) Ry, (∃y) Sy, ~ (∀y) (Ry ∨ Sy)}

b. {(∃y) Ry, ∨ (∃z) Sy, (∃x) ~ Rx, (∃x) ~ Sx}

c. {(∀y) (Hy ⊃ Gy), (∀y) (Iy ⊃ Jy), (∀y) (Gy ⊃ ~ Jy)}

d. {(∀y) (Jay ≡ Kay), ~ Jab, ~ Kba}

e. {~ (∀w) (Mw ⊃ Nw), ~ (∀y) ~ (Mw ⊃ Nw)}

3. a. Is the following set quantificationally consistent? Explain.

{La, Lb, Lc,, Ld, Le, Lf, ~ (∀y) Ly}

b. What is the minimum size U.D. for which the statements in the set must be expanded in order to satisfactorily show that the set of quantificationally consistent? Explain why.

Keywords

Alonzo Church result: There is neither now nor will there be any effective method of deciding for every statement in Predicate Logic whether a statement is quantificationally true, or quantificationally false, or quantificationally indeterminate.

Extension of a predicate: The set of those things in the U.D. that a predicate picks out.

Interpretations: Models which require interpretations of predicates and constants *with respect to* a universe of discourse.

Quantificational consistency: To have at least one interpretation on which every member of a given set of statements is true.

Quantificational equivalence: To have the same truth value on every interpretation.

Quantificationally false: False on every interpretation.

Quantificational inconsistency: To have no interpretation on which every member of a given set of statements is true.

Quantificationally indeterminate: Neither quantificationally true nor quantificationally false.

Quantificationally true: True on every interpretation.

Truth-functional expansion: The expansion of a quantified statement in terms of equivalent truth-functional formulations.

CHAPTER 12

PREDICATE LOGIC: DERIVATION

12.1 Preliminaries

In this chapter, we shall learn how to demonstrate the validity of arguments in Predicate logic. We shall use a deduction system which uses essentially the same procedure as *formal derivation* (see Section 8.2). We shall make use of the same inference rules, but there will be *some new additions meant specially for quantified statements of Predicate logic.*

The total set of rules for formal derivation in Predicate logic will include:

- All the **inference and replacement rules** of Propositional logic
- **Four** additional inference rules: **UI**, **UG**, **EI** and **EG**.
- The **quantifier negation rules**

Inference and replacement rules of Propositional logic: While doing derivations in Predicate logic, there will be occasions when you need to use the derivation rules you learnt in Chapter 8 such as *Modus Ponens* (M.P.) and all the others. As before, you have to be cautious about them, and remember that some of them apply only to a whole statement, and not to a part of the statement.

The additional four new rules of Predicate logic: In addition, Predicate logic proofs will require you to know four more rules. We shall discuss these four rules in Section 12.2. Their abbreviated names are UI, UG, EI and EG.

These four rules are for *introducing and eliminating quantifiers.* When dealing with quantified statements in the proof, you have to know how to deal with the quantifiers, when to take them off, and when to insert them.

Among the four new rules, there are two rules for each kind of quantifiers, which are now described.

For universal quantifier:
UI: allows the elimination of the universal quantifier.
UG: allows us to introduce a universal quantifier.

For existential quantifier:
EI: allows the elimination of an existential quantifier.
EG: allows us to introduce an existential quantifier.

As is the case with the derivation rules of Propositional logic (see Section 8.3), the new derivation rules of Predicate logic are *argument forms* (see Section 8.1). They provide us valid argument forms to derive conclusions on the basis of *forms* of statements. And like the derivation rules of Propositional logic, they too are *truth–preserving*. That is, given the semantics developed for Predicate logic, the inference rules of Predicate logic will never lead us from truth to falsity.

It is important to remember that UI, UG, EI *apply to entire statements, and not to parts of statements*. However, EG is an important exception to this general description, *as it allows application to part of a statement also*.

Remember that applications of UI and EI will free certain variables because they remove quantifiers. Similarly, applications of UG and EG will bind certain variables because they add a quantifier. When using these rules, you need to be careful about freeing the right variable and also about binding the right variable.

The Quantifier Negation Rules (QN)

In abbreviated form, as introduced in Section 10.2, the QN rules state, where 'ϕ' (Greek small letter 'phi') stands for any property symbol:

$$(\forall y)\ \phi y \equiv \sim (\exists y) \sim \phi y$$

$$(\forall y) \sim \phi y \equiv \sim (\exists y)\ \phi y$$

$$(\exists y)\ \phi y \equiv \sim (\forall y) \sim \phi y$$

$$(\exists y) \sim \phi y \equiv \sim (\forall y)\ \phi y$$

The QN rules are the equivalences between expressions in Predicate logic. They represent the contradictory relation between the classical categorical statements. They are intuitive and relatively easier to understand.

In Section 12.2, we want to focus on the four new derivation rules. These are a bit difficult for beginners. For, they come with several important restrictions or *caveats*. In order to make it easier for a beginner to follow, we shall introduce the rules first in Section 12.2. The restrictions on them will be explained separately in Section 12.3.

12.2 The Four Rules of Inference: UI, UG, EG, and EI

Universal Instantiation (UI)

The **Universal Instantiation (UI)** rule allows inference from a universal claim to its specific instance. Symbolically, it may be represented as:

$$\text{UI:}\quad \frac{(\forall\mu)\,\phi\mu}{\therefore \phi\nu} \quad \text{OR} \quad \frac{(\forall\mu)\,(\phi\mu \supset \psi\mu)}{\therefore \phi\nu \supset \psi\nu} \quad \begin{matrix}\text{Premise}\\ \text{Conclusion}\end{matrix}$$

In either version, given a universally quantified statement, the rule allows us to infer a specific instance of it. In this symbolic presentation of UI, do not feel intimidated by the Greek letters ϕ (*phi*) and ψ (*psi*). They, as before (see Section 10.2), refer to *any two* predicate symbols. The Greek letters μ (*mu*) and ν (*nu*), on the other hand, stand for individual symbols to which the predicates are to be attributed. Note that μ stands for *any* individual variable which is universally quantified in the premise. But the ν in the conclusion can be *any individual symbol*, either an individual constant like '*a*' or an individual variable such as '*y*'. We present the rule in two versions to emphasize that the universally quantified premise may have different forms. The premise could very well be a universally quantified statement such as $(\forall x)\,Fx$ or a bit more complicated, e.g. $(\forall x)\,(\sim Fx \vee Gx)$.

Thus, the premise states that for anything in a given domain it has the property 'ϕ' (first version), or if it has the property 'ϕ', then it has 'ψ' (second version). Given this, the rule UI allows us to infer that this is true also for any individual 'ν' within the domain: 'ν' too has the property 'ϕ', or if 'ν' has 'ϕ', then it has 'ψ'. If 'ν' happens to be a specific individual referred to by a proper name or by a definite description, then we need to instantiate it with an individual constant. If it happens to refer to a non-specific entity (something or someone indefinite), then it may be instantiated as an individual variable.

Thus, given a universally quantified statement such as

$$(\forall x)\,(Mx \supset Fx)$$

we may use the rule UI on it in the following way:

- ✓ First, remove the universal quantifier.
- ✓ Next, replace the resulting free variable either by a constant or a variable.

In this case, by UI we may validly infer *any* of the following:

$Ma \supset Fa$	replacing the freed variable by an individual constant	**permissible**
$My \supset Fy$	replacing the freed variable by an individual variable	**permissible**
$Mx \supset Fx$	replacing the freed variable by *itself*	**permissible**

Let us now consider the following example of a derivation in Predicate logic which uses UI.

Example 1

1. $(\forall x)(Mx \supset Fx)$
2. Mc $\quad$ $/ \therefore Fc$
3. $Mc \supset Fc$ $\quad$ **1, *UI***
4. Fc $\quad$ 3, 2, *M.P.*

On line 3 of Example 1, we have used UI on line 1 and instantiated the universal generalization. In Example 1, we also see how a proof in Predicate logic combines the Predicate logic derivation rules with the Propositional logic derivation rules. Note that in Example 1 on line 3, when we are using UI, our choice of c as the instantiating constant is already determined. For, Mc is already there on line 2 and no other constant or variable will allow us to use M.P. on line 4 as we have done here. But if we were not so constrained, then on line 3, our choice for instantiation could be any constant or variable, even the variable x. On line 3, after instantiation, we have a statement $Mc \supset Fc$, which is not a quantified statement but is a truth-functional compound. So, we can safely use the rules of truth-functional Propositional logic such as M.P. on this statement.

Note also that we were able to use UI on line 1 because the universal quantifier on that line ranges over the entire statement. Had it been the case that the universal quantifier ranged only over a part of the statement, then we would not have been able to use UI. For, we *cannot* use UI only on a selective part of a statement even if it is a universally quantified part. For example, the UI *cannot be applied* to the following statement:

$$(\forall x)\, Mx \supset (\forall y)\, Fx$$

to obtain by UI *any* of the following expressions

$$Ma \supset (\forall y)\, Fx \quad \times \textbf{ wrong!}$$

$$(\forall x)\, Mx \supset Fa \quad \times \textbf{ wrong!}$$

For, that will be an application of UI to a part of a statement. Similarly, it is *incorrect* to apply UI to the statement:

$$\sim [(\forall x)\, (Mx \supset Fx)]$$

to get

$$\sim (Ma \supset Fa) \quad \times \textbf{ wrong!}$$

For, $\sim [(\forall x)\ (Mx \supset Fx)]$ is not really a universally quantified statement. It is a negation. Thus, the universal quantifier in that statement does not range over the negation sign and thus it does *not* range over the *entire statement*.

Your instantiation by UI should be consistent and uniform, and not random and selective. For example, if you apply UI for the expression:

$$(\forall x)\ ((Mx \vee Nx) \supset Fx)$$

it will be a *wrong* application of UI if you produce the following statement:

$$(Ma \vee Na) \supset Fy \quad \times \textbf{ wrong!}$$

For, by removing the universal quantifier by UI, you have freed all the occurrences of x in that statement. In total there are three occurrences of x in that statement. The Universal instantiation rule requires that you instantiate *each* of these three occurrences of that freed variable by the *same symbol.*

Here is one more example of a derivation which uses UI:

Example 2

1. $(\forall x) \sim Mx$		
2. $Gy \supset My$	$/ \therefore \sim Gy$	
3. **$\sim My$**		**1, *UI***
4. $\sim Gy$		3, 2, *MT*

Statement 1 in Example 2 is not a negation. It is a quantified statement which contains a negation. So, we could safely use UI in the statement. The rest of the proof is simply an application of MT.

Universal Generalization (UG)

The Universal Generalization (UG) is a rule of inference that allows us to add a universal quantifier. In symbols, it may be stated as:

$$\text{UG:} \quad \frac{\phi\nu}{\therefore\ (\forall\mu)\ \phi\mu} \quad \text{OR} \quad \frac{\phi\nu \supset \psi\nu}{\therefore\ (\forall\mu)\ (\phi\mu) \supset (\psi\mu)} \quad \begin{array}{l}\text{Premise}\\ \text{Conclusion}\end{array}$$

Specifically, the rule permits the derivation of a universally quantified statement from a substitution instance of it. The premise asserts that ν has the property ϕ or is ϕ. The ν in the premise has to be an individual variable, and *not* an individual constant. Given this premise, by UG we can generalize on v. That is, we can infer a universally quantified statement. Thus, given the statement.

$$Bx \supset Cx$$

we can apply UG in the statement by:

✓ First, adding a universal quantifier in front.

✓ Then by ensuring in the conclusion that every occurrence of the variable generalized on is bound by this newly introduced universal quantifier.

Thus, by applying UG on '$Bx \supset Cx$', we may obtain *any* of the following:

$(\forall y)\ (By \supset Cy)$	using bound variable 'y' in place of 'x'	**permissible**
$(\forall z)\ (Bz \supset Cz)$	using bound variable 'z' in place of 'x'	**permissible**

We can generalize using the same variable also. For example, on $Bx \supset Cx$, we can apply UG to obtain

$(\forall x)\ (Bx \supset Cx)$	using the same variable 'x'	**permissible**

Similarly, from *any* of the following expressions:

$$My$$
$$Mz$$
$$Mx$$

by UG we can get

$$(\forall x) Mx$$

To avoid *illicit generalization* and other problems, there are several restrictions on the use of this rule, these will be discussed in Section 12.3. At this point, let us mention that before the application of the UG on a line, you need to ensure that the 'v' is an *arbitrary sample* or *an arbitrary individual* from the domain. No specific information about that individual must be used for the generalization.

This means that you cannot apply UG *on an individual constant.* For, constants refer to very specific individuals in the domain. Thus, we *cannot* apply UG on the statement

$$(Ma \lor Na) \supset Fa$$

to obtain by UG the statement

$(\forall x)\ ((Mx \lor Nx) \supset Fx)$ × **wrong!**

Just because a, a specific individual, is F if a is either M or N, you cannot thereby legitimately conclude that all are F if they are either M or

N. Just because Sachin Tendulkar is a good cricketer, from that you cannot legitimately conclude that every human being is a good cricketer!

This also means that you have to ensure that the symbol you are generalizing on is a *randomly selected individual variable*. In this respect, the requirement for UG rule is like the requirement of generality for geometrical proofs. In order to prove a certain property of triangles, such as that the three angles of a triangle will add up to 180 degrees, the proof has to start from a given triangle. But in order to make a claim about *all* triangles, the proof cannot rest upon anything specifically applicable or unique to the given triangle. Thus, the usual starting point for a proof such as this is: *Let ABC be any triangle*. Similarly, since the rule claims that the result is completely general as it holds for every individual in the domain, UG requires that it be applied on an arbitrary variable.

You *cannot use* UG *on a part of a statement*. For example, if in your derivation you have a statement:

$$Fx \supset (\exists y)\, My$$

You *cannot* make a convenient use of UG that applies only to *Fx* and leaves the rest of the statement unaffected. That is, by UG you *cannot* legitimately obtain the following statement from it:

$$(\forall x)\, Fx \supset (\exists y)\, My \qquad \times \textbf{ wrong!}$$

A proper application of UG on $Fx \supset (\exists y)\, My$ should get you a universally quantified statement such as the following where the entire statement should be within the scope of the universal quantifier:

$$(\forall x)\, (Fx \supset (\exists y)\, My)$$

Here is an example of a proof which shows an application of UG:

Example 3

1. $(\forall x)\,(Mx \supset Nx)$		
2. $(\forall x)\, Mx$	$/ \therefore (\forall x)\, Nx$	
3. $My \supset Ny$		1, *UI*
4. *My*		2, *UI*
5. *Ny*		3, 4, *M.P.*
6. **$(\forall x)\, Nx$**		**5, UG**

On line 6 of Example 3, we have obtained a universally quantified statement, which is also our conclusion in that proof, by applying UG on line 5. On line 5 we have *Ny*, where *y* is an individual variable, not an individual constant.

Note that line 5, however, is a result from previous derivations. Previously, on lines 3 and 4 we have used the rule UI. Because UI can be applied on individual constants as well as on individual variables, at that point we had a choice of how we want the freed variable to be instantiated. We could have chosen an individual constant or a variable. Note, however, that if an individual constant were chosen on lines 3 and 4, on line 6 application of UG would have become a problem. So, a randomly picked variable *y* was used on lines 3 and 4 to leave open the possibility of applying UG on line 6. The rule of thumb, therefore, is that *if you are planning to use* UG *at a later stage, it is better to instantiate by individual variables while using* UI.

Here is another example of a proof which uses UG:

Example 4

1. $(\forall x)(Jx \supset (Wx \bullet Sx))$		
2. $(\forall x) \sim Sx$	$/ \therefore (\forall y) \sim Jy$	
3. $\sim Sy$		2, UI
4. $\sim Sy \vee \sim Wy$		3, Add
5. $\sim (Sy \bullet Wy)$		4, De. M
6. $\sim (Wy \bullet Sy)$		5, Com.
7. $Jy \supset (Wy \bullet Sy)$		1, UI
8. $\sim Jy$		7, 6, MT
9. $(\forall y) \sim Jy$		**8, UG**

Example 4 also shows the prudent use of a variable while doing UI on lines 3 and 7. Without these steps, the UG step on line 8 at the end of the proof would not have been possible.

Existential Generalization (EG)

The rule **Existential Generalization (EG)** allows us to infer an existentially quantified generalization from a substitution instance of it. Formally, we may symbolically represent it as

$$\frac{\phi\nu}{\therefore (\exists\mu)\,\phi\mu}$$

The process of application of EG is simple:

✓ Insert an existential quantifier.

✓ Ensure that at least one occurrence of the individual symbol that you are generalizing on is bound by the newly introduced existential quantifier.

The ν in the premise $\phi\nu$ in the symbolic form of the rule may be either an individual constant or an individual variable. Using EG, there is no restriction on what you may generalize from. Thus, if you have a statement such as:

$$Gu \bullet \sim Ku$$

Then, by applying EG on it, you may get

$$(\exists z)\ (Gz \bullet \sim Kz)$$

Note that you may also obtain the statement $(\exists z)\ (Gz \bullet \sim Kz)$ from the following:

$$Gb \bullet \sim Kb$$

Any of the following is a legitimate application of EG:

$$\frac{Ba}{\therefore (\exists z)\ Bz} \qquad \frac{By}{\therefore (\exists x)\ Bx}$$

In EG, you may generalize *from an individual constant* just as you may generalize *from an individual variable.* Suppose you know that it was Seema (the proper name of a specific individual) who got *A* grade in the last semester, from this you can rightly generalize that there is at least one person who got an *A* last semester. However, even if you did not know that it was Seema then all you know is that *someone* (non-specific individual) got an *A* in the last semester you can still rightly generalize that there is at least one person who got an *A* last semester.

There is an **important exception** about EG. Though it is a rule of inference, with EG you are allowed to replace *some* or *at least one* variable or constant, and not necessarily all. With other rules, you have to be careful not to apply it to parts of a statement. However, for EG, *this rule does not always require that every occurrence of a given individual variable or constant be generalized.* On this point EG differs significantly from UG. So, given the statement:

$$Gu \bullet \sim Ku$$

you *cannot* obtain by EG

$$(\exists z)\ Gz \bullet \sim Ku \qquad \times \textbf{ wrong!}$$

But you may obtain any of the following by a proper use of EG:

$$(\exists z)\ (Gz \bullet \sim Ku)$$

or $$(\exists z)\ (Gu \bullet \sim Kz)$$

or $$(\exists z)\ (Gz \bullet \sim Kz)$$

Similarly, the following derivations by EG are also proper:

$$\frac{Ba \vee Dy}{\therefore (\exists x)(Bx \vee Dy)} \qquad \frac{Ba \vee Dy}{\therefore (\exists x)(Ba \vee Dx)}$$

Here is an example of a proof in which EG has been used:

Example 5

1. $(\forall y) \sim Dy \quad /\therefore (\exists x)\, Dx$
2. Dz — 1, UI
3. $(\exists x)\, Dx$ — 2, EG

The last line of Example 5 shows EG as applied to a variable z on line 2. As explained above, EG could have been applied even if the symbol was an individual constant.

Existential Instantiation (EI)

The rule **Existential Instantiation (EI)** allows the inference of a specific instance from an existentially quantified premise. EI *cannot* be applied to a part of a statement. Given an existentially quantified statement as a whole line such as:

$$(\exists \mu)\, \phi\mu$$

EI allows us to remove the existential quantifier and to instantiate the subsequently free variable to obtain something like:

$$\phi v$$

The v in the ϕv in the instantiation, however, *must be a variable and not an individual constant*. Consider this: If all you know is that there is at least one person who got an *A* grade last semester, from that you cannot rightly conclude that it is Seema who got the *A*. Non-specific information cannot yield definite information about specific individuals without causing logical problems.

Formally, the rule EI may be represented as follows:

$n. \quad (\exists \mu)\, \phi\mu$

$\rightarrow o \quad \phi v$

$\quad .$

$\quad .$

$\quad s \quad p$

$n+1. \quad p \qquad n,\ o–s,\ EI$

The schematic form above may look a bit complicated to you, but it actually shows you schematically how the EI rule works in a derivation. An EI application is like a derivation within a derivation, as you have seen in the case of conditional proof (CP). It has to start from an existentially quantified line that has to be there, either as an already given premise or as a line derived from earlier lines. In the symbolic format, line n is this starting line. It stands for a given existentially quantified line within the derivation which asserts that there is at least one 'μ' which has the property 'ϕ'. On this line we may use EI.

EI starts *like a conditional proof with an assumption* on line o. Line o assumes that let ν be that individual that has the property ϕ. Note that ν is supposed to be an arbitrary individual variable, representing an unknown individual from the domain. The arrow, as in conditional proof, indicates the beginning of an assumption. Given the existentially quantified statement on line n, and given this assumption on line o, suppose you come to some conclusion p, which was your target. After reaching p, you can let go of the assumption and restate that p follows, as has been done on line $n + 1$. This discharging of an assumption, as in the conditional proof, is marked by drawing a horizontal line under the vertical line elongated from the bent arrow.

But the justification of the term $n + 1$ must be noted carefully. This is the culmination line or the endline for the EI. It asserts that p is derived from an assumption-based proof and the existentially quantified line by EI. On the right-hand side of line $n + 1$, there are three components separated by commas as the justification: n refers to the originally given existentially quantified statement which acts as the premise; the lines from o through s refer *as a block* to the further derivation made to arrive at p, and then mention of EI as the justifying rule at the end completes the justification.

Let us take an example of a proof in which EI is used to understand this format better:

Example 6

	1. (∃y) (Wy • Jy)	/∴ (∃x) Wx
→	2. Wu • Ju	
	3. Wu	2, Simp.
	4. (∃x) Wx	3, EG
	5. (∃x) Wx	**1, 2–4, EI**

In Example 6, line 1 is the only premise given. On line 2, EI begins with an instantiation of line 1, but there is no justification required at that line. Only the bent arrow indicates that it is an assumption. The existential quantifier has been removed on line 2, and the freed variable y is instantiated by another variable u. $(\exists x)$ Wx is the target line or the p. From line 2, the target is reached by applications of Simp. and EG. After reaching this line at line 4 by EG, we are now ready to discharge the assumption. On line 5, the assumption is discharged and the target line is *restated* with the help of EI. This line is justified by line 1 and the blocks 2-4 and by the rule EI.

A second example may be of some help:

Example 7

1. $(\forall z)(Tz \bullet Sz)$
2. $(\exists y)\, Ty$
3. $(\exists x)\, Sx \supset (\exists y)\, Ry$ $/\therefore (\exists y)\, Ry$
4. → Tw
5. $Tw \supset Sw$ — 1, UI
6. Sw — 4, 3, MP
7. $(\exists x)\, Sx$ — 5, EG
8. **$(\exists x)\, Sx$ — 2, 4–7, EI**
9. $(\exists y)\, Ry$ — 3, 8, MP

Note that in Example 6, p or the target line was the conclusion $(\exists x)\, Wx$ itself. However, Example 7 shows that p or the target line in an EI *does not necessarily have to be the conclusion of the proof*; it may very well be some intermediate line that you need for further derivation of the conclusion. In Example 7, the conclusion is $(\exists y)\, Ry$. Basically you need $(\exists x) Sx$ by EI to derive $(\exists y)\, Ry$ by MP on line 9. Other than that, the structural features of EI in Example 7 are as in Example 6. Line 2, an existentially quantified statement, i.e., the entire statement is within the scope of the existential quantifier, is used as the beginning point of an EI. The entire block of lines 4–7 has acted as the vehicle to get $(\exists x)\, Sx$ by EI.

This ends our introduction to the four new rules. Of course, the rules, specially the EI, have many restrictions. These are discussed and explained in the next section separately. Overall, you have some idea now about the four inference rules of Predicate Logic, of which UG and EG introduce quantifiers, and UI and EI remove quantifiers.

EXERCISE 12.2

1. Identify in each of these arguments which of the UI, UG, EI and EG rules has or have been used:

*a. Let x and y be any two numbers. It does not matter which order you add them, the result will be the same; i.e. $x + y = y + x$. Therefore, for all pairs of numbers, the result of their addition remains the same no matter in which order they have been added.

b. About 4% of residents of Sweden are Muslims. So, some residents of Sweden are Muslims.

c. Anyone who owns a computer uses it sometimes. So, there is at least one person, who owns a computer, uses it sometimes.

d. Every living animal has to eat. So, my pet will need food.

e. There exists at least one person who does not wash his or her dishes. Therefore, somebody does not wash one's own dishes.

*f. The womens' self-help group is running well in the three blocks of the district. So, the womens' self-help group is running well in some of the blocks of the district.

2. Fill in the lines in these derivations:

*a.
1. $(\forall y)\,(Py \supset \sim By)$
2. $(\forall y)\,(Ay \supset Py)$ $/ \therefore (\forall y)\,(Ay \supset \sim By)$
3. $Ax \supset Px$ 2, UI

⋮

6. $(\forall y)\,(Ay \supset \sim By)$

b.
1. $(\forall x)\,[(Cx \vee Dx) \supset (Ex \bullet Fx)]$
2. $(\forall x)\,(Cx \vee Dx)$ $/ \therefore (\exists y)\,Fx$

⋮

9. $(\exists y)\,Fx$ 8, EG

c.
1. $(\forall z)\,(Lz \supset Mz)$
2. $(\exists z)\,(Lz \vee Mz)$ $/ \therefore (\exists x)\,Mx$
3. $Lx \vee Mx$

⋮

8. $\sim Mx \supset Mx$ 7, 4, H.S.

⋮

12. $(\exists x)\,Mx$ 11, EG
13. $(\exists x)\,Mx$ 2, 3–12, EI

*d.
1. $(\forall x)\,(Rx \supset Sx)$
2. $(\exists x)\,(Rx \bullet Tx)$ $/ \therefore (\exists x)\,(Sx \bullet Tx)$
3. $Ru \bullet Tu$

⋮

10. $(\exists x)\,(Sx \bullet Tx)$ 8, EG
11. $(\exists x)\,(Sx \bullet Tx)$ 2, 3–9, EI

e.
1. $\sim (\exists x)\,(Ux \bullet \sim Wx)$

2. $\sim (\exists x)(Vx \bullet Wx)$ $\quad$ $/ \therefore \sim (\exists x)(Vx \bullet Ux)$
3. $(\forall x)(Ux \supset Wx)$ $\quad$ 1, QN
4. $(\forall x)(Vx \supset \sim Wx)$ $\quad$ 2, QN

⋮

10. $\sim (\exists x)(Vx \bullet Ux)$ $\quad$ 9, QN

3. Construct formal proofs of validity for each of the following arguments. Feel free to use conditional proof or any other strategy that you find convenient.

*a. 1. $(\forall y)[(Ky \bullet Jy) \supset Hy]$
2. $(\forall y)\, Ky$
3. Jd $\quad$ $/ \therefore Kd \bullet Hd$

b. 1. $(\forall z)\, Nz \vee (\forall z) \sim Oz$
2. $\sim (\forall z)\, Nz$
3. $(\forall z)\,(Mz \supset Oz)$ $\quad$ $/ \therefore (\exists z) \sim Mz$

c. Either Trisha must know the address or Neena knows the telephone number. It seems that no one knows the telephone number. So, someone must know the address. (*Ax*: *x* must know the address, *Tx*: *x* knows the telephone number, *t*: Trisha, *n*: Neena)

d. All tigers, if they are not too old, are dangerous. Sheru is not too old. So, Sheru, if a tiger, is dangerous. (*Tx*: *x* is a tiger, *Ox*: *x* is too old, *Dx*: *x* is dangerous, *s*: Sheru)

*e. 1. $(\forall x)[Cx \vee (Fx \bullet \sim Ix)]$
2. $(\forall x)\, Ix$ $\quad$ $/ \therefore (\exists x)(Ox \supset Cx)$

12.3 Restrictions on Quantifier Rules

The Predicate logic inference rules come with certain restrictions. Among the general restrictions, we have already mentioned that UI, UG, and EI apply *only to entire statements* and *not* to their parts.

There are also special restrictions that apply exclusively to some rules. For example, among the four new rules, EI and UG have special restrictions. UG allows a universal generalization that intuitively seems questionable and, similarly, EI allows an instantiation which also seems to raise certain questions. For understandable reasons, therefore, EI and UG have special restrictions that apply exclusively to them. In this section we shall enumerate these.

Special Restrictions on UG

Let us start with UG. As already mentioned, the **first restriction** is

Application of UG on an individual constant is prohibited.

In a U.D. of persons, where Cx stands for "*x is a world-class cricketer*" and *s* stands for '*Sachin Tendulkar*', it is a blatant illicit generalization if you apply UG as shown below:

Example 8

1. Cs
2. $(\forall x)\, Cx$ **1, UG × wrong!**

So, for each application of UG, first ensure that you are generalizing on an individual variable.

The **next restriction** is also prompted by the need to block illicit generalization. In a U.D. of natural numbers, where Ox stands for *x is odd*, the inference from $(\exists x)\ Ox$ to $(\forall x)\ Ox$ is clearly invalid. For, though there are some numbers which are odd, that does not and should not imply that every natural number is odd! Yet, that is what happens if we allow application of UG in the following case:

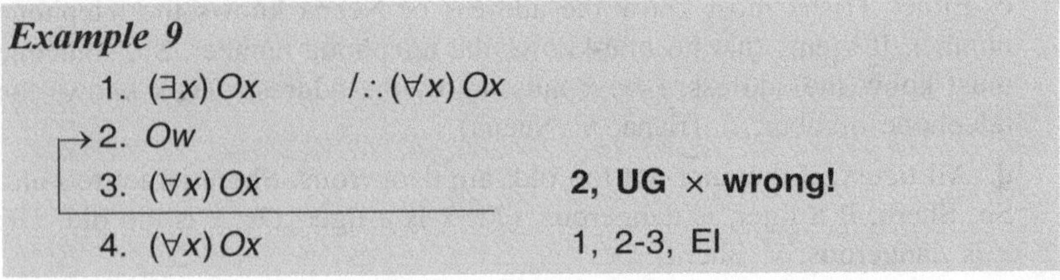

Example 9

1. $(\exists x)\, Ox$ $/ \therefore (\forall x)\, Ox$
2. Ow
3. $(\forall x)\, Ox$ **2, UG × wrong!**
4. $(\forall x)\, Ox$ 1, 2-3, EI

What went wrong? The basic mistake in this case is on line 3, where we have universally generalized on a variable that is *assumed* to have the property *O*. An assumption has value only within the scope of that assumption. Generalization on an assumed case of having a certain property, while relying on that assumption, is highly question-begging. It does not provide an independent ground for generalizing that every member in the domain has the same property. To prevent inferences based on illicit generalizations such as these, the second restriction on UG is that:

- Application of UG is prohibited on a variable that is free on a line that is either an undischarged assumption or is free within the scope of an assumption.

The '*w*' on line 2 in the above argument is a variable, but it is a variable that is free in an undischarged assumption as part of an EI procedure. It is also free within the scope of an assumption, because *all assumptions by default are within their own scope*. On line 3, UG should not be applied to it.

Does this mean that wherever assumptions are being made in the proof, either by CP or by EI or some other rule, we cannot ever use UG? No. You need to remember that *as long as* we are relying upon an assumption, i.e.

as long an assumption, is not discharged, *the variable used in that assumption* should not be universally generalized upon. Once the assumption is discharged, i.e., once we do not rely upon the assumption about a variable, we are free to use UG on it. So, it is permissible to use UG in the following case:

Example 10

1. $(\exists y)(Ay \bullet By)$	/ $\therefore (\forall y)(Cy \supset (\exists y) Ay)$	
→ 2. Cw		
→ 3. $Au \bullet Bu$		
4. Au	3, Simp.	
5. $(\exists y) Ay$	4, EG	
6. $(\exists y) Ay$	1, 3–5, EI	
7. $Cw \supset (\exists y) Ay$	2-6, CP	
8. $(\forall y)(Cy \supset (\exists y) Ay)$	**7, UG**	**permissible ✓**

We are also allowed to use UG within any proof strategy that requires making assumption *on any other variable that is not used in an assumption.* Introduction of assumptions is not the only way variables can be introduced to a proof. Often, variables appear in the proof by way of instantiation such as in UI. Application of UG is not restricted on these variables *even if they appear within a derivation based on an assumption.*

The **third restriction** on UG is that:

- The variable on which UG is applied must not be allowed to remain free in the resulting universally quantified statement.

The following is an example of an argument of what happens if this restriction is not followed. In an unrestricted UD, where *Txx* stands for *x is as tall as itself*, the following argument is clearly invalid:

Example 11

1. $(\forall y) Tyy$	
2. Txx	1, UI
3. $(\forall y) Tyx$	**2, UG × wrong!**
4. $(\forall x)(\forall y) Tyx$	3, UG

For, though everything is as tall as itself, from that it does not follow that any two objects in that domain are as tall as each other. The mistake happens on line 3 where all occurrences of the variable *x* were supposed to be bound by the universal quantifier by UG but its one occurrence remains free.

Special Restrictions on EI

As mentioned in Section 12.2 the **first restriction** on **EI**, is

- Instantiation by an individual constant is prohibited in **EI.**

The instantiating symbol must be a variable.

The **second restriction** adds to that:

- A variable introduced free by **EI** must not occur free previously in the proof. In other words, every fresh application of **EI** must introduce a new free variable.

Given below is an example of what happens when this restriction is flouted. In a UD of all natural numbers, where *Ox* stands for *x is odd* and *Ex* stands for *x is even*, the following is a clear case of invalidity:

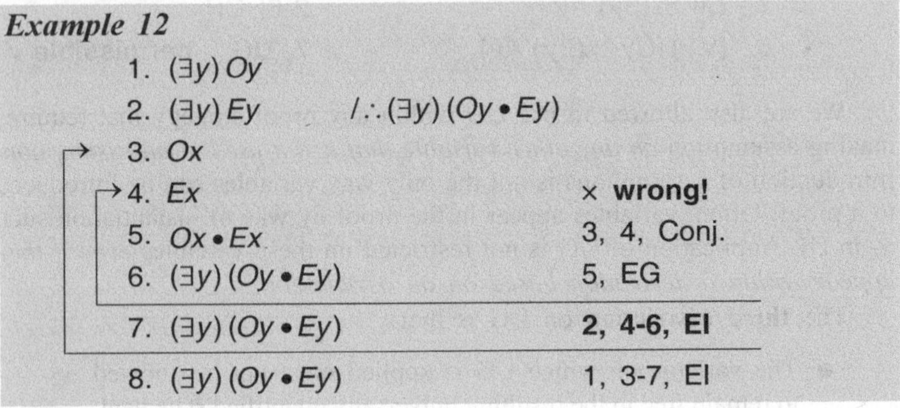

Example 12

1. (∃y) Oy
2. (∃y) Ey   /∴ (∃y) (Oy • Ey)
3. Ox
4. Ex   × **wrong!**
5. Ox • Ex   3, 4, Conj.
6. (∃y) (Oy • Ey)   5, EG
7. (∃y) (Oy • Ey)   **2, 4-6, EI**
8. (∃y) (Oy • Ey)   1, 3-7, EI

Just because some numbers are odd and some other numbers are even, it does not warrant to say that some numbers are both odd and even! The mistake in the above example originates from using the *same variable x* to instantiate for EI for the second time on line 4. However, *x* has been already used as a free variable once previously on line 3. Note that if on line 4 a variable other than *x* is chosen, then one cannot derive the wrong conclusion.

The **third restriction** is to prevent undesirable generalization on the variable freed by **EI**: It asserts that:

- The instantiated variable, introduced free by **EI**, must not occur free on line *p* in **EI**.

In an EI derivation, the target line is referred to as *p*. After reaching *p*, the EI assumption can be discharged. This restriction requires that on line *p* the variable introduced by instantiation must not run free. Otherwise, the chances are that the free variable may encourage invalid inferences. Here is an example of what happens when this restriction is violated. Consider a UD of all flowers, where *Rx* or stands for *x is red* and *Fx* for *x is fragrant*. In this context, the following is an invalid argument:

Example 13

1. $(\exists x)(Rx \bullet Fx)$ $/ \therefore (\forall x) Rx$
→ 2. $Rw \bullet Fw$
3. Rw 2, Simp.
4. Rw 1, 2-3, EI   × **wrong!**
5. $(\forall x) Rx$ 4, UG

Though there are some red flowers that are also fragrant, from that it does not legitimately follow that all flowers are red! The mistake arises because *w*, which is introduced as a free variable by EI on line 2 still occurs free on line *p*, i.e. on line 3, when the assumption has been discharged. As a result, the free variable again occurs on line 4. And, since *w* on line 4 no longer relies on any assumption made on that variable, application of UG on it on line 5 cannot be blocked.

This ends our discussion on the restrictions. The key to the level of success you achieve with the derivations in Predicate logic will depend on how well you have understood and followed these restrictions.

EXERCISE 12.3

1. Spot the errors in the following derivations. In each case, identify the line and the rule which has been wrongly applied, and explain the reasons why it is a mistake.

*a. 1. $(\exists x)(\forall y)(Hx \supset (Ny \vee Ty))$
2. Hy
→ 3. $(\forall y)(Hy \supset (Ny \vee Ty))$
4. $Hy \supset (Nm \vee Tk)$ 3, UI
5. $Nm \vee Tk$ 4, 2, MP
6. $(\exists x)(Nx \vee Tk)$ 5, EG
7. $(\exists x)(Nx \vee Tk)$ 2, 3–6, EI

b. 1. $(\forall y)(Ay \supset By)$
→ 2. $(\forall x) Ax$
3. $Aa \supset Ba$ 1, UI
4. Aa 2, UI
5. Ba 3, 4, MP
6. $(\forall x) Bx$ 4, UG
7. $(\forall x) Ax \supset (\forall x) Bx$ 2–6, CP

c. 1. $(\forall x)(\exists y)(Px \equiv Qy)$
   2. $(\exists y)(Px \equiv Qy)$ 1, UI
   → 3. $Px \equiv Qx$
   4. $(Px \supset Qx) \bullet (Qx \supset Px)$ 3, Equiv
   5. $(Px \supset Qx)$ 4, Simp
   6. $(\forall x)(Px \supset Qx)$ 5, UG
   7. $(\exists y)(\forall x)(Px \supset Qy)$ 6, EG
   8. $(\exists y)(\forall x)(Px \supset Qy)$ 2, 3–7, EI

d. 1. $(\forall y)(By \supset Dy) \supset Fa$
   2. $\sim (\forall x) Fx$
   3. $(\forall y)(By \supset Dy) \supset (\forall x) Fx$ 1, UG
   4. $\sim (\forall y)(By \supset Dy)$ 3, 2, MT
   5. $\sim (Bk \supset Dk)$ 4, UI

*e. 1. $(\exists x)(\exists y)(Hx \bullet Jy)$
   2. $(\forall y)((Hy \bullet Jy) \supset Ky)$
   → 3. $(\exists y)(Hx \bullet Jy)$
   → 4. $Hx \bullet Jx$
   5. $(Hx \bullet Jx) \supset Kx$ 2, UI
   6. Kx 5, 4, MP
   7. Kx 3, 4–6, EI
   8. Kx 2, 3–7, EI
   9. $(\exists y) Ky$ 8, EG

f. 1. $(\exists x)(Qx \bullet Rx)$
   2. $(\exists x)(\sim Qx \bullet Tx)$
   → 3. $Qa \bullet Ra$
   → 4. $\sim Qa \bullet Ta$
   5. Qa 3, Simp.
   6. $\sim Qa$ 4, Simp.
   7. $Qa \bullet \sim Qa$ 5, 6, Conj.
   8. $(\exists x)(Qx \bullet \sim Qx)$ 7, EG
   9. $(\exists x)(Qx \bullet \sim Qx)$ 2, 4–8, EI
   10. $(\exists x)(Qx \bullet \sim Qx)$ 1, 3–9, EI

g. 1. $\sim (\forall x) \sim Sx \supset (Sc \vee Kc)$
   2. $(\exists x) \sim Sx \supset (Sc \vee Kc)$ 1, QN

→ 3.	$\sim Sc \supset (Sc \vee Kc)$	
4.	$\sim\sim Sc \vee (Sc \vee Kc)$	3, Impl.
5.	$Sc \vee (Sc \vee Kc)$	4, DN
6.	$(Sc \vee Sc) \vee Kc$	5, Assoc.
7.	$Sc \vee Kc$	6, Taut.
8.	$(\exists x)\ (Sx \vee Kx)$	7, EG
9.	$(\exists x)\ (Sx \vee Kx)$	2, 3–8, EI

h. 1.	$(\forall x)\ [(Fx \supset Gx) \bullet \sim Ga]$	
2.	$(\exists x)\ [\sim Fx \bullet (\forall y)\ Dy] \supset (\forall z)\ Bz$	
→ 3.	Dw	
4.	$(Fa \supset Ga) \bullet \sim Ga$	1, UI
5.	$Fa \supset Ga$	4, Simp.
6.	$\sim Ga$	4, Simp.
7.	$\sim FA$	5, 6, MT
8.	$(\exists x) \sim Fx$	7, EG
9.	$(\forall y)\ Dy$	3, UG
10.	$(\exists x)\ [\sim Fx \bullet (\forall y)\ Dy]$	8, 9, Conj.
11.	$(\forall z)\ Bz$	2, 10, MP
12.	$Dw \supset (\forall z)\ Bz$	3–11, CP

*i. 1.	$(\forall y)\ (\exists z)\ (Tz \vee Uy)$	
2.	$(\exists z)\ (Tz \vee Uy)$	1, UI
→ 3.	$Tz \vee Uz$	
4.	$(\forall x)\ (Tx \vee Uz)$	3, UG
5.	$(\exists y)\ (\forall x)\ (Tx \vee Uz)$	4, EG
6.	$(\exists y)\ (\forall x)\ (Tx \vee Uz)$	2, 3–5, EI

12.4 The Rules of Replacement

As mentioned earlier, the **Quantifier Negation (QN) rules** are:

1. $(\forall y)\ \phi y \equiv \sim (\exists y) \sim \phi y$
2. $(\forall y) \sim \phi y \equiv \sim (\exists y)\ \phi y$
3. $(\exists y)\ \phi y \equiv \sim (\forall y) \sim \phi y$
4. $(\exists y) \sim \phi y \equiv \sim (\forall y)\ \phi y$

These four are the rules of replacement in Predicate logic. They tell us that you can change from a universal quantifier to the negation of an existential one and vice versa. They require deft handling of negation signs or removal of negation signs. For example, the universal quantifier $(\forall y)$ is replaceable by $\sim(\exists y)\sim$, and vice versa. The universal quantifier *followed by* a negation sign as in $(\forall y)\sim$ is replaceable by an existential quantifier with a negation sign *in front of it* as in $\sim(\exists y)$, and vice versa. Similarly, the existential quantifier $(\exists y)$ is replaceable by $\sim(\forall y)\sim$, and vice versa, and $(\exists y)\sim$ is replaceable by $\sim(\forall y)$, and vice versa.

You may also try to understand these rules intuitively. Everything has ϕ is equivalent to stating *it is not the case that there is at least one thing that does not have* ϕ, and the reverse is true as well. Similarly, *something does not have* ϕ, is equivalent to saying *it is not the case that everything has* ϕ, and vice versa.

As you have learnt in Propositional logic, these rules of replacement can be applied to entire statements as well as to parts of a statement to replace certain expressions in their equivalent expressions. Our Predicate Logic derivation system is complete without the QN rules, but they are useful for reducing the complexity and occasionally the length of a proof.

The following are some examples of how the QN rules may be applied:

Example 14

A 1. $(\forall x)\sim Lx$

2. $\sim(\exists x)\,Lx$ — **1, QN**

B. 1. $\sim(\forall x)\sim(\sim Lx \vee Mx) \supset (\exists y)\,Oy$

2. $(\exists x)(\sim Lx \vee Mx) \supset (\exists y)\,Oy$ — **1, QN**

In case A, the premise says that nothing has *L*. But the premise is a stand-alone quantified line. From this, by QN we derive *it is not the case* that something has *L*. This is expressed as $\sim(\exists x)$. In case B, however, the QN has been applied to part of a statement and an expression $\sim(\forall x)\sim$ has been converted by the QN to a more concise but logically equivalent expression $(\exists x)$.

Here is an example of a proof in which using QN is helpful:

Example 15

1. $(\forall x)\,Jx \supset (\forall y)\sim Oy$
2. $(\exists y)\,Oy$ — $/\therefore (\exists x)\sim Jx$
3. $\sim(\forall y)\sim Oy$ — **2, QN**
4. $\sim(\forall x)\,Jx$ — 1, 3, MT
5. $(\exists x)\sim Jx$ — **4, QN**

Given below is another example of a proof in which QN plays a crucial role:

Example 16

1. $(\exists x)(Mx \bullet Nx) \supset (\forall z)(Oz \supset Pz)$
2. $(\exists y)\, Jy \supset \sim (\forall x)(Mx \supset \sim Nx)$ $\quad /\therefore (\exists y)\, Jy \supset (\forall z)(Oz \supset Pz)$
3. $(\exists y)\, Jy \supset \mathbf{(\exists x)(Mx \bullet Nx)}$ **2, QN**
4. $(\exists y)\, Jy \supset (\forall z)(Oz \supset Pz)$ 3, 1, HS

Note that in Example 16 on line 3, QN has been applied to a part of line 2. The segment $(\forall x)(Mx \supset \sim Nx)$ is actually an *E* statement, and $\sim (\forall x)(Mx \supset \sim Nx)$ is comparable to the situation described in $\sim (\forall y) \sim \phi y$ of the QN rule. The negation sign in front of *Nx* ensures that every member of the domain does not have a certain property. We obtained $(\exists x)(Mx \bullet Nx)$ from this by applying the QN equivalence $(\exists y)\, \phi y \equiv \sim (\forall y) \sim \phi y$. After this application of QN, the proof becomes really easy and requires only one HS step.

If you still have some doubts, let us show you how $\sim (\forall x)(Mx \supset \sim Nx)$ is logically equivalent to $(\exists x)(Mx \bullet Nx)$. For the moment, let us keep the '$\sim (\forall x)$' part aside, and just take $Mx \supset \sim Nx$:

1. $Mx \supset \sim Nx$
2. $\sim Mx \vee \sim Nx$ 1, Impl.
3. $\sim (Mx \bullet Nx)$ 2, De M.

We find that $(Mx \supset \sim Nx)$ is actually equivalent to $\sim (Mx \bullet Nx)$. Let us now bring back the '$\sim (\forall x)$' part, and we have $\sim (\forall x)(Mx \supset \sim Nx)$, which is logically equivalent to $\sim (\forall x) \sim (Mx \bullet Nx)$. If we apply the QN equivalence $(\exists y)\, \phi y \equiv \sim (\forall y) \sim \phi y$ to this, then we get $(\exists x)(Mx \bullet Nx)$.

Here are two more examples of QN use:

Example 17

1. $\sim (\exists x)(Ux \bullet \sim Wx)$
2. $\sim (\exists x)(\sim Vx \bullet Wx)$
3. $(\forall x)(Ux \supset Wx)$ **1, QN**
4. $(\forall x)(Vx \supset \sim Wx)$ **2, QN**

We can use our intuitive understanding from Categorical logic to follow the QN replacements in Example 17. In this example, line 1 is actually a negation of an *O* statement. Without the negation sign in the front, $(\exists x)(Ux \bullet \sim Wx)$ is a categorical statement that *Some x – s that are U are not W* $\bullet \sim (\exists x)(Ux \bullet \sim Wx)$ is thus a negation of an *O* statement, and is equivalent to an *A* statement. Line 3 in Example 17 asserts it as an *A* statement with the help of the QN rule. Similarly, line 2 is a negation of an *I* statement, and is equivalent to an *E* statement. Line 4 asserts exactly this with the help of the QN rules.

12.5 Tips for Strategies

In Chapter 8, we found out how we can develop strategies or a series of planned moves for doing derivations in Propositional logic. In Predicate logic, the need for strategy is perhaps even greater. First, it has more complicated rules, and the proofs without a sound strategy can easily become unnecessarily long and inefficient. Second, there is practically no effective mechanical procedure, such as a truth table, for proving validity in Predicate logic. This makes derivation the only proper vehicle for proving validity for Predicate logic proofs. Well-formulated strategy can only diminish the chances of error in a derivation.

1. ✓ **Goal analysis:** Other than remembering the restrictions on UI, UG, EI and EG, we, as before, must use *goal analysis* as one of the tools. The conclusion that you are supposed to derive is the target or the goal and, as before, we have to look for intermediate steps which will lead us closer to this goal. The intermediate steps thus will be our sub-goals, the derivation of each of which will bring to the conclusion. Consider the following example:

Example 18

1. $(\forall x)(Ax \supset Bx)$ $/\therefore (\forall x)Ax \supset (\exists y)By$

Given the premise, it may seem that the only choice is to apply UI to it and obtain a line such as:

$$Ay \supset By$$

However, this line does not help us to get anywhere near our target line or the conclusion. For, we *cannot* selectively attach universal quantifier before *Ay* and an existential quantifier before *By* without breaking some rules. But that should not stop you from thinking of other alternatives. In fact, as in any derivation, you need to be resourceful. Everything that you have learnt about strategies in formal derivation for Propositional logic still very much applies here. So, feel free to use I.P., or C.P., or any other technique that you may find suitable.

Note that in this case your target line is not a quantified statement but a conditional statement. For derivation of a conditional, as in this case, a CP strategy may be very useful. So, you may start by assuming $(\forall x)Ax$. For, that will at least give you a starting point and also the antecedent that you are looking for in the target line.

Then your sub-goal will be how to derive $(\exists x)\ Bx$ from the assumption of $(\forall x)\ Ax$. If you can successfully handle this CP proof, you will have your target line after discharging the assumption. Thus at this point your strategy may look like:

1. $(\forall x)\ (Ax \supset Bx)$ $\quad / \therefore (\forall x)\ Ax \supset (\exists y)\ By$
2. Assume $(\forall x)\ Ax$

⋮

n. Show that $(\exists x)\ Bx$ follows

$n + 1$. Discharge the assumption and obtain the target line $(\forall x)\ Ax \supset (\exists x) Bx$ by *CP*

Once the details have been worked out, your derivation may look as in the following example:

Example 19

1.	$(\forall x)\ (Ax \supset Bx)$ $\quad / \therefore (\forall x)\ Ax \supset (\exists y)\ By$	
→2.	$(\forall x)\ Ax$	
3.	Ay	2, UI
4.	$Ay \supset By$	1, UI
5.	By	4, 3, MP
6.	$(\exists y)\ By$	5, EG
7.	$(\forall x)\ Ax \supset (\exists y)\ By$	2-6, CP

Note that, although UG has a restriction on generalizing on a variable which is within the scope of an assumption, EG has no such rule. Hence the EG application on line 6 is alright. Also, though EI has a restriction about not using a variable if it has already occurred free in the proof prior to the EI line, UI has no such restriction. Hence, on lines 3 and 4 we could use the same variable y for instantiation. Finally, note that if we had stopped at line 5 and had discharged our assumption, then we would have obtained a line as in the following:

$$(\forall x)\ Ax \supset By$$

Needless to say, this is not our target line. Moreover, application of EG on this line would have given us the expression.

$$(\exists y)\ [(\forall x)\ Ax \supset By]$$

And this would not bring us to our target line either. Therefore, EG on line 6 is very much required before you let go of the assumption.

2. ✓ **Which rule to apply first:** As a rule of thumb, remember that if in the derivation there is scope for applying both the rules UI and EI, *always use* EI *first*. For, EI has a restriction on previously used variables, but UI has none. Thus, if you apply UI first and use a variable, then you cannot use the same variable for EI next. And sometimes this stalls the proof completely. Here is a simple example of this:

Example 20

1. $(\forall z)(Fz \supset Hz)$
2. $(\exists y)\, Fy$ $\quad /\therefore (\exists y)\, Hy$

In Example 20, the two premises together clearly offer two choices: to do the UI first or the EI. Suppose that you choose to do UI first and by that you obtain:

3. $Fx \supset Hx$ $\quad$ 1, UI

Up to this point, you have not violated any rule. However, note that this eliminates the possibility of using the same *x* for applying EI on line 2 and obtain:

|→ 4. Fx $\quad$ 2, EI $\quad$ × **wrong!**

The point, however, is that unless you have *Fx*, your chances for getting *Hx* out by MP on line 3 is practically zero. On line 4, we are now forced to choose a variable other than *x* for EI, and no variable other than *x* can get us what our target line wants.

On the other hand, choosing to do EI first avoids all these difficulties and helps us construct a fairly simple proof as follows:

Example 21

1. $(\forall z)(Fz \supset Hz)$		
2. $(\exists y)\, Fy$	$/\therefore (\exists y)\, Hy$	
→ 3. Fx		
4. $Fx \supset Hx$		1, UI
5. Hx		4, 3, MP
6. $(\exists y)\, Hy$		5, EG
7. $(\exists y)\, Hy$		2, 3-6, EI

Of all the rules, EI is the most difficult for a beginner to apply. For, it requires a sub-derivation of its own. So, if you are planning to use EI in a proof, have a separate structure for this EI with the instantiated line as the beginning assumption and a sub-target line *p* as the end line. Then you can fill out the sub-derivation using other rules. But you have to be careful about which instantiating variable you are using for the EI.

3. ✓ **Keeping overlapping assumptions separate:** Sometimes in a single derivation you may have to use more than one assumption and, as you have seen before, proofs may have to be *nested* within each other. As you saw in Chapter 8, the scope of each of these assumptions need to be kept separate. *The last assumption must be discharged first*, and then its predecessor, and so on until the original or the first assumption is discharged at the very end. The following is an example of a proof which uses nested proof technique to use EI within a CP proof:

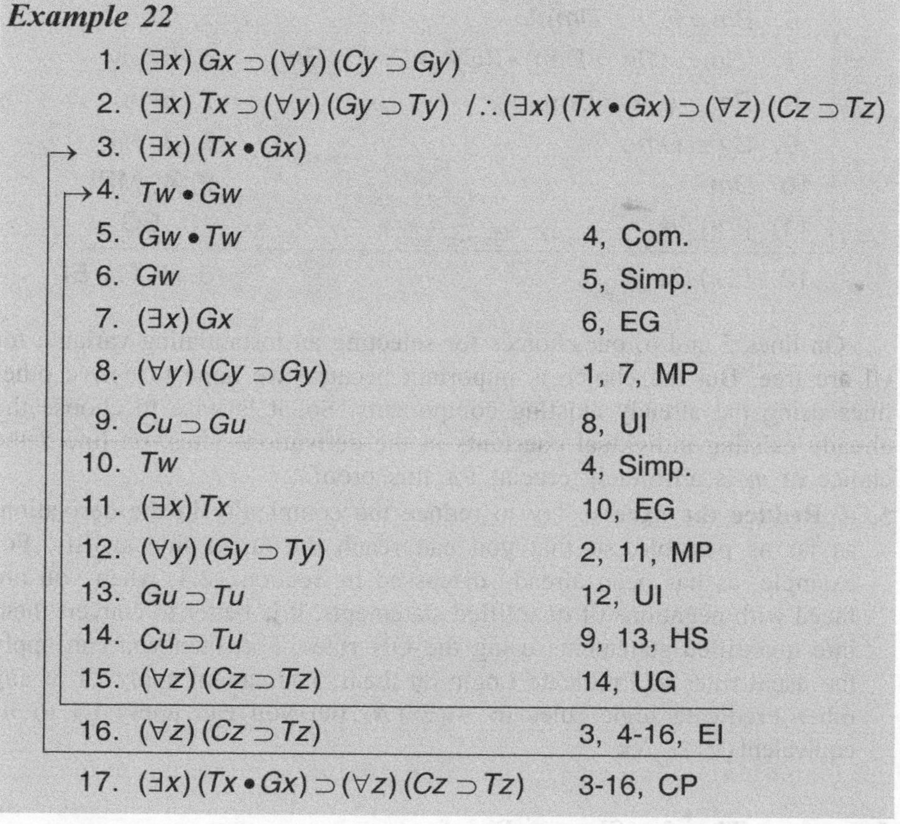

Example 22

1. $(\exists x)\, Gx \supset (\forall y)\,(Cy \supset Gy)$
2. $(\exists x)\, Tx \supset (\forall y)\,(Gy \supset Ty)$ $/\therefore (\exists x)\,(Tx \bullet Gx) \supset (\forall z)\,(Cz \supset Tz)$
3. $(\exists x)\,(Tx \bullet Gx)$
4. $Tw \bullet Gw$
5. $Gw \bullet Tw$ — 4, Com.
6. Gw — 5, Simp.
7. $(\exists x)\, Gx$ — 6, EG
8. $(\forall y)\,(Cy \supset Gy)$ — 1, 7, MP
9. $Cu \supset Gu$ — 8, UI
10. Tw — 4, Simp.
11. $(\exists x)\, Tx$ — 10, EG
12. $(\forall y)\,(Gy \supset Ty)$ — 2, 11, MP
13. $Gu \supset Tu$ — 12, UI
14. $Cu \supset Tu$ — 9, 13, HS
15. $(\forall z)\,(Cz \supset Tz)$ — 14, UG
16. $(\forall z)\,(Cz \supset Tz)$ — 3, 4-16, EI
17. $(\exists x)\,(Tx \bullet Gx) \supset (\forall z)\,(Cz \supset Tz)$ — 3-16, CP

This proof uses UG on line 15. You might think that this UG application violates a restriction because none of the assumptions are discharged yet. But, actually, it does not violate any restriction. On line 15, we have universally generalized on the variable *u* which was introduced by a UI application. This variable *u* is *not* part of any assumption that we are still relying upon while doing the UG on line 15. On line 4 we have used *w* as a variable used in EI assumption and on *w* we have not used UG at all in the proof.

4. ✓ **Using existing individual constants:** If some individual constants are already present in a proof, using them for UI could be helpful. Consider the following derivation:

Example 23

1.	$(\forall x)(\forall y)[Bx \equiv (Cy \supset Dx)]$	
2.	Bm	
3.	$(\exists z)\, Cz$ $/\therefore (\exists x)\, Dx$	
→ 4.	Cy	
5.	$(\forall y)[Bm \equiv (Cy \supset Dm)]$	1, UI
6.	$Bm \equiv (Cy \supset Dm)$	5, UI
7.	$(Bm \supset (Cy \supset Dm)) \bullet ((Cy \supset Dm) \supset Bm)$	6, Equiv.
8.	$Bm \supset (Cy \supset Dm)$	7, Simp.
9.	$Cy \supset Dm$	8, 2, MP
10.	Dm	9, 4, MP
11.	$(\exists x)\, Dx$	10, EG
12.	$(\exists x)\, Dx$	3, 4–11, EI

On lines 5 and 6, our choices for selecting an instantiating variable for UI are free. But the choice is important because we hope to derive other lines using the already existing components. So, it is wise to choose the already existing individual constants in the derivation. Thus, on line 5 the choice of *m* is absolutely crucial for this proof.

5. ✓ **Reduce the excess:** Try to reduce the complexity in the derivation, as far as possible, so that you can reach the target line swiftly. For example, as has been already discussed in Section 12.4, when you are faced with negations of quantified statements, it is better to convert them into quantified statements using the QN rules. For, then you can apply the usual rules of Predicate Logic on them. You cannot apply EI or any other Predicate logic rules to $\sim (\exists x)\, Nx$, but you can apply UI to its equivalent $(\forall x) \sim Nx$.

Important Tips for Shorter Proofs

Important: Note that since the proofs in Predicate logic will be longer, from now on use the following tips for shorter proof:

✓ Combine *DN*, *Com.*, with any step with or without referring. Thus, from *A*, you may go directly to $B \vee A$, which combines Add with Com. Or, from $\sim A \supset B$, we can now go directly to $\sim A \vee B$, combining Impl. and DN. Similarly, from $A \vee B$ and

~*B*, we can go directly to *A*, combining DS with Com.

✓ Add the following in your repertoire of rules of inferences:

Distribution of '⊃' (dist.): $A \supset (B \bullet C) \equiv (A \supset B) \bullet (A \supset C)$

Alternate version of Impl: $\sim (A \supset B) \equiv (A \bullet \sim B)$

EXERCISE 12.5

1. Construct a proof of validity for each of the following arguments:

*a. 1. $(\forall z)\ (Az \equiv Bz)$
   2. $(\forall x) \sim (Bx \vee \sim Cx)$ $\quad / \therefore \sim Ab$

b. 1. $(\forall x)\ Kx$
   2. $(\forall z)\ Lz$ $\quad / \therefore \sim (\exists y)\ (\sim Ky \vee \sim Ly)$

c. 1. $(\exists z)\ (Dz \bullet Fz)$
   2. $(\forall y)\ (Gy \supset \sim Dy)$ $\quad / \therefore (\exists z)\ (Fz \bullet \sim Gz)$

d. 1. $(\forall y)\ (Jy \supset Ky)$
   2. $(\forall z)\ [Kz \supset (Jz \supset \sim Lz)]$
   3. $(\forall x)\ [\ (\sim Mx \bullet Nx) \supset Lx]$ $\quad / \therefore (\forall x)\ [Jx \supset (Mx \vee \sim Nx)]$

*e. 1. $(\exists y)\ By \equiv (\exists x)\ Cx$ $\quad / \therefore (\exists y)\ [By \supset (\exists x)\ Cx]$

f. 1. $(\exists y)\ My \supset (\forall z)\ (Gz \supset Mz)$
   2. $(\exists z)\ Nz \supset (\forall y)\ (My \supset Ny)$
   3. $(\exists x)\ (Mx \bullet Nx)$ $\quad / \therefore (\forall x)\ (Gx \supset Nx)$

g. 1. $(\exists y)\ By \equiv (\forall x)\ Cx$ $\quad / \therefore (\forall x)\ [Bx \supset (\forall y)Cy]$

h. 1. $\sim (\forall z)\ (Iz \vee Cz)$
   2. $(\exists y) \sim Iy \supset (\forall z)\ (Jz \supset Cz)$ $\quad / \therefore \sim (\forall x)\ Jx$

i. 1. $(\forall y)\ (Dy \supset Ey)$ $\quad / \therefore (\forall y)\ [Fy \supset [(\forall z)\ (Fz \supset Dz) \supset Ey]]$

j. 1. $(\exists z)\ Az \supset (\forall y)\ [(Ay \vee Wy) \supset By]$
   2. $(\exists z)\ Az \bullet (\exists z)\ Bz$ $\quad / \therefore (\exists z)\ (Az \bullet Bz)$

*k. 1. $(\forall x)\ (Ex \supset Fx)$
   2. $(\forall x)\ (\sim Gx \vee Hx)$ $\quad / \therefore \sim (\exists x) \sim (Fx \supset Gx) \supset (\forall y)\ (Ey \supset Hy)$

l. 1. $(\forall x)\ [(Tx \vee Bx) \supset (Sx \bullet Cx)]$ $\quad / \therefore (\exists x)\ (Tx \vee Sx) \supset (\exists y)\ Sx$

m. 1. $(\exists w)\ Kw \supset (\forall y)\ [Uy \supset Ky]$
   2. $(\exists w)\ (Ow \bullet Pw) \supset (\forall y)\ (Ky \supset Py)$
   $\quad / \therefore (\exists x)\ [(Ow \bullet (Pw \bullet Kw)) \supset (\forall y)\ (Uy \supset Py)\ ]$

n. 1. $(\exists x)\ Kx \supset (\forall y)\ (Ly \supset My)$ $\quad / \therefore (\exists z)\ (Kz \bullet Lz) \supset (\exists w)\ (Kw \bullet Mw)$

o. 1. $(\exists x)[Cx \supset (\forall y)(Dy \supset Ey)]$ $/ \therefore (\forall z)(Cz \bullet Dz) \supset (\exists y)(Cy \bullet Ey)$

*p. 1. $(\exists y) Vy \supset (\forall y)(Uy \supset Wy)$

2. $(\exists x) Tx \supset (\exists y) Uy$ $/ \therefore (\exists x)(Vx \bullet Tx) \supset (\exists y) Wy$

12.6 Derivations with Multiple Quantifiers and Relational Predicates

The rules of inference of Predicate logic apply to the statements within the scope of more than one quantifier or to statements with relational predicates in the same way as they do to the less complex statements. However, since the level of complexity is more in these situations, you need to be more careful with multiple quantifiers and relational predicates. A few important things to remember are:

✓ If there are more than one quantifier present, remove a quantifier at a time, starting with the outermost.

✓ As you remove a quantifier, free and instantiate only that variable which was bound by the quantifier, leaving the rest of the variables intact.

✓ As you add a quantifier, bind and generalize only on that variable which will be within the scope of the newly introduced quantifier, leaving every other variable intact.

Thus, when you have a line such as

1. $(\forall x)(\exists y) Cxy$

If you are trying to remove the quantifier from this line, you must start with the UI since the outermost or the quantifier with the largest scope is a universal one. After the UI step on line 1, you are free to do the EI step to free the variable *y*. You are forced to follow this order.

Remember that applying UI on that line, you free and instantiate only *x*. So, your instantiation line may look like *any* of the following:

2. $(\exists y) Cxy$ (instantiation by the same variable)

or, 2′. $(\exists y) Czy$ (instantiation by some other variable such as *z*)

or, 2″. $(\exists y) Cay$ (instantiation by an individual constant such as *a*)

However, it would be a mistake in this case to instantiate *x* with *y*. For, then your instantiation line would be:

2‴. $(\exists y) Cyy$ × **wrong!**

This is a grave mistake because then the variable which is supposed to remain free after the UI step will become **accidentally bound** by the quantifier

(∃y), and that will affect the validity of the inference. In general, remember that to avoid the case of **accidentally binding the variables:**

✓ As you instantiate, it is *not* a good idea to use a variable which has occurred elsewhere on the same line. When a quantifier is removed by UI and EI, all the variables thus freed must remain free.

Similarly, when you are adding a quantifier to a line by UG or EG, always remember that a quantifier thus added will govern over the entire statement. Hence, the last quantifier added will be the one with the largest scope. For example, suppose on some line of your proof you have *Hwu* and your target line is (∃*y*) (∀*z*) *Hzy*, then your order of generalization must be:

i. *Hwu*
j. (∀*z*) *Hzu* i, UG
k. (∃*y*) (∀*z*) *Hzy* j, EG

Note that, as each quantifier has been added, the variable not bound has been left unbound. On line *j*, for example, *u* has been left alone while *w* has been bound by the universal quantifier. Note that on line *j*, *u* is still a free variable and when you are to bind it on line *k* by EG, you must choose some variable other than *z*, which already occurs on that line.

Given below is an example of a derivation with relational predicates, which emphasizes the importance of exercising caution while doing instantiation and generalization:

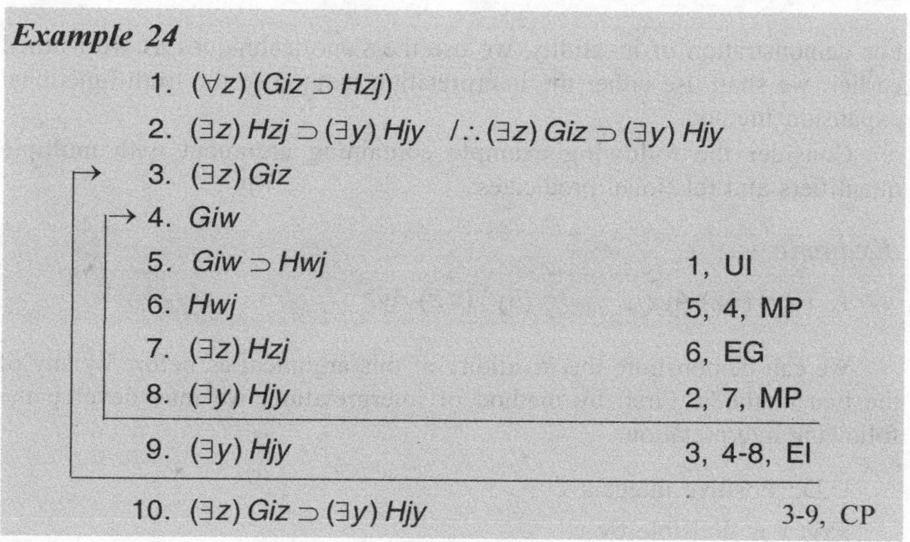

Example 24

1. (∀z) (Giz ⊃ Hzj)
2. (∃z) Hzj ⊃ (∃y) Hjy /∴ (∃z) Giz ⊃ (∃y) Hjy
3. (∃z) Giz
4. Giw
5. Giw ⊃ Hwj   1, UI
6. Hwj   5, 4, MP
7. (∃z) Hzj   6, EG
8. (∃y) Hjy   2, 7, MP
9. (∃y) Hjy   3, 4-8, EI
10. (∃z) Giz ⊃ (∃y) Hjy   3-9, CP

In Example 24, on line 3 we have begun a CP proof, where the aim is to assume (∃*z*) *Giz* and derive (∃*y*) *Hjy*. Within the CP, on line 4 the choice is clear, as we know that we need to do EI before UI. So EI is started using a fresh variable *w*. However, on line 5 as we are about to do UI on line 1, the choice of instantiating symbol becomes crucial. To fully utilize line 4 as part of an MP move, we choose to replace *z* by *w*. Without this instantiation the proof cannot progress. On line 6 we take *Hwj* out by MP, and note that on line 7 we derive (∃z) *Hzj* by EG. As we do EG, we bind only the free variable *w*, leaving the constant *j* untouched. On line 8 by MP we derive our target (∃y) *Hjy*.

It is perhaps better to recount at this point the violations on the rules that may lead to error:

- ✓ Do not use individual constants to do EI.
- ✓ Do not use individual constants to do UG.
- ✓ A variable that has occurred free in the proof prior to an EI line cannot be used for EI. For every new EI, you have to use a new variable.
- ✓ Do not use UG on a variable which is still within the scope of an assumption.
- ✓ The instantiated variable, introduced free by EI, must not occur free on line *p* in EI.
- ✓ Do not accidentally bind variables that are supposed to remain free.
- ✓ Do not free variables that are supposed to remain bound.

Invalidity

For demonstration of invalidity, we use the same techniques as we learned earlier: we shall use either the interpretation method or the truth-functional expansion method.

Consider the following example containing argument with multiple quantifiers and relational predicates:

Example

1. (∀y) (∃z) *Ayz* /∴ (∃y) (∀z) *Ayz*

We can demonstrate the invalidity of this argument as before by any of the two methods. First, by method of interpretation, we may develop the following interpretation:

U.D.: Positive integers
Fxy: *x* is divisible by *y*.

On this interpretation, the premise states that for every positive integer there is some number or other which it is divisible by. Even the prime numbers can be divided by themselves and by number 1. So, the premise is true. But the conclusion states that there is a positive number which is divisible by every number. This is false.

Second, we can also demonstrate the invalidity of the argument given above by the expansion method for a two-element universe: $\{a, b\}$.

The expansion of the premise is

$$(\forall y)\ (\exists z)\ Ayz \equiv (\exists z)\ Aaz \bullet (\exists z)\ Abz \equiv (Aaa \lor Aab) \bullet (Aba \lor Abb)$$

The expansion of the conclusion is

$$(\exists y)\ (\forall z)\ Ayz \equiv (\forall z)\ Aaz \lor (\forall z)\ Abz \equiv (Aaa \bullet Aab) \lor (Aba \bullet Abb)$$

The argument turns out to be invalid when the components have the following truth values:

Aaa	*Aab*	*Aba*	*Abb*
F	T	F	T

EXERCISE 12.6

1. Construct a proof of validity for each of the following arguments:

*a. 1. $(\forall y)\ (\forall z)\ Dyz$
   2. $(\exists y)\ (\forall z)\ (Dyz \supset Hzy)$ $\quad / \therefore (\exists x)\ (\forall z)\ Hzx$

b. 1. $(\exists y)\ (Ky \bullet (\forall z)\ (Lz \supset Myz))$
   2. $(\forall y)(Ky \supset (\forall z)\ (Nz \supset {\sim} Myz))$ $\quad / \therefore (\forall y)\ (Ly \supset {\sim} Ny)$

c. 1. $(\exists w)\ [Aw \bullet (\forall y)(By \supset Cwy)]$ $\quad / \therefore (\exists w)\ (Aw \bullet (Bk \supset Cwk))$

d. 1. $(\forall x)\ [Jx \supset (\exists y)\ (Jy \bullet Lxy)]$
   2. $(\exists x)\ [Jx \bullet (\forall y)[(Jy \bullet Lxy) \supset Oxy]]$ $\quad / \therefore (\exists x)(\exists y)\ [(Jx \bullet Jy) \supset Oxy]$

*e. 1. $(\exists u)\ (\forall v)\ [(\exists w)\ Avw \supset Avu]$
   2. $(\forall v)(\exists w)\ Avw$ $\quad / \therefore (\exists u)\ (\forall v)\ Avu$

f. 1. ${\sim} (\exists y)\ (Tym \bullet {\sim} Syn)$
   2. ${\sim} (\exists z)\ (Rzo \bullet Rnz)$
   3. $(\forall x)\ (Spx \supset Rxq)$ $\quad / \therefore {\sim} (Tpm \bullet Rqo)$

g. 1. $(\exists z)\ (\exists w)\ (Mzw \lor Nzw) \supset (\exists y)\ Oy$
   2. $(\forall z)\ (\forall w)\ (Oz \supset {\sim} Ow)$ $\quad / \therefore (\forall z)\ (\forall w) {\sim} Mzw$

h. 1. $(\exists y)\ [Cy \bullet (\forall z)\ (Dz \supset Fyz)]$
   $/ \therefore (\forall z)\ (Cz \supset Dz) \supset (\exists x)\ (Dx \bullet Fxx)$

i. 1. $(\forall x)\ [(\exists y)\ (Ayb \bullet Bxyb) \supset Cx]$
   2. $(\exists x)\ (Dxb \bullet Bxab)$ $\quad / \therefore (\forall x)\ (Dxb \supset {\sim} Cx) \supset {\sim} Aab$

*j. 1. $(\forall y)\ [(\exists z)\ [(\exists x)\ (Ax \bullet \sim Bx) \bullet Cyxz)] \supset Dy]$

2. $(\forall z)\ [(Fz \bullet Gaz) \supset (Cbza \vee Scza)]$

/ ∴ $(\exists z)\ ((Fz \bullet Gaz) \bullet (Az \bullet \sim Bz)) \supset [\ (\forall x) \sim Scxa \supset Db]$

2. Show that the following arguments are invalid:

*a. 1. $(\forall x)\ (\exists y) \sim Cxy$ / ∴ $(\exists x)\ (\forall y) \sim Cxy$

b. 1. $(\forall y)\ (\exists z)\ (Ay \supset Byz)$ / ∴ $(\exists y)(\forall z)\ (Ay \supset Byz)$

c. 1. $(\exists y)\ (\exists x)\ Myx$

2. $(\exists y)\ (\exists x)\ Nyx$ / ∴ $(\exists y)(\exists x)\ (Myx \bullet Nyx)$

d. 1. $(\forall x)\ (\exists y)\ (Axy \supset Bxy)$

2. $(\forall x)\ (\exists y)\ (Bxy \supset Cxy)$ / ∴ $(\forall x)\ (\exists y)\ (Axy \supset Cxy)$

e. 1. $(\forall x)\ (\forall y)\ (\exists z)\ Dxyz$ / ∴ $(\exists x)(\forall y)(\forall z)\ Dxyz$

12.7 Proof of Tautology

As we know from Section 8.8, theorems or tautologies are logical truths, the truths of which are provable *without* any contingent premises as added information. In Section 8.8, we saw how a proof of a tautology is a **zero premise proof.** In Predicate logic also, the proof of theorems or tautologies are proofs without any premise. However, the key difference with the tautologies of Propositional logic that most tautologies of Predicate logic cannot be proven by the truth-table analysis. For the tautologies of Predicate logic, the derivation of Predicate logic is the *only available method.*

Consider, for example, the logical truth:

$$(\forall x)\ Px \supset (\exists x)\ Px$$

which asserts that if everything in a domain has *P* then something in that domain has *P.* This is always true in a non-empty universe. Here is a zero premise proof of the tautology. As before, since there are no premises given, we have to rely upon either the CP or the IP for the proof. In this case, the conditional structure makes application of CP the obvious choice:

Example 25

Prove that: $(\forall x)\ Px \supset (\exists x)\ Px$

→ 1. $(\forall x)\ Px$	
2. Py	1, UI
3. $(\exists x)\ Px$	2, EG
4. $(\forall x)\ Px \supset (\exists x)\ Px$	1-3, CP

Here is another example:

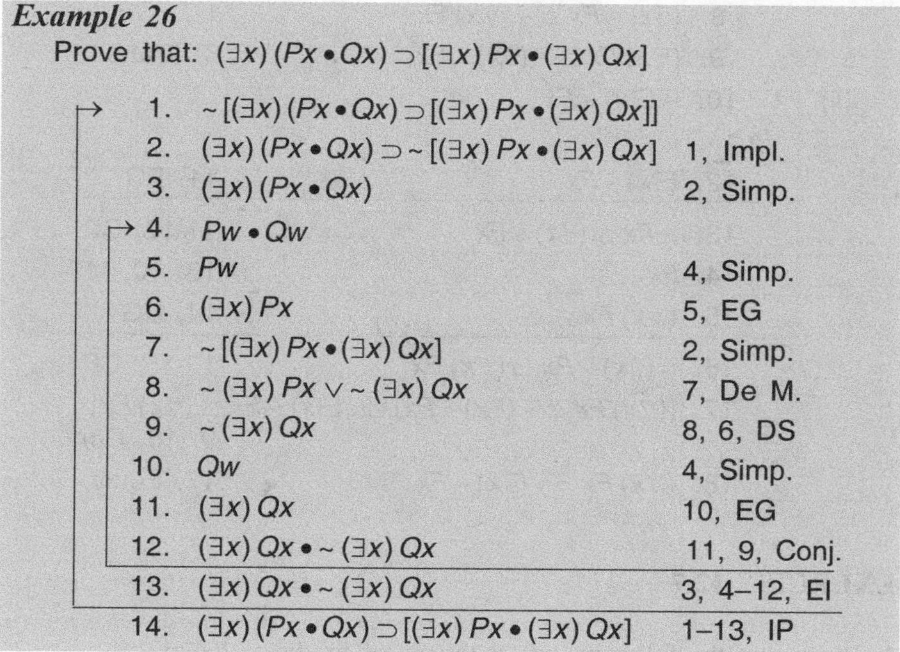

Example 26

Prove that: $(\exists x)(Px \bullet Qx) \supset [(\exists x) Px \bullet (\exists x) Qx]$

1.	$\sim[(\exists x)(Px \bullet Qx) \supset [(\exists x) Px \bullet (\exists x) Qx]]$	
2.	$(\exists x)(Px \bullet Qx) \supset \sim[(\exists x) Px \bullet (\exists x) Qx]$	1, Impl.
3.	$(\exists x)(Px \bullet Qx)$	2, Simp.
4.	$Pw \bullet Qw$	
5.	Pw	4, Simp.
6.	$(\exists x) Px$	5, EG
7.	$\sim[(\exists x) Px \bullet (\exists x) Qx]$	2, Simp.
8.	$\sim(\exists x) Px \vee \sim(\exists x) Qx$	7, De M.
9.	$\sim(\exists x) Qx$	8, 6, DS
10.	Qw	4, Simp.
11.	$(\exists x) Qx$	10, EG
12.	$(\exists x) Qx \bullet \sim(\exists x) Qx$	11, 9, Conj.
13.	$(\exists x) Qx \bullet \sim(\exists x) Qx$	3, 4–12, EI
14.	$(\exists x)(Px \bullet Qx) \supset [(\exists x) Px \bullet (\exists x) Qx]$	1–13, IP

In Example 26, we have chosen to use IP, i.e., to assume the negation of the theorem for obtaining a contradiction. Note that we may also use CP.

There can be theorems which are equivalences or have '$\equiv$' as their main connective. For this type of statements, it is easier to break the equivalence as two conditionals and prove by two separate CPs, and then conjoin the conditionals to prove equivalence. In the following example, we use this technique to prove *non-trivially*, i.e. without referring back to QN, that the QN rule $(\forall x) Fx \equiv \sim(\exists x) \sim Fx$ is a logical truth:

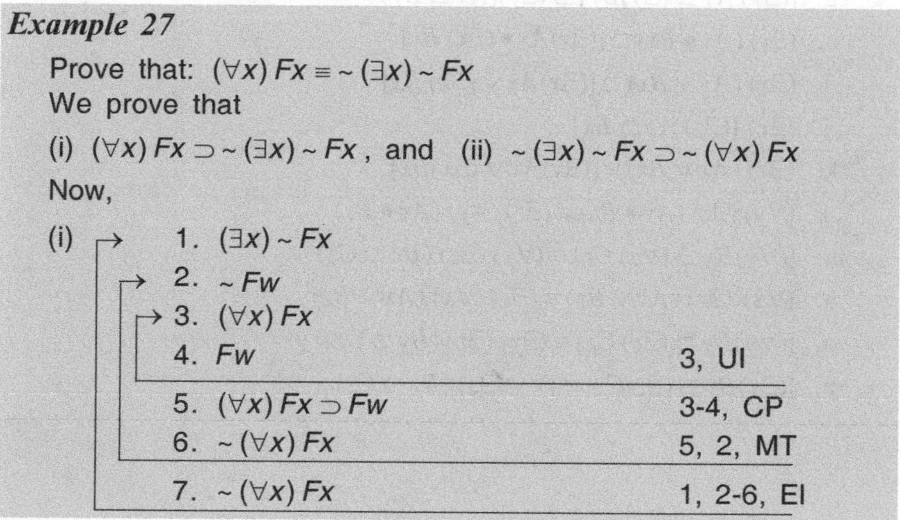

Example 27

Prove that: $(\forall x) Fx \equiv \sim(\exists x) \sim Fx$

We prove that

(i) $(\forall x) Fx \supset \sim(\exists x) \sim Fx$, and (ii) $\sim(\exists x) \sim Fx \supset \sim(\forall x) Fx$

Now,

(i)

1.	$(\exists x) \sim Fx$	
2.	$\sim Fw$	
3.	$(\forall x) Fx$	
4.	Fw	3, UI
5.	$(\forall x) Fx \supset Fw$	3-4, CP
6.	$\sim(\forall x) Fx$	5, 2, MT
7.	$\sim(\forall x) Fx$	1, 2-6, EI

	8. $(\exists x) \sim Fx \supset \sim (\forall x) Fx$	1-7, CP
	9. $(\forall x) Fx \supset \sim (\exists x) \sim Fx$	8, Trans.
(ii)	10. $\sim (\exists x) \sim Fx$	
	11. $\sim Fx$	
	12. $(\exists x) \sim Fx$	11, EG
	13. $\sim Fx \supset (\exists x) \sim Fx$	11-12, CP
	14. Fx	13, 10, MT
	15. $(\forall x) Fx$	14, UG
	16. $\sim (\exists x) \sim Fx \supset (\forall x) Fx$	10-15, CP
	17. $[(\forall x) Fx \supset \sim (\exists x) \sim Fx] \bullet [\sim (\exists x) \sim Fx \supset (\forall x) Fx]$	9, 16, Conj.
	18. $(\forall x) Fx \equiv \sim (\exists x) \sim Fx$	17, Equiv.

EXERCISE 12.7

1. Prove that the following are theorems of Predicate logic:

a. $(\forall x)(\forall y) Axy \equiv (\forall y)(\forall x) Axy$

b. $(\forall y)(By \supset (\exists x) Bx)$

*c. $(\forall z)(Az \supset Bz) \supset [(\forall y)Ay \supset (\forall y) By]$

d. $(\exists x) Ax \equiv (\exists y) Ay$

e. $(\forall x)(\exists y)(Ax \supset By) \supset [(\forall z)Az \supset (\exists y) By]$

f. $[(\forall y) Ay \vee (\forall y) By] \supset (\forall y)(Ay \vee By)$

*g. $[(\exists y) Ay \supset (\exists y)By] \supset (\exists y)(Ay \supset By)$

h. $(\exists x)(Ax \bullet Bx) \supset [(\exists x)Ax \bullet (\exists x) Bx]$

i. $(\exists x)(Ax \vee Bx) \supset [(\exists x)Ax \vee (\exists x) Bx]$

j. $(\exists x)[(\exists z) Az \supset Bx]$

k. $(\exists x)(Ax \vee Bx) \equiv [(\exists x)Ax \vee (\exists x)Bx]$

l. $(\forall y)(\exists z)(Ay \bullet Bz) \equiv (\exists z)(\forall y)(Ay \bullet Bz)$

m. $[(\forall y)By \supset (\forall z) Cz] \equiv (\forall y)(\exists z)(By \supset Cz)$

n. $(\forall x)(\exists z)(Ax \vee Bz) \equiv (\exists z)(\forall x)(Ax \vee Bz)$

o. $[(\forall y)By \supset (\exists z) Cz] \equiv (\exists y)(\exists z)(By \supset Cz)$

p. $[(\exists y)By \supset (\exists z)Cz] \equiv (\forall y)(\exists z)(By \supset Cz)$

Part C

INDUCTION

CHAPTER

INDUCTIVE REASONING

13.1 Introduction

From this chapter onwards, our focus will be on **induction**. In earlier chapters, we have briefly introduced you to induction as a type of logical reasoning. In the Informal Logic section, we also showed how induction as a reasoning is different *in kind* from deduction (see Section 2.4). Let us start afresh for a more detailed introduction to induction.

Induction is a particular kind of logical reasoning. It is a type of logical reasoning in which we proceed from *known* premises or from observed cases to infer about *unknown* or *unobserved* cases. That is, we do not draw the conclusion by analyzing only what is already explicitly stated or implied by the given premises. In induction, we try to infer something new or something that is not covered by the premises.

A usual format for induction is as given below:

The usual format of inductive arguments

1. Case 1: ϕ
2. Case 2: ϕ
3. Case 3: ϕ

⋮ ⋮

n Case n: ϕ

$n+1$. Therefore, Case $n+1$ also will be a ϕ case

You observe case$_1$, case$_2$ …case$_n$. For example, you see a black crow one day, two more black crows the next day, and then again more on another day… Based on these observations, you *induce* the conclusion that case $_{n+1}$, the next crow you will see will also be black, or that all crows are black.

The conclusion of an inductive argument is either a conclusion about a future or unobserved case, as in the case of next crow being also black. Or, it could be a generalization or a universal statement. For example, you may also conclude that all crows are black. These generalizations based on induction are called **inductive generalizations**. Some examples of inductive generalization are:

1. All human beings are mortal.
2. No mammals are cold blooded.
3. Plants get their nourishment from soil and sunlight.

Inductive leap: A very important and unique characteristic of induction is the **inductive leap** which is a leap or a jump from the known to the yet unknown or from the cases observed so far to the yet unobserved cases. The usual format for inductive arguments involves the **inductive leap**. Every time we reason inductively, we make an uncertain leap from the probable premises to a new but probable conclusion.

Inductive reasoning: This is reasoning which uses induction. Given below are some examples of common conclusions that we routinely draw by inductive reasoning:

Example 1

1. Tomorrow the Sun will rise.
2. If I post a letter, it will reach its destination.
3. Next time I breathe, I shall not breathe pure Nitrogen.
4. Objects made of glass break easily.

Each of statements 1–4 is a conclusion reached by inductive reasoning. From what we have observed or learnt in the past, we have made claims about something that is not yet observed or known or universally about a class of objects. Everyday in our life we have seen the Sun to rise, and before us many generations have seen it to rise with the beginning of a new dawn. But no one has seen tomorrow. Yet, on the basis of what we have seen, or known from our ancestors, we may claim that tomorrow the Sun will rise again.

Similarly, we know from my own past experience and also from the similar experiences of others, that the postal system will deliver the letter that we shall post next time to its destination, as it has done in the past. The letter is not yet posted, and no one has seen the future; yet we draw the conclusion about the unobserved future case routinely. Each of 1-4 is an example of conclusion based on inductive reasoning.

Inductive logic: This is a system of logic that applies to the kind of reasoning mentioned above. **Inductive arguments** are arguments based on inductive reasoning. Here are some examples of inductive arguments which display the inductive leap that uniquely characterizes inductive reasoning.

Example 2

5. Every book written by Chaudhuri is funny. So, if anything is a book written by Chaudhury, it is funny.
6. All students of IIT Kharagpur so far observed have black hair. So, the next batch of fresh students of IIT Kharagpur also will have black hair.
7. For the past ten years in August, we have had rain at least once every day for twenty days on the average. So, coming August will also show the same weather pattern.

Probabilistic character of inductive logic: Note that the truth of the conclusion in each of these arguments (5-7 above) in Example 2 is not *guaranteed.* Strictly speaking, the conclusion *does not follow* even if you know that the premises are true. The premises in each case provide us some good basis to draw the conclusion, but they do *not* provide us a conclusive basis. That is, they do not provide us enough basis for claiming that the conclusion *must follow*.

Consider Examples 6 and 7 above. You may have seen enough past batches of students of IIT Kharagpur with black hair to conclude the same is going to happen for the next batch. Still you cannot entirely rule out the possibility that the natural hair colour of some student in the future could be different.

Similarly, weather prediction contains an element of uncertainty. Though your premise may be a large database that contains the weather data of August in a certain region for the last ten years, still it does not provide you *conclusive certainty* to claim that your prediction *must* be right. For, there are so many factors involved in weather pattern that are prone to sudden changes, and with a minute but sudden change in any of them, the outcome may be different.

In Example 5, you may think that the situation is somewhat less uncertain. For, the premise is based on test of every book written by certain author. Arguments of this kind are a special type of induction called **induction by simple enumeration** (see Section 13.2). But even in this case, an element of uncertainty remains though it may be miniscule in comparison. For, even though every book by Chaudhury so far has delighted us by being funny, there is no guarantee that his next book will continue to do so. For, many authors like to diversify and try out a new line of writing once in a while. There is no guarantee that the author will continue to write only the same kind of books. All we have, in each of the arguments cited above, is a *probabilistic support* from the premise for the conclusion.

This point constitutes one of the major differences between induction and deduction. Deduction holds the promise of conclusive evidence. Validity for a deductive argument is an all-or-none situation. If even the smallest amount of doubt remains about the validity of a deductive argument, we have no choice but to call it invalid. That is not the case with induction. In a good deductive argument, the conclusion *must* be true if the premises are true (sound), and the conclusion follows (valid). However, even for *good* inductive arguments, the conclusions *cannot* be claimed as necessarily true or must be true, even if all their premises are true. Their conclusions as a rule contain information that is not contained in the premises. All we can expect from the premise of an inductive argument is *some degree of probabilistic support* for its conclusion. Better inductive arguments will provide **stronger probabilistic support** for their conclusion, and worse inductive arguments will provide **weaker probabilistic support** for their conclusion. But, none of them can deliver absolute certainty.

Thus, if you want to use the deductive standard on inductive arguments, you will be disappointed. There will always be an element of risk in even the best of the inductive arguments. But such is the nature of inductive arguments. Through the inductive leap, we try to gain new knowledge. We take the risk of uncertainty and even error to attain new knowledge. As mentioned earlier, some inductive leaps are safer than others. Inductive arguments with established or known to be true premises can yield stronger inductive support for their conclusions. But they cannot ever deliver certainty, nor are they meant to deliver certainty.

Does this feature make inductive arguments unusable? Not at all. On the contrary, we routinely rely upon inductive arguments such as the ones mentioned above and many others like these. We count upon them *knowing that they are at best probable*. Apart from the use of induction in our every day life, it is also used in sciences. In science, induction is used widely whenever a conclusion is drawn from a finite number of observed cases. The element of probability in these conclusions are accepted with the conclusions.

Some of the indicator words for induction are: *Probably, usually, tends to support, likely, very likely, almost always, may, might, sometimes*.

Non-monotonic character of inductive logic: Deductive reasoning is **monotonic**. 'Monotonic' roughly means that additional information will have *no* bearing on the truth of the conclusion. For example, finding another sample of warm-blooded mammal will not change the **validity** of the deductive argument: All mammals are warm-blooded, and so is a human being since a human being is a mammal.

But Induction is different from Deduction because it is **non-monotonic**. New information can change the strength of an inductive argument. Finding more samples of warm-blooded mammals, for example, can further strengthen the inductive conclusion that mammals are warm-blooded. Similarly, finding an instance of a mammal which is not warm-blooded, can also affect the strength of the same conclusion. The importance of additional information is always a relevant consideration in inductive reasoning.

From this chapter onwards, we shall try to understand induction and its special nature as a type of reasoning, and also learn about its different types. We shall also look into its strong points and weak points to learn how to evaluate these probability based arguments.

EXERCISE 13.1

1. What are the typical characteristics of Induction?

2. How is Induction different from deduction? Will an invalid deductive argument be acceptable as a weak inductive argument? Explain with your own examples.

3. Which of these are inductive patterns of reasoning? Justify your claim in each case.

a. I cannot cook. I have tried twice earlier, and both cases were disasters.

b. "…In every country of the world, all of a sudden the weather forecasting computer models are failing. Over the past years, China has installed 74 sets of the world's advanced Doppler weather radar with 87 per cent put into operation. But in the last year all on a sudden the weather forecasting computer models have failed so badly that China has decided to install thirty more of the devices rapidly this year with a satellite launched later last year expected to start its operations soon. In India, for example, scientists were astonished at the National Center for Medium Range Weather Forecasting by the deviation of the weather from that predicted by the Doppler reports. In Russia, authorities are just perplexed with bizarre patterns of snow falls. In America, the weather forecasters are similarly perplexed in their inability to tell people what will happen next day. This is the same story echoed in every part of the world from India to America".

—Staff Reporter, *India Daily*, Jan. 30, 2005.

c. I know Burundi as a country also will have a flag since every country has a flag.

d. If the battery is dead, the car will not start. So, the battery provides the energy to the engine.

e. Every time I ate prawns, my throat would get itchy and rashes would come out on my face. I must be allergic to prawns.

f. Investments in shares are known to be risky. So, I should not invest in shares if I want to avoid risky investments.

g. Each year, 1,82,000 women all over the world are diagnosed with breast cancer and 43,300 die. One woman in eight either has or will develop breast cancer in her lifetime. In addition, 1,600 men will be diagnosed with breast cancer and 400 will die this year.

13.2 Induction by Simple Enumeration

Inductive arguments are traditionally classified as **perfect** and **imperfect induction**. Perfect induction is also known as **induction by enumeration**. Inductive arguments are said to be *perfect* or by *enumeration* when *each* of the observed samples for the induction is *checked* or *examined individually,* and in each case the induced conclusion is found to be true. Enumeration roughly means counting. So, when all your samples to be observed are counted and listed and observed, your induction is by enumeration. For example, let us say that you want to induce that: all students in a certain class, say Class XII, owns a pen. Note that your intended conclusion is a **generalization**, i.e., you want to conclude a *universal conclusion about every member in a certain class.* We may restate your conclusion also as:

If x is a student of a particular class, then x owns a pen.

The process of arriving at a universal conclusion from facts about particular samples is called **inductive generalization**. It is a standard feature of inductive arguments, and particularly of induction by enumeration. Let us now assume that this class of students, about which you want to induce, has 27 students. In order to have a perfect induction in this case, we need to exhaustively examine whether each of the 27 students owns a pen or not. When every examined student is found to own a pen, you may conclude by induction by simple enumeration that all students of Class XII own a pen each. This is an inductive generalization that is certain because every possible case has been actually examined.

Aimed conclusion: If x is a student of Class XII, then x owns a pen.

Observed samples: Student 1 of Class XII owns a pen.
Student 2 of Class XII owns a pen.
⋮
Student 27 of Class XII owns a pen.

Induction by enumeration: All students of Class XII own a pen.

Take another example. Suppose you want to induce that in a certain apartment complex, each owner of an apartment pays income tax. Again, a perfect induction in this case would require counting the total number of samples you need to observe, and then examining each case individually before concluding. The inference schema that it follows is:

All the observed A-s are B-s.
____
Therefore, all A-s are B-s.

This is the simplest kind of inductive reasoning and is considered to be the foundation of other types of inductive reasoning.

However, as you may have already realized, the exhaustive examination of every sample is unfortunately always not possible. Though by exhaustive enumeration of each instance you may achieve an ideal amount of conclusive evidence often, for various reasons, this is simply not possible. Consider, for example, the situation in which you may need to induce about *all* stars in the universe, or about *all* cats, or about *all* herbivorous animals. Surely, and I hope you will agree, you cannot in your own lifetime exhaust *all* the samples that you need to observe to make inductions in cases such as these.

Consider also the following cases of inductive generalizations:

Dogs bark.

Butterflies come out of cocoons.

Drinking polluted water causes stomach infections

People are happy when their needs are met.

Of course, we cannot possibly examine *every* single dog, or *every* individual butterfly that was, is and will be. Similarly, we cannot ever exhaustively observe every single case of consumption of polluted water or the satisfaction level of each and every person. Yet, we do hold these generalizations. Perfect induction or induction by simple enumeration yields high certainty, but is rather limited in its scope. We need to learn how to deal with **imperfect inductions**. We need to learn how to infer safely within reasonable limits where induction cannot be done by simple enumeration. In the next two sections, we will find out about two important kinds of inductive reasoning that are by nature imperfect: reasoning by analogy and causal reasoning. There we shall also discuss what the methodological constraints must be in order to have reliable inductive arguments in less than perfect situations.

In Sections 13.3 and 13.4, however, we will learn about two other kinds of induction: **statistical induction** and **mathematical induction**.

13.3 Statistical Induction

Induction is used widely in statistics. Statistics is often required to project an estimate about an entire population from the observed samples of a number of its members. For this purpose, a version of induction by enumeration may be used. For example, suppose that there is a basket of mangoes in front of you. It contains 10 mangoes. You have already tasted five of them, and you found each of them still unripe. From the number of tasted samples, you can now project a ratio about the entire basket of mangoes by induction by enumeration: that 50% of the mangoes in the basket are unripe.

Though this was a case of induction by enumeration, every statistical induction need *not* be based on induction by enumeration. Without checking every single sample in the population, one may still make statistical projections.

Suppose again that a basket of mangoes is in front of you. But this time you yourself want to buy the entire basket of mangoes. Suppose that the shop owner allows you to taste some samples before you purchase them. Let us also suppose that you picked four mangoes from the basket to taste, and you found out that two out of these four mangoes that you have tasted are ripe and sweet. Now, it is neither desirable nor possible that you nibble each and every mango from the basket before you make the decision to purchase. So, at some point you will want to project an inductive generalization about the mangoes in the basket: all mangoes in this basket are good/bad. No matter what you conclude, how safe is your conclusion?

Clearly, you can only make an estimate based on probability. The likelihood of the correctness of the induction will depend upon how you answer the following conditions:

- Was the pool of samples tested large enough in proportion to the population?
- Was the samples distributed enough to represent the population?

One of the safeguards for statistical induction is to ensure that the pool of samples is **large enough in proportion to the population to be tested.**

If there are only 10 mangoes in the basket, then whatever your conclusion is about the mangoes, it will have a higher level of probabilistic support on the basis of sampling 4 out of 10. But if the basket contains 250 mangoes, then sampling of only 4 will not provide a very convincing support for your conclusion. The *ratio* of the sample size that are tested or examined must be significant to the whole population. The greater the size of the observed or tested samples is in proportion to the actual population, the greater will be the probability of the conclusion based on it.

Another safeguard is to ensure that the samples tested are **representative** of the population. In our mango example, the worth of your conclusion will depend upon how well the four mangoes that you have tested represent the entire batch of mangoes in the basket. If they are not well distributed in the population, then the samples will be **biased** and the likelihood of truth of your conclusion gets affected.

For instance, suppose that the four mangoes that you tasted and smelled were all from the top of the basket. If the fruit seller has put only a few ripe and sweet mangoes on the top of the basket, then your conclusion about the whole batch based upon the four mangoes taken from the top is likely to be incorrect.

Or, take another example. Suppose you want to find out what percentage of the people on the street uses credit cards. Suppose you asked 40 people during the lunch hour, and found that only two of them use credit cards. From this, you may conclude that very few people in the city use credit cards. But suppose that a closer examination of the people you interviewed shows that for some reason most of the people you have asked are teenagers. Since a high percentage of teenagers does not truly represent a city's overall population, unknowingly you have resorted to **biased sampling**. Biased sampling is a particular case of information sampling in which the samples are limited in their variety and reveal very little information about the actual nature of the situation.. Your sample interviewees should have included proportionate number of people from each group that constitute a city's diverse population, such as people from different age groups who are eligible to use credit card, and also people from different genders and professions.

The point is that statistical estimations are of inductive nature. If you can, you may ensure the certainty of your estimation by induction by simple enumeration. However, even in the case of imperfect inductions, if you take sufficient safety precautions about the samples that are tested, it is very much possible to make reliable statistical generalizations of inductive nature about the entire population.

13.4 Mathematical Induction

Mathematical induction is a very powerful proof method, very effectively used in mathematics and also in formal logic.

Ordinary induction, as we know, is a leap into uncertainty beyond what is certified by the premises. So, in general, inductions are supposed to be 'probabilistic' by nature. Mathematical inductions, on the other hand, yield certain conclusions and are actually deductive in nature. However, it has enough similarity with the ordinary induction to be called a kind of induction. It is like an induction because:

> It starts from a small sample and usually from one item. Then it generalizes about a whole class. In the context of mathematics, the class is usually infinite.

To the uninitiated, this may seem obviously invalid and similar to an illegitimate move like illicit generalization. However, a closer look at the method may remove all such doubts. Mathematical induction operates with a small sample, but also with *a rule about the unexamined cases* in the whole class. This rule becomes the key to make claims about the unexamined members of the class.

In arguments by mathematical induction, usually there is a *theorem* that we wish to prove about a whole class. The proof begins by proving the theorem about some member, usually one member, in the class. But in order to complete the proof, the entities or items, or the members of the class, about whom we wish to prove something (let us say, we wish to prove a characteristic of the class) must be arranged in a series such that each item has a *position in the series*. If you are dealing with numbers, then consider them as a number series so that there has to be a *first* number, then a *second*, then a *third* in the series, and so on. For, in this kind of proof we need to be able to talk about an item and its successor in the series, or about its predecessor in the series.

> Suppose you want to prove some statement P that $P(n)$ is true about all n-s starting from $n = 1$. Your series needs to be arranged as
>
> $$n_1, n_2, n_3, \ldots$$
>
> We can talk about n_2 and its successor in the series n_3, or about n_3 and its predecessor n_2.

After this, proofs by mathematical induction consist of just two steps, which may be used repetitively for the entire series. Where the items that we wish to consider all occur in a series S, and the theorem that we wish to prove is a statement *P*, the proof by mathematical induction will be of the following form:

1. Prove that *P* holds for the first member of the series *S* or for S_1. This is the minimal case or the basis. Accordingly, it is called the **basis clause.**
2. For every member in *S*, *if P* is true about S_n, then *P* is true for S_{n+1} (the successor) also.

   [In other words, for each member in *S if P* is true of every predecessor member in the series, then *P* is true of that number also.]

   This is the *rule* about the class in general. This is known as the **induction step**. On this step we try to show that the property of '*P* being true about it' is **hereditary**, i.e., if a member in the series has it, then its successor also has it. [Alternatively, for any member in series, if all its predecessors have it, then that number too will have it.]

3. Conclusion: Therefore, *P* holds true of every member in *S*.

As said before, though it is called induction, mathematical induction is actually deductive by nature. All arguments of the above-mentioned form have to be valid. The link between the premises and the conclusion is of deductive nature. The conclusion does not say anything that is *not* contained in the premises. Step 1, or the basis clause, establishes that the theorem holds for the minimal case, the first member. By step 2, the induction step, then we can claim that it holds for the successor of the first member namely, the second number. A repeated application of the induction step on the second number shows that it has to hold for the third member as its successor, and then for the fourth, and so on, for all the members in the series.

Alternatively, one may also use mathematical induction as follows:

In step 1, one proves that *P* is true about all members *before* the second number. In the induction step or step 2, one needs to show that *P* holds true of the second member. Because it holds true of first and second number, by repeated application of the induction step, *P* holds for the third number, and then for the fourth, and so on for all members in the series.

Because of its admission of repeated application of the induction step, often it is referred to as a process comparable to 'climbing a ladder':

Step 1: Climb on to the first rung of the ladder.
Step 2: Climb from the current rung to the next rung.

Without the first step or the basis clause, you cannot get started. Without the induction step, you cannot get beyond the first rung. But a combination and repetition of the two steps make you climb the entire ladder and take you to a new height.

Note that validity of arguments of by mathematical induction is certain. However, only those that have true premises will be sound. Also note that one may need a finite number of steps in this kind of proof to prove something about an infinite number of members in a series. Next to mathematics, application of mathematical induction is frequent in computer science and mathematical logic.

EXERCISES 13.2–13.4

Determine the type of reasoning in the following passages and decide what can be justifiably induced from each of them:

1. In 1761, Dr. John Hill, a London physician, recorded an early observation linking tobacco (specifically, snuff) and cancer. By 1836, it was known that there is a causal link between smoking and lung cancer. 2004 studies show that 90% of cases of lung cancer in men, and 80% in women, were also smokers. Some recent 2004 studies, however, also show that a cigarette smoker has 10% less chance of getting lung cancer.

***2.** All the dogs in my neighbourhood are small. I have seen them all. So, dogs are small animals.

3. For any positive integer $n, 1+2+\cdots n = n(n+1)/2$. For, $1 = 1\times(2)/2$, and, if it is true for 1, then it is also true for 2.

4. "There was once upon a time a census officer who had to record the names of all householders in a certain Welsh village. The first that he questioned was called William Williams; so were the second, third, fourth,...

At last he said to himself: "This is tedious; evidently they are all called William Williams. I shall put them down so and take a holiday." Bertrand Russell, *History of Western Philosophy*, first Published 1945, p. 543.

5. 98% of the stereo equipments supplied by Bright Industries were found to be without defect in the last month. The same supplier has been asked to supply 5% more equipment next month. It is expected that the ratio of the defect-free equipment will remain the same or close to same with the increased volume of supply.

6. 60% voters in the pre-election polls were found to be sympathetic to candidate A. In the actual elections, the percentage of voters sympathetic to candidate A may rise.

***7.** Every even number is the sum of two prime numbers.

8. There is a 75% match between fibres on the victim's clothing and fibres on the seat of the defendant's car. The victim probably was at some point in the defendant's car on the last day of her life.

13.5 Uniformity of Nature and Problem of Induction

Induction of any kind has to rely upon an *assumption*: that the future will follow a course of action that it followed in the past. While carrying out an induction, we assume that nature will act uniformly as in the past. For example, we assume that in fruit-bearing trees, fruits will follow the flowers as they have done in the past. The sun will rise tomorrow as it has risen every day in the past. Mammals will be born from mammals as they have in the past. Certain events will continue to cause other events as they have in the past. This assumption, that the future events will uniformly follow the past, is known as **uniformity of nature.** I call it an assumption because there is no empirical way to verify whether this really holds or not.

If we reflect upon this assumption, we shall find that it forms the backbone for any kind of induction. Without it, we cannot make any claim or prediction of any sort about an unobserved, or unknown, event. When we reason inductively that the next crow we see will also be black, our premise is the past observations of crows being black. However, together with this premise there is a crucial background assumption that all of a sudden the color of the crow will *not* get changed. Similarly, when we inductively reason that it will rain because there are dark black clouds in the sky, again our implicit faith is on the assumption of uniformity of nature. If, since we last observed, the black clouds cease to be indicators of rain, then we shall no longer have no probabilistic basis for making any kind of claim about what to expect.

David Hume, a philosopher whose views in this regard are very important, saw a problem for induction in this assumption. He posed questions that can be framed as follows.

David Hume
(1711–1776)

How do human beings form opinions or conclusions about matters of fact that they have not yet observed?

Undoubtedly, we normally have many opinions or conclusions about matters that we have not directly observed. We know, for example, that tomorrow the Sun will rise, the next time we shall breathe there will be oxygen in the air; if we drop a glass on a hard floor it will break, when next winter comes we will have to wear woollen clothes, etc.

There are things that we know by observation through our sensory organs. For example, if I see that there is a book on the table, then I know that it is there. If it was there yesterday and I saw it, then today by consulting my memory I know that it is there. But how do we know about things that we have neither directly observed by any of our sensory organs nor know by remembering?

Hume answered this question by drawing our attention to the fact our previous experiences play a part in the formation of such knowledge. He stated that knowledge of unobserved matters must come to us somehow from experience. Imagine someone who has never seen glass before or has never handled it, how will he or she know that it is fragile, or that it will break, when dropped from a certain height on a certain kind of floor?

He claimed that out of the past experiences we arrive at opinions about the unobserved *by induction.*

We argue that *so far in our experience* we have seen glass to break when dropped from a certain height on a certain kind of floor.

Then we conclude that the next glass thus dropped will also break.

From all our discussion above, we recognize the pattern of induction in this. So, Hume's answer was that our knowledge is extended to matters unobserved only by induction. Whether we agree or disagree with him is another issue. But Hume contended in the above fashion.

Given this, he thought the next legitimate question to ask is:

How safe or justified is our faith in thus proceeding by induction to form opinions about induction?

Hume thought, as explained above, that **uniformity of nature** plays the role of a crucial but hidden premise in this process. *If* something occurs regularly or uniformly in nature, then we can expect the next instance of a certain kind that will follow will be like others in the past. Or, if the occurrences that take place regularly in the past take place the same way in nature (i.e., are not freak accidents), then they will hold also in the future.

Hume thought that there is room to raise skeptical worries about this faith of ours in the **uniformity of nature.** How do we know that uniformity of nature will hold? What reason do we have to place faith in uniformity of nature? He argued that we have no good reason at all. After all, uniformity of nature has been seen to work in the past, but its unobserved behaviour in future is not known. Hence, we cannot settle this question by direct observation or experience. Also, it is quite possible to imagine that tomorrow we might find the opposite happening. It is entirely possible that the regularities that we have so far observed (summer following winter, heat causing perspiration, etc.) may not hold in future. Moreover, if we have still to believe in uniformity of nature, then our best option perhaps is to use an inductive inference of the following type:

In the past so far, uniformity of nature has been known to hold.
Therefore, next time in future, uniformity of nature will also hold.

But as discussed above, uniformity of nature serves as a hidden premise in induction. To rely upon induction to establish our faith in uniformity of nature will be blatantly circular. Every induction uses uniformity of nature, and for that reason no inductive argument can justify uniformity of nature as an inductive conclusion.

Thus, Hume concluded, there is no *non-circular*, good reason for us to feel justified about using induction. If we have been successful in our inductive reasoning so far, and the water has quenched our thirst and the fire has produced heat, then we have been lucky. But as such, our usage of induction must come with the caveat that it ultimately is not a certain process. Note that Hume does not urge us to reject induction. His point simply is that we can have rational beliefs, such as opinions about unobserved matter by induction, even when we cannot provide any conclusive or convincing reason for it. This, I believe, is an important lesson to learn.

We should proceed to learn more about inductive reasoning and its important types in the next sections with this cautionary advice in mind. Hume's problem of induction should keep us aware about precautions and measures that we need to adopt before floating an inductive claim.

Keywords

Biased sampling: A particular case of information sampling in which the samples are limited in their variety and reveal very little information about the actual nature of the situation.

Imperfect induction: Inductions which are not done by simple enumeration.

Induction: A special type of logical reasoning in which we proceed from known premises or from observed cases to infer about unknown or unobserved cases.

Induction by simple enumeration: A special case of induction when *each* of the observed samples for the induction is *checked* or *examined individually* and in each case the induced conclusion is found to be true.

Inductive arguments: Arguments which primarily use induction.

Inductive generalization: Generalizations or universal conclusions based on induction. It is also a process of arriving at a universal conclusion from facts about particular samples.

Inductive leap: A unique characteristic of induction. A leap or a jump from the known to the yet unknown or from the cases observed so far to the yet unobserved cases

Inductive logic: Logic applicable only to inductive arguments.

Inductive reasoning: Reasoning based on induction.

Mathematical induction: A powerful proof procedure which yield certain conclusions and are actually deductive in nature.

Monotonic: Monotonic in the context of logical reasoning roughly means that additional information will have *no* bearing on the truth of the conclusion.

Perfect induction: Same as induction by simple enumeration.

Statistical induction: Induction used in statistics with quantitative tools.

Uniformity of nature: The assumption or belief that the future events in nature will uniformly follow the past events.

CHAPTER 14

ARGUMENT BY ANALOGY

14.1 Argument by Analogy as a Type of Inductive Argument

Analogy is a comparison, or a way to match the likenesses between items, or entities, or situations. To draw an analogy between two or more items is to indicate their *similarities* in certain aspects.

Two items are called **analogous** when they are found to have commonalities. For example:

Example 1

1. The gold coin was to the ancient kingdoms what paper notes are to India.

Gold Coin

Paper Currency Notes

2. In a battery-operated direct current (DC) electrical circuit, the battery is *analogous* to a pump in a water circuit: the pump takes in water at low pressure and ejects it in high pressure, and the battery takes in low voltage charge and ejects high voltage.

3. Ernest Rutherford proposed that the atomic structure is *like* the planets: electrons orbiting the nuclei just as the planets orbit around the Sun.

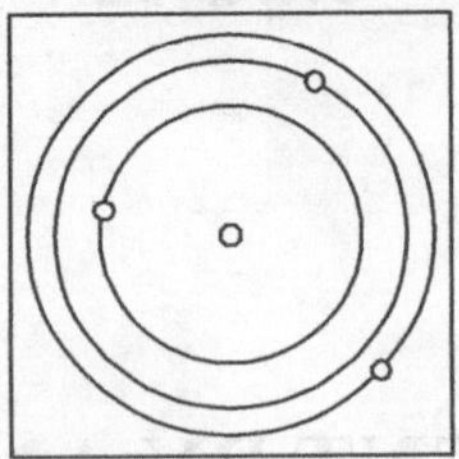

Planetary model

Each of the Examples 1-3 shows analogy between two items. The point of Example 1 is to show the common purpose that the gold coins in ancient times used to serve and the paper notes do these days; namely, serve as the currency or the unit of exchange for transfer of goods and services in trade or in economic activities. Similarly, in Example 2, the similarity between the function of the battery and the function of a water pump is drawn out to show that they are analogous in this respect. In Example 3, it is claimed that the orbits of the planets around the Sun and the arrangement of the atoms around the nucleus are similar. In each case, our attention has been drawn to a certain aspect of similarity that the objects under consideration have.

Analogies can be of two kinds:

- Literal
- Metaphorical

A **literal analogy** is to compare between items that are factually or logically similar. For example, two geographical locations may be compared to one another, such as two deserts may be compared for the daytime temperatures. Or, two coastal areas may be compared for analogous conclusions about their ecosystems. Similarly, the transportation system of big cities which have above 10 million population may be literally compared to each other for a comparative evaluation, as you can see in Example 4.

***Example 2* of literal analogy**

4. The Metro of Paris is *like* the Metro rail of Kolkata: crowded, but the easiest way to travel in a big city without facing the traffic congestion.

Often, quantitative problems make use of literal analogy between groups of numbers. For example, quizzes may ask to complete the sequence:

$$2:4, 5:10, 16:?$$

The idea is that the respondent will use the two groups, '2 : 4' and '5 : 10', as the source to find the suitable pair for 16. Ideally, the first question to solve this problem is to ask: What is common between '2 : 4' and '5 : 10'? Once you have found out that the basic similarity between the groups is that the first number in the pair is the exact half of the second number, then figuring out the answer is easy. The answer 32 will come as a conclusion of this piece of analogical reasoning by a literal analogy. 32 is to 16 what 4 is to 2 and 10 is to 5.

A **metaphorical** or **figurative analogy**, on the other hand, is a non-literal analogy. The similarities are created by imagination or are only figurative. Often, two entirely dissimilar items are compared to create imagery. For example, a city's transportation system may be compared figuratively or metaphorically to the arteries in the human body. The city's transportation system is certainly not literally like arteries which carry blood from the heart around the body. Yet, in a figurative sort of way, the two are comparable. Just as the arteries carry blood around the body, the transport system carries people around the city.

A metaphorical analogy is often used for the purpose of a lively description or to create an impressive image in the mind of the reader. Consider the lyrics of a song by *ABBA* (a Swedish rock band) which used the vivid imagery of nature to draw a figurative analogy with the onward flow of life and urges one to move on:

> Like a roller in the ocean
> Life is motion, move on.
> Like a wind that is blowing,
> Life is flowing, move on.

The similes and metaphors used in literature also belong to this category. Given below are some examples of poetic usage of analogy:

***Example 3* (similes and metaphors)**

5. "I wandered lonely as a cloud" *Daffodils*—Wordsworth
6. "All the world's a stage, and all the men and women are merely players..." *Macbeth*—Shakespeare.
7. "Life is a tale told by an idiot, full of sound and fury, signifying nothing" *Macbeth*—Shakespeare.
8. "Now the kingly monsoon season has come with its clouds containing raindrops like elephants in its convoy, and with flashes of lighting as its banners and flags, and with the thunders of thunderbolts as its percussive drumbeats, thus this rainy season has come to pass, radiantly shining forth like a king,..." *Meghdoot* —Kalidasa.

Metaphorical or poetic analogy may be effective to arouse certain feelings and imagery, but for logical purposes literal analogy is more important.

Argument by analogy or **analogical reasoning** is argumentation which employs analogy. It is a basic kind of human reasoning that is used in widely different fields such as science, literature, politics, law and moral considerations. It is used to gain new knowledge, or to predict future course of action, or to explain the unfamiliar.

If you ask me about which computer I use, and I tell you that I have had excellent computing support from a computer of a certain company, you may infer that if you buy a computer of the *similar* kind from the *same* or *similar* company, you may also get the *same* or *at least similar* experience.

Your conclusion is based on the analogy or the similarity that you perceive between the two situations. Of course, the conclusion is not absolutely certain, but still may be acceptable to you.

Or, suppose that you are new in a city and you have to get train tickets. If you have previous experience of booking train tickets at a railway ticket counter, then you may count upon that experience and conclude that in the new city also the system of ticket purchase will be same or at least similar. In that case, you will draw a conclusion on the basis of your observation that the situations are analogous.

Children learn a lot of things by watching their parents. In fact, we are encouraged from our childhood to profit from the experience of others. This too is an extended form of analogical reasoning. By watching others, we learn what would be a fitting response or a coping strategy for us to adopt in *similar* situations. This is the reason teachers are supposed to solve some problems in the classroom in front of the students. The idea is to give the students an opportunity to learn how to solve *similar* problems by themselves.

If the analogy is metaphorical or figurative, often people do not intend to use it for the purpose of argument. That is, they do not want to make any logical claim about what follows from that analogy. For instance, in Example 5, when Wordsworth says that he wandered lonely as a cloud, he does not want to impose a conclusion upon us. It is a poetic comparison to evoke a beautiful image and at the same time to highlight the freedom and the loneliness of his walks. But the literal analogy adds value to the argument. People find it easier to understand literal analogies and to respond to them in a critical manner. Since metaphorical analogies are open to interpretation, it is difficult to argue about their logical value. However, often people also use figurative analogy to persuade others. The logical aim of using an analogy is to compare and relate something *unfamiliar* or *unknown* to something *similar* that is more familiar or known, so that some conclusion can be made about the unknown or the unfamiliar.

The **format for an analogical argument** often is as follows:

Basic Format of an Analogical Argument

Premise 1: A and B both have the characteristic *u*.

Premise 2: A is known to have the characteristic *v*.

Conclusion: Therefore, B too is likely to have *v*.

The idea is to argue from the similarity of two things in certain respects to their similarity in some unknown respect.

Different people use different terminology to identify the components in an analogical argument. However, a common terminology used is:

- The **source:** The source is the information that one is familiar with and uses as the basis for drawing conclusion.
- The **target**: The target is the less familiar information that one wants to infer.

The terms **basic similarity** and **inferred similarity** are also used for this purpose. The characteristic *u* in the format shown, for example, is the **basic similarity**, or the known similarity. Based upon that, the characteristic *v* in B is the **inferred similarity**.

The format given above is illustrated in the following example:

Example 4

The buffalo and the bison both are herbivorous animals (eat grass, herbs, and leaves).
The buffalo is a ruminating animal.
So, the bison too is likely to be a ruminating animal.

'Being herbivorous' is the basic similarity in this example, whereas 'being a ruminating animal' is the target similarity. Analogical argument may be based upon more than one similarity. In such cases, the format will be as follows:

Format of an Analogical Argument

Premise 1: A and B are similar in aspects *u,v,x,y* and *z*.

Premise 2: A is known to have the characteristic *p*.
Conclusion: B is likely to have the characteristic *p*.

The aspects *u, v, x, y* and *z* are referred to as the **basic similarity** or similarity that is known. The characteristic *p* in B is the **inferred similarity**, something that was not known but was concluded by analogy.

Example 5

The buffalo and the bison both are herbivorous animals, living in the plains and have horns.
The buffalo is known to be a mammal.
So, the bison too is likely to be a mammal.

Reasoning by analogy is used quite often and effectively in the law courts in the form of *citing a precedent*. By legal definition, a precedent is created by a previous court decision which provides an example for settling *similar* legal issues later. The lawyer needs to identify the earlier case or cases that are relevantly similar and also the ruling given in those cases as a *precedent* or *precedents*. Then she needs to establish whether the similarities between the precedent and the case in hand are important enough to argue that same decision should be followed in the case on hand.

A lot of important policy decisions, such as decisions about tax reformations, or budget allocations, in a nation are sometimes taken on the basis of analogy with other nations in the similar stage of development. For example, when Nation A finds that increased national expenses in family welfare has increased the national productivity in a different nation B with similar economy, it may decide to adopt the same policy in its next budget allocation with the expectation of the same positive result.

In medical research, analogical reasoning provides the strong ground for conducting experimentation on animals such as monkeys, chimpanzees, when the medicine is meant for the benefit of the human beings. Experimental drugs are tested on these animals on the assumption that they are relevantly similar to human beings to provide some basis to conclude about the effect of the drug on a human body.

These and many other propositions may be supported with reasoning from analogy. Here is a sample of analogical argument used recently by one US politician who believed that the Bush administration was not handling the aftermath of Iraq war of 2004-2005 very efficiently:

Iraq Analogous to Vietnam

"Vietnam was much longer, but we can see the same kind of thinking that got us involved in Vietnam and refused to change course. It's so obvious to anyone that what we're doing in Iraq in terms of the occupation is not working."

—Eliot Engel, Democrat representative from Bronx, Friday, July 11, 2003 reported by Elaine S. Povich, *Newsday.*

The analogy is supposed to evoke the unpleasant association with Vietnam to warn the American public about the undesirable aspect of the Iraq occupation. It is not meant to be conclusive, and is not demonstratively valid. Yet, analogies such as these are commonly used in reasoning to persuade people and public decision makers.

Given below is another example of argument by analogy. The author uses the established idea of survival of the fittest in the evolutionary theory to explain how some tools and other artifacts designed by the humans continue to be used by generations of humans:

Survival of an Artifact and Survival of a Species

"From the vast pool of human-designed variant artifacts, a few are selected to become part of the material life of society. In nature it is the ability of the species to survive that counts—the fact that the organism, and especially its kind, can thrive and reproduce in the world in which it finds itself. The artifact may also be said to survive and pass on its form to subsequent generations of made things. This process requires the intervention of human intermediaries who select the artifact for replication in workshop or factory."

—George Basalla, *The Evolution of Technology*, 1988, Cambridge University Press, p. 137.

The conclusions of these arguments by analogy are not demonstratively valid, but they are not invalid either. All they claim is some probabilistic credibility.

The relation between argument by analogy and induction is close. Argument by analogy is considered as an important kind of inductive arguments.

1. **The inductive leap:** In analogical argument the basic inductive leap is always present. The transition from premises to conclusion of an

analogical argument shows the leap from the known or familiar cases to the unknown but similar case.

2. **Similarity as a basis:** The ground that it uses is the similarity or resemblance between the comparable cases. This observation of similarity between the cases observed and the unknown case is also present in induction.
3. **Probabilistic nature:** The conclusion of an analogical argument is never certain. All its premises can offer is a degree of probabilistic support for its conclusion.

However, one may still draw a distinction between the two in the following way. Most commonly, in the case of analogical reasoning, the comparison is made between relatively small number of items: two or three. In the case of induction, however, the observed cases that build the premise base are supposed to be numerous.

EXERCISE 14.1

1. Identify which of the following contain analogical arguments and which use analogy in a non-argumentative way. Justify your answer.

   *a. Businessmen are like blood-sucking vampires.

   b. The world is a complex system like a watch. A watch cannot come by pure accident. It is a piece of artifact that is made with a clever design by someone intelligent, with each of its parts put there for a purpose. The world is far more complicated than a watch. So, it too could not have come by accident. Someone with a clever design and a whole lot more intelligence must have created it.

   c. Newspaper reports are like weather reports. We do not blame the weather reports when they report the weather as bad. Why then blame the reporters for the bad news?

   d. Just as postal mail is delivered to your mailbox, e-mail is delivered to your account.

   *e. War and robbery are rather similar: the same intrusion, violence involved with taking what belongs to another. If one needs to be stopped, why not the other?

   f. In 1999, in *Biswas Vs. Metropolitan Hospital*, The Calcutta High Court decided in favour of Biswas and awarded him Rs. 5,00,000 as compensation for harm inflicted on him during a careless surgery in the hospital. A similar case was also decided in favour of the patient in 2002. It is likely in the present case also the Judge could give his verdict in favour of the patient suffering from injury due to negligence of hospital staff.

g. The cell membrane is like the offensive line in football. It wants to let the striker with the football go out, without letting the opponents in.

h. An eye is like a camera, with the pupil as the aperture, and an inverted image on the retina acting as the film.

i. Reading computer manuals without the hardware is as frustrating as reading manuals without the software.

—Arthur C. Clarke

j. The empiricists are like the ant; they only collect and use. The rationalists resemble the spiders, who make cobwebs out of their own substance. The scientist is like the bee; it takes a middle course; it gathers material from the flowers, but adapts it by a power of its own.

—Francis Bacon, *Novum Organum, XCV*, 1620.

2. Determine which of the following are the literal analogies and which are figurative or metaphorical analogies. Justify your answer.

a. Life is like a box of chocolates.

b. The admission process of Government College A should work well in Government College B, because their student size and administration size are similar.

*c. ". . For answers successfully arrived at are solutions to difficulties previously discussed, and one cannot untie a knot if he is ignorant of it."

—Aristotle

d. "Knowledge always desires increase: it is like fire, which must first be kindled by some external agent, but which will afterwards propagate itself." —Samuel Johnson.

*e. If Bobby could pass the test, so can Rishav. They followed the same books and took the same classes.

f. "Nature's first green is gold...nothing gold can stay." —Robert Frost.

g. "Smaller animals tend to have higher metabolic rates, just as the engines of small cars tend to turn over at a higher rate than those of larger cars" —British Biologist Richard Dawkins.

h. Rats and human beings have a nervous system that includes a developed brain. When injected with new medicine Alpha, 80% of the rats went into toxic shock. A similar fate could wait for human beings if they too are injected with it.

14.2 Evaluation of Arguments by Analogy

Arguments by analogy, as mentioned earlier, by nature are never certain. As is the nature of inductive arguments, premises of the analogical arguments can at best provide probabilistic support for the conclusion. Still, among themselves, some analogical arguments are better than others. The better ones are considered to be based on **strong analogies**, and the worse ones are considered to be based on **weak analogies**. Accordingly, there can be **strong analogical arguments** and **weak analogical arguments**.

(i) **Strong analogical argument**: Based on strong analogy, the premises provide strong probabilistic support for the conclusion.

(ii) **Weak analogical argument**: Based on weak analogy, the premises provide weak probabilistic support for the conclusion.

When analogical arguments are too weak to support the conclusions they want to assert, it is a failure of the analogy. The analogy could be misapplied or may be misleading. The **fallacy of false analogy** is the general name for the failure of an analogical argument to support its conclusion adequately.

But this does not by itself explain what makes the analogy go weak or strong when used as the central point for formulating an argument. What we need to know is what the factors are which can weaken or strengthen an analogical argument. Awareness about them can help us improve and safeguard analogical arguments against possible objections. Also, these may be used as the criteria to evaluate the strength or the weakness of analogical arguments.

Given below are eight points which may be used as criteria to evaluate analogical arguments.

1. Fair Comparison

It is a basic rule for analogical arguments to keep the comparison fair and within reasonable limits. Things of *similar kind* should be compared. Games may be compared to other games, mammals with other mammals, soft drinks with other soft drinks, and artifacts with other artifacts. If the kinds or the types of the things being compared are too different, they can weaken the analogy being drawn, and as a result can impair the argument based on that analogy.

The most common fallacy associated with reasoning from analogy is to base one's conclusion on a **comparison of dissimilar cases**. For example, it would be an unfair comparison to draw an analogy between speed of a hand-driven cart and the speed of a racing car. Though both are vehicles, they are too dissimilar when compared for speed capacities. Similarly, the analogy between an elephant and a table is bound to break down. Though both may have four legs, they are of two entirely different kinds.

While considering what would count as the *similar kinds* or *types*, one needs to be careful because sometimes a superficial similarity may be mistakenly considered as the basis to identify a kind or a type. Consider the following example:

***Example 6* (a false analogy based on dissimilar cases)**

Whales and blue sharks both live in water.
Blue sharks are cold-blooded creatures.
So, the whales too are cold-blooded creatures.

In the example of whales and blue sharks, the analogy breaks down because the similarity that both the creatures live under water is shallow. Ultimately, they are incomparable because, even if whales live in water, they are mammals and like all mammals are warm-blooded. The blue sharks, on the other hand, belong to the fish group and like all fish are cold-blooded. So, when we claim similarity of kinds between the items you are considering for an analogical argument, we need to show further that the similarity in question is not a superficial or unimportant one, and also that for our conclusion the similarity in question is important.

For example, suppose you want to conclude that the human beings in the distant future also will be mortal. Your premise for that is that the future human beings will be biologically similar to the human beings in the past and in the present. The biological similarity between the human beings over time is an important similarity. It is also relevant for your target analogy of mortality: you wish to claim that because they are biologically similar, the future human will be mortal just like the present or past human beings. In this case, the similarity of kinds reinforces your analogy, and, consequently, provides a strong support for the analogical argument.

But, even among the similar kinds there can be individual differences. We have all heard about how apples cannot be compared to oranges. You may ask: why not? After all, they are both fruits, and belong to the same type. But note that there are enough differences between apples and oranges. Oranges belong to the citrus group of fruits, and have a distinct colour, taste and smell; the apples, on the other hand, have their own distinct smell, colour and smell. Being a fruit only separates them from the non-fruit categories. But when compared to each other *as fruits*, there are too many differences. To call them analogous is to overlook a host of important differences that exist between them.

You may ask: Taking individual differences into account, can we ever make a non-controversial claim about similarities between two items? Will there not always be individual differences between them? Even two oranges may have differences, one may be an orange from Florida, USA, and another may be from Nagpur, India. There could be individual differences between them also, which may create hurdles for making a comparison between them. Similarly, two people, two mammals, or two games are never exactly similar. Can we then ever hope to find the 'similar kinds' to satisfy the criterion that we are considering?

Because of concerns such as the above, some people are of the opinion that arguments based on analogy can never be sound. But then, as said earlier, when dealing with analogical arguments, our goal is not to attain deductive soundness. All we want is a reasonable amount of probabilistic support. And for that, we need to look into both similarities and differences between the compared items before we can decide whether they are *similar enough* to be comparable. This means that we have to understand *similarity as a notion relative to differences*. This relative notion of 'similarity' brings us to two criteria that we now discuss.

2. Do the Similarities Outweigh the Differences?

In the foregoing discussion, it was mentioned that between any two things similarity has to be understood in a relative sense. Unless they are exactly similar, two items usually will have both similarities and differences. The important question to ask, therefore, before one may use the analogy as the ground for a conclusion, is: Do the similarities between the items outweigh their differences? In order to answer this question satisfactorily, a comparative estimate between the similarities and differences needs to be done before we can call two items 'analogous' or 'similar'. For example: Suppose you wish to compare two tribal cultures, one from the Pantanol region of Brazil and another from South-Eastern part of West Bengal, India. Before declaring the two cultures as analogous, or before drawing any conclusion from the claimed analogy, we need to do a thorough comparison between their similarities and differences. We need to compare *as many facets* as possible, for example, the religious belief systems of the two cultures, their social practices such as marriage, funeral, celebration of festivals, and the role of men and women in the society.

The similarities can be said to outweigh the differences if:

(i) The number of ways in which they are similar are **greater** than the number of ways in which they are different,

(ii) The ways in which they are similar are **more relevant** than the ways in which they are dissimilar.

Satisfaction of either of these conditions will strengthen the analogy and will increase the likelihood of a conclusion based on that analogy. But it is desirable to have both the conditions satisfied. For, there are situations when a mere comparison of number of similarities and differences may not show their relative worth. For example, suppose that you are thinking about buying a pair of shoes for yourself. Suppose also that the salesman brings to you two separate pairs, which look very similar, and are priced very closely, but are made by two different companies. If you count the number of their similarities, then you might find that there are more ways in which they are similar than they are dissimilar. For example, they are very similar in colour, weight, pattern and soles. However, suppose that one of the pairs is made by a company which has a long-standing goodwill in the market, whereas the maker of other pair is not at all known in the shoe industry. For your decision, this one difference may become more important and relevant than the number of similarities that you may have observed between them.

On the other hand, suppose that between the shoes, there are differences but they appear to be minor in nature, e.g. suppose that one pair comes in a red box and the other in a blue box. If you consider the difference in the colour of the shoebox is not as important in comparison to the similarities the shoes have, you can claim that the shoes for all practical purposes are analogous, because similarities of the shoes outweigh their dissimilarities.

3. Do the Differences Outweigh the Similarities?

Dissimilarities between the items under consideration can weaken an analogical argument. So, while making an analogy, it is very important to be aware of the differences, if any. If there are differences, the success of an analogical argument will depend upon showing convincingly that the differences are neither significant nor great in number to override the similarities. Similar to the point made in connection to point 2, the differences can be said to outweigh the similarities if

(i) the number of ways in which they are dissimilar are greater than the number of ways in which they are similar;

(ii) the ways in which they are dissimilar are more relevant than the ways in which they are similar.

In short, differences between the items being compared **undermine** an analogical argument. If the differences can be shown to be more in number or more important than the similarities claimed, the analogy will be weaker. As a result, the argument based on that analogy will suffer from lack of support.

Note that a strategy in trying to undermine an analogical argument is to highlight the differences between the cases in question. For example, suppose that you are comparing two developing nations, A and B, and trying to predict their economic future. Suppose that the two nations share many similarities, such as in their number of population, area, mineral reserve, and you know that A is going into economic recession. Based on these observations, suppose you conclude that nation B too will go into economic recession. This conclusion may lack the support of the analogy drawn if, for example, you overlook the fact that in comparison to the population of nation A, most of the population of B are highly skilled, efficient and productive contributors to the society. This one difference may be a key difference. It is important from the point of view of prediction of economic future. For, the economic role that a population plays can be vital for the total economic outcome for a nation. It is possible that in spite of their similarities in other respects, this difference alone can lead B to a comparatively better economic future than A.

4. How Relevant Are the Similarities Observed?

While preparing for an analogy, it is better to keep an eye on how *relevant* the similarities observed are. A single relevant similarity can tilt the balance in favour of the argument than a whole bunch of irrelevant dissimilarities.

Suppose that you want to compare the performances of two students in a test for a comparable grade. If the similarity between them ends with the fact that they both use blue ink pen, then that similarity has no relation on the quality of their answers, based on which the grade is to be awarded. On the other hand, if their answers are similar in content, in the organization and analysis of the content, in accuracy and in writing style, then certainly these similarities will matter in order to consider them as analogous. For, these similarities are relevant for the qualitative judgement that is needed for deciding which grade to give to them.

How does one define what is relevant? This answer is decided by the situation in which the comparison takes place. One has to first decide what the *target analogy* is. For example, in the above example of the two students, the target analogy is the comparable grade: that they may both get an A (or 9 out of 10). When judging how relevant a similarity is, one needs to find out what bearing a certain observed similarity has vis-à-vis the target similarity. In the example above, the similarity that both the students have used blue ink becomes an *irrelevant* factor because our target is to award them an analogous grade and for that the colour of the ink has no relevance. But, if, for example, our target was to compare how the answers of both the students look, then the colour of the ink would be considered as a relevant similarity.

Example 7 **(irrelevant similarity)**

Target: Two students deserve similar grade.

Source: Both students have used blue ink pen.

Sometimes, the relevance of a factor is decided upon its causal connection to the attempted conclusion. If a similarity is causally contributive towards the target analogy, then it is considered as relevant. For example, in the example where the future human beings are claimed to be mortals because they are analogous to present human beings, the factor of same or similar biological composition in both cases becomes a relevant factor. For, the biological composition is viewed as *causally responsible* for the mortality.

5. How Many Cases of Similarity have been Observed?

Analogical arguments are inductive by nature. Like any inductive argument, it matters for analogical argument how many times the source similarity has been observed in the past. The larger the number of cases observed in the past the stronger is the support for the target analogy.

If my claim is based on just one observation, it is possible that the similarity in the next case may not be there. Suppose that I have read only one book by an author and I thought it was a rather interesting piece of work. If on that basis, I want to claim that other books by the same author will give me the same pleasant experience, I might be heading towards disappointment. On the other hand, if I have read several books by the same author, and each time I had a satisfying reading experience, I shall have better and stronger probabilistic support for my conclusion, that other unread books by the author, because they are written by the same author, will give me similar experience.

Having said this, it also must be mentioned that though the number of instances observed always matter, the number of instances are not connected by an exact ratio to the probability of the conclusion. Reading *five books* by the same author and having similar reading experience certainly contribute positively towards the probabilistic support for the conclusion about unread books by the same author. But, the probability of that conclusion will not be exactly *five times* higher than the probability of a conclusion based on reading only one book by the author. The number of observed cases of source similarity should be taken into consideration along with the considerations mentioned in points 1-4 above.

6. How Varied are the Circumstances?

It is important to also note whether the cases of similarity observed in the past have been observed in varied circumstances. If the similarity is observed repeatedly in the past in not only numerous occasions but also *under varied situations*, the stronger the claim of source analogy becomes, and, as a result, it reinforces the claim of target analogy. On the other hand, if the past experiences of similarity is restricted only to a specific circumstance, the chances are that the analogy may be weak. That is, possibility remains that the similarity observed applies only to certain situations and cannot be generalized. For example, suppose that I have read five books by the same author, and have always had the pleasant experience, but the books are on five different subjects. Suppose also that one of them is a drama, another a collection of short stories, and the rest are novels. This variety of genre, literary style and content in the writings of the same author help to boost my confidence on the conclusion by analogy that the unread works by the same author, no matter what their subject or style is, will also be a source of joy for me.

***Example 8* (varied instances of similarity)**

Book 1: Read drama, on family relations, pleasant reading, written by Author A.

Book 2: Read collection of short stories, miscellaneous topics, pleasant reading, written by Author A.

Book 3: Read short novel, a love story, pleasant reading, written by Author A.

Book 4: Read long novel, on a historical event, pleasant reading, written by Author A.

Book 5: Read long novel, on womens' status, pleasant reading, written by Author A.

Target: Next work by Author A will also be pleasant reading.

If, on the other hand, my pleasant experience of reading the author's work is limited to only his dramas, it is possible that my analogical argument to what to expect from his other kinds of literary works may fail.

7. What is the Nature of the Conclusion?

The success of an analogical argument also depends upon the kind of conclusion it wants to advocate. The analogical arguments, as has been already mentioned, cannot guarantee conclusive certainty. Their conclusions are thus probabilistic claims. It is better to remember this inherent characteristic of analogical arguments while advancing a conclusion. Otherwise, the argument may suffer from an overreaching claim that it cannot support.

For example, I subject my analogical argument to possible objection if I boldly conclude that because I have liked the performance of an actor in the past, next time I watch a movie in which he has acted, his performance *must* be good. The premises, which contain facts about my past experiences, cannot guarantee the necessity expressed by the 'must'. On the other hand, they provide a reasonable amount of support for a more sober claim: that it is *likely* that the performance of this actor in the next movie will be good. It is better to tone down the claim of certainty in the conclusion of an analogical argument in favour of a more guarded probabilistic claim.

Also, it always helps the conclusion of an analogical argument if additional premises can be brought in to bolster the probabilistic support provided by its original premises.

8. How to Safeguard against Disanalogy?

A **disanalogy** is a difference that is relevant and has the power to weaken an analogical argument. Since disanalogies have this capacity to harm an analogical argument, it is an additional strength for an analogical argument if it is well prepared against potential disanalogies. Anything that can defend the argument against a disanalogy is a point of strength for the argument.

Points 1–7 mentioned above can also be effectively used to safeguard an analogical argument from possible disanalogies:

a. Ensuring a basic similarity between the items under comparison
b. Establishing that the similarities override the differences
c. Establishing that the differences do not override the similarities
d. Establishing that the similarities are relevant
e. Ensuring that the number of instances observed are sufficiently large
f. Ensuring that the instances observed are varied enough
g. Making a claim that is appropriate to the supporting capability of the premises.

EXERCISE 14.2

1. Analyze the following analogical arguments and evaluate their worth by the eight criteria that you have learnt in this chapter.

*a. ...knowledge must continually be renewed by ceaseless effort if it is not to be lost. It resembles a statue of marble which stands in the desert and is continually threatened with burial by the shifting sand. The hands of service must ever be at work, in order that the marble continue to lastingly shine in the sun. To these serving hands mine shall also belong.

—Albert Einstein, On Education, 1950

b. Somebody who only reads newspapers and at best books of contemporary authors looks to me like an extremely near-sighted person who scorns eyeglasses. He is completely dependent on the prejudices and fashions of his times since he never gets to see or hear anything else. And what a person thinks on his own without being stimulated by the thoughts and experiences of other people is even in the best case rather paltry and monotonous. There are only a few enlightened people with a lucid mind and style and with good taste within a century. What has been preserved of their work belongs among the most precious possessions of mankind. We owe it to a few writers of antiquity (Plato, Aristotle, et al.) that the people in the Middle Ages could slowly extricate themselves from the superstitions and ignorance that had darkened life for more than half a millennium. Nothing is more needed to overcome the modernist's snobbishness.

—Albert Einstein

c. The tree of liberty must be refreshed from time to time with the blood of patriots and tyrants. It is its natural manure.

—Thomas Jefferson, 1787

d. Happiness is like a butterfly which, when pursued, is always beyond our grasp, but, if you will sit down quietly, may alight upon you.

—Nathaniel Hawthorne (1804–1864)

e. ...intellectual agnosticism is, in reality, very close to cowardice. The agnostic who claims that his is the more courageous course, that it is easy to jump to a conclusion but hard to keep one's head and 'see clearly' despite the mists of passion and prejudice—this man is deceiving himself. It is, on the contrary, easy to reflect on the complexity and many-sidedness of the issues that confront one, and to conclude that no man is capable of seeing the whole truth. What is hard is to hold the evidence clearly in mind and keep it there, persistently turning it over and integrating it until the conclusion emerges.

—James J. Gibson

f. A chronic lack of pleasure, of any enjoyable, rewarding or stimulating experiences, produces a slow, gradual, day-by-day erosion of man's emotional vitality, which he may ignore or repress, but which is recorded by the relentless computer of his subconscious mechanism that registers an ebbing flow, then a trickle, then a few last drops of fuel—until the day when his inner motor stops and he wonders desperately why he has no desire to go on, unable to find any definable cause of his hopeless, chronic sense of exhaustion.

—Ayn Rand, *The Voice of Reason*, p.104

g. Science is built up with facts, as a house is with stones. But a collection of facts is not more a science than a heap of stones is a home.

—Henri Poincaré

h. No social system can stand for long without a moral base. Project a magnificent skyscraper being built on quicksands: while men are struggling upward to add the hundredth and two-hundredth stories, the tenth and twentieth are vanishing, sucked under by the muck. That is the history of capitalism, of its swaying, tottering attempt to stand erect on the foundation of the altruist morality."

—Ayn Rand, *Capitalism: The Unknown Ideal*

*i. There is no gambling like politics. Nothing in which the power of circumstance is more evident.

—Benjamin Disraeli

j. Drops in separation could only fade away, drops in co-operation made the ocean, which carried on its broad bosom the ocean greyhounds. ...A drop torn from the ocean perishes without doing any good.

—Mahatma Gandhi

k. There is something which unites magic and applied science while separating both from the 'wisdom' of earlier ages. For the wise men of old the cardinal problem had been how to conform the soul to reality, and the solution had been knowledge, self-discipline, and virtue. For magic and applied science alike the problem is how to subdue reality to the wishes of men: the solution is a technique; and both, in the practice of this technique, are ready to do things hitherto regarded as disgusting and impious—such as digging up and mutilating the dead.

—C.S. Lewis

2. For each of these following analogical arguments, four additional premises are suggested below. Decide for each additional premise whether its addition will make the argument more probable or less probable, or will have no effect. Justify your answer.

(i) You have seen two movies by Director Zekis, and you found each of them interesting and profound. You are planning to go and see another movie by Zekis tonight expecting a good cinematic experience. You find out that:

a. Zekis is script writer of the present movie, but the director is Iftekar.

b. Zekis has done painstaking research for tonight's movie.

c. Tonight's movie will start at 6 p.m. as did the last two of movies of Zekis.

d. The two previous movies by Zekis were on war and crime, and tonight's movie is on streetfights.

*(ii) Prof. Batra has stayed in the Petri Pumpa Hotel every semester she has taught at Orresund University, and there every time she has found the food enjoyable, the service courteous, and the room spacious and comfortable. This year Prof. Batra has also written to her contacts to book the same hotel for her stay. Suppose that:

a. The Petri Pumpa Hotel is now under a different owner and a new manager.
b. She stayed in the hotel in a suite once, in a single room twice, and in a top floor penthouse once.
c. On her last stays she had reached the hotel from the station, but this time she will reach it from the airport.
d. The façade of the hotel is now blocked by a big new, high-rise, shopping mall which has come up only recently.

(iii) Sashi had bought fruits from the vendor at the fruit stall near the crossing three times before this and did not like their quality. Today, again he decided to buy from the same man, fearing the same disappointment. Suppose that:

a. The fruit stall has changed hands and there is a new vendor now in the same stall.
b. Sashi bought bananas before but today he wants to buy grapes.
c. The last three times Sashi bought apples, bananas and mangoes.
d. The vendor is wearing a red shirt today.

(iv) Parijat has seen some people buying lottery tickets before, and has seen pictures of winners of other lotteries in the newspapers. Recently her neighbour has won third prize in a state lottery. This month she decides to buy a lottery ticket for herself from an agent whose advertisement says that he has sold winning tickets before. Parijat argues that she has some probability to win. Suppose that:

a. The lottery ticket that Parijat wants to buy is a high value ticket which is sold only to 100 persons.
b. Just after the purchase Parijat comes to know that there will be 5000 small prizes for lottery in addition to the usual prizes.
c. The lottery agent sometimes sells spurious lottery tickets just to make money.
d. The chance of winning for the lottery ticket that Parijat has bought is 1: 25,000.

(v) Jonaki has sat for four admission tests before and she found the question papers on the average wanted long answers from memory. Since she cannot memorize so much, she found the tests a bit difficult.

Tomorrow is the admission test for her favourite course, but she is a bit nervous that this time also she will find the test difficult and may not be selected. Suppose that:

a. The four admission tests that she took were all in Economics and tomorrow's test is also in Economics.
b. The course that she will give the test for tomorrow is known to be very different from that taught in the usual colleges. In this course creative questions are asked in the admission test and the test allows for individual differences in the answers.
c. Her previous tests were in Ancient History, Medieval History, Political Science and World History.
d. The admission test will be an objective test with multiple choices.

Keywords

Analogical reasoning: Argumentation which employs analogy.

Analogy: A comparison, or a way to match the likenesses between items, or entities, or situations.

Argument by analogy: Same as analogical reasoning.

Disanalogy: A difference that is relevant and has the power to weaken an analogical argument.

Fallacy of false analogy: General name for the failure of an analogical argument to support its conclusion adequately.

Literal analogy: A kind of analogy. To compare between items that are factually or logically similar.

Metaphorical or figurative analogy: Another kind of analogy. The points of comparison are based on a metaphor or non-literal ground.

Strong analogical arguments: Analogical arguments with strong probabilistic support.

Weak analogical arguments: Analogical arguments with weak probabilistic support.

CHAPTER 15

ARGUMENT BY CAUSAL REASONING

15.1 Causal Reasoning: Its Nature

Causal reasoning is a very important kind of inductive reasoning. By causal reasoning, we mean reasoning from the presence of events of one sort known as the *causes* to the presence of events known as *effects* of the previous kind of events, and vice versa. The following are the examples of conclusions based on some sort of causal reasoning:

***Examples* (of causal conclusions)**

1. The Tsunami of December 26, 2004 *has caused* terrible damage to life and property.
2. Reckless driving *causes* accidents.
3. Lack of Fluoride in drinking water *make* teeth become unhealthy.
4. Strenuous and continuous physical exercise *does produce* substantial amount of endorphins in the body which creates a feeling of well-being.
5. Throat or nasal obstruction *make* people snore.

Causal reasoning is coming to causal conclusions when we have reason to believe that events of a certain kind are systematically and causally linked to another group of events. Using it, we may try to predict the presence of effect from the cause, or of the cause from the effect.

Consider the following examples of causal reasoning:

***Examples* (of causal reasoning)**

6. Since there is Malaria in the region, there must be *Anopheles* female mosquitoes in the region.

7. If I turn the ignition key, the car will start.
8. Symptoms of this patient indicate that he is suffering from a heat stroke, so he may have been exposed to the hot sun for a long time.

In Examples 6 and 8, we can see how the cause and its presence have been inferred from the presence of the effect on the basis of a known causal connection. The presence of Anopheles female mosquitoes is drawn as a conclusion from the known presence of Malaria. The mosquitoes are known to be the carrier of Malaria parasites. Exposure to sun is inferred as the cause from the observation of symptoms of a heat stroke. In Example 7, the effect is expected from the presence of a cause. The starting of the car is expected to follow as an effect of turning the ignition key.

Connection of Causal Reasoning to Induction

Causal reasoning, as mentioned above, is a kind of inductive reasoning. The inductive leap, which is a distinctive characteristic of inductive reasoning, is evident in causal reasoning as well. From past observation or knowledge of a causal connection, a new conclusion is drawn about a case that is not yet known and is uncertain. The probabilistic nature of inductive reasoning is also present in causal reasoning. Causal conclusions come with varied degree of probability. The conclusion of Example 6 about Malaria and Anopheles mosquitoes shows a higher degree of confidence than the conclusion of Example 8.

In addition, causal reasoning typically relies on a premise that affirms the assumption or knowledge of a causal connection. This premise is crucial for the induction of its conclusion in the present case. This can be seen from the examples cited above.

In Example 6, note that only the effect, or the case of Malaria in hand, is what is known or is observed. The presence of the special type of mosquito as the cause, on the other hand, is not known or observed, but is *inferred*. The knowledge about the causal connection between the disease and its carrier acts as the *bridge* between what is known and what is not yet known. It acts as the link between the *already known* causal knowledge base and the observed case in hand. This is an inductive leap from the known to the unknown, from the certain to something that is new and uncertain. But in the case of causal reasoning, this leap is made possible by the premise that affirms the knowledge of a causal connection. This crucial premise lends the strong probabilistic support that the argument needs to justify the conclusion.

Analysis of Example 6

(i) **Crucial premise of causal knowledge:** Mosquito bites by female Anopheles mosquitoes are known as the cause of Malaria. (As seen in the past, causal knowledge based on past observations).

(ii) **Directly observed new case:** This is a case of Malaria.

(iii) **Conclusion by induction:** This case of Malaria too is caused by female Anopheles mosquito bites. (from parts 1 and 2)

Similarly, in Example 7 above in which the car is expected to start from the turning of the ignition key, the conclusion follows as an inductive leap on the back of a causal assumption. The past experiences are known, but the outcome of the current case is still not known. The crucial premise about assumption or information of a causal connection is formed by past experiences in numerous cases in which the turning of the ignition key has been seen as the cause, and the starting of the car as the effect. And in the current case the effect, the starting of the car, is expected with some reasonable degree of probability. This too is an instance of an inductive leap. Without the premise about the causal connection, this leap is not possible. With the premise of causal connection, the leap becomes justifiable. For, in the past, it has been found repeatedly that turning of the ignition key may have started the car.

Thus, the premise about the causal knowledge, or information about a causal connection, is crucial for inductive causal arguments. However, like all inductive arguments, this premise cannot deliver certainty. It can only add degrees of probability for the argument. As we all know, it remains possible in Example 7 that this time due to some internal problem in the engine, the car may not start by simply turning the ignition key. Knowing the past connection between the two events help us to predict how the car will behave next time, but it does not provide us certainty.

To summarize, causal reasoning has the following characteristics:

- Inductive leap
- Probabilistic nature of its conclusion
- Knowledge of causal connection used as a crucial premise

For all practical purposes, causal reasoning is both useful and important. Knowledge of causal connection gives us some power to predict or prevent certain occurrences. For example, if I want to avoid Malaria or heat stroke, the knowledge about their causes will give me some advantage to take preventive measures against mosquito bites or against long exposure in the hot sun. Similarly, if a nation wants to prosper, knowing the causal factors leading to national prosperity can help it go the right direction. Overall, using causal information in reasoning allows us to have some control over our environment and events occurring all around us.

David Hume, a philosopher whose name we have cited in the earlier section in the context of problem of induction, observed that knowledge about causal relations and reasoning based on it alone can give us the confidence to go beyond what we can directly observe by our sensory organs or can store as memory. The information by direct observation or by memory is limited. Causal reasoning allows us to overcome that limitation. Borrowing one of Hume's examples, we can try to understand the point as follows.

Suppose that by a strange turn of events you find yourself deserted in a desolate island where you think you are the only person around. If you then find a watch lying around, you will conclude that some other human being besides yourself must have been there or is still there. You directly see only the watch, and certainly do not see any other human being. Yet, you argue, the watch could not have gotten to that island by itself. Someone must have been the *cause* of its being there. You use that causal knowledge to transcend what you can directly observe and create knowledge for yourself.

Causal reasoning is considered also as a powerful way to establish evidence for a claim. Suppose you return to your room after the whole day and find a set of footprints that you know are not yours and that you have not seen when you left, you can claim that someone else must have entered your room in your absence. If you are asked to substantiate this claim, your causal reasoning, that the footprints must have been caused by someone who has been to the room, is sufficient as evidence.

We use causal reasoning quite often. But we need to also remember that it is not easy to establish a causal relation between two events. David Hume, who maintained that our beliefs in induction do not have any conclusive evidence, also held that our beliefs in causal connection between two events come to us naturally but are *unjustifiable* under close scrutiny.

In the following sections, we shall learn about what constitutes as evidence for a causal relation and what does not. We shall also learn about the methods by which we can establish causal connection. However, in the next section, we shall learn what we mean by a *cause*, or what we mean when we say something is the *cause* of another.

15.2 Cause

For the occurrence of an event, certain conditions are responsible. For example, to make acid rain (rain which contains acid and is a dangerous kind of pollution) possible, there have to be emissions of gases and smoke from factories and cars which burn fossil fuels such as coal, petroleum, and the sulphur present in the fuel has to mix with the oxygen in the air to create sulphur dioxide, and with the nitrogen to create nitrogen oxide, and then these have to go into the air and become acid which come down mixed with the rain. For the occurrence of acid rain, all of these conditions are responsible.

Necessary Condition

It is common to distinguish between necessary and sufficient conditions for the occurrence of an event. A necessary condition for the occurrence of an event is a condition, in the absence of which the event cannot occur. In other words, if some condition *c* is the necessary condition for the event *e*, then if *c* does not happen, then *e* cannot happen. For example, without oxygen in the air, human beings cannot breathe and therefore cannot survive. If a human being has to survive, there has to be oxygen in the air. Thus, a condition *c* is the **necessary condition** for event *e* if, if *c* does not occur, *e* cannot occur.

Sufficient Condition

A sufficient condition *c*, on the other hand, for an event *e* is a condition that, if *c* happens, then *e* has to happen. The presence of *c* should be sufficient to make *e* happen.

The difference between a sufficient and a necessary condition is important. For example, oxygen in the air is the necessary condition for the survival of a human being, but it is *not* a sufficient condition for the survival of a human being. The presence of oxygen alone in the air does not suffice for the survival of a human being. Even if there is oxygen in the air, a human being may still not survive because of lack of food or water.

It is easier to identify a necessary condition for an event rather than identifying its sufficient condition. You can say that there is usually **a set**

of necessary conditions for the occurrence of an event. For example, the presence of oxygen, access to food and water, a certain range of temperature etc.—all of these may be part of the set of necessary conditions for the survival of the human being. When taken together, **a complete set of necessary conditions constitutes the sufficient condition for an event.** It is the complete set of necessary conditions of event *e*.

Given this preliminary distinction of conditions, now we need to find out what the term *cause* means. It is used in many different ways to convey many different senses, which include the necessary and sufficient conditions. In the remaining part of this section, some of these different senses of cause will be discussed. But, it should also be kept in mind that there is *no* single definition of cause that covers all these varied uses of the word "cause".

Cause as Necessary Condition

A cause is often understood as the necessary condition. For instance, if you want to prevent an undesirable or unpleasant event, you want to remove or avoid its *cause* as the necessary condition. If you consider the entry of the Malaria parasites in the human body as the *cause* of Malaria, in the sense that *if the entry is not there, Malaria will not be there*, then you are regarding it as the necessary condition for the occurrence of Malaria. Your strategy for avoidance of Malaria will include the avoidance or removal of that condition.

Cause as Sufficient Condition

However, a cause is also understood as the sufficient condition, if by cause one means the *producer* or *bringer* of an event or an effect. Suppose that a car has crashed and you want to find out what *caused* the crash. If so, you are searching for some event or events which have made the crash happen, and in that sense you are searching for the sufficient condition for the crash.

Cause as Probable Cause

The word 'cause' is also used in the sense of a *probable cause* such that when a condition probabilistically has a causal role to bring about a certain effect or outcome. In itself it may not be a sufficient condition, but it may be one of the factors to cause the effect.

In law, the concept of *probable cause* is used as evidence. For example, the event of a pedestrian walking recklessly in the middle of heavy traffic in itself is not a sufficient condition to bring about traffic accidents, but it certainly is a *probable cause* for traffic accidents. It provides enough reason to believe that it caused the traffic accidents, should there be any.

Cause as the Critical Factor

Another usage of the word 'cause' is as a *critical factor*. Though there may be many factors contributing to the occurrence of an event, but one of them may make a significant impact on the event. Its presence or absence can lead to the presence or absence of the event.

For example: C*ooking at a certain temperature is a critical factor for destroying parasites and bacteria that may be there in food stuff.* In this sense, one may say that cooking is the *cause* of destruction of parasites and bacteria found in food. Its absence may create food-borne illnesses, and its presence may avoid many such illnesses.

Classification of Cause as Proximate and Remote

Traditionally, there have been many classification of cause. One of them is cause as a *proximate cause* or as a *remote cause.* In a chain of events, a lot of conditions may together lead to another event. However, some of these conditions may be related in different ways to the event than the other.

A *proximate cause* is a condition which produces the effect under consideration directly, in virtue of its own action, without using the action of any other intervening factors. It also may be the closest to the effect in the chain of causal events leading to the effect. For example, for boiling water, heat is the proximate cause as it directly causes the action.

A *remote cause*, on the other hand, is the condition which requires the intervention of some other factor to cause the effect. When my hand turns the heater on which boils the water, that action of mine is a remote cause for the boiling of the water.

Classification of Cause as Total or Partial

A cause can be understood as a total cause or as a partial cause. When the entire effect is produced by the action of event *e*, *e* is the total cause for the effect. Whereas, if only a part of the entire effect can be attributed to a particular cause, then it is a partial cause. For example, everyone who worked in a team which completed a project successfully is a *partial* cause of the successful completion of the project. But, if I alone am responsible for the successful completion of the project, I am the *total cause* of these effects.

15.3 Mill's Methods of Causal Analysis

As mentioned earlier, reasoning by induction on the basis of knowledge of causal connection is very common and useful for us. However, establishing a causal connection between two events, *A* and *B*, is not easy. As Hume argued, we may see two events regularly following in a certain sequence. A match is struck, and a light appears. But we never actually directly observe the striking of the match to *cause* the fire. Our observation is only limited to the observation of a change in our environment: a light has appeared where there was no light before. Given this limitation, the key question to ask is: "How do we establish that a relation of cause and effect is before us?"

In 1843, in his book *A System of Logic,* John Stuart Mill, an English philosopher, proposed *five methods* in answer to this question. These five methods are now known as *Mill's Methods for causal analysis* of a relation between two events. Mill, in his classic formulation, however, named them as **canons of induction**. Though he did not invent these methods, Mill was certainly the one to provide an exposition of them in a systematic manner. The wide usage of these methods as methodological tools can still be seen in different areas such as physical sciences, social sciences, and life sciences.

The five methods are:

1. Method of Agreement
2. Method of Difference
3. Joint Method of Agreement and Difference
4. Method of Residues
5. Method of Concomitant Variation

In what follows, we shall learn about each of these methods and also about how to apply them.

It will help to us remember that the first four methods are **negative** or **eliminative** in character. They are good at eliminating what cannot justifiably be considered as cause. But there are situations where none of these methods is applicable, i.e., where situations do not allow for elimination of certain factors. For example, in usual experiments the factors of gravitation, heat, friction, etc., cannot be totally eliminated. They can be only studied in varying degrees. To study such phenomena, the last method, viz. Method of Concomitant Variation, can be very effectively used.

Method of Agreement

Mill's formulation of the method is as follows:

If two or more instances of a phenomenon under investigation have only one other circumstance (antecedent or consequent) in common, that circumstance is the cause (or an indispensable part of the cause) or the effect of the phenomenon.

What it means is this: if in all cases under investigation there is a *common factor* present, i.e. there is one circumstance or factor *in which all the cases agree*, then that factor or circumstance is the *cause* if it is present prior to the case, or is the effect if it is present after the case. The method of agreement is to look for a factor that all the cases under investigation agree on. The agreement serves as the basis for connecting it either as a cause or as an effect to the case under investigation.

Suppose that you are investigating the cause of an event, say, occurrence of Malaria. Your investigation covers several cases of Malaria. Suppose that 47 of the cases have happened in Thailand, 50 in Uganda, 41 in Bangladesh, and 30 in Vietnam. In these 168 instances of Malaria, there are 88 men, 45 women and 35 children. The age of the victim varies from 3 years to 71 years, and the living conditions, habits, surroundings also vary. But suppose that, in spite of many individual differences in their special circumstances, in every case you find that there are Anopheles mosquitoes in the region and, prior to the occurrence of Malaria, the victims have invariably slept without mosquito nets. Everything else varies about the instances, but these factors emerge as the common factor among all the cases.

This gives us the following important points to consider:

1. 168 instances in which the circumstances of the victims invariably sleeping without mosquito nets and the presence of Anopheles mosquitoes in the region are seen *in conjunction* with Malaria. **(Repeated observation of regular conjunction)**
2. 168 instances of Malaria in which the circumstances of the victims invariably sleeping without mosquito nets and the presence of Anopheles mosquitoes in the region are seen *as invariably present*. **(Discovery of the invariable factor)**

According to the method of Agreement, Malaria is the common *effect* in all these cases and, as the only antecedent factors on which the 168 cases agree, the factors of sleeping without mosquito nets and the presence of Anopheles mosquitoes are the cause or indispensable part of the cause of Malaria.

The method of Agreement looks for a common factor, or a common kind of phenomenon, or a common set of circumstances. Or, it tries to show that *wherever* event *e* has occurred, a condition *c* either has preceded or has followed. In other words: (a) Every case of *e* is also a case *c* happening prior to it. or, (b) Every case of *e* is also a case *c* happening after it.

Its use in scientific discoveries cannot be disputed. A search for a common factor led scientists to discover tobacco use (smoking or chewing) as a leading cause for oral cancer. A similar search helped to uncover the air-borne transmission pathway of Tuberculosis bacteria from the infected person to another.

Before agricultural science came as a discipline, a lot of agriculture-related causal discoveries were based on observation of agreement. Farmers saw year after year that the common factor of the presence of certain insects, such as bees, help the propagation of the plants by carrying the pollen from one plant to another. Similarly, they discovered that the other insects act as vectors for carrying plant-diseases from one plant to another.

However, the method of Agreement has limitations. Mill himself observed that the method *by itself* is not adequate to establish causal relation. For, he maintained, there can be **plurality of causes**. There can be more than one cause for one event. Basically, the Method of Agreement looks for a common factor in the instances and then it tries to attribute the commonality as a causal factor. However, *it is not necessary that there will always be a common factor*. An effect may sometimes be produced by cause A, sometimes by B, and sometimes by C. For example, high blood pressure in a human being may be sometimes caused by physical characteristics inherited from ancestors, sometimes by stress, and sometimes by food habits. It is not true therefore that one effect must always be connected with one case, or that every phenomenon must always be produced by the same condition or set of conditions. Given this possibility of plurality of causes, by method of Agreement we cannot be certain that we have found *the cause*.

Consider the following:

Plurality of Causes: Example

The cause for C_1 is being explored:

Suppose that we have found two sets of instances:

Set 1: the antecedent events A_1, A_2, A_3 were found to precede consequent events C_1, C_2, C_3.

Set 2: the antecedent events A_1, A_4, A_5 were found to precede consequent events C_1, C_4, C_5.

According to the method of Agreement, you may claim that A_1, being the common factor, is the cause of C_1. But this conclusion becomes false once we entertain the possibility of plurality of causes. For, it is possible that in set 1 C_1 was caused by A_3 and in set 2 C_1 was caused by A_4; whereas A_1 had *nothing at all* to do with C_1 in either of the cases. There is no reason to presume that C_1 must be caused in both cases by the same cause. This is what Mill called the **characteristic imperfection of Method of Agreement**. It always makes possible that what you may have concluded by the Method of Agreement alone may not be correct.

In addition, there are other problems for the application of the Method of Agreement. The circumstances may not always be so neatly and conveniently arranged to help us isolate *only one* factor among many. The phenomena may be so mixed together that no such isolation may be possible, and it may also be difficult to tell which one is the cause and which is the effect. For example, gene studies are excellent tools for finding weapons against various diseases that affect us. However, because of the extremely complex nature of the genetic material, it is not at all easy to isolate and establish that a particular gene is responsible for a particular disease or a disorder.

Also, it is possible that by the Method of Agreement more than one common factors are found to be present in the instances. In that case, the Method of Agreement will not be able to help us decide which of these, if at all, is causally more significant to the case under consideration.

In addition to the factor of plurality of the causes, these pose as difficulties for achieving certainty with the application of the Method of Agreement. What the Method of Agreement can do, however, is to strengthen the probability in favour of a certain condition by repeated observation of its invariable presence. But it cannot single handedly deliver the cause.

Method of Difference

Mill's formulation of the method is as follows:

> *If an instance in which a phenomenon occurs, and an instance in which it does not occur, have every other circumstance in common save one, that one (whether consequent or antecedent) occurring only in the former, the circumstance in which alone the two instances differ is the effect, or the cause, or an indispensable condition of the phenomenon.*

The aim is to find the crucial difference while noting the agreements. This means tshat we need to compare the *instances in which the event under examination occurs* with *instances in which the event under examination does not occur*. If there is one factor present among the cases in which the event occurs, and absent among the cases in which the event does not occur, and if everything else is just the same between two sets, then we have spotted a key difference. The Method of Difference allows us to causally connect that different factor to the event under examination. Consider the following example:

***Example* (of Method of Difference)**

The cause for C_1 is being explored:

Set 1 observed: The antecedents A_1, A_2, A_3 observed to be followed by consequents C_1, C_2, C_3.

Set 2 observed: The antecedents A_2, A_3 observed to be followed by consequents C_2, C_3.

Also observed: That A_1 is present in the set 1, where C_1 or the event under investigation is present, and A_1 is absent in the set 2 where C_1 or the event under investigation is also absent.

Conclusion by Method of Difference: A_1 is the cause of C_1.

Suppose that in a whole room full of people, only three people did not become unconscious. The *only difference* between these three and the rest is that these three who did not become unconscious did not drink the cold beverage that was served, but everyone else in the room drank it. Applying the Method of Difference, we can claim that consumption of that drink is the cause of loss of sense in all those people. Similarly, we can prove that loss of sense is the effect of consumption of that drink.

In everyday life, we use the Method of Difference without being aware of it. In fact, many of our opinions about our surrounding are formed by this method. For example, the Sun gives light and heat. Consider yourself standing first in the Sun, and then immediately afterwards in the shade. You notice the difference you feel in skin temperature and also observe the amount of light present around you. From that, you can conclude that the Sun is causally connected to light and heat. Similarly, our common observations that heat causes sweat, water quenches thirst, a painkiller cures a headache, etc. can be analyzed as applications of the Method of Difference.

Of course, the Method of Difference has a very important role in controlled scientific experiments. In the controlled settings of experimental environment, *only one* condition is altered while keeping all the other various factors the same. The aim is to observe the *critical difference* the alteration makes on the environment. From this, causal inferences are made about the effect produced and the introduction or the withdrawal of that one particular condition. For example, if a cross-cultural study shows that the rate of stomach cancers in Japan is on the rise, and in the USA the rate is dropping, *everything else being the same*, it may be possible to identify that an environmental factor or life-style is responsible for the difference. Using the Method of Difference, we can argue that that factor may be causally responsible for the higher incidence of cancer cases in one country, and its absence may be connected to the lower incidence of stomach cancer in another country.

In this context, we may remember Galileo's simple but effective experiment to show that air has weight. Galileo first weighed a container filled with normal air. Then he filled the same container with compressed air and weighed it again. The weight showed increase. Since the remaining conditions were the same, it was concluded that the increased weight can only be due to the increased amount of air in the container. Hence, air has weight.

The discovery of the connection of cause and transmission route of **Bubonic Plague** to the rats provides an interesting example of the use of Method of Difference.

In 1907, the Bubonic Plague hit San Francisco, USA. Bubonic Plague, or 'Black Death', was known to have a great toll in Europe and parts of Asia in earlier centuries, but in 1907, it came to the shore of another continent. It is said that infected Chinese sailors brought it to the American shore as early as 1899, but it was not detected at that time.

By 1894, Shibasaburo Kitasato and Alexandre Yersin had independently but simultaneously identified the 'germ' or the bacillus that causes Bubonic Plague. So, it was already known that the disease is caused by some 'germ'. But people thought the 'germ' infected through food or open wounds. Accordingly, disinfection campaigns were carried out to clean the sewers with carbolic acid. However, instead of curbing it, this measure fuelled the spread of the disease more as it dislodged the rats which lived in the sewer. But at that time that was the state of the information they had.

The connection of Bubonic Plague with rats was noticed in 1894 by physician Mary Miles who had reported the widespread death of rats in plague epidemics observed in Canton, China. But as this showed mere Agreement between the presence of dead rats and the presence of Plague epidemic, the observation was not found conclusive. People thought that the rats probably died after catching the infection from the infected people. But in 1905, a British Commission confirmed what Paul Louis Simmond had discovered by observation and experiment in 1895: that rat fleas from plague-infected rats can jump onto a human being (earlier thought impossible), that the fleas look for a new host once the rat is dead, and that once on the human being the fleas can bite other human beings, and the Plague bacillus is transmitted to a human being through the flea-bites.

The situation in San Francisco in 1907 provided a conclusive proof for this connection. In 1906, a devastating earth quake razed San Francisco. It not only made people homeless but also made the rats homeless. In the year that followed, people had to stay in refugee camps while the reconstruction of the city went on. This helped the rat and rat-flea infestations to grow. In 1907, the Bubonic Plague took 122 lives. Armed with the observation of the simultaneous presence of rats and Plague cases, and the information from the research literature, San Francisco city officials carried out another kind of campaign. They offered reward for catching and killing rats. It worked very well to halt the epidemic in 1909.

As you may have noticed, the city officials created a *crucial difference* by motivating people to catch and kill rats. With the absence of the rats, came the absence of the Plague. This was observed in conjunction with the epidemic situation where rat infestation existed along with the Plague.

The Method of Difference has some limitations too. For example, it is not always possible to make sure that *exactly one circumstance* at a time has been changed. This is particularly true in experiments in life sciences. In drug research, for instance, it is common to have inconclusive preliminary studies, particularly for this reason. Still the Method of Difference has wide usage.

It is particularly common in science to utilize the lesson learnt from the Method of Difference to *refute* or *disconfirm* a hypothesis. Typically, it is argued that *if* the hypothesis *were* true, then the presence of a certain actor or condition should result in a significant or crucial difference, but if no significant difference is observed, the hypothesis is questionable.

Consider, for example, the 'memory loss' study[1] by Alan Preece and his colleagues in University of Bristol.

> The 'memory loss' study experiment was meant to test the claim that use of mobile phones causes memory loss. The research team fixed a device that mimicked microwave emissions of digital or analogue mobile phones to the left ears of 36 volunteers. The volunteers were found to recall words or pictures shown on a computer screen regardless of whether the device was on or not. Though Preece did not want to comment on what long-term use of mobile phones would cause, but he concluded that his studies show that use of mobile phones at least have no immediate effect on short-term memory.

Finally, it needs to be mentioned that the Method of Difference does *not* suffer from the possibility of plurality of causes. In the case of method of Agreement, the doubt always remains whether an event A_1, though always present with event C_1, is ever a cause or an indispensable condition for it. However, in the case of Method of Difference, the factor which creates the crucial difference by its presence and its absence, is clearly to be considered as one of the causes, *even if there might be more than one cause.*

Joint Method of Agreement and Difference

Mill's formulation of the method is:

> *If (1) two or more instances in which a phenomenon occurs have only one other circumstance (antecedent or consequent) in common, while (2) two or more instances in which it does not occur (though in some important points, they resemble the former set of instances) have nothing else in common save the absence of that circumstance—the circumstance in which alone the two sets of instances differ throughout (being present in the first set and absent in the second) is the effect or the cause, or an indispensable part of the cause, of the phenomenon.*

[1] Alan Preece,"Effect of a 915 MHz mobile phone signal on cognitive function in man", International Journal of Radiation Biology, 1999, Vol. 75, 447–456.

The Joint Method, as its name suggest, combines the insights from the Method of Agreement and the Method of Difference. In Mill's formulation of it as given above, clause (1) essentially refers to Method of Agreement. For, according to it we need to look for that one common factor that is invariably present with the phenomenon under investigation among the instances. Clause (2), on the other hand, wants to ensure that the same common factor is *absent* throughout in another set of instances along with the *absence* of the phenomenon under investigation. Thus, two separate set of observed instances are required by this method. In one set, the correlation between the presence of the phenomenon under investigation and the presence of a common factor is to be searched for. In another set, the correlation between their absences is to be searched for. For example, consider the following two sets of instances given below:

Example **(of the Joint Method)**

Set 1 (Agreement in presence)	**Set 2** (Agreement in absence)
Case 1: $\mathbf{A_1}$, A_2, A_3	Case 1: A_3, A_4, A_5
$\mathbf{C_1}$, C_2, C_3	C_4, C_5, C_6
Case 2: $\mathbf{A_1}$, A_6, A_7	Case 2: A_2, A_8, A_9
$\mathbf{C_1}$, C_7, C_8	C_9, C_{10}, C_{11}

Agreement in presence and agreement in absence constitute the basis for claiming a causal relation in the Joint Method. In the above given example, note that in set 1, A_1 is the present throughout with C_1 when no other factor has remained the same. In set 2, the absence of both is the only common factor among the instances. Given this, we can say that A_1 is the cause of C_1. Since each of the Methods of Agreement and Difference provide some probability for the conclusion, the Joint Method benefits from both, and provides a higher probability.

The Joint Method has a special advantage. If the second set can be made exhaustive with other probable causes for a certain phenomena, then it serves as a tool to refute any hypothesis of plurality of causes. For example, if you find that whenever and wherever you eat shrimp, you feel sick, this alone gives you some basis for thinking that eating shrimp is the cause of that particular sickness. However, suppose that with shrimp, in at least one of those dinners you also had coconut, egg, and hot mango pickles. One way to force the conclusion, that shrimp eating is causing the sickness, is to have another set of observations at dinners where shrimp is not served, but each of coconut, egg, and hot mango pickles is served. Finding that you are not getting sick at any of the second set of dinners has some force to establish that shrimp is the cause of your sickness.

The 1954 Salk Polio Vaccine Field Trial conducted in the USA may be cited here as an important example of the Joint Method.

By the early 1950s, Salk had already finished the development of a killed-virus vaccine for Polio, but a field trial was needed to judge its effectiveness. For this purpose, two groups were created, treatment group who were given the vaccine and the control group who were not given the treatment. It was important for the two groups to be similar in important aspects. In selected areas of the country in selected schools children in the second grade were chosen as the treatment group, and in the same schools students from first and third grade were chosen as control group. All those who were given the vaccine produced antibodies but none became afflicted by Polio, whereas Polio was seen to occur only among those who were not given the vaccine. The test was considered as successful. The administration of the vaccine and the significant reduction of Polio cases were consistently observed in the treatment group, and the absence of Vaccine and significant occurrences of Polio were observed in the control group.

We may also cite as example the case of identification of Thalidomide as a cause of unusual congenital malformations.

In Germany in 1959, the first and the only case was reported of an extremely unusual birth defect: a malformation in a newborn resulting in missing or shortened limbs. By 1961, the cases had increased by 200 times. It was found that Thalidomide, a sleeping pill, was first introduced in Germany in 1956. Some pregnant women were prescribed Thalidomide to treat certain symptoms. It was noted that before Thalidomide was introduced, there were no cases reported or cited of same or similar unusual malformations. With the introduction of Thalidomide in the consumer market, the unusual cases occurred and continued. This led to the 1961 proposal that use of Thalidomide by the pregnant women is the cause of certain birth defects in their newborns.

Method of Residues

Mill's formulation of the method is:

> *Subduct from any phenomenon such part as previous inductions have shown to be the effect of certain antecedents, and the residue of the phenomenon is the effect of the remaining antecedents.*

According to this method, if we have a range of factors believed to be the causes of a range of effects, and we have reason to believe that all the factors, except one factor C_1, are causes for all the effects, except one, E_1, then we should infer that C_1 is the cause of the remaining effect E_1.

In this case the phenomenon under investigation is assumed to be an effect. It is also assumed that the phenomenon can be studied in parts. For example, phenomenon A is supposed to be consisting of parts B and C. If we know that both D and E are antecedents of A, the Method of Residue tells us that if we know that *B* is caused by *D*, then we can conclude that *E* is the cause of *C*. We must also know how to "add" the separate contributions of known causal factors like *D* and *E*. The method therefore deals with complex causes and complex effects.

The discovery of argon may be considered as an example of this method.

In 1894, Sir W. Ramsay heard in a lecture by Lord Rayleigh that nitrogen isolated from the air had a density slightly higher than that of nitrogen prepared from chemical sources. Rayleigh claimed that this might be due to the presence of a light impurity in the latter. But Ramsey thought that this might be the case due to a heavy impurity in atmospheric Nitrogen: a yet unrecognized element in the air. He conducted experiments on the atmospheric Nitrogen to isolate the 'impurity'. While the rest of the factors were accounted for, he found one new gas, the existence of which was still not accounted for and yet which had some weight. Thus, Argon gas was discovered as the residue gas which caused the extra weight in atmospheric Nitrogen.

The method of Residue requires the examination of one instance, whereas the previous three methods require the examination of two or more instances. The Method of Residue also assumes that part of the causal explanation for the phenomena is already known, whereas in the previous three methods there is no such assumption. Given that the phenomenon in question fits the required description given in the Method of Residue, the conclusion follows as an inductive claim which connects two remaining factors causally, but with some degree of probability.

Method of Concomitant Variation

Mill wrote:

> *Whatever phenomenon varies in any manner wherever another phenomenon (consequent or antecedent) varies in some particular manner [no other change having occurred] is either a cause or effect of that phenomenon [or is connected with it through some fact of causation].*

The Method of Concomitant Variation allows us to ground our causal reasoning in the observation of proportionate change or **concomitant variation** between two phenomena. If two events are so related that everything else being the same, the variation in one is reflected proportionately by the variation in another, then by this method we can conclude inductively that the antecedent event is probably the cause of the consequent event. The idea can be stated also in terms of certain properties of two phenomena. The variation in the properties of both phenomena is observed to vary in a certain proportionate manner.

Suppose that you find that the *harder* you exercise, the *longer* the pains in your body endure, according to this proportionate variation you may claim that the exercise in this case probably is the cause of your body aches. In many other common cases where we suspect that a causal connection exists, we may find that changes in the degrees or magnitudes of one are uniformly associated with changes in the degrees or magnitudes of another. For example, the more stressed one is, the higher the blood pressure may rise. Without realizing, children also may learn to form their own inductive conclusions using this method. For example, a child learns that her mirror image is actually she herself. The process, however, may be based on concomitant variation. The more she moves her hand, the more the image in the mirror moves its hands; and the closer she comes to the mirror, the mirror image too comes closer. These may be the beginning of her learning to deal with her own mirror image.

Correlational studies are helpful in establishing important concomitant variations. For example, observation of concomitant variations is very important in studying the causal role of certain food. If meat consumption is shown to vary concomitantly or proportionately to colon cancer, then we can draw an inductive conclusion about meat-eating and its causal effect on our health. If the physicians cannot ask people to completely eliminate meat from their diet (some people may not want to), at least this gives us enough ground to ask for moderation in meat consumption.

The method has wide usage. Advertising departments of big business houses, for instance, may decide to put their advertisements on a certain TV channel in a certain time slot after the market research shows that there is a positive concomitant variation between showing an advertisement at that hour on that channel and an increase in sales volume of a product. Similarly, the method supports the well-known correlational approach in empirical research. Social scientists, for instance, may notice that people with higher income are also people with higher education. Suppose that a regression analysis reveals that eighty percent of the variation in educational status is "explained" by corresponding variation in economic status. This strong association between the two variables suggests that there may be a causal relationship between the two facts. Though it may not tell us which is the cause of which, the strong association suggests that there is a causal relationship.

A recent research study may be cited here as an example.

A study conducted by Dr. Kirsten Wisborg and her colleagues in Denmark, and published in British Medical Journal (Feb. 2003; 326: 420), found that pregnant women who drink eight or more cups of coffee a day run more than twice the risk of stillbirth compared with women who do not drink coffee. During the period 1989–96, 18,478 pregnant women were surveyed who came for delivery at Aarhus University Hospital. The study predicted that compared to the women who did not drink any coffee, women who drank four to seven cups a day had an 80% increased risk of stillbirth, and women who drank eight or more cups a day had a 300% increased risk. The conclusion was that drinking too much coffee during pregnancy raises the chances of stillbirth.

Similarly, there have been claims from scientists on the basis of observed co-variation. Scientists have noticed that sunspots follow a cycle to form on Sun's surface. But the closer the cycle is to its peak, the higher the disturbances become in high frequency radio transmissions on the earth.

The method of concomitant variation can be easily regarded as a purely quantitative method. In this respect, it is unique among Mill's methods. For, none of the other methods are so evidently quantitative in nature. Its applicability to the correlational studies of quantifiable phenomena, therefore, cannot be overlooked.

Also, Mill's method permits the concomitant variation to be a variation of "in any manner". That is, it covers the cases of variations which are *parallel*: increase in one event parallel to an increase in another event, or decrease in parallel to decrease in another event. But it also covers the cases of *inverse variation*: increase of one while the decrease of another. For example, economists see the relation between supply and pricing in an unregulated market as a relation of inverse ratio. The more abundant the supply of a product becomes, the lower the price will be. Or, the more frequently the oil is changed in the engine, the less the wear will be on its pistons. Or, in these days of global warming, we have learnt that the higher the temperature is in Earth's atmosphere, the lesser the concentration of ozone will be in the upper layers of the atmosphere.

However, we need to also remember that there can be concomitant variations that are purely coincidental. Every pattern of concomitant variations, therefore, is not a safe basis for inference of causal connection. We may observe that the more we pray for global peace, the higher the international tensions become. But this does not give us any causal basis to infer that our prayer is somehow causally connected to the escalation of the global conflicts. It is possible to have cases of purely fortuitous but non-causal patterns of occurrences. For example, the moment you remembered someone, you got a phone call from that person; or, you open a book randomly and then on that randomly opened page you find the solution of the problem you were seeking. These are known as *chances* or *pure coincidences*. Mill's method does not refer to such eventualities.

Still, inferences from concomitant variation must be dealt with caution. Mill's method requires us to take note of *all* cases of variations between two events, "wherever" and "in any manner" they happen. This is simply not possible. Hence, we can only observe a handful of cases and form an inductive generalization out of these observations. This itself leaves room for uncertainty in the conclusion, as the probability of a negative instance in which the two events do not vary concomitantly cannot ever be ruled out. Moreover, just because two events co-vary, it does not mean that one is the cause of another. The classic example is that of thunder and lightning: the brighter the flash of lightning is, the stronger the boom of thunder is. But actually, neither is causally connected. They are the co-effects of a common cause: the discharge of electricity in the air. Finally, concomitant variation does not cover all cases of causation. There can be two events, A and B, where A is the cause of B, but changes in A may show no corresponding significant variation in B.

15.4 Limitations of Mill's Methods

Mill's five methods explained in Section 15.3 hold promises for providing basis for our causal inductive reasoning. Many of these rules represent some of the basic principles that we use implicitly in causal reasoning in everyday life. However, though their utility or wide usage cannot be denied, Mill's methods have certain limitations. While using them, it is important to remember these limitations. Their role in scientific analysis of causes is not as important or as extensive as Mill had believed.

Regarding Mills Methods, at least two important questions may be asked:

1. Do these methods help us to discover a causal relation in a given situation?
2. Do these methods help us to establish or justify that there is a relation of cause and effect in front of us?

Mill thought that his rules could provide answers to both the questions, that is, they can serve as ways of discovering causal hypotheses, and also serve as ways of testing causal claims once they have been arrived at. In both the cases, Mill overestimated the power of his methods.

Mill's critics point out that the rules presuppose that we already have a list of possible causes as candidates to consider. But the rules themselves do not tell us how to come up with such a list. In reality this would depend on our knowledge or informed guesses about likely causes of the effects. Thus, in the context of discovery of causes, Mill's Methods are not as helpful as Mill assumed them to be.

This leaves the question open as to which *two or more* phenomena or *circumstances* are we have to focus upon from the myriads that we normally see to pay attention to find *agreement*, or *difference*, or *both*, or *co-variation*. Since all possible circumstances cannot be considered, we need to be selective about which circumstances are need specially attention. And this judgment about which phenomena are to be specially attended to, could be pure guess or informed guess, depending on the status of available information at that time. But both are prone to error. For example, for a long time in Medieval Europe, certain mental disorders were thought to be effects of demonic possession or possession of spirits or of witchcraft. With this presupposition, records were kept of the behaviour of the affected, and then on that basis inductive generalizations were drawn to guide what used to be thought of as therapeutic measures. This dependence of inductive methods on the underlying hypotheses or beliefs shows that the methods cannot by themselves reveal to us what the cause is in a given situation.

Does this mean that Mill's Methods are better for justifying or establishing causal relations, once we have managed somehow to propose a causal hypothesis? Even regarding this, there are reservations. As we have indicated, while discussing each method, there are certain difficulties for the application of these methods. For example, the Method of Agreement or the Method of Difference requires us to identify cases which have *one and only one circumstance in common* or cases which have *everything else in common.* If we take these expressions in Mill's formulations of methods literally, then clearly we cannot proceed. For, in real life such cases are impossible to find. Between two events, numerous factors may be common; similarly, between two events numerous differences may hold. In fact, it is not possible in practice to observe every single instance of two phenomena to come to the conclusion that they agree or differ in exactly the same circumstance.

Even if we do not take these expressions literally, there can be difficulties for application. For, supposing that what Mill meant was only factors *relevant* to a causal analysis of a phenomenon are to be studied, the interpretation of what constitutes the *relevance* in a particular situation may jeopardize the examination. As a result, the fairness or correctness of our conclusions from this investigation may be compromised.

Consider the current debate about the controversial case of "cold fusion".

In 1989, Stanley Pons and Martin Fleischmann of the University of Utah announced their discovery of "cold fusion": the fusion of atoms at normal temperatures. It is well known that under extremely high temperatures and extreme pressure as happens in the core of a star, or in a very specialized set-up such as in a nuclear power plant, atomic nuclei collide and fuse, releasing energy that can act as limitless source of power. The "cold fusion" claims that atoms can be fused in room temperature. The implication of this claim is enormous. In the days when fossil fuels are becoming scantier as sources of electricity and power, "cold fusion" can solve the power generation problem. Each household could produce its own electricity by "cold fusion" created on a tabletop. However, the 1989 claim of Pons and Fleischman met with ridicule as researchers from MIT Plasma Fusion Centre claimed that the high energy gamma ray spectrum, which Pons and Fleischman had claimed to have observed in their experiment, could not have resulted from the reaction they described. On this basis, the experiment of Pons and Fleischman was rejected as irreproducible, and idea of "cold fusion" therefore became equivalent to a bogus claim.

Only recently in 2005, other scientists and scientifically oriented eminent persons such as Arthur C Clarke have drawn our attention to the fact that the idea of "cold fusion" may not be as absurd an idea as it was made out to be in 1989. Part of explanation of the ridicule that "cold fusion" received was a preconceived notion that "cold fusion" is an improbability. With this presupposition, if we approach the results of Pons and Fleischman, we shall only see what we think are relevant in the situation. The other factors, even if they are present, might be overlooked as a result. For example, now it is being pointed out that the claim of MIT Plasma Fusion Centre researchers about refutation of the Fleischmann/Pons neutron-gamma ray interaction does not completely rule out the possibility that cold fusion might be occurring. The Utah experimenters also reported observing other phenomena, such as an energy increase of four times over that supplied to the experimental apparatus, a result obtained by complicated heat measurements. The MIT Center results offered no insight regarding the possibility or impossibility of these other claims.

The point here is that there are scientists who think that the 'cold fusion' experiment was too summarily rejected when not all 'relevant' factors for the success of the experiment were given equal weightage.

These limitations of Mill's Methods in a way underscore the difference between deduction and induction once more. Because of the probabilistic uncertainty inherent in inductive methods, applications of these methods must always be done with an open mind. We can always suppose that there could be alternative causal hypotheses that might challenge or refute our own hypothesis. In fact, it would be wiser to use these methods to formulate *more than one* causal hypothesis, and then subject them to further testing.

In spite of their limitations, Mill's Methods are very powerful tools. They are not tools for discovery of causes or proofs to provide conclusive evidence. Nonetheless, they are good indicators of causally related phenomena, when the hypothesis they work with correctly identifies the relation. They are good tools in a controlled experimental set-up, where already well-formed causal hypotheses are tested for either confirmation or refutation.

EXERCISE 15.4

1. Analyze the following reports, explaining which of Mill's Methods is used. Decide in each case using the limitations of the Methods whether it establishes a causal connection.

a. Scientists at an influential California agency have concluded that second-hand smoke causes breast cancer. The 1,200-page report analyzes new data on the extent of Californians' exposure to second-hand smoke and more than 1,000 studies of health effects from second-hand smoke.

Chemicals in cigarette smoke cause breast cancer in rats; the chemicals are found in human breast tissue. Recent studies of groups of women show a breast cancer-smoking link. The California scientists who concluded that second-hand smoke causes breast cancer and whose report is likely to be approved next week by a review panel were persuaded by "the weight of evidence."

Much of that evidence was newer, better studies, says Melanie Marty, the section chief with the Office of Environmental Health Hazard Assessment who supervised the report. "What you want is multiple studies that show an effect," she says. "As time has gone by, more and more have shown an effect."

Marty's team looked at older studies that "didn't ask enough questions to figure out who was really exposed (to second-hand smoke) and who wasn't." But in six recent studies that were careful to take women who'd been exposed out of control groups, the risks went up, she says.

—*USA Today*, March 8, 2005.

*b. Researchers at the Health Effects Institute have reconfirmed the relationship between premature death and fine particulate matter originally demonstrated in the two most important particulate matter and mortality studies in the USA; the Harvard Six Cities Study and the American Cancer Society Study (ACS). The two landmark studies were a primary basis for the U.S. EPA's actions in 1997 establishing a national ambient air quality standard for fine particulate matter. The Six Cities Study was a prospective long-term study, to examine chronic (long-term) health effects of air pollution. The ACS study was a larger study, encompassing cities throughout the United States, with more statistical strength. Both studies were fully reanalyzed by Health Effects Institute after industry called the original methods into question. Results of the reanalysis vindicate both studies and confirm the robust quality of the original data and analysis. Results from the reanalyzed Harvard Six Cities Study, which tracked 8,111 adults in six cities in the Northeast and Midwest United States for 14 years, show a 28% higher chance of premature death due to particulate matter (PM) between the most polluted and least polluted cities. The reanalysis of the ACS study, which originally tracked 552,138 adults in 154 cities in all states from 1982-1989, found an 18% higher risk.

Dr. Morton Lippmann and his colleagues at the New York University School of Medicine attempted to identify and characterize components of PM and other air pollution mixtures that were associated with excess daily deaths and elderly hospital admissions in and around the area of Detroit, Michigan. The study used publicly available data for 1985–1990 and 1992–1994, including measures of several different PM components as well as other air pollutants. Statistical models were used to weigh the strength of one pollutant or two pollutants concurrently. Models using three or more pollutants were not attempted owing to the difficulty of separating the effects of pollutants that rise and fall closely together, or are correlated. To better assess relationships between pollutants and health outcomes, the authors evaluated the extent to which (1) air pollutants tended to vary together in space and time, (2) results depended on the specific location where pollutants were sampled, and (3) results were influenced by multiple hospital admissions of some individuals in the study population during the study period. The main statistical method used was Poisson regression, with a generalized additive model to adjust for the effects of time-trend meteorologic differences, and other variables.

—"Association of Particulate Matter Components with Daily Mortality and Morbidity in Urban Populations", Morton Lippman *et al. Clean Air*, August 1, 2000.

c. Detective Bejbarua started querying people who were there on the crime spot. He talked to seven of them, calling each one individually for a personal interview. He asked each one to describe the crime scene as he or she has seen it, and as each one talked, he took notes and also recorded their narration on audiotapes. Later he sat down with the tapes and notes and discovered that at some point or other in the narration each of the seven interviewed has mentioned seeing a tall man wearing a long coat leaving the scene in a hurry. In his report, he commented that the "tall man with a long coat" is the prime suspect in this case.

d. Researchers said that mutations in the gene, called *UBQNL1*, may raise risks for the common, late-onset form of the disease that comprises more than 90 percent of Alzheimer's cases. The gene, located on chromosome 9 is only the second gene ever linked to late-onset disease. The lead researcher is Rudolph Tanzi, a Professor of Neurology at Harvard Medical School, and director of the Genetics and Aging Research Unit at Massachusetts General Hospital, USA. The findings appear in the March 3 issue of the *New England Journal of Medicine*. Tanzi, who in 1996 identified one of the early onset genes, *Presenilin 2*, now believes his team at Harvard has isolated a second gene associated with late-onset disease.

Working first with a group of 437 families, each with two first-degree relatives affected by Alzheimer's, the researchers specifically looked at genes on chromosome 9. They eventually zeroed in on genes producing a protein called "ubiquilin". "The reason we specifically looked at ubiquilin was because it binds to and interacts with the early onset gene, *Presenilin 2*," Tanzi explained. The researchers hit pay dirt: Variants in a ubiquilin-linked gene, *UBQLN1*, were significantly associated with incidence of late-onset Alzheimer's in affected families.

A separate analysis, this time in 217 sibling pairs — where one had Alzheimer's but the other didn't — further strengthened the association, as did autopsy evidence from brains affected by Alzheimer's, the researchers found. They say that their goal is not the identification of one or two genes, but the identification of a much larger collection of mutations that together might better predict a person's overall risk to become affected with Alzheimer's disease.

— *New England Journal of Medicine*; March 2, 2005,
University of California, Irvine, news release.

e. Kidney disease is the most common cause of secondary hypertension (high blood pressure). Even subtle disruptions in kidney function play a role in most (if not all) cases of high blood pressure and increased injury to the kidneys. This injury can eventually cause malignant hypertension, stroke or even death.

In normal people, when there's a higher intake of sodium chloride (salt), the body adjusts. It excretes more sodium without raising arterial pressure. However, many outside influences and kidney problems can lead to reduced capability to excrete sodium. If the kidneys are less able to excrete salt with normal or higher salt intake, chronic increases in extracellular fluid volume and blood volume result. This leads to high blood pressure. When higher levels of hormones and neurotransmitters that directly cause blood vessels to narrow are also present, even small increases in blood volume are compounded. (This is due to the smaller area through which the blood is forced to flow.) Although the increases in arterial pressure lead the kidneys to excrete more sodium, which restores the sodium balance, higher pressure in the arteries may persist. This shows the important link between kidney disease and high blood pressure.

f. Does Coffee/Caffeine consumption contribute to high blood pressure? Despite previous controversy on the subject, most researchers now conclude that regular coffee and caffeine use has little or no effect on blood pressure. Studies reviewed in the Progress in Cardiovascular Diseases indicate that while first-time caffeine use may produce immediate, minimal changes in blood pressure, these changes are transient. No changes in blood pressure appear to occur in regular users of caffeine. A 1991 study published in the British Medical Journal reached the same conclusion and indicated that restricting caffeine did not reduce blood pressure in people with mild hypertension. A number of studies that have looked at people with normal blood pressure (published in the Archives of Internal Medicine and the American Journal of Nutrition) have concluded that caffeine does not contribute to hypertension.

In 1997, the Sixth Report of the National Institutes of Health's Joint National Committee on Prevention, Detection, Evaluation and Treatment of High Blood Pressure concluded that, "no direct relationship between caffeine intake and elevated blood pressure has been found in most epidemiologic surveys."

g. After renting the new apartment, Vibha found that she can hear the drone from the highway nearby. She decided that the drone can come from three possible sources: window in the kitchen, the windows in the attic and the thin, rickety screen door to the yard. She got the door to the yard changed, and closed the windows in the attic. She concluded that muffled sound that she can still hear from the highway probably comes from the kitchen window.

h. We know that human activities—primarily the burning of fossil fuels—have increased the greenhouse gas content of the earth's atmosphere significantly over the last century. Carbon dioxide is one of the most important greenhouse gases, which trap heat near the planet's surface.

We also know that the earth has become warmer over the last century. The Intergovernmental Panel on Climate Change (IPCC), a group established by the World Meteorological Organization (WMO) and the United Nations Environment Programme (UNEP), reports that the average surface temperature of the earth has increased during the twentieth century by about 0.6° ± 0.2°C. (The ± 0.2°C means that the increase might be as small as 0.4°C or as great as 0.8°C.) It is warmer today around the world than at any time during the past 1000 years, and the warmest years of the previous century have occurred within the past decade. We think human activities have played a causal role in the increase in global temperature.

*i. Asian populations that regularly consume green tea have lower overall rates of cancer. In 1994, researchers from the Shanghai Cancer Institute compared green tea drinkers to non-drinkers in a large population study in China. They found that in non-smokers, drinking green tea was associated with fewer cancers of the esophagus.

Since that time, scientists have been trying to ascertain exactly why green tea drinkers are less likely to develop cancer and how green tea works in the human body. What is known is that research conducted in the last few years suggests that green tea may be effective in helping to prevent a wide variety of cancers in humans, including cancers of the bladder, colon, esophagus, pancreas, rectum, and stomach. Studies released in 2004 support these findings with even greater evidence of green tea's value in the fight against cancer. One study investigated the effects of treatment with different concentrations of green tea on induced lung tumours in female mice. A treatment with 0.6% green tea preparation significantly reduced lung tumor multiplicity and also inhibited angiogenesis, the development of new blood vessels required by tumors in order to grow.

A second study, the Prostate Cancer Prevention Trial, investigated green tea's positive effects against the most commonly diagnosed visceral cancer in US men, with more than 230,000 newly diagnosed cases in 2004 alone. The trial cited considerable data supporting the use of green tea and other substances as "promising agents" in the prevention of prostate cancer. A study published in March 2004 explored the use of dietary components which are capable of inhibiting human cancer cell growth without affecting normal cell growth—specifically, EGCG's effects on breast cancer cells. EGCG was found to inhibit the actions of telomerase, an enzyme that prolongs the life span of cancer cells by maintaining the end portions of the tumour cell chromosomes. The Mayo Clinic study showed that EGCG from green tea prompted leukemia cells to die in eight of ten patient samples tested in the laboratory.

The evidence supporting green tea's role in cancer prevention is so overwhelming that the Chemo-prevention Branch of the National Cancer Institute has initiated a plan for developing tea compounds as chemopreventive agents in further human trials.

j. After seeing a reddish colour in the water, the municipality suspected the presence of some bacteria. When the water treatment lab confirmed the presence of coliform bacteria in the water sample, the municipality decided to treat the water tank with chlorine. After chlorination, the officials waited for five days before sending another water sample from the tank for testing for the presence of the bacteria. The water treatment lab tested and informed that they cannot detect the presence of bacteria anymore in the water sample. However, the officials still noticed the reddish colour in the water even after the chlorination. They concluded that the colour is coming from the iron bacteria which have infiltrated the water-bearing formation.

k. While it was a speeding Ford *Ikon* driven by Shiv Sena supremo Bal Thackeray's personal assistant Ravindra Mhatre that killed two persons on Mumbai's roads in September 2002, it was Bollywood star Salman Khan's speeding Toyota *Land Cruiser* that killed one pavement dweller and injured four others in Mumbai. Among the most high profile of such celebrity accidents in the past was the one involving Admiral S. M. Nanda's grandson Sanjeev whose speeding B.M.W. allegedly killed five persons and maimed one in 1999.

What was common in all three cases was the involvement of the powerful "C" segment cars (sedans and above) or UVs (utility vehicles) that went out of control while being driven at high speed. In all three cases, the accidents happened during the poor visibility hours of the night causing fatalities of innocent victims.

While rising disposable incomes, easy installment schemes and economic liberalization have made the big, powerful sedans and utility vehicles affordable to the Indian upper middle classes, their "mismatch" with lax driving discipline and regulation, bad roads and poor traffic planning are resulting in accidents. Transportation experts say that a "mismatch factor" is clearly visible on Indian roads through a deathly cocktail of better cars, bad roads, poor driving habits, poor regulation, high speed expressways and badly maintained vehicles.

Contributing a paper on "Dimensions of Road Safety" in the *Indian Journal of Transport Management* published by the Pune-based Central Institute of Road Transport (CIRT), authors B. Vithaldas Prabhu and S. Murali maintained that although the road transportation sector was growing vigorously, the mismatch factor between better cars and bad roads was also responsible for its share of accidents.

Prabhu (off campus faculty, Birla Institute of Technology and Science, Pilani) and Murali (Deputy General Manager, planning and quality, Ashok Leyland, Hosur Karnataka) said that the mismatch factor needs to be studied in greater detail to acquire a better understanding of rising accidents on Indian roads. According to the authors, the road accident fatality rate per 10,000 vehicles stands at 16.84 against the world average of 10 and the number of fatalities annually was over 85,000 presently against 15,000 in 197.

—*Times of India*, "Faster Cars = More Accidents?", March 28, 2005.

l. Two new studies on the effects of lead exposure to be released this week suggest that the toxin commonly found in household paints made before 1960 may stunt normal brain growth and could contribute to patterns of violent crime. Researchers who have reviewed the two studies caution that they are both preliminary and do not establish a firm causal link between lead exposure and aberrant behaviour. But they say the results go to the heart of scientific research on the subject.

In one of the first experiments of its kind, Baltimore's Kennedy Krieger Institute for Children found in a two-year study that relatively low levels of lead fed to a colony of nursing mother rats in their drinking water caused brain abnormalities in their offspring that stunted their sensory perception.

Experts say the research, which appears today in the Proceedings of the National Academy of Sciences, may have implications for human brain development since lead tends to have similar effects in animals and young children.

In the second study, a private consulting group working under contract for the U.S. Department of Housing and Urban Development used computers to track lead consumption in paint and gasoline over the past century and uncovered a striking coincidence. As the amount of lead released into the environment in paint and auto exhaust rose and fell through the decades, so did a broad range of reported violent crimes—including rape, robbery, assault and murder—a researcher at ICF Consulting in Fairfax, Virginia, found.

—"Studies suggest link between lead, violence Experiment on rats indicates exposure hinders brain growth; Analysis tracks lead, crime",

— Jim Haner, *Baltimore Sun Staff,* May 9, 2000.

m. There are approximately 40,000 people in the United States living with multiple myeloma and 14,000 new cases of multiple myeloma are diagnosed each year, thus making it the second most common blood cancer. Multiple myeloma is a cancer involving important immune (infection-fighting) cells called plasma cells. In multiple myeloma, cancerous plasma cells produce abnormal and excessive antibodies that do not have the ability to properly fight infection. In addition, the cancerous plasma cells accumulate in the bone marrow, suppressing the normal formation and function of other cells that are necessary for normal production of blood cells and immune functions. The excessive accumulation of cancer cells in the bone marrow ultimately leads to the formation of tumors in the bone and to the breakdown of bone. Standard treatment for multiple myeloma is chemotherapy. Results from several trials presented at the International Myeloma Workshop involved treatment with thalidomide in patients with multiple myeloma who had a cancer recurrence following standard therapy or had stopped responding altogether to conventional therapies. In these trials, the addition of dexamethasone, a steroid, to thalidomide improved anti-cancer responses compared with thalidomide alone. Significant responses occurred in 30% to 70% of patients with an average duration of response lasting 7–8 months.

Results from one clinical trial conducted by researchers from M.D. Anderson Cancer Center compared thalidomide alone to thalidomide plus dexamethasone for the treatment of newly diagnosed patients with multiple myeloma. Anti-cancer responses were achieved in 36% of patients receiving only thalidomide and in 72% of patients receiving thalidomide plus dexamethasone.

The results from all of these studies suggest that thalidomide may become an important component in the treatment of multiple myeloma. Thalidomide is not currently approved by the FDA for treatment of multiple myeloma treatment.

— *Multiple Myeloma Cancer News, Blood*, Vol. 96, 2000

n. In the cities along the Houston Ship Channel, 17,346 people died of respiratory complications between 1993 and 1999, according to the 1999 vital statistics report from the Texas Department of Health Bureau.

The cities of Baytown, Deer Park, La Porte, Pasadena and Channelview make up Southeast Houston and are home to the largest number of petrochemical plants and oil refineries in the state. Of the 809 chemical plants in the area, 89 percent handle hazardous waste. "Petrochemical plants have the ability to pollute the air and water with toxic particles if not properly monitored," said the United States Environmental Protection Agency. The agency also affirmed that coal combustion, a common practice at oil refineries, releases zinc and arsenic in toxic doses.

In Southeast Houston, 184 plants were reported to the EPA for having released toxins from their chemical processes and 219 plants were reported for having released toxic pollution into the air. Another 138 plants in Southeast Houston have permits from the EPA to discharge waste into the local water source. Dr. Kristin L. Fraser, a physician and journalist for Postgraduate Medicine magazine, defines Chronic Obstructive Pulmonary Disease as a "mixed group of common respiratory diseases united by the presence of persistent airflow limitation."

In 1999, the Texas Department of Health Bureau reported that 5.1 percent of the Southeast Houston population died from chronic obstructive pulmonary complications and that the disease was the fourth largest cause of death in the area.

Keywords

Causal reasoning: A very important kind of inductive reasoning in which the presence of *causes* is inferred from the presence of *effects* and vice versa.

Necessary condition: A condition in the absence of which the event cannot occur.

Partial cause: If only a part of the entire effect can be attributed to a particular cause, then that particular cause is a partial cause.

Plurality of causes: The possibility that there can be more than one cause for one event.

Proximate cause: A condition which produces the effect under consideration directly, without any other intervening factors. It also may be the closest to the effect in the chain of causal events.

Remote cause: A condition which requires the intervention of some other factor to cause the effect.

Sufficient condition: A condition for event e such that if it happens, then e has to happen.

Total cause: When the entire effect is produced by the action of event e, e is the total cause for the effect.

CHAPTER 16

PROBABILITY AND INDUCTION

16.1 Understanding Probability

We have been discussing induction and its probabilistic nature without specifying how to understand probability. This section is devoted for a basic understanding of probability.

History of Probabilistic Logic

The mathematical study of probability owes its origin to two Frenchmen: **Blaise Pascal** and **Pierre de Fermat** who lived in the middle of the 17th century. Since then till early 19th century, probability theory as a mathematical theory was primarily applied in two areas: to gambling to assess the risk factor and to assess mortality rates of a population for actuary estimation for life insurance premiums. In early 19th century, **Pierre Laplace** showed how probability theory could be applied also to a broad range of other kinds of problems. Today, its application is widely acknowledged in sciences, business, political strategies, medical diagnoses, and many other areas of our life. During the course of its development, the study of probabilities has

Blaise Pascal

Pierre de Fermat

been considered by various researchers as a type of logic. **George Boole** was the first to openly treat it as part of logic in *The Laws of Thought* (1854). **John Venn** did the same in his *The Logic of Chance* (1876).

The rigorous deductive formal system that we now call *Quantificational Logic* or *Predicate Logic*, developed by Frege, Russell and Whitehead, encouraged many to try whether a similar formal system could be developed also for inductive reasoning. The aim was to extend the deductive paradigm to the case of inductive arguments. That is, in deductive logic the validity was shown to be the product of the logical structure of the statements involved, as we have seen in the discussion of truth-functional validity in the earlier chapters in this book. Some logicians took this emulation of the deductive paradigm too seriously. They tried to specify inductive probabilities exclusively in terms of syntactic structure of inductive premises and inductive conclusions. So, in that system every statement allowed a certain syntactically specified degree of probabilistic support for each of the other statements within the system. Probability was considered as a logical relation between a premise or *evidence statement* (or a set of evidence statements) and a conclusion, in virtue of which relation having grounds for the evidence statements can be understood as constituting grounds for accepting the conclusion. Early attempts of this kind were in the works of John Maynard Keynes in his *Treatise on Probability* (1921) and of Rudolf Carnap in his *Logical Foundations of Probability* (1950). In these efforts, **Bayes' theorem**, which is a theorem in probability, occupies a major role in formulating how evidence comes to bear on hypotheses.

Now it is held that this notion of following deductive paradigm in inductive probabilities and in relation between premise and conclusion of inductive arguments is essentially a mistake. It is now accepted that mere syntactic logical structures cannot be the sole factors to determine the degree to which the premises would support the conclusion. Nor can they by themselves help us to decide which inductive arguments are good and which are bad. There are other factors to be taken into consideration, such as *prior probability*, to decide the worth of inductive support for a hypothesis. *Prior probability* means how plausible a hypothesis is by itself, even before the evidence for it is brought in. Syntactic logical structures do not help us to assign any value to *pre-evidential prior probabilities*.

While the Carnap-Keynes line of thinking was developing, at about the same time an alternative conception of probabilistic inductive reasoning also took root. This is now referred to as **Bayesian subjectivist** or **personalist approach**. It views inductive probability as a part of a larger normative theory, called **Bayesian Decision Theory**. The central idea is that the strength of agent's desires for various outcomes should combine with the strengths of his beliefs about claims about the world to produce optimal rational decisions. Bayesian inductive logic tries to show this and justifies its claims by showing that it leads to optimal decisions among various risky alternatives.

It consistently interprets inductive probability functions as subjective belief strengths of ideally rational agents.

Today, Bayesian inductive logic is most closely associated with subjectivist theory of belief and decision though elements of the inductive logic of the Keynes-Carnap type sometimes influence it. One of the most important applications of inductive logic is the confirmation or refutation of scientific hypotheses. It is expected of inductive logic to explain the notion of evidential support for all sorts of hypotheses such as "This is a new case of tuberculosis" to hypotheses about fundamental theories such as the Quantum Mechanics.

Three Ways to Understand Probability

Probability is a study of randomness or randomly occurring events. The word 'random' means "unpredictable", but it does not mean the same as 'haphazard'. Random events are not perfectly predictable, but they may have long-term regularities that we can quantify and describe using probability. Also, probability applies to those events about which we can specify all possible outcomes.

How in a fair toss a coin will land is a classic example of a random event. We cannot perfectly predict whether the coin will land as heads or tails. But its long-term average behaviour is predictable. In repeated tosses, the fraction of times it will land as heads will settle down to 50 per cent.

What does it mean when we say that a fair coin toss has a 50 per cent probability to land in heads? There are at least three ways to understand the meaning of that statement. Three standard answers come from three standard probability theories. These are now described.

(i) *A priori* theory of equally likely outcomes. In this theory, probability has to do with indistinguishable outcomes. If a given event or experiment has n possible outcomes, then this theory assumes that all these outcomes should be equally likely. If a coin is balanced well and the toss is fair, this theory assumes that there is no reason for it to land heads in preference to tails. So, according to this theory, the probability that the coin lands heads is equal to the probability that the coin lands tails, and both are 100/2 = 50 per cent. (This rules out the outcomes that the coin does not land at all or lands but is balanced on its edge.)

In this theory, the general formula for determining the probability of an event occurring under a given set of conditions is: (a) to know the exact number of total possible outcomes, and (b) to assign equal likelihood to each of these outcomes, unless there is reason to believe that one is more likely to happen than the other, and (c) to divide the number of ways in which the event can occur by the total number of things that could occur, or by the total number of outcomes possible. If there are 10 items listed on a food menu, and the situation allows only one choice by a person, then in every case of a choice from the menu, there are 10 equipossible outcomes. If I am asked to choose from this menu, my probability of choosing item number 6 is 1 over 10, or 1/10.

(ii) The relative frequency theory. In this theory, probability is the limit of frequency with which an event occurs in a set of repeated trials. So, according to this theory, to say that a fair coin toss has a 50 per cent probability to land in heads is to mean that if you toss the coin over and over again, the ratio of the number of times the coin lands heads to the total number of tosses will approach a limiting value of 50 per cent as the number of tosses increases. Relative frequencies are considered to be always between 100 per cent and 0 per cent.

In general terms, in this theory, probability may also be understood as the relative frequency with which members of a class exhibits certain property. For example, an ornithologist may wish to know the probability of spotting a snowy owl in a certain region. If 100 past observations of bird watchers in that specific region are examined, and in 18 of them sighting of a snowy owl is mentioned, then the probability of the sighting of a snowy owl is assigned 18 per cent.

The connection of this theory with empirical research is quite obvious. First of all, to find the relative frequency, trial runs are required and repeated observations are to be made. Also, note that the probabilities are relative to the observed *reference class*. If probability of sighting a snowy owl where none exists will be quite different from the probability of sighting it where it is known to exist. Fixing or finding an appropriate reference class requires some empirical search.

(iii) Subjective theory of probability. Subjective theory of probability measures probability by the agent's 'degree of belief' that an event will occur. A subjective probability describes an individual's personal judgement about how likely a particular event is to occur. It is not based on any precise computation but is often a reasonable assessment by a knowledgeable person.

A person's subjective probability of an event describes his/her degree of belief in the event.

According to this theory, to say that a fair coin toss has a 50 per cent probability to land in heads is to say that *I believe* that it will happen in half of the cases. The Subjective theory is particularly useful in assigning meaning to the probability of events that in principle can occur only once. Since there is no guarantee of repeated occurrence, it is difficult to use in these cases either of theory of relative frequency or theory of equally possible outcome. Consider, for example, the question: What is the probability of a Tsunami of the scale of 2004 Asian Tsunami happening in Indian ocean before 2020?

The classical theorists such as Laplace, Keynes and De Morgan have regarded probability as *measuring the degree of rational belief.* Probability is assigned to an event according to the degree to which a rational believer believes that it will occur. Or, probability may be assigned to a statement according to the degree of which a rational believer may believe in it. The term 'rational believer' refers to a believer who is supposed to act ideally following the usual and expected norms of rationality. For example, a rational believer is expected not to endorse inconsistency in his beliefs knowingly.

To assign probability value, in this theory a scale 1 to 0 is usually used, where '1' represents highest point in the scale and '0' the lowest point. In other words, 1 signifies certainty and 0 impossibility. Various fractions or percentages or real numbers are used to project the values in between these two extremes. However, it is *not always* the case that an in-between probability can be expressed or associated by a real number.

When one is completely convinced about something, the measure of one's degree of rational belief about it, or its probability, is assigned as 1. Since absolute certainty often eludes us, it is good enough probability to have a *probability close to 1.* For example, the probability of Sun rising tomorrow morning is *close to 1.* When one is completely convinced that an event cannot occur, its probability value is 0. For example, the probability of a rational person believing that a number above 10 can be both odd and even is 0. On the other hand, in a fair game with properly shuffled deck of cards, the probability of a 'Diamond' card showing up in the first deal is 13 out of 52, or 1/4. We know that the deck has total 52 cards with 13 Diamond cards in it. So, in an honest game and deal, the probability of a Diamond card showing up on the first deal is exactly 13 out of 52, or 1/4, or 0.25, or 25 per cent.

For Keynes, basic probabilities were to be *intuited*, though he held what were intuited as objective, i.e., not as subjective. Once we have an intuited stock of probabilities, using the general formula above, we can arrive at other probabilities by argument.

To summarize, each of the three probability theories assign different meanings to probability claims. Each theory has situations where it is most natural and advantageous to use it, and similarly each has its limitations.

16.2 A Simple Probability Calculus

A calculus of probability can be used for computing probabilities of events (or of statements describing events). Where P is the probability and e is some event, the notation $P(e)$ will be used to signify the probability of e.

1. If two events or statements p and q are assigned probabilities, then so are all of their logical (or Boolean) combinations formed with *not*, *and*, and *or* as in $\sim p$, $p \bullet q$, and $p \vee q$.

2. Similarly, if two events or statements p and q are assigned probabilities, then so is the **conditional probability** of q *given* p:

$$P(q/p)$$

Conditional probability is the probability of an event q assuming that another event p has occurred. The unconditional probability or the probability of the event q alone may be different. But given the condition, viz., the occurrence of p, the conditional probability of q may show a different value. Conditional statements or if-then statements may be approached in this way. For example, you might be interested in finding out the probability of a steel plant increasing its steel production capacity by 10 per cent *if* iron-ore supplies increase by 5 per cent.

Or, for example, you might be wondering about: What is the probability that the total of two dice will be greater than 8 *given that* the first die shows a 6? This can be calculated by considering the outcomes for which the first die is a 6. Given that the first die shows a 6, then we need to determine the proportion of these outcomes from two dice that total more than 8. The second die can show 6 different outcomes, but *only* 4 out of these will add with the first die to make more than 8; namely, 6 and 3, 6 and 4, 6 and 5, and 6 and 6. Therefore, the probability of getting a total greater than 8, *given that* the first die is 6 = 4/6 or 2/3. It can be also written as

P (the probability of getting a total greater than 8/the first die is 6) = 2/3

3. We shall consider $P(p) = 0$ *iff* p cannot be true, and $P(p) = 1$ *iff* p cannot be false.

For example: In a fair coin and a fair toss, P (show heads on this toss and not show heads on this toss) = 0.

4. Negation may be understood in the following way:

$$P\,(not-p) = 1 - P\,(p)$$

Where maximum probability is 1, subtracting the probability value of p from 1 will give us the probability value of not-p. *Example*: Suppose that P (coin will land heads on this toss) is 0.5. Then P (coin will not land heads on this toss) is $1 - 0.5 = 0.5$. Given that tails come up on a toss *iff* heads do not come up, then P (tails on this toss) = 0.5.

5. Joint occurrences or conjunction: When calculating the probability of a complex event which may include many component events as parts, calculation of probability of the complex event will require taking into consideration the probabilities of the component events. For example, calculation of a nation reaching a goal of self sufficiency on its 25th anniversary of independence will require consideration and calculation of the component events such as the nation not losing its independence, not suffering from natural catastrophes, a controlled population growth, etc.

When we are considering the probability of occurrence of more than one event, as in the example above, we may find the occurrence of the events being linked to each other, or alternatively as unconnected. Let us suppose that we are trying to determine the probability of two events, p and q. When we ask the probability of both p *and* q occurring, we are asking about the probability of their **joint occurrence**. For example, you might be wondering about the probability of it raining in Mumbai and the probability of traffic jam in that city. Or, you might be considering the probability of class being cancelled today, and the probability of geese flying over your hostel on the same day. In both cases you are asking for a probability of their conjunction. Probability of **conjunction** may be approached in two different ways, as explained now.

When considering joint occurrences, it is pertinent to further ask whether the occurrences of two events are dependent on each other, or independent. Two occurrences of events are **independent** if the occurrence or non-occurrence of any of them has no effect on the occurrence of the other. The probability of one does not get affected by the probability of the other. In terms of probability calculus, we can express independence as follows:

$$P\,(p) \text{ is independent of } P\,(q) \textit{ iff } P\,(p/q) = P\,(p)$$

For example, if two coins are tossed, the probability of the coin landing on heads on the second toss will not be affected by the probability of the coin landing on heads on the first toss. These are independent.

But, there can be **joint occurrence of independent events**. For example, what is the probability of class being cancelled and of geese flying over your hostel today? The events, under normal circumstances, are presumed to be independent. In that case, the probability of their joint occurrence is the *product of their individual probabilities*. This is known as the **product theorem for independent events**. It may be stated in general terms as follows:

$$P\,(p \text{ and } q) = P(p) \times P\,(q)$$

Where p and q are independent events, the probability of their joint occurrence will be the product of their individual probabilities. For example, if the probability of today being Friday is 1/7, and the probability of geese flying over your hostel or dormitory today is presumed to be 1/10, then the probability of today being both a Friday and a day when geese fly over your hostel will be $1/7 \times 1/10 = 1/70$.

The product theorem may be generalized to cover the joint occurrence of *any* number of independent events. If you are considering four independent events, p, q, r and s and their joint occurrence, for example, the formula will be equally applicable. The probability of their joint occurrence will be:

$$P\,(p \text{ and } q \textit{ and } r \textit{ and } s) = P(p) \times P(q) \times P(r) \times P(s)$$

However, not all events are independent. So, while considering joint occurrences, it is important to also talk abut **joint occurrences of dependent events**. Suppose we wish to find out the probability of a traffic jam in Mumbai given that it is a rainy day there. The two events are seen as related, and the search for the probability of their joint occurrence is also through this dependent relation.

The **product theorem for dependent events** is

$$P\,(p \text{ and } q) = P(p) \times P(p/q) \quad \text{[read } (q/p) \text{ as } q \textit{ if } p]$$

For example, let us consider what the probability, of a six-sided die showing an even number and a 6, will be. Suppose that the probability of any given side being shown on any given throw of a six-sided die is 1/6. So, P (this throw shows a 6) = 1/6. The probability of this throw showing as even (as 2, 4 or 6) is 1/2. So, P (this throw shows even) = 1/2. Then,

P (this throw shows even *and* this throw shows a 6)

$= 1/2 \times (1/6 / 1/2) = 1/2 \times 1/3 = 1/6.$

Similarly, if you know P (raining in Mumbai) = 1/3, and the P (Traffic jam in Mumbai) = 1/2, then P (raining in Mumbai *and* traffic jam in Mumbai) $= 1/3 \times (1/2 / 1/3) = 1/2.$

6. Alternate occurrences or disjunction: Where p and q are two events, if you are searching for the probability of their alternative occurrence, then you are searching for the probability of either p occurring or q occurring. From our previous discussion on disjunctions, we know that 'either-or' may be understood in two different ways. It may be understood as **exclusive disjunction** (where occurrences of two events are mutually exclusive) or as **inclusive disjunction** (where occurrences of two events are not mutually exclusive).

Where p and q are two mutually exclusive events, P (p or q) is understood to hold in the sense of exclusive disjunction. The general formula for computing the probability of alternative occurrence of two mutually exclusive events is to *simply add their individual probabilities*. This is known as the **addition theorem for mutually exclusive events**. It may be expressed as

$$P(p \text{ or } q) = P(p) + P(q)$$

For example, P (heads on this toss) is 0.5, and P (tails on this toss) is 0.5, and there cannot be both heads and tails on a single toss. That is, these are mutually exclusive events. They can only occur alternatively in a mutually exclusive way. So, according to the above formula, P (heads on this toss or tails on this toss) $= 0.5 + 0.5 = 1$.

In case the alternative occurrences are **not mutually exclusive**, i.e., are **inclusive disjunctions**, the above addition theorem cannot be applied directly. It can, however, be determined in any of the two following ways:

a. Analyze the favourable cases as mutually exclusive cases and then apply to them the addition theorem.
b. Or, determine the probability of none of the events occurring, and then obtain the probability of their alternative occurrence by using the Negation formula to subtract the probability value from 1.

Addition Rule

The addition rule is a result used to determine the probability that event A or event B occurs or both occur. The result is often written as follows, using the set notation:

$$P(A \cup B) = P(A) + P(B) - P(A \cap B)$$

where

$P(A) =$ probability that event A occurs

$P(B) =$ probability that event B occurs

$P(A \cup B) =$ probability that event A or event B occurs

$P(A \cap B) =$ probability that event A and event B both occur

Sometimes, the application of probability calculus may lead to a result that is counterintuitive or even paradoxical because of unknown factors that may show up in real life. Other times it could be a fault of judging the probability mistakenly. Yet other times a combination of several factors may lead to a paradox and may require serious solutions. Consider, for example, the following paradox.

The Lottery Paradox[1]

Suppose that in a fair lottery, one ticket has been drawn from a pool of 1000 tickets. Then for each ticket, the probability that that ticket will win is 1 in 1000. Let us suppose that the tickets are numbered in a series as T_1, T_2, T_3,.... up to T_{1000}. Now, $P(T_1) = 1/1000$ or 0.001. Note that the same is true for each of the other tickets from T_2 to T_{1000}. It follows from the probability calculus that the probability of T_1 *not* winning is $1 - 0.001 = 0.999$. In other words, $P(\text{not} - T_1) = 0.999$. Again, note that the same will hold for T_2 to T_{1000}.

How justified are we in believing that T_1 will *not* win? A probability of 0.999 or 999 out of 1000 seems a high probability sufficient for justification. If we agree on that, in that case, the belief that T_1 will *not* win is a justified belief. But since T_2 will *not* win also has exactly the same probability 0.999, it too is a justified belief. And so is the belief that not – T_3, not T_4, ... not T_{1000}.

If we accept further that if one is justified in believing all the conjuncts of a conjunction, then one is justified in believing the conjunction itself, then a problem shows up. It amounts to saying that none of the tickets in this lottery is likely to win. But that cannot be the case! Since every ticket in a lottery cannot be a loser, $P(\text{not } T_1 \text{ and not } T_2 \text{ and } \ldots \text{ and not } T_{1000})$ must be 0, which is impossible. So, even if we follow the probability calculus and believe in each statement separately, the probability of their conjunction turns out to be completely counterintuitive!

Various solutions have been suggested to evade the paradox. For example, Kyberg suggested that it is the result of a faulty conjunction principle. One could reject the principle that justified belief in each conjunct of a conjunction implies a justified belief in the conjunction. Just because one is justified in believing in p and in q, that does not imply one is justified in believing in p and q.

The lottery paradox does, however, raise a question about the connection of probability with justification for a belief. Justification for holding a belief is the subject matter of Epistemology, which is a special branch of philosophy. Lehrer[2], a renowned epistemologist, proposed to solve the paradox by rejecting one of its key suppositions that high probability of a belief is sufficient for its justification. Lehrer maintains that the only thing that can serve as evidence to support the acceptance that p is the other things that one accepts. In the lottery case, the various results of the draw have been

[1] Developed first in Kyburg, H. (1961) 'Conjunctivitis'. *Probability and the Logic of Rational Belief*, Middletown, Conn.: Wesleyan University Press. A similar structure may be seen in the Preface Paradox, Makinson, D.C. (1965) 'The Paradox of the Preface', *Analysis* 25: 205–7.

[2] Lehrer, K. (2000). *Theory of Knowledge*, 2nd ed., Westview Press, Boulder, Colorado.

considered as independent, each belief that a certain ticket will not win was assigned a high value of 0.999 but was claimed as a justifiable belief. But actually justifiability cannot be computed merely on the basis of probabilities, but also on what other information or belief one may have. The assumption that one of the tickets will not win affects the probability of another not winning. It diminishes the probability that another will not win. We need to see the beliefs as being related and accordingly compute their probability as dependent events. For example, P (T_1 will not win/T_2 will not win) = 998/999, which is less than 999/1000. The information that not T_2 is (negatively) relevant to the information that not T_1.

16.3 Bayes' Theorem

Bayes's Theorem gains its name from the posthumously published masterwork of Thomas Bayes, *An Essay Toward Solving a Problem in the Doctrine of Chances* (1764). *Bayes' theorem* is a mathematical formula that is used mostly for determining conditional probabilities. It features very importantly in Subjective Theory of Probability as applied in statistics, epistemology, or in inductive logic.

We seem to have various degrees of confidence in different statements. There are certain things about which we feel absolutely confident, e.g. that if it is 5 p.m. now, then in two hours it will be 7 p.m. But, we are not that confident about other statements: that the candidate I have voted for will win, or the lottery ticket she has purchased will win. These varying degrees of confidences or of subjective beliefs are known as subjective probabilities. Bayes' theorem assumes that for a rational person, we can determine the subjective probabilities quantitatively.

Bayes' Theorem states:

$$\mathrm{P}\,(H/I) = \mathrm{P}\,(I/H)$$

where H is a hypothesis and I is pertinent information. In words, it means that the probability of the hypothesis H *given* a body of information I is the *inverse probability* of the body of the information I given the hypothesis H.

Another form of Bayes' theorem is

$$\mathrm{P}\,(H/I) = \frac{\mathrm{P}\,(H) \times \mathrm{P}\,(I/H)}{[\mathrm{P}\,(H) \times \mathrm{P}\,(I/H) + [\mathrm{P}\,(\sim H) \times \mathrm{P}\,(I/\sim H)]}$$

In this form, Bayes' theorem is particularly useful for inferring causes from their effects since it is often fairly easy to discern the probability of an effect given the presence or absence of a putative cause.

The second form of Bayes' theorem may be understood using the example of a medical diagnosis. Suppose, as a medical doctor, you think that a woman W has TB. Your hypothesis or H is: W has TB. Your H is conditional upon a body of information I, that a certain diagnostic procedure says that W has TB. But you also know that the diagnostic procedure sometimes gives a 'false positive report', i.e. it incorrectly diagnoses someone having TB when the person does not have it. This is called a 'false positive report'. But most of the time it correctly identifies the disease. Now, given that this diagnostic procedure states that W has TB, what is the probability of your hypothesis H, that W has TB? You can determine that using Bayes' theorem as follows.

Suppose that: The unconditional probability of your H, that a woman of W's age in a certain population has TB, is 0.0002 or 1 in every 5000. $P(H) = 0.002$. So, $\boldsymbol{P(\sim H) = 1 - 0.0002}$

Your information (I) is that a diagnostic procedure has stated that W has the disease.

Let us suppose that in a certain population the diagnostic procedure correctly identifies 90 per cent women having TB. Then, $\mathbf{P(I/H) = 0.9}$.

Let us further suppose that the probability of the diagnostic procedure giving false positive report, or incorrectly identifying TB in women who do not have it, is 0.0005 per cent or 5 in every 1000. So,

$$\mathbf{P(I/\sim H) = 0.0005}.$$

Our task is: to find $P(H/I)$, or the probability of a woman such as W has TB given that the test says she does.

Bayes' theorem says:

$$P(H/I) = \frac{P(H) \times P(I/H)}{[P(H) \times P(I/H) + [P(\sim H) \times P(I/\sim H)]}$$

From the above, we know that:

$$P(H) \times P(I/H) \text{ is} : 0.0002 \times 0.9 = \mathbf{0.00018}$$

We also know that:

$$\mathbf{P}(\sim H) = 1 - 0.0002 \quad \text{and} \quad P(I/\sim H) = 0.0005$$

Therefore,

$$\mathbf{P}(\sim H) \times \mathbf{P}(I/\sim H) = (1 - 0.0002) \times 0.0005$$

and

$$\mathbf{P}(H) \times \mathbf{P}(I/H) + [\mathbf{P}(\sim H) \times \mathbf{P}(I/\sim H)]$$

$$= 0.00018 + (1 - 0.0002) \times 0.0005 = \mathbf{0.005179}$$

Putting it all together, we get

$$\mathbf{P}(H/I) = \frac{0.00018}{0.005179} = 0.0348 \text{ or less than } 4\%$$

This shows that less than 4 per cent women who have been diagnosed with TB in that population actually have TB! Therefore, you may conclude that from that diagnostic procedure, though you had confirmation for your hypothesis *H*, the conditional probability is low that *W* actually has TB!

We shall not go into further details about Bayes' theorem in this text. The theorem has been used in various forms and in various contexts. Those who are interested to know more about it and its applications may consult the books cited at the end of this section.

In Chapter 17, we shall look into the hypothesis formation in theories of science and the role of inductive logic in it.

EXERCISE 16.3

*1. If a six-faced die is rolled once, what is the probability of rolling an even number?

2. If a six-faced die is rolled once, what is the probability of rolling a 4?

3. What is the probability of rolling *at least* 3?

*4. What is the probability of getting heads every time in two tosses of a coin?

5. What is the probability of getting a total of ≤ 8 when two six-faced dice are rolled and the first one already shows a 5?

6. Four children put their own name on a piece of paper and each puts the paper inside an envelope. Now there are four envelopes inside, each of which there is a piece of paper with a name. At the end, each child is asked to pick up the envelope with his or her name on it and no one is allowed to pick up more than one envelope. What is the probability of each child picking up the envelope with his or her own name?

7. If you are trying to get a candy or lozenge from a box which contains 3 red candies, 5 orange candies and 4 green candies, what is the probability that you get a red candy?

8. What is the probability of getting head at least once in two tosses of a coin?

*9. What is the probability of drawing either a king or a Hearts card in a single draw from a pack of 52 cards?

Further Reading on Bayes' Theorem

Earman, J. (1992). *Bayes or Bust?* Cambridge, Mass., MIT Press.

Edwards, A.W.F. (1972). *Likelihood.* Cambridge: Cambridge University Press.

Glymour, Clark. (1980). *Theory and Evidence*. Princeton: Princeton University Press.

Hacking, Ian. (1965). *Logic of Statistical Inference*. Cambridge: Cambridge University Press.

Hartigan, J.A. (1983). *Bayes Theory*. New York: Springer-Verlag.

Kaplan, M. (1996). *Decision Theory as Philosophy*. Cambridge: Cambridge University Press.

CHAPTER 17

SCIENCE, HYPOTHESIS, AND INDUCTION

17.1 Scientific Hypothesis

A **hypothesis** is commonly understood as a *tentative explanation for an observed fact or a phenomenon, or a scientific proposal that can be tested by further investigation*. It may be also understood as something *taken to be true for the purpose of argument* or investigation. In this sense, a hypothesis is an assumption. For example, when in 1865, Gregor Mendel observed the garden peas and their pattern of inherited traits, he formed a number of hypotheses, such as:

1. In the organism there are two factors which determine the appearance of a characteristic.
2. The organism inherits these factors from its parents, one each from each parent.
3. Each is transmitted from generation to generation as a constant, unchanging unit.

Or, Copernicus formed the following hypothesis: The Earth revolves around the Sun. This was against the conventional wisdom of his time, that the Earth is stationary and the Sun revolves around the Earth. Or, a geologist may make a hypothesis about the age of a certain strata of earth: that it is 24 million years old.

In science, a hypothesis is worthy of acceptance or credibility only if there is enough evidence for it. The truth or falsity of a scientific hypothesis is not to be dogmatically or uncritically settled. Further and further investigations are supposed to uncover more and more evidence either in favour of it, or against it. On the basis of the evidence obtained, both the evidence for and against the hypothesis are weighed to evaluate and decide whether it is acceptable. Until confirmed by repeatedly done independent experiments, a hypothesis is never considered as a possible scientific theory. For instance, between 1856 and 1863, Mendel was known to cultivate and test some 28,000 pea plants which brought forth two theories of how character traits are inherited. However, it was only in the early 20th century that his ideas were truly accepted as a theory of heredity with enormous implications for genetic research in the subsequent days.

A scientific hypothesis must have at least two features:

- It must be testable.
- It must be falsifiable.

Testability

A remarkable characteristic of a scientific hypothesis is that it is **testable.** To say that a hypothesis is testable is to accept the possibility that a prediction made on the basis of the hypothesis will confirm or refute it. We also have to accept the possibility that the results will remain consistently the same no matter who or where the testing takes place. Science proceeds by making observations on nature. If a hypothesis does not generate any observational test, then it is **untestable**. An untestable hypothesis is not scientific. For example, if *x* proposes that a process *P* can turn any stone into gold, but also claims that *P* can work only if *x* alone does it, then by usual criterion it is a non-testable, and hence non-scientific hypothesis. Similarly, one might form a hypothesis that our world is surrounded by unobservable creatures with whom we cannot ever have contact. This hypothesis may be true or false. But it is entirely untestable, as there are no observations that a scientist can make to tell whether or not this hypothesis is correct.

Falsifiability

Testability alone does not make a hypothesis scientific. It must also be **falsifiable.** In this context, it is important to understand what exactly an observation or a prediction does to a hypothesis in terms of confirmation or non-confirmation. It may seem apparent that the more positive or supportive instance we find in favour of a hypothesis, the more confirmed it will be. For example, one may think that the more black crows that we see, the more confirmed the hypothesis “All crows are black” becomes. But actually that is not the case.

We have to remember that since future is uncertain and *all* possible evidence for a hypothesis can never be completely accumulated the absolute confirmation of a hypothesis can never perhaps be truly attained. Even when the supporting evidence for it is very strong, the possibility always remains that in the future something may question it. Even though you may have seen thousands of black crows, the element of doubt remains. All it will take is the sighting of one non-black crow, and you cannot rule out the possibility that next time you will not see one. Thus, establishing the absolute confirmation of a hypothesis is never certain. In addition, there may be errors in the empirical testing process itself. On the other hand, a counter-instance or counter-evidence to the hypothesis, if well-examined, may falsify the hypothesis indisputably. It is relatively easier to establish that a hypothesis has been falsified. Falsifiability is important because a falsified hypothesis provides greater advance in understanding than does a hypothesis that is supported. For this reason, **Karl Popper** maintained that the authentic characteristic of a scientific hypothesis is not mere testability, but its **falsifiability**. According to Popper, a truly scientific hypothesis should be falsifiable in the sense of being able to generate predictions that are not merely confirmable but can identify situations which would unequivocally falsify them.

A *hypothesis* is a limited statement or an explanation which is relative to specific situations. For example, when you find that your pen does not write, you may say that your first hypothesis is that the ink or the refill is finished.

In scientific contexts, the term **model** is reserved for hypotheses which have been known to have at least limited validity. For example, in Physics the 'Bohr model of the atom' is well known, in which, using an analogy to the solar system, the electrons are described as moving in circular orbits around the nucleus. This is not an accurate depiction of what an atom "looks like," but the model succeeds in a limited sense. Or, from Newton up to recent time, a 'mechanistic model' used to be the paradigm for explaining physical phenomena.

A **scientific theory**, on the other hand, is a hypothesis or a group of related hypotheses, which has gained credibility through repeated experimental tests. In Physics, these theories often acquire the status of a law, as in 'laws of nature'. Accepted scientific theories and laws shape and mould our understanding of the universe and serve as the basis or exploring less well-understood areas of knowledge. Theories are not easily discarded; new discoveries are first assumed to fit into the existing theoretical framework. It is only when, after repeated experimental tests, the new phenomenon cannot be accommodated that scientists seriously question the theory and attempt to modify it.

17.2 Testing of a Hypothesis

In the case of scientific prediction, a prediction need not be an event in future as in an astrological prediction. It may be an event or a response or a reaction to an action that is happening right now. Thus, if you have taken enough precaution to make your hypothesis falsifiable, then in an experiment you can predict:

If the hypothesis is true, then
(a) ________ should happen
(b) when conditions … are manipulated

This prediction plays a key role in formulating a test of the hypothesis. The blank space in (a) names the expected response or reaction or the **dependent variable.** The blank in (b) is the **independent variable** that you manipulate in a controlled set-up. For example, you may claim that in your experiment if your hypothesis, medicine *A* controls disease *D*, is true, then the mortality rate of the control group of mice would decrease if the mice are given nutrients *N*. A prediction of this kind gives indications of what would make your hypothesis false. This indication of the possibility of being false is the falsifiability condition. The people interested in your research would watch out for the mortality rate of a particular group of mice and check whether it is decreasing. If what you have predicted to happen does not happen, then we have some evidence that shows that your hypothesis may be rejected. Note that if what you predicted does happen, then all you know is that you have not been able to reject your hypothesis. It does not get confirmed, but remains falsifiable.

As an example, consider the hypothesis that 1 kg of feather and 1 kg of iron will reach the ground at the same time when dropped from the same height if there is no air resistance. This is a scientific hypothesis as it is testable and falsifiable: Testable because in a vacuum chamber (for guaranteeing the elimination of air resistance) we can try dropping them. Falsifiable because it will be falsified if someone shows that these two objects did not reach ground at the same time and the difference was not due to air resistance.

Falsifiability is one of the reasons why in Statistics testing of a hypothesis focuses on a **Null hypothesis** or H_0. The Null hypothesis is often the testable prediction which is the *exact opposite* of what you actually wish to find out. The **Alternative hypothesis**, or H_1, is the testable prediction that you actually want to find out. The Null hypothesis is contrasted with the Alternative hypothesis to see which one is more supported by the statistical evidence found. It is a **rival hypothesis** purposely kept in the study for fair comparison. One tries to reject that rival or opposite hypothesis rather than directly seeking for confirmation of one's own hypothesis. For example, if you are trying to hold a clinical test on a new medicine, your Null hypothesis will be:

H_0: This new medicine is no better than on average from the old medicine.

The Alternative hypothesis will be:

H_1: This new medicine on the average is better than the old medicine.

In statistics, the testing of a hypothesis is seen as a matter of conditional probability. You want to find out what the probability of your results or data are *given that* the Null hypothesis is true. The objective is to find sufficient evidence to reject the Null hypothesis and to proceed towards establishment of your Alternative hypothesis. All statistical test is done on the Null hypothesis, and never on the Alternative hypothesis. Your statistical data will either enable you to reject the Null hypothesis or will fail to enable you to reject the Null hypothesis. Even when you have failed to reject the Null hypothesis, it does not mean that you have found it to be true. It only indicates that the Null hypothesis *may be true*. In social sciences, statistical testing of a hypothesis has become the norm.

In non-statistical contexts, a hypothesis is usually tested many, many times to see whether the results are consistently reproducible. Research is peer-reviewed and is usually retested by other scientists. In Chapter 15, we mentioned about the recent controversy about cold fusion. In 1989, Stanley Pons and Martin Fleischmann of University of Utah announced their discovery of cold fusion: the fusion of atoms at normal temperatures. This claim was later rejected on the ground that scientists from a MIT Lab (MIT Plasma Fusion Center) could not replicate all the results in the experiment that Pons and Fleischman had claimed to have discovered.

Testing of a hypothesis may be **direct** or **indirect**. To determine directly whether it is cold outside, one can always go outside and check. To tell whether the vehicle in front of my car will turn left or right at the next intersection, I need to only keep looking at it. Or, a new physical particle may be 'observed' under special circumstance.

But in most cases, the hypotheses are not directly testable. For example, it is not possible in the same sense to directly test the hypothesis, that extra-terrestrial creatures came to earth in the ancient times and changed the course of history of humankind. Or, for example, Avogadro's hypothesis that equal volumes of gases, at the same temperature and pressure, contain equal numbers of molecules, is not directly testable either. Or, suppose you have formed the hypothesis that the rate of radioactive decay process requires the existence of a new particle.

Indirect testing involves two components: (a) Some directly testable statements need to be deduced from the proposed hypothesis, and (b) then these conclusions are directly tested. If they are found true, they indirectly provide some support for the original hypothesis. If they are found false, then they show that the original hypothesis is false. Thus, the reasoning follows the *Modus Tollens* structure: If the hypothesis is correct, then B, C, D (all directly testable) will be the case. B, C, D, are not the case; so, the original hypothesis too cannot be the case.

But indirect testing is not conclusive in nature. The deduction from the original hypothesis may require the support of auxiliary on additional premises. Defects or faults in these additional premises may show up in the deduction of the conclusions and affect their truth. For example, an indirect testing of a hypothesis that a certain death was caused by a predator animal such as a tiger, may lead to the formation of a directly testable claim deduced from this hypothesis: if there were such an animal, then there would have been footprints. Suppose that no footprints are found. Does this show that the original hypothesis is false? The deduced conclusion seemed to rely on certain assumptions which may not be appropriate. For example, it assumes that the floor is suitable for identification of footprints, but perhaps it is not; or may be the prints have been destroyed by rain or erased by something else. There should have been footprints, but their absence does not really show the falsity of the said hypothesis. Thus, indirect testing always leaves room for doubt.

Only after a hypothesis has been tested, it may, then be accepted, or rejected, or modified.

17.3 The Scientific Method

From the observation of the actually conducted scientific researches, it is possible to formulate an idea of steps in a scientific method. A *scientific method* is a method or a process by which scientists, collectively or individually, try to understand and represent a reliable, consistent and non-arbitrary view of a phenomenon in the world. Hypothesis formation and its gradual testing occupy very important roles in this method.

The scientific method is basically supposed to have the following steps:

Observation and identification of a problem: A good scientist is also a good observer. She has to see, hear, smell, and in other ways notice things around her. She can also come to notice things by reading or studying about them. Newton, for example, already knew about the works of Copernicus, Galileo and Kepler, before he came up with his new observations on the Theory of Motions.

Observation can reveal a puzzling event, or a phenomenon, or a 'problem' for which a satisfactory or adequate explanation is required. For example, the scientist may observe that in a certain region of a country, the number of Thalassemia patients is significantly high. Or, she may observe that the stars seem to twinkle more when seen from a lakeside. Identification of a problem based on empirical observation is the crucial first step in the scientific method.

However, observation alone does not guarantee that a 'problem' will be detected. Many must have observed green peas plants before and after

Mendel. But to Mendel alone, the 'problem' of explaining inherited attributes 'appeared'. Thus, recognition of a 'problem' as a problem is the first step in any scientific investigation.

Formulation of a hypothesis: With the observation and identification of a 'problem' comes the responsibility of proposing an explanation for it. Usually, the scientific investigator forms some preliminary idea about what could be its explanation. An assumption is floated as a *tentative explanation.* This is known as the **formation of a hypothesis.**

It is very rare to come up with a complete and accurate explanation of a 'problem' at the first attempt. Usually, some **preliminary hypotheses** are formed. For example, the Thalassemia investigator may form the rudimentary idea that in a particular region the high incidence of Thalassemia may be connected to the fact of marriages only within a certain community, in that region. For formation of preliminary hypotheses, some previous knowledge or prior beliefs are required. A hypothesis cannot be formed out of nothing.

However, it is entirely possible to be completely wrong while forming a preliminary hypothesis. For example, for centuries, ordinary people have tried to make sense of how frogs can appear out of nowhere in the mud of the river. In ancient times, people of Egypt noted that every spring the flooded river Nile not only gives rise to crops but also to frogs where there were none in the drier times! In many parts of Europe, people noted that mice appear in locked cabinets! For centuries this led people to believe that there can be *spontaneous generation* of living organisms: living organisms can be generated from non-living objects. The recipe of Jan Baptista van Helmont (1577–1644) for mice was to put some clothes with a few kernels of grains in a pot or a barrel and within 21 days mice would appear in that container!

Errors such as these emphasize the need for further investigations and further testing of preliminary hypotheses. Since it is possible to be wrong particularly at the preliminary stage of the investigation, forming a plausible hypothesis is an important step in scientific investigation.

In Section 17.2, while discussing about testing of a hypothesis, we have already mentioned the following factors:

(a) *Further investigation to collect more facts.* This usually is a time-consuming process of **repeated observation**. Sometimes it requires an increase in the population size observed. Mendel, as mentioned earlier, is known to have observed 28,000 pea plants for seven years. Sometimes, it may require **experiments**: observation under controlled situation. Note that experiments cannot be conducted without some preliminary hypothesis in mind.

(b) *Formation of more and more refined hypotheses.* Testability and falsifiability may be used as determinants for how to improve on the formation of the hypothesis. Louis Pasteur disproved the hypothesis of spontaneous generation of microbes from air by showing that in special, boiled flasks, microbes do not appear. His claim was that the microbes come from the cells of organisms on dust particles in the air, but not from the air. Rejection of unuseable ideas, or repudiated thoughts, and constant modifications of the hypothesis are important factors at this stage.

(c) *Formation of an explanatory hypothesis.* Through this process, the scientist finally arrives at a formed hypothesis which, on the whole, appears to him to make sense as the explanation of the 'problem' at hand. There is no rule of thumb on how to reach this stage. However, for some, the coherence of the proposed explanatory hypothesis with other known theories seem to be a decisive factor. For others, there may be other reasons.

Prediction of consequence: A well-formed hypothesis will not explain certain range of facts but also may point to new facts beyond the problem at hand. These new facts are further consequences that can be 'deduced' from the truth of the hypothesis. The consequences, if they hold true, in a way provide some support for the hypothesis, and can also cast doubt on it if they do not hold true.

Christian Doppler (1803–1853) proposed that the perceived change of frequency in light and sound waves was due to the relative motion of the source and the observer. If that is the case, then sound from a moving object would sound different to a stationary observer. That was a testable prediction from a hypothesis.

Albert Einstein made the famous prediction that if the theory of relativity is true, then massive bodies can cause space-time to curve and starlight would bend under gravity. Guglielmo Marconi's hypothesis was that radio signals can travel between two points even when there is a physical obstacle in between them. He used the prediction that his servant will be able to receive the radio signal sent from a distance of 3 kilometres with a hill in between.

Conducting experiments to verify prediction: In every experimental science, experiment is regarded as the supreme factor and experimental verification of hypothetical predictions is considered absolutely necessary.

For example, Christian Doppler in 1845 arranged to have trumpets played from a moving train. As predicted, the pitch heard from the stationary position on the ground sounded higher than what was played. The effect came to be known as the *Doppler effect.*

Arthur Eddington led an expedition to the island of Principe to observe a total solar eclipse. His observations of stars near the Sun at that time (not ordinarily visible because they were too close to the Sun) of solar eclipse lent support to Einstein's conclusion from general theory of relativity that light rays would bend when subjected to a strong gravitational field.

Marconi's servant was able to fire his rifle after receiving the radio signal from a distance of 3 km with a hill in between.

History of science shows that experimental evidence sometimes has been instrumental for discarding accepted scientific theories. We all know that in the field of astronomy, the earth-centred theory of the planetary orbits, which has been held as the truth for centuries, was overthrown by the Copernican hypothesis, in which the Sun was placed at the centre of a series of concentric, circular planetary orbits. Later, however, even this hypothesis was modified. For, measurements of the planetary motions were found to be compatible with the notion of orbits being of elliptical shape, not circular. Subsequently, it has been further revised with more new observations.

In Biology, Pasteur's experiments helped reject the *spontaneous generation* hypothesis which was held for ages. Galileo Galilei's experiment with rolling balls helped to disprove the Aristotelian theory of motion, in which motion was conceived on the idea of a non-moving Earth.

So, the role of experiments in deciding the worth of a scientific hypothesis cannot be questioned. But, at the same time, we must also remember that, though experiments are crucial in the scientific method, they are not completely error-free. Therefore, the evidence that they offer also are not always beyond all doubt.

This ends our discussion of the steps that are supposed to be in a scientific method. In the remaining part, I shall briefly mention how experiments may suffer from errors and how to avoid the errors.

Random errors in experiments: Errors in experiments may appear from several sources. First, instruments of measurement may be responsible for some errors. Any measurement device is prone to error. You may have observed that even simple weighing scales can show errors. Three different measurements, closely succeeding each other in time, on the same scale under essentially the same conditions may show different weights! If simple measuring devices such as a weighing scale is subject to error, it is understandable how measurements from complex devices used in a scientific research laboratory may be subject to errors of imprecision and inaccuracy. The imprecision inherent in measuring instruments is the source of such errors. This type of error has the equal probability of producing a measurement numerically higher or lower than the 'true' value. If the items you have brought to weigh shows 1 kilo 200 gms as the weight on an imprecise weighing scale, chances are equal that the actual weight of the items could be either higher or lower. Thus, this kind of error is called **random error**.

Non-random errors in experiments: There is also non-random or systematic error, due to factors which bias the result in only one direction. A systematic shift may displace the mean of the distribution from its original value. In contrast to random errors that may be either negative or positive and whose direction cannot be predicted, systematic errors are in one direction and cause all the test results to be either high or low.

Total error is the net or combined effect of random and systematic errors on the results. A test result might be affected due to both random and systematic errors. Because laboratories typically only make a single measurement for each test, it is important to be aware of this possibility.

No measurement and, therefore, no experiment, can be perfectly precise. At the same time, in science there are standard ways of estimating and, in some cases, reducing these errors. We now give a list of different cautionary measures that are supposed to be routinely done to reduce the errors mentioned above in experiments..

(i) A **replication experiment** provides information about random error and is performed by making measurements on copies of same test samples within a specified period of time (usually within an analytical run) e.g. within a day, or over a period of a month. The aim is to provide a good estimate of the total imprecision.

(ii) An **interference experiment** gives information about the constant systematic error caused by the lack of specificity of the method.

(iii) A **recovery experiment** provides information about the proportional systematic error caused by a competitive reaction.

(iv) A **comparison of methods experiment** is primarily used to estimate the average systematic error observed with real samples, but can also reveal the constant or proportional nature of that error.

It is important to determine the accuracy of a particular measurement and, when stating quantitative results, **to quote the measurement error**. A measurement without a quoted error is meaningless. The comparison between experiment and theory is made within the context of experimental errors. Given the experimental evidence, the scientists ask: How far is the standard deviation in the results from the theoretical prediction? Have all sources of systematic and random errors been properly estimated?

In addition to these errors, there are subjective factors from the side of the experimenter or the scientist, which may vitiate the experiment. Some of these are:

(i) **Subjective bias:** When testing an hypothesis or a theory, the scientist may have a preference for one outcome or another, and it is important that this preference not to affect the results or their interpretation. The *most fundamental* error is to mistake the hypothesis for an explanation of a phenomenon without performing experimental tests. History shows that there have been many instances when scientists and ordinary people have committed this error.

(ii) **Selective attention to data:** A common mistake in experiment is to ignore or eliminate data which do not support the hypothesis. Ideally, the experimenter should be open-minded, i.e. she should be open to the possibility that the hypothesis may be correct or incorrect. Sometimes, however, a scientist may have a strong belief that the hypothesis is true (or false), or may be in a hurry due to internal or external pressure to get a specific result. In that case, there may be a psychological bias to find 'something wrong', such as systematic effects, with data which do not support the scientist's expectations, while data which do agree with those expectations may not be checked as carefully. The lesson is that all data must be handled in the same way.

The scientific method attempts to minimize the influence of the scientist's bias on the outcome of an experiment. One way to do this is have open discussions. In a field where there is active experimentation and open communication among members of the scientific community, the biases of individuals or groups may cancel out because experimental tests are repeated by different scientists who may have different biases. In addition, different types of experimental set-ups have different sources of systematic errors. Over a period spanning a variety of experimental tests (usually at least several years), a consensus develops in the community as to which experimental results have stood the test of time.

We shall end this discussion with a few observations. *First*, the 'scientific method' is thought to be exclusively associated with science. It is generally thought of as being used only by scientists and by no one else! That is not the case in reality. It simply reflects cautionary measures needed in the process of human inquiry that pervades our life on many different levels. If the light on your table does not work, how do you try to figure out its cause? What do you do when you know you must arrive at a distant place within a very short time for a crucial interview? The process that you go through to solve these 'little' problems could involve the essentials of the 'scientific method'. Of course, systematic experimentation separates science from many of our other activities. A lawyer in the court has to produce evidence and can offer only argument for it without any hope of replicating the evidence repeatedly, or by predicting a confirming or refuting consequence. However, the mind which works behind the method to find out the truth about things remains the same in all these activities. *Second*, we have described the method in phases as if it is an algorithm to follow, leading to scientific discovery. This description in terms of separate components of the method was done mainly to help your understanding of the method. Actually, it is a very complex process. While the method appears simple and logical in description, there is perhaps no more complex question than that of knowing how we come to know things.

17.4 Application of Inductive Probabilities for Evaluation of Scientific Hypothesis

From a formal inductive logic, it is expected that it should be applicable, among other things, to the confirmation or refutation of scientific hypotheses. It is expected that it should be able to show how to weigh the evidence for a hypothesis. If necessary, it should also be able to determine the right choice among two or more competing hypotheses. Thus, for inductive logic, application to scientific hypotheses is an important feature.

Consider the confirmation of a hypothesis H_2 as a matter of selecting from a set of mutually incompatible, preferably exhaustive, set of hypotheses or theories such as $\{H_1, H_2, H_3, ...\}$ on a certain subject in a specific field. For example, suppose that you are considering the origin of this universe and the set of alternatives are {The Big Bang hypothesis is right, The Big Bang hypothesis is not right}. Or, suppose that you are investigating why the dinosaurs became extinct, your set is {Lack of food hypothesis, Huge meteorite hypothesis, or severe weather change hypothesis}. Or, it could be a case of medical diagnosis {This patient has Cancer, this patient does not have Cancer.}

Supposing that there are finite number of alternatives to consider, for evidence of a hypothesis we look into the scientific experiment or observation. Let us call the description of this experiment or observation and its conditions *d*. Let the letter 'e' represent the evidential outcome of *d*. Scientific hypotheses assume certain background information or auxiliary hypotheses. Let us call these background factors *b*.

In probabilistic inductive logic, the evidential value of a hypothesis h_i will depend upon its **likelihood** under certain conditions. A likelihood may be understood as a support functional probability:

$$P[e/(h_i \times b \times c)].$$

It states how likely or probable *e* is to occur given the hypothesis h_i, and *b* and *c*. Likelihood that arises from clear statistical claims is often called **direct inference likelihoods**. They are supposed to be completely objective. Likelihoods such as these may be solved using the conditional probability as we have learnt while discussing simple probability calculus in Section 16.2. Or, it may be approached on the basis of Bayes' theorem which has been discussed in Section 16.3.

However, not all hypotheses are entirely statistical by nature. As Carnap explained, different types hypotheses require different evaluation criteria. A universal hypothesis such as "All swans are white" is best tested by seeking a single exception. In contrast, a **statistical law**, such as "Almost all swans are white" or "99 per cent of swans are white" requires a statistical test that compares observed frequencies to hypothesized frequencies. Theoretical and empirical hypotheses call for contrasting evaluation techniques and standards. For example, a hypothesis from theoretical physics may concern properties that are not directly measurable and that must be inferred indirectly, and it may be judged more on simplicity and scope than on accuracy of fit to observations.

In the case of selection of a hypothesis of a non-statistical nature among similar alternatives, a qualitative estimation of the evidential support of such a hypothesis is required. Given that evaluation of evidential support of a hypothesis cannot be absolutely objective, Kuhn[1] described *five factors* by which we can still judge a good scientific theory:

1. Accuracy
2. Simplicity
3. Consistency
4. Scope
5. Fruitfulness

In the remaining part of this section, we shall describe these criteria:

(i) Accuracy: Accuracy has a quantitative aspect. But it need not be restricted to only quantitative sciences. Biases of personal and social nature, systematic oversights can equally vitiate the explanatory ability and predictive power of a hypothesis in any field. Thus, they can compromise the probability of a hypothesis being correct.

(ii) Simplicity: William of Occam, a 14th-century English philosopher, developed a metaphysical principle **Occam's Razor** as a methodological tool of arriving at the truth of a matter: Entities are not to be multiplied beyond necessity. This is sometimes stated as: The simplest answer is the one most likely to be correct. It is also known as the **maxim of parsimony**.

Occam's Razor is an imperfect rule of thumb, but often it does select correctly among hypotheses that attempt to account for the same observations. Though the 'simplest answer' is not necessarily the one most easily comprehended, often it is the one with the fewest assumptions, or it is the most elegant idea. Ptolemy's hypothesis that the earth was at the centre of the universe and every other heavenly body was moving around it could explain many celestial observations. That is why it survived for so many centuries. But in order to explain it needed so many other auxiliary notions. For example, he supposed *deferents* were large circles centred on the Earth, and *epicycles* were small circles whose centres moved around the circumferences of the *deferents*. The Sun, Moon, and the planets moved around the circumference of their own *epicycles*. In the movable eccentric, there was one circle; this was centred on a point displaced from the Earth, with the planet moving around the circumference. Even with all these, Ptolemy could not fully account for all observed planetary phenomena. Therefore, he exhibited brilliant ingenuity by introducing still another concept. He supposed that the Earth was located a short distance from the centre of

[1]Kuhn, Thomas, 'Objectivity, Value Judgement, and Theory Choice', in *The Essential Tension. Selected Studies in Scientific Tradition and Change*. Chicago, University of Chicago Press: 1977.

the deferent for each planet and that the centre of the planet's deferent and the epicycle described uniform circular motion around what he called the *equant*, which was an imaginary point that he placed on the diameter of the *deferent* but at a position opposite to that of the Earth from the centre of the *deferent*, i.e., the centre of the deferent was between the Earth and the equant. Ptolemy further supposed that the distance from the Earth to the centre of the *deferent* was equal to the distance from the centre of the *deferent* to the *equant*. At the end, however, this entire intricate model was rejected because of the comparative simplicity of the Copernican hypothesis.

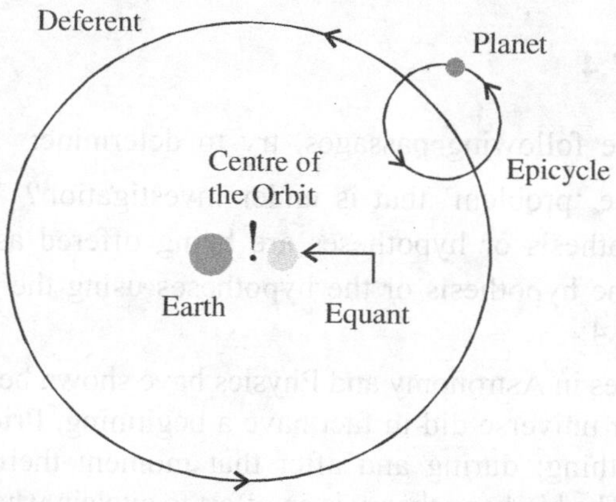

(iii) Consistency: The hypothesis should be consistent with relevant concepts that have already been accepted, or else it will face the formidable hurdle of either overthrowing the established wisdom or uneasily co-existing with incompatible hypotheses. Theories in science are not rejected readily or without controversies. For, usually a considerable data or evidence is accumulated in favour of a theory of over time. Often, new works are known to revisions or modifications on the past established theories.

However, there are notable exceptions too. Sometimes, new revolutionary ideas or hypotheses, inconsistent and incompatible with older theories, take the field by storm and simply replace them. The older Newtonian theory suffered the same fate in the hands of Einstein's Relativity Theory.

(iv) Scope: Comprehensive explanatory power of a hypothesis is another important criterion in its favour. A hypothesis, which only accounts for the observations that inspired it, has little value. In contrast, a hypothesis with a broad explanatory power inspires confidence through its ability to find order in formerly disparate types of observations. Also, a hypothesis with broad scope tends to be more amenable to diversified testing. Newton's Law of Gravitation, for example, could explain in one sweep, simple events such as an apple falling to the orbital motions of planets.

(v) Fruitfulness or **utility:** Kuhn [1977] says simply that "a theory should be fruitful of new research findings: It should, that is, disclose new phenomena or previously unnoted relationships among those already known." Most hypotheses seek to disclose previously unnoticed relationships. Yet some do not lead anywhere, sparking no further research except the confirmation or refutation of that specific conjecture. In contrast, a hypothesis is considered better if it adds value in terms of scientific progress. Hypotheses are valued also because of their exciting implications for a variety of new research directions or for its impact on the flow of science.

EXERCISE 17.4

1. In each of the following passages, try to determine:

a. What is the 'problem' that is under investigation?

b. What hypothesis or hypotheses are being offered as its explanation?

c. Evaluate the hypothesis or the hypotheses using the criteria discussed in Section 17.4:

*(i) Discoveries in Astronomy and Physics have shown beyond a reasonable doubt that our universe did in fact have a beginning. Prior to that moment there was nothing; during and after that moment there was something: our universe. The big bang theory is an effort to explain what happened during and after that moment. Our universe is thought to have begun as an infinitesimally small, infinitely hot, infinitely dense, something—a singularity. Where did it come from? We don't know. Why did it appear? We don't know. After its initial appearance, it apparently inflated (the "Big Bang"), expanded and cooled, going from very, very small and very, very hot, to the size and temperature of our current universe. It continues to expand and cool to this day and we are inside of it. This is the Big Bang theory.

What are the major evidences which support the Big Bang theory?

First, we are reasonably certain that the universe had a beginning.

Second, galaxies appear to be moving away from us at speeds proportional to their distance. This is called *Hubble's Law*, named after Edwin Hubble (1889–1953) who discovered this phenomenon in 1929. This observation supports the expansion of the universe and suggests that the universe was once compacted.

Third, if the universe was initially very, very hot as the Big Bang suggests, we should be able to find some remnant of this heat. In 1965, Radioastronomers Arno Penzias and Robert Wilson discovered a 2.725 degree Kelvin (–454.765 degree Fahrenheit, –270.425 degree Celsius) Cosmic Microwave Background Radiation (CMB) which pervades the observable universe. This is thought to be the remnant which scientists were looking for. Penzias and Wilson shared the 1978 Nobel Prize for Physics for their discovery.

Finally, the abundance of the "light elements" Hydrogen and Helium found in the observable universe is thought to support the Big Bang model of origins.

Is the standard Big Bang theory the only model consistent with these evidences? No, it's just the most popular one. Internationally renowned Astrophysicist, George F.R. Ellis explains:

> People need to be aware that there is a range of models that could explain the observations….For instance, I can construct you a spherically symmetrical universe with Earth at its centre, and you cannot disprove it based on observations….You can only exclude it on philosophical grounds. In my view there is absolutely nothing wrong in that. What I want to bring into the open is the fact that we are using philosophical criteria in choosing our models. A lot of cosmology tries to hide that.

In 2003, Physicist Robert Gentry proposed an attractive alternative to the standard theory, an alternative which also accounts for the evidences listed above. Dr. Gentry claims that the standard Big Bang model is founded upon a faulty paradigm (the Friedmann-Lemaitre expanding-space-time paradigm) which he claims is inconsistent with the empirical data. He chooses instead to base his model on Einstein's static-space-time paradigm which he claims is the "genuine cosmic Rosetta." Gentry has published several papers outlining what he considers to be serious flaws in the standard Big Bang model. Other high-profile dissenters include Nobel laureate Dr. Hannes Alfvén, Professor Geoffrey Burbidge, Dr. Halton Arp, and the renowned British astronomer Sir Fred Hoyle, who is accredited with first coining the term "the Big Bang" during a BBC radio broadcast in 1950.

(ii) The ice fields of Mount Kilimanjaro in Tanzania have given up remarkable new information about the African climate stretching back more than 11,000 years. Cores drilled into the glaciers high up on the peak support earlier evidence that there were three catastrophic droughts on the continent in the intervening period. Professor Lonnie Thompson, from Ohio State University, US, collected six cores from the mountain.

The ice columns were investigated for deposits trapped in the yearly snowfalls that built up the glaciers. By checking these markers against other historical records, Thompson and his colleagues were able to construct a climate 'history book'. The cores show much of the past 11,000 years to have been generally wetter and warmer than the present, but they also show evidence for three major droughts—8,300, 5,200 and 4,000 years ago—the last of which went on for 300 years.

The research, published in the journal *Science*, also reinforces predictions in 2003 that rising temperatures—if they persist—could clear the mountain's ice completely within two decades. By using global positioning from satellites, aerial maps and an array of stakes placed on the ice fields, the researchers have been able to confirm that Kilimanjaro's white cap is retreating in extent and volume. In February 2001, Professor Thompson said the rate of retreat could see the mountain completely ice free within 20 years. He said the latest work had not changed that assessment. This could cause difficulties for local people whose economies depend in part on the melt waters coming from the mountain and who also benefit from the influx of tourists drawn to the beauty of the white-capped tropical peak.

But Thompson's colleague Dr. Douglas Hardy, from the University of Massachusetts at Amherst, (US), cautioned against jumping to conclusions about global warming: "... Kilimanjaro's glaciers have little in common with mid-latitude Alpine glaciers, and we must accept that simple explanations are not always possible."

—BBC News World Edition, "Kilimanjaro ice 'archive'", *Science/ Nature*, Oct. 18, 2002.

(iii) Some scientists have proposed the idea that the 'great dying' at the boundary of the Permian and Triassic Periods 250 million years ago could have occurred quite abruptly—the result of environmental changes brought on by the impact of a giant space rock. The Permian-Triassic mass extinction killed off about 95% of all marine species and about three-quarters of all land families. It is a similar argument to the one put forward to explain the demise of the dinosaurs at the much later date of 65 million years ago.

But it is an argument that has struggled to find favour. The prevailing theory is that *several factors*—including supervolcanism and extensive climate warming—combined over thousands of years to strangle the planet's biodiversity.

A joint UK-Chinese team tells *Nature* magazine the disaster that befell the planet 250 million years ago must have happened in phases. Their conclusion is based on the abundance of 'organic fossils' found in rocks at Meishan in southern China. These suggest there were at least two episodes to the mass die-off that saw up to 95% of lifeforms disappear. "And this fits with a growing body of literature that now points to a complex sequence of changes on Earth," — Richard Pancost, from the University of Bristol, UK, told the BBC News website.

The new data from China is based on the traces left in rocks by cyanobacteria. These photosynthetic, mostly single-celled organisms existed in vast blooms in the Permian oceans. They are one of the major groups of phytoplankton, which form the basis of the marine food chain. However, the phytoplankton not eaten by higher organisms would have fallen to the seafloor over time to be incorporated into the sedimentary rocks we see today. And chemical components in their cell membranes have left tell-tale signs of their past existence.

Specifically, a lipid molecule, known as 2-methylhopane, has left ring structures in the Meishan rock. "These ring structures are the 'hydrocarbon skeleton'—that is how we would refer to them—and they can be preserved for a very long time," explained Dr. Pancost. The research team sees two peaks of abundance in the Chinese rocks which are believed to indicate periods immediately following biotic crises in the oceans—times when the collapse of higher marine lifeforms allowed the cyanobacteria populations to boom. "What we think happened was that the grazing pressure changed," explained Dr. Pancost. "A lot of the fauna that went extinct went through larval stages that would have fed on the phytoplankton. "Changes in the faunal assemblages would have changed predation patterns, and this led to the phytoplankton prospering."

—BBC News, UK Edition, "Great extinction came in Phases", April 1, 2005.

(iv) Why does the Earth have so much water in comparison to other planets? Earth has a lot of visible water—oceans cover 70 percent of its surface. But another 10 oceans' worth of water may be entombed deep inside it. How the water got here is a matter of debate. Some researchers suggested that comets or asteroids brought it to an initially dry Earth. This explanation has been largely ruled out since the geochemical signature of Earth's water doesn't match those of comets and asteroids. More likely, our planet is wet simply because it formed from water-covered materials. Computer simulations suggest that when Earth began forming from dust particles 4.5 billion years ago, it was surrounded by clouds of hydrogen and oxygen that could have reacted together and deposited layers of water onto the particles' surface. As bits of dust came together and formed into the early Earth, the water was trapped and eventually became incorporated into the planet's rocky interior. Some of that water may have eventually reached the surface through volcanoes. Earth is not the only world that formed wet. Venus too apparently had water but lost it. Mars may still have more water than Earth, locked up in its permafrost and ice caps. The giant planets, such as Jupiter, and their satellites also have lots of water. In the giant planets, it is in the vapour form; the interiors of their moons may consist largely of water ice.

(v) 65 million years ago the dinosaurs, suddenly became extinct, but before that they have ruled the earth for more than 200 million years. What caused their extinction? There has been some suggestion of an epidemic that took their lives. Meteorological studies have suggested that perhaps a sudden climate change was the cause. As a result of the frequent volcanic activity in the relatively newly formed earth, a thick cloud cover did not allow sunlight to warm up the air. The Earth suddenly became much colder and the creatures died because they could not cope with the change of climate. Others have suggested that a huge meteorite crashed onto Earth and caused havoc in weather and as a consequence the dinosaurs died. Yet another suggestion is that the mammals became competitors for food with dinosaurs. The dinosaurs with their large bodies could not sustain themselves.

Of these, two main suggestions are considered seriously: the volcanic theory and the meteorite theory. In the late 1970s, Luis and Walter Alvarez (father and son), along with a team of scientists from the University of California, were making a study of the rocks around the K-T boundary in Gubbio, Italy. In particular, they were looking at an unusual layer of clay at the boundary point which contained an unusual spike in the amounts of the rare element iridium. This spike revealed that the levels of iridium contained in the clay were roughly 30 times the normal levels. Iridium is an extremely rare element, so its discovery in 'large' amounts indicates that something serious happened. There are 2 sources of iridium, the main source comes from outer space in the form of cosmic dust which is constantly showering the planet. A second source is the Earth's core when there are eruptions of certain types of volcano. It is believed that the iridium, plus many other rare elements, were carried down and concentrated into the Earth's core while the Earth was still largely molten. During this time certain types of primitive chondritic meteorites were formed where no concentration could have taken place due to rapid cooling. This means that it is possible that within the primitive chondritic meteorites there could be reasonable levels of iridium. From this information it can be seen that there are only two possible theories to explain the increased presence of iridium in the clay layer—either an asteroid strike or a massive volcanic eruption.

Of the two more serious theories, perhaps the most well-supported theory is about the impact of a large asteroid type body. It is a well-known fact that throughout the history of the planet there have been many thousands of impacts, some large and some small. In 1990, a scientist called Alan Hildebrand was looking over some old geophysical data that had been recorded by a group of geophysicists searching for oil in the Yucatan region of Mexico. Within the data he found evidence of what could have been an impact site. What he 'found' was a ring structure 180 km in diameter which was called Chicxulub. The location of this structure was just off the northwest tip of the Yucatan Peninsula. The crater has been dated (using the 40Ar/39Ar method) as being 65 million years old. The size of the crater is comparable to that which would have been caused by an impacting body with a diameter of roughly 10 km. So we now have some proof of the asteroid theory. We know that a chondritic meteorite with a diameter of 10 km contains enough iridium to cause a spike. We also know that about 65 million years ago there was an impact of a large object. The big question is what were the results, and how did they effect the dinosaurs.

(vi) "Some five decades after *Principia Mathematica*, David Hume dreamt of a scientific psychology in which mathematical laws would govern the mental realm, just as Newton's laws governed the material realm. The universal force of gravitation, whereby bodies attract in proportion to their masses, would be replaced by a universal force of association, whereby ideas attract in proportion to their similarity. The dynamics of matter would be paralleled by a dynamics of mind.

Thomas Hobbes took this calculating activity itself as his model of the mechanisms of mental operation. Perhaps, thought is symbolic computation, the rule-governed manipulation of symbols inside the head. Seventeenth-century speculation became twentieth-century science. Hobbes's idea evolved into the *computational hypothesis* (CH) that cognitive agents are basically digital computers. Perhaps, the most famous rendition is Newell and Simon's (1976) doctrine that "A physical symbol system has the necessary and sufficient means for general intelligent action." They proposed this hypothesis as a "law of qualitative structure," comparable to the cell doctrine in Biology or plate tectonics in Geology. It expresses the central insight into the research paradigm which has dominated cognitive science for some 40 years.

In recent years, however, the Humean alternative has been gaining momentum. One of the most notable developments has been the rise of connectionism, which models cognition as the behaviour of dynamical systems and often understands those models from a dynamical perspective. Equally significant is the emergence of cognitive neuroscience, and within it, the increasing prevalence of dynamical theorising. Dynamics forms the general framework for growing amounts of work in psychophysics, perception, motor control, developmental psychology, cognitive psychology, situated robotics and autonomous agents research, artificial intelligence, and social psychology. It is central to a number of general approaches, such as ecological psychology, synergetics, and morphodynamics. The *dynamical hypothesis* (DH) is the unifying essence of dynamical approaches to cognition. It is encapsulated in the simple slogan, "cognitive agents are dynamical systems".

—Tim van Gelder, "The Dynamical Hypothesis in Cognitive Science".

(vii) A diet rich in certain antioxidants, such as vitamins C and E, may help prevent Alzheimer's disease, according to the results of two new studies. Scientists have known for some time that certain proteins accumulate in the brains of Alzheimer's patients, leading to nerve cell damage. Exactly what causes the toxic plaques to form has not been established, but researchers posit that the so-called free radicals—highly reactive, naturally occurring molecules that damage cellular structures—play a role. If so, it would stand to reason that antioxidants, which have the ability to bind and inactivate these destructive radicals, can combat the plaques. The new findings, published today in the *Journal of the American Medical Association,* may strengthen that case.

In the first study, Marianne Engelhart of the Erasmus Medical Center in Rotterdam, the Netherlands, and her colleagues observed more than 5,000 Dutch subjects aged 55 and older. The team recorded the dietary habits of the participants at the beginning of the study and repeatedly examined them for signs of dementia in the years that followed. Out of the original test group, 197 individuals developed Alzheimer's. Comparing the types of foods eaten by patients with and without the disorder, the investigators found that smokers who consistently dined on foods rich in vitamins C and E were less likely to fall victim to the disease than were smokers who did not have high-antioxidant diets. Nonsmokers did not exhibit this pattern. The team notes that smoking may itself increase the production of free radicals, and thus spur Alzheimer's progression. If so, antioxidants may help offset that additional risk by reducing the smoker's larger load of free radicals.

In the second study, Martha Morris of Rush-Presbyterian St. Luke's Medical Center in Chicago and her colleagues examined 815 of the city's residents, all aged 65 and older. They found that dietary vitamin E intake was associated with a reduced risk of developing Alzheimer's, but only in patients lacking the APOE E4 gene variant associated with the disease. Notably, for subjects in that subset who ranked in the top fifth of vitamin E intake, the risk of the disease was 67 per cent lower than that of participants in the bottom fifth. Neither team observed a positive effect from vitamin supplements.

"These two studies do not provide the final answer as to whether antioxidant vitamins are truly protective against [Alzheimer's]," Daniel J. Foley of the National Institute of Aging in Bethesda, Maryland, and Lon R. White of the Pacific Health Research Institute in Hawaii, write in accompanying editorial. "Nonetheless, the idea that vitamin E and vitamin C might have beneficial effects on the underlying AD process makes sense." Studies tracking a greater number of people for a longer period of time may produce more telling results.

—Rachael Moeller, Studies Suggest Antioxidants may Protect against Alzheimer's, *Scientific American*, June 26, 2002.

Keywords

Falsifiable: Being able to generate predictions which can identify situations which would unequivocally falsify them.

Falsifiability condition: Indication of the possibility of circumstance in which the hypothesis could be found false.

Hypothesis: A tentative explanation or an assumption.

Model: A hypothesis which has been known to be true at least in limited number or type of cases.

Random error: Error in experiments that show up due to inherent imprecision in measuring devices.

Scientific theory: A hypothesis, or a group of related hypotheses, which has been confirmed through repeated experimental tests.

Systematic error: Non-random error in experiments due to factors which bias the result in only one direction.

Testable: A hypothesis that is verifiable.

APPENDICES

APPENDIX A

LOGICAL PARADOXES

Logical paradoxes are puzzles or perplexing statements which seem to indicate highly counter-intuitive possibilities, such as contradictory conclusions. They appear to be meaningful and true, yet they baffle us and seem to challenge our reasoning skills and our orderly way of logical understanding. Hence they provoke us to resist them and tease the logically and the mathematically inclined the more. Their presence in the literature is abundant and some of them are handed down to us from the ancient times. Given below is an overview of some of the more famous paradoxes.

Eubulides of Miletus (approx. 4th BCE), a logician belonging to the Megarian school in ancient Greece, and a worthy rival of Aristotle, is attributed a number of interesting logical paradoxes which still have not lost their charm, such as the Liar paradox, the Argument from the Heap, or The horned man[1].

The horned man is about asking someone:

Do you still have horns on your head?

This is certainly a tricky question which requires a well-thought out answer. For, a straight 'No' in this case may imply that "now I do not, but earlier I used to have horns", which is an unwelcome suggestion. It is similar to the more recent question:

Have you stopped beating your wife?

A straight 'no' only further confirms the aspersion hidden in the question and a straight 'yes' may carry the undesirable insinuation that earlier you used to beat your wife. A careful "No, and I never have" as an answer

[1] See for a discussion, Kneale, W. and Kneale M. 1968, *The Development of Logic*, Clarendon Press, Oxford, p. 114.

perhaps can save the face in both these cases. This is one of the cases in which the riddle rests on the way the question is phrased. The way the question has been expressed holds the key to the puzzle why a straightforward 'yes' or 'no' does not answer the question, but only helps to make the question more pointed.

Argument from the Heap has been already discussed as a fallacy in this book in Section 3.2, and for that reason has not been covered here.

The **Liar paradox** is famous. Its complexity comes from its self-reference. Eubulides reportedly had put it in this way:

A man says that he is lying. Is what he says true or false?

Suppose that X says:

I am lying.

Let us call this statement *S*. Is *S* true or false? Note that if *S* is true, then X is lying when making the statement *S*. For, X is lying about his lying, so what he says is false. And if *S* is false, then it is false that X is lying, and then what X is telling is the truth. This paradox seems to question all our cherished notions about truth and falsity, as it leads to a contradiction from either of the only two possibilities.

The earliest credit for the **Liar paradox** goes to Epimenides, a 6th BCE Greek Philosopher, who himself was from Crete and therefore a Cretan, and who is quoted as saying:

All Cretans are liars.

However, many consider that Epimenides' statement is not really paradoxical. For, if it is a lie, it only makes Epimenides a liar; it does not make all his fellow Cretans liars. On the other hand, a simpler version of the Liar paradox seems to very effectively defy any attempt of assigning it a truth value:

This statement is false.

If the statement above is true, then what it says is true, hence it is false. And if it is false, then what it says is false, hence it is true. According to some logicians, the best way to resist this paradox is to give up the notion of **bivalence**, according to which there are two and only two truth-values: truth and falsity, and every statement has to be either true or false, one or the other. *Intuitionistic propositional logic*, for example, rejects the assumption that every statement has to be true or false and allows for statements which may be *neither true nor false*. Also, a formal system of logic which uses *three-values* (e.g. C.S. Peirce's truth, falsity and indeterminate) or more than three values (see Appendix C below for *many-valued or multivalent logic)* begins by rejecting the principle of bivalence.

A discussion on logical paradoxes remains unpardonably incomplete if Zeno's name is omitted from it. Zeno (approximately 490 BCE), in defense of the philosophy of Parmenides, wrote a book of paradoxes to mainly show that rejection of conclusions of Parmenides on motion or change or monism leads only to absurd conclusions. However, over the millennia that have passed, many of **Zeno's paradoxes** continued to baffle us and steadfastly refused to be resolved. In 19th CE, as modern mathematics developed new resources, more difficulties arose from these paradoxes which required the new resources for resolution. Zeno's book was supposed to contain more than 40 paradoxes, from which those which have survived are all reported from secondary sources. Here we can mention only one of the more famous paradoxes and will ask you to look up other sources to know more about Zeno and his paradoxes.

Achilles and the tortoise: Suppose that Achilles, the fastest runner, is chasing a tortoise (well known for its slow pace). Achilles is moving at 1 m/s speed and the tortoise at 0.1 m/s, but the tortoise has started out 0.9 m ahead of Achilles. Will Achilles be able to catch up the tortoise? We with our all our common sense think that he obviously will after 1s; Zeno, however, does not think so. For, he argues, Achilles as the pursuer first has to come up to the point where the tortoise started from, but by that time the tortoise will crawl to another point, and again Achilles has reach this new point and again by that time the tortoise will move to yet another new point. So, everytime Achilles reaches the point the tortoise was at, the tortoise by its motion will create a new distance that Achilles will have to catch up with. So, first he has to travel the 0.9 m distance, then an additional 0.09 m, and then another 0.009 m and so on. Though the distance each time will be a finite distance, Achilles will have to do infinite number of catch ups, which makes the task unending. Therefore, contrary to all ordinary expectation, Zeno concludes that Achilles will never be able to catch the tortoise.

What does this paradox show? Some maintain that it only shows that the our commonsensical concept of motion is paradoxical. Others have argued that it shows something about mathematics; namely, that ordinary mathematics fails to describe this run intelligibly and, in general, does not apply well to space and time. However, in 19th CE, Russell and other mathematicians and philosophers contended that modern mathematics can solve this problem and that this paradox shows nothing about modern mathematics. Clearly, the paradox brings in the idea of a series which has no final member. If we consider **Cantor's theory of the Transfinites**, then Zeno's series of finite distances refers to ordinal numbers and is a mathematically legitimate series. But others have argued that there is something wrong about that mathematical way of understanding the series. Though Zeno's paradox has no pernicious result for modern mathematics, they claim that it really talks about a *supertask*, i.e., a task which requires an infinite number of actions to complete it and therefore cannot be completed. They contend that every completable task cannot be described as a sum of infinity of finite tasks, though that is how mathematics would describe it.

Hence, Achilles' run, no matter if we try understand it using modern mathematics, is actually a *supertask* that cannot be completed. Thus, Zeno's point holds true.

In recent times, **Russell's paradox** is one of the very famous logical paradoxes (see also Chapter 4 for a discussion on this paradox). At the turn of the 19th CE, Set theory caught the attention of everyone concerned with mathematics and it seemed promising to many as a foundation on which the entire mathematics can rest such that everything in mathematics would be explainable in set theoretical terms. Frege (if you have read the Chapter 4 you already know) was trying to derive all of mathematics from a few axioms of Logic. For this project, he was actually trying to define numbers in terms of sets and their members.

Usually, if one is trying to describe a thing or an object in terms of a set, the common practice is to refer to a common property by which it belongs as a member to a set of other things or objects with that common property. For example, *x is P* is understood to mean *Px*, and then a set of all objects which are *P* can be written as $(\forall x)\,Px$ (for all *x*, *x* is *P*). Russell's paradox attacks this core tenet of a naïve set theory to show that this condition for identifying a set is not a coherent one, and hence not everything is explainable in terms of a set and its members.

To appreciate this paradox, consider a set of all sets which are not a member of itself. Some sets are members of themselves as, for example, the set of all non-chairs. Being a non-chair itself, the set is a member of itself. But some sets are not members of themselves. For instance, the set of all flowers is not a flower itself, hence it is not a member of itself. But what about the set of all sets that are not members of themselves? Is it a member of itself? If it is, then it cannot be a member of itself; and if it is not, then by the nature of the set it should be a member of itself. Thus, it is a member of itself if and only if it is not a member of itself! Hence, the paradox arises.

Russell is said to have discovered his paradox in 1901, while working on his *Principles of Mathematics* (1903). Independently, Cesare Burali-Forti, an assistant to Giuseppe Peano, also had discovered a similar paradox in 1897 when he noticed that since the set of ordinals is well-ordered, it too must have an ordinal. However, this ordinal must be both an element of the set of all ordinals and yet greater than every such element. Unlike Burali-Forti's paradox, Russell's paradox does not involve the mathematical entities of either ordinals or cardinals, but it utilizes instead only on the primitive notion of set. It has provoked much work in philosophy, logic, mathematics and set theory and theories on foundations of mathematics. As you may recall from our discussion in Chapter 4, when Russell communicated this paradox to Frege, Frege felt defeated and left his earlier views on logic and mathematics. Russell, since his project in his *Principles of Mathematics* was somewhat similar to that of Frege, himself was concerned about this paradox and how it affects the set theory. His own attempt at resisting the paradox came in the form of his **Theory of Types**. Realizing that self-reference is at the core of this paradox, Russell proposed that we can avoid the paradox by arranging all statements in a hierarchy of types. The first level or the lowest type will the statements about the individuals or entities that are not sets, and then the next higher type will be the sets of these individuals or objects, and then the next higher type will be the sets of sets of individuals. If we restrict the use of predicates or properties *only to things of the same level or the same type*, then we can avoid this paradox. The set of all sets that are not members of themselves is *not* of the same *type* or at the same level as the sets that are not members of themselves. So, the same predicate which decides the membership criterion for the lower level cannot and should not apply to the higher level.

Russell's attempt to resolve the paradox has been criticized as being too *ad hoc* to be satisfactory. Other notable attempts at resolving this paradox had been from David Hilbert, Luitzen Brouwer and Frank Zermelo. Overall, this paradox and the responses to it had helped logic and mathematics to grow as a formal systems. A paradox similar to that of Russell was proposed by Cantor in the context of sets and power sets. In more popular way, Russell's paradox is often presented as the **Barber problem**:

Suppose there is a barber who shaves all and only those men who do not shave themselves. If the barber is a shaved man, then does the barber shave himself? If he does, then he does not, for, he does not shave anyone who shaves themselves. If he does not, then he does!

The key difference between the Barber problem and Russell's paradox, however, is that one may still dismiss the Barber problem by rejecting that such a barber exists. Given the naïve theory of sets, there is no similar way to reject a set of sets.

It is perhaps befitting to mention **Gödel's theorems** in this context which seem to show that in any standard, sufficiently equipped, formal system some statements can be constructed which are true but which are not provable *within* that formal system. For example, the consistency of that system is not provable within that system, similarly sme self-referential statements may not be provable within the system. However, the paradoxical thing about Gödel's theorems is that they seem to suggest that we can *prove* that something is *unprovable*!

Is there any escape from these deadlock situations? Some suggest that paradoxes may be resolved by prohibiting all self-referential statements. This solution is inadequate; for, it may eliminate many harmless statements from our language while not being able to eradicate those paradoxes which are not rooted in anything self-referential. Tarski and others have suggested that the flaw is somewhere in assumptions we make about the natural language. He suggested a hierarchy of languages, such as:

Object language: O
Metalanguage M: at this level we can refer to O and use expressions such as 'true in O' or 'false in O'
Meta-metalanguage M': at which level we can refer to M and use expressions such as 'true in M' or 'false in M'.

Thus, he prescribes a relative use of 'true' or 'false' with respect to a certain level. However, **Saul Kripke**, a noted philosopher, pointed out that this hierarchical ascription of truth values entirely misses the fact that even ordinary empirical statements belonging to the sae level can turn out to be paradoxical if the circumstances are not in favour. For example, suppose that

A says: All of B's utterances are true
B says: All of A's utterances are false

Then B's utterance is false if true, and true if false! Kripke's proposal was to accept that some statements may be meaningful without being either true or false.

On the other hand, others, looking at the survival ability of the paradoxes and the failure of some of greatest geniuses at resolving them, have concluded that we need to accept contradictions and accommodate our traditional logic accordingly. For example, Graham Priest in his theory of **Dialetheism** argues powerfully for the existence of true contradictions. Protagonists of **Paraconsistent logic** (see Appendix C below) argue that the law of contradiction has no place as a theorem in logic, as there can be statements which are both true and false. They claim that paradoxes thrive on the law of contradiction. They argue that if we remove this law, then the contradictions resulting from the paradoxes will not have the huge repercussion in logic as it is thought to have.

SUGGESTED FURTHER READING

Beall, J.C. (2004). *Liars and Heaps: New Essays on Paradox*. Oxford: Oxford University Press.

Beall, J.C. and Bas C. van Fraassen (2003). *Possibilities and Paradox. An Introduction to Modal and Many-Valued Logic*. Oxford: Oxford University Press.

Priest, Graham, Richard Routley, and Jean Norman, Eds. (1990). *Paraconsistent Logic.* Munich: Verlag.

Sainsbury, R.M. (1995). *Paradoxes*. Cambridge: Cambridge University Press.

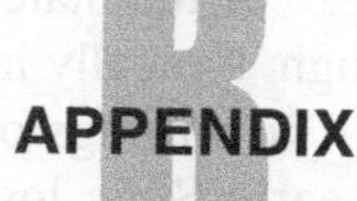

APPENDIX

PHILOSOPHICAL CONTROVERSY WITH 'if-then' AND '$\supset$'

When '$\supset$' or material conditional was introduced as one of the basic connectives in Section 5.2 of this book, it was briefly mentioned that it is controversial whether or not, and how far, the '$\supset$' with its unique truth table truly represents the *if-then* as we understand it in our everyday use of language. Here a summary is presented to acquaint you with the extent and the depth of the controversy.

In our everyday language statements with *if-then* structure have widely different usages, such as:

(a) *As indicative conditionals*: The antecedent and consequent are supposed to be in the *indicative mood*. For example:

If Ravi is in Kolkata, then he is in Grand Hotel.

(b) *As subjunctive conditionals*: The antecedent and consequent are supposed to be in the *subjunctive mood* describing contrary-to-fact scenarios or what *could have happened* if something *were* the case. For example:

If I could fly, I would have gone home by now.

(c) *As statements which are not really not conditional at all*: These statements use the if-then, but do not really express a fact which is dependent on an antecedent such as:

If you are hungry, then there is food in the fridge.

Regarding the first two kinds of statements, there have been vigorous debates recently about whether the indicative and the subjunctive conditionals have the same truth conditions, and if the same logic of conditionals apply to both; and if not, then where exactly the line has to be drawn. Type (c) 'if-then' structures, for obvious reasons, are not part of this debate.

However, there is a long-standing controversy[2] in the western logic on whether the truth-functional '⊃' or the material conditional truly represents the indicative conditionals though, typically in standard two-valued sentential logic, that has been the claim. The writings of Diogenes Laertius and Sextus Empiricus in 3rd CE refer to early Stoic logicians debating over this issue in ancient Greece. Philo of Megarian School of Logic (to be distinguished from its contemporary rival Peripatetic School of Logic of Aristotelian tradition) is said to have claimed that a 'sound' (read 'true') conditional is the one that does *not* begin with a true antecedent and end with a false consequent. Translated in the symbolic language of logic of today, the condition clearly is $\sim (p \bullet q)$ [Not (p and not–q)]. Or, in truth-table form the *only* undesirable falsity condition is

p	q
T	F

On every other possible situation, Philo's conditional is true. Thus understood, Philo's approach matches exactly with that of today's truth-functional approach. All one requires to check in a Philonian conditional is whether the antecedent is false, or the consequent is true, or both [$(\sim p \vee q)$, where '$\vee$' is an inclusive 'or']. Sextus Empiricus further attributes to Philo the following:

> ...there are three ways in which a conditional may be true, and one in which it may be false. For, a conditional is true when it begins with a truth and ends with a truth like "if it is day, it is light"; and true also when it begins with a falsehood and ends with a falsehood, like "If the earth flies, the earth has wings", and similarly a conditional which begins with a falsehood and ends with a truth is itself true, like "if the earth flies, the earth exists". A conditional is false only when it begins with a truth and ends with a falsehood, like "If it is day, it is night". (As cited in Kneale and Kneale, 1968, p. 130)

Sextus Empiricus reports of at least three other opposing views to this conception of a conditional, which are attributable to the eminent logicians of those times. At least one of them, ascribed to Chryssipus, maintained that the relation between the antecedent and the consequent of a conditional is far stronger than how Philo envisages it and demanded that a conditional be 'sound' only when *the contradictory of the consequent is incompatible with the antecedent*.

Boethius, a latin logician born in Rome in 470 CE, also noted that the connection between the antecedent and the consequent of a conditional

[2] For a more comprehensive historical coverage of this debate, see Chhanda Chakraborti, 'There is something about indicative conditionals', *Journal of Indian Council of Philosophical Research,* XX, 3, 145–86, 2003.

statement differs in nature. For, he observed, sometimes a conditional is true because of a necessary connection and sometimes because of some empirical, contingent factors. Influnced by this way of thinking, subsequently logicians in medieval Europe, such as Peter Abelard (1079–1142) and William Ockham (1287–1347), proposed different kinds of *classifications of conditionals* based on the different factors which in their views *made a certain kind of conditional true*. Clearly, the medieval logicians did not treat all conditionals alike as their Greek predecessors did, nor did they try, like the Greeks, to provide a single theory that provides the truth condition for all conditionals.

In modern times, the Philonian conditional was rediscovered as the material conditional, the symbol for which is the '⊃' (the *horseshoe* or the *hook*). As you already know from the earlier chapters of this book, a material conditional $p \supset q$ behaves exactly like the Philonian conditional; it is false only when the p (antecedent) is true but the q (consequent) is false, and it is true in every other possible circumstance. Typically, the account for material conditionals of the form $p \supset q$, complete with truth conditions, is offered as the account for the conditionals.

The Philonian truth functional conditional re-entered the modern logic through the seminal work of Gottlob Frege (1848–1925). Frege, whose work in logic (particularly his system of derivation and his ideas of quantification and variables) is the fountainhead for today's symbolic logic, was the first to clearly enunciate the notion of truth functionality of these conditionals. Philo, though he attributed the same truth conditions to his conditional, was never explicit whether he meant the truth conditions of his conditional as the *function* of the truth conditions of its components. For Frege, the truth functionality of the material conditionals was an operational necessity. Treating them as truth functional easily resolves the problem of determining truth values of statements such as these. All one needs is to find out the truth values of the component statements, and then use these as the basis for computing the truth value of the entire statement with the help of a generalized formula such as the truth table mentioned above.

Charles Sanders Peirce was one of the first to point out that the calculus of Frege-Russell's material conditional "...produces results which seem offensive to common sense" (Peirce, 1933, p. 279). Among other things, he observed that it is too easy for a material conditional to be true. The falsity of the antecedent or the truth of the consequent: either way it becomes true. Peirce used the following subjunctive conditional which he clearly considered as counter-intuitive to prove his point:

> If the Devil were elected president of the United States, it would prove highly conducive to the spiritual welfare of the people. (Peirce, 1933, p. 279)

His point seems to be that (17), according to the truth-functional analysis, comes out to be true specifically because of the least likelihood of the antecedent.

After the publication of the *Principia Mathematica*, Vol. 1 (Russell and Whitehead, 1910), C.I. Lewis also voiced a similar concern that Russell and Whitehead's "algebra of logic" produces "two somewhat startling theorems", namely:

> ...(1) a false proposition implies any proposition, and (2) a true proposition is implied by any proposition. (Lewis, 1912, p. 522)

These results subsequently have come to be known as the **paradoxes of material implication**. It is held as paradoxical that:

> A false statement materially implies any statement whatsoever. Thus, if p is false, then $p \supset q$ must be true, irrespective of what q happens to be.
>
> A true statement is materially implied by any statement whatsoever. Thus, if q is true, then $p \supset q$ must be true, irrespective of what p happens to be.

These results can be easily shown as counter-intuitive in the context of indicative conditionals. For instance, the following apparently nonsensical conditionals will have to be accepted as true simply by virtue of their either having a false antecedent or a true consequent, or both:

> If $2+2=5$, then Thailand is in Europe.
>
> If $2+2=5$, then Thailand is in Asia.

For that matter, we find it odd to declare the following indicative conditional true also though both of its components are true:

> If $2+2=4$, then Thailand is in Asia.

In the 1950s, when the ordinary language movement in Philosophy was taking shape, Strawson, an English philosopher (b.1919–) associated with the movement, objected to the treatment of indicative conditionals as material conditionals. He claimed that there were important differences between the *if-then* construction of the indicative conditionals and the $\supset$, such as in the circumstances in which we would primarily (or in a standard fashion) use them. For example, he claimed that, unlike the material conditionals, the *if then* construction is typically used in circumstances where there has to be an element of doubt regarding the truth or falsity of the antecedent and the consequent. Moreover, although the material conditionals $p \supset q$ and $p \supset \sim q$ are consistent with each other (when p is false), Strawson argued that the ordinary indicative conditionals 'if p then q' and 'if p then not-q' cannot be considered consistent in the same way. Consider, for instance:

If it rains, then the match will be cancelled.

If it rains, then the match will not be cancelled.

If two people assert these two statements separately about the same match, they would be considered as disagreeing or contradicting with each other.

In defense of the truth-functional treatment of the indicative conditionals, a group of recent theories claim that the truth conditions of a conditional, i.e. conditions which make it true, must be differentiated from its assertion-conditions, i.e., conditions in which it is usually asserted. Also, they claim that the truth conditions must be distinguished from whatever *implied* inferences that an asserted statement may generate.

In 1967 in his William James lectures entitled "Logic and conversation", H.P Grice was the first philosopher to propose a theory of *conversational implicatures* to claim that there are implied meanings, apart from the conventional meaning, of an utterance that come out in a conversational context as a result of our following certain conversational rules. For example, consider the following conversation between two persons, A and B:

A: Where is the nearest grocery shop?

B: Oh! But today is Sunday.

In this apparently impertinent reply of B, you might find the answer that, though there could be grocery shops nearby, they are all closed on a Sunday. But this is not what B *said*, and that is not what B said he means. Yet, this is what you may conclude from B's saying what he said in reply to A in the conversational context. Assuming that B fully understood what he was being asked, his answer seems to generate this *implied* answer or the conversational implicature.

There is no need to go in the details of the theory of conversational implicatures here, but through this theory of conversational implicatures, Grice developed an argument that the implicatures or suggestions that a conditional may generate are *not* part of its core meaning. According to Grice, whenever we use the *if then* construction in natural language, as pointed out by Strawson, we seem to expect and indicate that there is some sort of "connection" between the antecedent and the consequent, whereas there is no such requirement in the use of a '⊃'. However, that extra indication, Grice claims, is just a "conversational implicature" that the *if then* construction generally carries, and *has nothing to do with its truth conditions*. In Grice's view, the truth conditions of an indicative conditional are exactly the same as those of the material conditional. Although this is an attractive proposal, the problem with this Gricean answer is that it does *not* explain (Edgington, 1995, p. 245), why one has to *believe in* a conditional as true when all one knows is that the antecedent is false or just that the consequent is true. Comparatively speaking, there is no such problem of dearth of reasons for believing in '$p \supset q$' as true when all we know is that p is false. The difference, therefore, remains.

In his book *Conditionals* (Jackson, 1987), Frank Jackson has presented another supplemented defense. Like Grice, Jackson too claims that the 'if-then' and '⊃' do not differ in their truth conditions. However, they differ in their *assertibility conditions*. There is a special condition for asserting an indicative conditional; namely, that the belief in the conditional will have to be *robust with respect to the truth of its antecedent*. It clearly is not enough to have high probability for high assertability. The sentence also must be *robust* in the sense of being able to retain its probability value under the emergence of some new, pertinent information. Suppose that my sole basis for saying "If Smith is in London, then he is attending a meeting" is that I have almost certain information that Smith is *not* in London. In that case, in Jackson's view, the assertability of the sentence becomes questionable because the sentence is not *robust with respect to the truth of its antecedent*. If by chance Smith comes to London and if I do not know what Smith will do if he comes to London, my point of statement will be completely lost. The *if then* construction of indicative conditionals, according to him, is a syntactic device in our language to explicitly signal to the hearers that "If *A* then *B*" is *robust* with respect to *A*. That is, belief in the probability of "if *A* then *B*" will not go through a radical revision if one were to come to know that *A* indeed is the case. Therefore, in Jackson's view, it is not enough to know that the antecedent is false for asserting an indicative conditional. It has to be further tested whether the belief in the conditional will not be forsaken if one came to know that the antecedent is actually true. Thus, whatever differences that we may feel there are between the indicative and the material conditional, in Jackson's view, they all pertain to the difference in the asssertibility condition.

One of the problems with Jackson's response is that it leaves no explanatory ground in his theory to explain why at all the indicative conditional must have the same truth conditions as the material conditional. His theory does not help us to believe in the truth of the *if then* under the same circumstances in which a '⊃' is believable as true. For, it piles on more differences between the two by tagging a special assertability condition and special linguistic functions on to the *if then*. Jackson's indicative *if then* does not mean the same as '⊃', it does not imply the same as '⊃', and cannot even be asserted under the same circumstances. For all practical purposes, therefore, his indicative conditional is ultimately a very different entity from a material conditional. Why does it, then, have to have the *same* truth conditions as the '⊃'?

Just as there are theorists who support the truth-functional treatment of the indicative conditionals, there are others who oppose it. Robert Stalnaker, for example, has argued that the truth-functional treatment of indicative conditionals is inherently inadequate because the indicative conditionals have a very different set of *belief-conditions*. Ernest Adams has argued that an indicative conditional is not a proposition *per se*, it is not a truth-bearer; and that they only have *conditional probability*. We may borrow the words of Thomas Bayes to briefly explain what conditional probability is:

> The probability that two … events will both happen is … the probability of the first, [multiplied by] the probability of the second on the supposition that the first happens (Bayes, 1940, p. 378)

The conditional probability of "if *A* then *B*", where *A* and *B* are two dependent events, will be:

$$\text{Probability of } B \text{ given } A \text{ or } P\,(B/A) = \frac{P\,(A \text{ and } B)}{P\,(A)}$$

Adams also argues that certain argument forms, such as "$p \supset q$, and $q \supset r$, therefore, $p \supset r$" (known as *hypothetical reasoning*) or "$\sim (p \supset q)$, therefore p", which are considered as valid under the truth functional account, come out to have invalid instances as given below when ordinary language-indicative conditionals are used:

1. If Brown wins the election, then Smith will retire to private life. If Smith dies before the election, then Brown wins the election. Therefore, if Smith dies before the election, then Smith will retire to private life.
2. It is not the case that if John passes History, he will graduate. Therefore, John will pass History. (Adams, 1965, pp. 166-67)

These, according to Adams, bear clear evidence that the truth functional analysis of indicative conditionals is not tenable at all hence, the truth functional logic of '⊃' cannot be applied to the *if then* of ordinary indicative conditionals.

This debate is still not settled in philosophical logic. Therefore, there is ample scope of research on this issue. But we shall end this discussion here by mentioning how in the recent times experiments done in cognitive psychology have added another interesting dimension to the controversy. As mentioned elsewhere[3], some experiments (Johnson-Laird and Tagart, 1969) seem to suggest that people do not perceive the truth conditions of the indicative conditional as those of material conditional. The experimenters found that when subjects encountered the conditional in the *if p then q* natural language form, then they judged only the TT cases as true, TF cases as clearly false, but regarded FT and FF cases as *irrelevant*. Thus, this study, which was about how we understand implication or conditionals, exhibited that in people's perception the truth table for *if then* is strikingly different from that of the

---

[3] *Ibid.*

material implication. While this does not tell us which reading of the conditional, as the indicative or as the truth-functional material conditional, is correct, a claim such as this does raise questions about how much of our truth-functional understanding is acquired or learnt and how much of it is innate or inherent in us. Others (Evans *et al.*, 1993) have claimed to have found significant difference in the use of *Modus Ponens* and *Modus Tollens* among the common people, a difference which, they claim, goes against a purely truth-functional interpretation of the indicative conditionals. How far the interpretations of these experimental results are to be trusted and how far they can be contested is still an open question. However, the aim of this Appendix at the whole, was to raise your awareness level. As a student of Logic, while you are learning about the truth-functional '⊃', you should be aware of the subtler philosophical points so as not to blindly accept it as a proper substitute of the 'if-then' of the ordinary language, without a pause.

SUGGESTED FURTHER READING

Adams, E.W. (1965). The logic of conditionals. *Inquiry*, 8, 166–97.

Bayes, Thomas. (1940). An essay towards solving a problem in the doctrine of chances, *in* Deming, W.E. Ed., (1940). Originally published in *Transactions of the Royal Society of London,* 53, 1763, 370–418.

Evans, J.St.B.T., Newstead, S., and Byrne, R.M.J. (1993). *Human Reasoning: The psychology of deduction*. Hillsdale, USA: Lawrence Erlbaum Associates.

Jackson, F. (1987). *Conditionals*. London: Basil Blackwell.

Jackson, F. Ed., (1991). *Conditionals*. Oxford: Oxford University Press.

Johnson-Laird, P.N. and Tagart, J. (1969). How implication is understood. *American Journal of Psychology*, 2, 367–73.

Kneale, W. and Kneale, M. (1968). *The Development of Logic*: Oxford, Clarendon Press (1984 reprint).

Lewis, C.I. (1912). Implication and the algebra of logic. *Mind*, 21, 522–31.

Lewis, D. (1976). Probabilities of conditionals and conditional probabilities, *Philosophical Review*, 85, 297–315. Reprinted in Jackson, Ed., (1991), 76–101.

Lewis, D. (1986). Probabilities of conditionals and conditional probabilities II. *Philosophical Review*, 5, 581–89. Reprinted in F. Jackson Ed., (1991), 102–10.

Peirce, C.S. (1933). *Collected Papers*. Cambridge, Mass., Harvard University Press.

Sanford, D.H. (1989). *If P, Then Q: Conditionals and the Foundations of Reasoning.* New York, Routledge.

Stalnaker, R.C. (1991a). A theory of conditionals, *in* F. Jackson, Ed., *Conditionals* (pp. 28–45). Oxford, Oxford University Press. Originally published in Studies in Logical Theory, *American Philosophical Quarterly,* Monograph 2: 98–112.

Stalnaker, R. (1991b). Indicative conditionals, *in* F. Jackson Ed., *Conditionals.* Oxford, Oxford University Press, 136–54.

Strawson, P.F. (1974). *Introduction to Logical Theory.* London: Methuen.

APPENDIX

ALTERNATIVE LOGICS IN WESTERN SYSTEM

At present, traditional logic or the Formal First Order Logic is no longer considered the only logic possible. It is just one of the many kinds of logic available among many viable alternatives. We can mention here only about some of these alternatives. The aim is to acquaint you to the diversity that is present in the field of logic today. It is also to contest the common misconception that there is only one kind of logic.

Since **Informal Logic** has already been discussed in some detail in this book, some of the other varieties of logic are:

- Many-valued logic
- Fuzzy logic
- Non-monotonic logic
- Modal logic
- Paraconsistent logic

The list is not intended to be exhaustive, but it refers to some of the important recent developments in systems of logic. You will find a brief description of each of the above-mentioned kind of logics below.

Usually, these alternative logic systems have emerged because of two reasons:

1. The proponents of the system reject some of the fundamental postulates of classical formal truth-functional logic.
2. Or, a domain in which logic needs to be applied has special features that call for certain accommodations and changes in the classical logic.

Many-valued Logics

The main difference of these logics from classical logic is that many-valued logics do *not* adhere to the Principle of Bivalence, that is, they do *not* accept that the number of truth values must be restricted to only two: truth and falsity. Instead, they allow for a larger set of truth values. Some more recent examples will be:

- Kleene's **three-valued system** which uses 'undefined' as the third value
- Belnap's Relevance Logic which uses **four-valued system**.

After the discovery of his unpublished notes[4], C S Peirce is now accepted as the pioneer in three-valued logic. In his notes, Peirce experimented with three symbols representing truth values: *V*, *L*, and *F*. He associated *V* with '1' and 'T', indicating truth, *F* with '0', and 'F', indicating falsehood, and *L* with '1/2' and '*N*', indicating perhaps an intermediate or unknown value.

Many-valued logics have important contributions and applications in widely diverse fields such as linguistics, philosophy, hardware design, and artificial intelligence.

Fuzzy Logic

This logic is based on the theory of Fuzzy Set by Lotfi Zadeh[5]. Roughly speaking, a fuzzy set allows each of its members to have a *degree of membership*. Similarly, in fuzzy logic, the components of a statement may be assigned *degrees of truth* such that in a context a statement may be *more true* than another. The truth degrees may range from *being absolutely true* to *being absolutely false,* with a range of intermediary discrete values in between, some of which may overlap. This is particularly convenient in case of statements involving imprecise or vague concepts such as 'hot', 'rich', 'tall', 'bald', etc., as in statements such "He is tall". Fuzzy logic has extensive applications in areas such as fuzzy control, fuzzy computation. Its basic difference with traditional logic is that the traditional way is to ascribe truth or falsity absolutely. A statement is supposed to be true or false, with no other possibilities in between. Just as some cases cannot be described as simply black or simply white, but in terms of some in between shades

[4]See Dipert, Randall (1995) "Peirce's Underestimated Role in the History of Logic." *In* Kenneth Ketner (Ed.) *Peirce and Contemporary Thought*. New York: Fordham University Press. See also Fisch, Max and Atwell Turquette (1966), "Peirce's Triadic Logic." *Transactions of the Charles S. Peirce Society* **11**, 71–85.

[5]Zadeh, L., Fuzzy sets. *Information and Control*, **8**, 338–353, 1965.

of grey, similarly fuzzy logic allows us to respond to the need for truth-value ascription in terms of degrees.

Non-monotonic Logic

A key assumption of classical first order logic is that a deductive argument, if *valid*, cannot become invalid with *new information*. Classical logic is monotonic in the sense that if in it a conclusion *C* can be inferred from a set of premises $\{P\}$, then *C* can also be inferred from a set of premises $\{S\}$, which contains $\{P\}$ as a subset. The validity of an argument is considered to be impervious to the change of time and its effect on the availability of information. This is exactly the point of departure for non-monotonic logic, which believes that conclusions of arguments are *tentatively* warranted on the basis of a given knowledge base. Since this base is subject to change, this logic allows the right to retract a conclusion or a change of opinion about the status of an argument (valid or invalid) with the emergence of further information in the knowledge base or in the premise set.

Modal Logic

Modal expressions are expressions such as 'necessarily' or 'possibly'. Modal logic is the study of behaviour of expressions 'it is neccesary that' or 'it is possible that', or their negations, in deductive reasoning. The philosopher, Saul Kripke is considered as the founder-figure of this logic.

Paraconsistent Logic

Traditionally, contradiction is considered as a property of two statements which cannot be true together and which cannot be false together. Paraconsistent logic rejects this to claim that in certain situations two propositions which are considered as contradictory in this classical sense may be both held as true in some sense (as in some belief situations, or in scientific theories). Classical logic also accepts contradiction as an undesirable trait which trivializes the consequence relation; anything can follow from contradictory premises. Paraconsistent logic challenges this logical principle of classical logic. In their view, all that follows from an inconsistent set of premises need not be trivial. They argue that there actually are theories (in natural science, for example) which exhibit inconsistent premises, when axiomatized. For instance, if it is true that an electron orbits the nucleus of the atom without radiating energy (Bohr's theory), then it is inconsistent with Maxwell's equations that an electron which is accelerating in orbit must radiate energy. Together, they form a part of the theory of atoms, which is successful and is not at all trivial, contrary to the expectation of classical logic.

Importance of paraconsistent logic also holds if there could be situations when *true contradictions* can hold, i.e., a statement A and its negation can both be true. Celebrated Buddhist logician, **Nagarjuna** of the Madhayamika School refers to situations such as these in his logic of *Sunyata.* **Graham Priest** in recent times also had done important work in **Dialetheism** to argue for true contradictions. From such true statements, only true conclusions can follow validly. The case for paraconsistent logic is also argued from its applications. For example, in the field of information processing by a computer, paraconsistent logic is preferable for automated theorem proving. For, due to data entry errors or because of collection of data from multiple sources, it is quite common for the computer to contain inconsistent information. This has drawn attention from computer scientists, specially from those involved in the work with automated theorem-proving. Though there are techniques to detect the latent inconsistencies, each one has its limitations and none can guarantee to predict consistency. In Artificial Intelligence or AI, applications of paraconsistent logic have been found to be particularly useful for research on *belief revision.*

SUGGESTED FURTHER READING

Belnap, N.D., Jr. (1992) A useful four-valued logic: How a computer should think, *Entailment: The Logic of Relevance and Necessity*, Vol. II, A.R. Anderson, N.D., Belnap, Jr. and J.M. Dunn, Princeton University Press, first appeared as *A Useful Four-valued Logic*, *Modern use of multiple-valued logic*, J.M. Dunn and G. Epstein, Eds., (1977), D. Reidel Publishing Company, Dordrecht, and How a computer should think, *Comtemporary Aspects of Philosophy*, G. Ryle, Ed., (1977), Oriel Press.

Besnard, P. and Hunter, A. Eds., (1998), *Handbook of Defesible Reasoning and Uncertainty Management Systems*, Vol. 2, *Reasoning with Actual and Potential Contradictions*, Kluwer Academic Publishers, Dordrecht.

Priest, G., Routley, R., and Norman, J., Eds., (1989). *Paraconsistent Logic: Essays on the inconsistent*, Philosophia Verlag, München.

Priest, G., (2002). Paraconsistent logic, *Handbook of Philosophical Logic* (2nd ed.), Vol. 6, D. Gabbay and F. Guenthner (Eds.), Kluwer Academic Publishers, Dordrecht, pp. 287-393, 2002.

APPENDIX

METATHEORY

Completeness

Completeness in logic is understood as an attribute or property of a formal system such that for a system which has this property it will be a contradiction if a statement is introduced but cannot be derived from the axioms of the system. So, if a logical system is complete, then if a statement is true, it can be derived from the axioms of that system. This is the notion of completeness in its *strongest* sense.

Conceptually, it is the *reverse* notion of **soundness** of a logical system. If a logical system is sound, then every statement that is derivable in that system is true. Completeness, on the other hand, claims that if a system is complete then every true statement is derivable in that system.

A very famous theorem on completeness was proved by Kurt Gödel in 1929. Gödel's **Completeness theorem** is *not* to be confused with another famous result by the same person: Gödel's Incompleteness theorem which shows that the formal proofs of Mathematics are inherently limited. Simply put, Gödel's Completeness theorem states:

> In first-order predicate calculus, every universally valid statement (formula) can be derived from its axioms and the rules of inference.

The expression "universally valid" in this context means a statement that is true in every possible universe of discourse or domain and with every possible interpretation. A proof such as this shows that the axioms and the rules of inference of the system are **complete**. For, they can prove every universally valid statement.

There are other *weaker* senses of completeness which are utilized in logic, such as in Modal Logic. The weaker sense of completeness makes claims about what is provable in a certain domain with certain interpretations.

Completeness, clearly, is a very important requirement for any logical system, but it is not at all easy to demonstrate. Its proof requires more sophisticated techniques than the ones discussed in this book. However, you can acquire these skills at an advanced stage of your logic studies. At this point, you may remember that with the supplementation of rule of conditional proof and indirect proof, the axioms and rules of sentential logic and predicate logic are both sound and complete in their respective domains.

APPENDIX E

INDIAN LOGIC

Early Indian Logic, which developed independently of the West, is said to have originated about 200 BCE or so. The *Nyāya-Sutra* authored by *Gautama Akshapada,* which dates from around 1st or 2nd CE, was thought to be one of the earliest logic texts. This text is associated with the Nyāya philosophical tradition of India. Scholars, however, now think that two earlier texts have been merged in this text: one on rules and principles of debate, and the other on general philosophical issues in metaphysics and epistemology.

Ancient Indian logic is said to have originated, at least partly, from the need to properly evaluate debates. The art of philosophical disputation or *Vāda-vidyā* was practiced extensively in ancient India, particularly in the post-Upanishadic period. The aim was to defend or refute certain interpretations of the Vedas and Upanishads and scriptures. The popularity of philosophical debates was not confined only to the Hindu tradition at that time. Historians mention that even the Buddhist and Jain texts refer to many technical terms about the art of debate. In the Greek writings, there is reference to the 'gymnosophists' of India who, as a profession, would go from place to place and engage themselves in debates. According to scholars (see, for instance, Matilal, 1997, 1998), there was a connection between the origin of Indian logic with the extensive practice of debating prevalent at that time: Indian Logic emerged from a felt-need to have a well-reasoned, systematic discussion. In the Nyaya-Sutra, three kinds of debates were identified:

1. Good debate or *Vāda* in which the proof and refutation of thesis and antithesis are based on proper evidence (pramāna) and without contradicting any background or already established assumptions (*siddhānta*)
2. Devious or sly debate, or *Jalpa*, in which the proof and refutation

use unfair, measures such as hair-splitting empty pedantry (*chala*), false rejoinders (*jāti*) and defeat situations (*nigraha-sthāna*).

3. Purely destructive or refutation-only debate or *Vitanda,* in which no positive counter-thesis is proved.

The Nȳaya-sutra offered a **five-step inference pattern** for those who want to engage in an honest, friendly, fair, and balanced debate or *Vāda.* This five-step inference schema (see Appendix F below) is known as the *classical five-membered inference pattern for proper argumentation.* The concern clearly was to promote the notion and the practice of a *good* debate, and to differentiate it from the pointless, destructive debates (e.g., *vitanda*).

Among the traditional schools of thought in ancient India, the *Nyāya system* devoted itself more to the careful study of Logic than any other system. For over ten centuries, the focus was on identification and classification of fallacies, and on resolution of disputes. From 14th Century CE, with the New Nyaya school, Logic became more formal. Logicians came up with a novel idea of universal quantification, rules for sentential logic etc. By 18th century CE, the creativity in New Nyaya school diminished.

Indian Logic also boasts of Buddhist Logic and Jaina Logic. Among the renowned Buddhist logicians, we shall mention a few: Nagarjuna who possibly lived in 2nd or 3rd CE, Vasuvandhu, whose name is associated with the development of the Yogachāra school of Buddhism, his disciple Dinnāga (480–540 CE), who is considered as one of the greatest Indian logicians, and his commentator Dharmakirti who authored *Pramana-varttika, Pramana-viniscaya,* and specially *Nyāya-bindu.*

The seven-fold method of conditionally valid predications or the (*Sapta-bhangi-naya-vāda*)* is considered as an important element in the Jain system. The theory of multiplicity of viewpoints (*Anekāntavāda*) is an integral part of Jain logic. Some of the notable names in Jain Logic are: Siddhasenadivakara (5th A.D.), Akalanka (8th A.D.), Abhayadeva, and Hemachandra.

SUGGESTED FURTHER READING

Ganeri, J., Ed., (2001). *Indian Logic: A reader*. Curzon Press, UK.

Matilal, B.K. (1997). *Logic, Language, and Reality: Indiān Philosophy and Contemporary Issues*. Motilal Banarasi Dass, New Delhi (reprint).

________. (1998). *The Character of Logic in India.* J., Ganeri and H. Tiwari (Eds.). Oxford: Oxford University Press.

*The ' ā ' is the 'a' with diacritical mark. It is to be pronounced as a long 'a' (aa).

APPENDIX

F

INFERENCE IN THE NYAYA SYSTEM

The **Nyāya tradition** is one of the six well-known ancient, traditional philosophical traditions in India. Out of the six, the Nyaya school of thought is better known for its extensive works in logic and on argumentation. In this section, we shall get an overview of how the Nyaya tradition treated the subject of inference.

The widely used terminology for inference is a*numāna*. A*numāna* literally means 'after knowledge'. The reference is to the knowledge that follows from (or is after) the directly observed. Suppose you have spotted some smoke rising from a faraway mountain-top. The distance between you and mountain is considerable, and all you *saw* was smoke on the mountain top. But you *inferred* that there must be fire on the mountain-top. You never actually saw the fire. You inferred the *unseen* fire on the mountain-top based on the *seen* evidence of smoke in the same place. Why? Because earlier many times you may have seen smoke associated with fire, as for example, in the kitchen. This is an example, of inferential knowledge or a*numāna*. The basic idea is that an object is inferred to have a certain property on the ground that it is observed to have another property.

Let us now take a look at how the Nyaya tradition classifies different types of a*numāna*. First of all, it is said that a*numāna* can be of two types:

- **For the sake of oneself** (their term is *svarthanumāna*, i.e., *sva-artha-anumāna*)
- **For the sake of others**, as in a dialectical or debate situation where you have to prove what you inferred and also show how you have inferred it (their term is *parārthānumāna,* i.e., *parārtha-anumāna*)

The 'inference for the sake of oneself' is an inference drawn in one's own mind as a result of repeated observation earlier. You see the smoke on the mountain top and in your own mind you draw the conclusion that there must be fire at the top. It is a rather casual process.

However, the 'inference for the sake of others' is not an informal matter. It requires demonstration of the inferential process as well as the evidence or ground for making the inference. For the sake of demonstration, according to the ancient Nyaya logic, the proper formulation of your inference should have *five* parts. It is technically known as the five-membered inference or argument schema. The classical example of this five-membered (*Pancha-avayava*) inference schema is given in the following table.

Technical name of the part	**Explanation**	**Example**
Pratijñā	The tentative thesis to be proved	That the mountain-top has fire.
Hetu	The reason cited	Because it has smoke.
Udāharana	Mentioning an example of earlier seen cases	Cases of smoke are known to be cases of fire as seen in the kitchen.
Upanaya	Application of reason and example to the case in hand	The smoke, which is known to be associated with fire (as seen in the kitchen), is seen coming out of the mountain-top.
Nigamana	Final assertion of the thesis to be proved	Therefore, the mountain-top has fire.

It is a schema for proper reasoning among debaters who are engaged in a fair, friendly and balanced argumentation or *Vāda.* Inference here means a cognitive process by which the knower wants to arrive at a correct knowledge.

Note that in this format *Pratijñā* and *Nigamana* are the same statements. What you aim to prove is stated twice, once in the beginning and again in the end. This is required because, in the beginning, you need to clearly state what the aim of your inference is, and in the end, when all the steps have been laid out, you restate it for closure. *Pratijñā* announces what you are set to demonstrate, and *Nigamana* is the statement of the conclusion after the demonstration.

The example is not a simple example. It is an example which is fundamentally important for the inference. It connects a crucial generalization (Cases of smoke are cases of fire) which acts as the spine of the inference, and an easily observable, or well-known instance. Smoke and fire have been found associated in the kitchen also.

Vātsyāyana, the first commentator of the *Nyāya Sutra*, interpreted this schema as an analogical reasoning, or an inference based on similarity. The case of mountain and the case of kitchen are comparable or similar simply because they share the *hetu* or reason as same property: 'because they have smoke'. *Vātsyayāna* did not consider the example or *udāharana* as greatly important because he thought its function was merely to exhibit the relationship that exists between the two properties of 'having smoke' and 'having fire'.

But, as we have noted in our discussion of analogical reasoning in Chapter 14 of this book, there is an obvious difficulty in making resemblance the sole ground of an inference. Mere similarity between two cases, *A* and *B*, is not a sufficient ground for inferring that *B* too must have a property that *A* has, unless it is shown separately that the aspect in which the two cases resemble is a *relevant aspect.* Two cases may resemble trivially or in ways that may not be pertinent for the drawing of the conclusion. You may wish to infer that a horse also has dewlap (a loose hanging flap of skin from the neck) like a cow, because a horse is similar to a cow in having four legs. But it will be a false proof. The property of 'having four legs' is not a relevant property for drawing the conclusion about 'having a dewlap'. Then why should one be allowed to infer analogically on its basis? If one does, it will be a false proof which cannot rule out the possibility of its being invalid (*jāti*).

The five-membered inference schema in itself does not have any safeguard to stop undesirable inferences based on superficial or irrelevant similarities. It is Buddhist logician Dinnāga (480–540 CE) who first pointed out for further elucidation of what a good Hetu should have. He stated that a good *Hetu* must satisfy three conditions:

a. It must occur in the case to be proved. Thus, 'having smoke' must exist in the mountain.
b. It must occur in cases which are relevantly similar to the case to be proved.
c. It must not occur in counter-example or cases which are not at all similar to the case to be proved.

This argument schema has frequently been discussed and considered, and compared with Aristotle's syllogism or the mathematical logic, by both Indian and European scholars. The aim was to understand it and to evaluate it with comparison to western logic. Earlier European scholars, such as Henry Colebrooke, identified this as the *Indian syllogism*, as compared to Aristotelian syllogism (see Chapter 9 of this book). He and other scholars compared this schema to *Barbara*, an Aristotelian syllogism in the first figure. On this understanding, the five-membered inference schema is simply:

All cases of 'having smoke' are cases of 'having fire'.

This (mountain) is a case of 'having smoke'.

Therefore, it (mountain) is a case of 'having fire'.

However, recent scholars find this 'western' interpretation of the Indian inference schema a bit forced and contrived. For, the conclusion of the Indian schema proves something about a single case, and thus draws only a singular proposition as the conclusion. However, Aristotelian syllogistic forms such as *Barbara* can only deal with universal or particular categorical propositions which are positive or negative in character. Stanislaw Schayer, who was a pupil of Lukasiewicz, the famous mathematical logician, gave another slightly different interpretation. But he also showed that the authentic Aristotelian and traditional syllogisms did not provide a suitable basis for the interpretation of Indian syllogistic theory.

Ganeri, a recent scholar on Indian Logic, has rightly pointed out that the early European scholars approached Indian logic with little knowledge about many other complexities and developments in Indian Logic such as the *Navya Nyāya*, and with a presumption of intellectual superiority (Ganeri, 2001). It also is a fact that the western scholars approached Indian Logic with the only tools that they had, namely, Western Logic. It is possible that they projected elements of their own philosophical legacy onto the Indian thought systems while trying to understand them.

In the *Nyāya-sûtra* of Aksapada Gautama, inference has been classified as: 1. A *priori* (*purvavat*, from cause to effect) 2. A *posteriori* (*sesavat*, from effect to cause) and 3. From analogy (*samanyato-drsta*, perception of homogeneousness, that is, the recognition of the subject as being referable to some class, and as being therefore liable to have predicated of it whatever may be predicable of the class).

SUGGESTED FURTHER READING

Ganeri, J. (2003). Ancient Indian Logic as a theory of case-based reasoning. *Journal of Indian Philosophy*, Vol. 31, pp. 33–45.

Ganeri, J., Ed., (2001). *Indian Logic*: *A Reader*, Richmond, Surrey: Routledge.

*The 'n' with a curl on top of it should be pronounced as the nasal 'n' (as in 'gnosis'), and the 'u' with a carat mark on top is the long 'u' as in 'oo'.

APPENDIX G

DYNAMIC LOGIC AND TEMPORAL LOGIC

In this part, we want to introduce you to relatively recent developments in logic. **Dynamic Logic** is a kind of multi-modal logic, which was introduced by Vaughan Pratt in the 1970s. Dynamic Logic (DL) is a formal system to reason about computer programs. Traditionally, this means starting with a system of formalized correctness specifications and then proving rigorously and formally that these specifications are met by a certain computer program. Among the other considerations that fall into this category are: how to determine that two computer programs are equivalent, how to compare the expressive power of various programming constructs, etc.

There are numerous formal systems which have been proposed for these purposes. Several of them combine propositional logic, predicate logic, modal logic with algebra of events. A major difference between Predicate Logic and Dynamic Logic is that in Predicate Logic truth values are considered as **static** or **fixed**. The truth value of a formula or well-formed expression in Predicate Logic is determined by an assessment of its free variables in a specified context or universe of discourse. Within that discourse, the truth-value of the formula, once fixed, does not change. But in Dynamic Logic, the context is formed by computer programs which are syntactic structures. The task of the programs is to change the value of variables, and hence it allows for a dynamic or changeable interpretation of truth values of its formulas. If, while working with natural numbers a program initializes its variable x as $x = x + 1$, then the truth value of "x is divisible by 4" will naturally change. Dynamic Logic allows for that change and then tries to formalize a logical system.

Temporal logic, on the other hand, stands for any system of rules and symbolism for representing, and reasoning about, propositions qualified in terms of time. It is sometimes also used to refer to *tense logic*, a particular modal logic-based system of temporal logic introduced by Arthur Prior in the 1960s and subsequently further developed by logicians and computer scientists. Temporal Logic is used as a formal system for approaching philosophical issues about time. It is also used as a framework for understanding the semantics of temporal expressions in natural language such as "There will be a battle tomorrow". In artificial intelligence, it has been used as a language for encoding temporal knowledge in a computer for decoding expressions such as 'after', 'before' as in "open the gate *after* checking if $x = 15$", and in computer science it has been used as a tool for handling the temporal aspects of the execution of computer programs.

In temporal logic, the insights of Predicate Logic are sometimes used. For example, the statement "The excavators at Mohenjodaro, Sind, discovered the Indus Valley civilization in 1920" can be understood using the method of Predicate Logic. The temporal dimension '1920' may be captured by adding to the predicates an extra argument-place filled by an expression designating a time. For example:

> Discovered (excavators at Mohenjodaro, Sind, the Indus Valley civilization, 1920)

Or, a constant 'now' can be used to indicate the present moment of time, and temporal ordering relation 'earlier than' may be used to formulate formal expressions.

APPENDIX H

BASIC SET THEORY

Set

George Cantor, the famous German mathematician and also one of the principal contributors to set theory, defined a *set* as any collection of definite, distinct objects that are experienced or perceived by us, or thought of by us.[1] This means that he viewed a set as a collection of any kind of objects that we normally observe or we can conceive of.

Let us try to understand this notion of a set. For our purpose, we shall understand a set as *a collection, or a list, or a class of things*. For example, you may consider the entire collection of audio cassettes that you own as a set. Or, if you wish, you may consider the collection of some of your audio cassettes, e.g. the cassettes of *Sarod* recitals by Ustad Amjad Ali Khan, as a set. Similarly, you may consider the items in the drawer of your table as a set.

Intuitively, we distinguish between objects or things, and collection of things. For example, we differentiate between flowers and collection of flowers, e.g. the class of Petunias, the class of Marigolds. A set, as mentioned, is a collection of things or objects. However, by convention, a set is also regarded as a single object. A set is a mathematical entity, which though itself a collection of objects, is nonetheless an object.

The convention of expressing a set in writing is to write with curly brackets { }. So, the set of audio cassettes that you own may be written as:

{all audio cassettes owned by you}

---

[1]Cantor, George, 1955 (1915). *Contributions to the Founding of the Theory of Transfinite Numbers*. Philip Jourdain (Editor and Translator), Dover, New York.

Elements or Members of a Set

The items that are entered or considered as *in* the set are called the **elements** or **members** of that set.

The elements may be anything. As Cantor mentioned, anything that we see or can be thought of may qualify as an element of a set. So, supposing that the drawer of your table contains 1 pencil, 2 pens, 2 greeting cards, and a calculator. Then the set of items in the drawer of your table contains all of these pens, pencil, card and calculator as its elements or members. This set may be expressed as:

{pencil, pen_1, pen_2, greeting card_1, greeting card_2, calculator}

Note that the elements or members are written inside the curly brackets with each one separated from the other by a comma.

Similarly, the set of odd numbers may be written as

{1, 3, 5, 7, 9, 11...}

Note that, as is shown by the set of odd numbers, some sets may have *infinite number* of elements. The dots after the comma indicate that the set elements go on infinitely.

There are different ways to describe a set. In the examples of sets given above, we have described a set by making a list of the members in the set. That is, we have explicitly mentioned the elements within the curly brackets. This is one kind of procedure.

It is also possible to describe a set using some kind of common property or class property among its elements. For example, consider the following:

$\{x : x \text{ is a mammal}\}$ = the set of mammals

What the expression '$\{x : x \text{ is a mammal}\}$' means is that it is a set of any (and all) x, such that x has the property of being a mammal. This is what we mean by the set of mammals. In this sense, a class is a specific type of a set which uses the class property shared by its elements as the defining characteristic. Other examples of sets expressed in terms of some class property or category could be:

$\{x : x \text{ is an Indian university}\}$ = the set of Indian universities

$\{x : x \text{ is a prime number}\}$ = the set of prime numbers

Not all sets are, however, classes. There is no rule about what may qualify as elements. So, sets may be formed by randomly putting or listing some items together. For example, the following collection of arbitrarily selected items is also a set:

{Mt. Everest, City of Agra, the number 21}

Let us call this set M. Then,

$$M = \{\text{Mt. Everest, City of Agra, the number 21}\}$$

Note that M is a collection and a set but, strictly speaking, it is not a class.

The '$\in$' and the '$\notin$'

In the language of set theory, to write that Mt. Everest is a member (or element) of M or it 'belongs to' M, usually the belongs to symbol '$\in$' is used. Thus, the expression 'Mt. Everest is a member of M' in the language of set theory becomes

$$\text{Mt. Everest} \in M$$

By definition,

where A is any set, $x \in A$ *iff* x is an element of A.

The symbol '$\notin$' is used to express 'not an element of'. So, if we consider the above-mentioned set M, then the number 22 is not an element of M. We can express this in the language of set theory as

$$22 \notin M$$

By definition, where A is any set, $x \notin A$ *iff* x is *not* an element of A.

Using these symbols, we can now write:

$$7 \notin \{\text{even numbers}\}$$
$$\text{Rakesh} \in \{\text{Himesh, Rakesh}\}$$

Note that as in the case of objects, *a set can also be an element of another set*. For example, where $A = \{1,2,\{1\}\}$,

$$1 \in A$$
$$2 \in A$$

and also the set $\{1\} \in A$

The Empty Set

According to set theory, not all sets have members. The empty set is the set which has *no* members.

The axiom of empty set is one of the axioms in Zermelo-Frankel set theory:

Empty set axiom: $(\exists A)\ (\forall x)\ x \notin A$

It is postulated that there *exists* a set A such that for any x, x is *not* an element of A. Such a set, which has no members, is called the empty set or the **null set**. By convention, an empty set is written as '∅' or as '{ }'.

For example, the set of all four-sided triangles is an empty set. Similarly, the set of natural numbers that is not divisible by itself is an empty set. It is important to note that the empty set is *not* equivalent to nothing. Rather, it is a set. However, by definition, it has no members.

You may think that the empty set is of no use. On the contrary, it plays a significant role in many set-theoretic theorems. By set operations, a surprising array of new sets can be constructed from the empty set. For example, we can form the set $\{\varnothing\}$ whose only member is $\varnothing$.

Note that $\varnothing \neq \{\varnothing\}$, i.e. the empty set and the single-membered set of empty set are not identical. Principle of extensionality, which is discussed below, shows that they cannot be identical; for, their members are not identical. For, $\varnothing \notin \varnothing$ but $\varnothing \in \{\varnothing\}$.

We can also form other non-empty sets out of the empty set such as $\{\{\varnothing\}\}$, $\{\{\{\{\varnothing\}\}\}\}$.

Cardinality of Sets

Cardinality of a set indicates the number of elements in a given set. Each set is supposed to have distinct, unique elements. When M = {Mt. Everest, City of Agra, the number 21}, we have a three-member set. That is, the cardinality of M is 3. Symbolically we express this as

$$|M| = 3$$

You can easily come up with examples of set with different cardinalities, e.g. two-membered or four-membered sets.

Two sets can be compared in terms of their cardinality. When M = {Mt. Everest, City of Agra, the number 21}, and $N = \{1, 2, 3\}$, the cardinality of M and N are said to be identical, as they both have three elements. Symbolically, we express this as $|M| = |N|$.

A set A is said to have cardinality greater than set B if, for every element of B, we can find an element in A, but not the converse.

We can also express the situation depicted in Fig. H.1 as set B has cardinality less than set A.

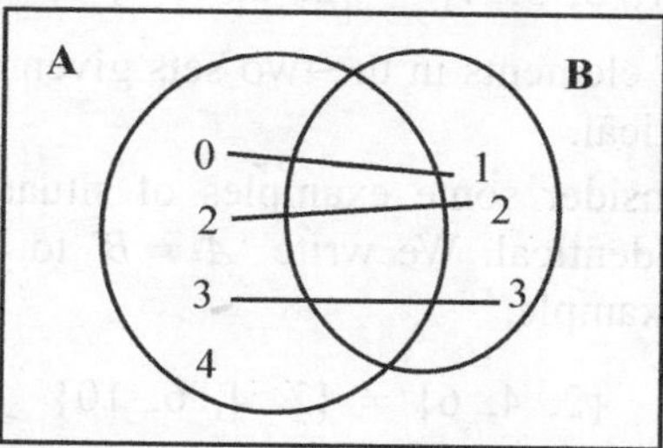

Fig. H.1 ***A* has greater cardinality than *B*.**

As we saw above, some sets can have infinite number of elements. For example, the set of all even numbers, the set of all odd numbers, the set of all natural numbers, etc. Note that the set of even positive numbers {2, 4, 6, …} has the same cardinality as the set of natural numbers {1, 2, 3, …}. Both are infinite.

The cardinality of the empty set, because it has no members, is zero. The cardinality of {∅}, however, is not zero. It is a one-membered set.

Principle of Extensionality

Simply put, this principle states that if two sets have exactly the same members, then they are identical. That is, the Principle of extensionality states that for any two sets A and B:

$$(A = B) \equiv [(x \in A) \equiv (x \in B)]$$

Given any two sets A and B, A and B are identical *iff* every member of A is a member of B, and every member of B is also a member of A. In other words, $A = B$, *iff* x is a member of A *iff* it is also a member of B. Thus,

$$\{2, 4, 6, 8\} = \{x : x \text{ is an even number and } x < 10\}$$

A set is uniquely and solely determined by its elements, i.e., a set is characterizable only in terms of its elements. There is no other way. Any two sets are different *iff* their elements are different. On the other hand, any two sets are identical *iff* their elements are identical. The same thought is expressed by the principle of extensionality.

Note that while considering the identity of two sets, the order in which the elements are presented in a set does not matter. Thus,

{Gandhi, Nehru, Radhakrishnan} = {Nehru, Radhakrishnan, Gandhi}

Since the elements are the same, the two sets are identical.

Similarly, while considering the identity of two sets, each *unique* element is counted. Repeated occurrence of an element is not considered as the occurrence of a new element. Thus,

$$\{1, 2, 3, 4\} = \{2, 2, 1, 4, 3, 1\}$$

Though the number of elements in the two sets given above differs, actually the two sets are identical.

Now, we may consider some examples of situations when we cannot consider two sets as identical. We write '$A \neq B$' to express that "A is not identical to B". For example,

$$\{2, 4, 6\} \neq \{2, 4, 6, 10\}$$

For, 10 is a member of one of the sets but is not the member of the other. Similarly,

{Gandhi, Nehru, Radhakrishnan} $\neq$ {Manmohan Singh, Nehru, Gandhi, Subhas Bose}

Uniqueness of Empty Set

Note that we can apply this principle of extensionality to establish that there can be *only one* empty set. Since an empty set has no elements, if there were two empty sets, they would be indiscernibly identical. Any two such sets must *coincide*. Thus, the empty set is unique. Because of its uniqueness, logicians speak of empty set as 'the' empty set, instead of saying 'an' empty set.

Subset

For any two sets A and B, A is said to be the *subset* of B *iff* every element of A is also an element of B. Consider all the houses in your street. They form a set. Let us call that set A. Now, consider all the houses in your city or town. They too form a set that we'll call B. Note that all the houses in set A, as they are also included among the houses in your city or town, are contained in B also as members. This is when we can say that A is the subset of B.

In the language of set theory, we express 'A is the subset of B' as:

$$A \subseteq B$$

Symbolically, the subset relationship may be expressed as follows:

$$A \subseteq B \equiv (\forall x)\ [(x \in \mathrm{A}) \supset (x \in B)]$$

$A \subseteq B$ *iff* for any x, if x is a member of A, then x is a member of B.

Consider, for example the following:

$\{a, e\} \subseteq \{a, e, i, o, u\}$
$\{133, 61\} \subseteq \{222, 141, 61, 8, 433, 133\}$
$\{x\text{: } x \text{ is a dog}\} \subseteq \{x\text{: } x \text{ is a mammal}\}$
$\{x\text{: } x \text{ is a river}\} \subseteq \{x\text{: } x \text{ is a water body}\}$

Two rather interesting conclusions about subsets follow:

(i) Any given set is a subset of itself. i.e.

For any set A, $A \subseteq A$.

For, every element in A, by definition, is also an element in A.

(ii) The empty set is the subset of any set A, i.e.

$$(\forall A)\ \varnothing \subseteq A$$

For, the empty set has no elements. It vacuously holds true that *if* x is a member of the empty set, then x is also a member of A.

If $A \subseteq B$, then we can also say that A is *included* in B, or that B *includes* A. This inclusion relation in the context of subsets is not to be confused with the membership relation. For, if we want to know if $A \in B$, then we look for A as a single element among the members of B. On the other hand, if we want to know if $A \subseteq B$, then we look, not for A as a single object, but for all elements in A, and check if they are also elements of B.

For example,

$$\varnothing \subseteq \varnothing \text{ but } \varnothing \notin \varnothing$$

Similarly,

$$\{\varnothing\} \in \{\{\varnothing\}\} \text{ but } \{\varnothing\} \not\subset \{\{\varnothing\}\}$$

If we understand subset relationship as explained, then you will also see that subset relationship is *transitive*. If $A \subseteq B$, and $B \subseteq C$, then $A \subseteq C$. However, $A \subseteq B$ holds if *every* member of A is also a member of B. In other words, if even one element of A is not an element of B, then A cannot be a subset of B. So, if $A = \{1, 2, 3\}$, and $B = \{1, 2, 4\}$, then $A \not\subset B$ (A is not a subset of B) as $3 \in A$ but $3 \notin B$.

Any set will have one or more subsets. In fact, if any given set A has n elements, then A will have 2^n subsets.

Proper Subset

A set A is said to be a *proper subset* of set B (symbolically $A \subset B$) *iff* it is a subset of B and B is not identical to A, i.e.,

$$A \subset B \equiv (A \subseteq B) \bullet (A \neq B)$$

Note that if A is a proper subset of B, every member of A is a member of B, but every member of B is not be a member of A. You can also understand this relationship by pondering over the following fact. Every set is a subset of itself, but no set is a proper subset of itself.

For example,

$$\text{Set of dogs} \subset \text{Set of mammals}$$
$$\{1, 2, 5\} \subset \{1, 2, 3, 4, 5\}$$

Power Set

If we collect all the subsets of a set A in one collection, then we shall have the *power set* ($\mathcal{PA}$) of A.

For any set A, there exists a set B whose members are exactly the subsets of A.

Power set axiom: $(\forall A)\ (\exists B)\ (\forall x)\ ((x \in B) \equiv (x \subseteq A))$

For example, if $A = (1, 2, \{1\}\}$,

$\mathcal{P}(\mathcal{A}) = \{\varnothing, \{1\}, \{2\}, \{\{1\}\}, \{1,2\}, \{1, \{1\}\}, \{2, \{1\}\}, \{1, 2, \{1\}\}\}$

Note that the empty set is a subset of any set. So, it has a place in every power set, regardless of what the set is.

Thus,

$$\mathcal{P}\{\varnothing\} = \{\varnothing, \{\varnothing\}\}$$

$$\mathcal{P}\{0, 1\} = \{\varnothing, \{0\}, \{1\}, \{0,1\}\}$$

Set Operations

From a given set or from given sets, there are number of ways in which new sets may be formed. The operations which lead to construction of new sets from the existing ones are listed below.

Union: A new set may be constructed out of the 'union' of two existing sets. Simply put the union of any two sets A and B is another set C which contains all the members of A and also all the members of B. Consider the situation when you take all the items from drawer A and also take all the items from drawer B and put them all together in drawer C. That is how we may understand the union of sets.

The symbol for union is '$\cup$'. It A and B are any two sets, $A \cup B$ represents their union. Thus,

$$A \cup B = \{x: x \in A \text{ or } x \in B\}$$

If A = {Taj Mahal, Qutab Minar} and $B = \{16, 17, 18\}$, then

$$A \cup B = \{\text{Taj Mahal, Qutab Minar, } 16, 17, 18\}$$

If $A = \{155, 166\}$ and $B = \{155, 166\}$, then

$$A \cup B = \{155, 166\}$$

In general, for any given set A, $A \cup A = A$.

The union operation works similar to the operator '$\vee$' in propositional logic. The union of set *A* and *B* is the set of all things that are either member of *A* or of *B*, or of both. If $A = \{1, 2, 3\}$ and $B = \{2, 4, 5\}$, then

$$A \cup B = \{1, 2, 3, 4, 5\}$$

Note that '2' belongs to both sets *A* and *B*. However, there is no need to write it twice in the new set $A \cup B$. All we need for $A \cup B$ is to list all the elements of *A* and *B* without duplication.

Similarly, for example, if *A* = {all the towns in West Bengal State} and *B* = {all the towns in Orissa state}, then

$A \cup B$ = {all the towns that are either in West Bengal state or in Orissa state}

Note that it is a basic property of union that union is commutative:

$$A \cup B = B \cup A$$

Furthermore, for any given set *A*, $A \cup \varnothing$ (the empty set) $= A$. For, the empty set does not have any member. Therefore, union with the empty set does not add any members to the elements of a given set.

Intersection: While learning about 'union', we used the examples of items in your two drawers and saw how the union operation allows us to 'add' all the items in both drawers to arrive at a new set. For 'intersection', let us use the example of the same two drawers in your table. However, this time we look only for the elements that these two drawers have *in common.* If you find any item or items that are common to both of them, you have an example of intersection.

The symbol used for intersection is '$\cap$'. Given any two sets, *A* and *B*, their intersection, i.e., the elements they have in common, is denoted by $A \cap B$. Thus,

$$A \cap B = \{x: (x \in A) \bullet \{x \in B)\}$$

For example, where $A = \{33, 37, 38, 41\}$, and $B = \{23, 33, 41, 51\}$, the elements that they have in common are 33, and 41. Thus,

$$A \cap B = \{33, 41\}$$

If *A* = {Panini, Aryabhatt, Varahamihir} and *B* = {Panini, Jaimini, Vyasa}, the

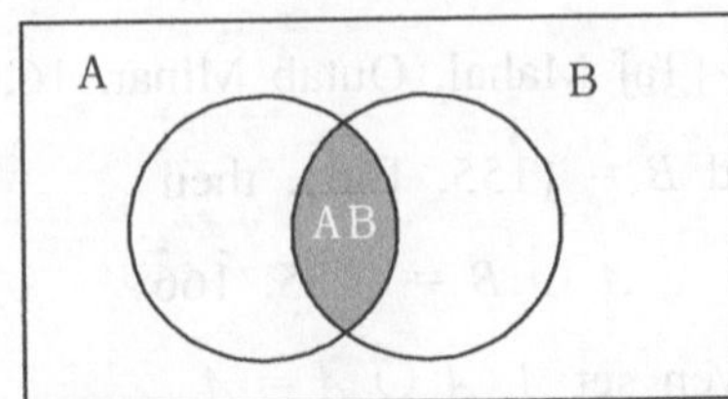

Fig. H.2 The shaded area *AB* shows that $A \cap B$.

$$A \cap B = \{\text{Panini}\}$$

Now suppose $A = \{1, 2, 617\}$, and $B = \{316, 312, 312\}$, then $A \cap B$ is an empty set. For, there is no element that is common to both A and B. In case any two sets A and B have nothing in common, i.e., when $A \cap B = \varnothing$, A and B are said to be **disjoint sets.**

Note that the intersection of a set with itself is the set itself. In general, for any set A,

$$A \cap A = A$$

However, for any set A, the intersection with the empty set will result in empty set. For, if A is a non-empty set, there shall be no common element between it and the empty set. On the other hand, if A is the empty set itself, even then since the set is empty, there is no question of there being any common element. So, the result will be the empty set. Thus, the general tenet is that:

$$A \cap \varnothing = \varnothing$$

Also note that it is a basic property of intersection that for any two sets A and B,

$$A \cap B = B \cap A$$

If you have understood the concept of intersection, it should be also evident to you that the intersection set is a *subset* of any of the two sets from which it was constructed. Where $A = \{33, 37, 38, 41\}$, and $B = \{23, 33, 41, 51\}$, we saw above that $A \cap B = \{33, 41\}$. Every element of this new set $A \cap B$ is a member of set A. Similarly, every element of this new set $A \cap B$; namely, either 33 or 41, is also a member of set B. In this sense, $A \cap B$ is a subset of set A. For the same reason, it is also a subset of B. Thus, in general we can say that where A and B are any two given sets,

$$A \cap B \subset A$$
$$A \cap B \subset B$$

Note that where $A = \{33, 37\}$ and $B = \{41, 38, 33, 37\}$, i.e., where $A \subset B$, there $A \cap B = A$. In fact, in general it is true that for any two sets A and B,

$$\text{If } A \subset B, \text{ then } A \cap B = A$$

However, in case of union, a significantly different result holds:

$$\text{If } A \subset B, \text{ then } A \cup B = B$$

Consider again, for example $A = \{33, 37\}$ and $B = \{41, 38, 33, 37\}$. $A \subset B$, therefore, $A \cup B$ will produce the set of all elelments from both sets. Since A is a subset of B, its elements are already contained in B. Therefore, $A \cup B = B$.

Relative complement: For any sets A and B, the relative complement $A - B$ is:

$$A - B = \{x : (x \in A) \bullet (x \notin B)\}$$

Algebra of Sets

The study of the above-mentioned set operations, Union—intersection, and relative complementation—goes by the name of "Algebra of Sets".

The following rules which hold for any given set are some of the basic facts of algebra:

Commutative Laws

$$A \cup B = B \cup A$$
$$A \cap B = B \cap A$$

Associative laws

$$A \cup (B \cup C) = (A \cup B) \cup C$$
$$A \cap (B \cap C) = (A \cap B) \cap C$$

Distributive laws

$$A \cup (B \cap C) = (A \cup B) \cap (A \cup C)$$
$$A \cap (B \cup C) = (A \cap B) \cup (A \cap C)$$

De Morgan's laws

$$C - (A \cup B) = (C - A) \cap (C - B)$$
$$C - (A \cap B) = (C - A) \cup (C - B)$$

Identities involving the empty set

$$A \cup \varnothing = A$$
$$A \cap \varnothing = \varnothing$$
$$A \cap (C - A) = \varnothing$$

Since the basic set theory is included in this book as an appendix, problems or exercises have not been included. However, in Chapter 9 on Aristotelian Syllogistic Logic, plenty of exercises are given, in which the set theoretic concepts and principles may be applied.

SOLUTIONS TO SELECTED EXERCISES

CHAPTER 1

Section 1.1

2. a. No reasoning involved.

e. There is reasoning involved in this passage. Someone is trying to claim that death penalty is justifiable and in support the person has cited one of the usual reasons.

4. The etymological meaning of 'logic' has to be derived from the root of the word, which is Greek. The English word 'logic' comes from the Greek word *Logos* which means reasoned discourse or a systematic study. According to this, logic also means a systematic study.

But this does not give us any information about what logic is about or what is its subject matter. 'Biology', on the other hand, gives a clue about its subject matter: 'Bio' or life. For logic, the absence of any clue to the subject matter is supposed to be a clue in itself. For, logic is a reasoned study about reason and its application.

Section 1.2

3. The Law of Non-contradiction states: Nothing can be both 'a' and 'not–a' at the same time, everything being the same. For example, nothing can be both white and non-white at the same time, everything else being the same.

If we allow a violation of this law, then it should become possible for a thing to be both 'a' and 'not–a' at the same time, with everything remaining the same. If so, then the thing has to be both 'a' and 'not–a'.

This is a direct violation of the Law of Excluded Middle, which says that everything must be either 'a' or its negation, with no Middle or in-between possibilities.

CHAPTER 2

Section 2.1

3. a. Not a claim, it is an exclamatory statement that cannot be properly called true or false.

d. A claim which can be found out to be true or false.

Section 2.2

1. a. False. Arguments are always more than a mere set of claims. They must exhibit a special relationship, that of conclusion and supporting premises, among the claims which constitute the set of claims.

g. True. See point No. 6 in Section 2.2.

2. c. In standard format:

Each person has a right to liberty and property

∴ The government should leave individual citizens free to exchange their labour and property as they freely choose.

h. In standard format:

1. History in the strict sense is dependent on human testimony.
2. This is not available with respect to the development of the world of life.
3. The only evidence available is that provided by the fossils.

∴ We must be satisfied with something less satisfactory.

Section 2.3

1. b. Yes, it contains an argument.

The conclusion marker 'therefore' is present in the last statement "Therefore, if an industry pollutes, it is only fair to make it pay for the damages caused". Also, overall there is a specified structure among the statements in this passage that shows that one of the claims is a conclusion and the rest are premises towards that.

g. Not an argument. It does not contain any indicator words and also there is no premise-conclusion relation among the statements used.

Section 2.4

2. b. *Deductive argument.* The premises contain all the facts and the conclusion 'simple' brings out what is already given in the premises. If the premises are true, in this case the conclusion must be true. Therefore, we will call it a deductive argument with 'good' justification.

f. *Inductive argument.* The generalization that TV watching is linked to obesity is the result of observing and researching many instances, as the reference to numerous studies bear out. There is an inductive leap from the cases observed to a universal claim.

Section 2.5

1. b. The close connectivity between countries can (G) lead to undesirable economic consequences. Although (D) close connection between countries promises greater economic growth, it may (G) also cause undesirable economic fluctuation. Like a plague, any adverse economic condition or implementation of one economic policy by one country could be (G) easily transmitted to another.

Section 2.6

1. a. First, we mark the statements as: Research findings are often questionable [1]. Due to pressure of meeting deadlines, external and internal competitions, researchers often cannot be as careful as they should be [2]. Little errors slowly mount up and as a result the data becomes unreliable [3].

The first statement is the conclusion. The diagram is as follows:

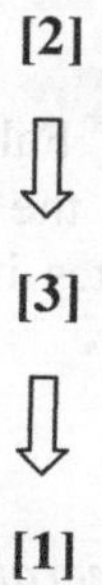

g. If I take the train to Oviedo, I arrive at Oviedo quite late [1]. Arriving late means reaching my hotel could be a problem [2]. On the other hand, if I fly to Oviedo, I have to buy the air-tickets now [3]. Buying air-tickets now will mean I have to check their prices first [4]. So, whichever transport I use, I shall reach Oviedo [5].

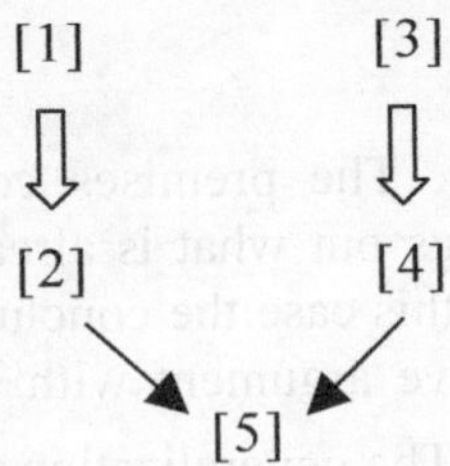

Section 2.7

1. a. True. By definition, an argument, if it is sound, has to be valid and in addition has to have all true premises. Thus, by definition a sound argument must be valid.

   e. False. For, it is possible that an argument with all true premises and true conclusion may be invalid. That is, it is possible that the truth of the conclusion may not follow from the truth of the premises. If it is possible for the argument to be invalid, it is possible that it is unsound.

   Example: Bangkok is the capital of Thailand and Dhaka is the capital of Bangladesh. So, New Delhi is the capital of India.

   j. False. For, it is possible that the argument may have a false conclusion, and argument with all true premises but a false conclusion will be invalid. And if invalid, it cannot be sound.

CHAPTER 3

Section 3.1

2. Incorrect. It is an example of Fallacy of Division. Just because the colour black can be applied to the whole pen, it does not mean every physical molecule that constitutes it must individually be black also.

Section 3.2

b. *Example of illicit or hasty generalization fallacy.* Only three instances have been seen, and a universal claim has been made. It is also an example of *Post hoc, ergo propter hoc* or the fallacy of false cause. It is an unwarranted assumption based on coincidences. Just because Preetpal was present on three occasions when bad luck fell on me, I should not jump to a causal conclusion that he is the cause of my bad luck.

g. It is an example of Fallacy of Appeal to Common Practice or to the Popularity of the Belief. The fact that most people do or believe something does *not* make an action or a belief right or acceptable.

CHAPTER 4

1. b. True.

f. False. Greek logicians were known even before Aristotle.

CHAPTER 5

Section 5.2

1. b. Not simple. It is a compound statement made of two statements joined by the connective 'and'.

Four of us can go by car <u>and</u> *the rest can take the train.*

e. Simple statement because it has no other simple statement as a structural component present in it.

2. In propositional logic, 'simple' statement means structurally simple statements. This means only that the statement does not contain any other statement as a component. 'Simple' in this sense does not mean simplicity in meaning. Many structurally simple statements can have complex meaning, 'Simple' also does not mean that the statement will have to be short in length. It only means that when its composition is analyzed, there will be no other statement present as its constituent.

Section 5.3

1. A monadic or unary connective can connect only one statement at a time. A dyadic or binary connective can, on the other hand, connect at most two statements at a time. 'Not' is the only monadic connective among the five connectives used in propositional logic. The rest, 'and', 'or', 'if-then', and 'if and only if' are dyadic or binary connectives.

5. a. True. The possibility remains that a material conditional may be false with a true antecedent, *if it also has a false consequent.* According to the truth table of a material conditional, it is false when its antecedent is true but its consequent is false.

f. True. A '$\vee$' is true when both its disjuncts are true.

Section 5.5

3. Three truth values: true, false, and undecided.

4. a. True. For, we know C is true, and this makes $D \vee C$ true, and since $D \vee C$ is the consequent, it makes the whole statement, which is a material conditional, true. For, a material conditional with a true consequent is always true. Note that once we know that C is true, it does not matter in this case what value the unknown D has.

e. We know that $A \bullet B$ is false as A is true and B is false. Now, D is unknown, which means it can be either true or false. Therefore:

Possibility 1: Suppose that D is true, then $D \equiv (A \bullet B)$ will be false as $T \equiv F$ is false.

Possibility 2: Suppose that D is false, then '$D \equiv (A \bullet B)$' will be true as $F \equiv F$ is true.

So, the answer to this question is to cite both of these possibilities. Note that the truth value of the whole statement can still be determined even when the truth value of D is unknown.

l. False, as the second conjunct will be false.

Section 5.7

1. a. False. '$p \bullet r$' is false, so that makes the conditional with $p \bullet r$ as the antecedent true, and $q \vee r$, both being false, will be false. $T \equiv F$ is false so the truth value of the whole statement will be false.

e. False, because the conjunct $\sim [(p \vee q) \bullet (p \vee r)]$ will be false and a conjunction with a false conjunct will be false.

Section 5.8

1. d. The main connective is '~'. The rest of the statement is within its scope.

Section 5.9

1. b. $M \supset G$

2. a. At least one of Aveek, Balaram and Champa will win.

e. At most one of Aveek, Balaram and Champa will win.

3. a. $\sim I \bullet (P \vee C)$

g. $I \supset (J \vee (Q \bullet P))$

Section 5.10

1. a. $\sim N \bullet \sim T$ or $\sim (N \vee T)$

i. $(A \supset H) \equiv (C \bullet S)$

CHAPTER 6

Section 6.1

1. a. There will be 2^5 or $2 \times 2 \times 2 \times 2 \times 2 = 32$ rows, as there are five distinct atomic components in the statement.

3. a.

H	K	$H \bullet K$[1]	$K \supset H$	$H \supset (K \supset H)$[2]	$1 \bullet 2$
T	T	T	T	T	T
T	F	F	T	T	F
F	T	F	F	T	F
F	F	F	T	T	F

4. a. Translation: $\sim I \supset \sim B$. In the truth table below, in order to keep the sequence of logical relation correct, we have put I before B in the reference columns.

I	B	$\sim I$	$\sim B$	$\sim I \supset \sim B$
T	T	F	F	T
T	F	F	T	T
F	T	T	F	F
F	F	T	T	T

Section 6.2

1. b. Not an actual statement, it is a statement form composed exclusively of statement variables.

4. b. False. For, a conjunction is true only when both its conjuncts are true. Having a tautology as one of the conjuncts ensures that one of the conjuncts will be true, but it does not ensure what the value of the other conjunct will be.

e. True. Follows from the definition of a tautology.

Section 6.3

1. a. True. Both are tautologies, as can be seen from the following truth tables:

p	$p \bullet p$	$p \supset (p \bullet p)$
T	T	T
F	F	T

p	q	$\sim q$	$q \vee \sim q$	$p \supset (q \vee \sim q)$
T	T	F	T	T
T	F	T	T	T
F	T	F	T	T
F	F	T	T	T

2. d. Contingent statement form, as can be seen from the following truth table:

q	$q \supset q$	$(q \supset q) \supset q$
T	T	T
F	T	F

Section 6.4

1. a. Invalid argument, as there is one F in the final column.

H	J	K	$\sim J(3)$	$\sim K(4)$	$H \supset J$	$K \bullet (H \supset J)(1)$	$J \equiv H(2)$	$(1 \bullet 2) \bullet 3$	$((1 \bullet 2) \bullet 3) \supset 4$
T	T	T	F	F	T	T	T	F	T
T	T	F	F	T	T	F	T	F	T
T	F	T	T	F	F	F	F	F	T
T	F	F	T	T	F	F	F	F	T
F	T	T	F	F	T	T	F	F	T
F	T	F	F	T	T	F	F	F	T
F	**F**	**T**	**T**	**F**	**T**	**T**	**T**	**T**	**F** ⇦
F	F	F	T	T	T	F	T	F	T

f. Valid argument. Its truth table is as follows:

A	C	~A	~C	A≡C	~(A≡C)	~A≡C	(A≡C)∨ (~ A ≡ C)[1]	~A≡~C	(~A≡~C)∨ ~ (A ≡ C)[2]	[1]⊃[2]
T	T	F	F	T	F	F	T	T	T	T
T	F	F	T	F	T	T	T	F	T	T
F	F	T	F	F	T	F	F	F	T	T
F	T	T	T	T	F	T	T	T	T	T

Section 6.5

1. c. Argument shown invalid under the truth value assignments as shown below in the shorter truth table:

X	Y	U	V	(X ⊃ Y) • (U ⊃ V)	Y ⊃ V	X ⊃ U
T	T	F	T	T • T	T	F

o. The shorter truth table below shows one of the possible truth value assignments on which the argument will be invalid:

A	B	C	G	K	L	M	K ⊃ (A • B)	~ L ∨ ~ M	L ⊃ (K ∨ C)	C ⊃ (B ⊃ M)	G ⊃ (A ⊃ K)	~ (K ≡ G)
T	T	F	T	T	F	T	T	T	T	T	T	F

Section 6.6

1. d. Inconsistent set. The truth table below shows that there is no row on which each statement is true.

T ⇩	R	~T	~R	T≡R ⇩	~T∨ ~R ⇩
T	T	F	F	T	F
T	F	F	T	F	T
F	T	T	F	F	T
F	F	T	T	T	T

2. e. The set is consistent. There is at least one possible truth value assignment on which every member of the set will be true and we can construct this row by a shorter truth table:

A	D	E	A ≡ ~ D	~ D ⊃ (E • A)	~ (~ A ∨ ~ E)
T	F	T	T	T	T

Section 6.8

1. f. $H \supset (I \supset J)$ and $(H \supset I) \supset J$ are not logically equivalent. We prove this by the truth table method as follows:

⇩ ⇩

H	I	J	$I \supset J$	$H \supset (I \supset J)$	$H \supset I$	$(H \supset I) \supset J$
T	T	T	T	T	T	T
T	T	F	F	F	T	F
T	F	T	T	T	F	T
T	F	F	T	T	F	T
F	T	T	T	T	T	T
F	T	F	F	T	T	F
F	F	T	T	T	T	T
F	F	F	T	T	T	F

A comparison of the final columns of the statements shows that they are not logically equivalent.

2. f. The statements $V \bullet (P \vee L)$ and $(V \bullet P) \vee L$ are not logically equivalent. The shorter truth table shows that they have different truth values under the identical truth value assignments:

L	P	V	$V \bullet (P \vee L)$	$(V \bullet P) \vee L$
T	T	F	F	T

3. c. The translation for the two statements are:

(i) The inflation rate will not increase provided the economy is flourishing. $E \supset \sim I$

(ii) If the economy is not flourishing, then the inflation rate will increase. $\sim E \supset I$

We show by shorter truth table method that they are *not* logically equivalent as they show different truth values under identical truth value assignments:

E	I	$E \supset \sim I$	$\sim E \supset I$
T	T	F	T

CHAPTER 7

Sections 7.1–7.2

2. Decomposition in the context of truth trees means breaking down a compound statement to literals. Literals in this context means an atomic component such as a simple statement '*B*' or its negation such as '~*B*'. Thus, decomposition would mean breaking a statement down to simple statements and their negations.

A decomposition rule lists the basic truth conditions of a connective or a compound statement formed by that connective. So, the rule tells us when and under which truth value assignment or assignments the connective or the compound formed out of it will be true.

4. b. False. An open tree means a tree which has at least one completed open branch. This means there has to be at least one branch which has been completely decomposed with every decomposable statement being decomposed and the branch open. This does not rule out the possibility of there being some other closed branches. For example, consider the following tree:

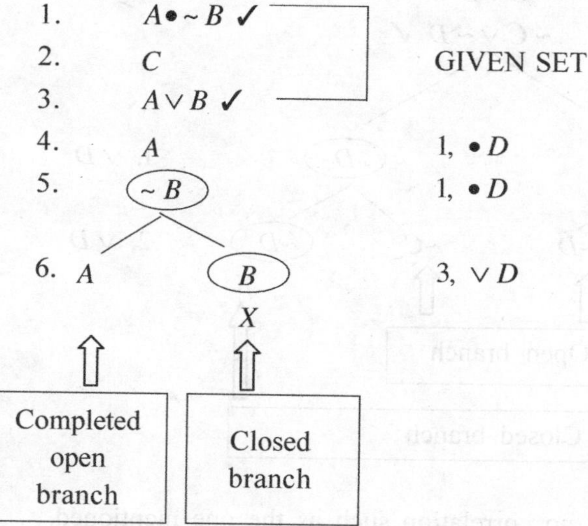

4. d. False. There is no rule that a truth tree must have more than one branch. Since branching or non-branching depends on the nature of the statements that one has to decompose, it is entirely possible that the trunk or the root of the tree continues and becomes the only branch. In other words, it is possible for a truth tree to have only one branch.

Consider the following example:

1.	$B \bullet C$ ✓	GIVEN SET
2.	$A \bullet D$ ✓	
3.	$\sim K \bullet A$ ✓	
4.	B	1, $\bullet D$
5.	C	1, $\bullet D$
6.	A	2, $\bullet D$
7.	D	2, $\bullet D$
8.	$\sim K$	3, $\bullet D$
9.	A	3, $\bullet D$

Section 7.3

1. a. This tree will not result in a closed tree. It will have some closed branches. But since every branch is not closed, the tree cannot be called a closed tree. Consider the following tree:

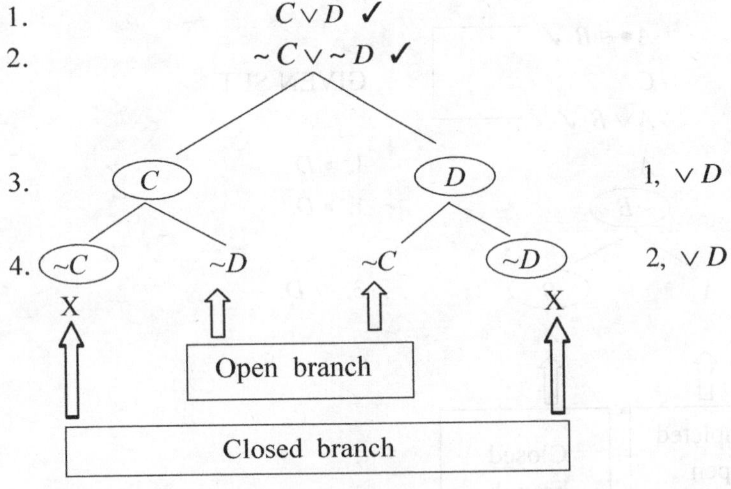

2. a. False. There is no correlation such as the one mentioned.

Section 7.4

1. a. The tree for $(M \bullet N)$, $(M \bullet \sim N)$ will be closed as shown below. Therefore, the set is inconsistent.

1.	$M \bullet N$	✓
2.	$M \bullet \sim N$	✓

3. M — 1, $\bullet D$
4. N (circled) — 1, $\bullet D$
5. M — 2, $\bullet D$
6. $\sim N$ (circled) — 2, $\bullet D$

×

Closed branch

d. The tree will be open as shown below by the tree. Therefore, the set is consistent.

1. $M \bullet N$ ✓
2. $(M \vee (\sim N \bullet O))$ ✓
3. M — 1, $\bullet D$
4. N (circled) — 1, $\bullet D$
5. M | $\sim N \bullet O$ ✓ — 2, $\vee D$
6. | $\sim N$ (circled) — 5, $\bullet D$
7. | O — 5, $\bullet D$

X

One of the branches of this tree is closed as it contains both N and $\sim N$. But the other branch is open. From it we can recover the partial truth value assignments as follows:

M	N
T	T

Under these truth values, the set will be consistent no matter what the truth value of O is.

Section 7.5

1. c. *Testing for contradiction*:

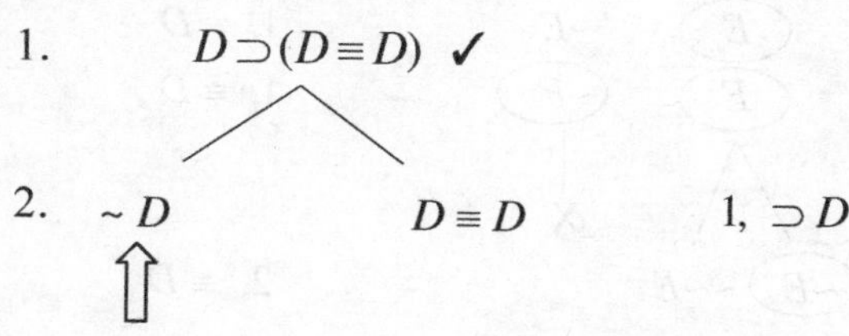

1. $D \supset (D \equiv D)$ ✓
2. $\sim D$ | $D \equiv D$ — 1, $\supset D$

⇧

Thus, the statement is not a contradiction.

Testing for tautology:

1. $\sim[D \supset (D \equiv D)]$ ✓

2. D — 1, $\sim\supset D$

3. $\sim(D \equiv D)$ ✓ — 1, $\sim\supset D$

4. D | $\sim D$ — 3, $\sim\equiv$

5. $\sim D$ | D — 3, $\sim\equiv$

X | X

Since the negation of the statement has resulted in a closed tree, the statement is a tautology.

2. c. True, as can be seen from the tree above.

Section 7.6

1. c. The claim is false since the argument is invalid, as can be seen from the tree below with the premises and the negation of the conclusion:

Original argument: $(E \equiv F)$, $(\sim E \equiv G)$, $(\sim F \equiv H)$, therefore, $(\sim E \bullet \sim F)$

Negation of the conclusion: $\sim(\sim E \bullet \sim F)$

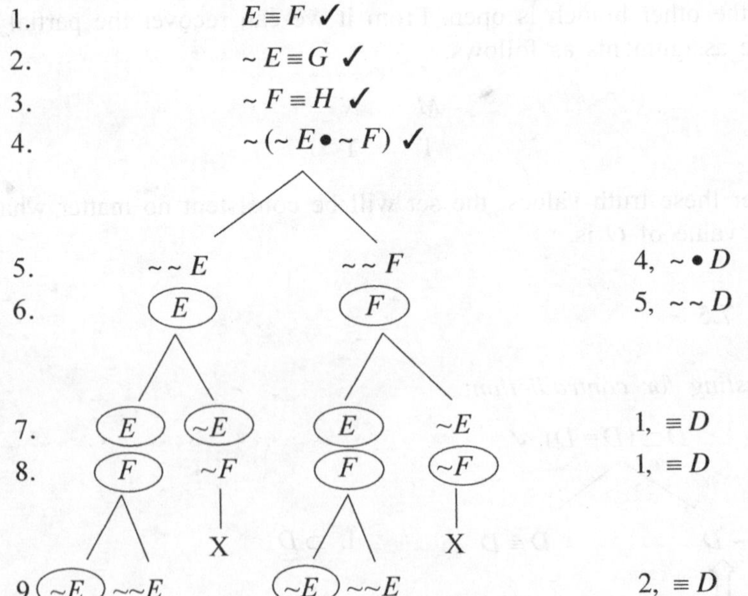

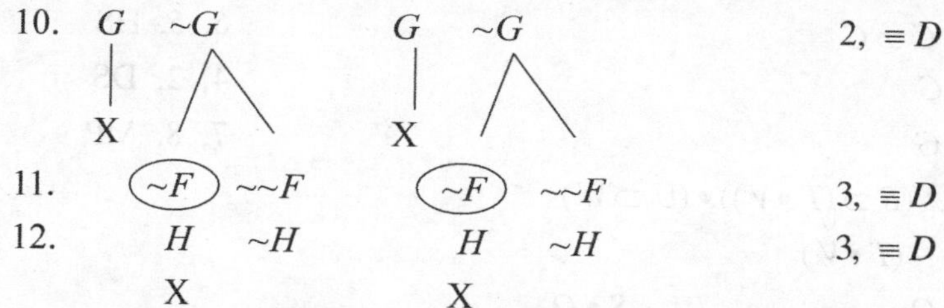

As there are completed open branches on this tree, the given argument is invalid, and a set of recovered partial truth values from its open branches is as follows:

E	*F*	*G*	*H*
T	T	F	F

Section 7.7

1. Yes, because logical equivalence would mean having identical truth conditions. This means there will not be any occasion when a contradiction of truth values will occur in any of the branches.

3. Yes, for the same reason as 1. In this case, the only difference would be that the tree would be for the statements for themselves and not for their compound made with '$\equiv$'. A tree for $\{(A \supset B), (\sim A \vee B)\}$ is a tree for both $A \supset B$ and $\sim A \vee B$.

CHAPTER 8

Section 8.3

A. A2.

1.	L	P
2.	$K \supset N$	P
3.	$\sim N$	P
4.	$\sim K$	2, 3, MT
5.	$L \bullet \sim K$	1, 4, Conj.

A5.

1.	$C \supset D$	P
2.	$\sim F$	P
3.	$D \supset E$	P
4.	$F \vee C$	P
5.	$E \supset G$	P
6.	$C \supset E$	1, 3, HS

	7. $C \supset G$	6, 5, HS
	8. C	4, 2, DS
	9. G	7, 8, MP
B. B1.	*1. $(S \supset (T \bullet V)) \bullet (U \supset W)$	
	2. $\sim (T \bullet V)$	
	3. Q $\quad / \therefore \sim S \bullet Q$	
	4. $(S \supset (T \bullet V))$	1, Simp.
	5. $\sim S$	4, 2, MT
	6. $\sim S \bullet Q$	5, 3, Conj.
B5.	1. $[(K \bullet P) \supset [K \supset (M \bullet N)]]$	
	2. $(K \bullet P) \bullet L$ $\quad / \therefore M \vee N$	
	3. $K \bullet P$	2, Simp.
	4. $K \supset (M \bullet N)$	1, 3, MP
	5. K	3, Simp.
	6. $M \bullet N$	4, 5, MP
	7. M	6, Simp.
	8. $M \vee N$	7, Add.
B10.	1. $K \vee \sim (B \vee R)$	
	2. $K \supset (L \equiv W)$	
	3. $\sim (B \vee R) \supset (K \vee \sim T)$	
	4. $\sim (L \equiv W) \bullet \sim M$ $\quad / \therefore \sim T$	
	5. $\sim (L \equiv W)$	4, Simp.
	6. $\sim K$	2, 5, MT
	7. $\sim (B \vee R)$	1, 6, DS
	8. $K \vee \sim T$	3, 7, MP
	9. $\sim T$	8, 6, DS.

Section 8.4

A. A1.	1. $M \supset Q$	P
	2. $\sim M \vee Q$	1, Impl.
	3. $\sim (\sim\sim M \bullet \sim Q)$	2, De M.
	4. $\sim (M \bullet \sim Q)$	3, DN
A5.	1. $W \equiv X$	P
	2. $W \vee X$	P

3. $(W \bullet X) \vee (\sim W \bullet \sim X)$ — 1, Equiv.
4. $(W \bullet X) \vee \sim W] \bullet [(W \bullet X) \vee \sim X]$ — 3, Dist.
5. $[\sim W \vee (W \bullet X)] \bullet [(W \bullet X) \vee \sim X]$ — 4, Com.
6. $[W \supset (W \bullet X)] \bullet [(W \bullet X) \vee \sim X]$ — 5, Impl.
7. $W \supset (W \bullet X)$ — 6, Simp.

B. B1.

1. $\sim L \vee M$
2. $\sim N \supset \sim M$ — $/ \therefore L \supset N$
3. $L \supset M$ — 1, Impl.
4. $M \supset N$ — 2, Trans.
5. $L \supset N$ — 3, 4, HS.

B5.

1. $J \supset (K \supset L)$ — $/ \therefore K \supset (J \supset L)$
2. $(J \bullet K) \supset L$ — 1, Exp.
3. $(K \bullet J) \supset L$ — 2, Com.
4. $K \supset (J \supset L)$ — 3, Exp.

B10.

1. $\sim K \vee (J \equiv B)$
2. $\sim K \supset K$ — $/ \therefore (B \supset J) \bullet K$
3. $\sim\sim K \vee K$ — 2, Impl.
4. $\sim\sim K \vee \sim\sim K$ — 3, DN
5. $\sim\sim K$ — 4, Taut.
6. $J \equiv B$ — 1, 5, DS
7. $(J \supset B) \bullet (B \supset J)$ — 6, Equiv.
8. $(B \supset J) \bullet (J \supset B)$ — 7, Com.
9. $B \supset J$ — 8, Simp.
10. K — 5, DN
11. $(B \supset J) \bullet K$ — 9, 10, Conj.

Section 8.5

A. 1.

1. $(\sim R \bullet C) \supset (S \vee B)$
2. $\sim R \supset (S \supset V)$
3. $\sim R \bullet C$
4. $\sim B$ — $/ \therefore V$
5. $S \vee B$ — 1, 3, MP
6. S — 5, 4, DS
7. $\sim R$ — 3, Simp.

	8.	$\sim R \bullet S$	7, 6, Conj.
	9.	$(\sim R \bullet S) \supset V$	2, Exp.
	10.	V	9, 8, MP
A.5.	1.	$I \supset (O \supset E)$	
	2.	$(E \bullet R) \supset S$	
	3.	$\sim D \supset (R \bullet \sim S) \quad / \therefore I \supset (O \supset D)$	
	4.	$(I \bullet O) \supset E$	1, Exp.
	5.	$E \supset (R \supset S)$	2, Exp.
	6.	$(I \bullet O) \supset (R \supset S)$	4, 5, HS
	7.	$\sim (R \bullet \sim S) \supset \sim\sim D$	3, Trans.
	8.	$(\sim R \vee \sim\sim S) \supset \sim\sim D$	7, De M.
	9.	$(\sim R \vee \sim\sim S) \supset D$	8, DN
	10.	$(\sim R \vee S) \supset D$	9, DN
	11.	$(R \supset S) \supset D$	10, Impl.
	12.	$(I \bullet O) \supset D$	6, 11, HS
	13.	$I \supset (O \supset D)$	12, Exp.
A.10.	1.	$R \supset (H \bullet S)$	
	2.	$H \supset F$	
	3.	$(E \supset \sim K) \bullet \sim F$	
	4.	$H \supset (R \bullet \sim E) \quad / \therefore H \supset \sim E$	
	5.	$\sim H \vee (R \bullet \sim E)$	4, Impl.
	6.	$(\sim H \vee R) \bullet (\sim H \vee \sim E)$	5, Dist.
	7.	$(\sim H \vee \sim E) \bullet (\sim H \vee R)$	6, Com.
	8.	$\sim H \vee \sim E$	7, Simp.
	9.	$H \supset \sim E$	8, Impl.
A.15.	1.	$(T \supset R) \bullet (U \supset P) \quad / \therefore (T \bullet U) \supset (R \bullet P)$	
	2.	$T \supset R$	1, Simp.
	3.	$(U \supset P) \bullet (T \supset R)$	1, Com.
	4.	$U \supset P$	3, Simp.
	5.	$\sim T \vee R$	2, Impl.
	6.	$(\sim T \vee R) \vee \sim U$	5, Add.
	7.	$\sim U \vee (\sim T \vee R)$	6, Com.
	8.	$(\sim U \vee \sim T) \vee R$	7. Assoc.
	9.	$(\sim T \vee \sim U) \vee R$	8, Com.

10.	$\sim(T \bullet U) \vee R$	9. De M.
11.	$\sim U \vee P$	4, Impl.
12.	$(\sim U \vee P) \vee \sim T$	11, Add.
13.	$\sim T \vee (\sim U \vee P)$	12, Com.
14.	$(\sim T \vee \sim U) \vee P$	13, Assoc.
15.	$\sim(T \bullet U) \vee P$	14, De M.
16.	$[\sim(T \bullet U) \vee R] \bullet [\sim(T \bullet U) \vee P]$	10, 15, Conj.
17.	$\sim(T \bullet U) \vee (R \bullet P)$	16, Dist.
18.	$(T \bullet U) \supset (R \bullet P)$	17, Impl.

Section 8.6

1.1

1.	$R \supset (S \bullet T)$	
2.	$\sim S$	$/ \therefore \sim R$
→3.	R	
4.	$S \bullet T$	1, 3, MP
5.	S	4, Simp.
6.	$S \bullet \sim S$	5, 2, Conj.
7.	$\sim R$	3-6, IP

1.5

1.	$P \supset Q$	
2.	$R \supset P$	
3.	$R \vee (Q \bullet S)$ $/ \therefore Q$	
→4.	$\sim Q$	
5.	$\sim P$	1, 4, MT
6.	$\sim R$	2, 5, MT
7.	$Q \bullet S$	3, 6, DS.
8.	Q	7, Simp.
9.	$Q \bullet \sim Q$	8, 4, Conj.
10.	Q	4–9, IP

1.10

1.	$(R \vee N) \supset (P \bullet R)$	
2.	$N \supset P$	
3.	$\sim Q \supset (R \vee N)$	$/ \therefore Q \vee R$
→4.	$\sim(Q \vee R)$	
5.	$\sim Q \bullet \sim R$	4, De M.
6.	$\sim Q$	5, Simp.

7. $R \vee N$ — 3, 6, MP
8. $P \bullet R$ — 1, 7, MP
9. $R \bullet P$ — 8, Com.
10. R — 9, Simp.
11. $\sim R \bullet \sim Q$ — 5, Com.
12. $\sim R$ — 11, Simp.
13. $R \bullet \sim R$ — 10, 12, Conj.
14. $Q \vee R$ — 4–13, IP

Section 8.7

1.1
1. $C \supset D$ $\quad / \therefore [(D \supset E) \supset (C \supset E)]$
2. $D \supset E$
3. C
4. D — 1, 3, MP
5. E — 2, 4, MP
6. $C \supset E$ — 3–5, CP
7. $(D \supset E) \supset (C \supset E)$ — 2–6, CP

1.5
1. $P \supset (T \bullet S)$
2. $Q \supset (S \bullet W)$ $\quad / \therefore (\sim T \bullet \sim W) \supset (\sim P \bullet \sim Q)$
3. $\sim T \bullet \sim W$
4. $\sim T$ — 3, Simp.
5. $\sim T \vee \sim S$ — 4, Add.
6. $\sim (T \bullet S)$ — 5, De M
7. $\sim P$ — 1, 6, MT
8. $\sim W \bullet \sim T$ — 3, Com.
9. $\sim W$ — 8, Simp.
10. $\sim W \vee \sim S$ — 9, Add.
11. $\sim S \vee \sim W$ — 10, Com.
12. $\sim (S \bullet W)$ — 11, De M.
13. $\sim Q$ — 2, 12, MT.
14. $\sim P \bullet \sim Q$ — 7, 13, Conj.
15. $(\sim T \bullet \sim W) \supset (\sim P \bullet \sim Q)$ — 3–14, CP

1.10.
1. $P \vee [(K \supset P) \bullet (Q \supset P)]$
2. $M \bullet (K \vee Q)$ $\quad / \therefore P$

3. $\sim P$	
4. $(K \supset P) \bullet (Q \supset P)$	1, 3, DS
5. $(K \vee Q) \bullet M$	2, Com.
6. $K \vee Q$	5, Simp.
7. $P \vee P$	4, 6, CD
8. P	7, Taut.
9. $\sim P \supset P$	3–8,CP
10. $\sim\sim P \vee P$	9, Impl.
11. $P \vee P$	10, DN
12. P	11, Taut.

Section 8.8

1.5. Show that $(X \supset Y) \supset [(X \bullet Z) \supset (Y \bullet Z)]$ is a tautology

1. $X \supset Y$	
2. $X \bullet Z$	
3. X	2, Simp.
4. Y	1, 3, MP
5. $Z \bullet X$	2, Com.
6. Z	5, Simp.
7. $Y \bullet Z$	4, 6, Conj.
8. $(X \bullet Z) \supset (Y \bullet Z)]$	2–7,CP
9. $(X \supset Y) \supset [(X \bullet Z) \supset (Y \bullet Z)]$	1–8,CP

CHAPTER 9

Section 9.2

2. a. This is a disjunction or an 'either or' statements and is a truth-functional statement, but it is not a categorical statement. No class relationships are being affirmed or denied in it.

c. This is a categorical statement. Something, namely, "that they can be often wrong" is being attributed to 'weather predictions' as a class. Since no quantity term is mentioned, it is not in standard form of a categorical statement. It, nonetheless, is a categorical statement.

4. a. No authors are famous people. Alternatively, no famous people are authors.

Section 9.3

2. a. Some swimmers are not professionals.

d. No traitors are respectable persons. It may be also read as 'no respectable persons are traitors'.

3. b.

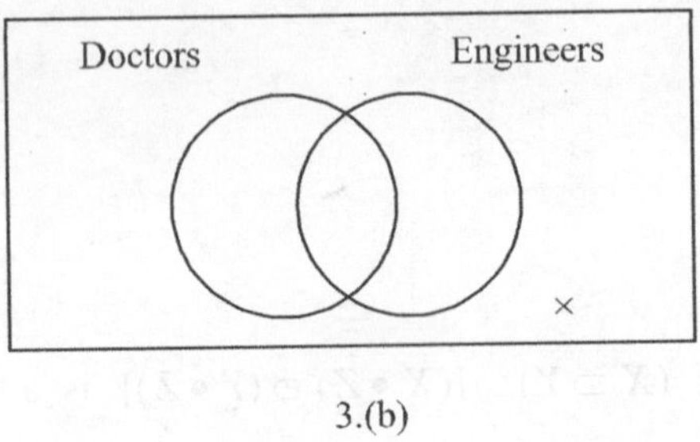

3.(b)

e.

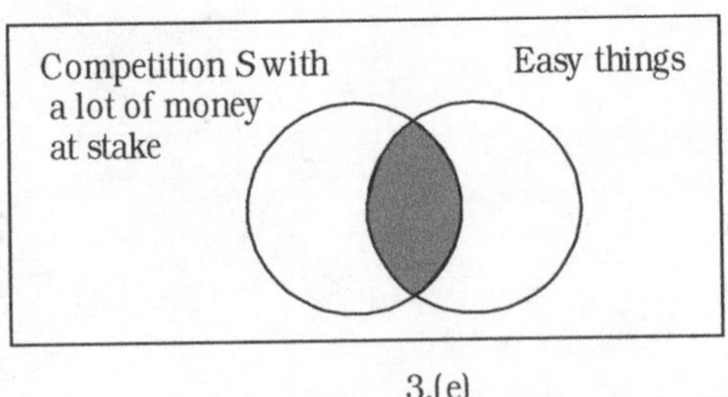

3.(e)

Section 9.4

2. a. If "All politicians are corrupt" is true, then:

(i) "No politicians are corrupt" is false, by contrariety relation.

(ii) "Some politicians are corrupt" is true, by subalternation.

(iii) "Some politicians are not corrupt" is false by contradiction.

c. If "Some reptiles are not poisonous" is false, then:

(i) "All reptiles are poisonous" is true, by contradiction.

(ii) "No reptiles are poisonous" is false, by subalternation.

(iii) "Some reptiles are poisonous" is true, by subcontrariety relation.

Section 9.5

1. a. 1. Some parrots are pet birds.

Conversion: Some pet birds are parrots.

Valid conversion on *I* statement, logically equivalent.

e. 1. All scholarly works are works of dedication.

It is an *A* statement, and *A* statements cannot be validly converted. A conversion by limitation may give us the statement: Some works of dedication are scholarly works. This is not exactly what the given statement says but it follows from what it states.

2. b. 1. Some philosophers are non-conformists.

Obversion: Some philosophers are not non-nonconformists or Some philosophers are not conformists. It is logically equivalent to the given statement.

g. 1. All businessmen are profit oriented.

Obversion: No businessmen are non-profit oriented.

It is logically equivalent to the given statement.

3. a. 1. Some light-bulbs are not blue things.

Contraposition: Some non-blue things are not non-light bulbs.

Or, Some non-blue things are light bulbs.

Logically equivalent to the given statement.

h. Given statement is an *I* statement and Contraposition on *I* statement is not valid.

4. a. Given that "All traders are investors" is true:

1. All non-investors are non-traders	must be true,by contraposition.
2. Then, no non-investors are non-traders	must be false, by contrariety relation.

g. Given that "All traders are investors" is true,

1. Some traders are investors	— True, by subalternation from given
2. Some investors are traders	— True, conversion on 1
3. Some investors are not non-traders	— True, obversion on 2

∴ The truth value of 'No investors are non-traders' cannot be determined. For, by subalternation from the truth of an 'O' statement, nothing can be said about the truth value of the corresponding 'E' statement.

5. a. Given: No politicians are honest (people) — True

1. No honest (people) are politicians.	— True, by conversion on given

∴ 2. Some non-politician are not non-honest (people)	— Must be true, by contraposition by limitation on 1.

g. Given that "No politicians are honest" is true:

1. No honest (persons) are politicians	is true by conversion
2. Then, All honest (persons) are politicians.	is false by contrary relation.

6. a. Given that "Some animals are herbivores" is true:

1. Some animals are not non-herbivores	is true, by obversion on given.
2. Then, All animals are non-herbivores	is false, by contradiction relation.

j. Given that "Some animals are herbivores" is true:

1. Some herbivores are animals	is true, by conversion on given.
2. Then, Some herbivores are not non-animals	is true, by obversion

7. b. Given that "Some economists are not forecasters" is true:

1. Some economists are non-forecasters	is true, by obversion on given
2. Then, No economists are non-forecasters.	is false, by contradiction.

j. Given that "Some economists are not forecasters" is true:

1. Some economists are non-forecasters	is true, by obversion on given
2. Then, Some non-forecasters are economists.	is true, by conversion on 1.

Section 9.6

1. b. No sheep are hostile animals.

k. All Autumn days are short days.

t. Some people are people who have seen the Northern Lights.

Section 9.7

4. a. All good actors are astute observers of human life.

Some comic role artists are astute observers of human life.

Therefore, some comic role artists are good actors.

c. Some metals are conductors.

All copper alloys are metals.

Therefore, some copper alloys are conductors.

Section 9.8

A.1 Standard form:

All citizens are residents.

No foreigners are citizens

So, No foreigners are residents.

The Venn Diagram of this syllogism is as follows:

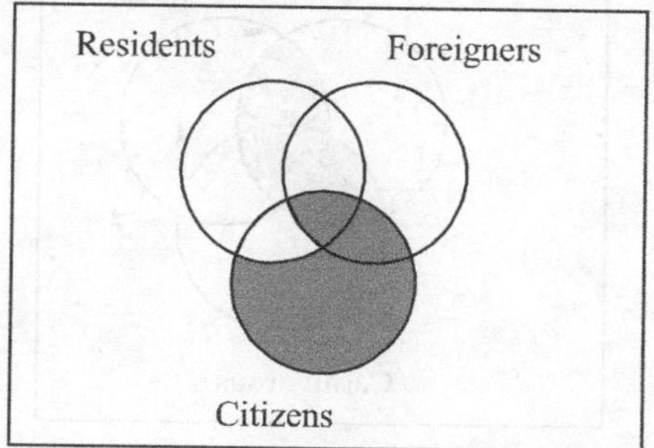

Since the overlapping area between Foreigners and Residents is not completely shaded, the conclusion "No foreigners are residents" does not follow. Therefore, the syllogism is *invalid.*

A.5 Standard form:

Some Indians are Christians

All residents of Kerala are Indians

So, some residents of Kerala are Christians.

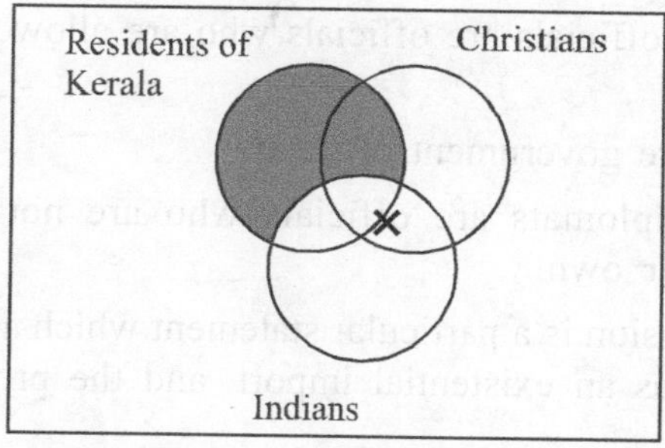

According to the premises, the 'X' lands on the border of the region overlapping between Christians and Indians. It is possible that it is in the region of "Residents of Kerala", but there is also the possibility that it may not fall within that region. If it does not, then the syllogism is invalid. Because of this element of possibility, the syllogism is *invalid*.

B1. Elephants are not tigers and no elephants are carnivorous, so no tigers are carnivorous.

Standard form:

No elephants are carnivorous.

No elephants are tigers.

So, No tigers are carnivorous.

The syllogism is *invalid* as can be seen from the following Venn Diagram:

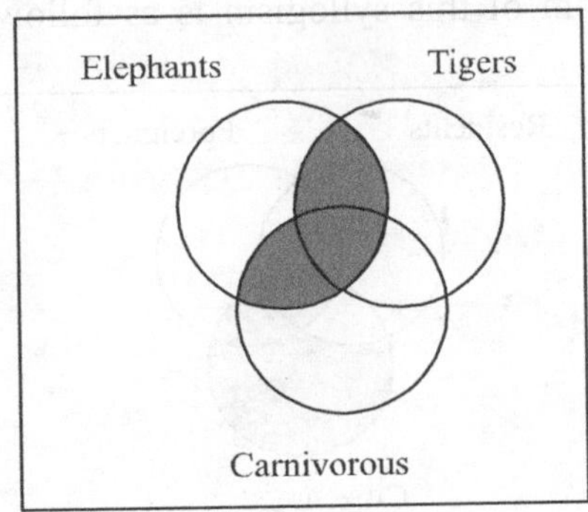

Since the overlapping region between "Tigers and Carnivorous" is not completely shaded, the conclusion does not follow from the premises.

Section 9.9

3. No government officials are allowed to run a business of their own, and all diplomats are government officials. Therefore, almost all diplomats are not allowed to own a business of their own.

   Standard form:

   No government officials are officials who are allowed to run a business of their own.

   All diplomats are government officials.

   Hence, some diplomats are officials who are not allowed to own a business of their own.

   Since the conclusion is a particular statement which according to Boolean interpretation has an existential import, and the premises are universal statements which according to Boolean interpretation do not have existential import, it will be an **existential fallacy** to infer anything about the truth or falsity of the conclusion from the premises. Thus, it will not be a valid inference after Boolean interpretation.

CHAPTER 10

Section 10.1

1. a. $(Rs \bullet Bs) \bullet \sim Is$

j. $Sa \equiv Ha$

3. No, it does not. In it a predicate 'being coextensive', is being attributed to the class of properties. Quantification and Predication of properties is not within the purview of First Order Predicate Logic.

Section 10.2

1. a. $(\exists x)\,(Bx \bullet (Ex \bullet \sim Ix))$

f. $\sim [(\exists x)\,(Bx \bullet Ex)]$

j. $(\forall x)\,(Ex \supset \sim Gx)$

2. a. $(\forall x)\,(Ax \supset Dx)$

h. $[(\forall y)\,(Ax \supset Dx)] \bullet \sim [(\forall x)\,(Dx \supset Cx)]$

or, $[(\forall x)\,(Ax \supset Dx)] \bullet (\exists x)\,(Dx \bullet \sim Cx)$

Section 10.3

1. c. Not all black persons are tall.

f. There is no one who is not subjected to the Law of Gravitation. Or, everyone is subjected to the Law of Gravitation.

Section 10.4

1. b. It is not a statement of Predicate logic, it is a truth functional compound made of a quantified statement and an atomic statement.

i. This is not a statement of Predicate logic, as the negation sign is not at an appropriate place. This disqualifies it from being a well-formed statement of Predicate logic.

2. a. A quantified statement, as the whole statement is within the scope of a quantifier.

g. It is a truth-functional compound. It is a material conditional with two quantified statements as its antecedent and consequent.

Section 10.5

1. b. $(\forall x)\,(Px \supset (Ox \bullet Ux))$

j. $[(\forall y)\,(Sy \supset Oy)] \bullet [(\forall x)\,(Ox \supset Sx)]$, or $(\forall y)\,(Sy \equiv Oy)$

2. a. $(\exists x)\,Fx \supset (\exists y)\,(Oy \bullet Iy)$

Section 10.6

1. a. $(\forall x)\,((Fx \bullet \sim (\exists y)\,Oy) \supset \sim Rx)$

h. $(\exists x)\,(Px \bullet Ox) \supset [(\exists y) \sim Fy \supset (\exists z)\,(Pz \bullet \sim Iz)]$

2. b. $(\forall x)\,(\forall y)\,[(Px \bullet Sxy) \supset \sim Hcy]$

f. $(\forall x)\,(Stx \supset Lsx)$

3. a. $\sim [(\exists x)\,(Nx \bullet (\forall y)\,(Ny \supset Lxy)]$

i. $(\exists x)\,(\exists y)\,[(Px \bullet (Py \bullet Cxy)) \bullet \sim Hxy]$

4. a. The grass on the other side looks greener.

Section 10.7

1. $(\forall x)\,(\forall y)\,[(Dx \bullet Py) \supset (Txy \equiv Tyx)]$

5. $(\exists x)\,(\forall y)\,(\exists z)\,[Sx \bullet (Py \supset ((Fz \bullet Hxz) \bullet Izy)]$

10. $(\exists x)\,[Gx \bullet [(\exists y)\,(Wy \bullet Sy) \bullet Iyx) \bullet (\exists z)\,(Mz \bullet Sz) \bullet Izx)]]$

15. $(Lrs \bullet Lsn) \bullet (\exists x)\,(Rx \bullet \sim [(\exists y)\,(\forall z)\,(Py \bullet Pz) \bullet Lyz)])$

Section 10.9

1. $(\exists x)\,[(Sxp \bullet Mx) \bullet (\forall y)\,(Syp \supset Iyx)] \bullet (\exists y)\,(\exists z)$
$[((Dyp \bullet Dy) \bullet (Dzp \bullet Dz)) \bullet \sim Iyz]$

4. $Krs \bullet (\forall y)\,(Kys \supset Iyr)$

CHAPTER 11

Section 11.1

1. a. False, as both disjuncts are false. The number 164 is neither a prime number, nor is it true that if 164 is a positive number then –2 is the square root of 1.

f. B is known to be false.

$\sim Sab$ is true because it is true that 1 is not the square root of 164. $(Pb \bullet Pa)$ is true because both 1 and 164 are positive numbers. Hence, $\sim Sab \equiv (Pb \bullet Pa)$ is true, therefore, $\sim [\sim Sab \equiv (Pb \bullet Pa)]$ is false.

Thus, $\sim [\sim Sab \equiv (Pb \bullet Pa)] \equiv B$ is true, with false statements on both sides of the '$\equiv$'.

2. a. Interpretation:

U.D.: Persons

Bxy: *x* is the brother of *y*

b: Ravana

a: Shurpanakha

$Bba \supset \sim Bab$ is true on this interpretation because if Ravana is the brother of Shurpanakha, then Shurpanakha is not the brother of Ravana.

3. b. Interpretation:

U.D.: Positive numbers

Bxy: *x* is divisible by *y*

Cxy: *x* is greater than *y*

a: the number 137

b: the number 237

$(Baa \bullet Cba) \supset (Bab \bullet Bba)$ is false on this interpretation, for it is true that 137 is divisible by itself and 237 is greater than 137. But it is false both that 137 is divisible by 237 and 237 is divisible by 137. Since the conditional has a true antecedent and a false consequent, it is false.

4. a. Interpretation:

U.D.: Set of positive integers

Lx: *x* is a prime number

c: the number 4

d: the number 5

$Lc \supset Ld$ is true, but $Ld \supset Lc$ is false on this interpretation. For, the number 4 is not a prime number, it makes *Lc* false. But 5 is a prime number and that makes *Ld* true. $Lc \supset Ld$ has a false antecedent on this interpretation, so it is true, but $Ld \supset Lc$ has a true antecedent and a false consequent on this interpretation so it is false.

5. a. The statement says: If someone is the father of another person, then someone is the parent of the other person. This is true, therefore, the statement is true.

e. The statement is false. Its antecedent is true, which says that there is at least one European. But its consequent is false, which says that every parent is a father. Since mothers are parents too, this makes the consequent false. Therefore, the statement is false.

Section 11.2

1. b. One-element U.D.: $\{b\}$, in this universe the expansion for $(\exists x)(\exists y)(Jxy \bullet Pb)$ is: $Jbb \bullet Pb$

2. b. Two-element U.D.: $\{a, b\}$, in this universe the expansion for $(\forall y)\, Hy \supset (\forall x)\, Ix$ is:

$$(Ha \bullet Hb) \supset (Ia \bullet Ib)$$

e. Two-element U.D.: $\{a, b\}$, in this universe the expansion for $(\forall y)(Fy \supset (\exists x)(Ixy \vee Iyy))$ is:

$$(Fa \supset \{(Iaa \vee Iaa) \vee (Iba \vee Iaa)\} \bullet (Fb \supset \{(Iab \vee Ibb) \vee (Ibb \vee Ibb)\}$$

3. a. The three-element U.D. is: $\{a, b, c\}$

The expansion of $(\exists x)\, Kx \bullet (\forall y)$ By is:

$$((Ka \vee Kb) \vee Kc) \bullet ((Ba \bullet Bb) \bullet Bc)$$

Section 11.3

1. a. Two-element universe: $\{a, b\}$

(i) $(\forall y)(Dy \supset Ey) \supset (\exists y)\, Fy$ is expanded as:

$$[(Da \supset Ea) \bullet (Db \supset Eb)] \supset (Fa \vee Fb)$$

(ii) $(\forall y)(Fy \supset Ey)$ is expanded as: $(Fa \supset Ea) \bullet (Fb \supset Eb)$

(iii) The conclusion is: $(\forall y)(\sim Dy \vee Ey)$. It is expanded as:

$$(\sim Da \vee Ea) \bullet (\sim Db \vee Eb)$$

The argument will be invalid on the following truth value assignments:

Da	*Ea*	*Fa*	*Db*	*Eb*	*Fb*
T	F	F	T	T	F

f. For a two-element universe: $\{a, b\}$, the expansion will be as follows:

(i) $(\exists x)\, Sx$ will be: $(Sa \vee Sb)$

(ii) $(\forall x)(Sx \supset Rxx)$ will be: $(Sa \supset Raa) \bullet (Sb \supset Rbb)$

(iii) $(\exists x)(\forall y)(Sx \bullet Rxy)$ will be: $[Sa \bullet (Raa \bullet Rab)] \vee [Sb \bullet (Rba \bullet Rbb)]$

The argument can be shown to be invalid on the following truth value assignments:

Sa	*Sb*	*Raa*	*Rab*	*Rba*	*Rbb*
T	F	T	F	T	F

Section 11.4

1. a. Proving $(\forall x)\, Hx \supset (\forall x)\, Gx$ not quantificationally true:

By Interpretation method:

U.D.: Human beings

Hx: *x* is mortal

Gx: *x* is cold blooded

$(\forall x)\, Hx \supset (\forall x)\, Gx$ is false on this interpretation as all humans are mortal but no humans are cold blooded.

By expansion for a two-element universe: $\{a, b\}$

$$(Ha \bullet Hb) \supset (Ga \bullet Gb)$$

where *Ha* and *Hb* are true, and *Ga* and *Gb* are false.

f. Showing that $(\forall y)\,(Dya \vee Ey) \supset [(\forall y)\, Dya \bullet (\forall y)\, Ey]$ is not quantificationally true:

By Interpretation method:

U.D.: Positive integers

Dxy: *x* is divisible by *y*

Ex: *x* is odd

a: The number 2

On this interpretation, the antecedent will be true, as any positive number is either divisible by 2 or is an odd number, but it is not true that all numbers are both divisible by 2 and are odd numbers.

By expansion for a two-element universe: $\{a, b\}$. The expansion is:

$$[(Daa \vee Ea) \bullet (Dba \vee Eb)] \supset [(Daa \bullet (Ea \bullet Eb)) \bullet (Dba \bullet (Ea \bullet Eb))]$$

The possible truth-value assignments on which it will be false are:

Ea	*Eb*	*Daa*	*Dba*
T	T	F	F

2. b. Showing that $[(\exists x)\, Hx \bullet (\exists x)\, Gx] \bullet \sim [(\exists x)\,(Hx \bullet Gx)]$ is not quantificationally false:

By Interpretation method:

U.D.: Positive integers

Hx: *x* is odd

Gx: *x* is even

On this interpretation the statement will be true because it is true that though there are odd numbers and even numbers, there is no number which is both odd and even.

By expansion on $\{a, b\}$:

$$[(Ha \vee Hb) \bullet (Ga \vee Gb)] \bullet \sim [(Ha \bullet Ga) \vee (Hb \bullet Gb)]$$

will be true when:

Ha	*Hb*	*Ga*	*Gb*
F	T	T	F

3. b. Showing that $(\exists x)(Lx \bullet Mx) \supset (\exists x) \sim (Lx \vee Mx)$ is quantificationally indeterminate by:

Interpretation method:

Interpretation 1: U.D.: Human beings:

Lx: *x* is six feet tall

Mx: *x* is blonde haired

The statement is true on this interpretation since, if there are six feet tall blonde persons, there are also persons who are neither six feet tall nor blonde haired.

Interpretation 2: U.D.: Human beings:

Lx: *x* is mammal

Mx: *x* is mortal

The statement is false on this interpretation because if there is at least one human who is both mammal and mortal, then it is false that there is a human who is neither.

By expansion: For a two-element universe $\{a, b\}$, the expansion will be:

$$[(La \bullet Ma) \vee (Lb \bullet Mb)] \supset [\sim (La \vee Ma) \vee \sim (Lb \vee Mb)]$$

It will be false when *La*, *Lb*, *Ma*, *Mb* are all true.

Section 11.5

1. b. Showing that $(\exists w)(Bw \bullet Cw)$, $(\exists w) Bw \bullet (\exists w) Cw$ are not quantificationally equivalent:

By interpretation:

U.D.: Animals

Bx: x is a cow

Cx: x is a fox

The statement $(\exists w)(Bw \bullet Cw)$ will be false on this interpretation, but $(\exists w)\, Bw \bullet (\exists w)\, Cw$ will be true.

The expansion method for $\{a, b\}$ is: $(Ba \bullet Ca) \vee (Bb \bullet Cb)$ will be false and $(Ba \vee Bb) \bullet (Ca \vee Cb)$ will be true when: *Ba* is *T*, *Ca* is *F*, *Bb* is *F* but *Cb* is *T*.

2. a. Showing that $\{(\exists y)\, Ry,\ (\exists y)\, Sy,\ \sim (\forall y)(Ry \vee Sy)$ are quantificationally consistent:

Interpretation method:

U.D.: Human beings

Rx: x is an African

Sx: x is Australian

On this interpretation, every member of the set will be true because, just as it is true that there are Africans and Australians, it is also true that it is not the case that every human being is either an African or an Australian.

Expansion for $\{a, b\}$:

$$(Ra \vee Rb),\ (Sa \vee Sb),\ \sim [(Ra \vee Sa) \bullet (Rb \vee Sb)]$$

The statements—all of them—will be true when *Ra* and *Sa* are false but *Rb* and *Sb* are true.

CHAPTER 12

Section 12.2

1. a. Universal generalization (UG). On two random but representative samples of numbers, a claim is based about the properties of addition. From this, by UG a universal claim is made about the whole class of numbers.

f. Existential generalization (EG). From the named three samples, a limited generalization is being made about 'some' cases.

2. a.

1. $(\forall y)(Py \supset \sim By)$		
2. $(\forall y)(Ay \supset Py)$	$/ \therefore (\forall y)(Ay \supset \sim By)$	
3. $Ax \supset Px$		2, UI
4. $Px \supset \sim Bx$		1, UI

5. $Ax \supset \sim Bx$		3, 4, HS
6. $(\forall y)(Ay \supset \sim By)$		5, UG

d.

1. $(\forall x)(Rx \supset Sx)$		
2. $(\exists x)(Rx \bullet Tx)$	$/ \therefore (\exists x)(Sx \bullet Tx)$	
→ 3. $Ru \bullet Tu$		
4. Ru		3, Simp.
5. $Ru \supset Su$		1, UI
6. Su		5, 4, MP
7. $Tu \bullet Ru$		3, Com.
8. Tu		7, Simp.
9. $Su \bullet Tu$		6, 8, Conj.
10. $(\exists x)(Sx \bullet Tx)$		8, EG
11. $(\exists x)(Sx \bullet Tx)$		2, 3–9, EI

3. a.

1. $(\forall y)[(Ky \bullet Jy) \supset Hy]$		
2. $(\forall y)\,Ky$		
3. Jd	$/ \therefore Kd \bullet Hd$	
4. Kd		2, UI
5. $Kd \bullet Jd$		4, 3, Conj.
6. $(Kd \bullet Jd) \supset Hd$		1, UI
7. Hd		6, 5, MP
8. $Kd \bullet Hd$		4, 7, Conj.

e.

1. $(\forall x)[Cx \vee (Fx \bullet \sim Ix)]$		
2. $(\forall x)\,Ix$	$/ \therefore (\exists x)(Ox \supset Cx)$	
→ 3. Ow		
4. Iw		2, UI
5. $Cw \vee (Fw \bullet \sim Iw)$		1, UI
6. $Iw \vee \sim Fw$		4, Add.
7. $\sim Fw \vee Iw$		6, Com.
8. $\sim Fw \vee \sim\sim Iw$		7, DN
9. $\sim (Fw \bullet \sim Iw)$		8, De M.
10. $(Fw \bullet \sim Iw) \vee Cw$		5, Com.
11. Cw		10, 9, DS
12. $Ow \supset Cw$		3–11, CP
13. $(\exists x)(Ox \supset Cx)$		12, EG

Section 12.3

1. a.

1. $(\exists x)(\forall y)(Hx \supset (Ny \vee Ty))$		
2. Hy		
→ 3. $(\forall y)(Hy \supset (Ny \vee Ty))$		⟸ ERROR!
4. $Hy \supset (Nm \vee Tk)$	2, UI	⟸ ERROR!
5. $Nm \vee Tk$	4, 2, MP	
6. $(\exists x)(Nx \vee Tk)$	5, EG	
7. $(\exists x)(Nx \vee Tk)$	2, 3–6, EI	

The first major mistake in this proof occurs on line 3 when, for a fresh application of EI, a variable y is chosen which has occurred free previous to line 3. Line 2 already has the free occurrence of y.

The other mistake occurs when on line 4 UI is applied selectively to instantiate only a few occurrences of y, and it is also used non-uniformly to instantiate first with constant m and then with k.

1. e.

1. $(\exists x)(\exists y)(Hx \bullet Jy)$		
2. $(\forall x)((Hy \bullet Jy) \supset Ky)$		
→ 3. $(\exists y)(Hx \bullet Jy)$		
→4. $Hx \bullet Jx$		⟸ ERROR!
5. $(Hx \bullet Jx) \supset Kx$	2,UI	
6. Kx	5, 4, MP	
7. Kx	3, 4–6, EI	
8. Kx	2, 3–7, EI	
9. $(\exists y)\,Ky$	8, EG	

The error in this proof is an error of application of EI. Every fresh application of EI must use a fresh or new variable. On line 4, a second EI proof is beginning, but for instantiation the same variable 'x' has been chosen which has already been used once on line 3 for the first EI.

i.

1. $(\forall y)(\exists z)(Tz \vee Uy)$		
2. $(\exists z)(Tz \vee Uy)$	1, UI	
→3. $Tz \vee Uz$	⟸	ERROR!
4. $(\forall y)(Tx \vee Uz)$	3, UG	⟸ ERROR!
5. $(\exists y)(\forall x)(Tx \vee Uz)$	4, EG	
6. $(\exists y)(\forall x)(Tx \vee Uz)$	2, 3–5, EI	

The first mistake in this proof occurs when on line 3, an EI proof is started and it instantiates 'Uy', which is not supposed to be instantiated, as it does not fall within the scope of the existential quantifier. EI is a rule for removing an existential quantifier and then replacing the variable made free by this removal. In this case, the variable '*z*' is freed by the removal of the existential quantifier, but not '*y*'. So, '*Uy*' should not have been instantiated as '*Uz*' on line 3.

Then, on line 4, UG is used selectively, generalizing on one occurrence of '*z*', but not on the other. UG cannot be selectively applied.

Section 12.5

1. a.

1.	$(\forall z)(Az \equiv Bz)$	
2.	$(\forall x) \sim (Bx \vee \sim Cx)$ $\quad / \therefore \sim Ab$	
3.	$\sim (Bb \vee \sim Cb)$	2, UI
4.	$Ab \equiv Bb$	1, UI
5.	$\sim Bb \bullet \sim\sim Cb$	3, De M.
6.	$\sim Bb$	5, Simp.
7.	$(Ab \supset Bb) \bullet (Bb \supset Ab)$	4, Equiv.
8.	$Ab \supset Bb$	7, Simp.
9.	$\sim Ab$	8, 6, MT

e.

1.	$(\exists y)\, By \equiv (\exists x)\, Cx$ $\quad / \therefore (\exists y)[By \supset (\exists x)\, Cx]$	
2.	$[(\exists y)\, By \supset (\exists x)\, Cx] \bullet [(\exists x)\, Cx \supset (\exists y)\, By]$	1, Equiv.
3.	$(\exists y)\, By \supset (\exists x)\, Cx$	2, Simp.
→4.	By	
5.	$(\exists y)\, By$	4, EG
6.	$(\exists x)\, Cx$	3, 5, MP
7.	$By \supset (\exists x)\, Cx$	4–6, CP
8.	$(\exists y)[By \supset (\exists x)\, Cx]$	7, EG

k.

1.	$(\forall x)(Ex \supset Fx)$	
2.	$(\forall x)(\sim Gx \vee Hx)$ $\quad / \therefore \sim (\exists x) \sim (Fx \supset Gx) \supset (\forall y)(Ey \supset Hy)$	
→3.	$\sim (\exists x) \sim (Ex \supset Gx)$	
4.	$(\forall x)(Fx \supset Gx)$	3, QN
5.	$Fx \supset Gx$	4, UI
6.	$Ex \supset Fx$	1, UI
7.	$Ex \supset Gx$	6, 5, UI
8.	$\sim Gx \vee Hx$	2, UI
9.	$Gx \supset Hx$	8, Impl.

10.	$Ex \supset Hx$	7, 9, HS
11.	$(\forall y)(Ey \supset Hy)$	10, UG
12.	$\sim(\exists x) \sim (Fx \supset Gx) \supset (\forall y)(Ey \supset Hy)$	3–11, CP

p.

1.	$(\exists y) Vy \supset (\forall y)(Uy \supset Wy)$	
2.	$(\exists x) Tx \supset (\exists y) Uy$	$/ \therefore (\exists x)(Vx \bullet Tx) \supset (\exists y) Wy$
3.	$(\exists x)(Vx \bullet Tx)$	
4.	$Vw \bullet Tw$	
5.	Vw	4, Simp.
6.	$(\exists y) Vy$	5, EG
7.	$(\forall y)(Uy \supset Wy)$	1, 6, MP
8.	$Tw \bullet Vw$	4, Com.
9.	Tw	8, Simp.
10.	$(\exists x) Tx$	9, EG
11.	$(\exists y) Uy$	2, 10, MP
12.	Uv	
13.	$Uv \supset Wv$	7, UI
14.	Wv	13, 12, MP
15.	$(\exists y) Wy$	14, EG
16.	$(\exists y) Wy$	11, 12–15, EI
17.	$(\exists y) Wy$	3,4–16, EI
18.	$(\exists x)(Vx \bullet Tx) \supset (\exists y) Wy$	3–17, CP

Section 12.6

1. a.

1.	$(\forall y)(\forall z) Dyz$	
2.	$(\exists y)(\forall z)(Dyz \supset Hzy)$	$/ \therefore (\exists x)(\forall z) Hzx$
3.	$(\forall z)(Dyz \supset Hzy)$	
4.	$(\forall z) Dyz$	1, UI
5.	Dyz	4, UI
6.	$Dyz \supset Hzy$	3, UI
7.	Hzy	6, 5, MP
8.	$(\forall z) Hzy$	7, UG (*Note*: 'z' is not free on line 3)
9.	$(\exists x)(\forall z) Hzx$	8, EG
10.	$(\exists x)(\forall z) Hzx$	2, 3–9, EI

e.

1. $(\exists u)(\forall v)[(\exists w)\,Avw \supset Avu]$
2. $(\forall v)(\exists w)\,Avw$ $\quad /\therefore (\exists u)(\forall v)\,Avu$
3. $(\forall v)[(\exists w)\,Avw \supset Avu]$
4. $(\exists w)\,Avw \supset Avu$ — 3, UI
5. $(\exists w)\,Avw$ — 2, UI
6. Avu — 4, 5, MP
7. $(\forall v)\,Avu$ — 6, UG
8. $(\exists u)(\forall v)\,Avu$ — 7, EG
9. $(\exists u)(\forall v)\,Avu$ — 1, 3–8, EI

j.

1. $(\forall y)[(\exists z)[(\exists x)(Ax \bullet \sim Bx) \bullet Cyxz] \supset Dy]$
2. $(\forall z)[(Fz \bullet Gaz) \supset (Cbza \vee Scza)]$
   $/\therefore (\exists z)((Fz \bullet Gaz) \bullet (Az \bullet \sim Bz)) \supset [(\forall x) \sim Scxa \supset Db]$
3. $(\exists z)((Fz \bullet Gaz \bullet (Az \bullet \sim Bz))$
4. $(\forall x) \sim Scxa$
5. $(Fz \bullet Gaz) \bullet (Az \bullet \sim Bz)$
6. $Fz \bullet Gaz$ — 5, Simp.
7. $(Fz \bullet Gaz) \supset (Cbza \vee Scza)$ — 2, UI
8. $Cbza \vee Scza$ — 7, 6, MP
9. ~Scza — 4, UI
10. $Cbza$ — 8, 9, Com., DS
11. $Az \bullet \sim Bz$ — 5, Com., Simp.
12. $(Az \bullet \sim Bz) \bullet Cbza$ — 11, 10, Conj.
13. $(\exists x)((Ax \bullet \sim Bx) \bullet Cbxa)$ — 12, EG
14. $(\exists z)[(\exists x)(Ax \bullet \sim Bx) \bullet Cbxz)]$ — 13, EG
15. $(\exists z)[(\exists x)(Ax \bullet \sim Bx) \bullet Cbxz)] \supset Db$ — 1, UI
16. Db — 15, 14, MP
17. Db — 3, 5–16, EI
18. $(\forall x) \sim Scxa \supset Db$ — 4–17, CP
19. $(\exists z)((Fz \bullet Gaz) \bullet (Az \bullet \sim Bz)) \supset [(\forall x) \sim Scxa \supset Db]$ — 3–18, CP

2. a. The expansion of $(\forall x)(\exists y) \sim Cxy$ is

$$(\sim Caa \vee \sim Cab) \bullet (\sim Cba \vee \sim Cbb)$$

The expansion of $(\exists x)(\forall y) \sim Cxy$ is: $(\sim Caa \bullet \sim Cab) \vee (\sim Cba \bullet \sim Cbb)$

The argument will be invalid under the truth value assignments:

Caa	*Cab*	*Cba*	*Cbb*
T	F	T	F

Interpretation: Human beings
Cxy: *x* is the child of *y*, so ~*Cxy*: *x* is not the child of *y*.

Section 12.7

1. c. Show that $(\forall y)(Az \supset Bz) \supset [(\forall y) Ay \supset (\forall y) By]$ is a theorem:

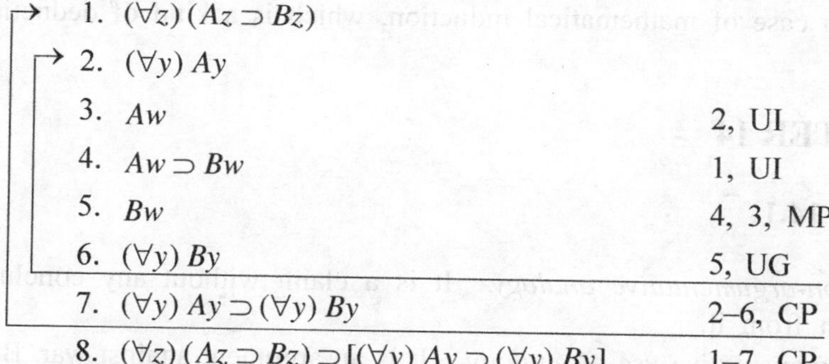

1. $(\forall z)(Az \supset Bz)$
2. $(\forall y) Ay$
3. Aw — 2, UI
4. $Aw \supset Bw$ — 1, UI
5. Bw — 4, 3, MP
6. $(\forall y) By$ — 5, UG
7. $(\forall y) Ay \supset (\forall y) By$ — 2–6, CP
8. $(\forall z)(Az \supset Bz) \supset [(\forall y) Ay \supset (\forall y) By]$ — 1–7, CP

g. Show that: $[(\exists y) Ay \supset (\exists y) By] \supset (\exists y)(Ay \supset By)$ is a theorem.

1. $(\exists y) Ay \supset (\exists y) By]$
2. $\sim (\exists y)(Ay \supset By)$
3. $(\forall y) \sim (Ay \supset By)$ — 2, QN
4. $\sim (Ay \supset By)$ — 3,UI
5. $Ay \bullet \sim By$ — 4, Impl.
6. Ay — 5, Simp.
7. $\sim By$ — 5, Com., Simp.
8. $(\exists y) \sim By$ — 7, EG
9. $(\exists y) Ay$ — 6, EG
10. $(\exists y) By$ — 1, 9, MP
11. $(\exists y) By \bullet (\exists y) \sim By$ — 10, 8, Conj.
12. $(\exists y)(Ay \supset By)$ — 2–11, IP.
13. $[(\exists y) Ay \supset (\exists y) By] \supset (\exists y)(Ay \supset By)$ — 1–12, CP.

CHAPTER 13

Sections 13.2–13.4

2. It is an inductive generalization based on personal observation. If it is true that the person has seen 'all' the dogs in his or her neighbourhood, then it is an induction by simple enumeration. But it certainly is not a good induction. The conclusion is about all dogs, and not just the dogs in the neighbourhood. For that conclusion, the inductive observations do not provide a strong support. To arrive at a conclusion about dogs not within the neighbourhood, more samples should have been observed.

7. It is a case of mathematical induction, which is a kind of deduction.

CHAPTER 14

Section 14.1

1. *a. Non-argumentative analogy.* It is a claim without any conclusion drawn from it.

e. Argumentative use of analogy. It is an argument against war. Based on an analogy with violent robbery, it points out that war has many of the traits, because of which we find robbery objectionable.

2. *c. Figurative analogy.* Aristotle is comparing difficulties that have not been previously discussed to knots which are not known to exist.

e. Literal analogy. Two persons are compared for what they actually are or have done.

Section 14.2

1. a. The edifice of knowledge is claimed to be analogous to a marble statue standing in a desert. The statue being made of marble is not subject to easy decay, so is knowledge. But it is subject to the threat of getting buried under the constantly shifting sand of the desert. Knowledge too is open to the threat of oblivion by getting buried under the shifting sands of time. Constant vigilance to clear the sand is necessary for the statue to remain visible and clear. Therefore, constant repair and tending is also needed to keep the body of knowledge remain visible and shining.

The author has used a figurative analogy to evoke a vivid image. The similarities, though are not many, are relevant. The target conclusion is to urge people to be constantly vigilant in the service of knowledge. For that purpose, the imagery used and the similarities are relevant. Thus, our criterion 4 is satisfied. But it does not have any safeguard against a possible disanalogy (criterion 8). For, there could be differences between a marble statue standing in a desert and a body of knowledge. For example, some one might argue that a statue left in the desert may be left there as it has outrun its utility, and thus being buried in the shifting sand is what it deserves. Einstein's argument has no protective measure against such disanalogies. An indication of the awareness of the differences or their relative unimportance to the similarities observed (criteria 2 and 3) would have helped, but its absence is conspicuous. This makes the analogy somewhat weak.

Also, as is the case with figurative analogy, only one instance has been used as the base for making an analogical claim, the claim is not based on observation of numerous instances. Nor is it based on observation of instances in many varied circumstances (criteria 5 and 6).

The conclusion however, is rather modest (criterion 7). It only wants to advance a prima facie case that knowledge require constant tending. Therefore, even though based on weak analogy, the argument conveys its message clearly.

i. The author's conclusion is: "Politics is more a matter of chance than any game of gambling." His premise is: "Power of circumstance is most evident in politics."

The points of analogy are: A game of cards, or any gambling game, is subject to chances. It is also subject to unpredictable circumstances which can alter its history. It is more so in the case of politics, which involves many people playing a similar gambling game. The number of unknown factors that can affect are also much higher in politics than in a gambling game. The stakes in a gambling game usually involve money. But in politics the stakes are money, fame, power and position in life. Moreover, change of circumstances in a gambling game can make one a winner or a loser. In politics, on the other hand, it can make a winner and a leader, or a loser and a defeated individual.

The similarities are literal. They are also fair and relevant by criteria 1 and 4. The similarities with a gambling game are used to show that politics involves more gambling than any gambling game itself. This shows that the author is aware of the differences between the cases, just as he is aware of the similarities (criteria 2 and 3).

The generalizations about gambling games in general to compare with a generalized claim about politics in general take care of criteria 5 and 6 to some extent, in terms of wide and varied observation.

The conclusion, however, is rather strong (criterion 7) and entertains no possibility of a disanalogy (criterion 8). This is a weakness in the argument. For example, it is possible to say that politics is a more crooked game than any gambling game, as in the former most factors can be manipulated leaving almost nothing to luck. On the other hand, a gambling game no matter how unfair, after all, has to let others win a few times in order to keep semblance of a fair game.

In the final analysis, however, the analogy is strong and it provides strong support to the argument.

2. (ii) a. less probable, criterion 3.
   b. more probable, criterion 6.
   c. no effect, irrelevant factor.
   d. may have no effect, the food and service and inside comfort may remain the same, and similarities may outweigh this difference-criterion 2.

CHAPTER 15

3. b. The phenomenon under investigation is the effect of a particulate matter in air on long-term health effects. The approach is a combination of various methods. The present study is a reassessment of data found by previous studies, but in the present study, the Method of Residue has been applied to measure the effect of distinct components of particulate matter separately. The method of concomitant variation also was used to study the results between the pollutants and the outcome on health. Finally, in combination, this is a joint method of agreement and the difference has been used to find out the rate difference between the highest and the lowest polluted cities.

   i. The studies mentioned in this report are studies of concomitant variations. For example, drinking green tea or green tea treatment with reduction in lung cancer tumour multiplicity, or green tea use and reduction in prostate cancer cases, etc. The aim of the studies is to establish some evidence to the causal role of green tea in reduction and prevention of different kinds of cancer cases. To that extent, the studies show significant concomitant relationship.

CHAPTER 16

1. Probability-favourable outcomes divided by total outcomes. The favourable outcome, in this case rolling an even number, and the number of possible outcomes are three: 2, 4, 6. But the number of total outcomes is six: 1, 2, 3, 4, 5, 6. Therefore, the probability of rolling an even number is 3/6 or 1/2.

4. The number of favourable outcomes in both tosses is one: both times head.

Number of total outcomes is 4: Head and head, head and tail, tail and head, and tail and tail. So, the probability of getting two heads in both tosses is: 1/4.

9. Let us define even $A =$ Drawing a king

$P(A) = 4/52$, since there are only 4 kings in the pack

Let us define event $B =$ drawing a Hearts card

$P(B) = 13/52$, since there are 13 Hearts cards in the pack

But we know that there is a card that both a king and a Hearts card, namely, King of Hearts.

Let us define that event as $A \cap B$ or A and B both occurring. $P(A \cap B) = 1/52$. So, in this case, the probability of either a king or a Hearts card or both, or $P(A \cap B)$, can be calculated by the Addition Rule for non-exclusive events:

$$P(A \cup B) = P(A) + P(B) - P(A \cap B)$$

Thus,

$$P(A \cup B) = 4/52 + 13/52 - 1/52 = 16/52 \text{ or } 4/13$$

CHAPTER 17

1. (i) a. What is the 'problem' that is under investigation? The data to be explained is how the universe began.

b. What hypothesis or hypotheses are being offered as its explanation?

The Big Bang theory is being offered as one of the explanations. It starts from the assumption of something, a singularity, very very dense and hot which, then the theory says, expanded or exploded (Big Bang) and gradually cooled down and became our universe of today.

There are other rival hypotheses to this. For example, the passage mentions Gentry's hypothesis.

c. Evaluate the hypothesis or the hypotheses using the criteria.

The Big Bang hypothesis provides an explanation for the problem under consideration. It gives us a reasonable explanation for how the universe came to be. It also has predictive power, which is confirmed by Hubble's law and the CMB radiation detection. Accepting the established theories of Physics, we can deduce the consequences: that if Big Bang were true, then galaxies would be moving away from us at speeds proportional to their distance, and we should be able to find some remnant of the immense initial heat that the hypothesis assumes, etc. These are testable and falsifiable consequences, which give credibility to the hypothesis.

The hypothesis also is simple as it does not presume anything other than the presence of a singularity. It is consistent with the relevant facts of cosmology which are already accepted, and it is wide in its 'scope' as it can explain other phenomena such as the observed expansion of the universe.

However, when deciding between conflicting hypotheses, we need some crucial evidence that helps us decide in favour of one of the hypotheses. In this passage, no such crucial evidence is allowed to the Big Bang hypothesis. In fact, it is mentioned that the same consequences can also fit in and corroborate other rival hypotheses. Thus, though it is a reasonable hypothesis, its exclusivity is not yet established.

INDEX